SPIDER-MAN 2099

WRITERS: PETER DAVID, EVAN SKOLNICK & IAN EDGINTON

PENCILERS: RICK LEONARDI, TOM GRINDBERG, CHRIS WOZNIAK, RON LIM & MALCOLM DAVIS

INKERS: AL WILLIAMSON, DON HUDSON, CHRIS IVY, JOHN LOWE & JIMMY PALMIOTTI

COLORISTS: KEVIN TINSLEY, GEORGE ROUSSOS, EVA GRINDBERG, MARIE SEVERIN, KEVIN SOMERS, JOE ANDREANI & TOM SMITH WITH STEVE BUCCELLATO & ROBBIE BUSCH

LETTERERS: RICK PARKER, STEVE DUTRO, DAVE SHARPE, ROD OLLERENSHAW & JON BABCOCK

ASSISTANT EDITORS: MATTHEW MORRA & LIA PELOSI

EDITOR: JOEY CAVALIERI

FRONT COVER COLORIST: THOMAS MASON
BACK COVER ARTISTS: CHRIS WOZNIAK & TOM SMITH

COLLECTION EDITOR: NELSON RIBEIRO ASSISTANT EDITOR: ALEX STARBUCK
EDITORS, SPECIAL PROJECTS: MARK D. BEAZLEY & JENNIFER GRÜNWALD
SENIOR EDITOR, SPECIAL PROJECTS: JEFF YOUNGQUIST
RESEARCH: GARY HENDERSON LAYOUT: JEPH YORK
PRODUCTION: COLORTEK & JOE FRONTIRRE
SVP OF PRINT & DIGITAL PUBLISHING SALES: DAVID GABRIEL

EDITOR IN CHIEF: AXEL ALONSO CHIEF CREATIVE OFFICER: JOE QUESADA
PUBLISHER: DAN BUCKLEY EXECUTIVE PRODUCER: ALAN FINE

SPIDER-MAN 2099 VOL. 2. Contains material originally published in magazine form as SPIDER-MAN 2099 #11-14 and ANNUAL #1, and 2099 UNLIMITED #1-3. First printing 2013. ISBN# 978-0-7851-8537-6. Published by MARVEL WORLDWIDE, INC., a subsidiary of MARVEL ENTERTAINMENT, LLC. OFFICE OF PUBLICATION: 135 West 50th Street, New York, NY 10020. Copyright © 1993, 1994 and 2013 Marvel Characters, Inc. All rights reserved. All characters featured in this issue and the distinctive names and likenesses thereof, and all related indicia are trademarks of Marvel Characters, Inc. No similarity between any of the names, characters, persons, and/or institutions in this magazine with those of any living or dead person or institution is intended, and any such similarity which may exist is purely coincidental. **Printed in the U.S.A.** ALAN FINE, EVP - Office of the President, Marvel Worldwide, Inc. and EVP & CMO Marvel Characters B.V.; DAN BUCKLEY, Publisher & President - Print, Animation & Digital Divisions; JOE QUESADA, Chief Creative Officer; TOM BREVOORT, SVP of Publishing; DAVID BOGART, SVP of Operations & Procurement, Publishing; C.B. CEBULSKI, SVP of Creator & Content Development; DAVID GABRIEL, SVP of Print & Digital Publishing Sales; JIM O'KEEFE, VP of Operations & Logistics; DAN CARR, Executive Director of Publishing Technology; SUSAN CRESPI, Editorial Operations Manager; ALEX MORALES, Publishing Operations Manager; STAN LEE, Chairman Emeritus. For information regarding advertising in Marvel Comics or on Marvel.com, please contact Niza Disla, Director of Marvel Partnerships, at ndisla@marvel.com. For Marvel subscription inquiries, please call 800-217-9158. **Manufactured between 8/2/2013 and 9/9/2013 by R.R. DONNELLEY, INC., SALEM, VA, USA.**

10 9 8 7 6 5 4 3 2 1

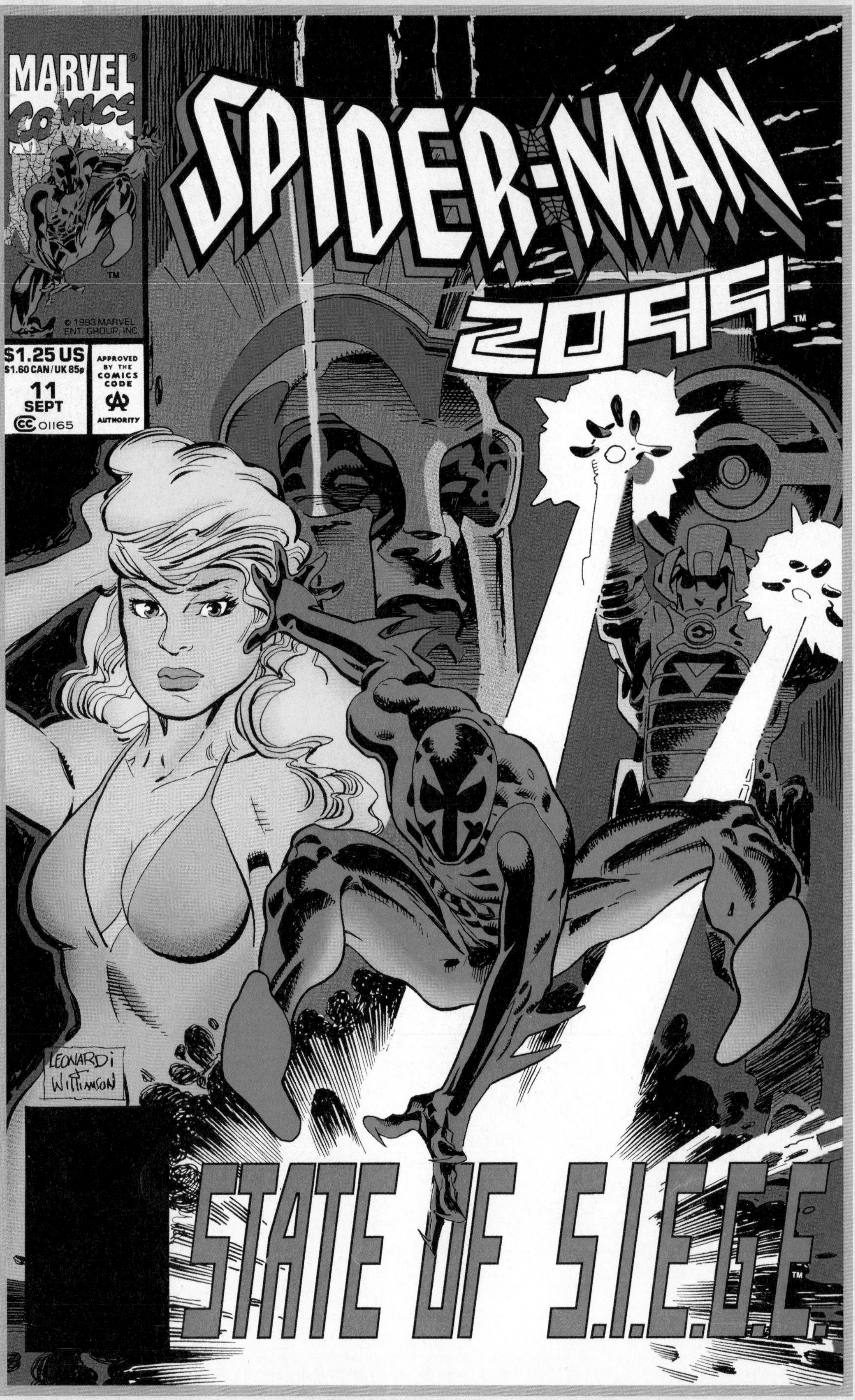

MARVEL COMICS
SPIDER-MAN 2099™
© 1993 MARVEL ENT. GROUP, INC.
$1.25 US
$1.60 CAN/UK 85p
11
SEPT
01165
APPROVED BY THE COMICS CODE AUTHORITY
LEONARDI WILLIAMSON
STATE OF S.I.E.G.E.™

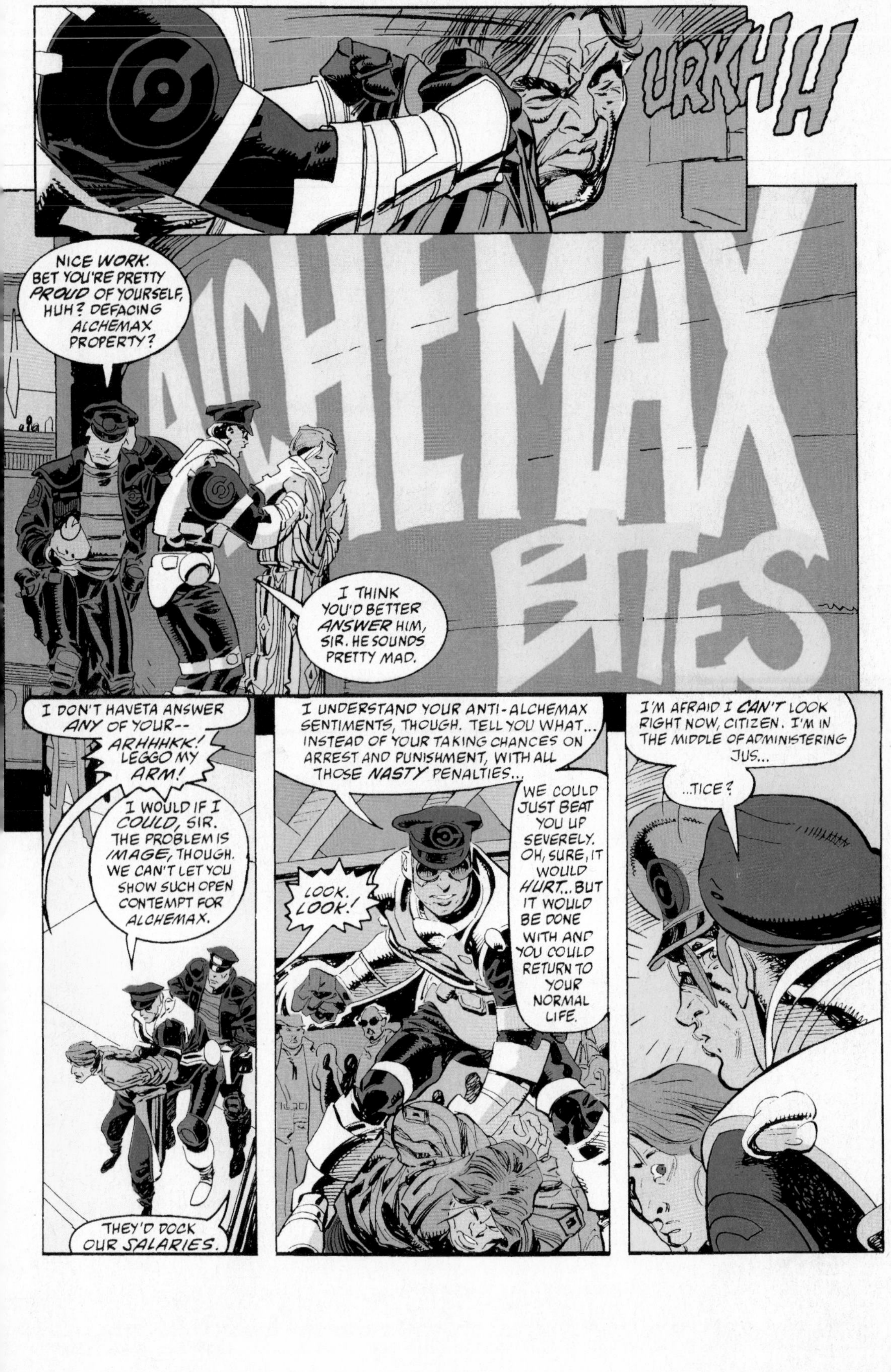
URKHH
NICE WORK. BET YOU'RE PRETTY PROUD OF YOURSELF, HUH? DEFACING ALCHEMAX PROPERTY?
ALCHEMAX BITES
I THINK YOU'D BETTER ANSWER HIM, SIR. HE SOUNDS PRETTY MAD.
I DON'T HAVETA ANSWER ANY OF YOUR-- ARHHHKK! LEGGO MY ARM!
I WOULD IF I COULD, SIR. THE PROBLEM IS IMAGE, THOUGH. WE CAN'T LET YOU SHOW SUCH OPEN CONTEMPT FOR ALCHEMAX.
THEY'D DOCK OUR SALARIES.
I UNDERSTAND YOUR ANTI-ALCHEMAX SENTIMENTS, THOUGH. TELL YOU WHAT... INSTEAD OF YOUR TAKING CHANCES ON ARREST AND PUNISHMENT, WITH ALL THOSE NASTY PENALTIES...
WE COULD JUST BEAT YOU UP SEVERELY. OH, SURE, IT WOULD HURT... BUT IT WOULD BE DONE WITH AND YOU COULD RETURN TO YOUR NORMAL LIFE.
LOOK. LOOK!
I'M AFRAID I CAN'T LOOK RIGHT NOW, CITIZEN. I'M IN THE MIDDLE OF ADMINISTERING JUS...
...TICE?

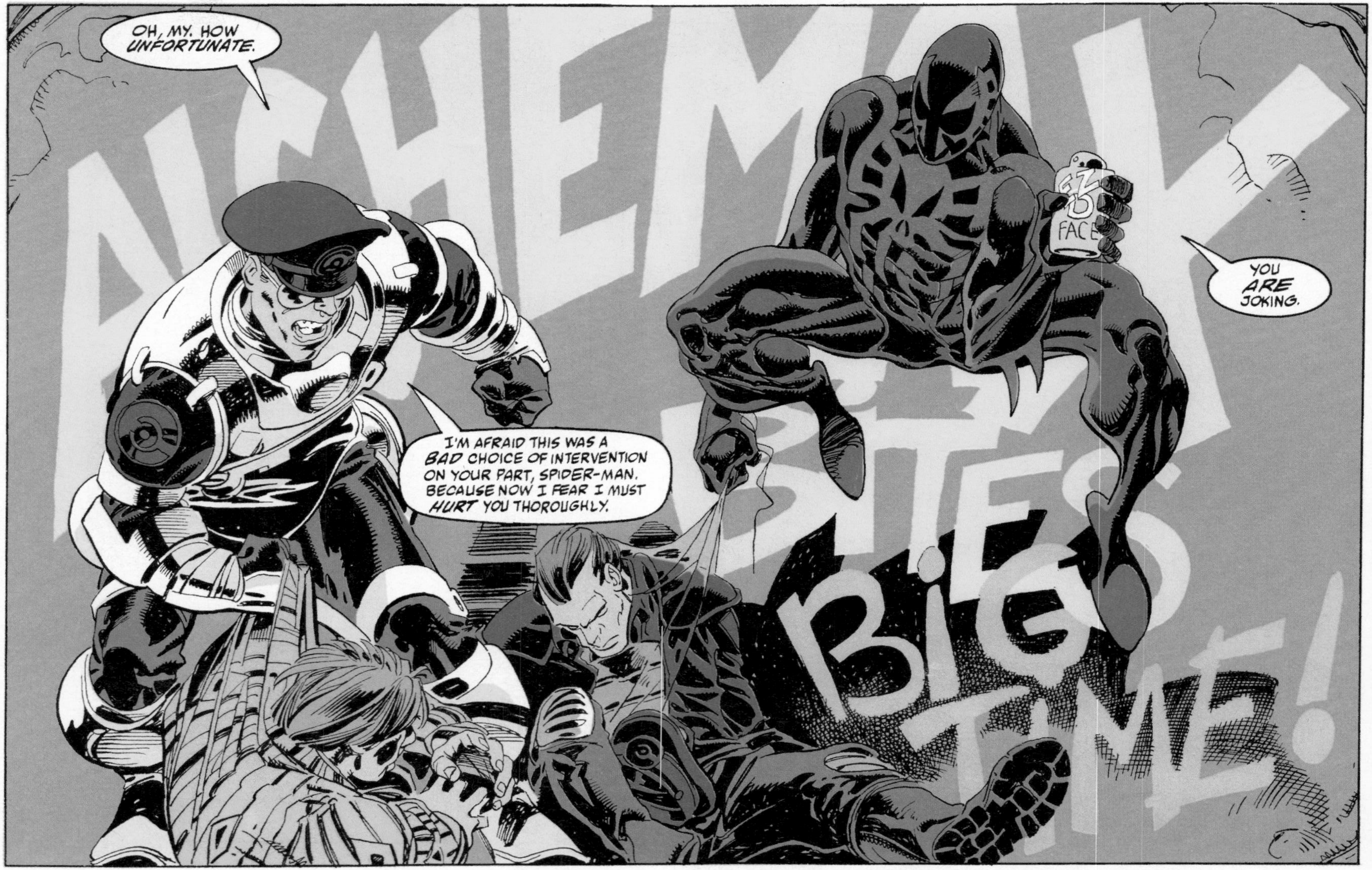
OH, MY. HOW UNFORTUNATE.
I'M AFRAID THIS WAS A BAD CHOICE OF INTERVENTION ON YOUR PART, SPIDER-MAN. BECAUSE NOW I FEAR I MUST HURT YOU THOROUGHLY.
YOU ARE JOKING.
BIG TIME!

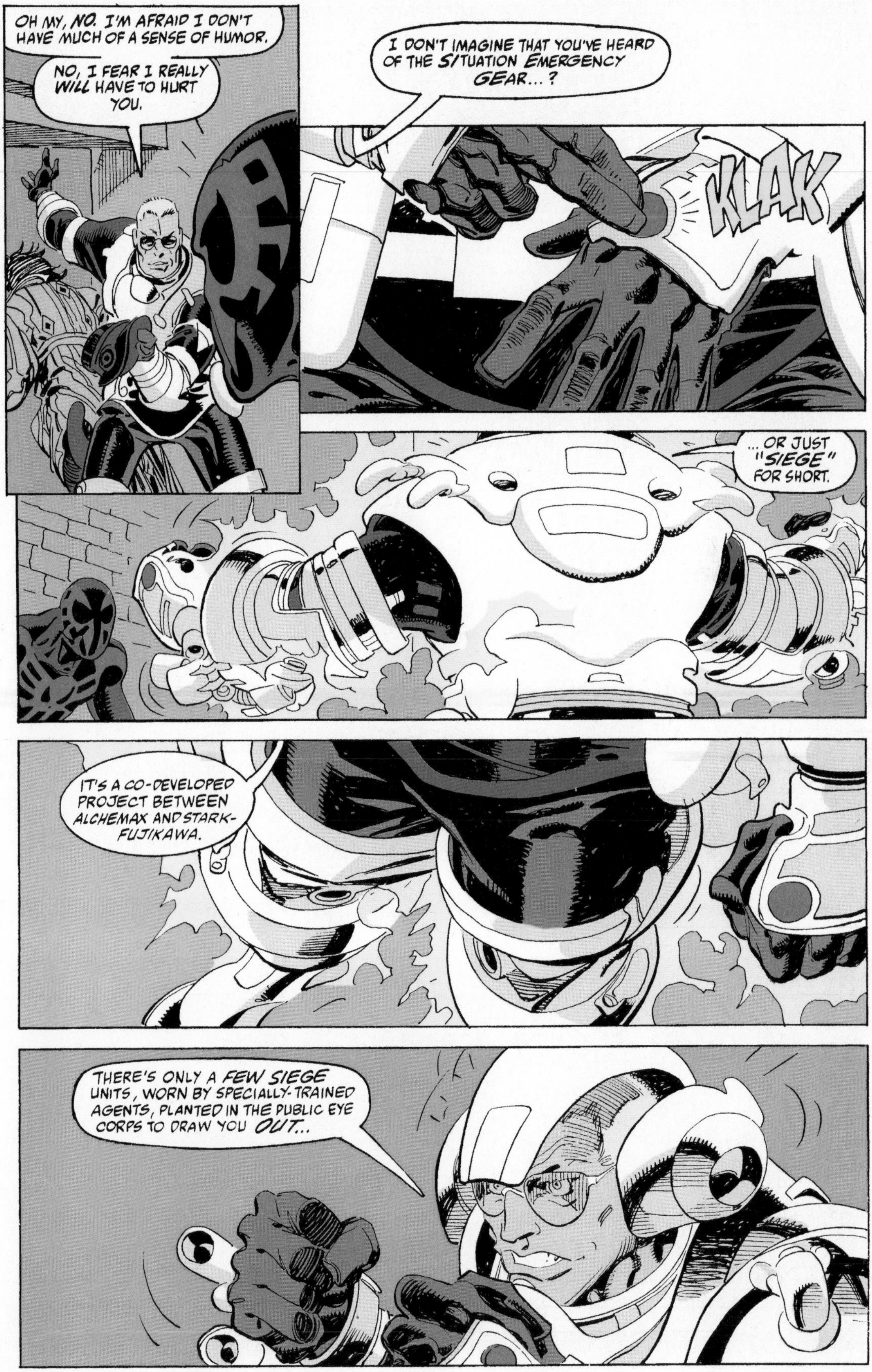
OH MY, NO. I'M AFRAID I DON'T HAVE MUCH OF A SENSE OF HUMOR.
NO, I FEAR I REALLY WILL HAVE TO HURT YOU.
I DON'T IMAGINE THAT YOU'VE HEARD OF THE SITUATION EMERGENCY GEAR...?
KLAK
...OR JUST "SIEGE" FOR SHORT.
IT'S A CO-DEVELOPED PROJECT BETWEEN ALCHEMAX AND STARK-FUJIKAWA.
THERE'S ONLY A FEW SIEGE UNITS, WORN BY SPECIALLY-TRAINED AGENTS, PLANTED IN THE PUBLIC EYE CORPS TO DRAW YOU OUT...

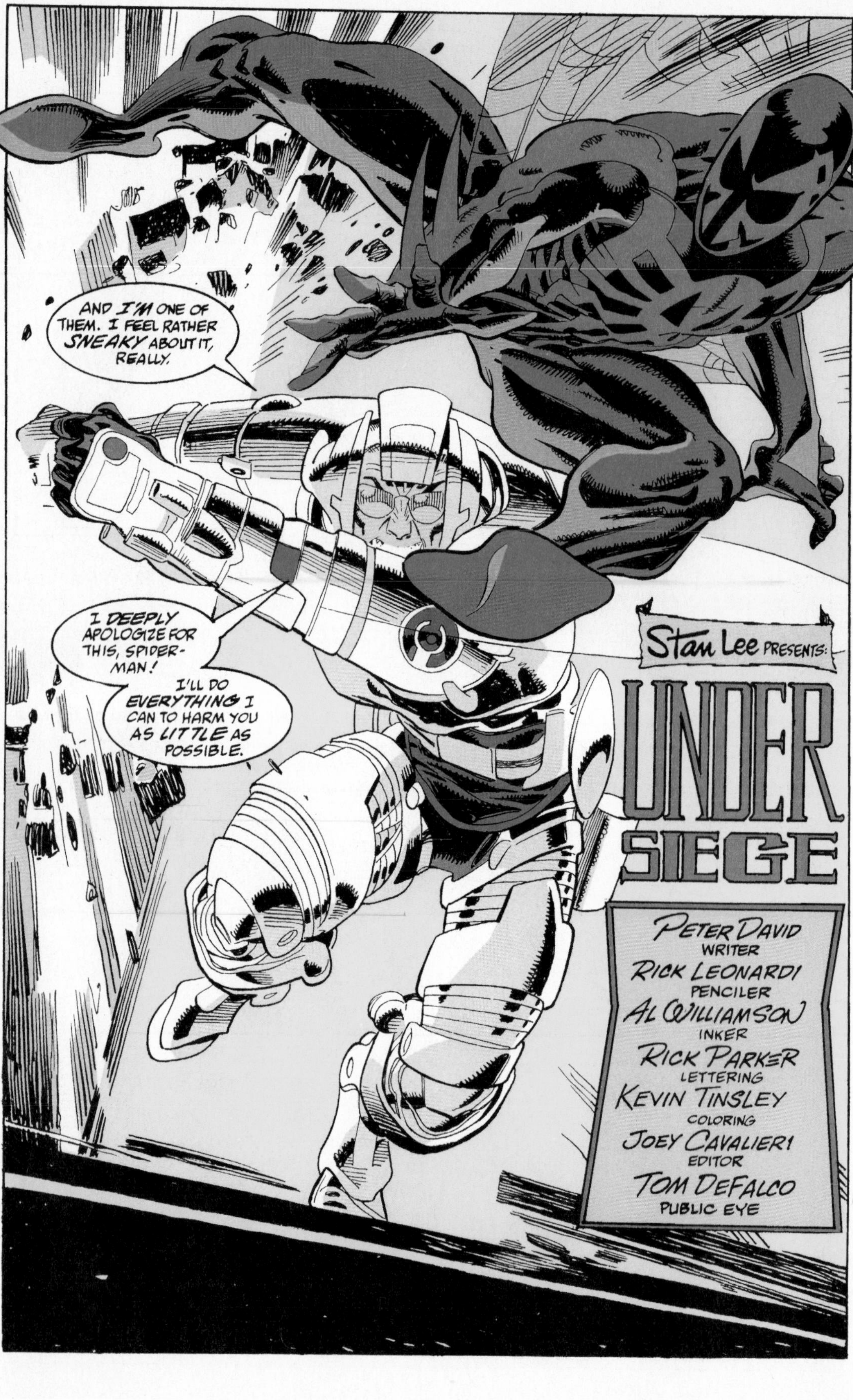
AND I'M ONE OF THEM. I FEEL RATHER SNEAKY ABOUT IT, REALLY.
I DEEPLY APOLOGIZE FOR THIS, SPIDER-MAN!
I'LL DO EVERYTHING I CAN TO HARM YOU AS LITTLE AS POSSIBLE.
Stan Lee PRESENTS:
UNDER SIEGE
PETER DAVID WRITER
RICK LEONARDI PENCILER
AL WILLIAMSON INKER
RICK PARKER LETTERING
KEVIN TINSLEY COLORING
JOEY CAVALIERI EDITOR
TOM DEFALCO PUBLIC EYE

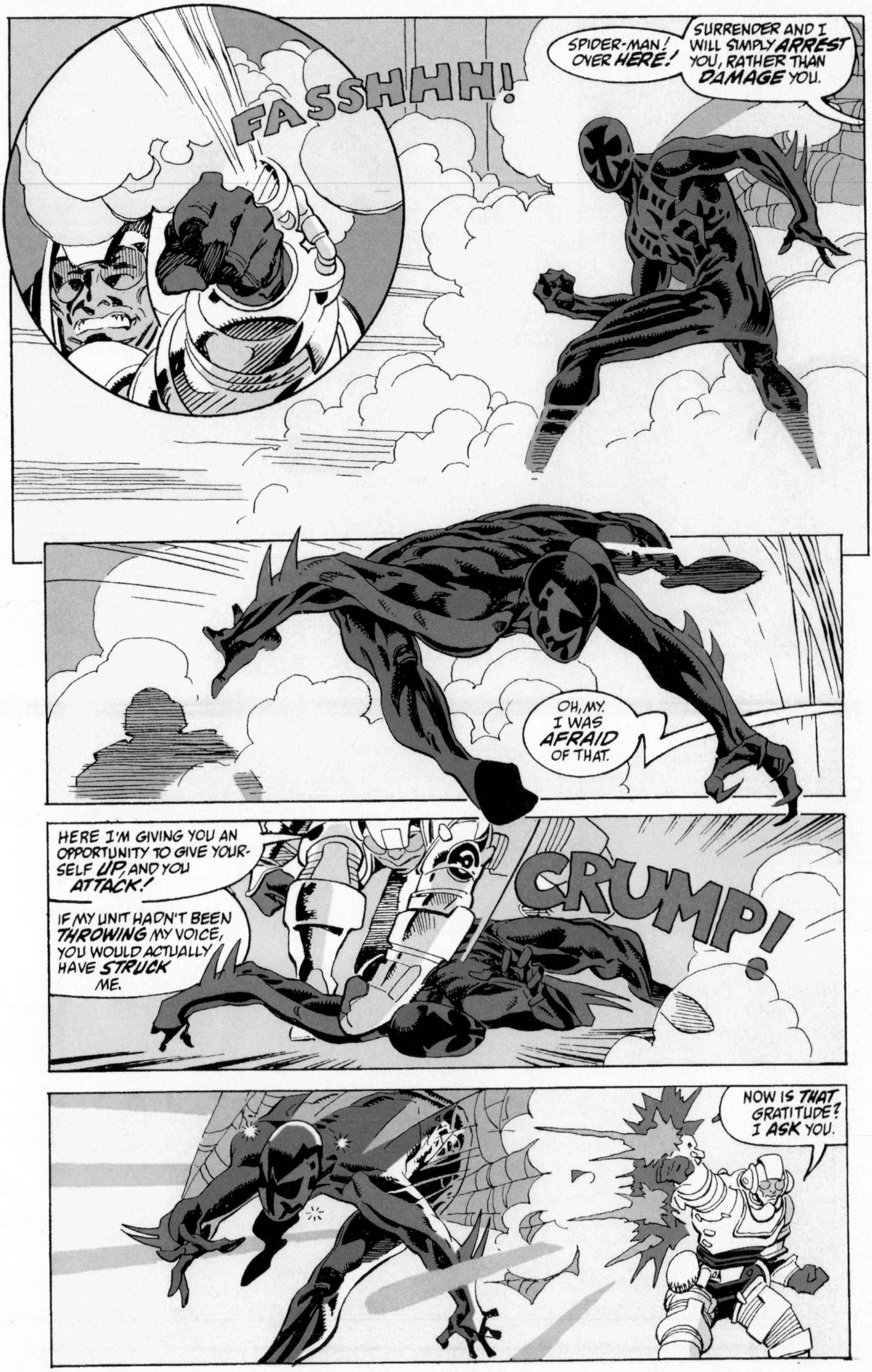
FASSHHH!
SPIDER-MAN! OVER HERE!
SURRENDER AND I WILL SIMPLY ARREST YOU, RATHER THAN DAMAGE YOU.
OH, MY. I WAS AFRAID OF THAT.
HERE I'M GIVING YOU AN OPPORTUNITY TO GIVE YOURSELF UP, AND YOU ATTACK!
IF MY UNIT HADN'T BEEN THROWING MY VOICE, YOU WOULD ACTUALLY HAVE STRUCK ME.
CRUMP!
NOW IS THAT GRATITUDE? I ASK YOU.

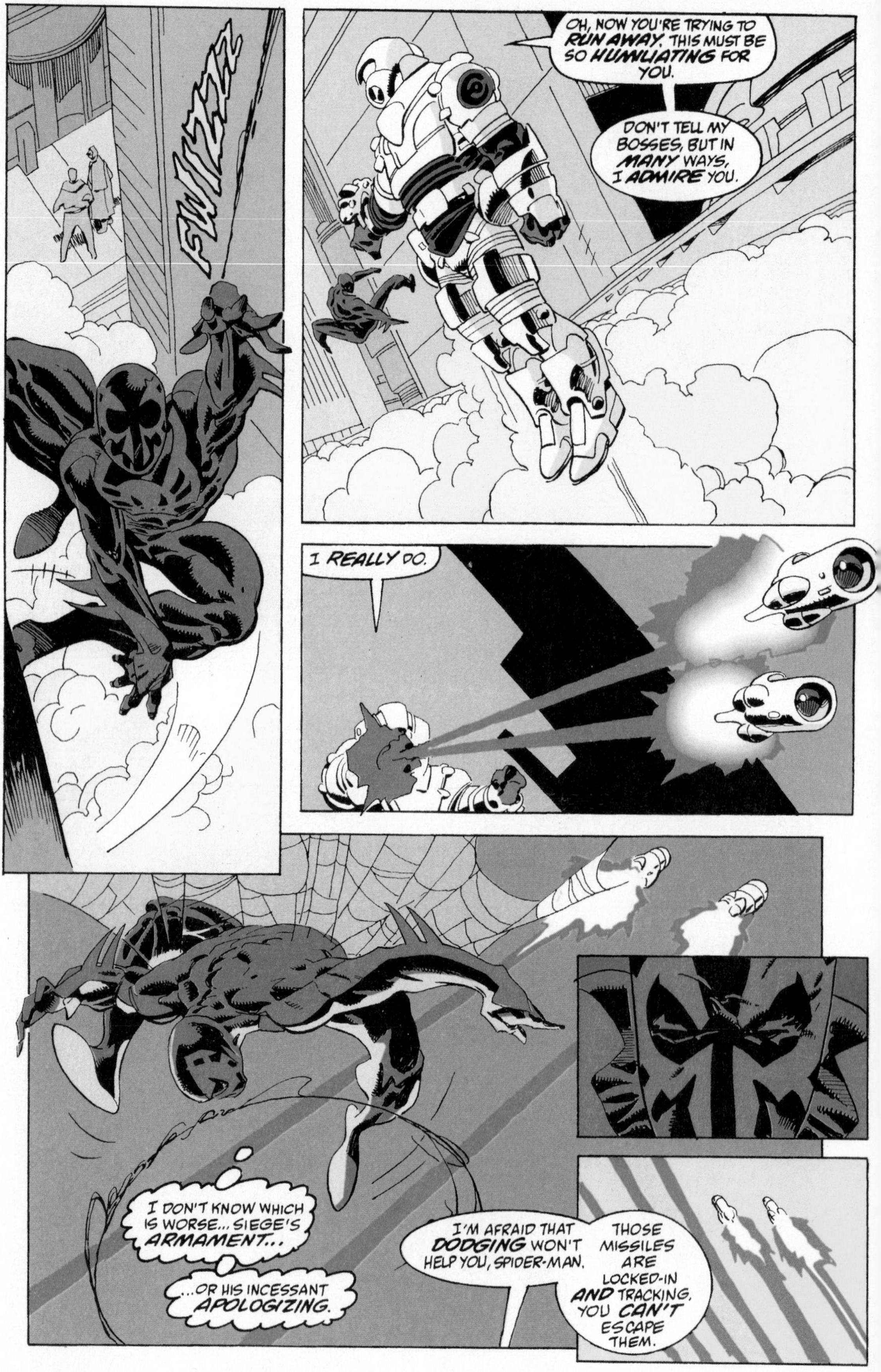
FWIZZZ
OH, NOW YOU'RE TRYING TO RUN AWAY. THIS MUST BE SO HUMILIATING FOR YOU.
DON'T TELL MY BOSSES, BUT IN MANY WAYS, I ADMIRE YOU.
I REALLY DO.
I DON'T KNOW WHICH IS WORSE... SIEGE'S ARMAMENT...
...OR HIS INCESSANT APOLOGIZING.
I'M AFRAID THAT DODGING WON'T HELP YOU, SPIDER-MAN.
THOSE MISSILES ARE LOCKED-IN AND TRACKING. YOU CAN'T ESCAPE THEM.

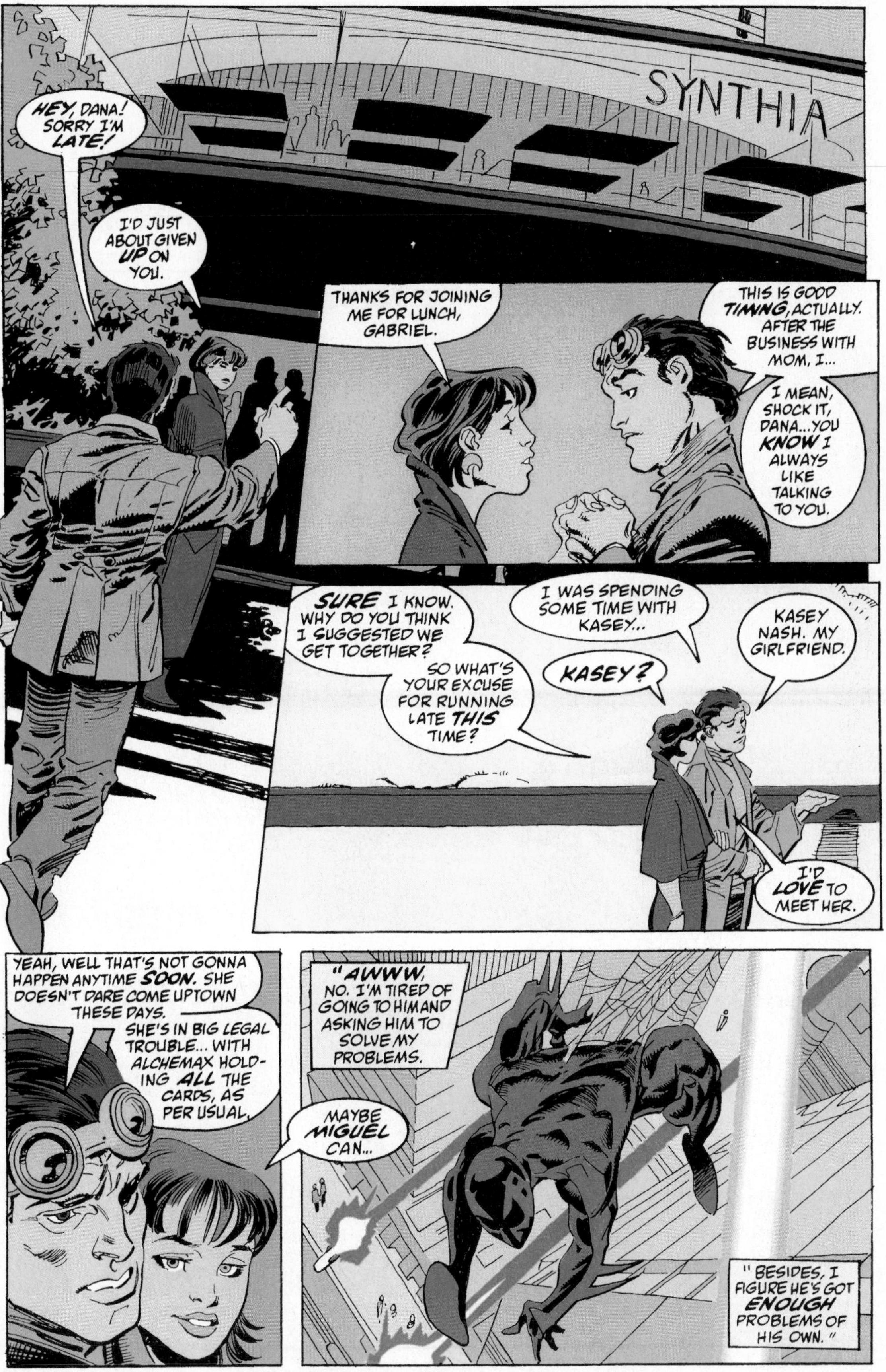
SYNTHIA
HEY, DANA! SORRY I'M LATE!
I'D JUST ABOUT GIVEN UP ON YOU.
THANKS FOR JOINING ME FOR LUNCH, GABRIEL.
THIS IS GOOD TIMING, ACTUALLY. AFTER THE BUSINESS WITH MOM, I...
I MEAN, SHOCK IT, DANA...YOU KNOW I ALWAYS LIKE TALKING TO YOU.
SURE I KNOW. WHY DO YOU THINK I SUGGESTED WE GET TOGETHER?
SO WHAT'S YOUR EXCUSE FOR RUNNING LATE THIS TIME?
I WAS SPENDING SOME TIME WITH KASEY...
KASEY?
KASEY NASH. MY GIRLFRIEND.
I'D LOVE TO MEET HER.
YEAH, WELL THAT'S NOT GONNA HAPPEN ANYTIME SOON. SHE DOESN'T DARE COME UPTOWN THESE DAYS.
SHE'S IN BIG LEGAL TROUBLE... WITH ALCHEMAX HOLDING ALL THE CARDS, AS PER USUAL.
MAYBE MIGUEL CAN...
"AWWW, NO. I'M TIRED OF GOING TO HIM AND ASKING HIM TO SOLVE MY PROBLEMS.
"BESIDES, I FIGURE HE'S GOT ENOUGH PROBLEMS OF HIS OWN."

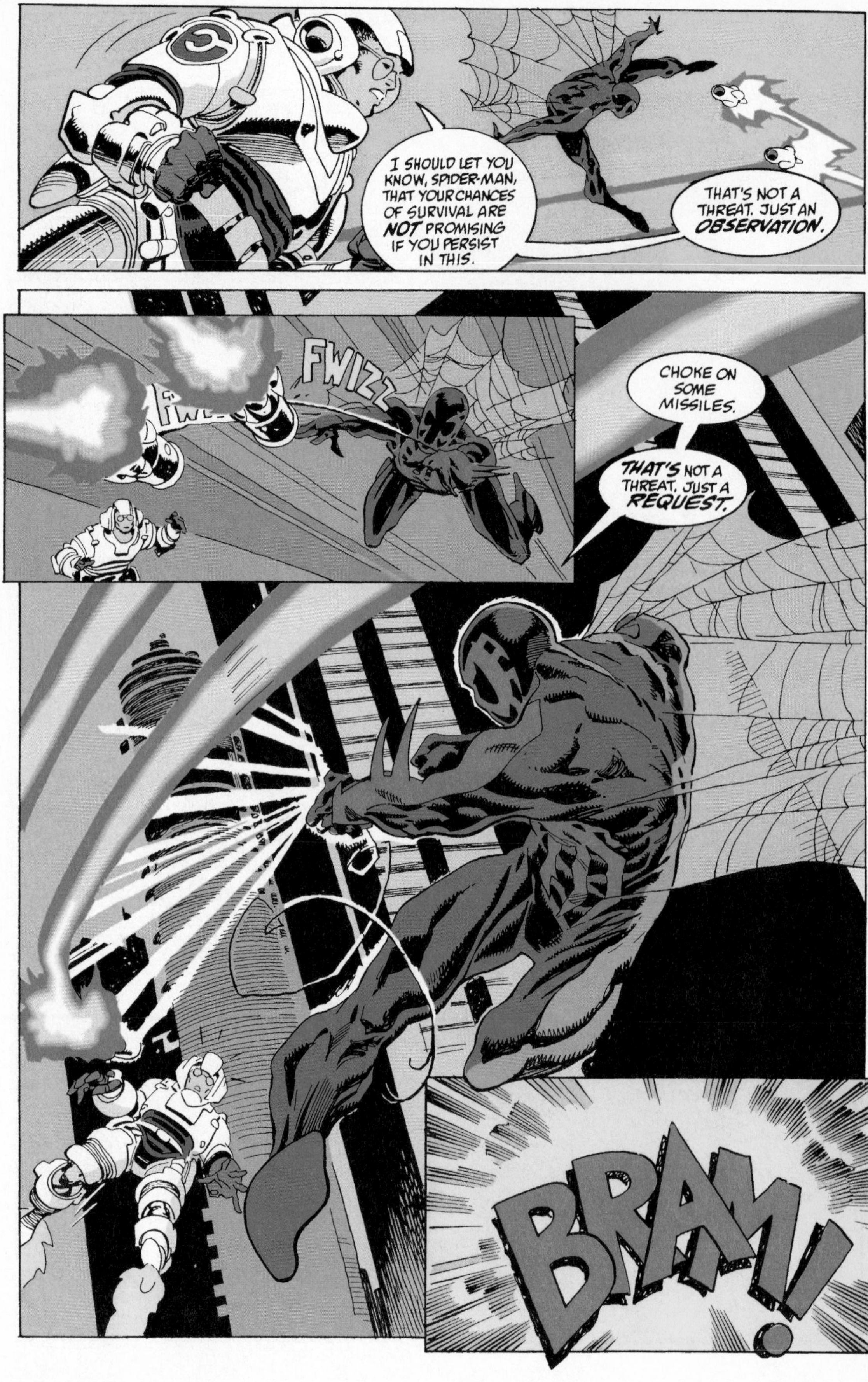
I SHOULD LET YOU KNOW, SPIDER-MAN, THAT YOUR CHANCES OF SURVIVAL ARE NOT PROMISING IF YOU PERSIST IN THIS.
THAT'S NOT A THREAT. JUST AN OBSERVATION.
FWIZZ
CHOKE ON SOME MISSILES.
THAT'S NOT A THREAT, JUST A REQUEST.
BRAM!

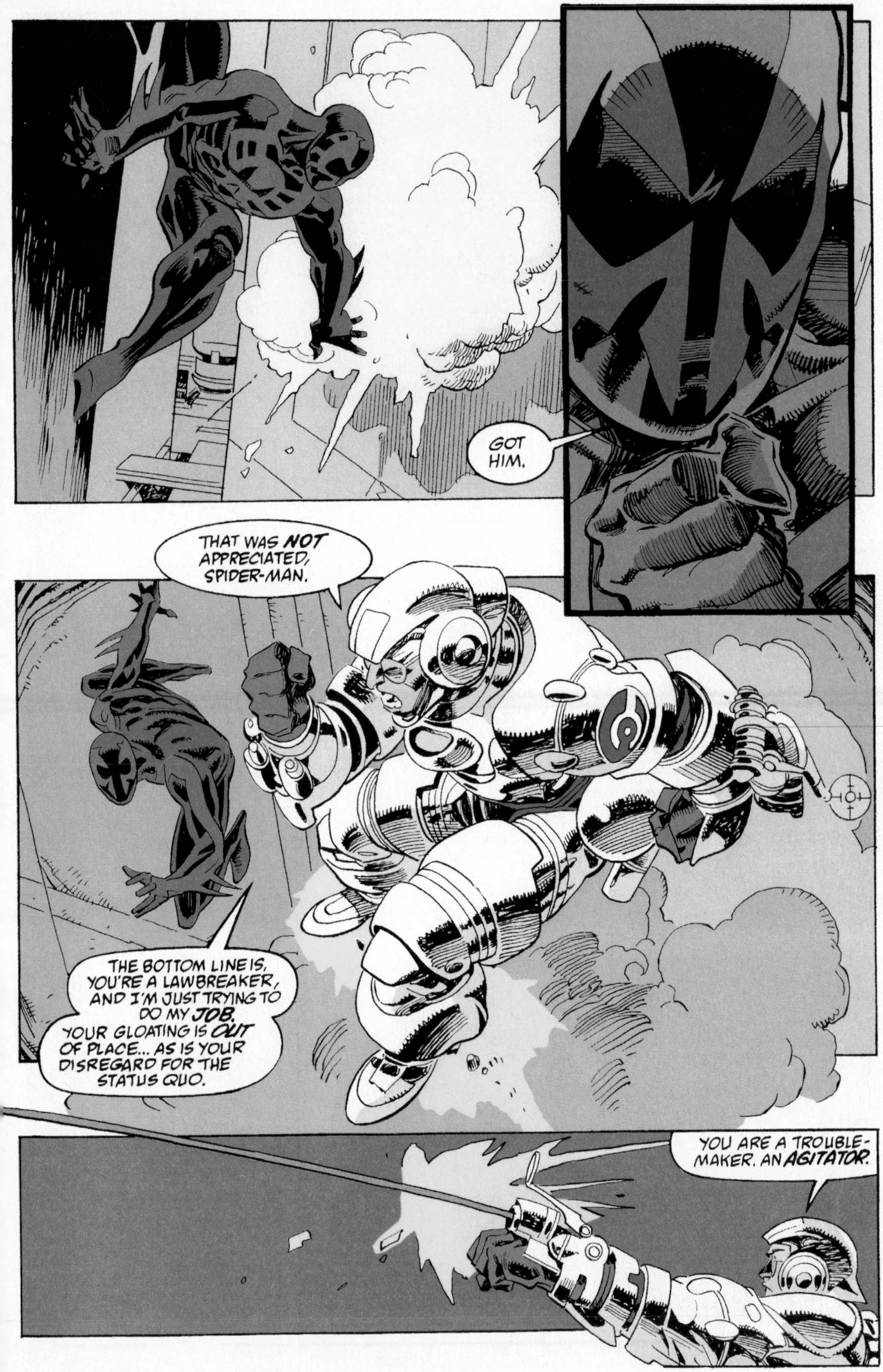
GOT HIM.
THAT WAS NOT APPRECIATED, SPIDER-MAN.
THE BOTTOM LINE IS, YOU'RE A LAWBREAKER, AND I'M JUST TRYING TO DO MY JOB. YOUR GLOATING IS OUT OF PLACE... AS IS YOUR DISREGARD FOR THE STATUS QUO.
YOU ARE A TROUBLE-MAKER. AN AGITATOR.

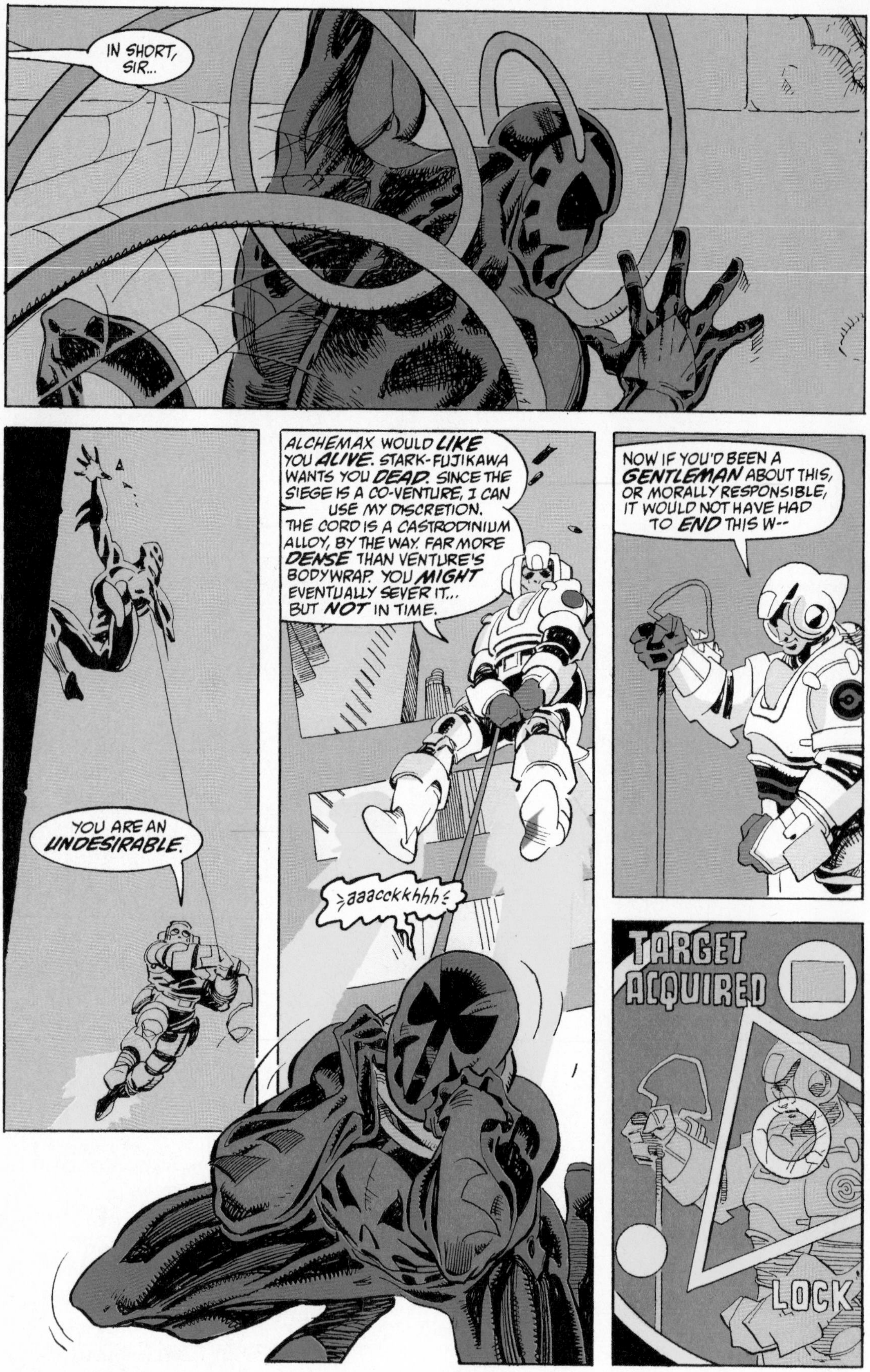
IN SHORT, SIR...
YOU ARE AN UNDESIRABLE.
ALCHEMAX WOULD LIKE YOU ALIVE. STARK-FUJIKAWA WANTS YOU DEAD. SINCE THE SIEGE IS A CO-VENTURE, I CAN USE MY DISCRETION.
THE CORD IS A CASTRODINIUM ALLOY, BY THE WAY. FAR MORE DENSE THAN VENTURE'S BODYWRAP. YOU MIGHT EVENTUALLY SEVER IT... BUT NOT IN TIME.
aaacckkhhh
NOW IF YOU'D BEEN A GENTLEMAN ABOUT THIS, OR MORALLY RESPONSIBLE, IT WOULD NOT HAVE HAD TO END THIS W--
TARGET ACQUIRED
LOCK

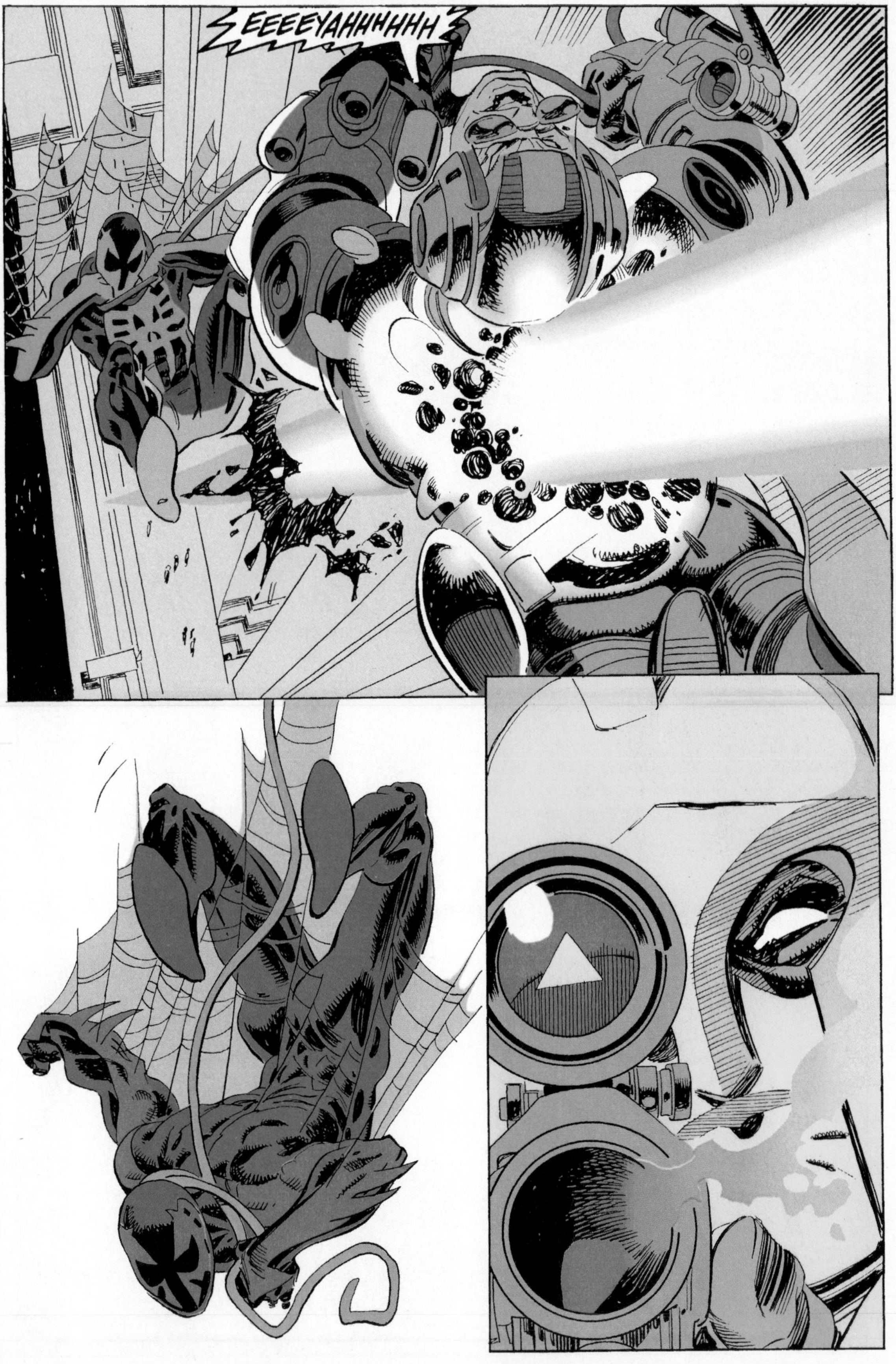
EEEEYAHHHHHH

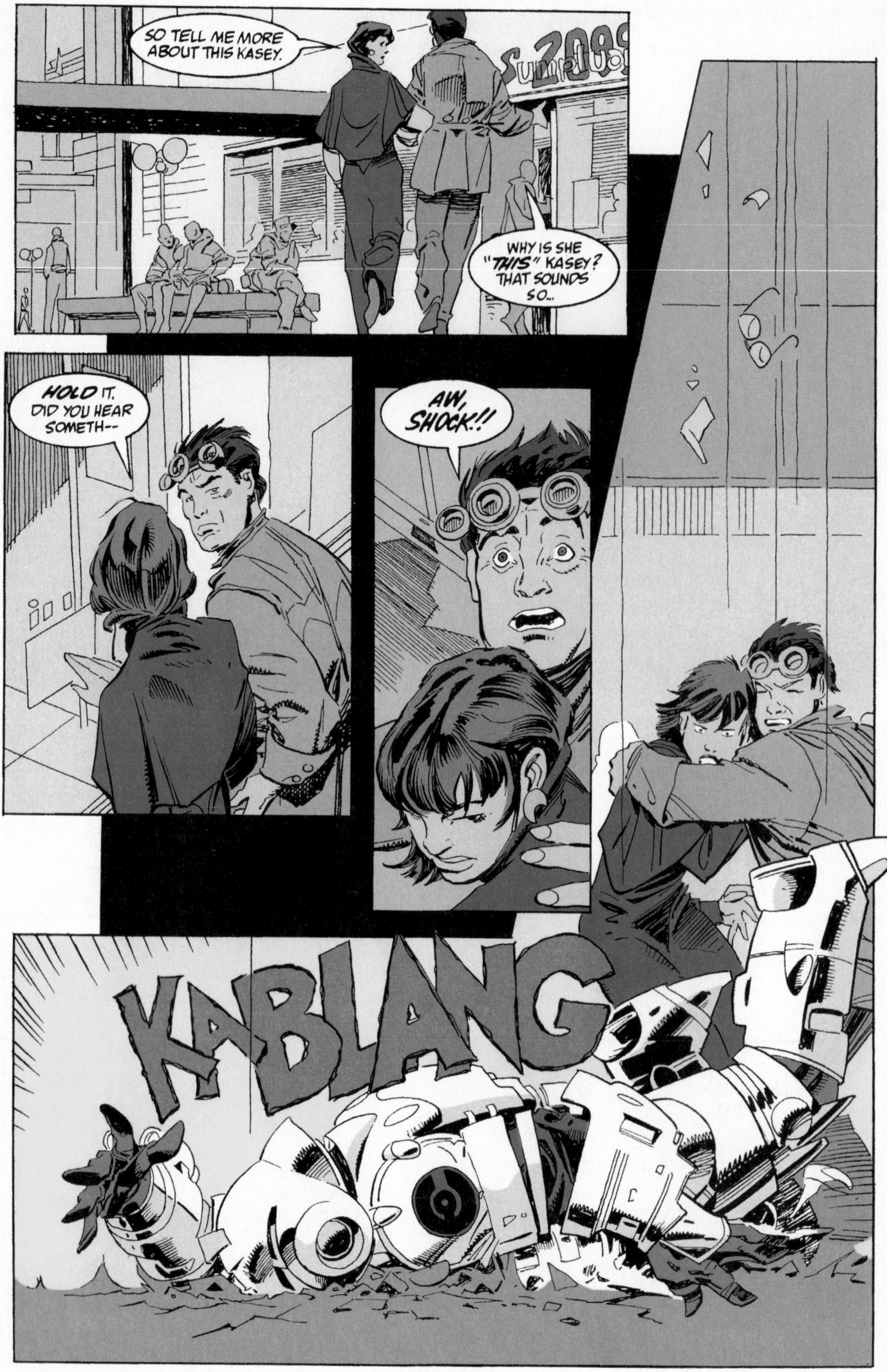
SO TELL ME MORE ABOUT THIS KASEY.
SUMP 2099
WHY IS SHE "THIS" KASEY? THAT SOUNDS SO...
HOLD IT. DID YOU HEAR SOMETH--
AW, SHOCK!!
KABLANG

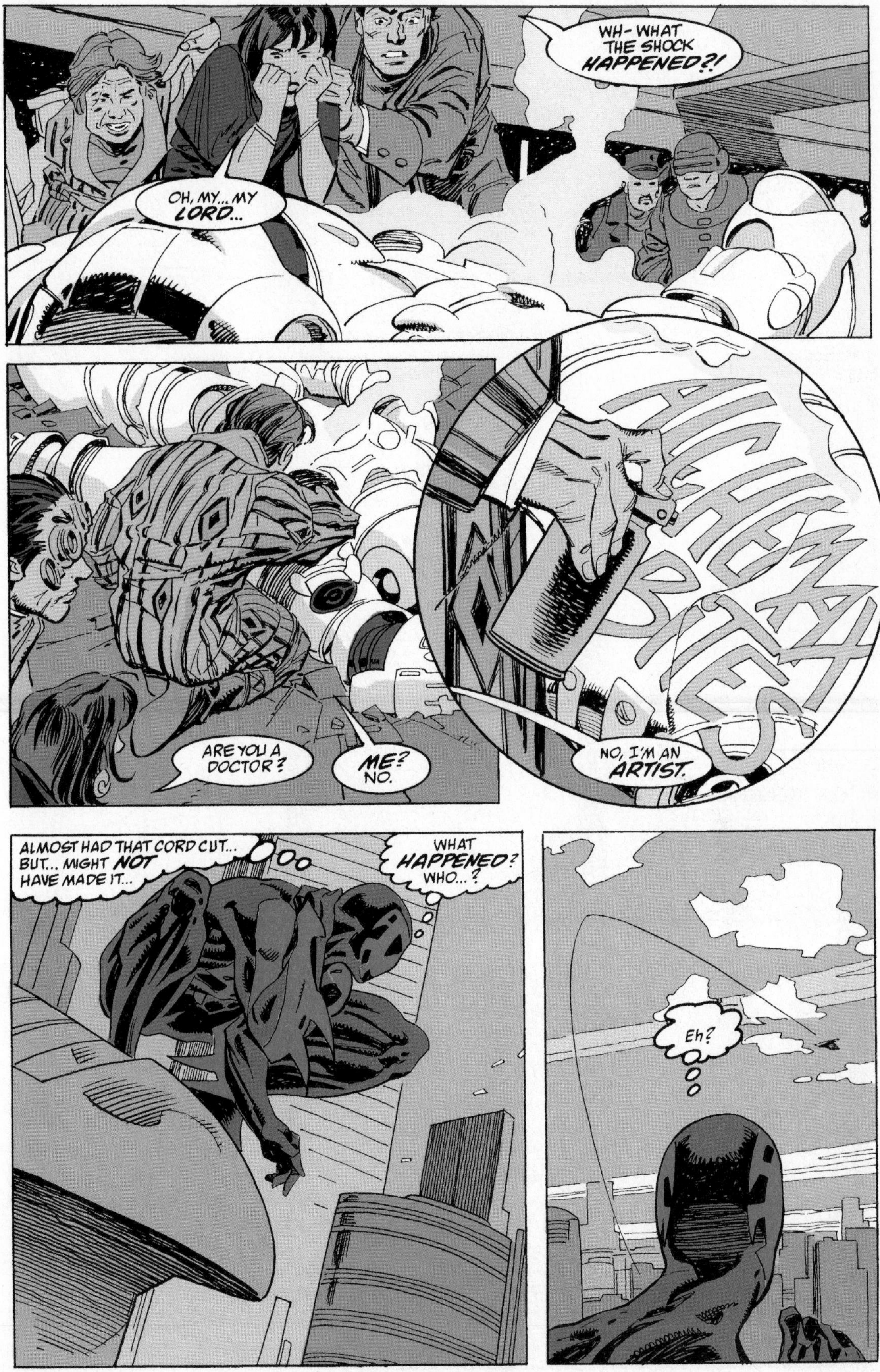
OH, MY... MY LORD...
WH- WHAT THE SHOCK HAPPENED?!
ARE YOU A DOCTOR?
ME? NO.
ALCHEMAX BITES
NO, I'M AN ARTIST.
ALMOST HAD THAT CORD CUT... BUT... MIGHT NOT HAVE MADE IT...
WHAT HAPPENED? WHO...?
Eh?

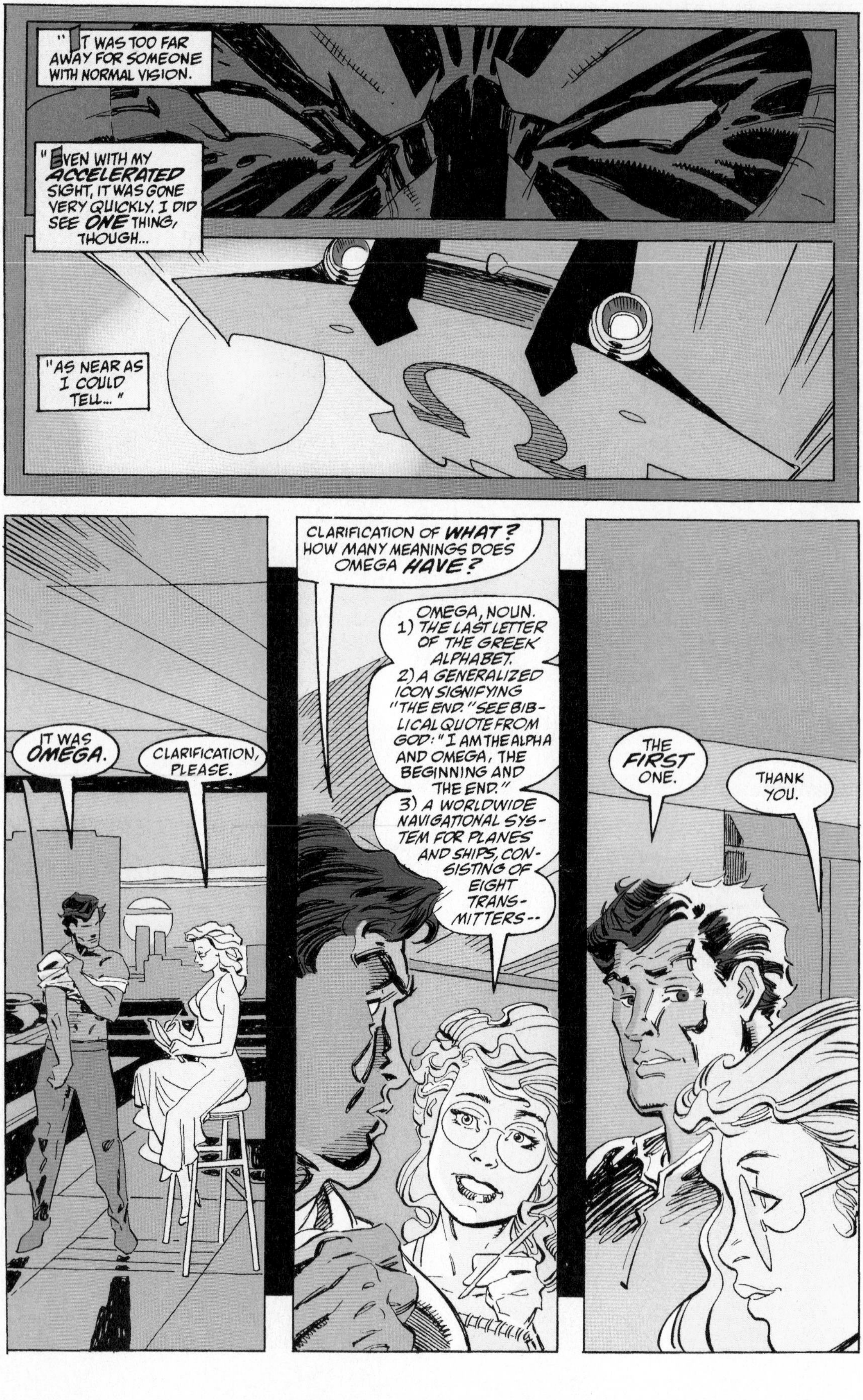

"IT WAS TOO FAR AWAY FOR SOMEONE WITH NORMAL VISION.
"EVEN WITH MY ACCELERATED SIGHT, IT WAS GONE VERY QUICKLY. I DID SEE ONE THING, THOUGH...
"AS NEAR AS I COULD TELL..."
IT WAS OMEGA.
CLARIFICATION, PLEASE.
CLARIFICATION OF WHAT? HOW MANY MEANINGS DOES OMEGA HAVE?
OMEGA, NOUN. 1) THE LAST LETTER OF THE GREEK ALPHABET. 2) A GENERALIZED ICON SIGNIFYING "THE END." SEE BIBLICAL QUOTE FROM GOD: "I AM THE ALPHA AND OMEGA, THE BEGINNING AND THE END." 3) A WORLDWIDE NAVIGATIONAL SYSTEM FOR PLANES AND SHIPS, CONSISTING OF EIGHT TRANSMITTERS--
THE FIRST ONE.
THANK YOU.

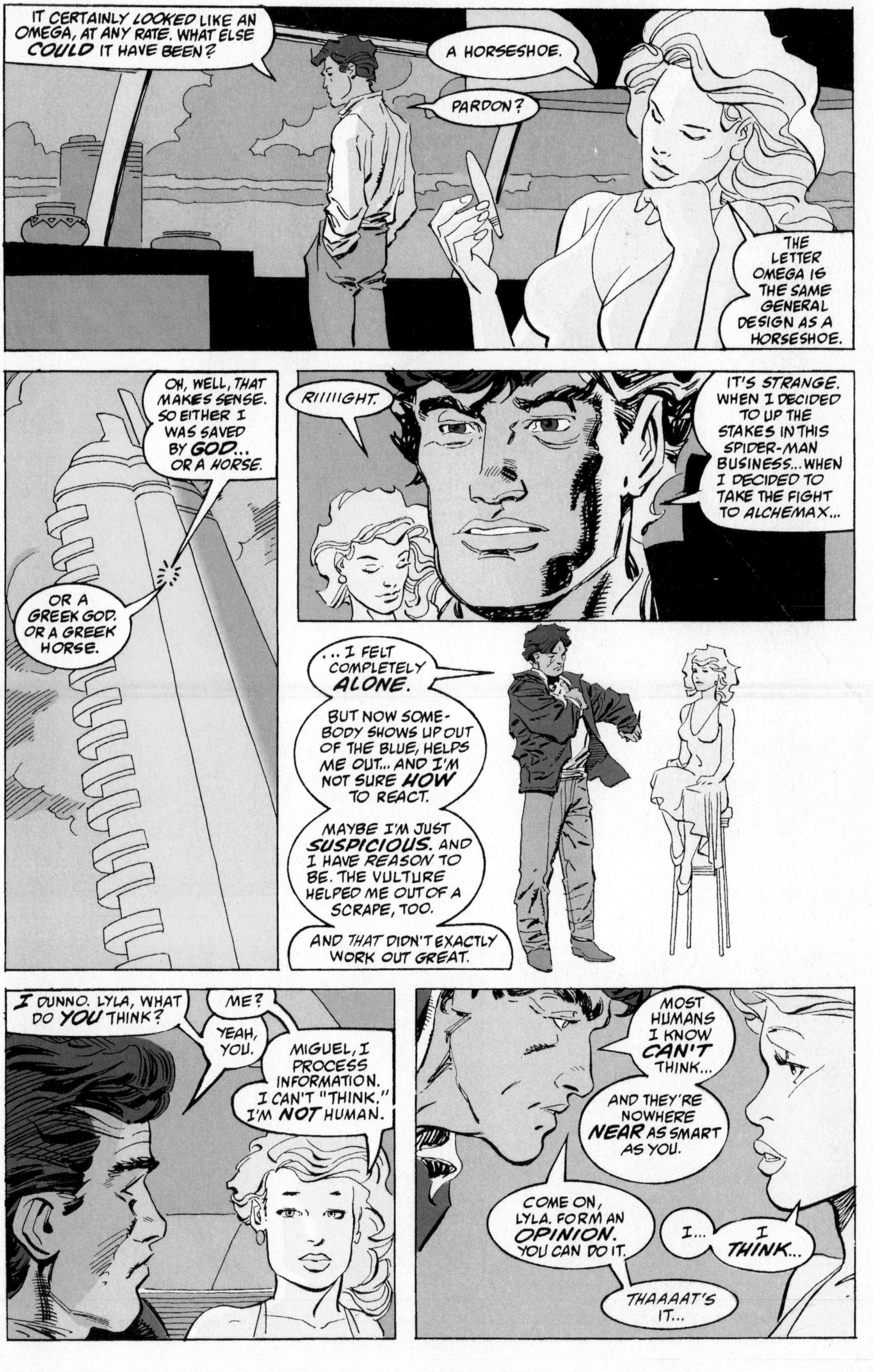

IT CERTAINLY LOOKED LIKE AN OMEGA, AT ANY RATE. WHAT ELSE COULD IT HAVE BEEN?
A HORSESHOE.
PARDON?
THE LETTER OMEGA IS THE SAME GENERAL DESIGN AS A HORSESHOE.
OH, WELL, THAT MAKES SENSE. SO EITHER I WAS SAVED BY GOD... OR A HORSE.
OR A GREEK GOD. OR A GREEK HORSE.
RIIIIIGHT.
IT'S STRANGE. WHEN I DECIDED TO UP THE STAKES IN THIS SPIDER-MAN BUSINESS... WHEN I DECIDED TO TAKE THE FIGHT TO ALCHEMAX...
...I FELT COMPLETELY ALONE.
BUT NOW SOMEBODY SHOWS UP OUT OF THE BLUE, HELPS ME OUT... AND I'M NOT SURE HOW TO REACT.
MAYBE I'M JUST SUSPICIOUS. AND I HAVE REASON TO BE. THE VULTURE HELPED ME OUT OF A SCRAPE, TOO.
AND THAT DIDN'T EXACTLY WORK OUT GREAT.
I DUNNO. LYLA, WHAT DO YOU THINK?
ME?
YEAH, YOU.
MIGUEL, I PROCESS INFORMATION. I CAN'T "THINK." I'M NOT HUMAN.
MOST HUMANS I KNOW CAN'T THINK...
AND THEY'RE NOWHERE NEAR AS SMART AS YOU.
COME ON, LYLA. FORM AN OPINION. YOU CAN DO IT.
I...
I THINK...
THAAAAT'S IT...

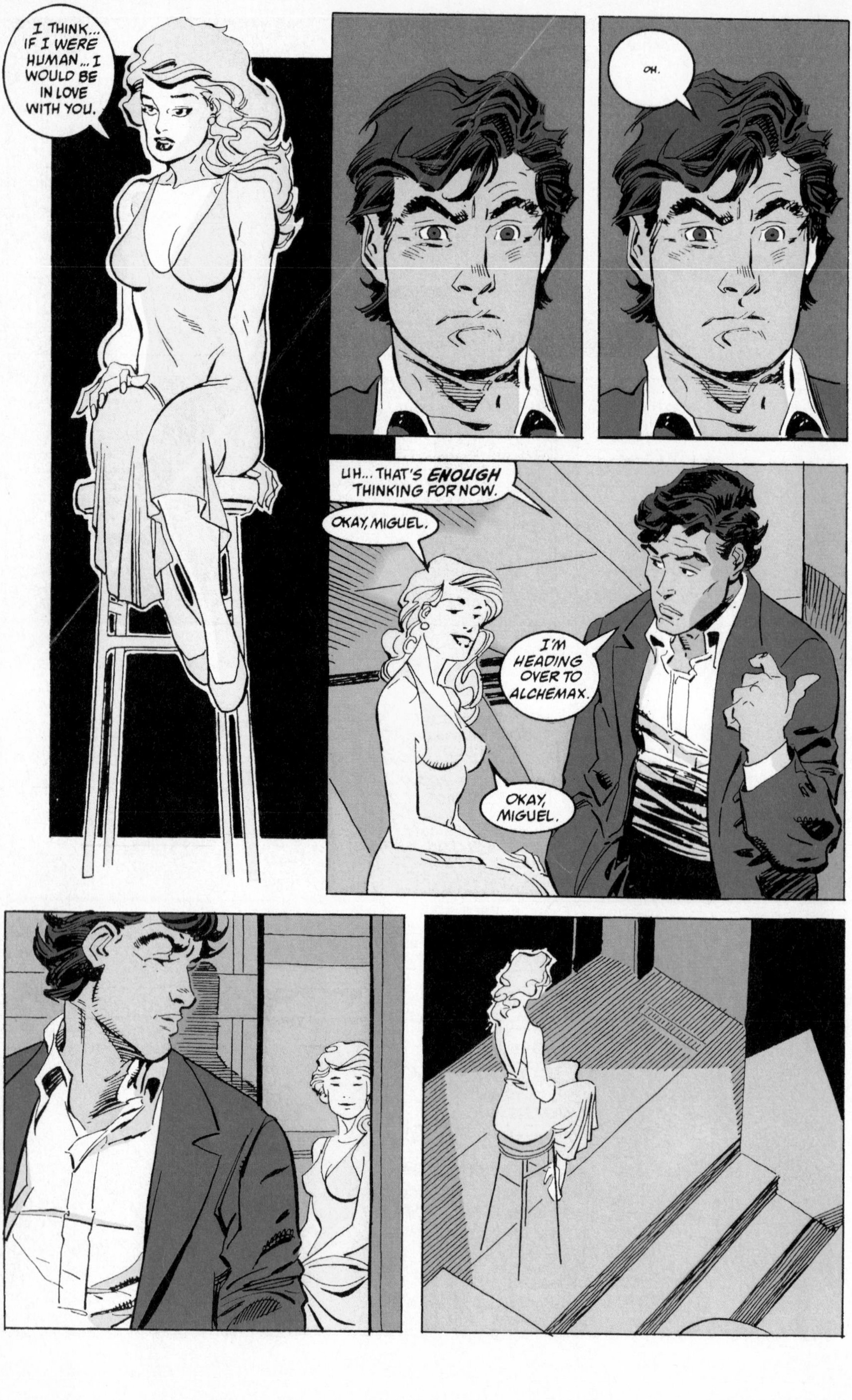
I THINK... IF I WERE HUMAN... I WOULD BE IN LOVE WITH YOU.
OH.
UH... THAT'S ENOUGH THINKING FOR NOW.
OKAY, MIGUEL.
I'M HEADING OVER TO ALCHEMAX.
OKAY, MIGUEL.

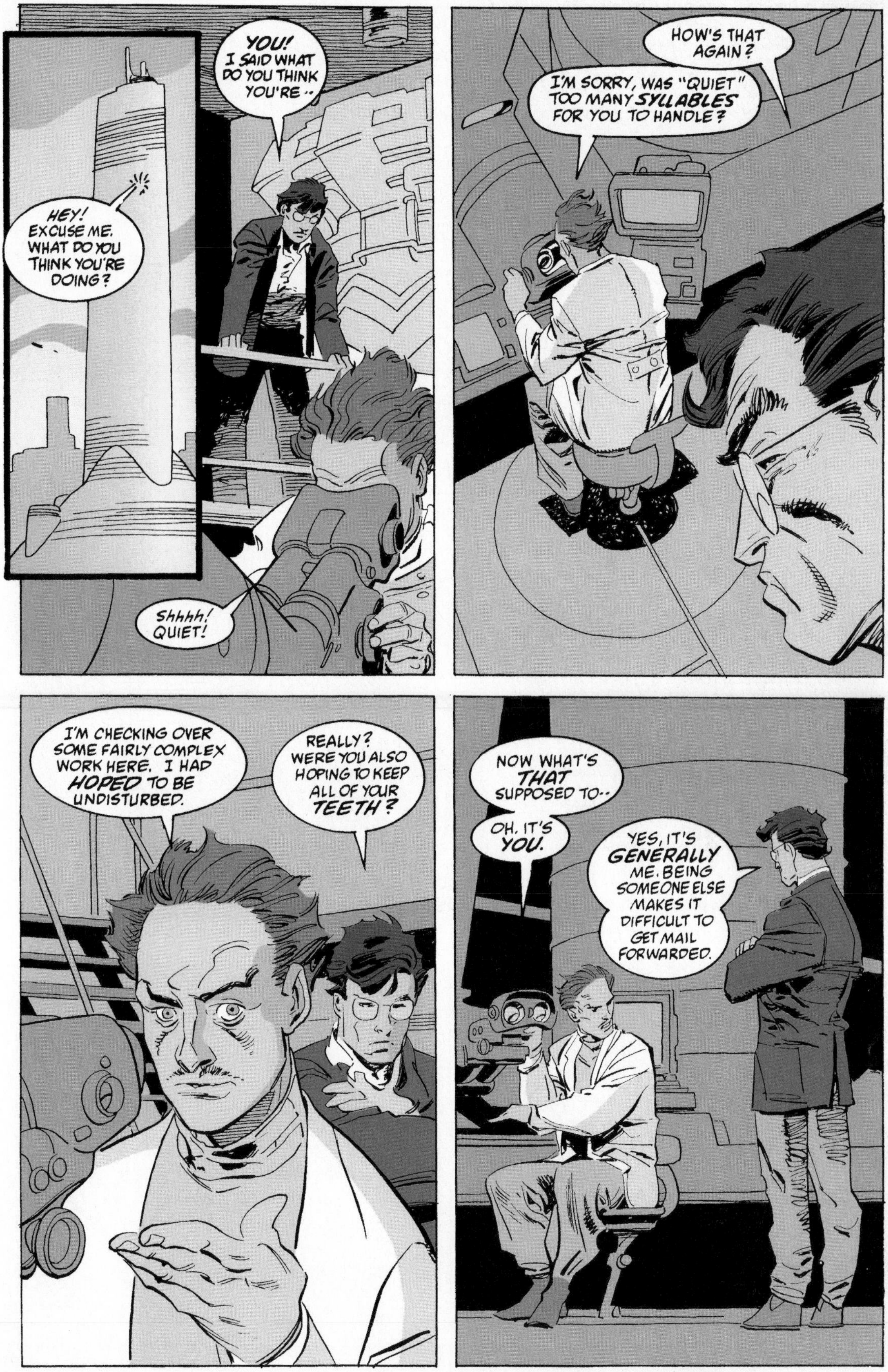

YOU! I SAID WHAT DO YOU THINK YOU'RE --
HEY! EXCUSE ME. WHAT DO YOU THINK YOU'RE DOING?
Shhhh! QUIET!
HOW'S THAT AGAIN?
I'M SORRY, WAS "QUIET" TOO MANY SYLLABLES FOR YOU TO HANDLE?
I'M CHECKING OVER SOME FAIRLY COMPLEX WORK HERE. I HAD HOPED TO BE UNDISTURBED.
REALLY? WERE YOU ALSO HOPING TO KEEP ALL OF YOUR TEETH?
NOW WHAT'S THAT SUPPOSED TO--
OH. IT'S YOU.
YES, IT'S GENERALLY ME. BEING SOMEONE ELSE MAKES IT DIFFICULT TO GET MAIL FORWARDED.

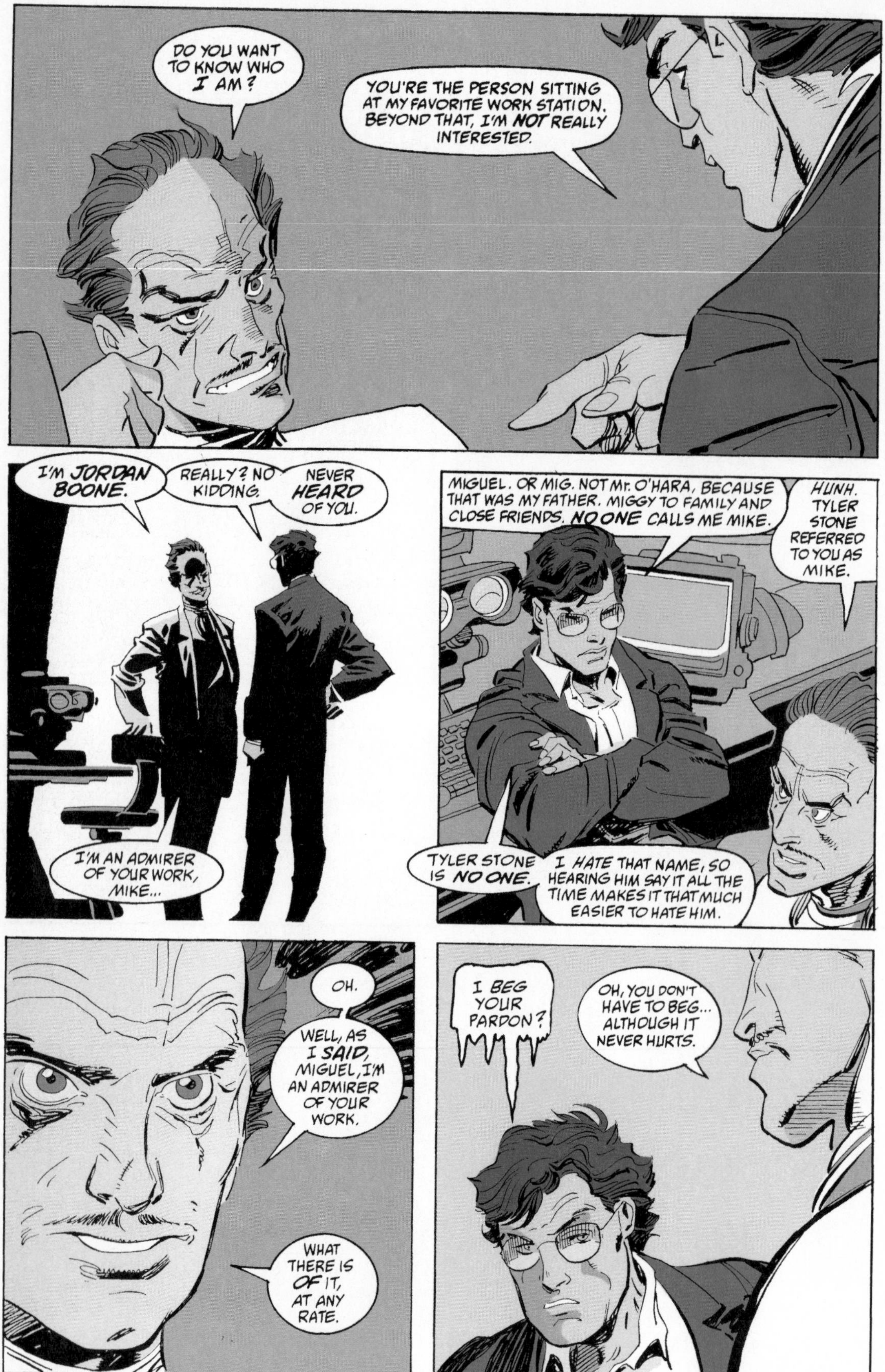
DO YOU WANT TO KNOW WHO I AM?
YOU'RE THE PERSON SITTING AT MY FAVORITE WORK STATION. BEYOND THAT, I'M NOT REALLY INTERESTED.
I'M JORDAN BOONE.
REALLY? NO KIDDING.
NEVER HEARD OF YOU.
I'M AN ADMIRER OF YOUR WORK, MIKE...
MIGUEL. OR MIG. NOT Mr. O'HARA, BECAUSE THAT WAS MY FATHER. MIGGY TO FAMILY AND CLOSE FRIENDS. NO ONE CALLS ME MIKE.
HUNH. TYLER STONE REFERRED TO YOU AS MIKE.
TYLER STONE IS NO ONE.
I HATE THAT NAME, SO HEARING HIM SAY IT ALL THE TIME MAKES IT THAT MUCH EASIER TO HATE HIM.
OH.
WELL, AS I SAID, MIGUEL, I'M AN ADMIRER OF YOUR WORK.
WHAT THERE IS OF IT, AT ANY RATE.
I BEG YOUR PARDON?
OH, YOU DON'T HAVE TO BEG... ALTHOUGH IT NEVER HURTS.

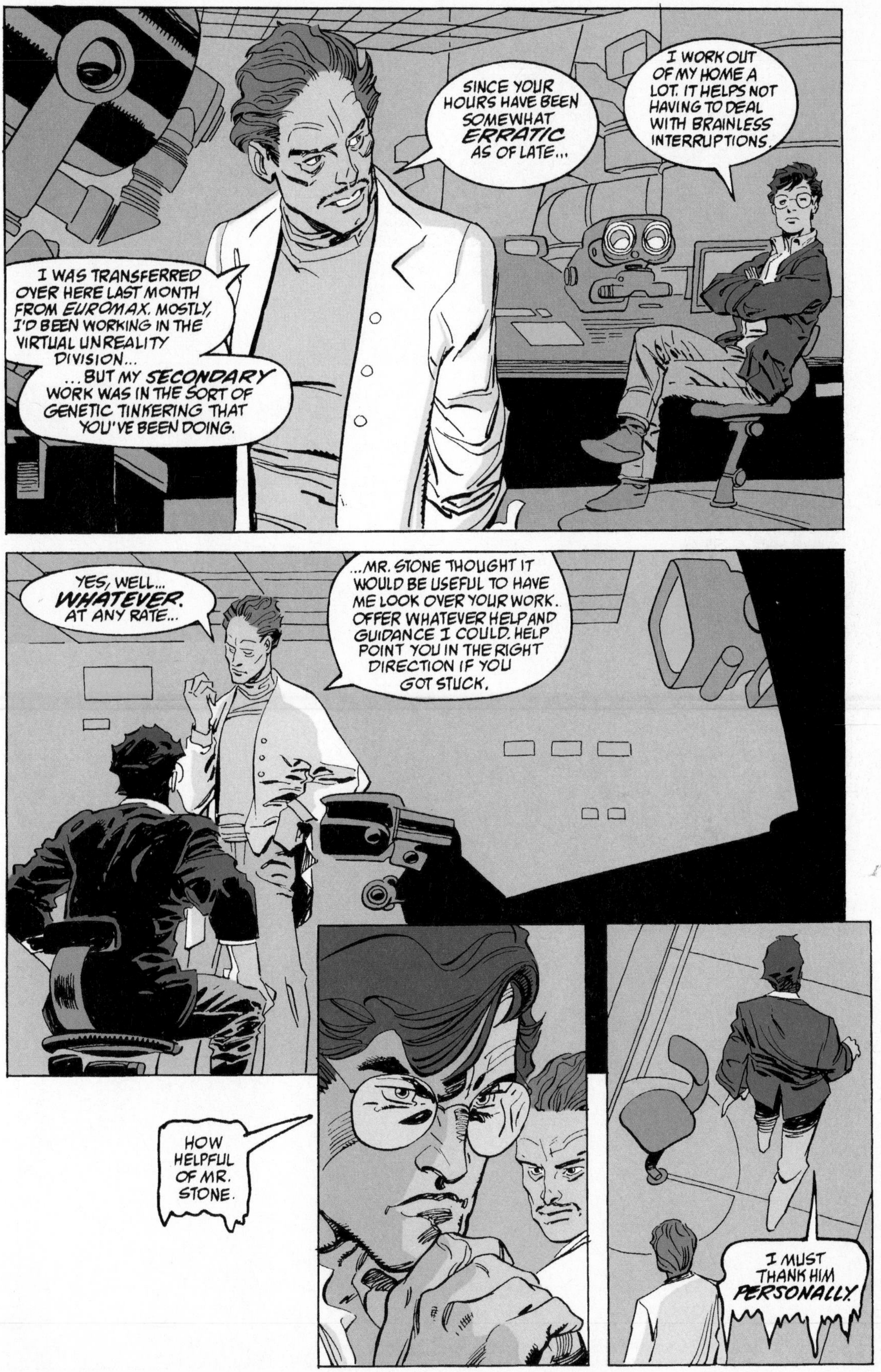

SINCE YOUR HOURS HAVE BEEN SOMEWHAT ERRATIC AS OF LATE...
I WORK OUT OF MY HOME A LOT. IT HELPS NOT HAVING TO DEAL WITH BRAINLESS INTERRUPTIONS.
I WAS TRANSFERRED OVER HERE LAST MONTH FROM EUROMAX. MOSTLY, I'D BEEN WORKING IN THE VIRTUAL UNREALITY DIVISION...
...BUT MY SECONDARY WORK WAS IN THE SORT OF GENETIC TINKERING THAT YOU'VE BEEN DOING.
YES, WELL... WHATEVER. AT ANY RATE...
...MR. STONE THOUGHT IT WOULD BE USEFUL TO HAVE ME LOOK OVER YOUR WORK. OFFER WHATEVER HELP AND GUIDANCE I COULD. HELP POINT YOU IN THE RIGHT DIRECTION IF YOU GOT STUCK.
HOW HELPFUL OF MR. STONE.
I MUST THANK HIM PERSONALLY.

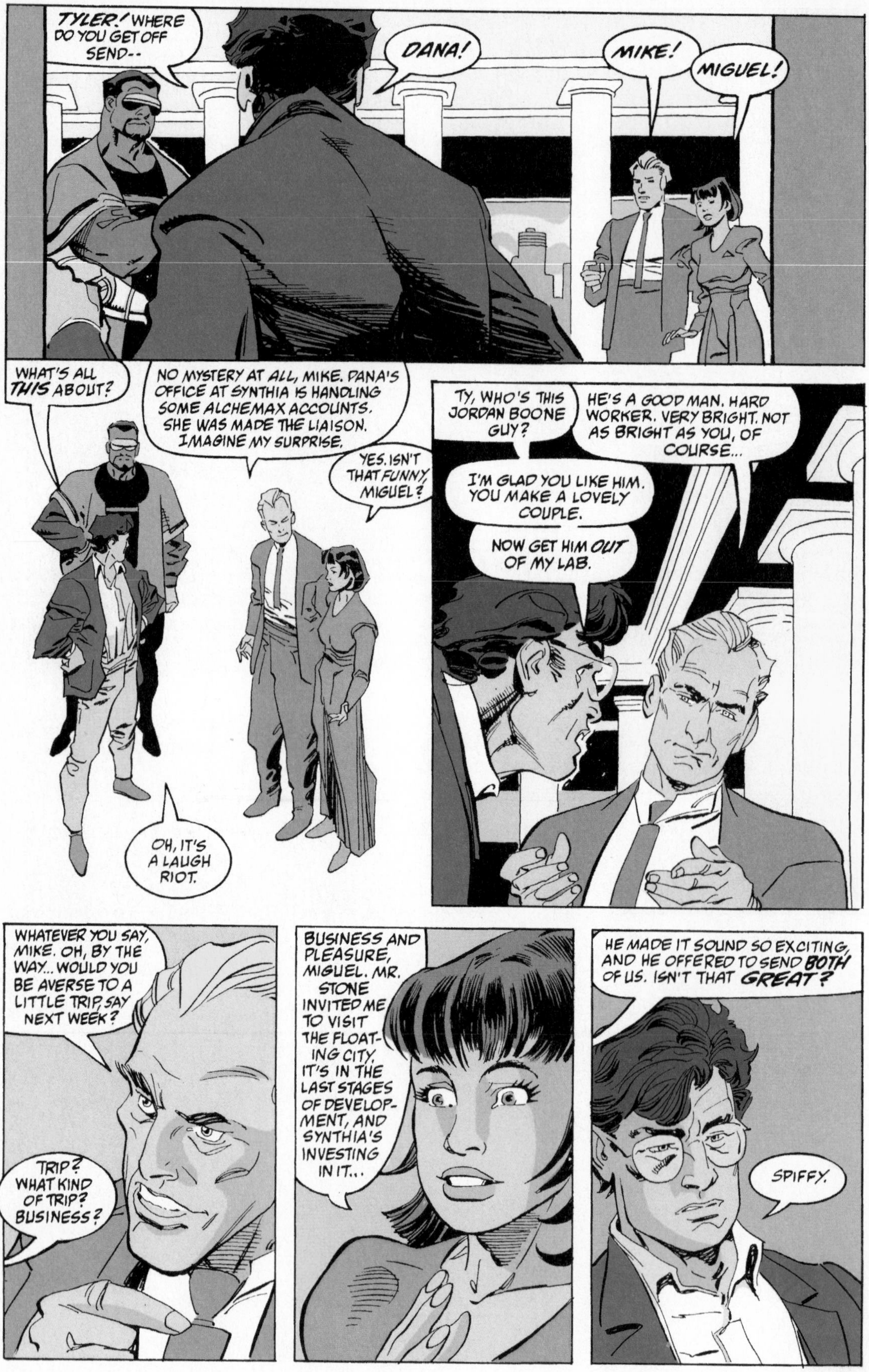
TYLER! WHERE DO YOU GET OFF SEND--
DANA!
MIKE!
MIGUEL!
WHAT'S ALL THIS ABOUT?
NO MYSTERY AT ALL, MIKE. DANA'S OFFICE AT SYNTHIA IS HANDLING SOME ALCHEMAX ACCOUNTS. SHE WAS MADE THE LIAISON. IMAGINE MY SURPRISE.
YES. ISN'T THAT FUNNY, MIGUEL?
OH, IT'S A LAUGH RIOT.
TY, WHO'S THIS JORDAN BOONE GUY?
HE'S A GOOD MAN. HARD WORKER. VERY BRIGHT. NOT AS BRIGHT AS YOU, OF COURSE...
I'M GLAD YOU LIKE HIM. YOU MAKE A LOVELY COUPLE.
NOW GET HIM OUT OF MY LAB.
WHATEVER YOU SAY, MIKE. OH, BY THE WAY... WOULD YOU BE AVERSE TO A LITTLE TRIP, SAY NEXT WEEK?
TRIP? WHAT KIND OF TRIP? BUSINESS?
BUSINESS AND PLEASURE, MIGUEL. MR. STONE INVITED ME TO VISIT THE FLOATING CITY. IT'S IN THE LAST STAGES OF DEVELOPMENT, AND SYNTHIA'S INVESTING IN IT...
HE MADE IT SOUND SO EXCITING, AND HE OFFERED TO SEND BOTH OF US. ISN'T THAT GREAT?
SPIFFY.

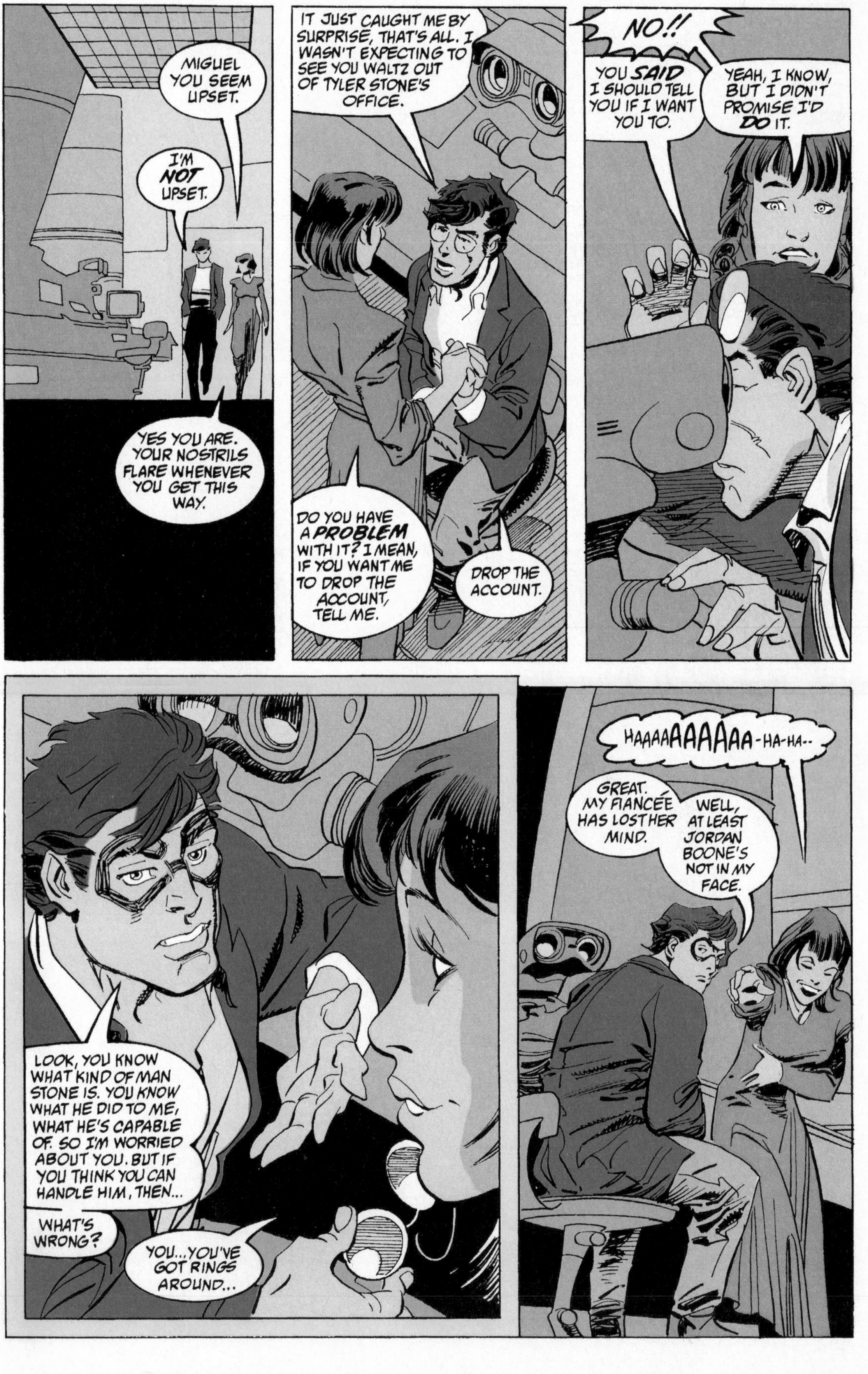
MIGUEL YOU SEEM UPSET.
I'M NOT UPSET.
YES YOU ARE. YOUR NOSTRILS FLARE WHENEVER YOU GET THIS WAY.
IT JUST CAUGHT ME BY SURPRISE, THAT'S ALL. I WASN'T EXPECTING TO SEE YOU WALTZ OUT OF TYLER STONE'S OFFICE.
DO YOU HAVE A PROBLEM WITH IT? I MEAN, IF YOU WANT ME TO DROP THE ACCOUNT, TELL ME.
DROP THE ACCOUNT.
NO!!
YOU SAID I SHOULD TELL YOU IF I WANT YOU TO.
YEAH, I KNOW, BUT I DIDN'T PROMISE I'D DO IT.
LOOK, YOU KNOW WHAT KIND OF MAN STONE IS. YOU KNOW WHAT HE DID TO ME, WHAT HE'S CAPABLE OF. SO I'M WORRIED ABOUT YOU. BUT IF YOU THINK YOU CAN HANDLE HIM, THEN...
WHAT'S WRONG?
YOU... YOU'VE GOT RINGS AROUND...
HAAAAAAAAAA-HA-HA--
GREAT. MY FIANCÉE HAS LOST HER MIND.
WELL, AT LEAST JORDAN BOONE'S NOT IN MY FACE.

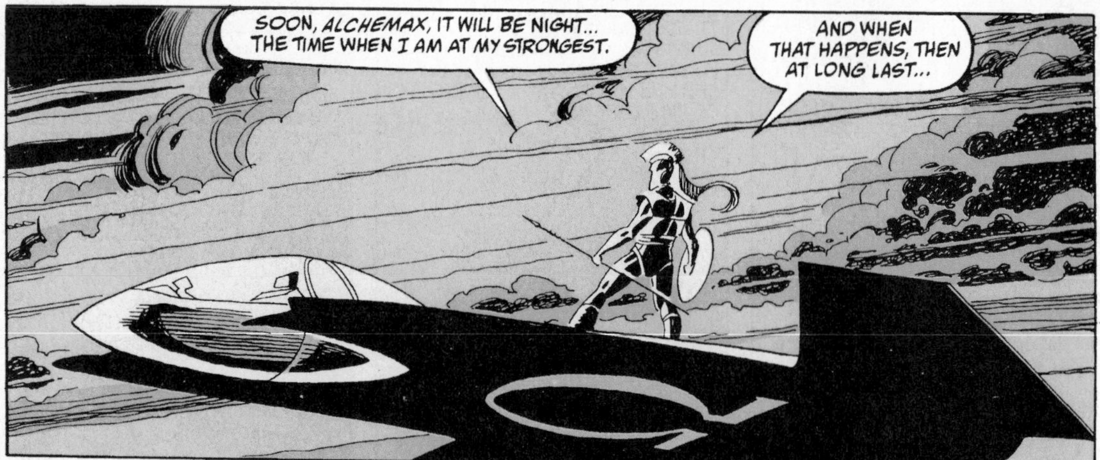
SOON, ALCHEMAX, IT WILL BE NIGHT... THE TIME WHEN I AM AT MY STRONGEST.
AND WHEN THAT HAPPENS, THEN AT LONG LAST...

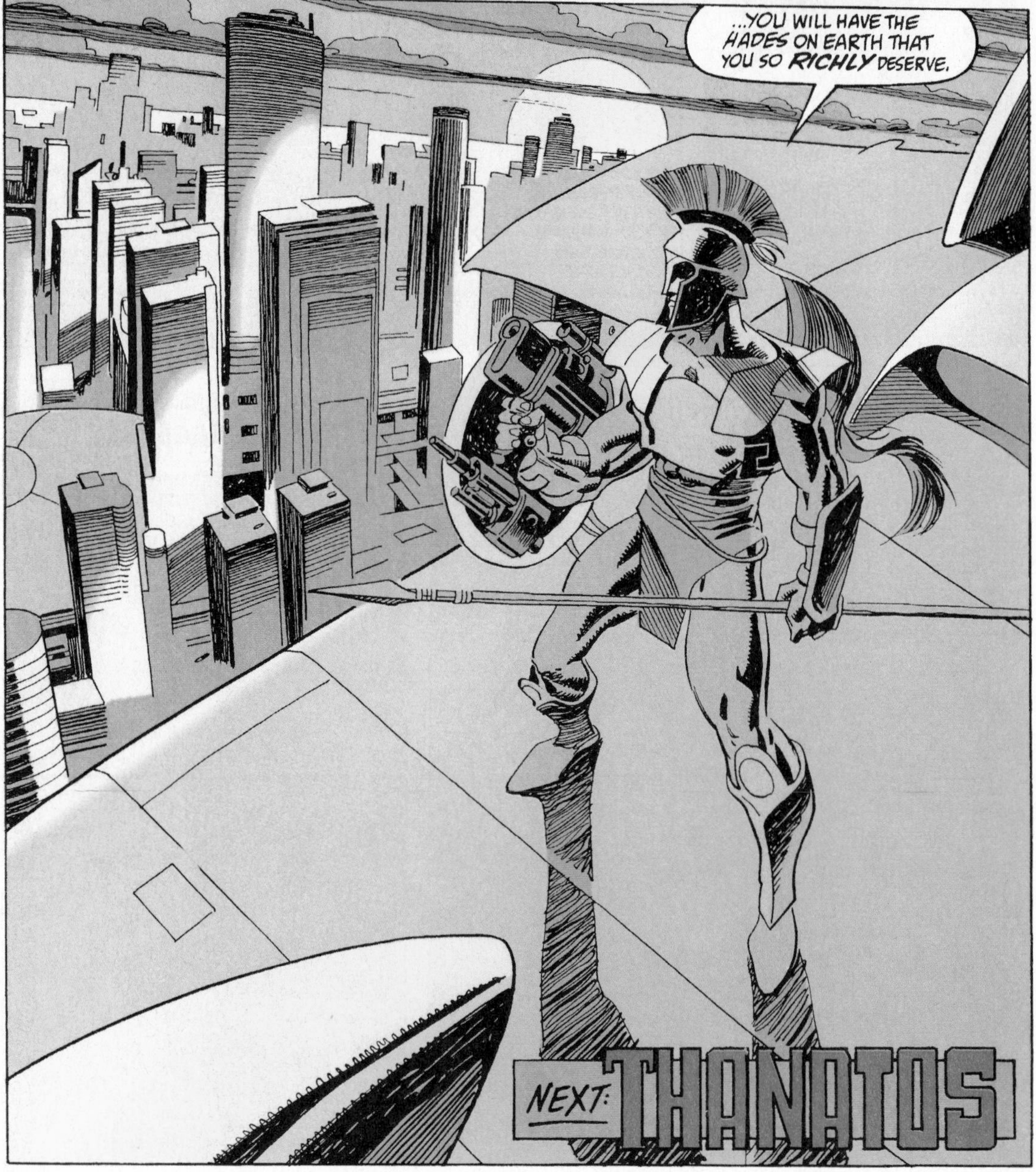
...YOU WILL HAVE THE HADES ON EARTH THAT YOU SO RICHLY DESERVE.
NEXT: THANATOS

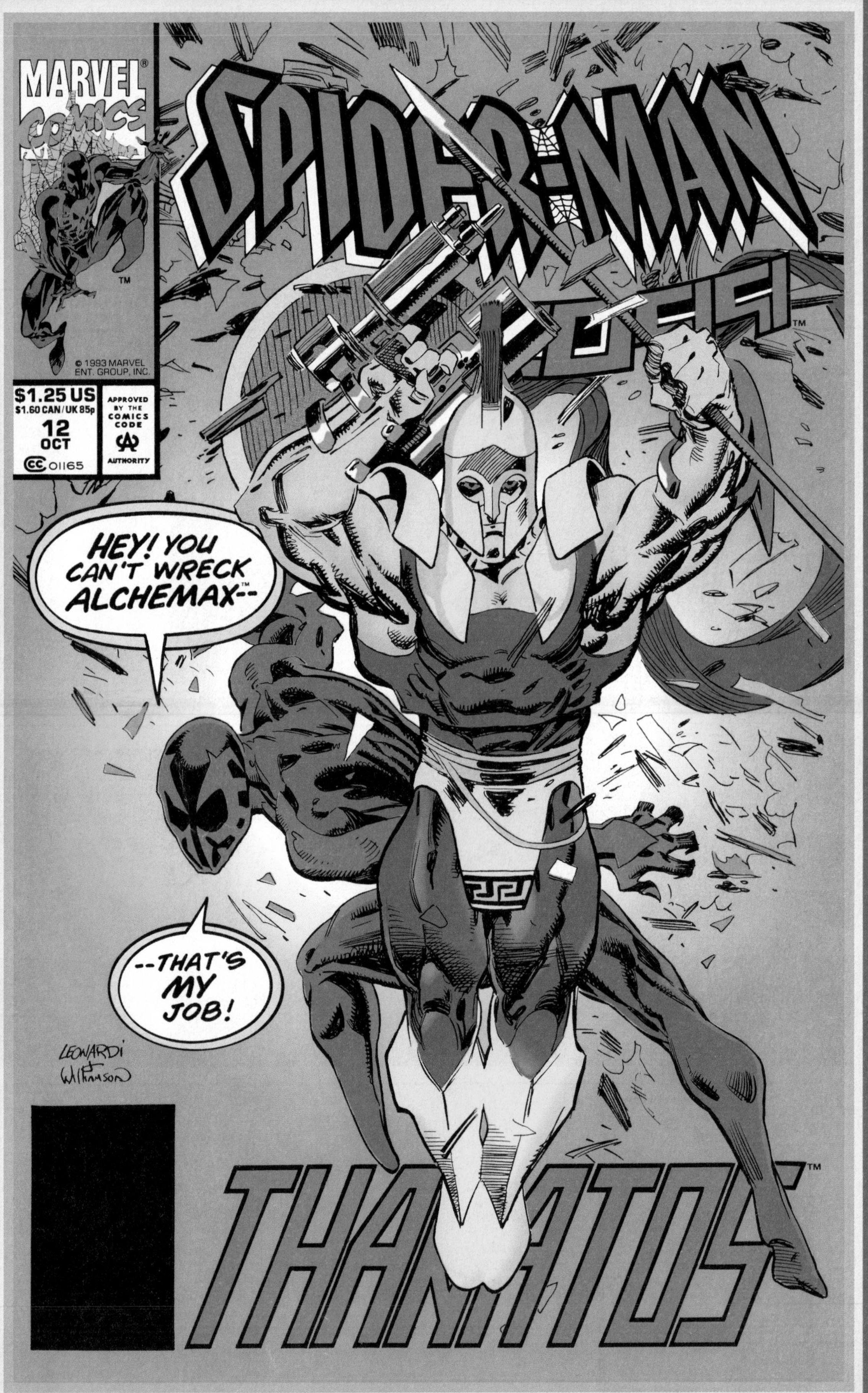
MARVEL® COMICS
SPIDER-MAN 2099™
© 1993 MARVEL ENT. GROUP, INC.
$1.25 US
$1.60 CAN/UK 85p
12
OCT
APPROVED BY THE COMICS CODE AUTHORITY
HEY! YOU CAN'T WRECK ALCHEMAX™--
--THAT'S MY JOB!
LEONARDI
WILLIAMSON
THANATOS™

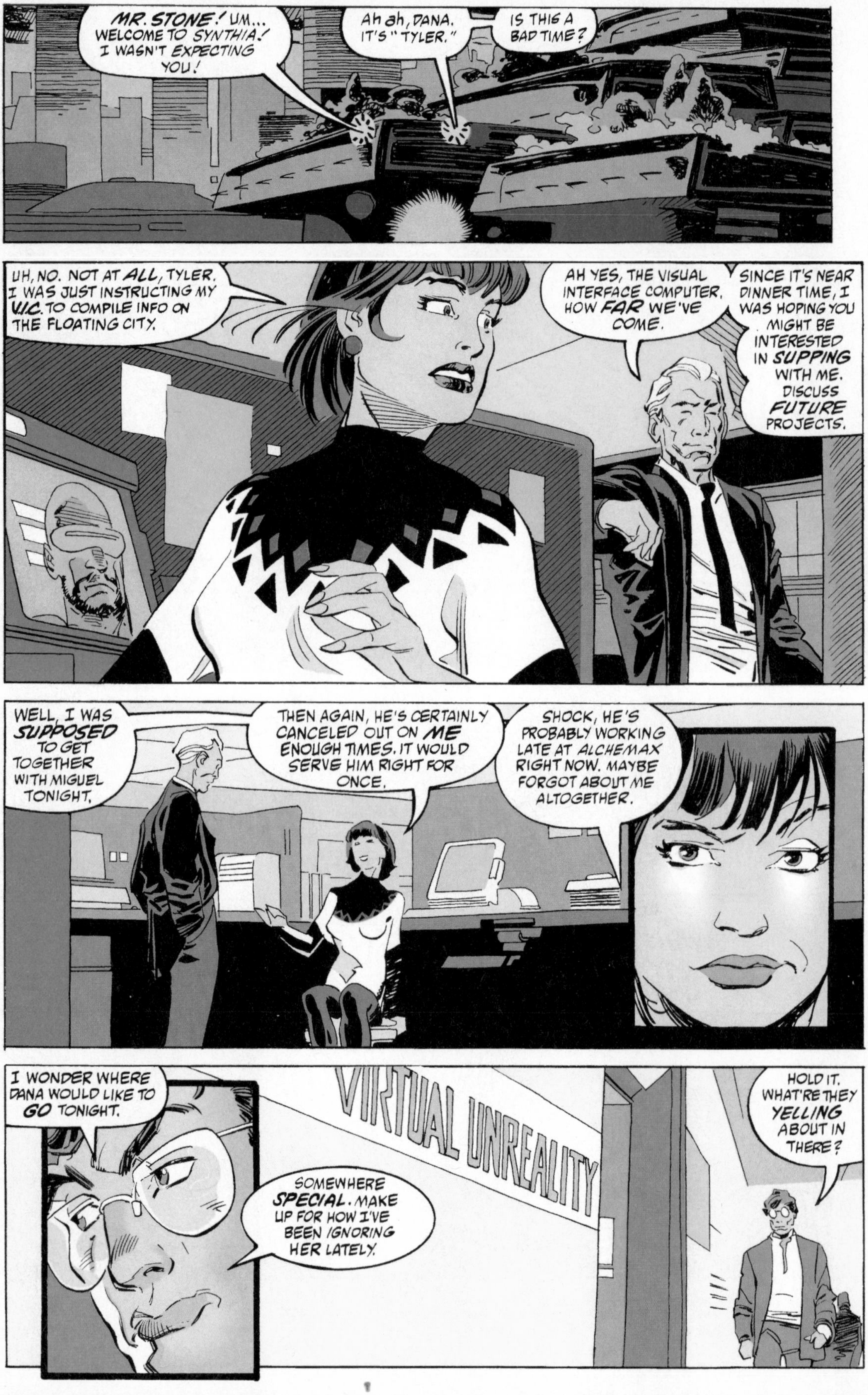
MR. STONE! UM... WELCOME TO SYNTHIA! I WASN'T EXPECTING YOU!
Ah ah, DANA. IT'S "TYLER."
IS THIS A BAD TIME?
UH, NO. NOT AT ALL, TYLER. I WAS JUST INSTRUCTING MY V.I.C. TO COMPILE INFO ON THE FLOATING CITY.
AH YES, THE VISUAL INTERFACE COMPUTER. HOW FAR WE'VE COME.
SINCE IT'S NEAR DINNER TIME, I WAS HOPING YOU MIGHT BE INTERESTED IN SUPPING WITH ME. DISCUSS FUTURE PROJECTS.
WELL, I WAS SUPPOSED TO GET TOGETHER WITH MIGUEL TONIGHT.
THEN AGAIN, HE'S CERTAINLY CANCELED OUT ON ME ENOUGH TIMES. IT WOULD SERVE HIM RIGHT FOR ONCE.
SHOCK, HE'S PROBABLY WORKING LATE AT ALCHEMAX RIGHT NOW. MAYBE FORGOT ABOUT ME ALTOGETHER.
I WONDER WHERE DANA WOULD LIKE TO GO TONIGHT.
VIRTUAL UNREALITY
SOMEWHERE SPECIAL. MAKE UP FOR HOW I'VE BEEN IGNORING HER LATELY.
HOLD IT. WHAT'RE THEY YELLING ABOUT IN THERE?

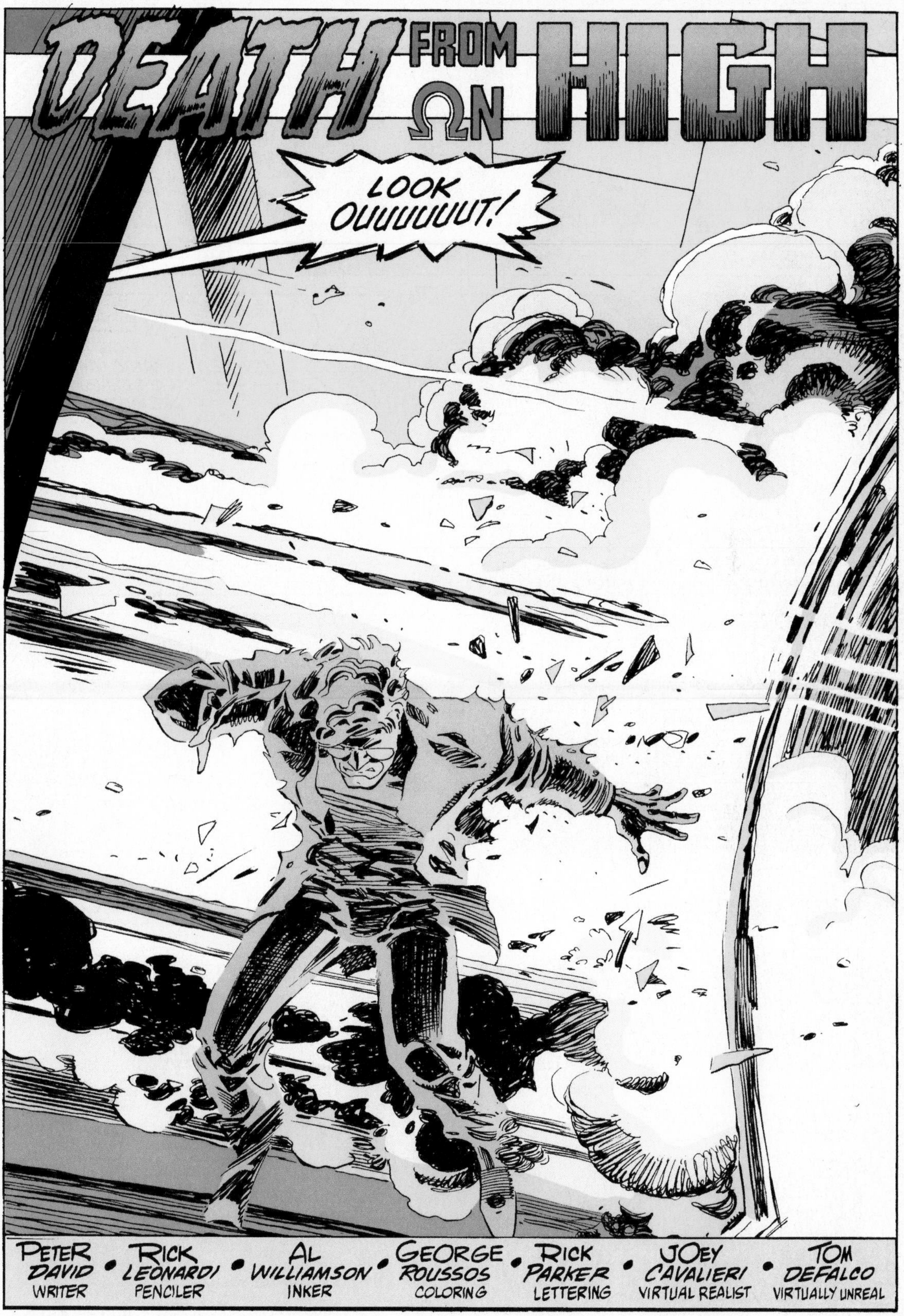
DEATH FROM ΩN HIGH
LOOK OUUUUUUT!
PETER DAVID WRITER • RICK LEONARDI PENCILER • AL WILLIAMSON INKER • GEORGE ROUSSOS COLORING • RICK PARKER LETTERING • JOEY CAVALIERI VIRTUAL REALIST • TOM DEFALCO VIRTUALLY UNREAL

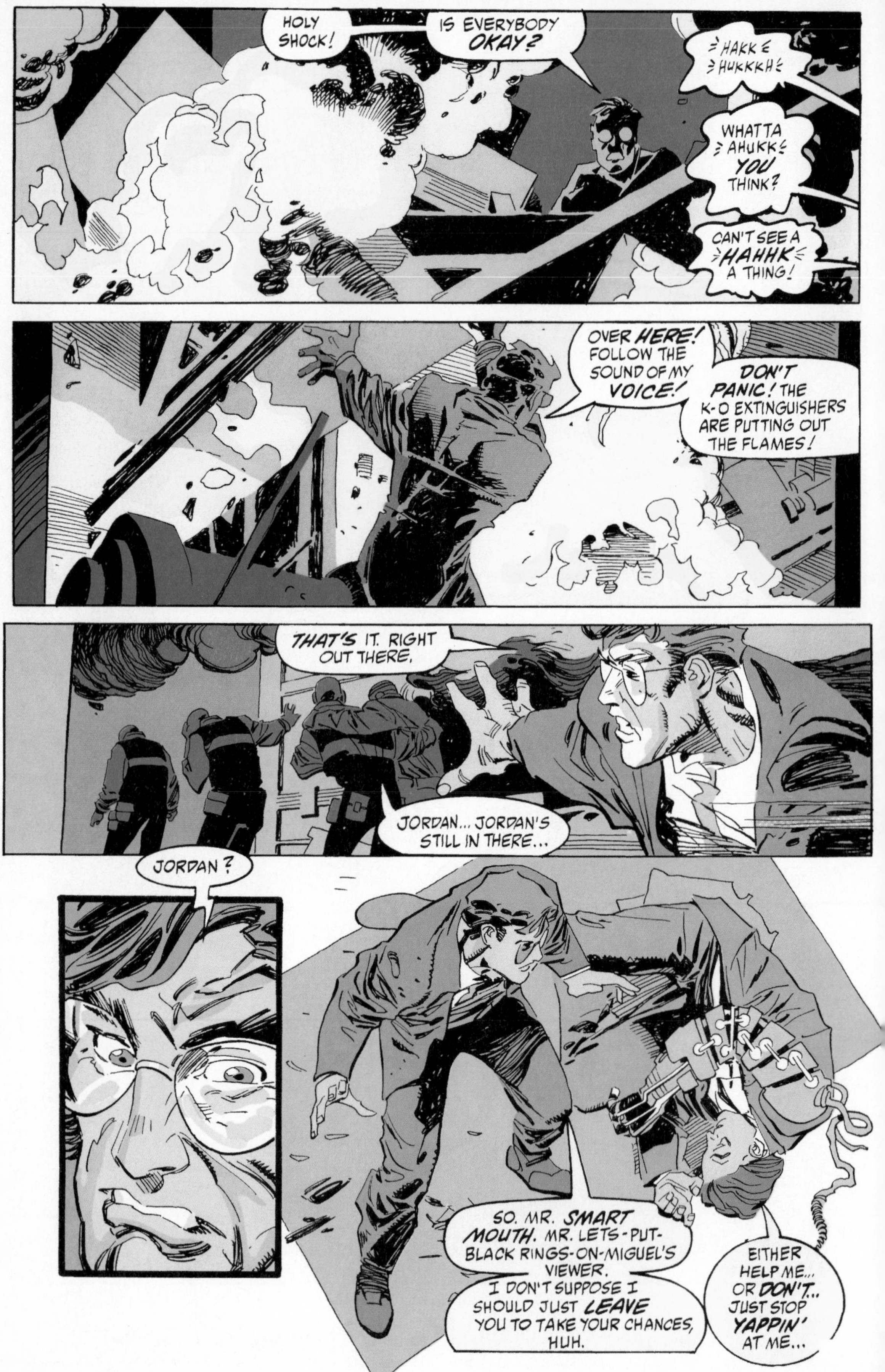
HOLY SHOCK!
IS EVERYBODY OKAY?
HAKK HUKKKH
WHATTA AHUKK YOU THINK?
CAN'T SEE A HAHHK A THING!
OVER HERE! FOLLOW THE SOUND OF MY VOICE!
DON'T PANIC! THE K-O EXTINGUISHERS ARE PUTTING OUT THE FLAMES!
THAT'S IT. RIGHT OUT THERE.
JORDAN... JORDAN'S STILL IN THERE...
JORDAN?
SO. MR. SMART MOUTH. MR. LETS-PUT-BLACK RINGS-ON-MIGUEL'S VIEWER.
I DON'T SUPPOSE I SHOULD JUST LEAVE YOU TO TAKE YOUR CHANCES, HUH.
EITHER HELP ME... OR DON'T... JUST STOP YAPPIN' AT ME...

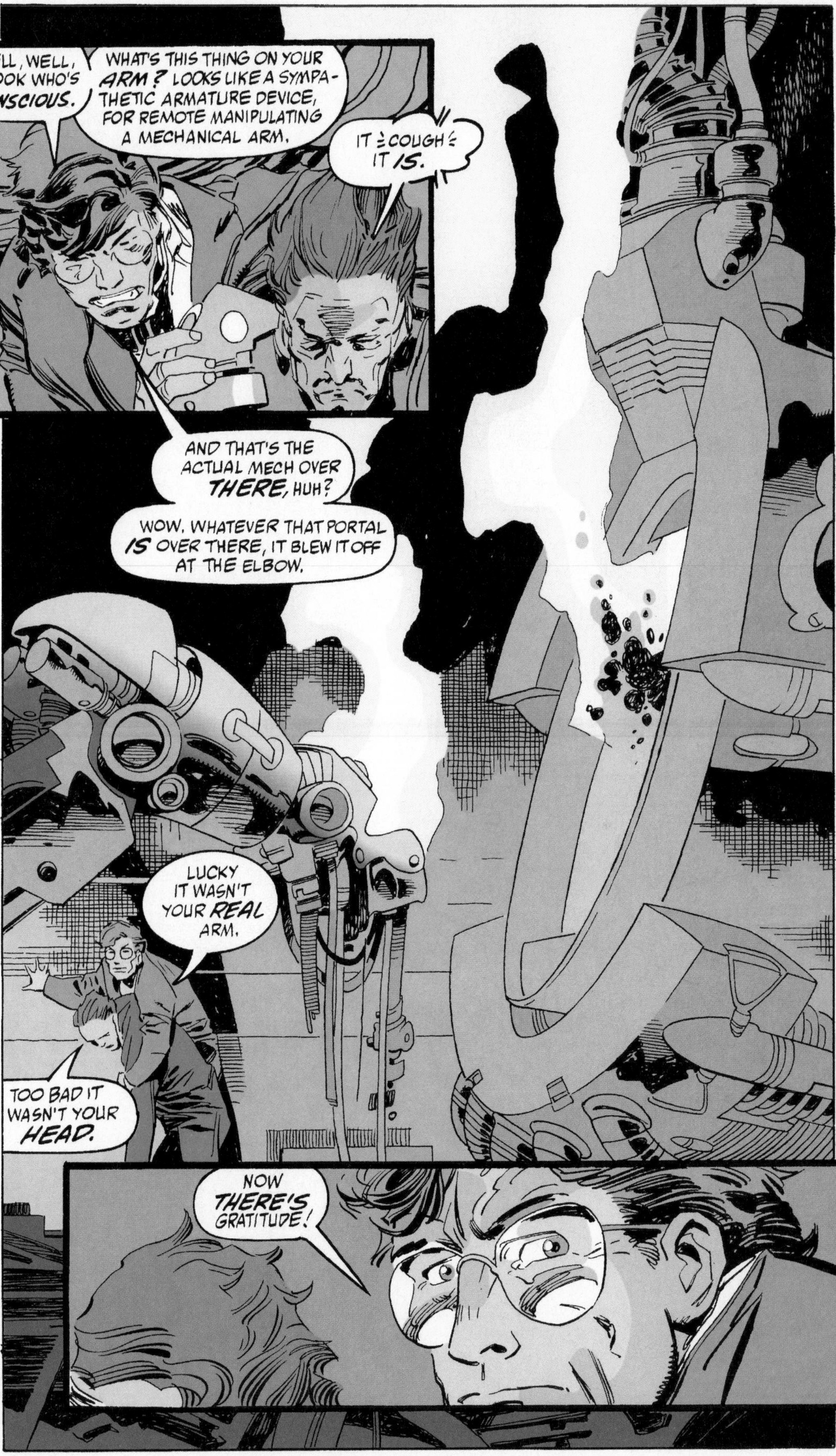
WELL, WELL, LOOK WHO'S CONSCIOUS.
WHAT'S THIS THING ON YOUR ARM? LOOKS LIKE A SYMPATHETIC ARMATURE DEVICE, FOR REMOTE MANIPULATING A MECHANICAL ARM.
IT =COUGH= IT IS.
AND THAT'S THE ACTUAL MECH OVER THERE, HUH?
WOW. WHATEVER THAT PORTAL IS OVER THERE, IT BLEW IT OFF AT THE ELBOW.
LUCKY IT WASN'T YOUR REAL ARM.
TOO BAD IT WASN'T YOUR HEAD.
NOW THERE'S GRATITUDE!

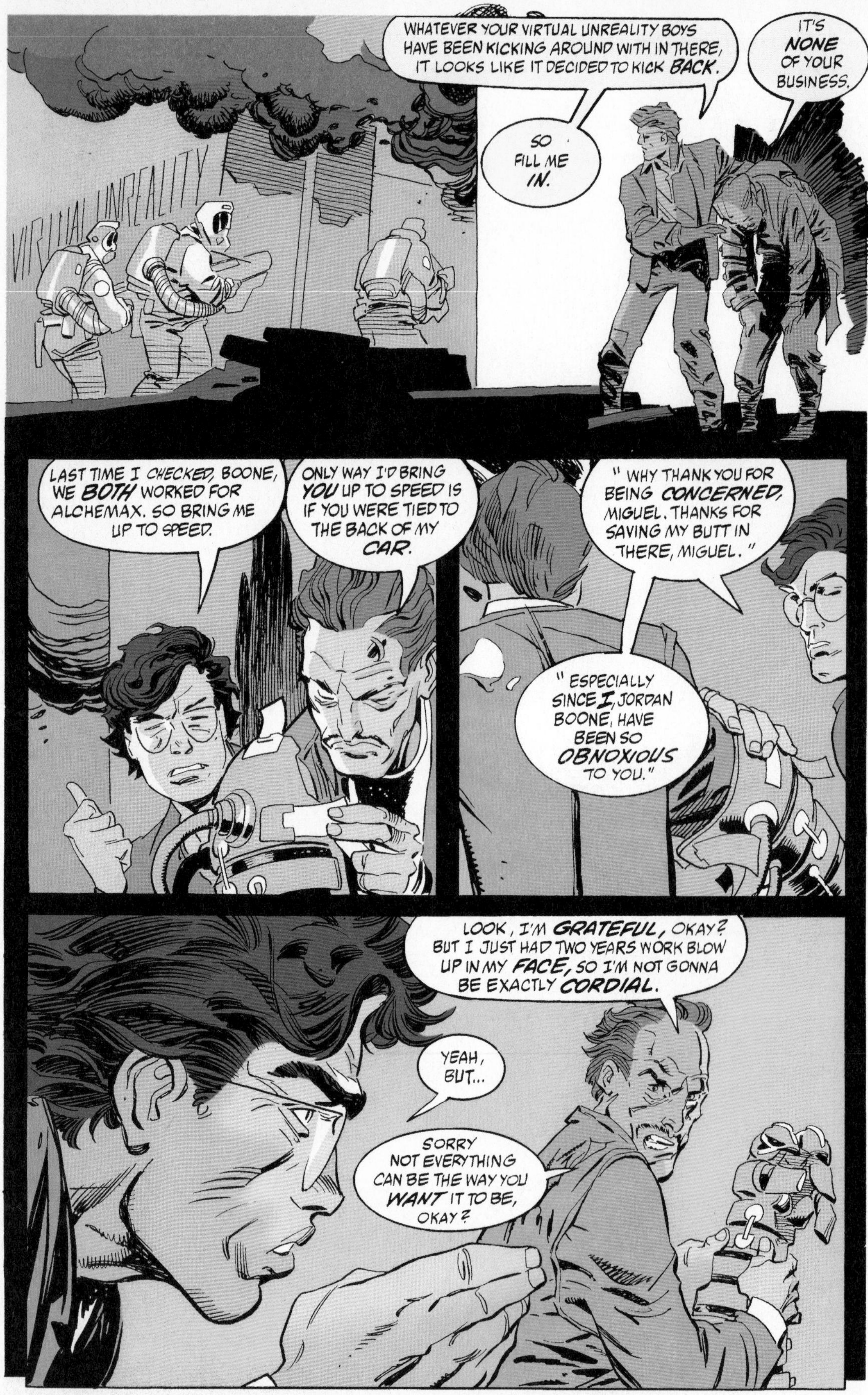
VIRTUAL UNREALITY
WHATEVER YOUR VIRTUAL UNREALITY BOYS HAVE BEEN KICKING AROUND WITH IN THERE, IT LOOKS LIKE IT DECIDED TO KICK BACK.
SO FILL ME IN.
IT'S NONE OF YOUR BUSINESS.
LAST TIME I CHECKED, BOONE, WE BOTH WORKED FOR ALCHEMAX. SO BRING ME UP TO SPEED.
ONLY WAY I'D BRING YOU UP TO SPEED IS IF YOU WERE TIED TO THE BACK OF MY CAR.
" WHY THANK YOU FOR BEING CONCERNED, MIGUEL. THANKS FOR SAVING MY BUTT IN THERE, MIGUEL."
" ESPECIALLY SINCE I, JORDAN BOONE, HAVE BEEN SO OBNOXIOUS TO YOU."
LOOK, I'M GRATEFUL, OKAY? BUT I JUST HAD TWO YEARS WORK BLOW UP IN MY FACE, SO I'M NOT GONNA BE EXACTLY CORDIAL.
YEAH, BUT...
SORRY NOT EVERYTHING CAN BE THE WAY YOU WANT IT TO BE, OKAY?

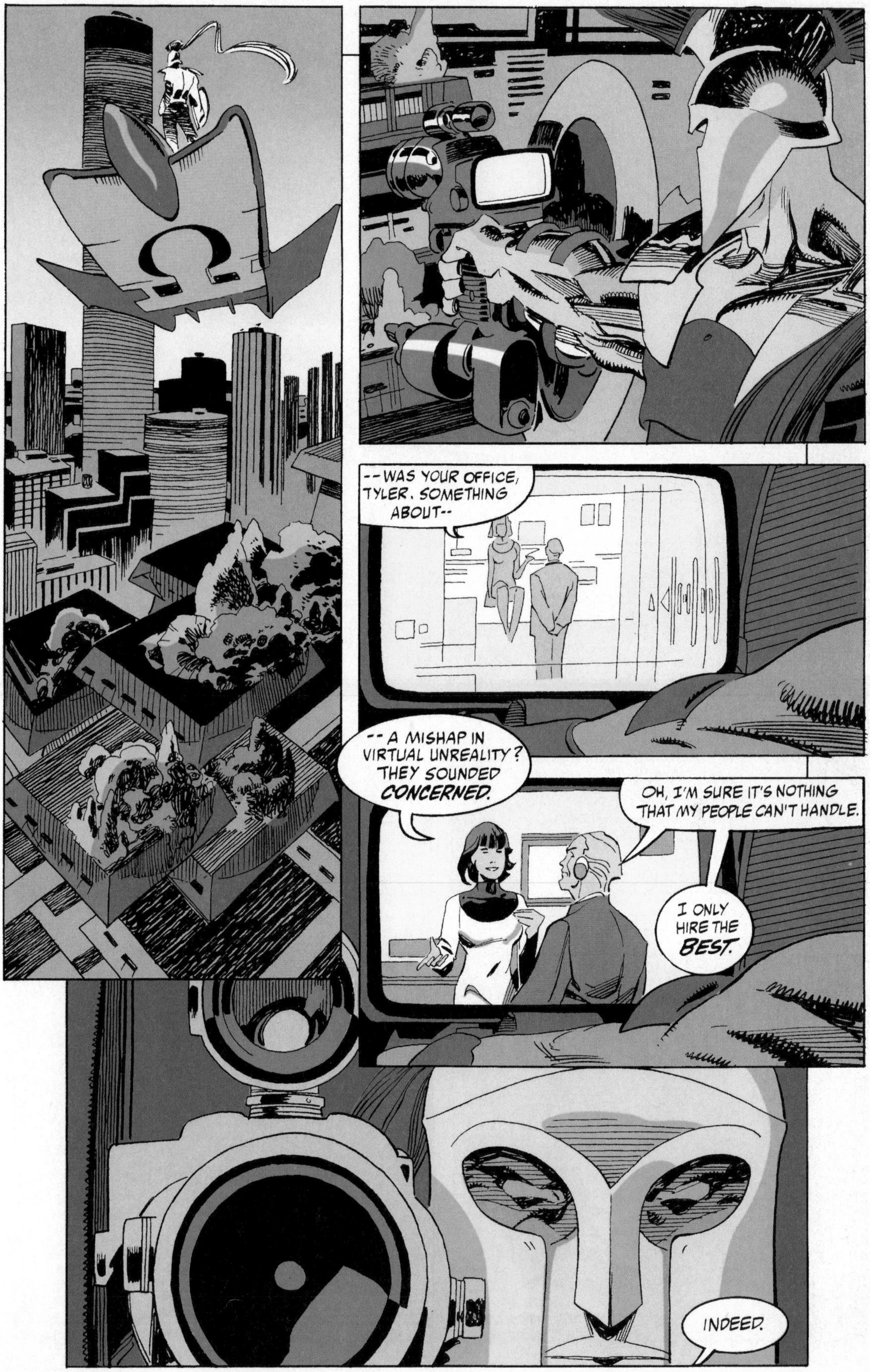
--WAS YOUR OFFICE, TYLER. SOMETHING ABOUT--
--A MISHAP IN VIRTUAL UNREALITY? THEY SOUNDED CONCERNED.
OH, I'M SURE IT'S NOTHING THAT MY PEOPLE CAN'T HANDLE.
I ONLY HIRE THE BEST.
INDEED.

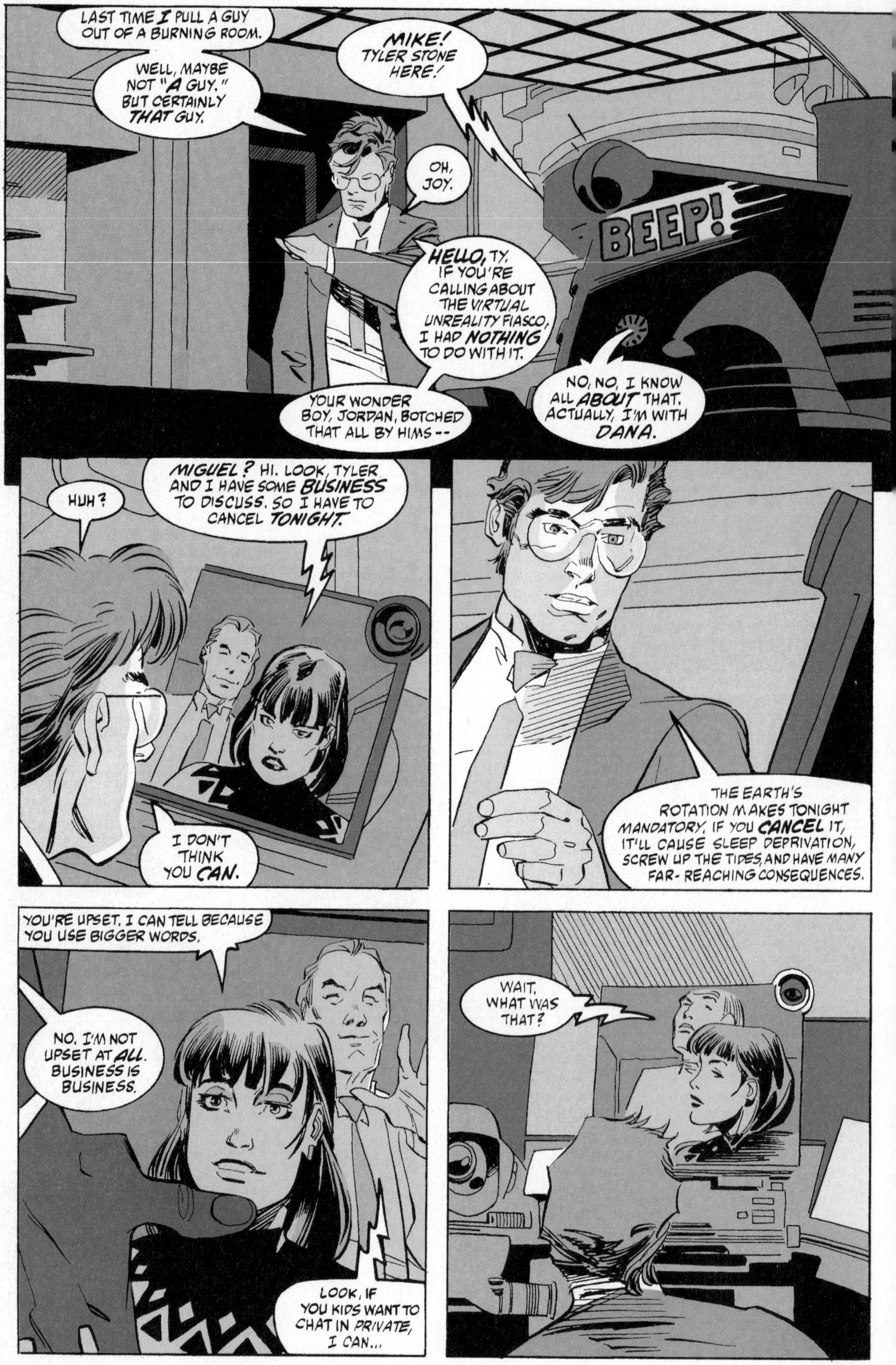
LAST TIME I PULL A GUY OUT OF A BURNING ROOM.
WELL, MAYBE NOT "A GUY." BUT CERTAINLY THAT GUY.
MIKE! TYLER STONE HERE!
OH, JOY.
BEEP!
HELLO, TY. IF YOU'RE CALLING ABOUT THE VIRTUAL UNREALITY FIASCO, I HAD NOTHING TO DO WITH IT.
YOUR WONDER BOY, JORDAN, BOTCHED THAT ALL BY HIMS--
NO, NO, I KNOW ALL ABOUT THAT. ACTUALLY, I'M WITH DANA.
HUH?
MIGUEL? HI. LOOK, TYLER AND I HAVE SOME BUSINESS TO DISCUSS. SO I HAVE TO CANCEL TONIGHT.
I DON'T THINK YOU CAN.
THE EARTH'S ROTATION MAKES TONIGHT MANDATORY. IF YOU CANCEL IT, IT'LL CAUSE SLEEP DEPRIVATION, SCREW UP THE TIDES, AND HAVE MANY FAR-REACHING CONSEQUENCES.
YOU'RE UPSET. I CAN TELL BECAUSE YOU USE BIGGER WORDS.
NO. I'M NOT UPSET AT ALL. BUSINESS IS BUSINESS.
LOOK, IF YOU KIDS WANT TO CHAT IN PRIVATE, I CAN...
WAIT. WHAT WAS THAT?

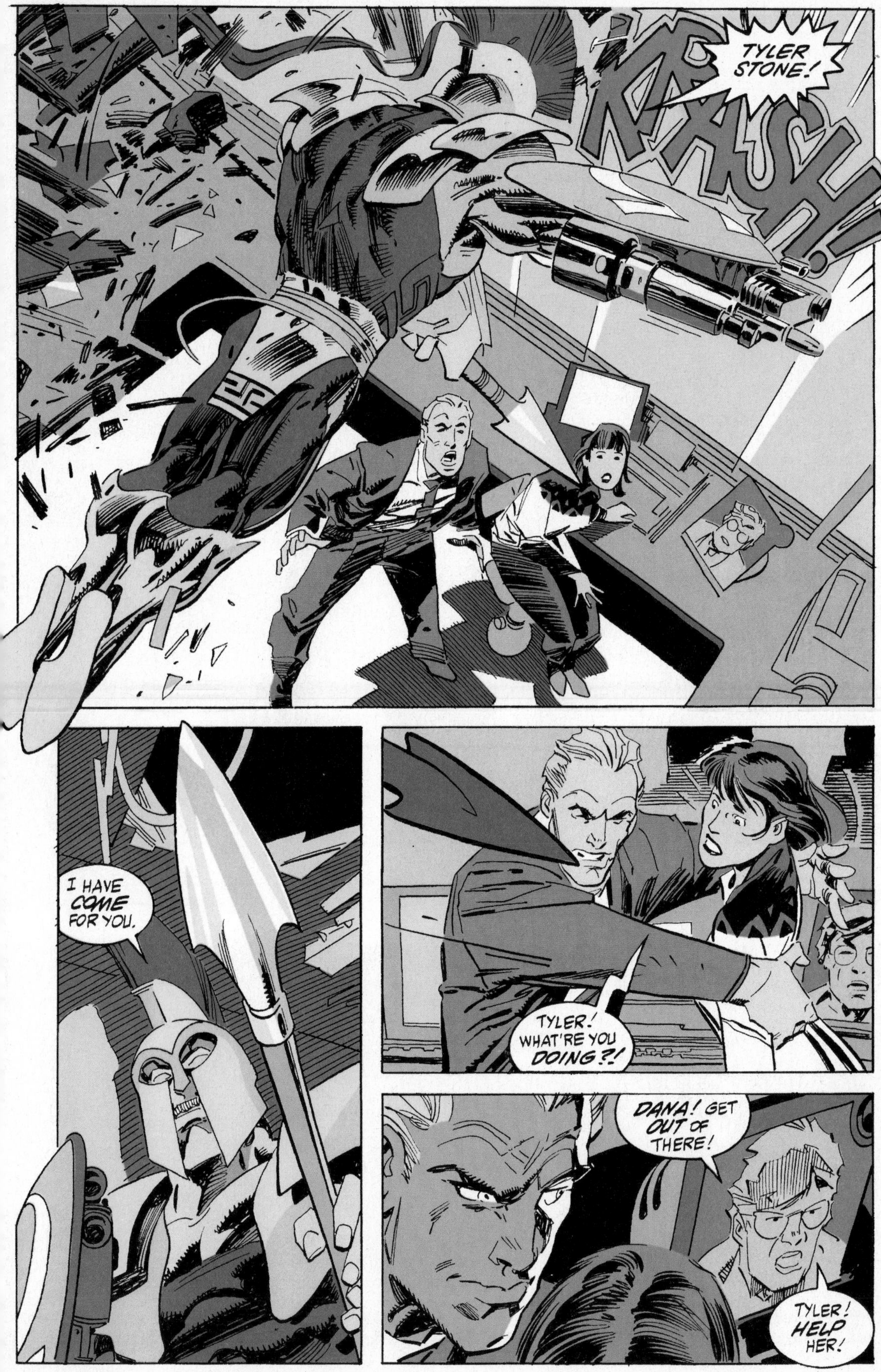
KRASH!
TYLER STONE!
I HAVE COME FOR YOU.
TYLER! WHAT'RE YOU DOING?!
DANA! GET OUT OF THERE!
TYLER! HELP HER!

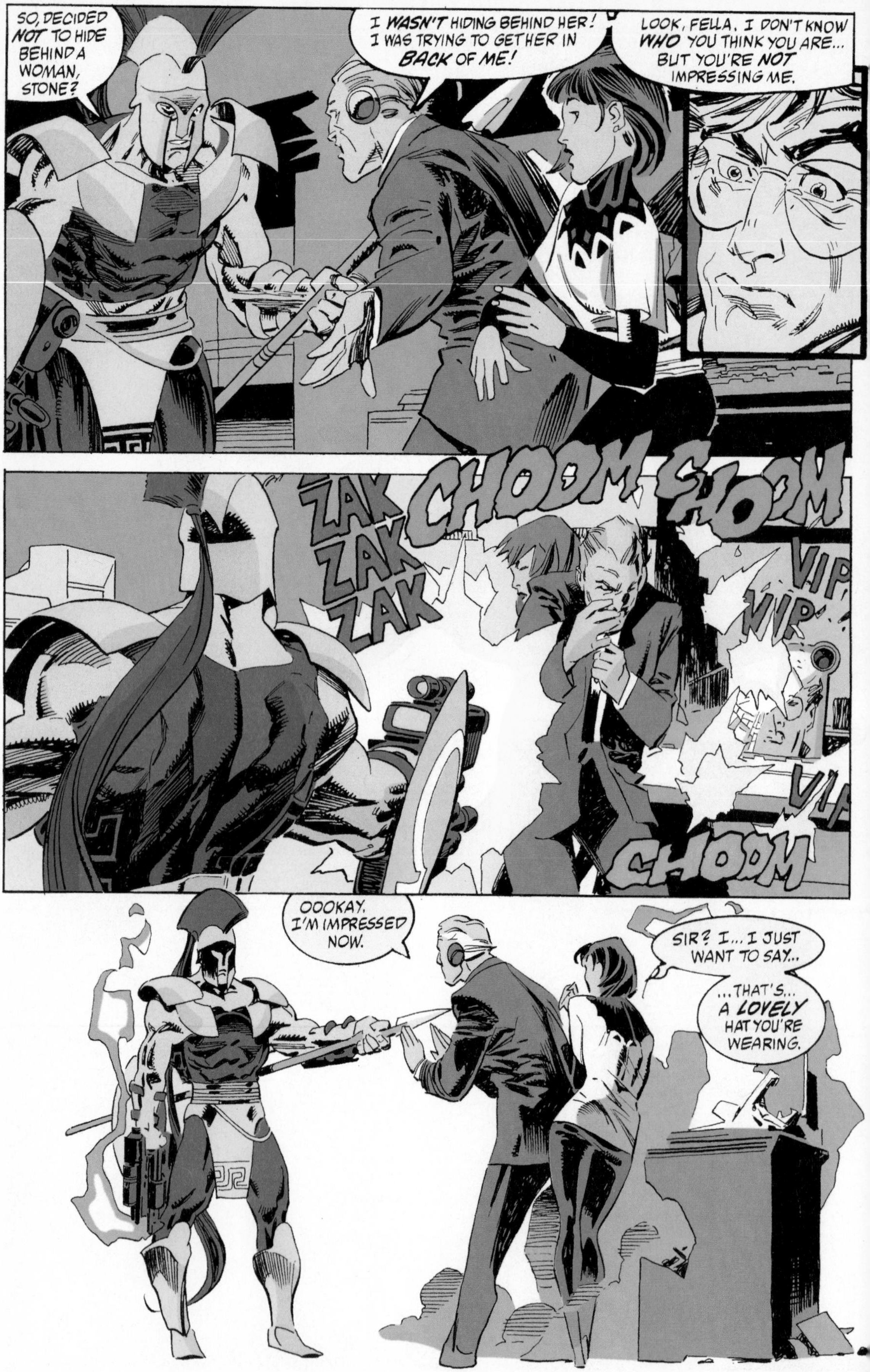
SO, DECIDED NOT TO HIDE BEHIND A WOMAN, STONE?
I WASN'T HIDING BEHIND HER! I WAS TRYING TO GET HER IN BACK OF ME!
LOOK, FELLA, I DON'T KNOW WHO YOU THINK YOU ARE... BUT YOU'RE NOT IMPRESSING ME.
ZAK ZAK ZAK
CHOOM CHOOM
VIP VIP
VIP
CHOOM
OOOKAY. I'M IMPRESSED NOW.
SIR? I... I JUST WANT TO SAY...
...THAT'S... A LOVELY HAT YOU'RE WEARING.

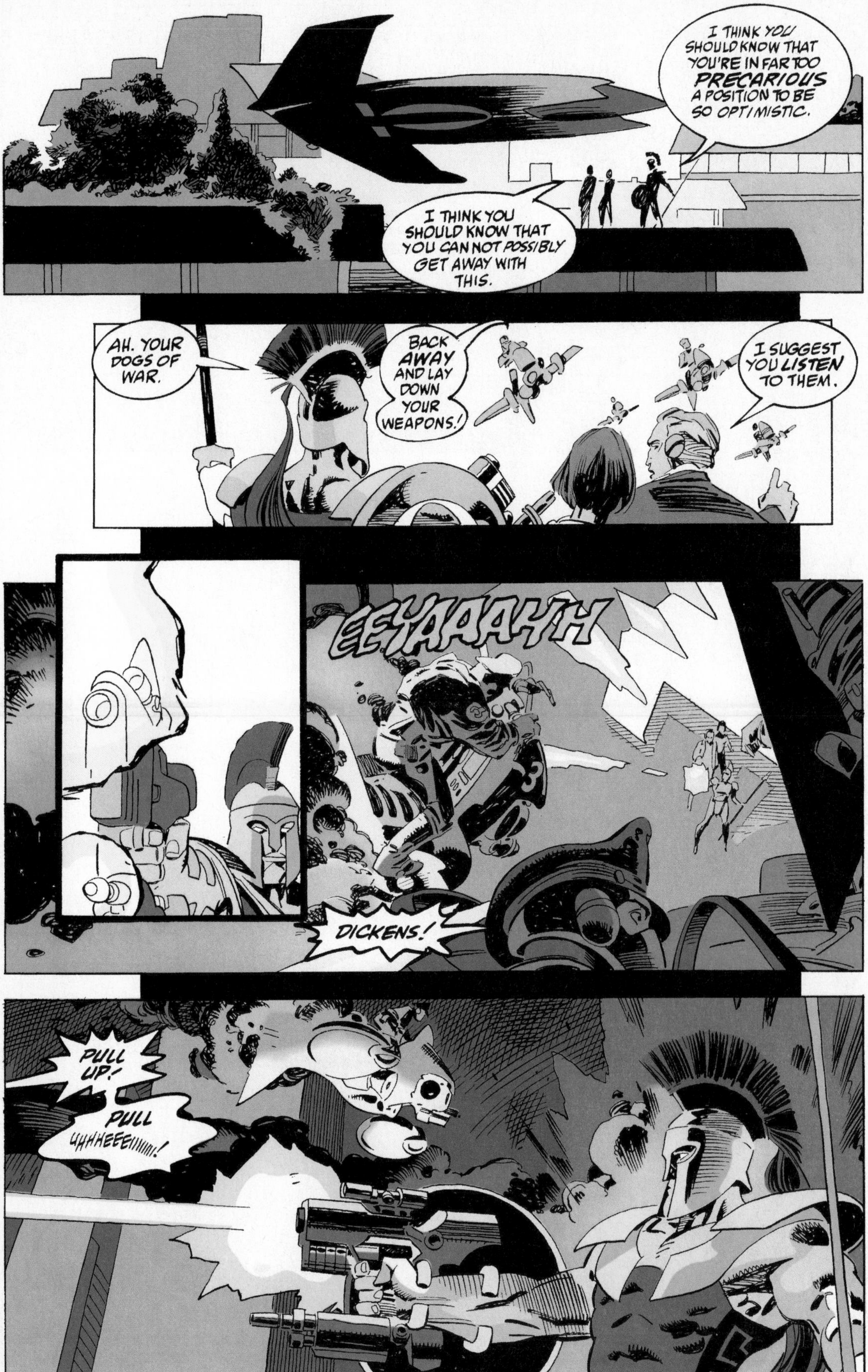
I THINK YOU SHOULD KNOW THAT YOU'RE IN FAR TOO PRECARIOUS A POSITION TO BE SO OPTIMISTIC.
I THINK YOU SHOULD KNOW THAT YOU CAN NOT POSSIBLY GET AWAY WITH THIS.
AH. YOUR DOGS OF WAR.
BACK AWAY AND LAY DOWN YOUR WEAPONS!
I SUGGEST YOU LISTEN TO THEM.
EEYAAAHH
DICKENS!
PULL UP!
PULL UHHHEEE!!!!!!!!

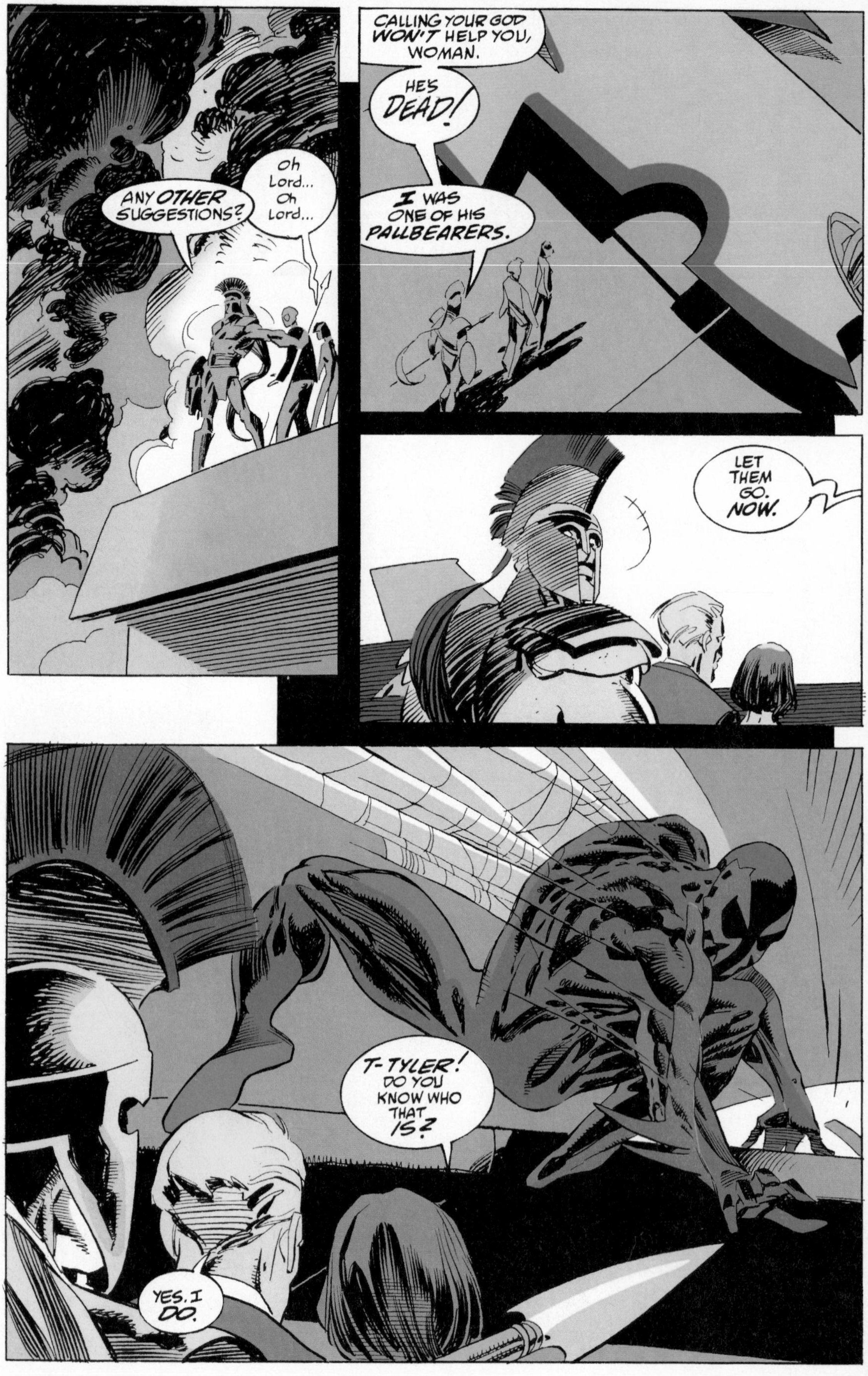
ANY OTHER SUGGESTIONS?
Oh Lord... Oh Lord...
CALLING YOUR GOD WON'T HELP YOU, WOMAN.
HE'S DEAD!
I WAS ONE OF HIS PALLBEARERS.
LET THEM GO. NOW.
T-TYLER! DO YOU KNOW WHO THAT IS?
YES. I DO.

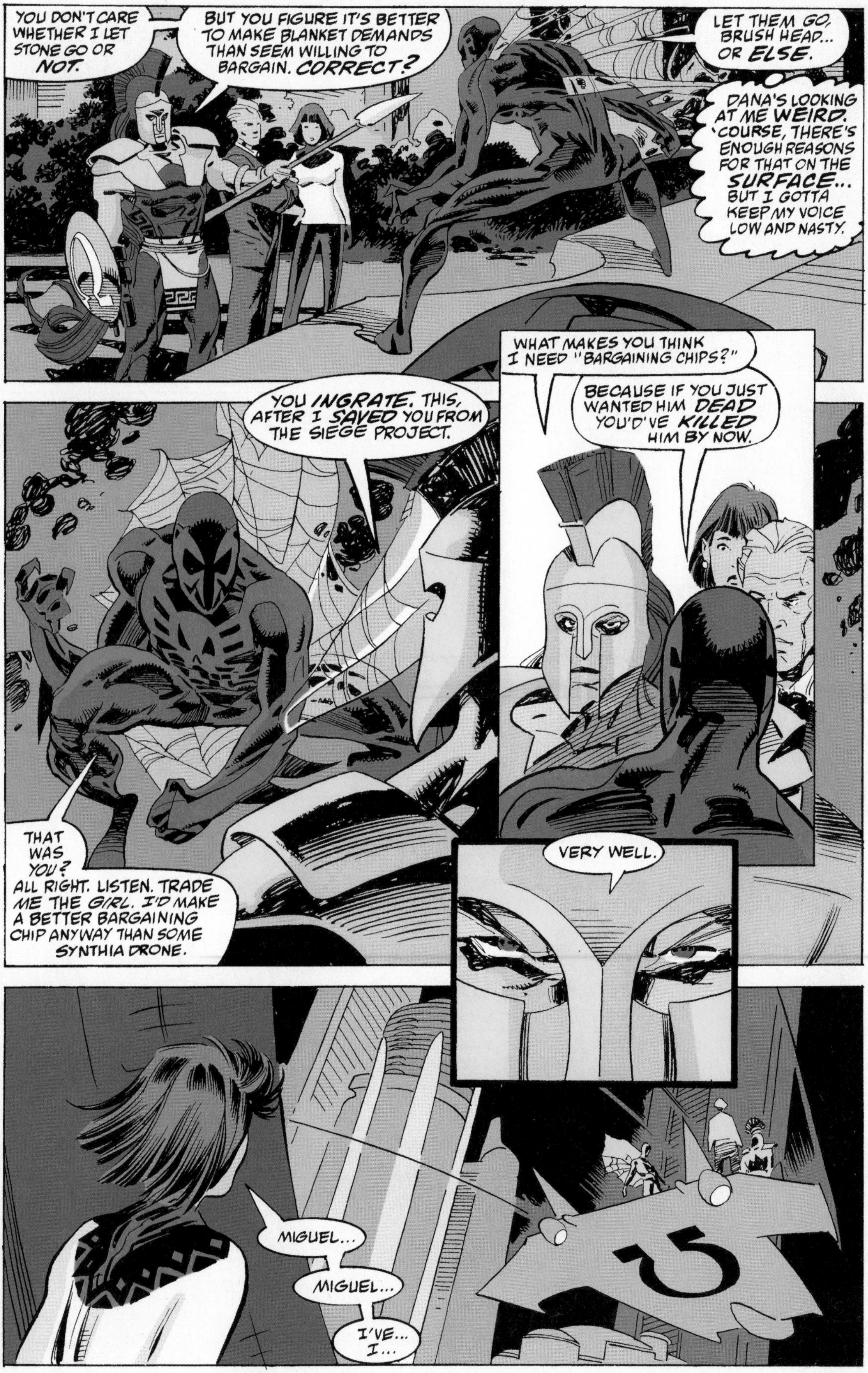
YOU DON'T CARE WHETHER I LET STONE GO OR NOT.
BUT YOU FIGURE IT'S BETTER TO MAKE BLANKET DEMANDS THAN SEEM WILLING TO BARGAIN. CORRECT?
LET THEM GO, BRUSH HEAD... OR ELSE.
DANA'S LOOKING AT ME WEIRD. 'COURSE, THERE'S ENOUGH REASONS FOR THAT ON THE SURFACE... BUT I GOTTA KEEP MY VOICE LOW AND NASTY.
YOU INGRATE. THIS, AFTER I SAVED YOU FROM THE SIEGE PROJECT.
WHAT MAKES YOU THINK I NEED "BARGAINING CHIPS?"
BECAUSE IF YOU JUST WANTED HIM DEAD YOU'D'VE KILLED HIM BY NOW.
THAT WAS YOU? ALL RIGHT. LISTEN. TRADE ME THE GIRL. I'D MAKE A BETTER BARGAINING CHIP ANYWAY THAN SOME SYNTHIA DRONE.
VERY WELL.
MIGUEL...
MIGUEL...
I'VE... I...

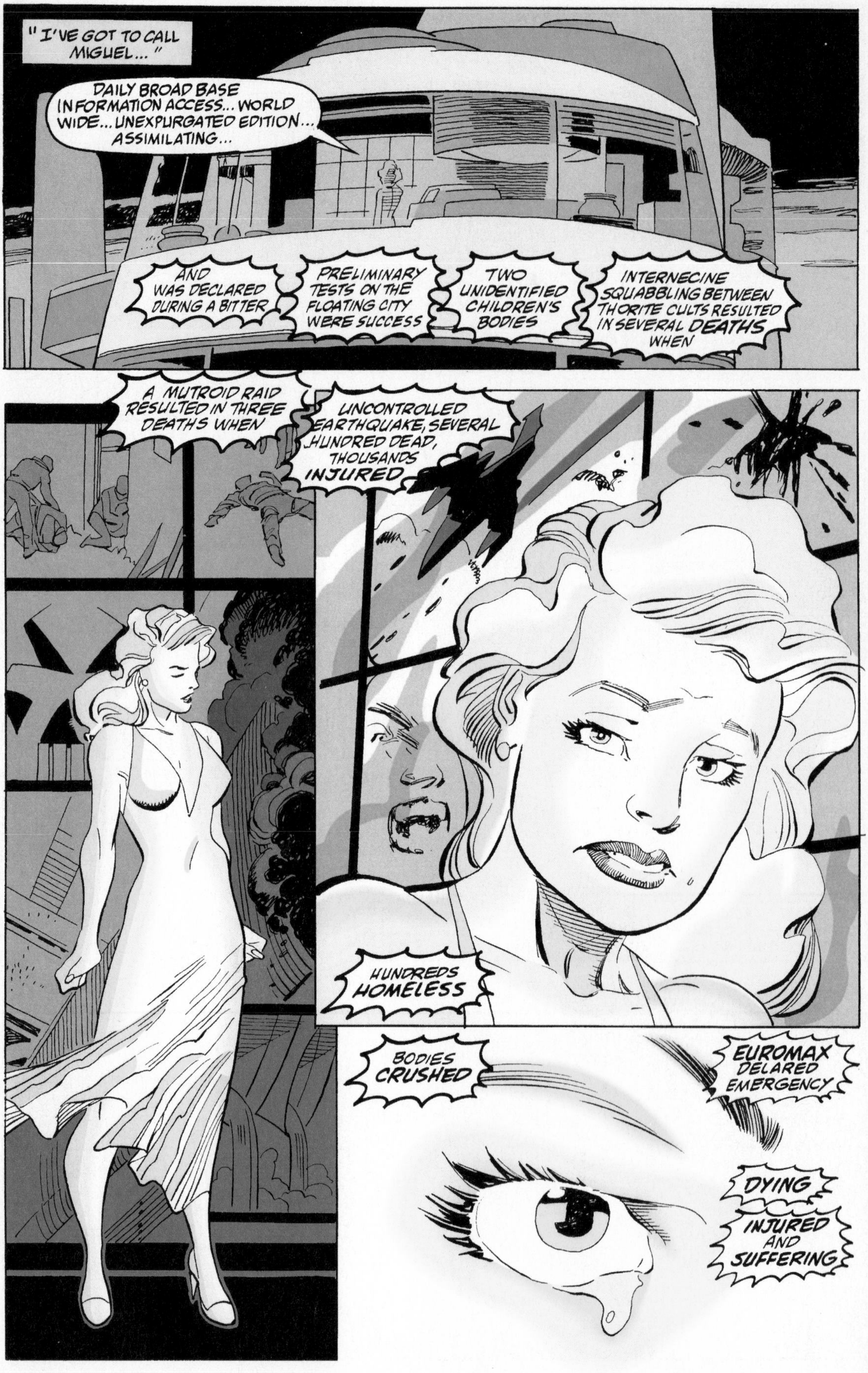
"I'VE GOT TO CALL MIGUEL..."
DAILY BROAD BASE INFORMATION ACCESS... WORLD WIDE... UNEXPURGATED EDITION... ASSIMILATING...
AND WAS DECLARED DURING A BITTER
PRELIMINARY TESTS ON THE FLOATING CITY WERE SUCCESS
TWO UNIDENTIFIED CHILDREN'S BODIES
INTERNECINE SQUABBLING BETWEEN THORITE CULTS RESULTED IN SEVERAL DEATHS WHEN
A MUTROID RAID RESULTED IN THREE DEATHS WHEN
UNCONTROLLED EARTHQUAKE, SEVERAL HUNDRED DEAD, THOUSANDS INJURED
HUNDREDS HOMELESS
BODIES CRUSHED
EUROMAX DELARED EMERGENCY
DYING
INJURED AND SUFFERING

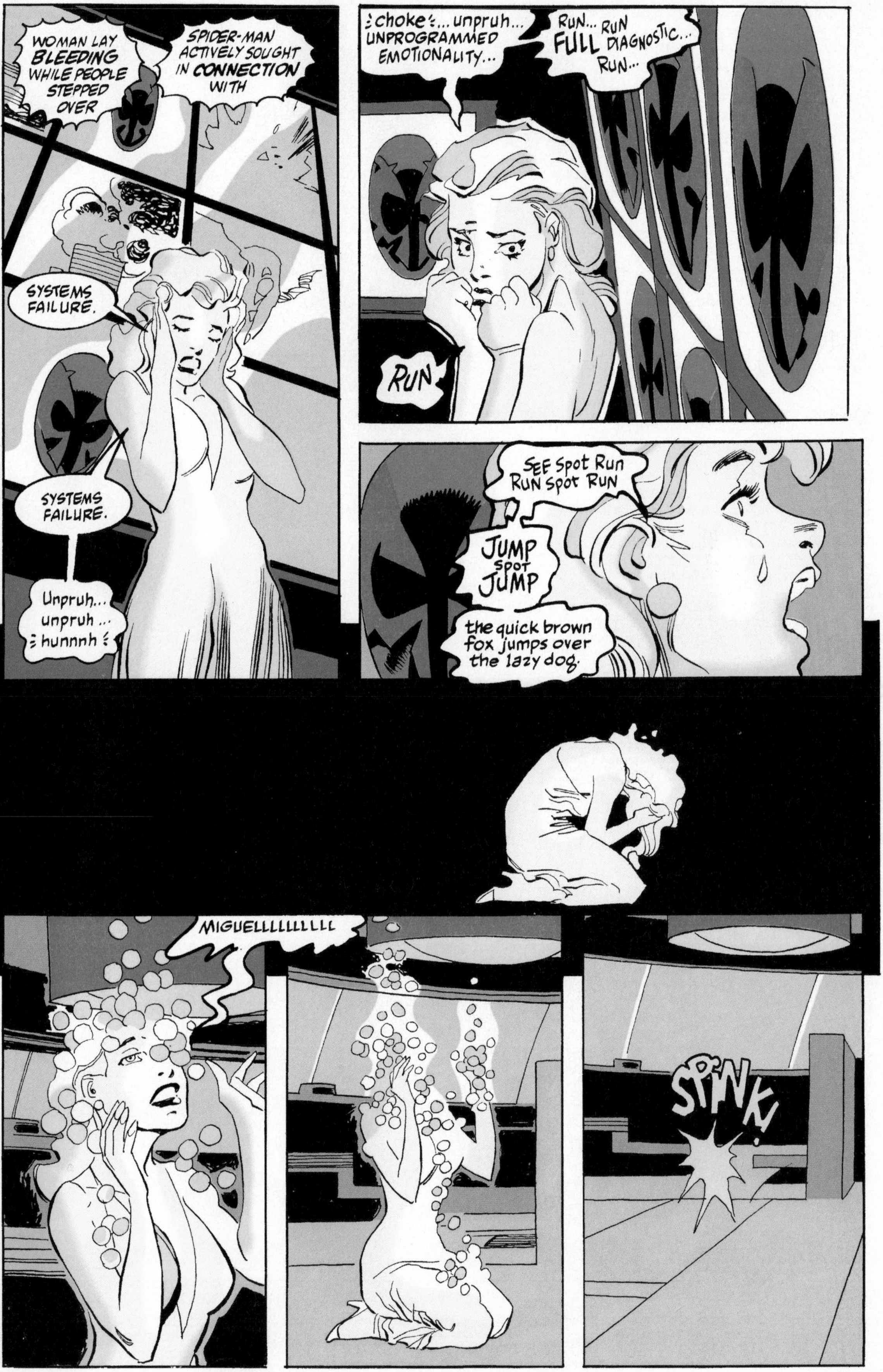
WOMAN LAY BLEEDING WHILE PEOPLE STEPPED OVER
SPIDER-MAN ACTIVELY SOUGHT IN CONNECTION WITH
SYSTEMS FAILURE.
SYSTEMS FAILURE.
Unpruh... unpruh... :hunnnh:
:choke:... unpruh... UNPROGRAMMED EMOTIONALITY...
RUN... RUN FULL DIAGNOSTIC... RUN...
RUN
SEE Spot Run Run Spot Run
JUMP spot JUMP
the quick brown fox jumps over the lazy dog.
MIGUELLLLLLLLLL
SPINK!

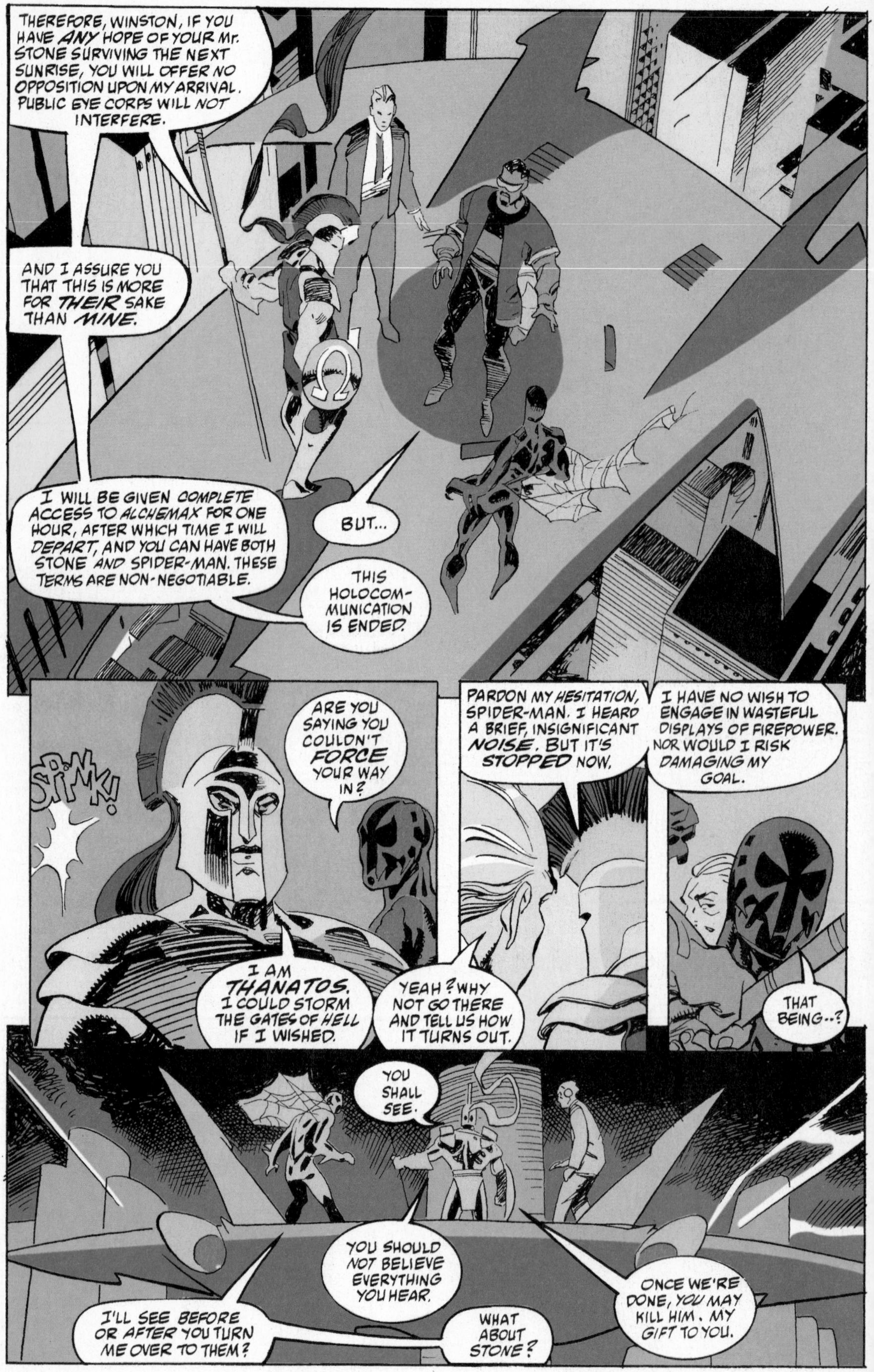
THEREFORE, WINSTON, IF YOU HAVE ANY HOPE OF YOUR Mr. STONE SURVIVING THE NEXT SUNRISE, YOU WILL OFFER NO OPPOSITION UPON MY ARRIVAL. PUBLIC EYE CORPS WILL NOT INTERFERE.
AND I ASSURE YOU THAT THIS IS MORE FOR THEIR SAKE THAN MINE.
I WILL BE GIVEN COMPLETE ACCESS TO ALCHEMAX FOR ONE HOUR, AFTER WHICH TIME I WILL DEPART, AND YOU CAN HAVE BOTH STONE AND SPIDER-MAN. THESE TERMS ARE NON-NEGOTIABLE.
BUT...
THIS HOLOCOM-MUNICATION IS ENDED.
SPINK!
ARE YOU SAYING YOU COULDN'T FORCE YOUR WAY IN?
I AM THANATOS. I COULD STORM THE GATES OF HELL IF I WISHED.
YEAH? WHY NOT GO THERE AND TELL US HOW IT TURNS OUT.
PARDON MY HESITATION, SPIDER-MAN. I HEARD A BRIEF, INSIGNIFICANT NOISE. BUT IT'S STOPPED NOW.
I HAVE NO WISH TO ENGAGE IN WASTEFUL DISPLAYS OF FIREPOWER. NOR WOULD I RISK DAMAGING MY GOAL.
THAT BEING..?
YOU SHALL SEE.
YOU SHOULD NOT BELIEVE EVERYTHING YOU HEAR.
I'LL SEE BEFORE OR AFTER YOU TURN ME OVER TO THEM?
WHAT ABOUT STONE?
ONCE WE'RE DONE, YOU MAY KILL HIM. MY GIFT TO YOU.

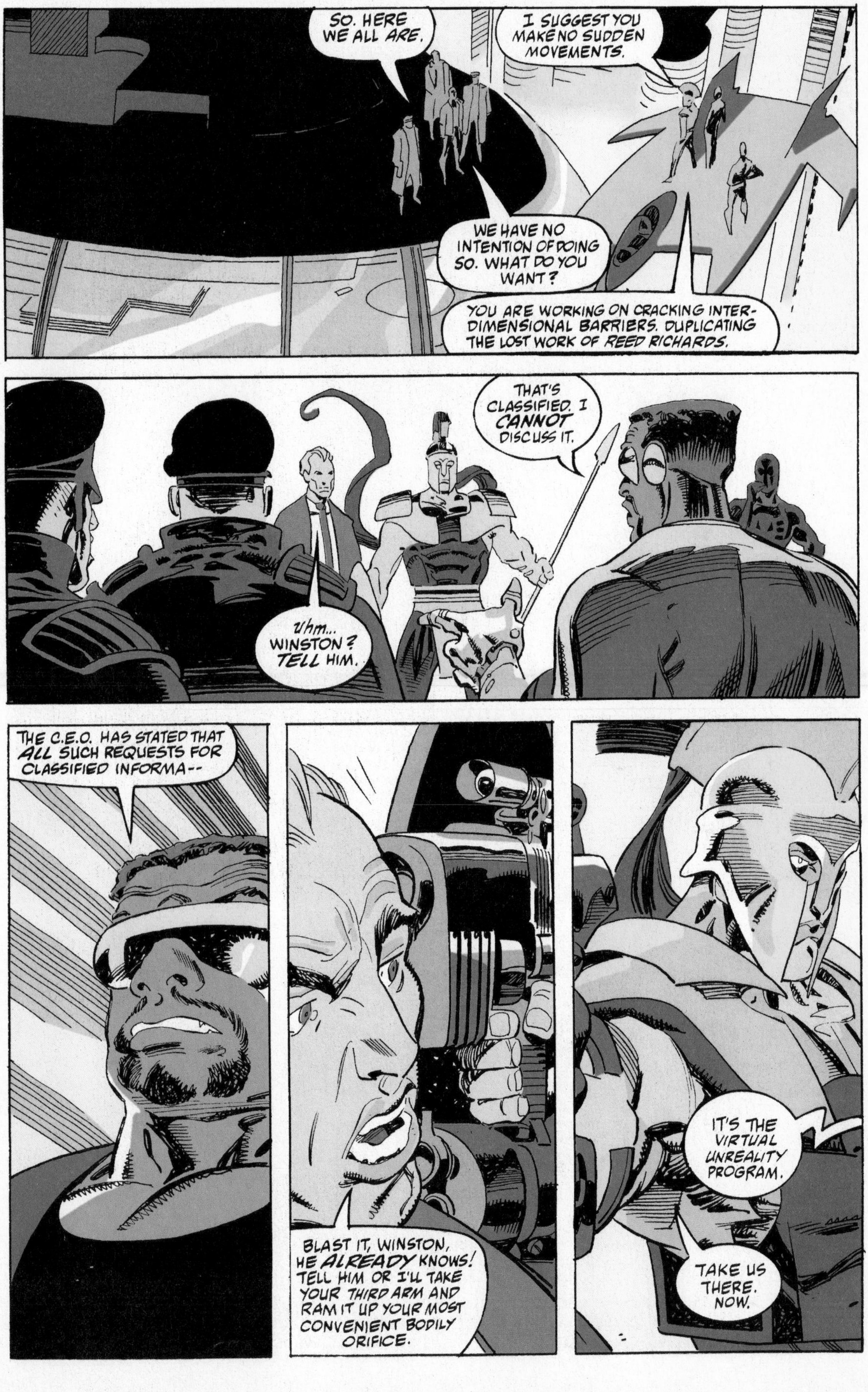
SO. HERE WE ALL ARE.
I SUGGEST YOU MAKE NO SUDDEN MOVEMENTS.
WE HAVE NO INTENTION OF DOING SO. WHAT DO YOU WANT?
YOU ARE WORKING ON CRACKING INTER-DIMENSIONAL BARRIERS. DUPLICATING THE LOST WORK OF REED RICHARDS.
THAT'S CLASSIFIED. I CANNOT DISCUSS IT.
Uhm... WINSTON? TELL HIM.
THE C.E.O. HAS STATED THAT ALL SUCH REQUESTS FOR CLASSIFIED INFORMA--
BLAST IT, WINSTON, HE ALREADY KNOWS! TELL HIM OR I'LL TAKE YOUR THIRD ARM AND RAM IT UP YOUR MOST CONVENIENT BODILY ORIFICE.
IT'S THE VIRTUAL UNREALITY PROGRAM.
TAKE US THERE. NOW.

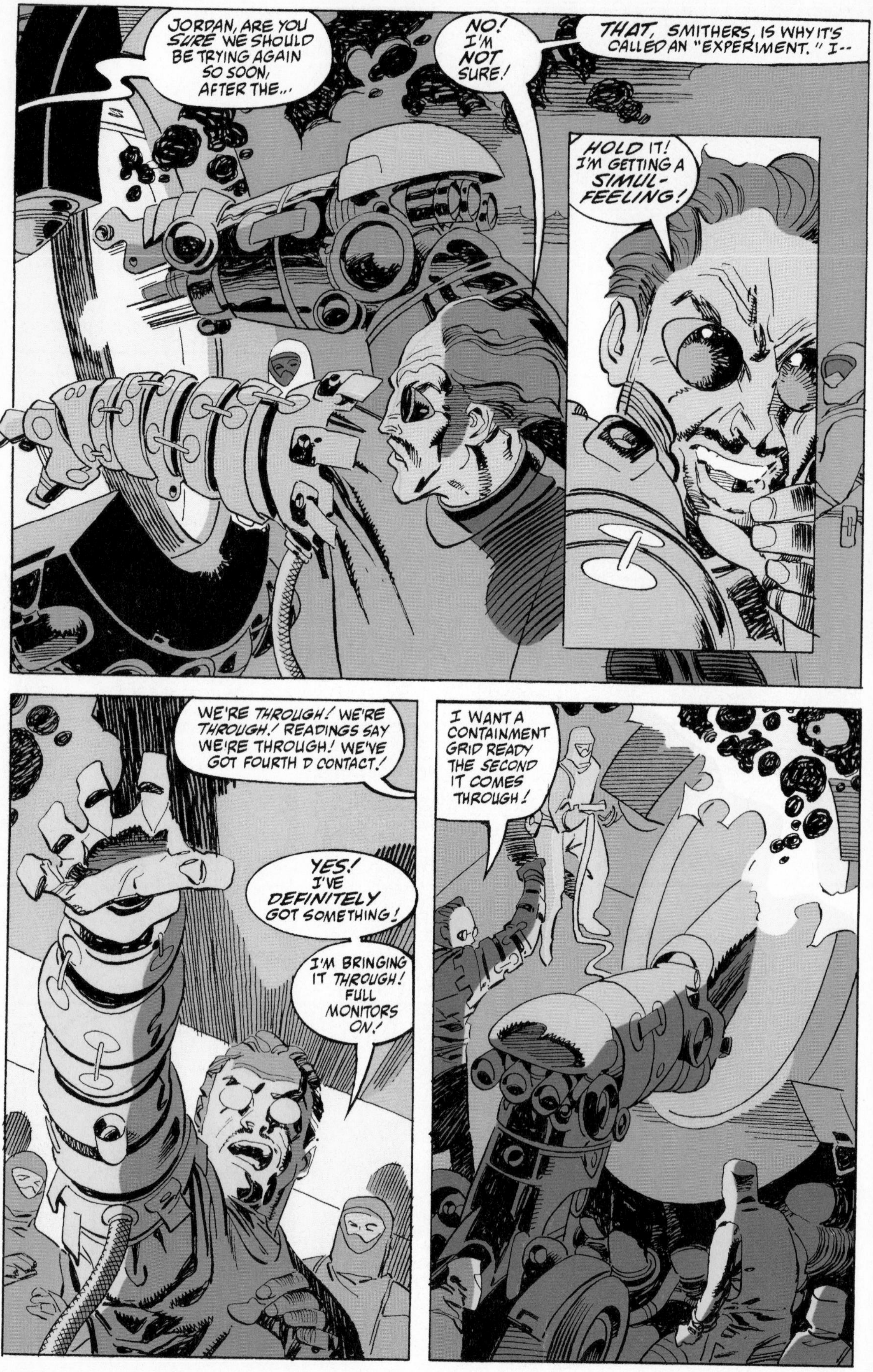
JORDAN, ARE YOU SURE WE SHOULD BE TRYING AGAIN SO SOON, AFTER THE...
NO! I'M NOT SURE!
THAT, SMITHERS, IS WHY IT'S CALLED AN "EXPERIMENT." I--
HOLD IT! I'M GETTING A SIMUL-FEELING!
WE'RE THROUGH! WE'RE THROUGH! READINGS SAY WE'RE THROUGH! WE'VE GOT FOURTH D CONTACT!
YES! I'VE DEFINITELY GOT SOMETHING!
I'M BRINGING IT THROUGH! FULL MONITORS ON!
I WANT A CONTAINMENT GRID READY THE SECOND IT COMES THROUGH!

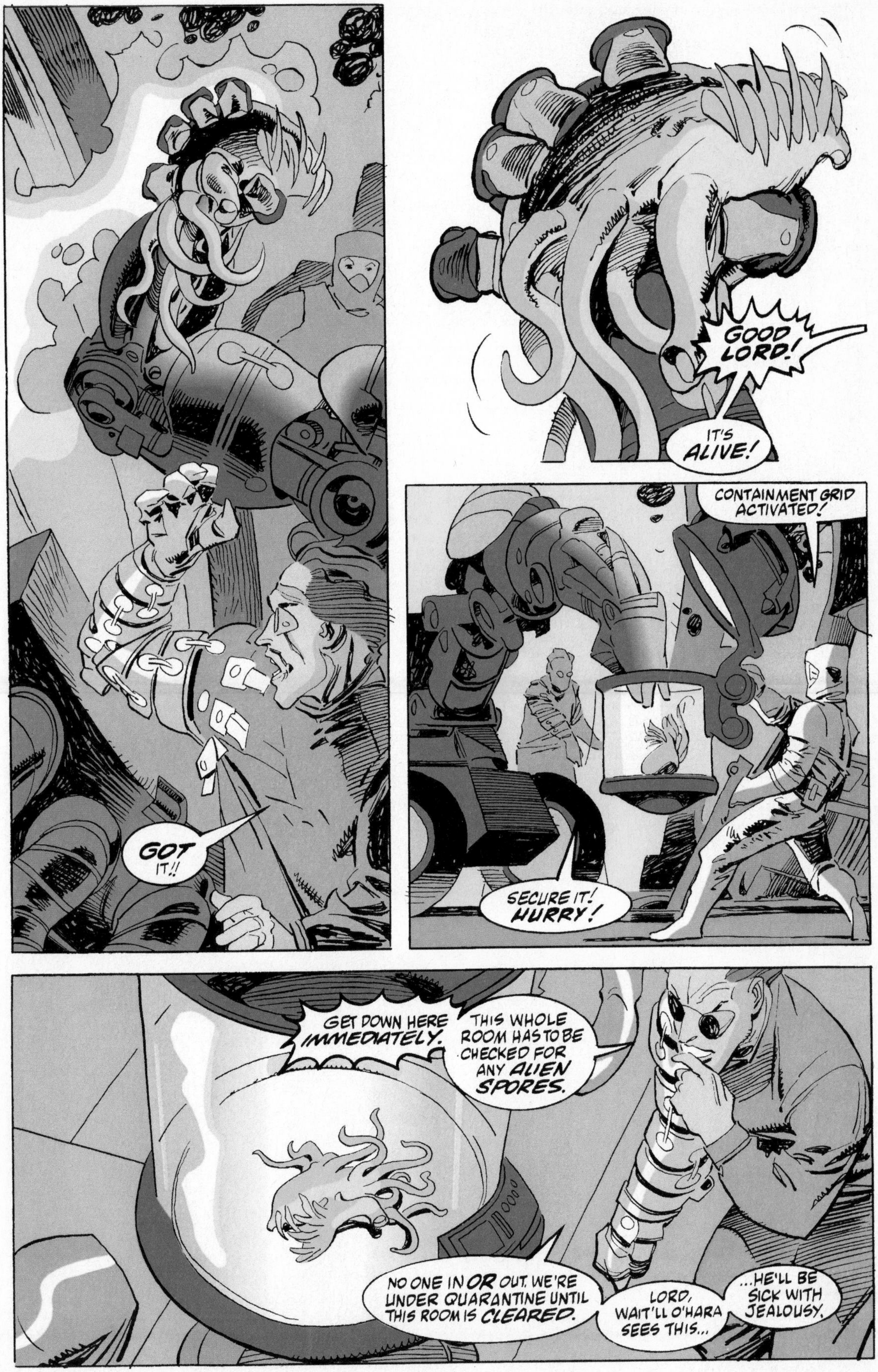
GOT IT!!
GOOD LORD!
IT'S ALIVE!
CONTAINMENT GRID ACTIVATED!
SECURE IT! HURRY!
GET DOWN HERE IMMEDIATELY.
THIS WHOLE ROOM HAS TO BE CHECKED FOR ANY ALIEN SPORES.
NO ONE IN OR OUT. WE'RE UNDER QUARANTINE UNTIL THIS ROOM IS CLEARED.
LORD, WAIT'LL O'HARA SEES THIS...
...HE'LL BE SICK WITH JEALOUSY.

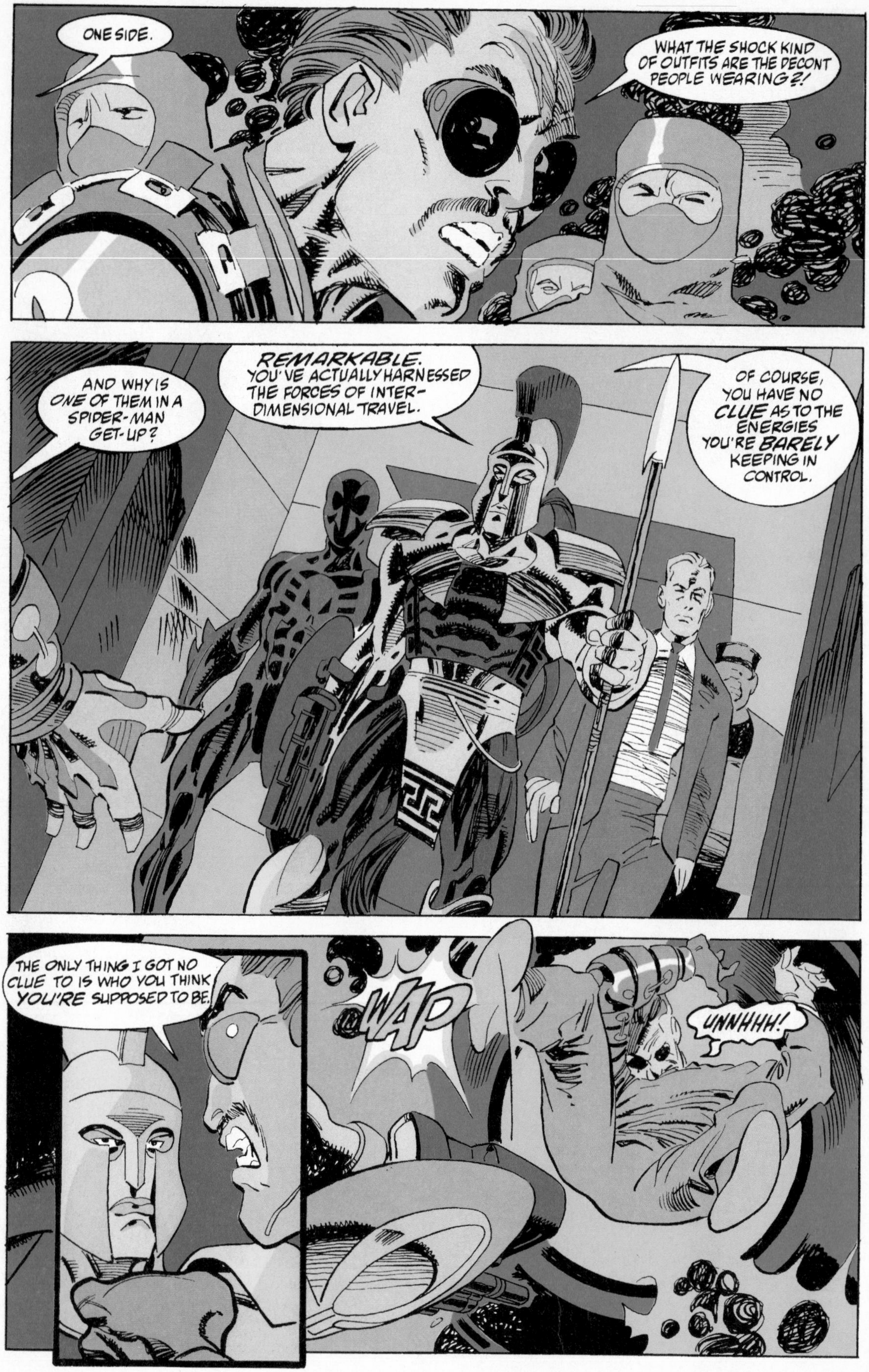
ONE SIDE.
WHAT THE SHOCK KIND OF OUTFITS ARE THE DECONT PEOPLE WEARING?!
AND WHY IS ONE OF THEM IN A SPIDER-MAN GET-UP?
REMARKABLE. YOU'VE ACTUALLY HARNESSED THE FORCES OF INTER-DIMENSIONAL TRAVEL.
OF COURSE, YOU HAVE NO CLUE AS TO THE ENERGIES YOU'RE BARELY KEEPING IN CONTROL.
THE ONLY THING I GOT NO CLUE TO IS WHO YOU THINK YOU'RE SUPPOSED TO BE.
WAP
UNNHHH!

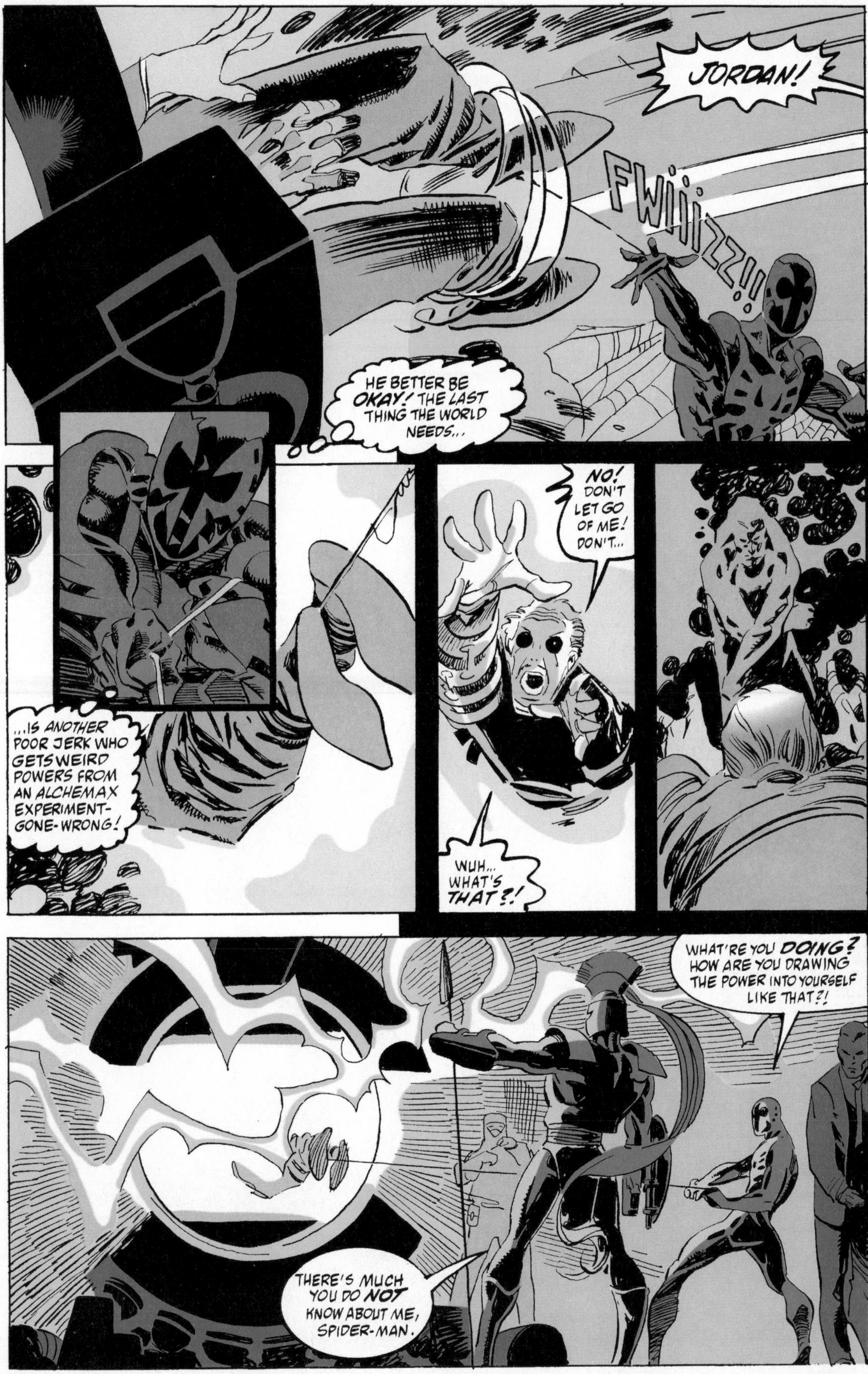

JORDAN!
FWIIJIZZZ!!
HE BETTER BE OKAY! THE LAST THING THE WORLD NEEDS...
...IS ANOTHER POOR JERK WHO GETS WEIRD POWERS FROM AN ALCHEMAX EXPERIMENT-GONE-WRONG!
NO! DON'T LET GO OF ME! DON'T...
WUH... WHAT'S THAT?!
WHAT'RE YOU DOING? HOW ARE YOU DRAWING THE POWER INTO YOURSELF LIKE THAT?!
THERE'S MUCH YOU DO NOT KNOW ABOUT ME, SPIDER-MAN.

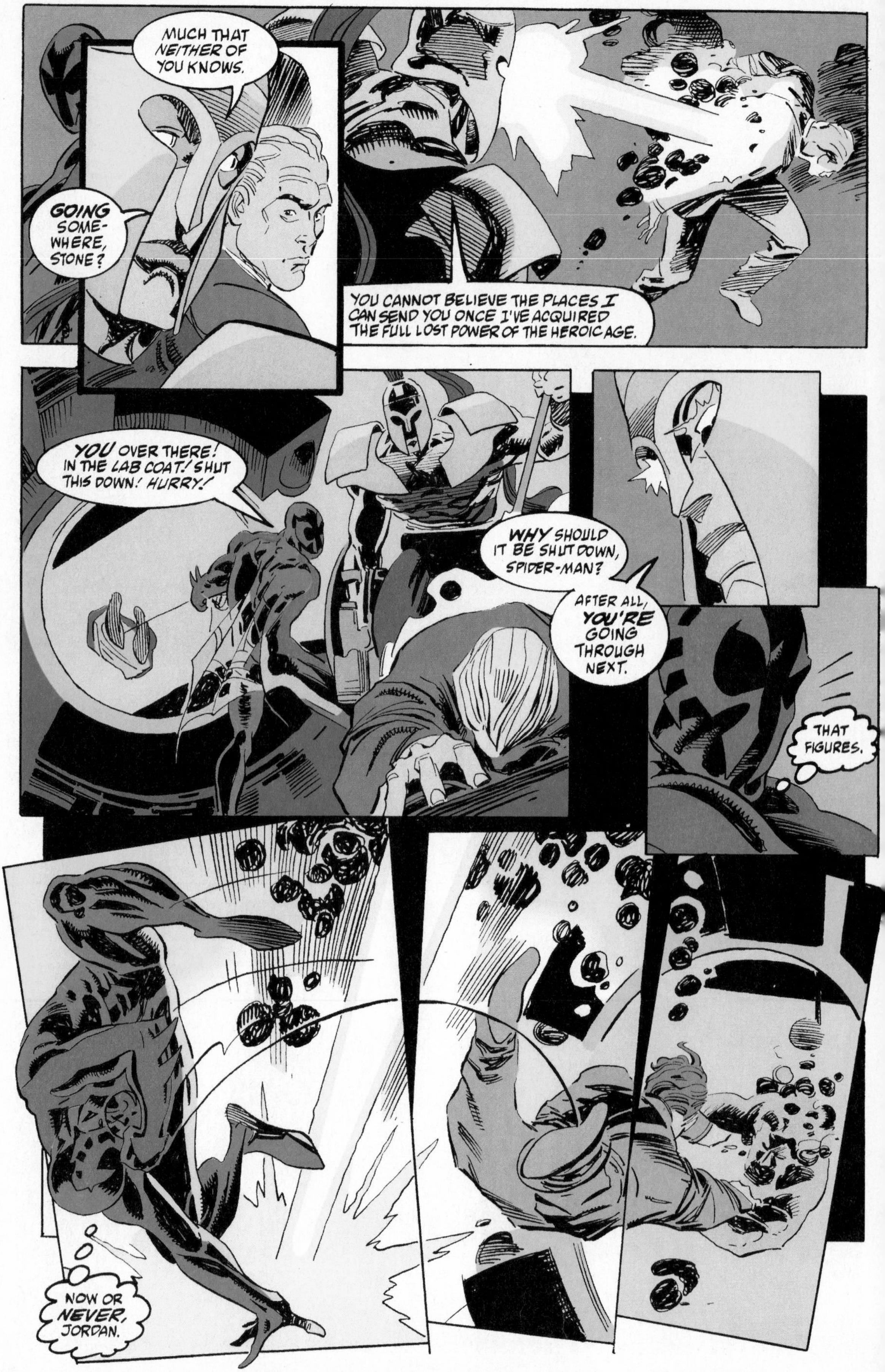
MUCH THAT NEITHER OF YOU KNOWS.
GOING SOME-WHERE, STONE?
YOU CANNOT BELIEVE THE PLACES I CAN SEND YOU ONCE I'VE ACQUIRED THE FULL LOST POWER OF THE HEROIC AGE.
YOU OVER THERE! IN THE LAB COAT! SHUT THIS DOWN! HURRY!
WHY SHOULD IT BE SHUT DOWN, SPIDER-MAN?
AFTER ALL, YOU'RE GOING THROUGH NEXT.
THAT FIGURES.
NOW OR NEVER, JORDAN.

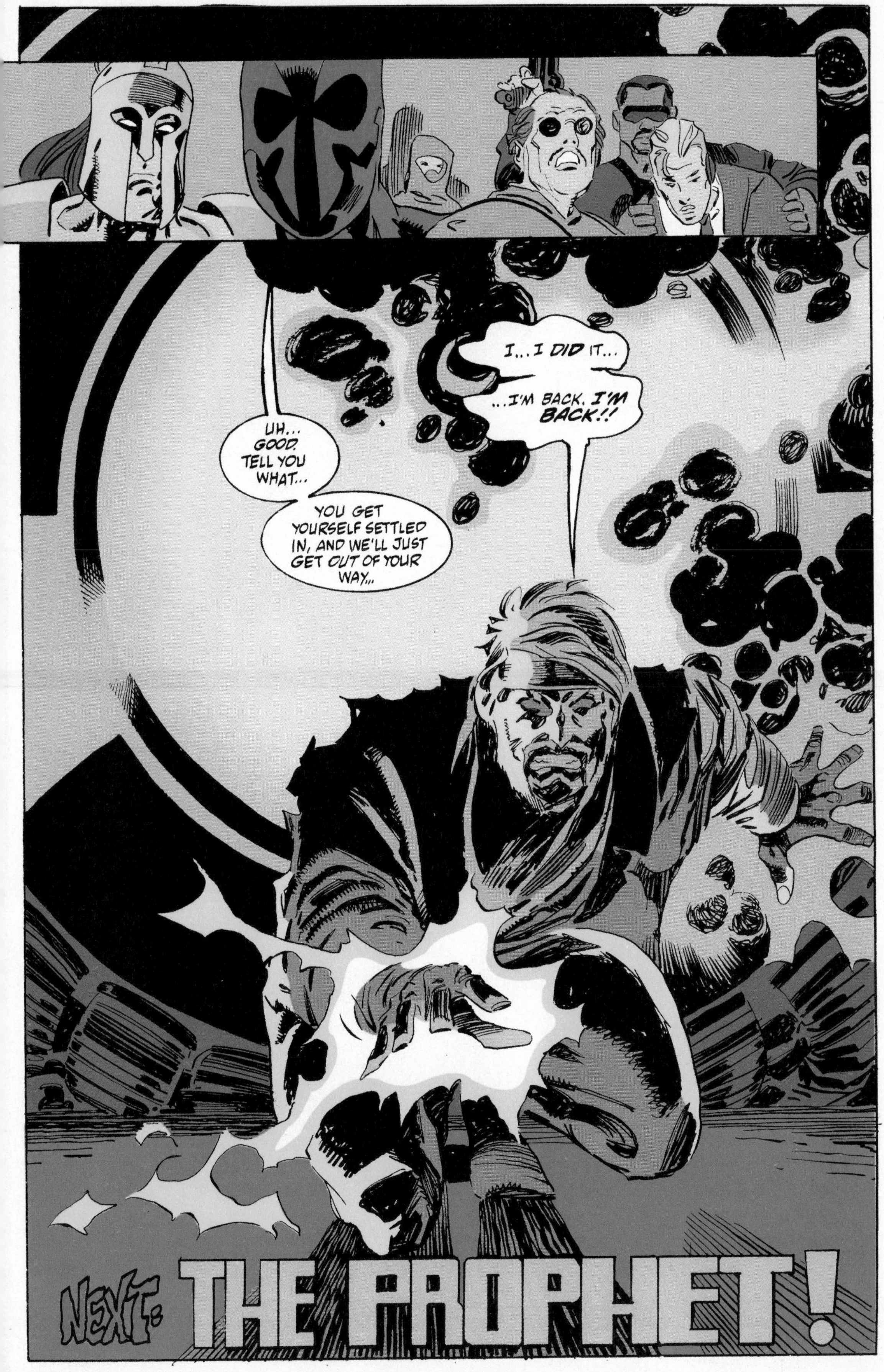
UH... GOOD. TELL YOU WHAT...
YOU GET YOURSELF SETTLED IN, AND WE'LL JUST GET OUT OF YOUR WAY...
I... I DID IT...
...I'M BACK. I'M BACK!!
NEXT: THE PROPHET!

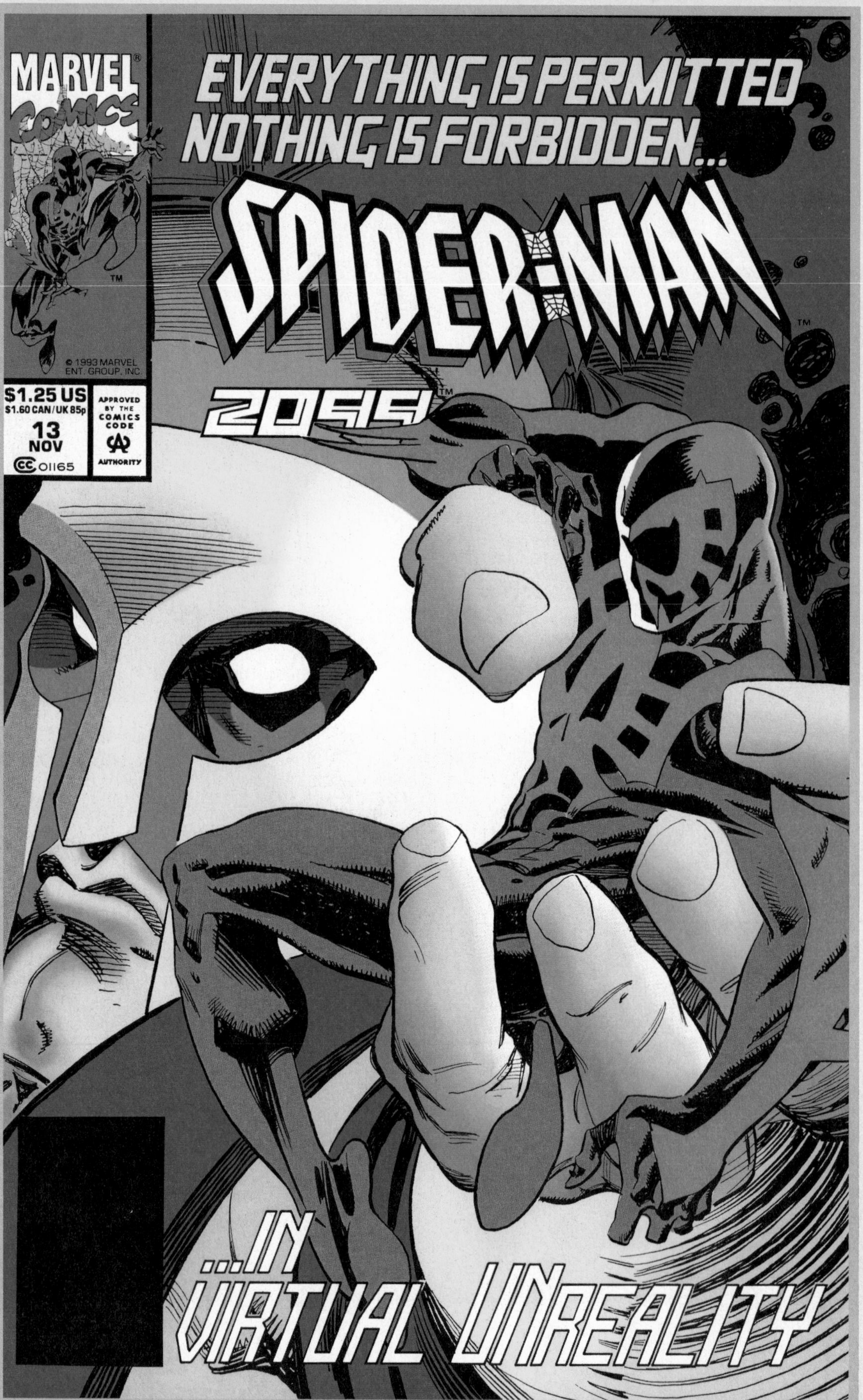

MARVEL COMICS
EVERYTHING IS PERMITTED
NOTHING IS FORBIDDEN...
SPIDER-MAN
2099
™
© 1993 MARVEL ENT. GROUP, INC.
$1.25 US
$1.60 CAN/UK 85p
13
NOV
CC 01165
APPROVED BY THE COMICS CODE AUTHORITY
...IN
VIRTUAL UNREALITY

Stan Lee PRESENTS:

Prophet AND Loss

| PETER DAVID WRITER | RICK LEONARDI PENCILS | AL WILLIAMSON INKS | RICK PARKER LETTERS | BUCCELLATO & ROUSSOS COLORS | JOEY CAVALIERI EDITOR | TOM DEFALCO EDITOR IN CHIEF |

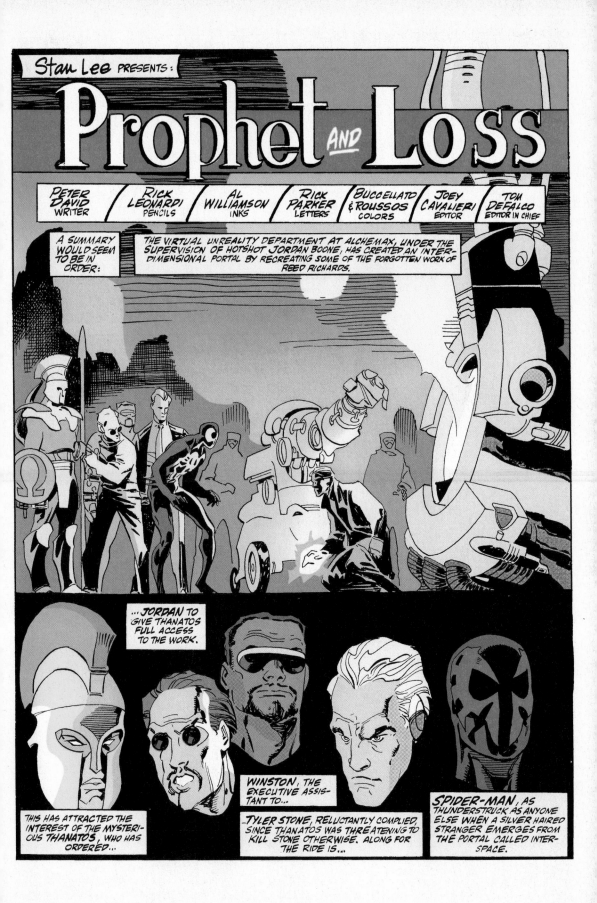

A SUMMARY WOULD SEEM TO BE IN ORDER:

THE VIRTUAL UNREALITY DEPARTMENT AT ALCHEMAX, UNDER THE SUPERVISION OF HOTSHOT JORDAN BOONE, HAS CREATED AN INTER-DIMENSIONAL PORTAL BY RECREATING SOME OF THE FORGOTTEN WORK OF REED RICHARDS.

...JORDAN TO GIVE THANATOS FULL ACCESS TO THE WORK.

THIS HAS ATTRACTED THE INTEREST OF THE MYSTERI-OUS THANATOS, WHO HAS ORDERED...

WINSTON, THE EXECUTIVE ASSIS-TANT TO...

...TYLER STONE, RELUCTANTLY COMPLIED, SINCE THANATOS WAS THREATENING TO KILL STONE OTHERWISE. ALONG FOR THE RIDE IS...

SPIDER-MAN, AS THUNDERSTRUCK AS ANYONE ELSE WHEN A SILVER HAIRED STRANGER EMERGES FROM THE PORTAL CALLED INTER-SPACE.

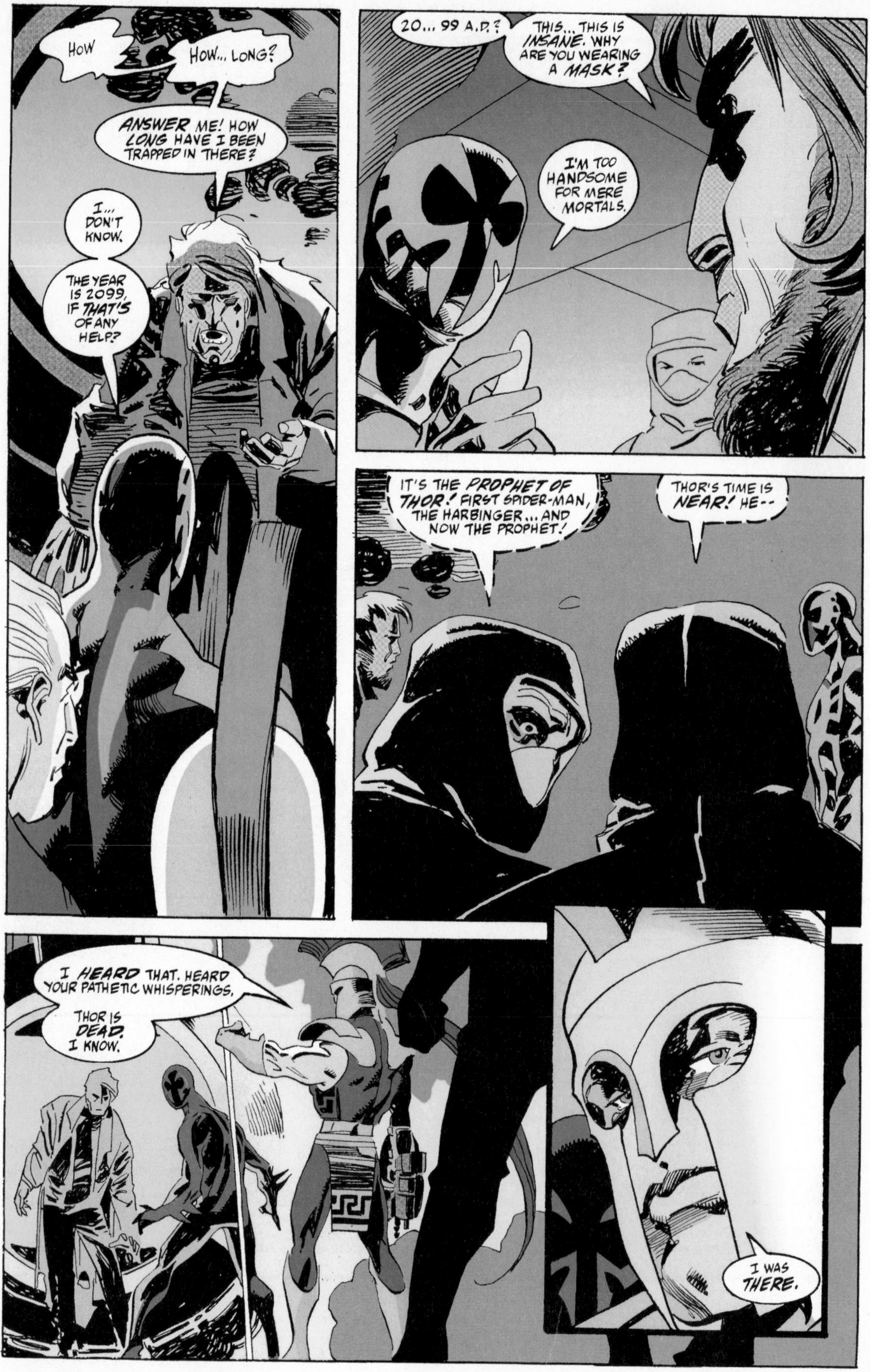
HOW
HOW... LONG?
ANSWER ME! HOW LONG HAVE I BEEN TRAPPED IN THERE?
I... DON'T KNOW.
THE YEAR IS 2099, IF THAT'S OF ANY HELP?
20... 99 A.D.?
THIS... THIS IS INSANE. WHY ARE YOU WEARING A MASK?
I'M TOO HANDSOME FOR MERE MORTALS.
IT'S THE PROPHET OF THOR! FIRST SPIDER-MAN, THE HARBINGER... AND NOW THE PROPHET!
THOR'S TIME IS NEAR! HE--
I HEARD THAT. HEARD YOUR PATHETIC WHISPERINGS.
THOR IS DEAD. I KNOW.
I WAS THERE.

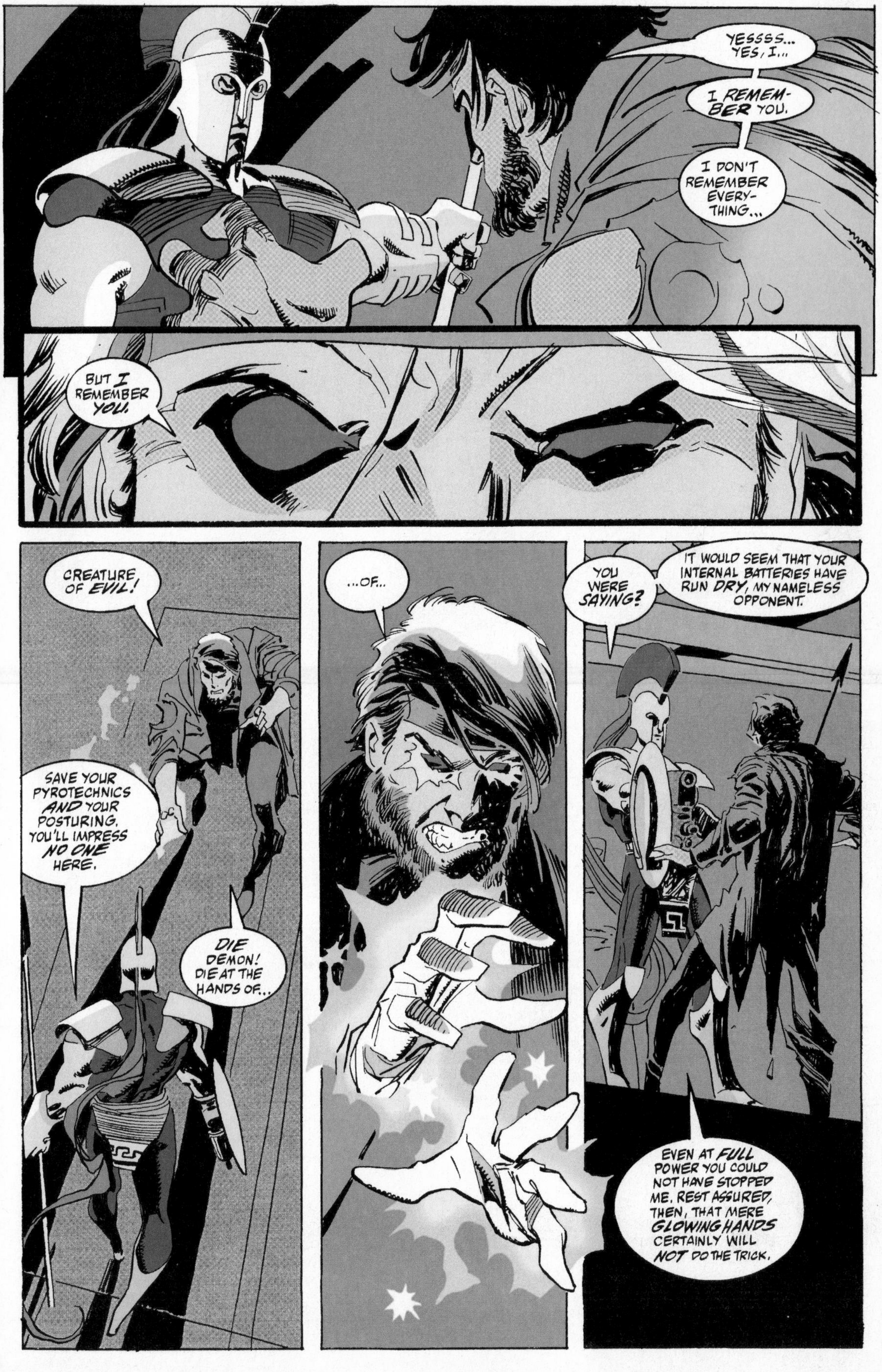
YESSSS... YES, I...
I REMEMBER YOU.
I DON'T REMEMBER EVERYTHING...
BUT I REMEMBER YOU.
CREATURE OF EVIL!
SAVE YOUR PYROTECHNICS AND YOUR POSTURING. YOU'LL IMPRESS NO ONE HERE.
DIE DEMON! DIE AT THE HANDS OF...
...OF...
YOU WERE SAYING?
IT WOULD SEEM THAT YOUR INTERNAL BATTERIES HAVE RUN DRY, MY NAMELESS OPPONENT.
EVEN AT FULL POWER YOU COULD NOT HAVE STOPPED ME. REST ASSURED, THEN, THAT MERE GLOWING HANDS CERTAINLY WILL NOT DO THE TRICK.

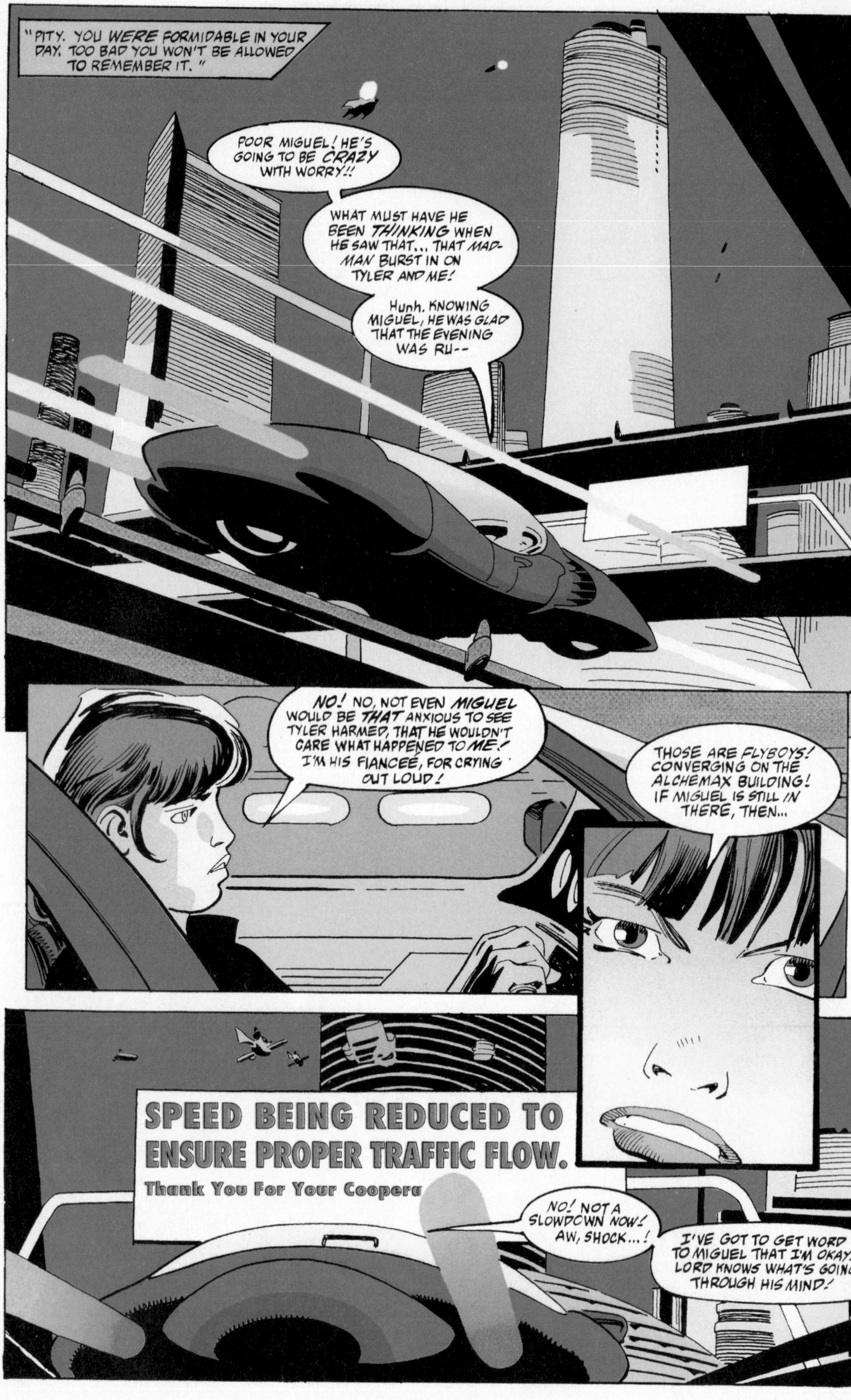
"PITY. YOU WERE FORMIDABLE IN YOUR DAY. TOO BAD YOU WON'T BE ALLOWED TO REMEMBER IT."
POOR MIGUEL! HE'S GOING TO BE CRAZY WITH WORRY!!
WHAT MUST HAVE HE BEEN THINKING WHEN HE SAW THAT... THAT MAD-MAN BURST IN ON TYLER AND ME!
Hunh. KNOWING MIGUEL, HE WAS GLAD THAT THE EVENING WAS RU--
NO! NO, NOT EVEN MIGUEL WOULD BE THAT ANXIOUS TO SEE TYLER HARMED, THAT HE WOULDN'T CARE WHAT HAPPENED TO ME! I'M HIS FIANCEE, FOR CRYING OUT LOUD!
THOSE ARE FLYBOYS! CONVERGING ON THE ALCHEMAX BUILDING! IF MIGUEL IS STILL IN THERE, THEN...
SPEED BEING REDUCED TO ENSURE PROPER TRAFFIC FLOW.
Thank You For Your Coopera
NO! NOT A SLOWDOWN NOW! AW, SHOCK...!
I'VE GOT TO GET WORD TO MIGUEL THAT I'M OKAY! LORD KNOWS WHAT'S GOING THROUGH HIS MIND!

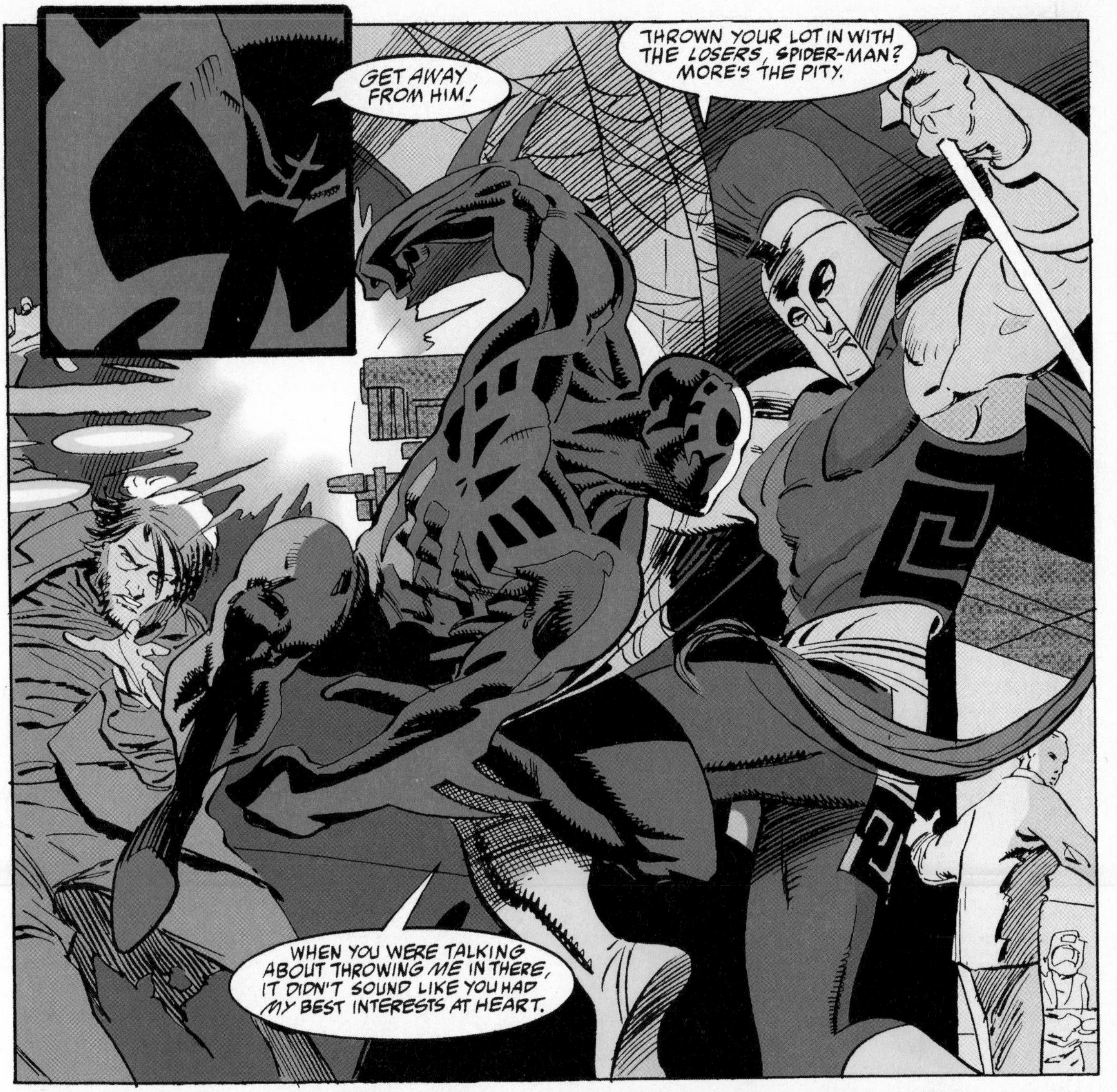
GET AWAY FROM HIM!
THROWN YOUR LOT IN WITH THE LOSERS, SPIDER-MAN? MORE'S THE PITY.
WHEN YOU WERE TALKING ABOUT THROWING ME IN THERE, IT DIDN'T SOUND LIKE YOU HAD MY BEST INTERESTS AT HEART.

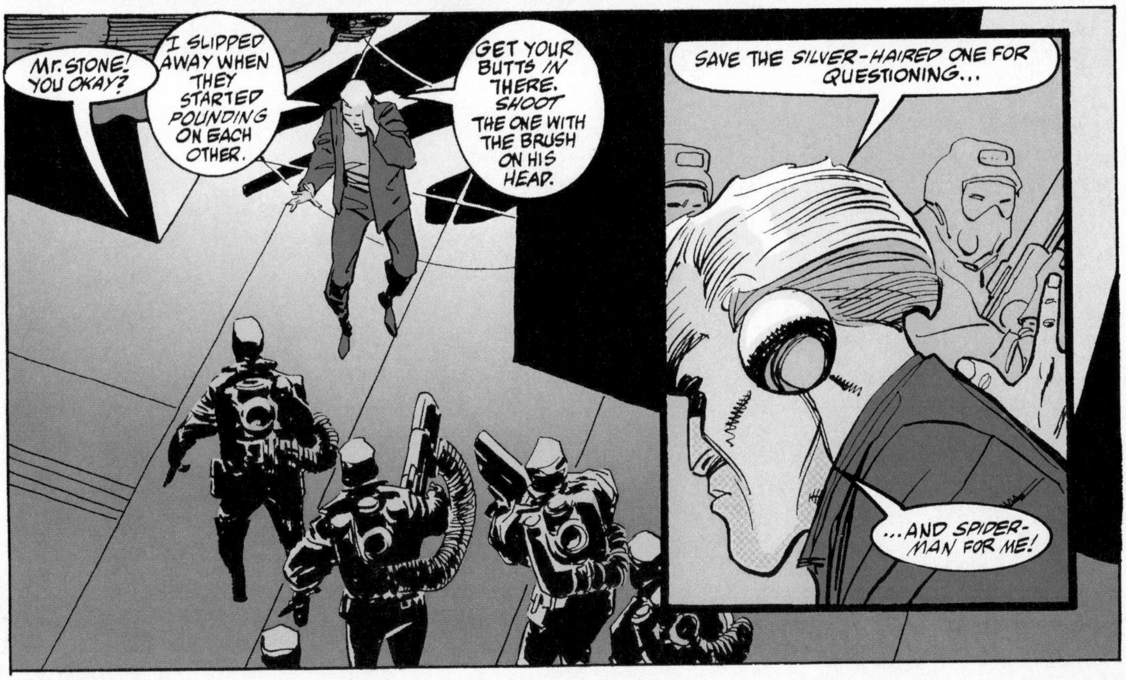
Mr. STONE! YOU OKAY?
I SLIPPED AWAY WHEN THEY STARTED POUNDING ON EACH OTHER.
GET YOUR BUTTS IN THERE. SHOOT THE ONE WITH THE BRUSH ON HIS HEAD.
SAVE THE SILVER-HAIRED ONE FOR QUESTIONING...
...AND SPIDER-MAN FOR ME!

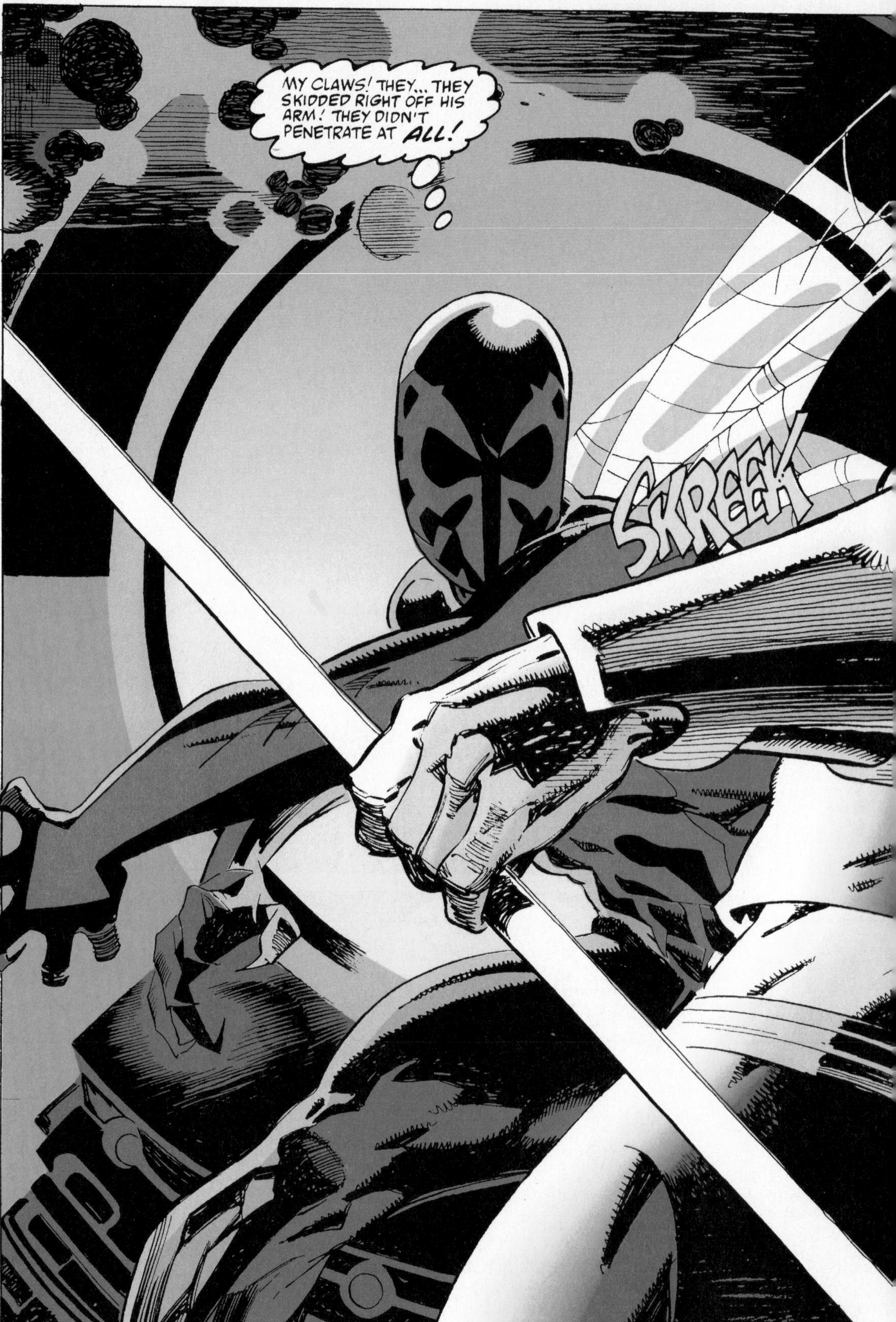
MY CLAWS! THEY... THEY SKIDDED RIGHT OFF HIS ARM! THEY DIDN'T PENETRATE AT ALL!
SKREEK

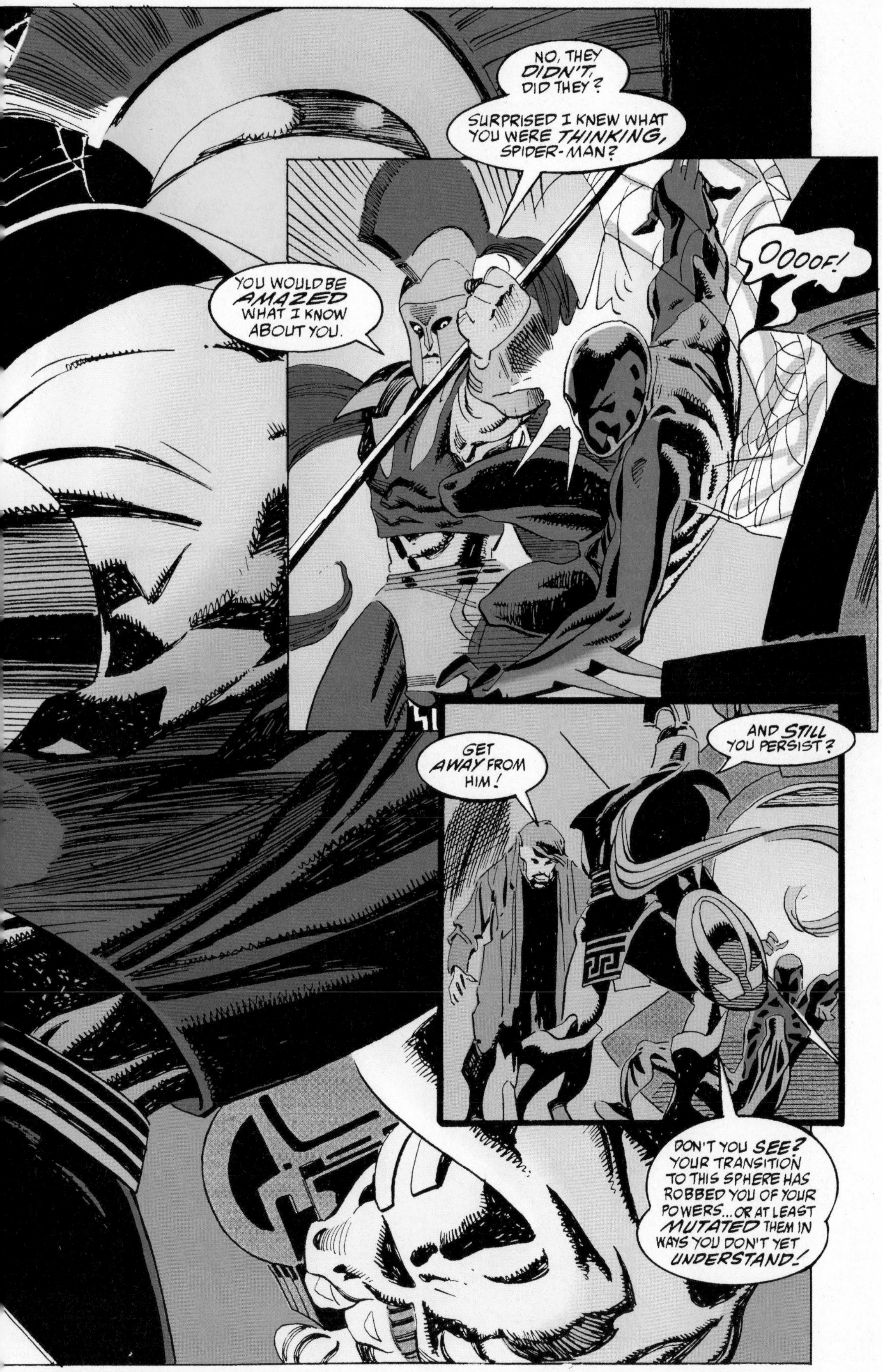
NO, THEY DIDN'T, DID THEY?
SURPRISED I KNEW WHAT YOU WERE THINKING, SPIDER-MAN?
YOU WOULD BE AMAZED WHAT I KNOW ABOUT YOU.
OOOOF!
GET AWAY FROM HIM!
AND STILL YOU PERSIST?
DON'T YOU SEE? YOUR TRANSITION TO THIS SPHERE HAS ROBBED YOU OF YOUR POWERS...OR AT LEAST MUTATED THEM IN WAYS YOU DON'T YET UNDERSTAND!

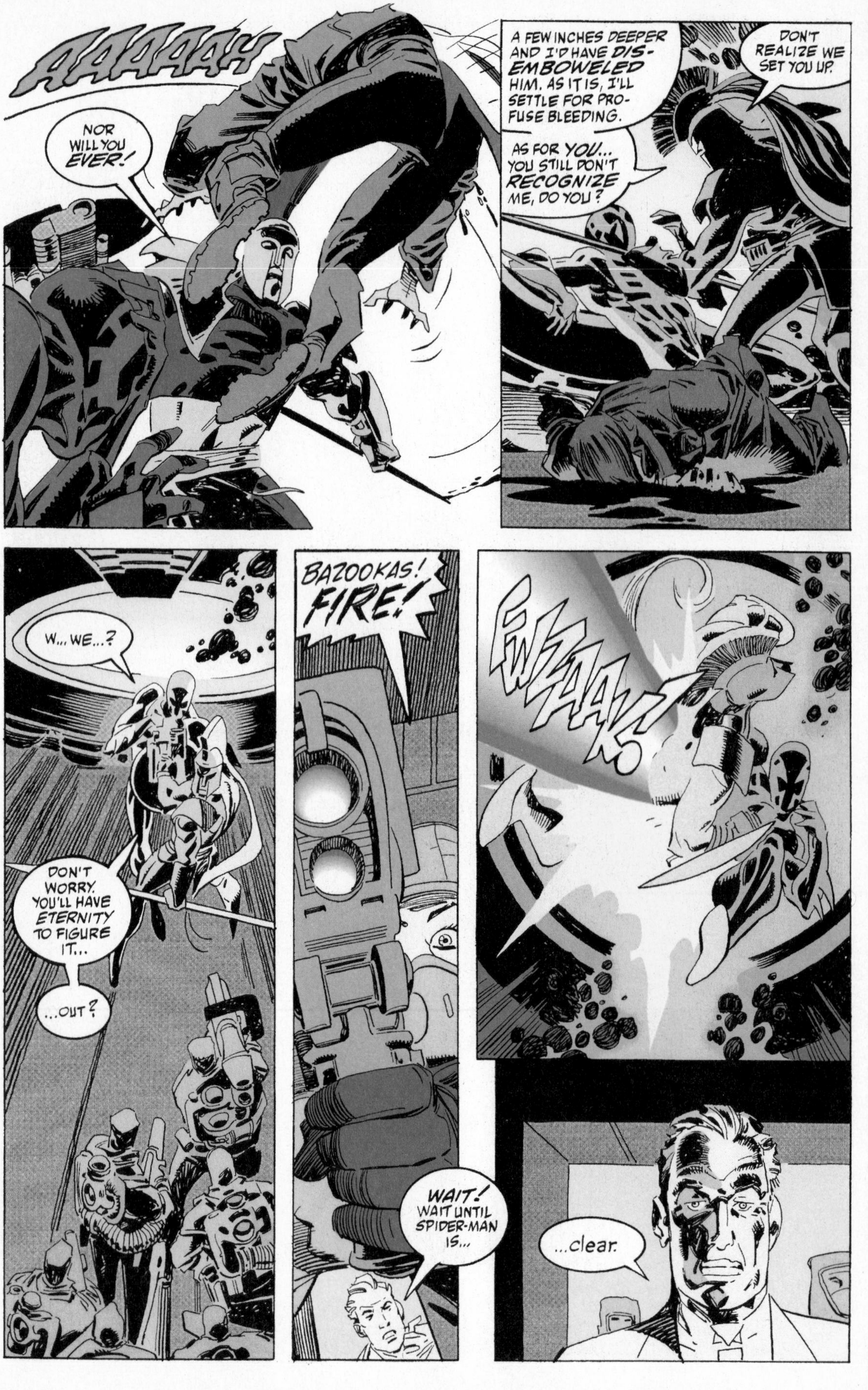
AAAAAH
NOR WILL YOU EVER!
A FEW INCHES DEEPER AND I'D HAVE DIS-EMBOWELED HIM. AS IT IS, I'LL SETTLE FOR PRO-FUSE BLEEDING.
AS FOR YOU... YOU STILL DON'T RECOGNIZE ME, DO YOU?
DON'T REALIZE WE SET YOU UP.
W... WE...?
DON'T WORRY. YOU'LL HAVE ETERNITY TO FIGURE IT...
...OUT?
BAZOOKAS! FIRE!
FWAAAK!
WAIT! WAIT UNTIL SPIDER-MAN IS...
...clear.

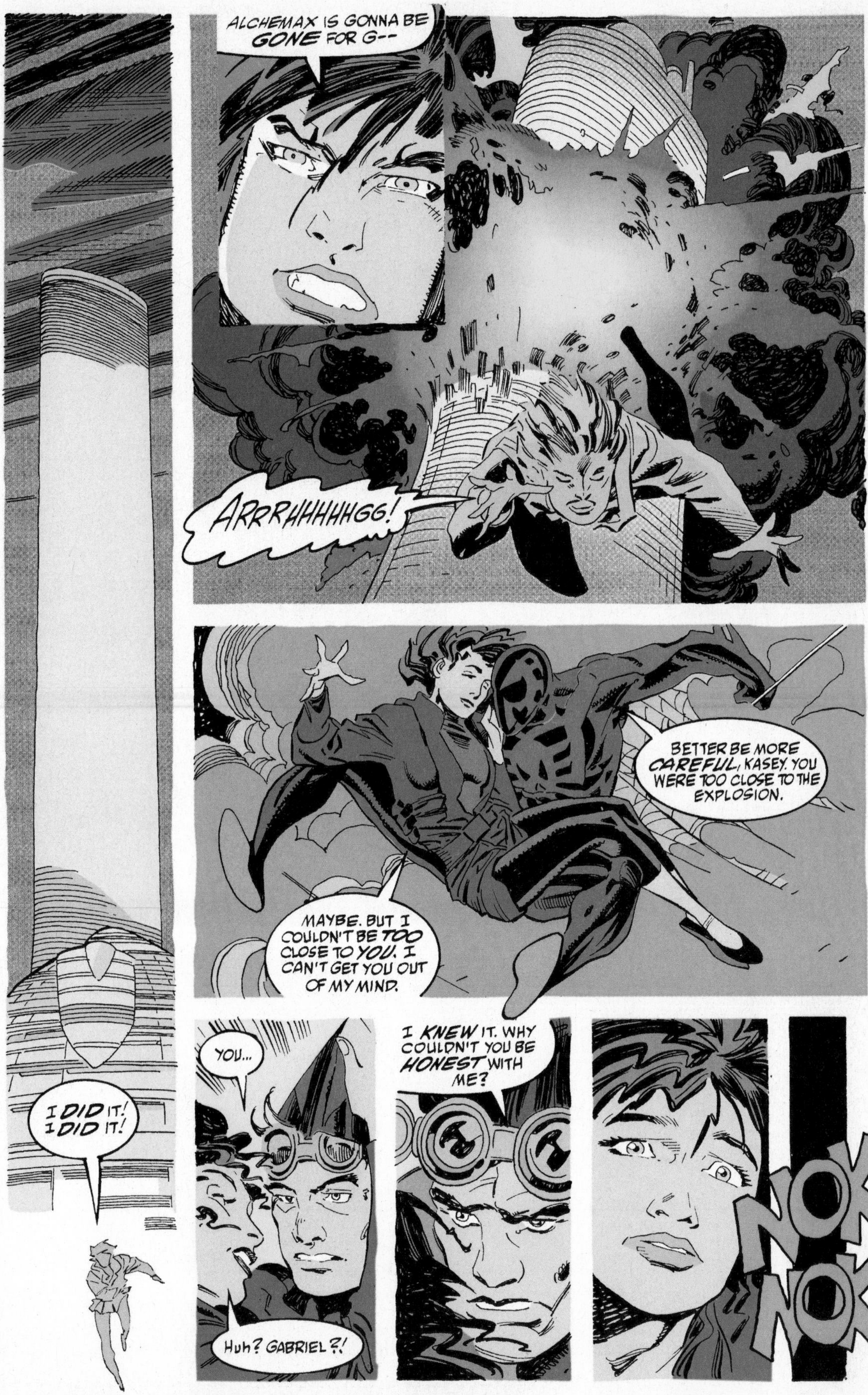

ALCHEMAX IS GONNA BE GONE FOR G--
ARRRHHHHHGG!
BETTER BE MORE CAREFUL, KASEY. YOU WERE TOO CLOSE TO THE EXPLOSION.
MAYBE. BUT I COULDN'T BE TOO CLOSE TO YOU. I CAN'T GET YOU OUT OF MY MIND.
I DID IT! I DID IT!
YOU...
Huh? GABRIEL?!
I KNEW IT. WHY COULDN'T YOU BE HONEST WITH ME?
NOK NOK

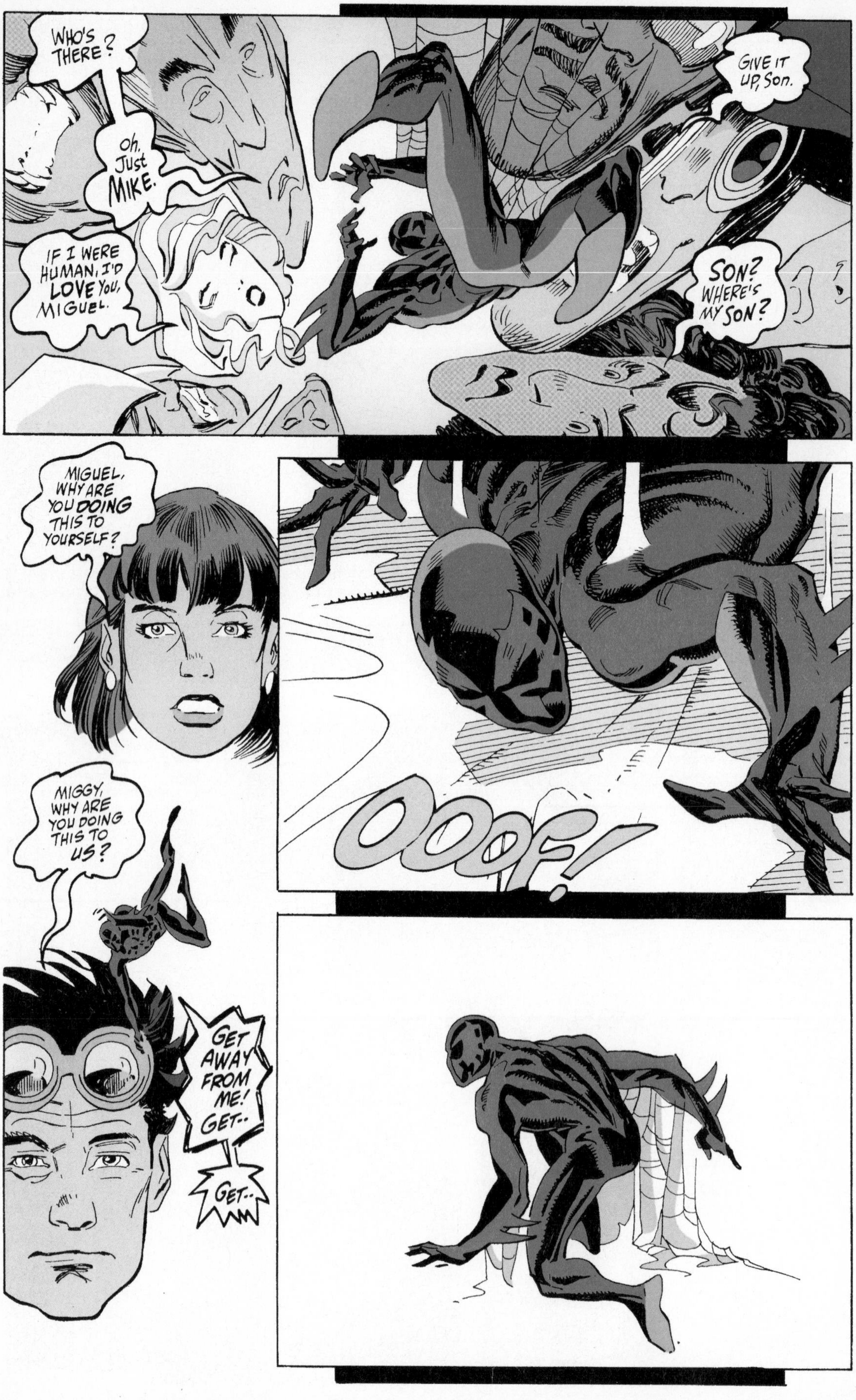
WHO'S THERE?
Oh, Just MIKE.
IF I WERE HUMAN, I'D LOVE YOU, MIGUEL.
GIVE IT UP, Son.
SON? WHERE'S MY SON?
MIGUEL, WHY ARE YOU DOING THIS TO YOURSELF?
OOOF!
MIGGY, WHY ARE YOU DOING THIS TO US?
GET AWAY FROM ME! GET..
GET..

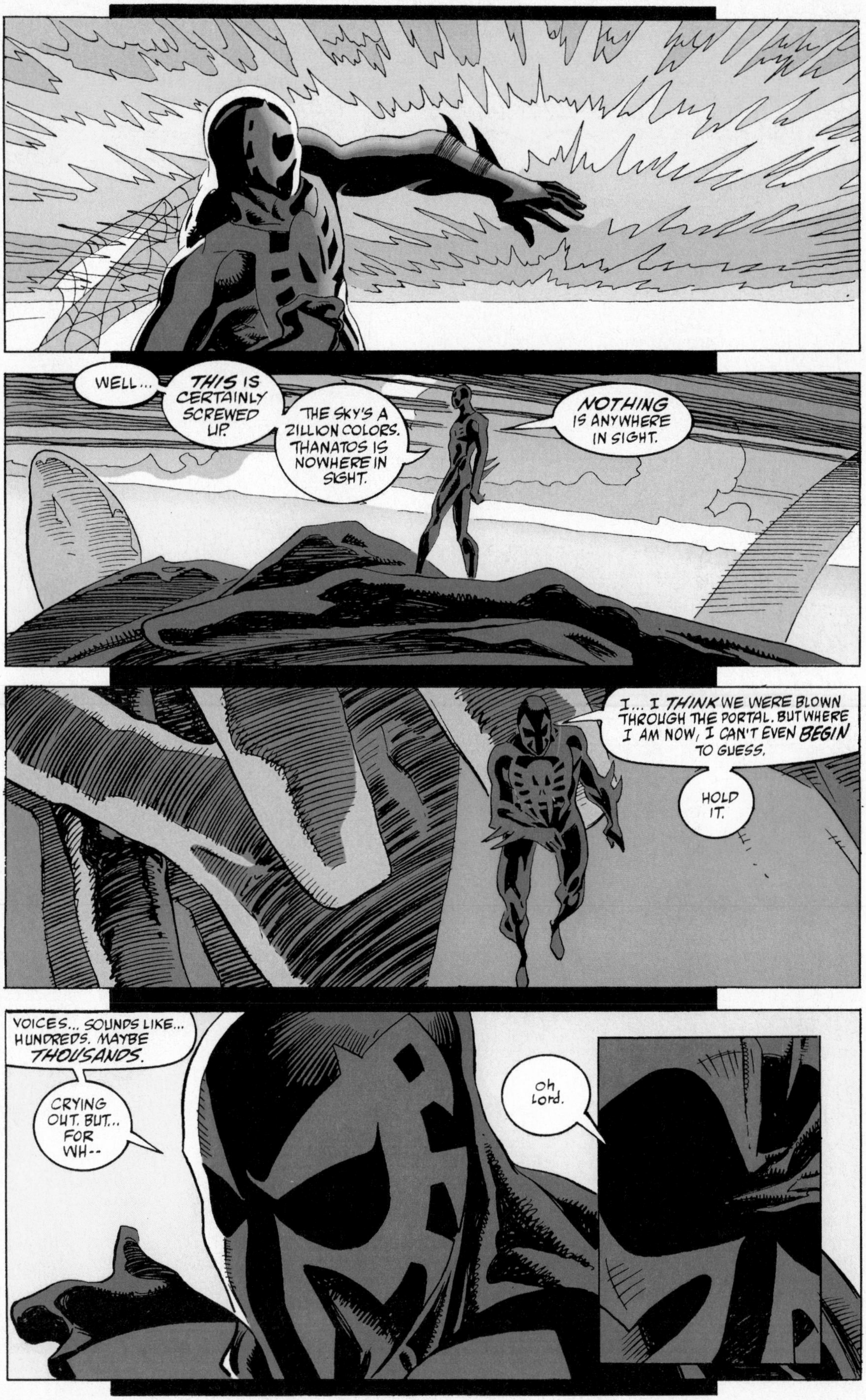

WELL...
THIS IS CERTAINLY SCREWED UP.
THE SKY'S A ZILLION COLORS. THANATOS IS NOWHERE IN SIGHT.
NOTHING IS ANYWHERE IN SIGHT.
I... I THINK WE WERE BLOWN THROUGH THE PORTAL. BUT WHERE I AM NOW, I CAN'T EVEN BEGIN TO GUESS.
HOLD IT.
VOICES... SOUNDS LIKE... HUNDREDS. MAYBE THOUSANDS.
CRYING OUT. BUT... FOR WH--
Oh Lord.

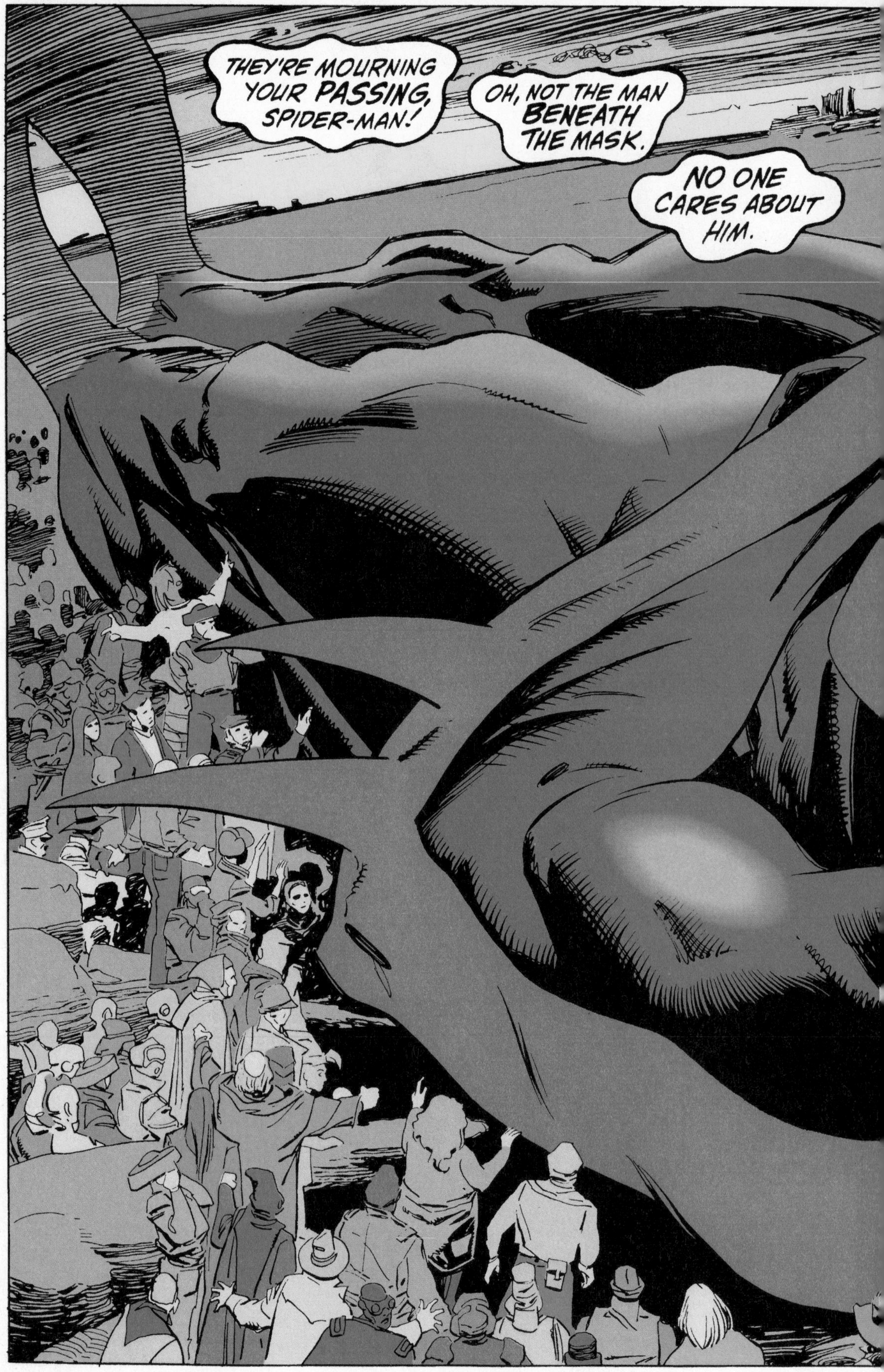
THEY'RE MOURNING YOUR PASSING, SPIDER-MAN!
OH, NOT THE MAN BENEATH THE MASK.
NO ONE CARES ABOUT HIM.

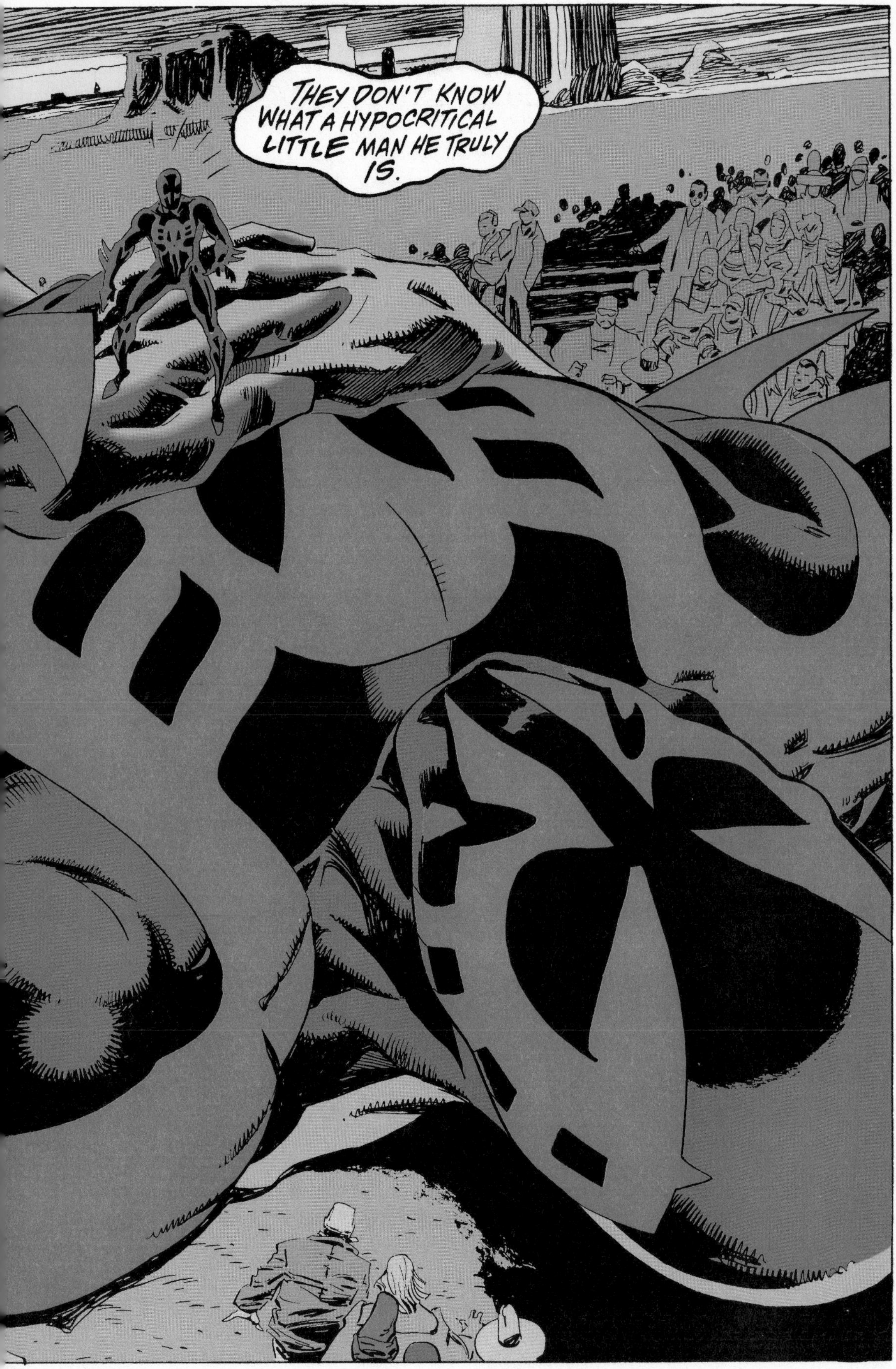
THEY DON'T KNOW WHAT A HYPOCRITICAL LITTLE MAN HE TRULY IS.

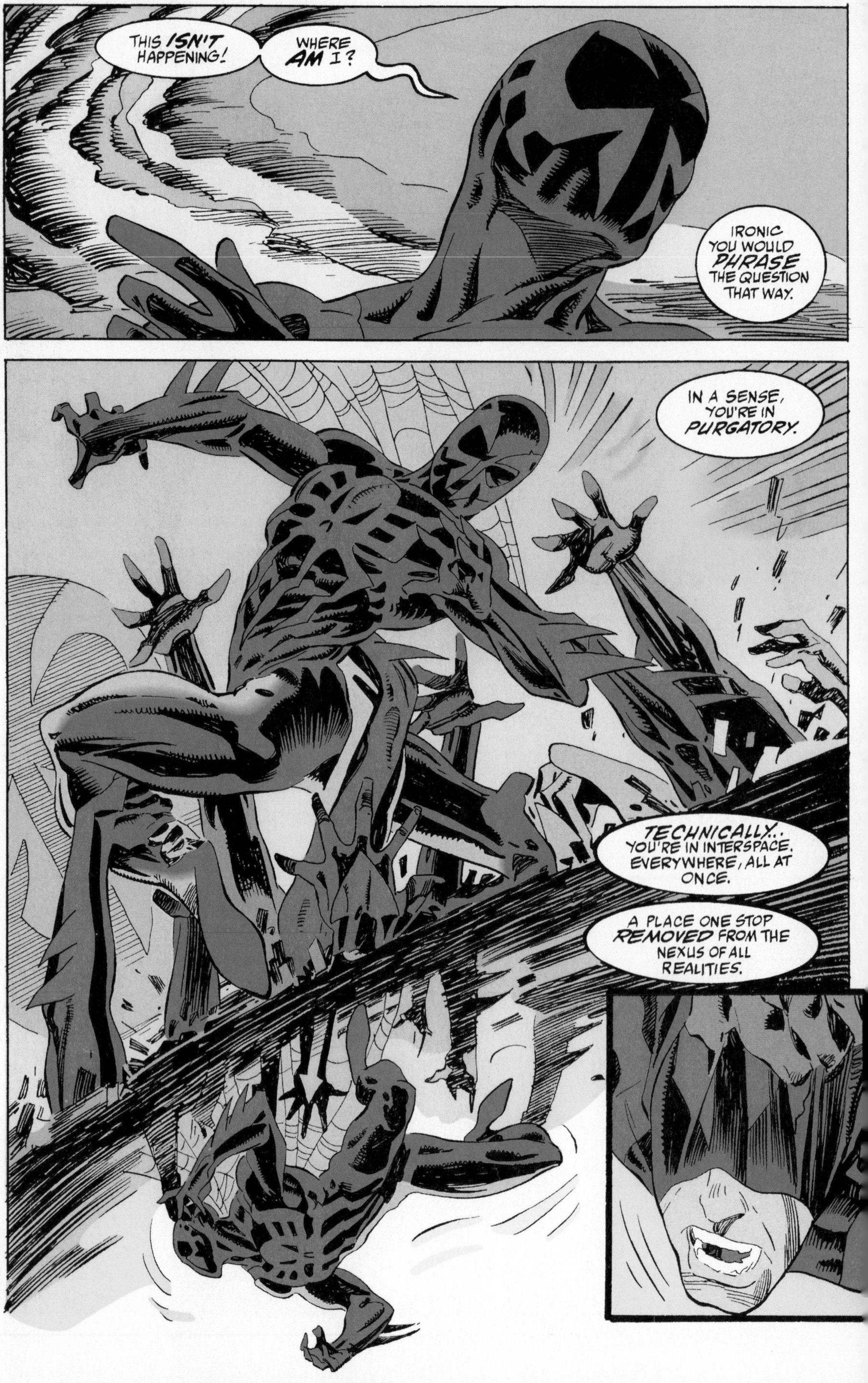
THIS ISN'T HAPPENING!
WHERE AM I?
IRONIC YOU WOULD PHRASE THE QUESTION THAT WAY.
IN A SENSE, YOU'RE IN PURGATORY.
TECHNICALLY... YOU'RE IN INTERSPACE. EVERYWHERE, ALL AT ONCE.
A PLACE ONE STOP REMOVED FROM THE NEXUS OF ALL REALITIES.

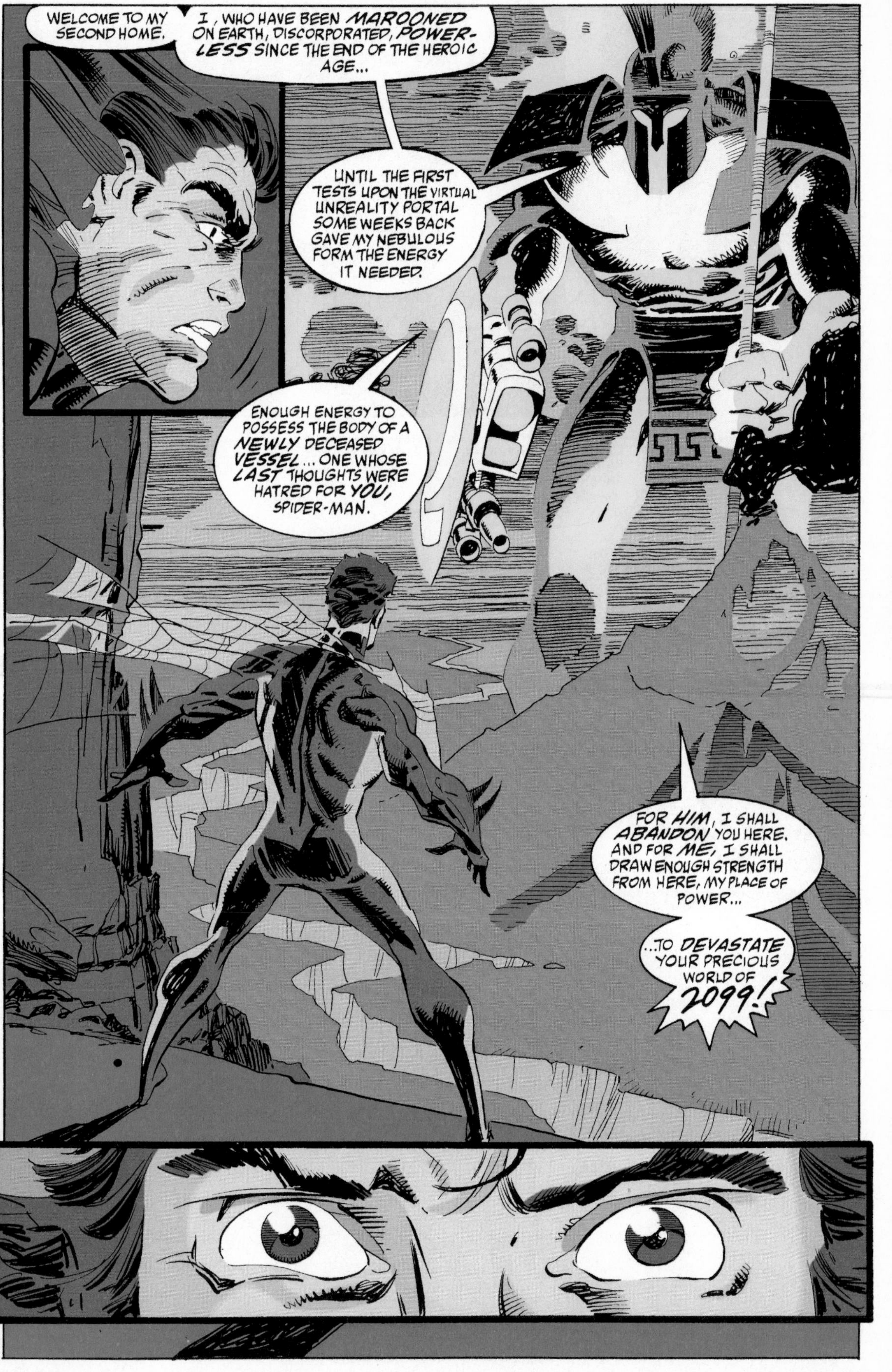
WELCOME TO MY SECOND HOME.
I, WHO HAVE BEEN MAROONED ON EARTH, DISCORPORATED, POWERLESS SINCE THE END OF THE HEROIC AGE...
UNTIL THE FIRST TESTS UPON THE VIRTUAL UNREALITY PORTAL SOME WEEKS BACK GAVE MY NEBULOUS FORM THE ENERGY IT NEEDED.
ENOUGH ENERGY TO POSSESS THE BODY OF A NEWLY DECEASED VESSEL... ONE WHOSE LAST THOUGHTS WERE HATRED FOR YOU, SPIDER-MAN.
FOR HIM, I SHALL ABANDON YOU HERE. AND FOR ME, I SHALL DRAW ENOUGH STRENGTH FROM HERE, MY PLACE OF POWER...
...TO DEVASTATE YOUR PRECIOUS WORLD OF 2099!

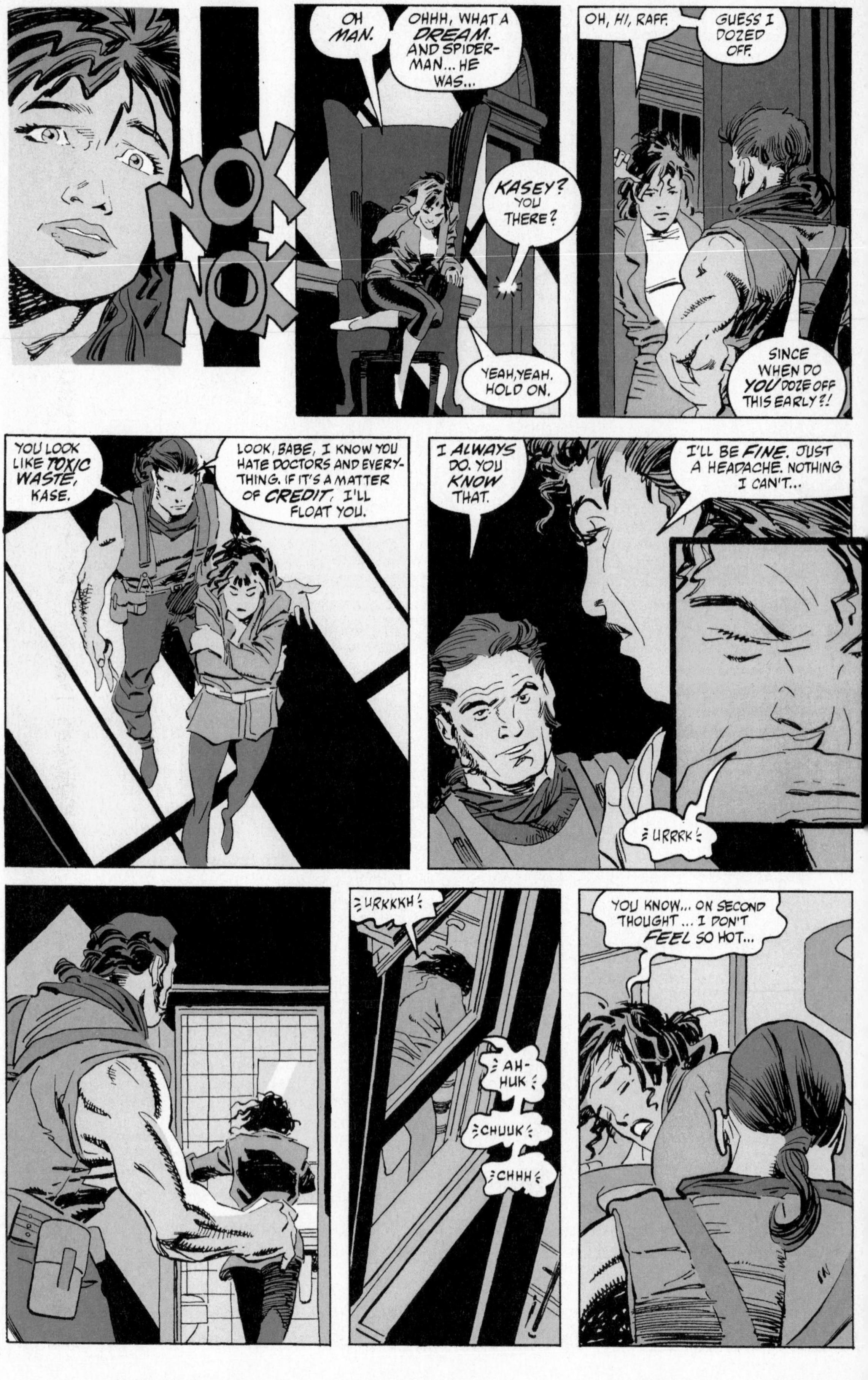
NOK
NOK
OH MAN.
OHHH, WHAT A DREAM. AND SPIDER-MAN... HE WAS...
KASEY? YOU THERE?
YEAH, YEAH. HOLD ON.
OH, HI, RAFF.
GUESS I DOZED OFF.
SINCE WHEN DO YOU DOZE OFF THIS EARLY?!
YOU LOOK LIKE TOXIC WASTE, KASE.
LOOK, BABE, I KNOW YOU HATE DOCTORS AND EVERYTHING. IF IT'S A MATTER OF CREDIT, I'LL FLOAT YOU.
I ALWAYS DO. YOU KNOW THAT.
I'LL BE FINE. JUST A HEADACHE. NOTHING I CAN'T...
URRRK
URKKKH
AH-HUK
CHUUK
CHHH
YOU KNOW... ON SECOND THOUGHT... I DON'T FEEL SO HOT...

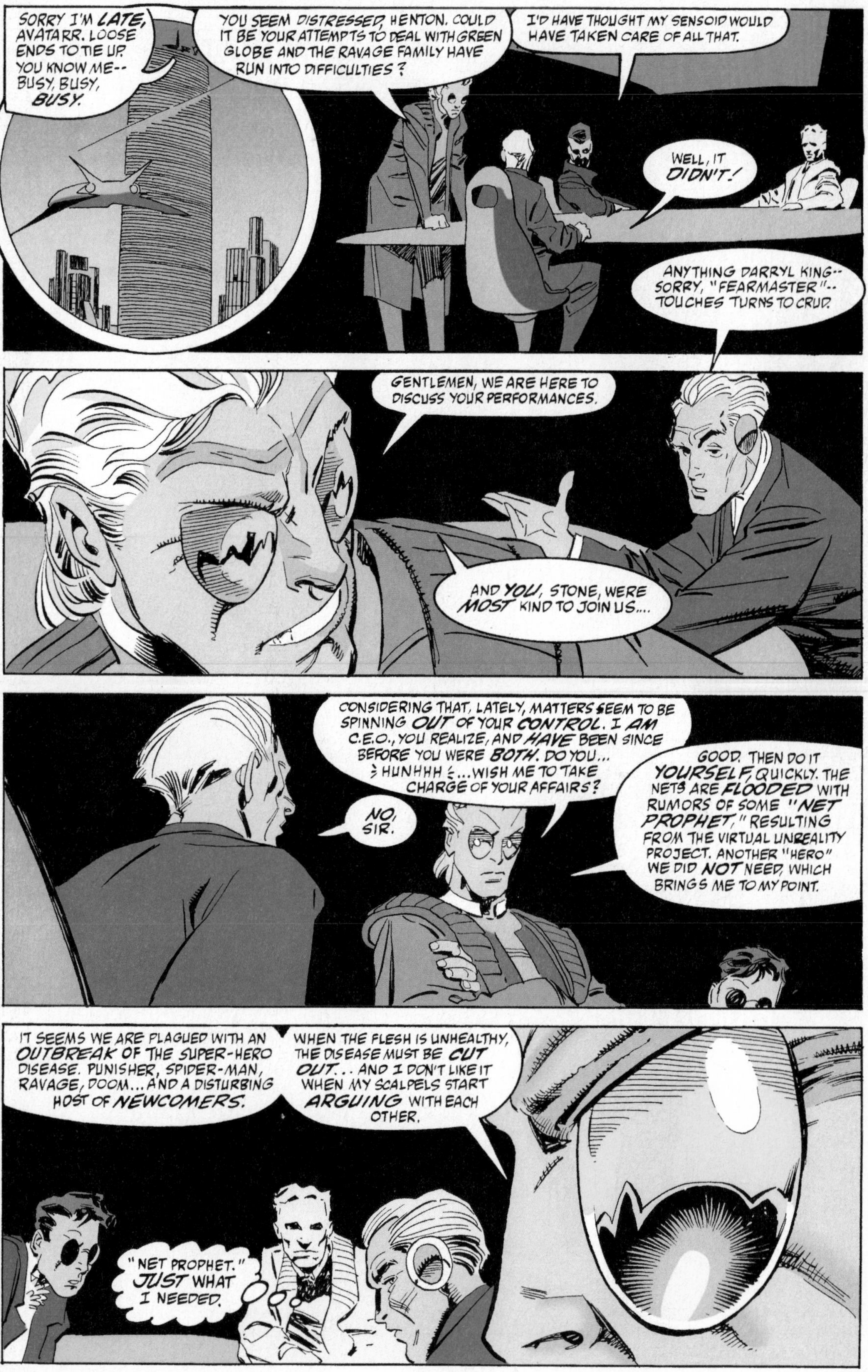
SORRY I'M LATE, AVATARR. LOOSE ENDS TO TIE UP. YOU KNOW ME-- BUSY, BUSY, BUSY.
YOU SEEM DISTRESSED, HENTON. COULD IT BE YOUR ATTEMPTS TO DEAL WITH GREEN GLOBE AND THE RAVAGE FAMILY HAVE RUN INTO DIFFICULTIES?
I'D HAVE THOUGHT MY SENSOID WOULD HAVE TAKEN CARE OF ALL THAT.
WELL, IT DIDN'T!
ANYTHING DARRYL KING-- SORRY, "FEARMASTER"-- TOUCHES TURNS TO CRUD.
GENTLEMEN, WE ARE HERE TO DISCUSS YOUR PERFORMANCES.
AND YOU, STONE, WERE MOST KIND TO JOIN US....
CONSIDERING THAT, LATELY, MATTERS SEEM TO BE SPINNING OUT OF YOUR CONTROL. I AM C.E.O., YOU REALIZE, AND HAVE BEEN SINCE BEFORE YOU WERE BOTH. DO YOU... HUNHHH ...WISH ME TO TAKE CHARGE OF YOUR AFFAIRS?
NO, SIR.
GOOD. THEN DO IT YOURSELF, QUICKLY. THE NETS ARE FLOODED WITH RUMORS OF SOME "NET PROPHET," RESULTING FROM THE VIRTUAL UNREALITY PROJECT. ANOTHER "HERO" WE DID NOT NEED, WHICH BRINGS ME TO MY POINT.
IT SEEMS WE ARE PLAGUED WITH AN OUTBREAK OF THE SUPER-HERO DISEASE. PUNISHER, SPIDER-MAN, RAVAGE, DOOM... AND A DISTURBING HOST OF NEWCOMERS.
WHEN THE FLESH IS UNHEALTHY, THE DISEASE MUST BE CUT OUT... AND I DON'T LIKE IT WHEN MY SCALPELS START ARGUING WITH EACH OTHER.
"NET PROPHET." JUST WHAT I NEEDED.

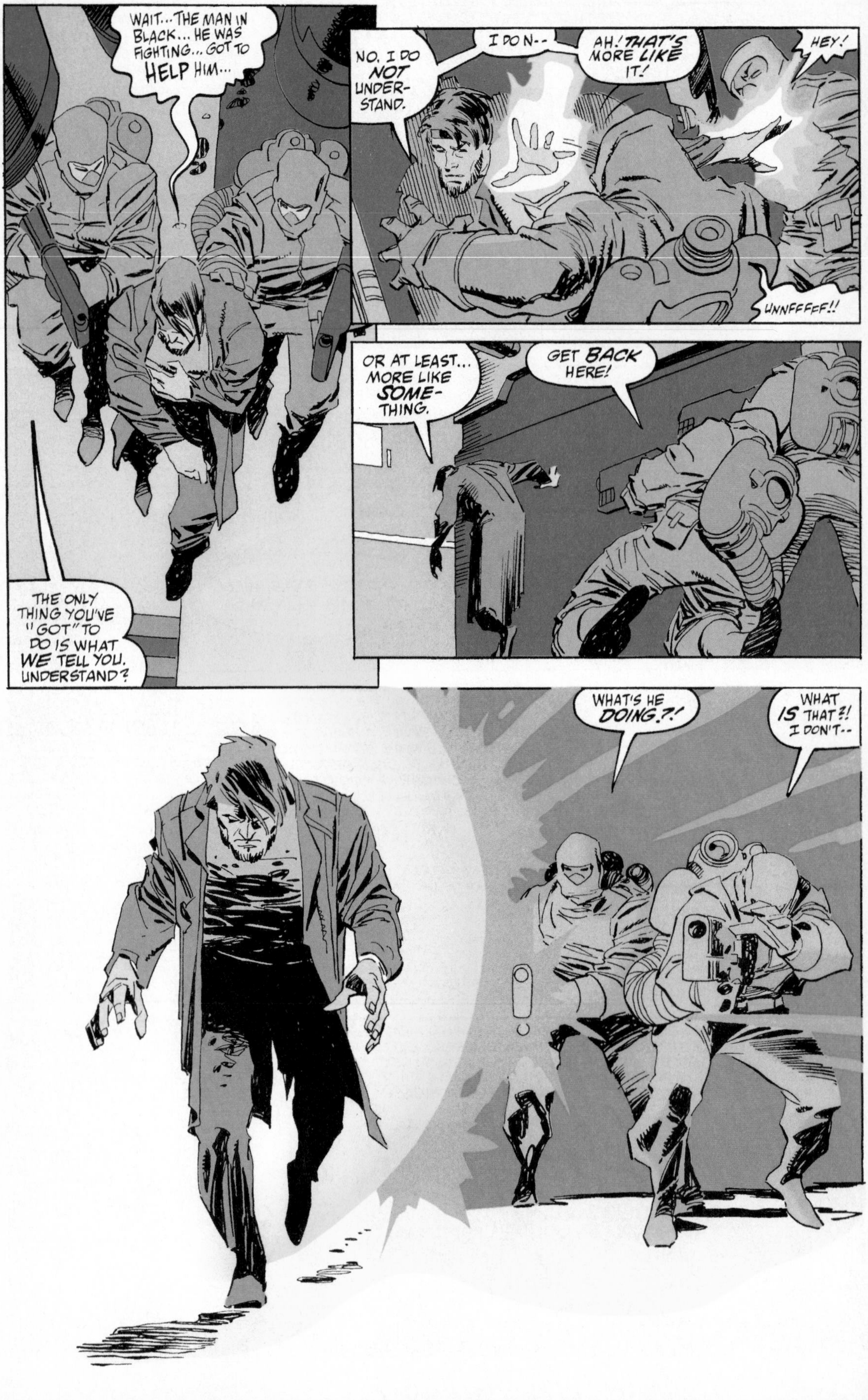
WAIT... THE MAN IN BLACK... HE WAS FIGHTING... GOT TO HELP HIM...
THE ONLY THING YOU'VE "GOT" TO DO IS WHAT WE TELL YOU. UNDERSTAND?
NO, I DO NOT UNDER-STAND.
I DO N--
AH! THAT'S MORE LIKE IT!
HEY!
UNNFFFFF!!
OR AT LEAST... MORE LIKE SOME-THING.
GET BACK HERE!
WHAT'S HE DOING?!
WHAT IS THAT?! I DON'T--
!

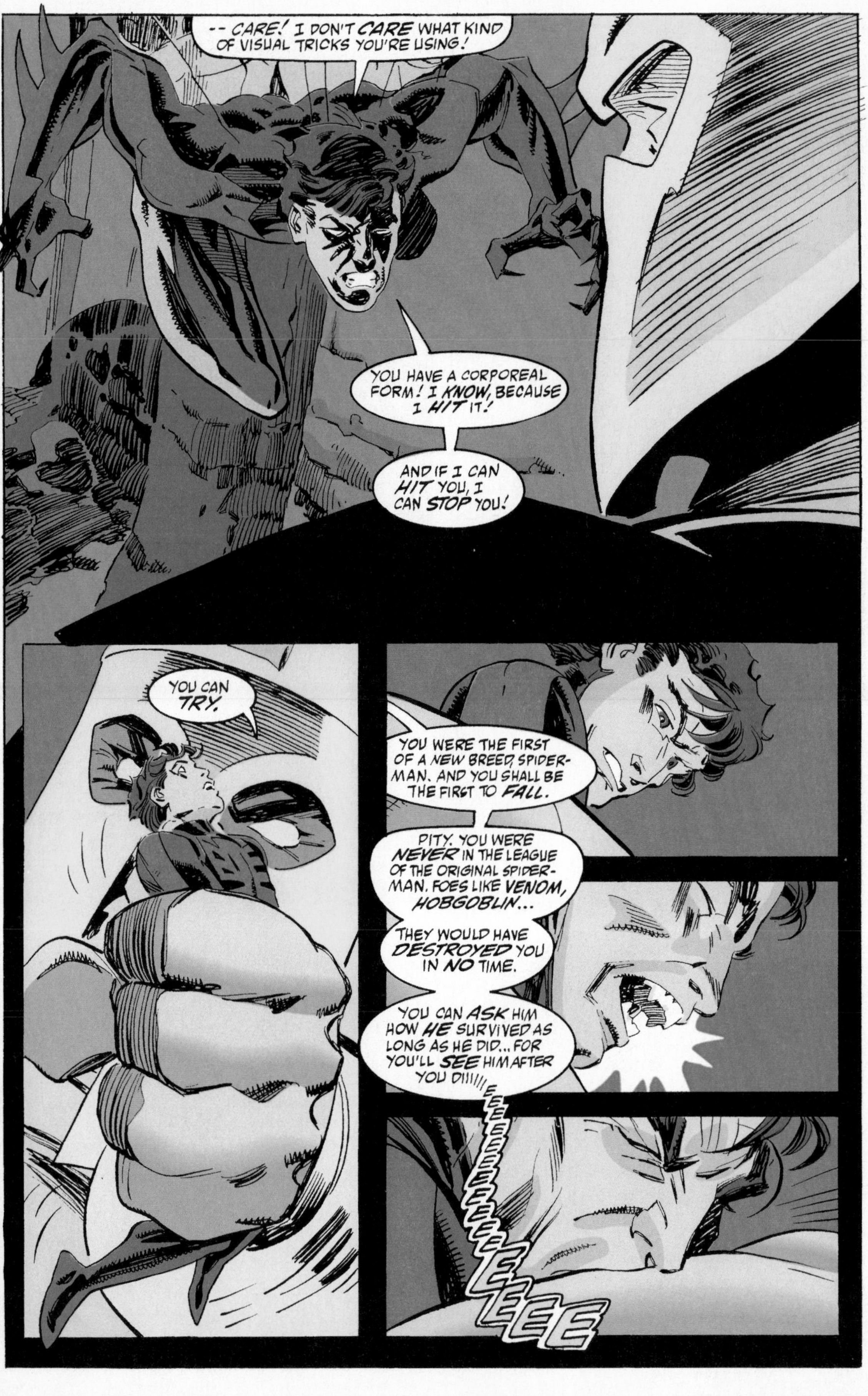
-- CARE! I DON'T CARE WHAT KIND OF VISUAL TRICKS YOU'RE USING!
YOU HAVE A CORPOREAL FORM! I KNOW, BECAUSE I HIT IT!
AND IF I CAN HIT YOU, I CAN STOP YOU!
YOU CAN TRY.
YOU WERE THE FIRST OF A NEW BREED, SPIDER-MAN. AND YOU SHALL BE THE FIRST TO FALL.
PITY. YOU WERE NEVER IN THE LEAGUE OF THE ORIGINAL SPIDER-MAN. FOES LIKE VENOM, HOBGOBLIN...
THEY WOULD HAVE DESTROYED YOU IN NO TIME.
YOU CAN ASK HIM HOW HE SURVIVED AS LONG AS HE DID... FOR YOU'LL SEE HIM AFTER YOU DIIIII
EEEEEEEEEEEEEEEE

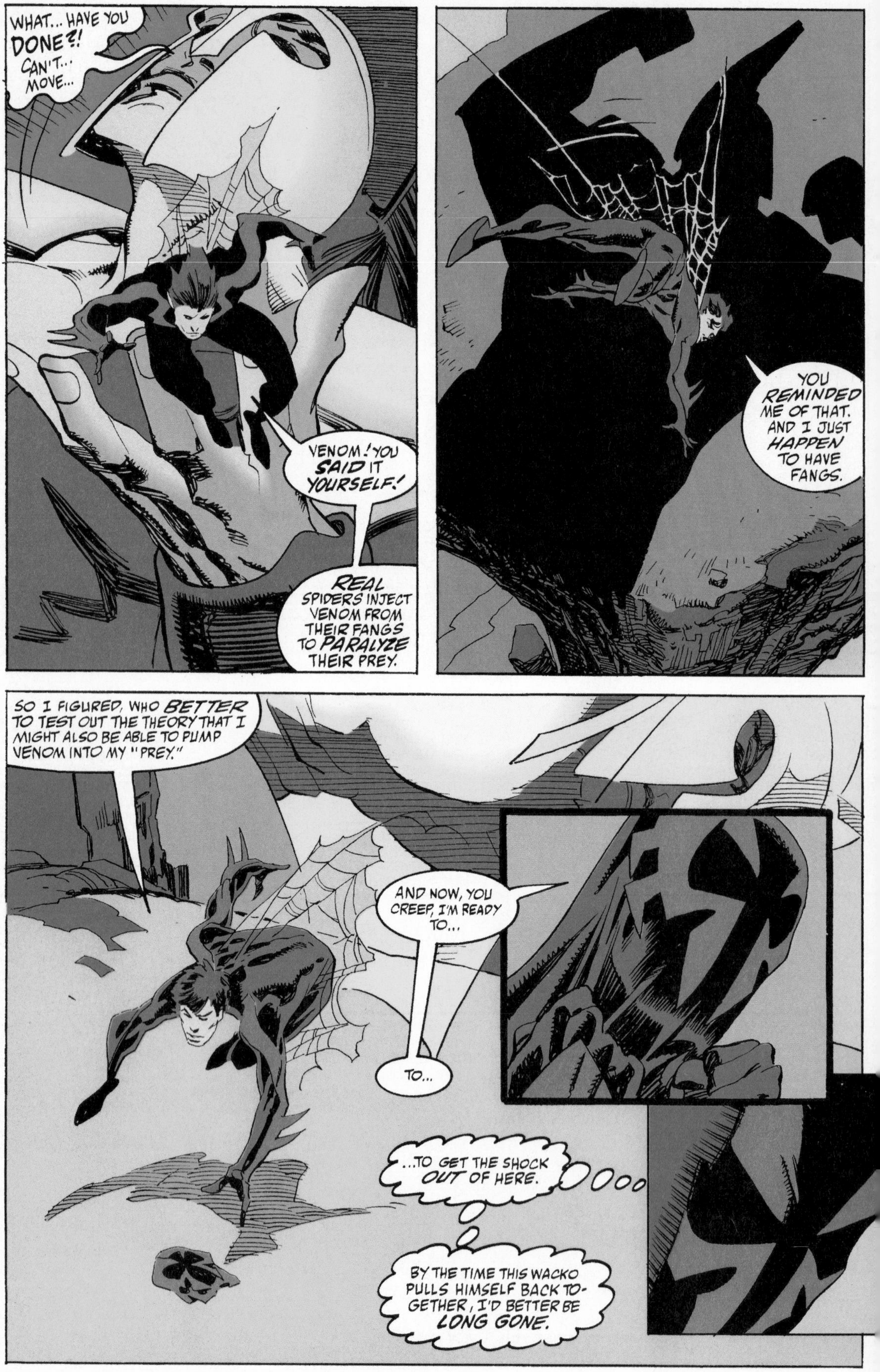
WHAT... HAVE YOU DONE?! CAN'T... MOVE...
VENOM! YOU SAID IT YOURSELF!
REAL SPIDERS INJECT VENOM FROM THEIR FANGS TO PARALYZE THEIR PREY.
YOU REMINDED ME OF THAT. AND I JUST HAPPEN TO HAVE FANGS.
SO I FIGURED, WHO BETTER TO TEST OUT THE THEORY THAT I MIGHT ALSO BE ABLE TO PUMP VENOM INTO MY "PREY."
AND NOW, YOU CREEP, I'M READY TO...
TO...
...TO GET THE SHOCK OUT OF HERE.
BY THE TIME THIS WACKO PULLS HIMSELF BACK TO-GETHER, I'D BETTER BE LONG GONE.

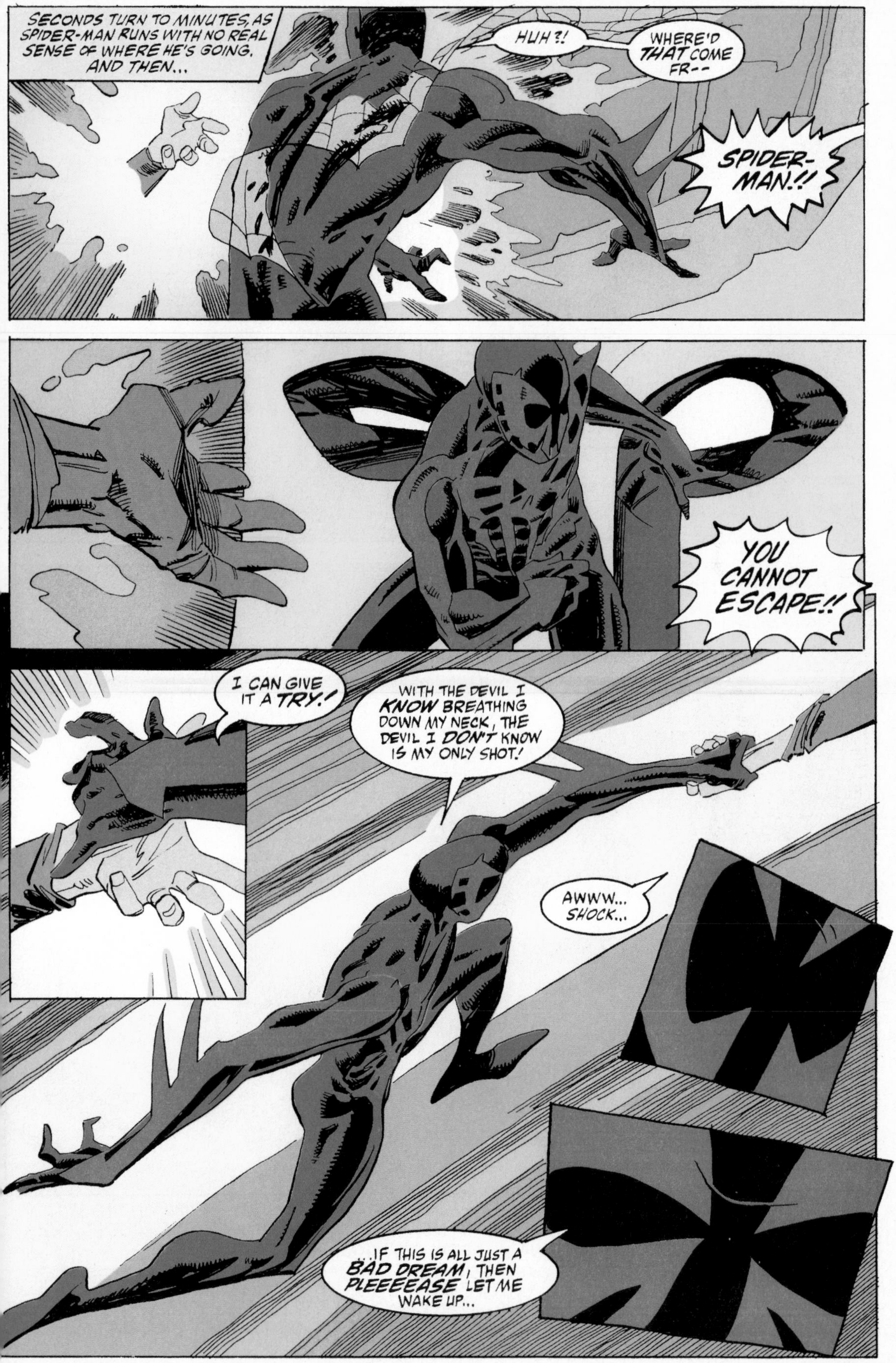
SECONDS TURN TO MINUTES, AS SPIDER-MAN RUNS WITH NO REAL SENSE OF WHERE HE'S GOING. AND THEN...
HUH?!
WHERE'D THAT COME FR--
SPIDER-MAN!!
YOU CANNOT ESCAPE!!
I CAN GIVE IT A TRY!
WITH THE DEVIL I KNOW BREATHING DOWN MY NECK, THE DEVIL I DON'T KNOW IS MY ONLY SHOT!
AWWW... SHOCK...
...IF THIS IS ALL JUST A BAD DREAM, THEN PLEEEEASE LET ME WAKE UP...

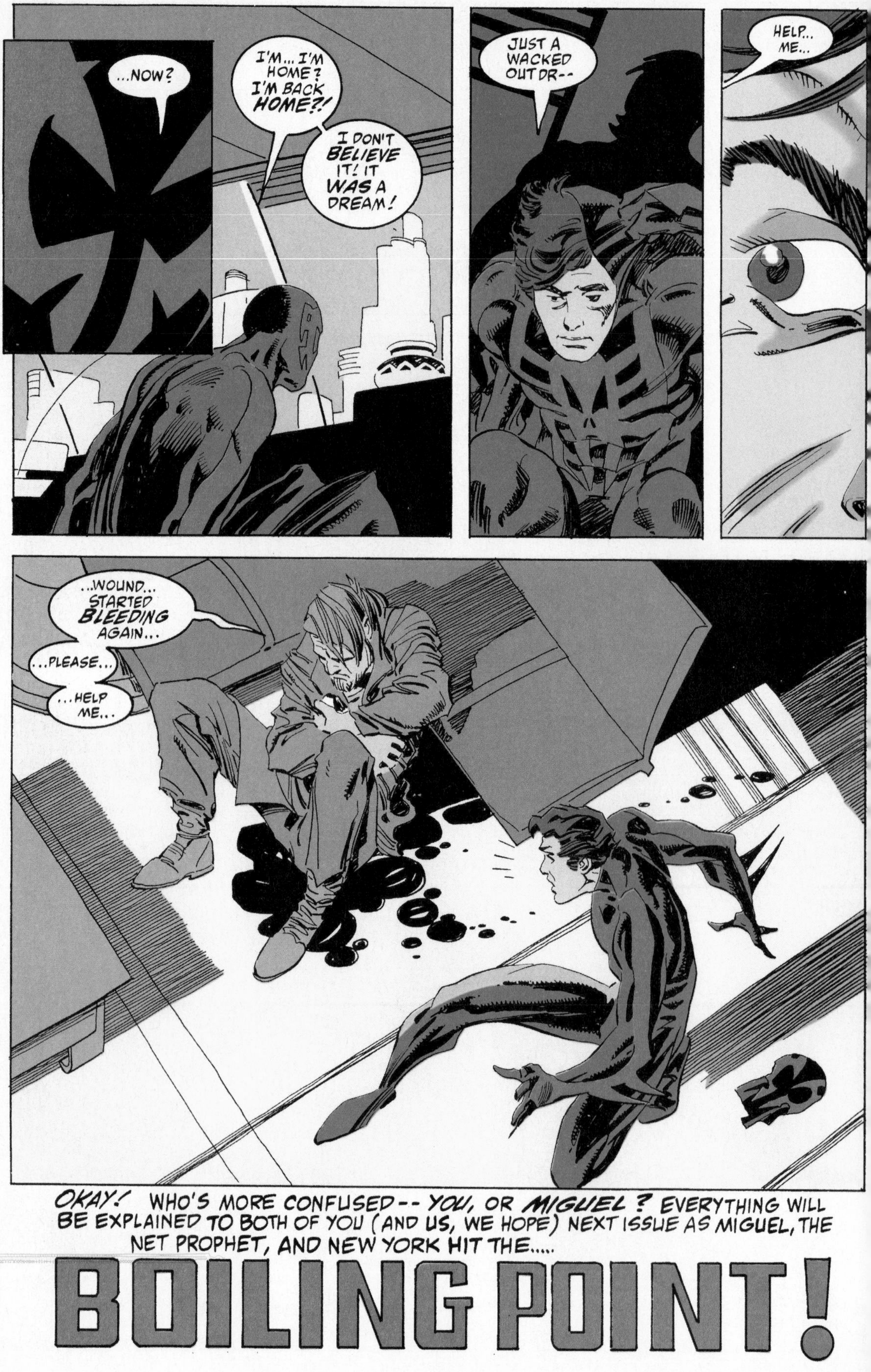
...NOW?
I'M... I'M HOME? I'M BACK HOME?!
I DON'T BELIEVE IT! IT WAS A DREAM!
JUST A WACKED OUT DR--
HELP... ME...
...WOUND... STARTED BLEEDING AGAIN...
...PLEASE...
...HELP ME...
OKAY! WHO'S MORE CONFUSED -- YOU, OR MIGUEL? EVERYTHING WILL BE EXPLAINED TO BOTH OF YOU (AND US, WE HOPE) NEXT ISSUE AS MIGUEL, THE NET PROPHET, AND NEW YORK HIT THE.....
BOILING POINT!

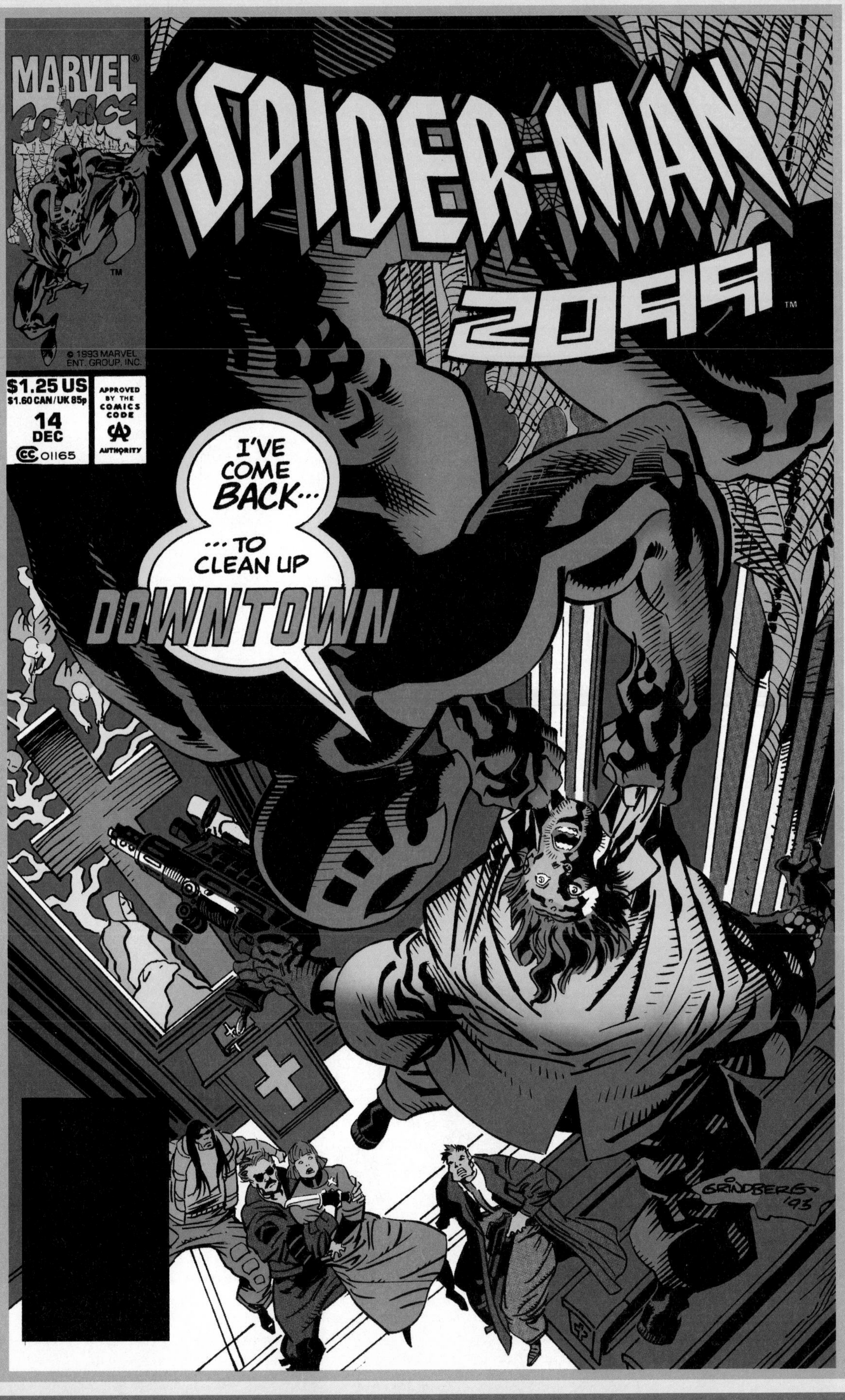
MARVEL COMICS
SPIDER-MAN 2099
© 1993 MARVEL ENT. GROUP, INC.
$1.25 US
$1.60 CAN/UK 85p
14
DEC
01165
APPROVED BY THE COMICS CODE AUTHORITY
I'VE COME BACK...
...TO CLEAN UP DOWNTOWN
GRINDBERG '93

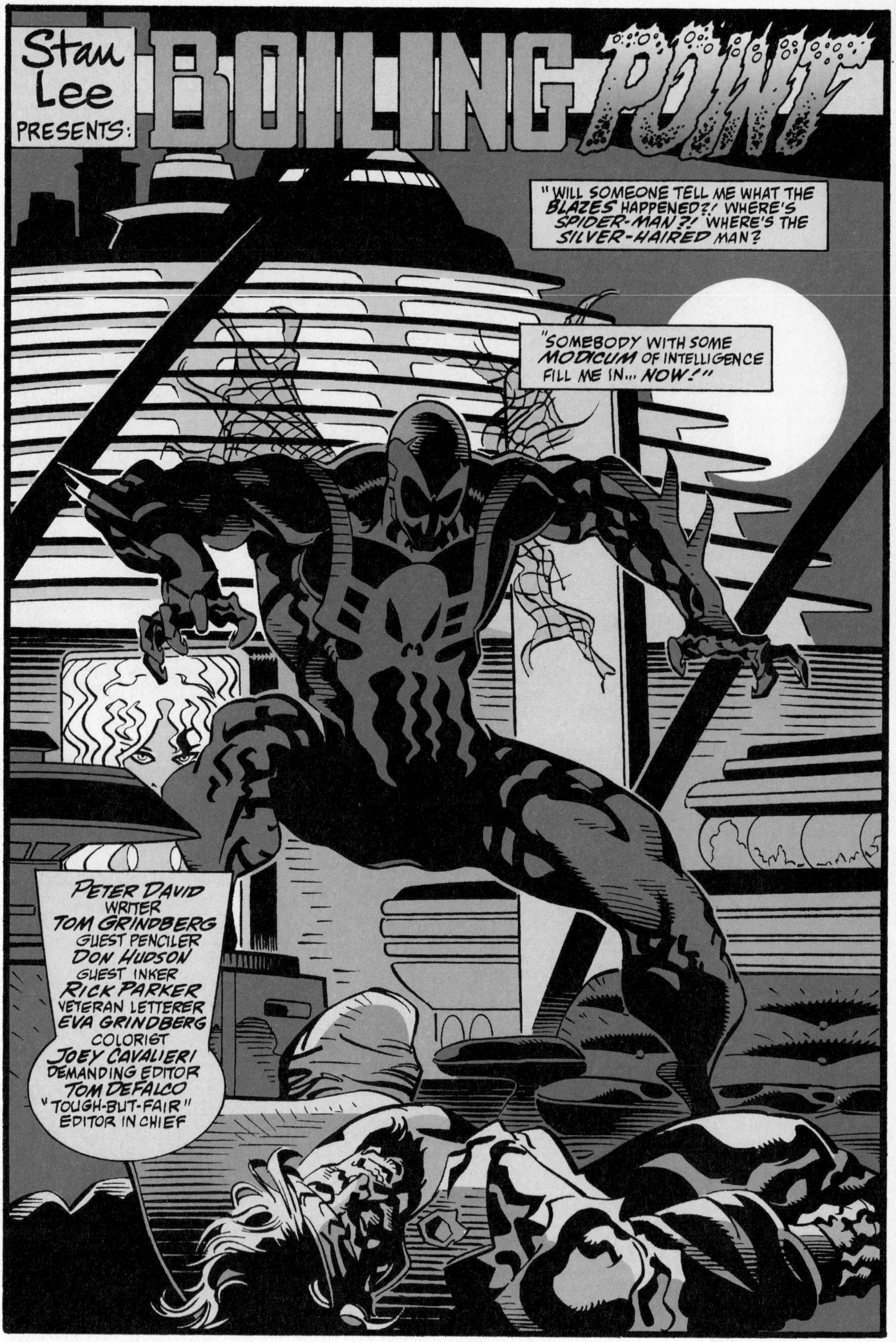
Stan Lee PRESENTS:
BOILING POINT
"WILL SOMEONE TELL ME WHAT THE BLAZES HAPPENED?! WHERE'S SPIDER-MAN?! WHERE'S THE SILVER-HAIRED MAN?
"SOMEBODY WITH SOME MODICUM OF INTELLIGENCE FILL ME IN... NOW!"
PETER DAVID WRITER
TOM GRINDBERG GUEST PENCILER
DON HUDSON GUEST INKER
RICK PARKER VETERAN LETTERER
EVA GRINDBERG COLORIST
JOEY CAVALIERI DEMANDING EDITOR
TOM DEFALCO "TOUGH-BUT-FAIR" EDITOR IN CHIEF

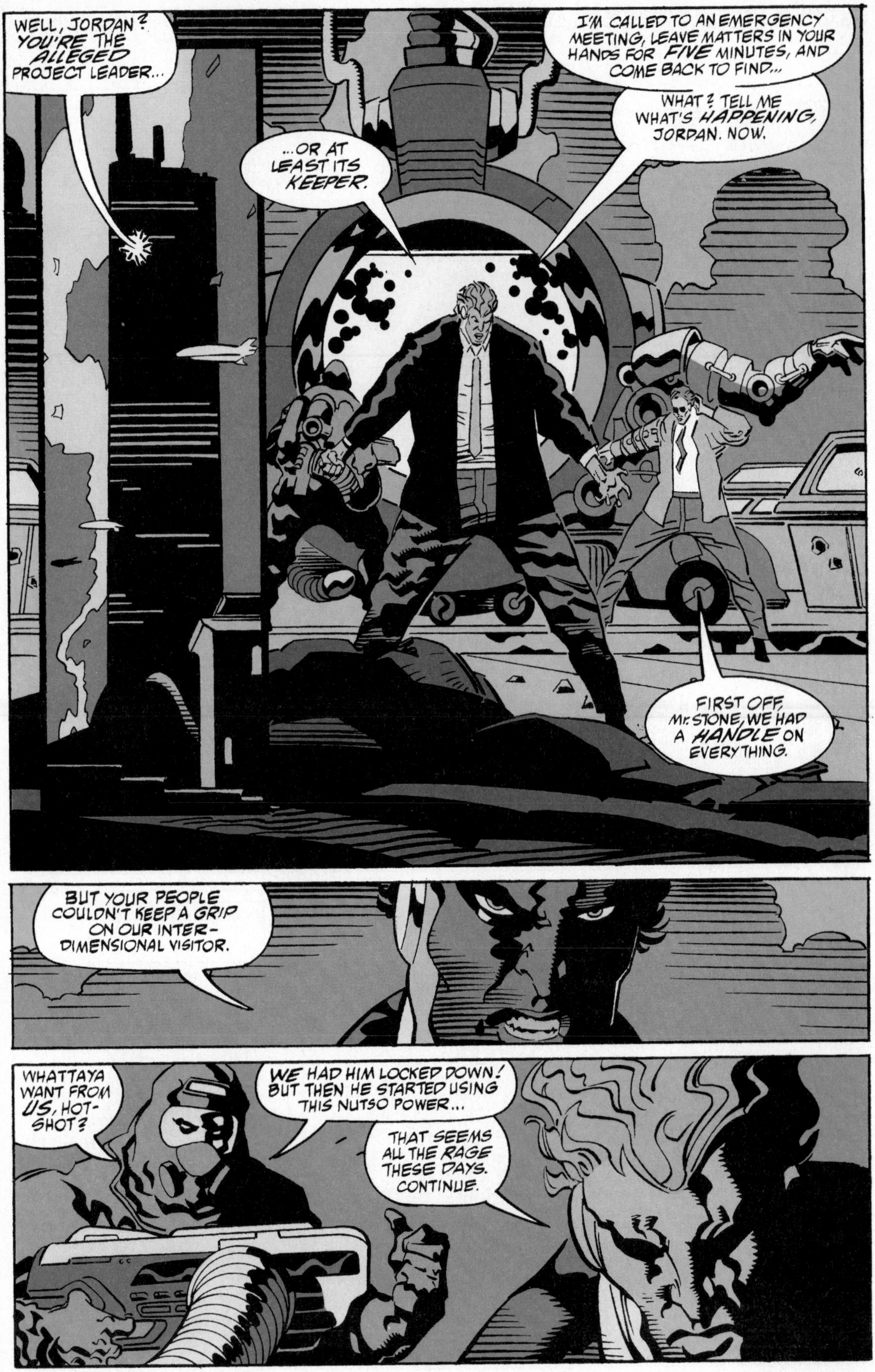
WELL, JORDAN? YOU'RE THE ALLEGED PROJECT LEADER...
...OR AT LEAST ITS KEEPER.
I'M CALLED TO AN EMERGENCY MEETING, LEAVE MATTERS IN YOUR HANDS FOR FIVE MINUTES, AND COME BACK TO FIND...
WHAT? TELL ME WHAT'S HAPPENING, JORDAN. NOW.
FIRST OFF, Mr. STONE, WE HAD A HANDLE ON EVERYTHING.
BUT YOUR PEOPLE COULDN'T KEEP A GRIP ON OUR INTER-DIMENSIONAL VISITOR.
WHATTAYA WANT FROM US, HOT-SHOT?
WE HAD HIM LOCKED DOWN! BUT THEN HE STARTED USING THIS NUTSO POWER...
THAT SEEMS ALL THE RAGE THESE DAYS. CONTINUE.

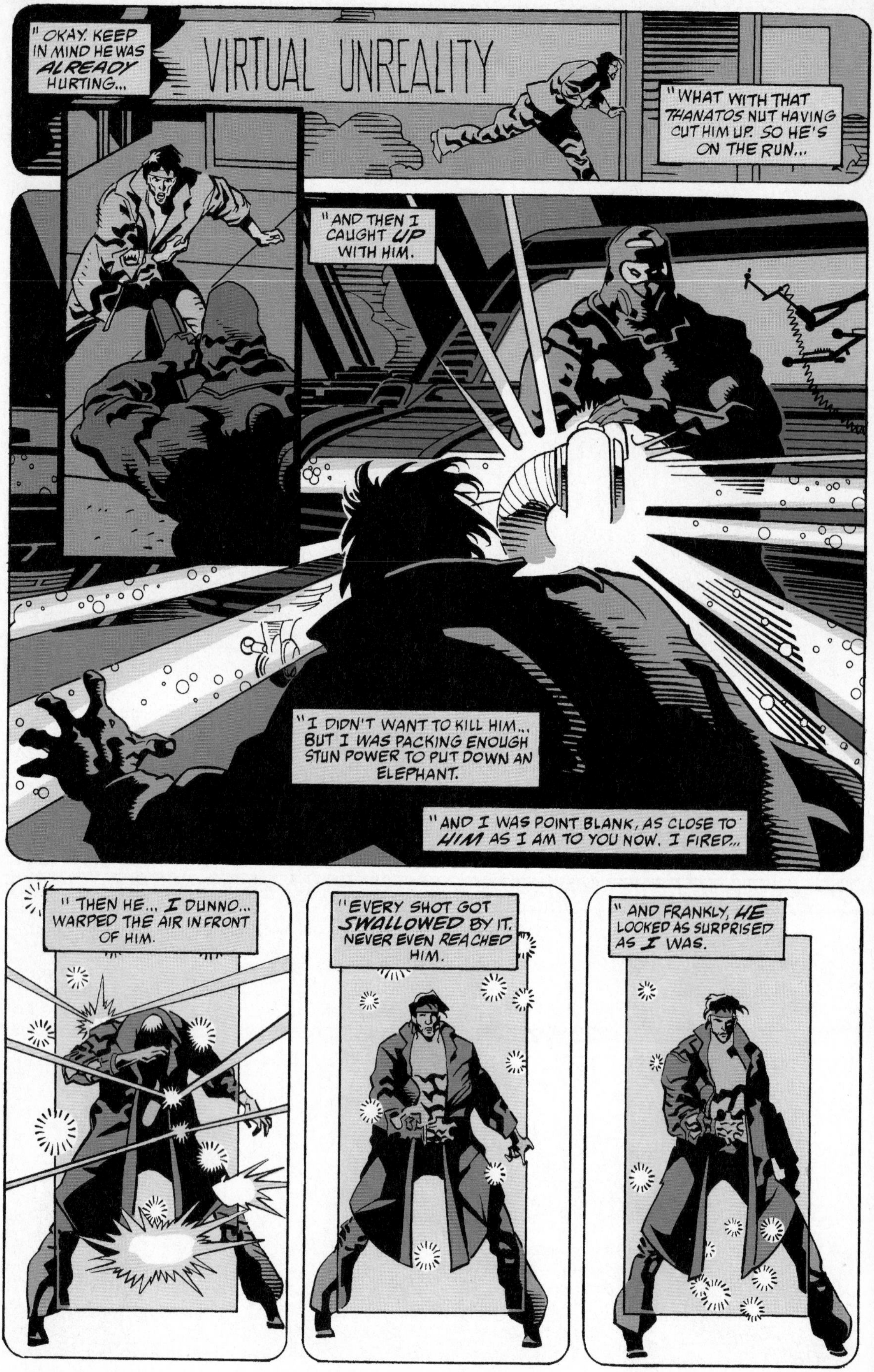
"OKAY. KEEP IN MIND HE WAS ALREADY HURTING...
VIRTUAL UNREALITY
"WHAT WITH THAT THANATOS NUT HAVING CUT HIM UP. SO HE'S ON THE RUN...
"AND THEN I CAUGHT UP WITH HIM.
"I DIDN'T WANT TO KILL HIM... BUT I WAS PACKING ENOUGH STUN POWER TO PUT DOWN AN ELEPHANT.
"AND I WAS POINT BLANK, AS CLOSE TO HIM AS I AM TO YOU NOW. I FIRED...
"THEN HE... I DUNNO... WARPED THE AIR IN FRONT OF HIM.
"EVERY SHOT GOT SWALLOWED BY IT. NEVER EVEN REACHED HIM.
"AND FRANKLY, HE LOOKED AS SURPRISED AS I WAS.

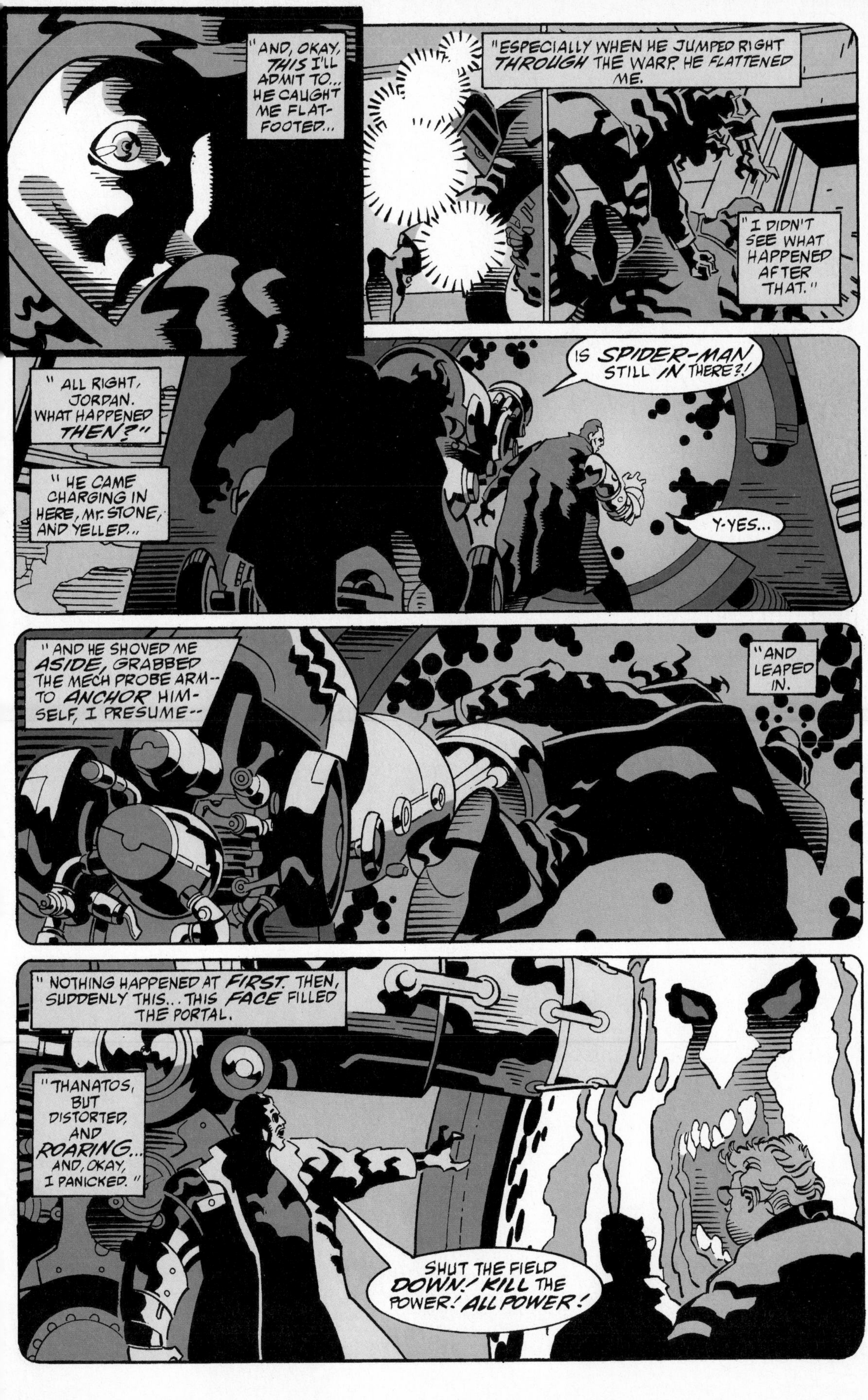
"AND, OKAY, THIS I'LL ADMIT TO... HE CAUGHT ME FLAT-FOOTED...
"ESPECIALLY WHEN HE JUMPED RIGHT THROUGH THE WARP. HE FLATTENED ME.
"I DIDN'T SEE WHAT HAPPENED AFTER THAT."
"ALL RIGHT, JORDAN. WHAT HAPPENED THEN?"
"HE CAME CHARGING IN HERE, MR. STONE, AND YELLED...
IS SPIDER-MAN STILL IN THERE?!
Y-YES...
"AND HE SHOVED ME ASIDE, GRABBED THE MECH PROBE ARM--TO ANCHOR HIM-SELF, I PRESUME--
"AND LEAPED IN.
"NOTHING HAPPENED AT FIRST. THEN, SUDDENLY THIS... THIS FACE FILLED THE PORTAL.
"THANATOS, BUT DISTORTED, AND ROARING... AND, OKAY, I PANICKED."
SHUT THE FIELD DOWN! KILL THE POWER! ALL POWER!

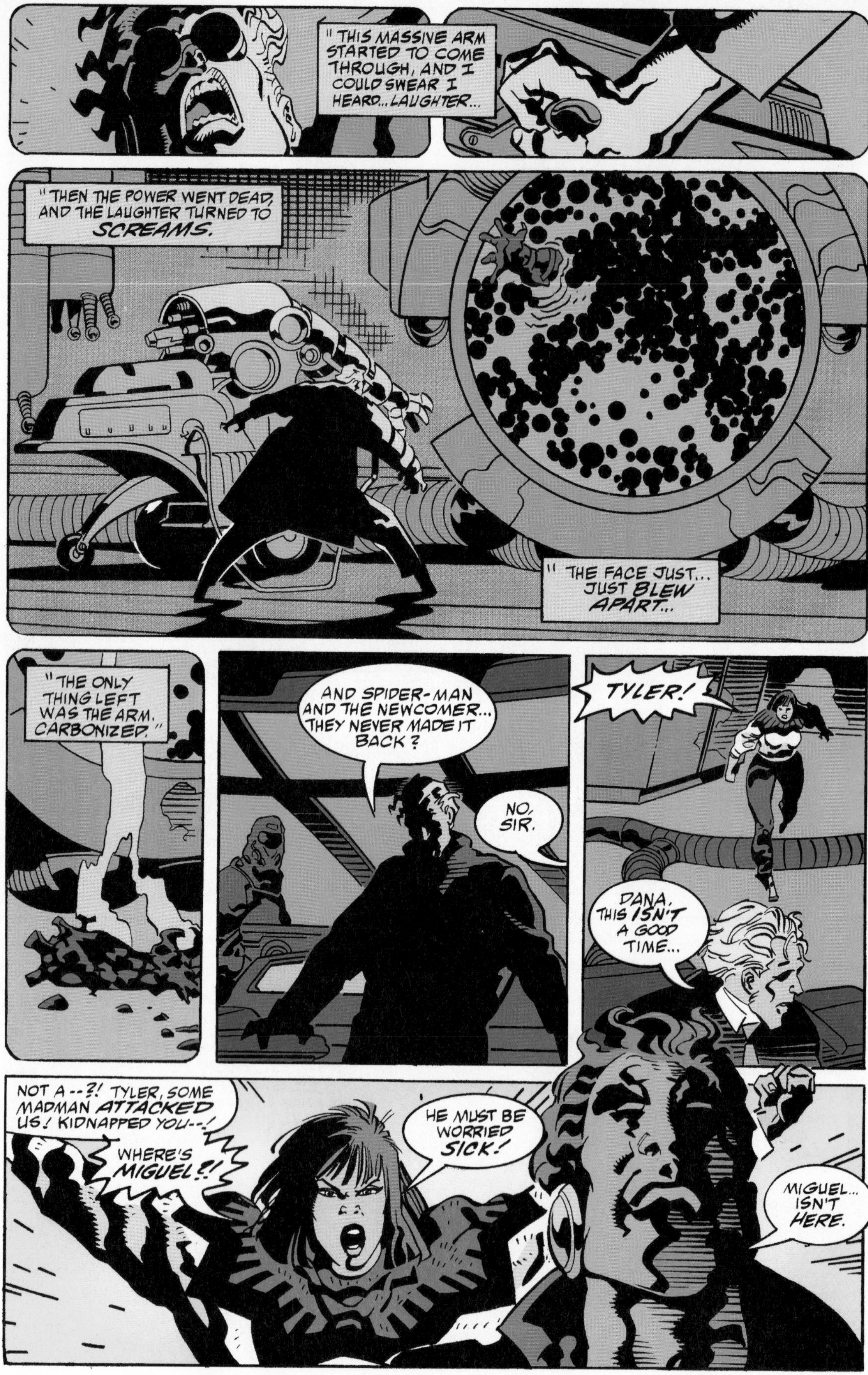
"THIS MASSIVE ARM STARTED TO COME THROUGH, AND I COULD SWEAR I HEARD... LAUGHTER...
"THEN THE POWER WENT DEAD, AND THE LAUGHTER TURNED TO SCREAMS.
"THE FACE JUST... JUST BLEW APART...
"THE ONLY THING LEFT WAS THE ARM. CARBONIZED."
AND SPIDER-MAN AND THE NEWCOMER... THEY NEVER MADE IT BACK?
NO, SIR.
TYLER!
DANA, THIS ISN'T A GOOD TIME...
NOT A--?! TYLER, SOME MADMAN ATTACKED US! KIDNAPPED YOU--!
WHERE'S MIGUEL?!
HE MUST BE WORRIED SICK!
MIGUEL... ISN'T HERE.

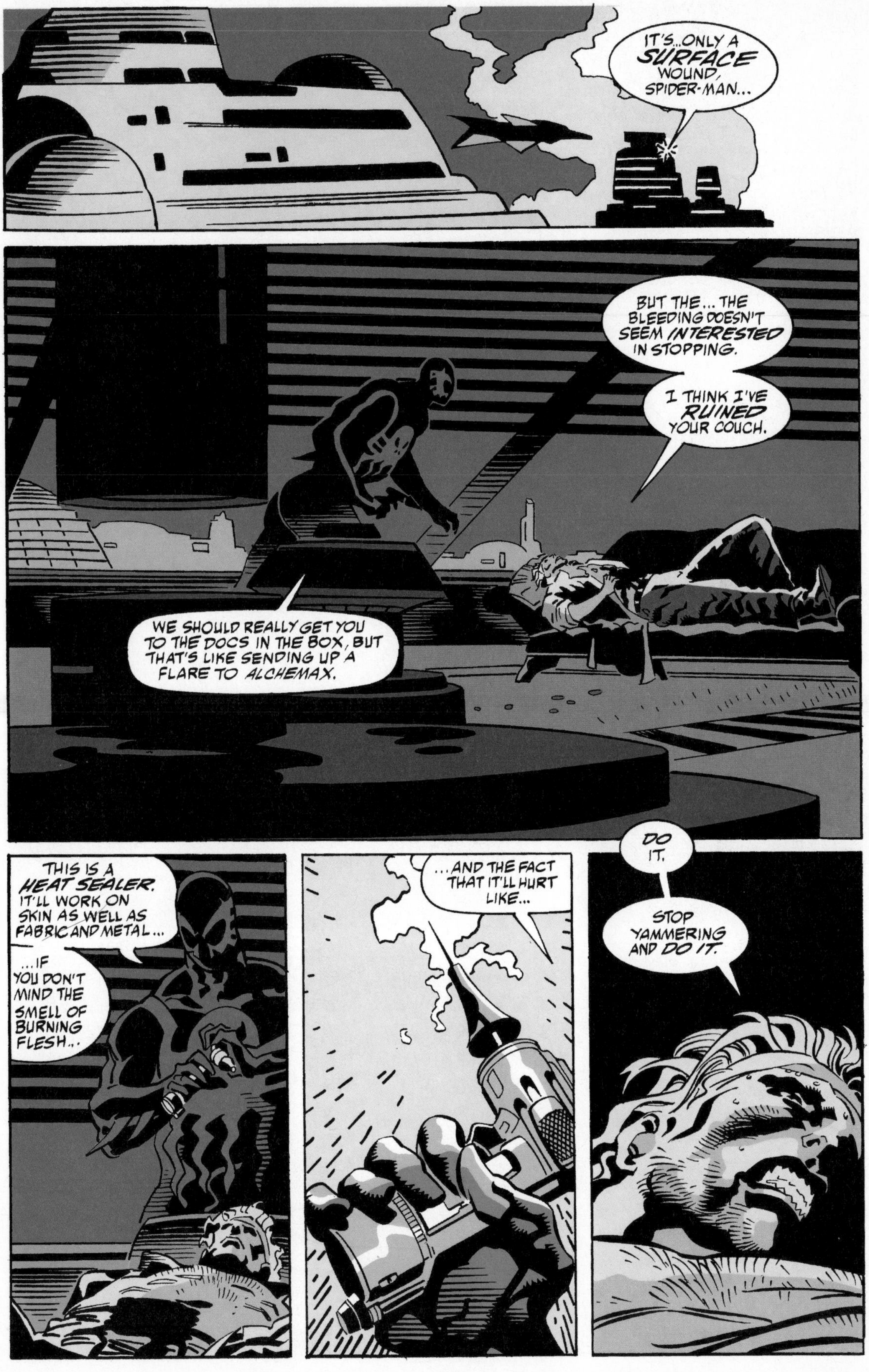
IT'S...ONLY A SURFACE WOUND, SPIDER-MAN...
BUT THE... THE BLEEDING DOESN'T SEEM INTERESTED IN STOPPING.
I THINK I'VE RUINED YOUR COUCH.
WE SHOULD REALLY GET YOU TO THE DOCS IN THE BOX, BUT THAT'S LIKE SENDING UP A FLARE TO ALCHEMAX.
THIS IS A HEAT SEALER. IT'LL WORK ON SKIN AS WELL AS FABRIC AND METAL...
...IF YOU DON'T MIND THE SMELL OF BURNING FLESH...
...AND THE FACT THAT IT'LL HURT LIKE...
DO IT.
STOP YAMMERING AND DO IT.

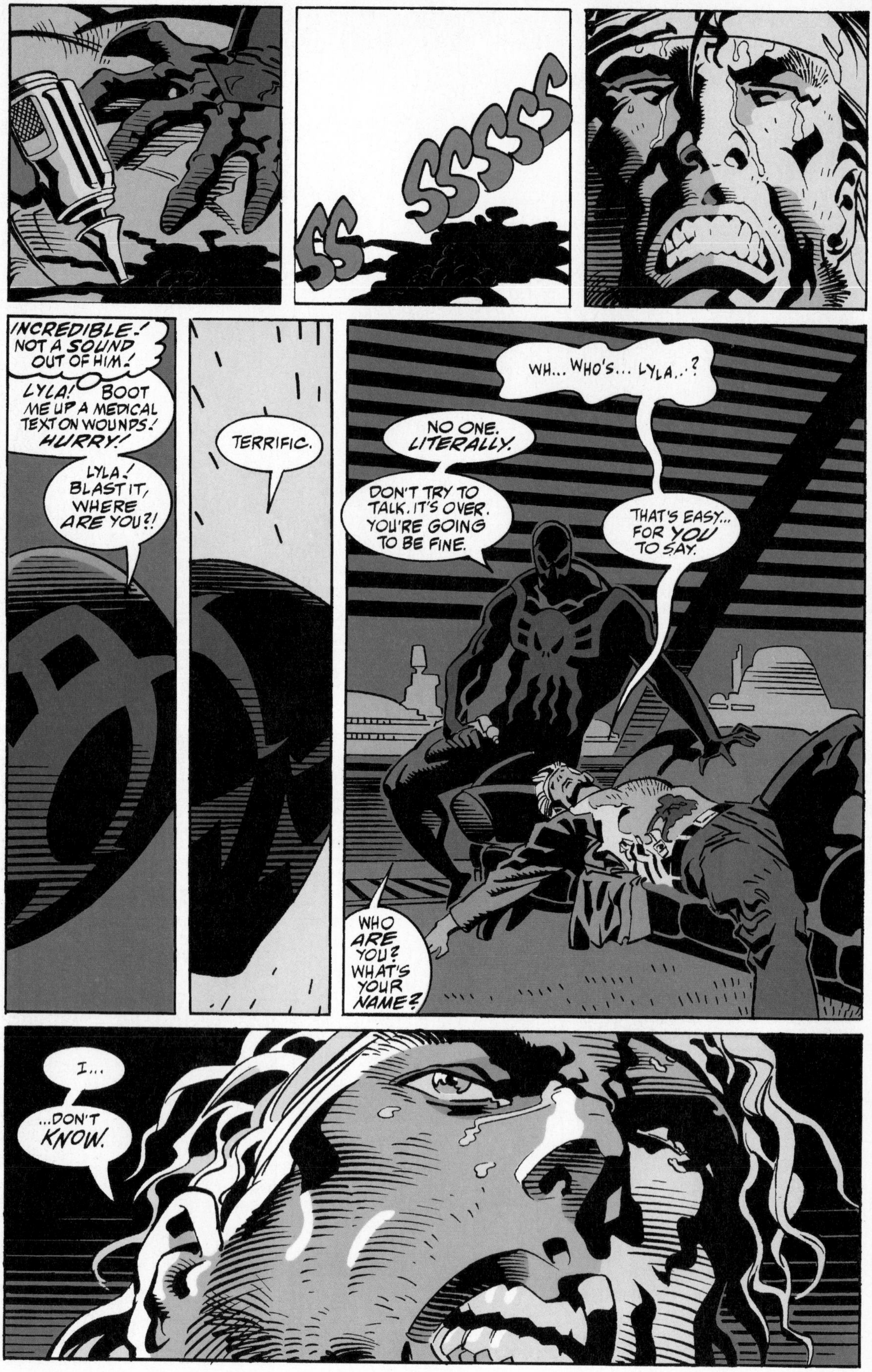
SS SSSSS
INCREDIBLE! NOT A SOUND OUT OF HIM!
LYLA! BOOT ME UP A MEDICAL TEXT ON WOUNDS! HURRY!
LYLA! BLAST IT, WHERE ARE YOU?!
TERRIFIC.
WH... WHO'S... LYLA...?
NO ONE. LITERALLY.
DON'T TRY TO TALK. IT'S OVER. YOU'RE GOING TO BE FINE.
THAT'S EASY... FOR YOU TO SAY.
WHO ARE YOU? WHAT'S YOUR NAME?
I...
...DON'T KNOW.

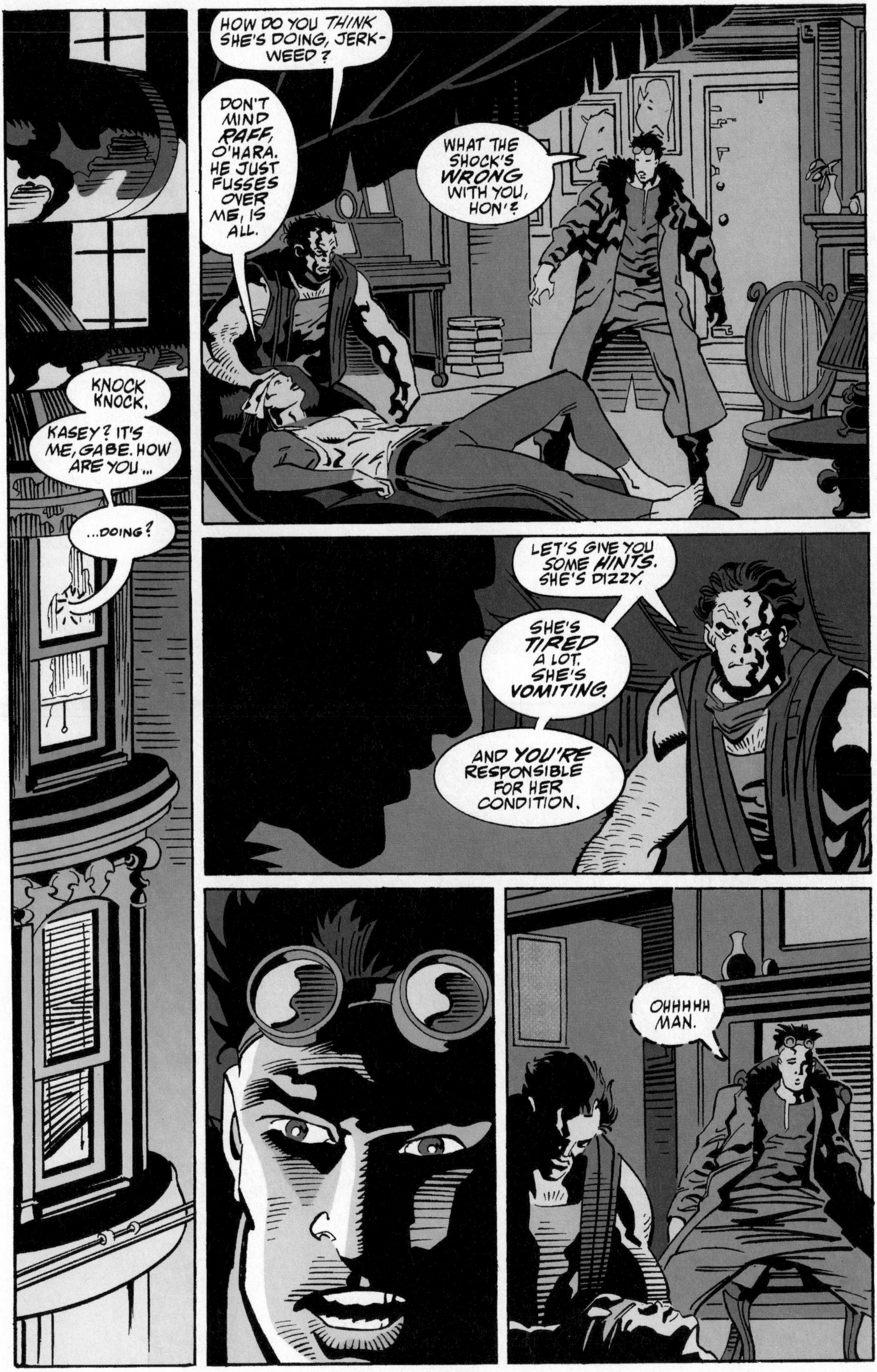
KNOCK KNOCK.
KASEY? IT'S ME, GABE. HOW ARE YOU...
...DOING?
HOW DO YOU THINK SHE'S DOING, JERK-WEED?
DON'T MIND RAFF, O'HARA. HE JUST FUSSES OVER ME, IS ALL.
WHAT THE SHOCK'S WRONG WITH YOU, HON'?
LET'S GIVE YOU SOME HINTS. SHE'S DIZZY.
SHE'S TIRED A LOT. SHE'S VOMITING.
AND YOU'RE RESPONSIBLE FOR HER CONDITION.
OHHHHH MAN.

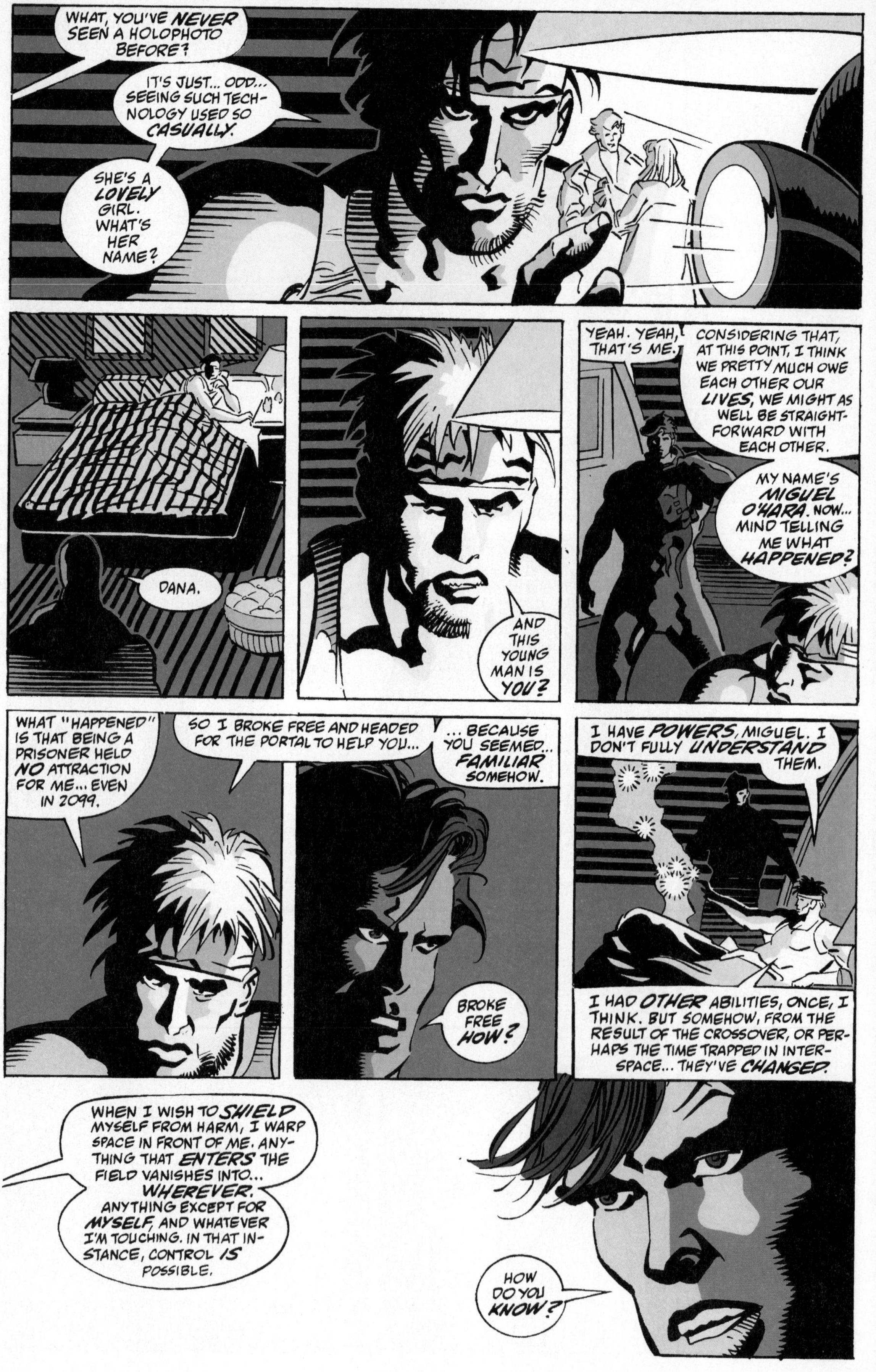

WHAT, YOU'VE NEVER SEEN A HOLOPHOTO BEFORE?
IT'S JUST... ODD... SEEING SUCH TECHNOLOGY USED SO CASUALLY.
SHE'S A LOVELY GIRL. WHAT'S HER NAME?
DANA.
AND THIS YOUNG MAN IS YOU?
YEAH. YEAH, THAT'S ME.
CONSIDERING THAT, AT THIS POINT, I THINK WE PRETTY MUCH OWE EACH OTHER OUR LIVES, WE MIGHT AS WELL BE STRAIGHT-FORWARD WITH EACH OTHER.
MY NAME'S MIGUEL O'HARA. NOW... MIND TELLING ME WHAT HAPPENED?
WHAT "HAPPENED" IS THAT BEING A PRISONER HELD NO ATTRACTION FOR ME... EVEN IN 2099.
SO I BROKE FREE AND HEADED FOR THE PORTAL TO HELP YOU...
... BECAUSE YOU SEEMED... FAMILIAR SOMEHOW.
BROKE FREE HOW?
I HAVE POWERS, MIGUEL. I DON'T FULLY UNDERSTAND THEM.
I HAD OTHER ABILITIES, ONCE, I THINK. BUT SOMEHOW, FROM THE RESULT OF THE CROSSOVER, OR PERHAPS THE TIME TRAPPED IN INTER-SPACE... THEY'VE CHANGED.
WHEN I WISH TO SHIELD MYSELF FROM HARM, I WARP SPACE IN FRONT OF ME. ANYTHING THAT ENTERS THE FIELD VANISHES INTO... WHEREVER. ANYTHING EXCEPT FOR MYSELF, AND WHATEVER I'M TOUCHING. IN THAT INSTANCE, CONTROL IS POSSIBLE.
HOW DO YOU KNOW?

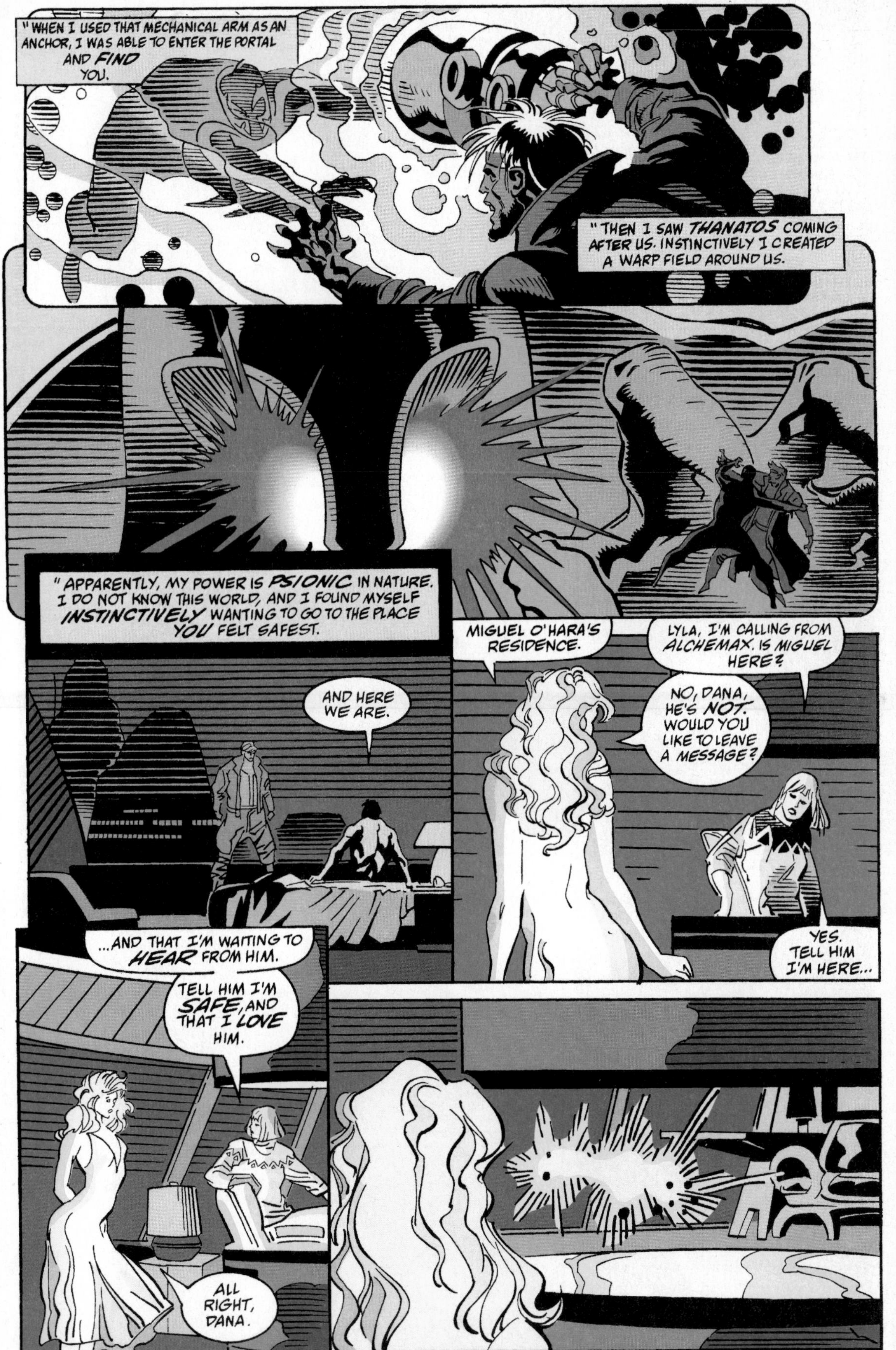
"WHEN I USED THAT MECHANICAL ARM AS AN ANCHOR, I WAS ABLE TO ENTER THE PORTAL AND FIND YOU.
"THEN I SAW THANATOS COMING AFTER US. INSTINCTIVELY I CREATED A WARP FIELD AROUND US.
"APPARENTLY, MY POWER IS PSIONIC IN NATURE. I DO NOT KNOW THIS WORLD, AND I FOUND MYSELF INSTINCTIVELY WANTING TO GO TO THE PLACE YOU FELT SAFEST.
AND HERE WE ARE.
MIGUEL O'HARA'S RESIDENCE.
LYLA, I'M CALLING FROM ALCHEMAX. IS MIGUEL HERE?
NO, DANA, HE'S NOT. WOULD YOU LIKE TO LEAVE A MESSAGE?
YES. TELL HIM I'M HERE...
...AND THAT I'M WAITING TO HEAR FROM HIM.
TELL HIM I'M SAFE, AND THAT I LOVE HIM.
ALL RIGHT, DANA.

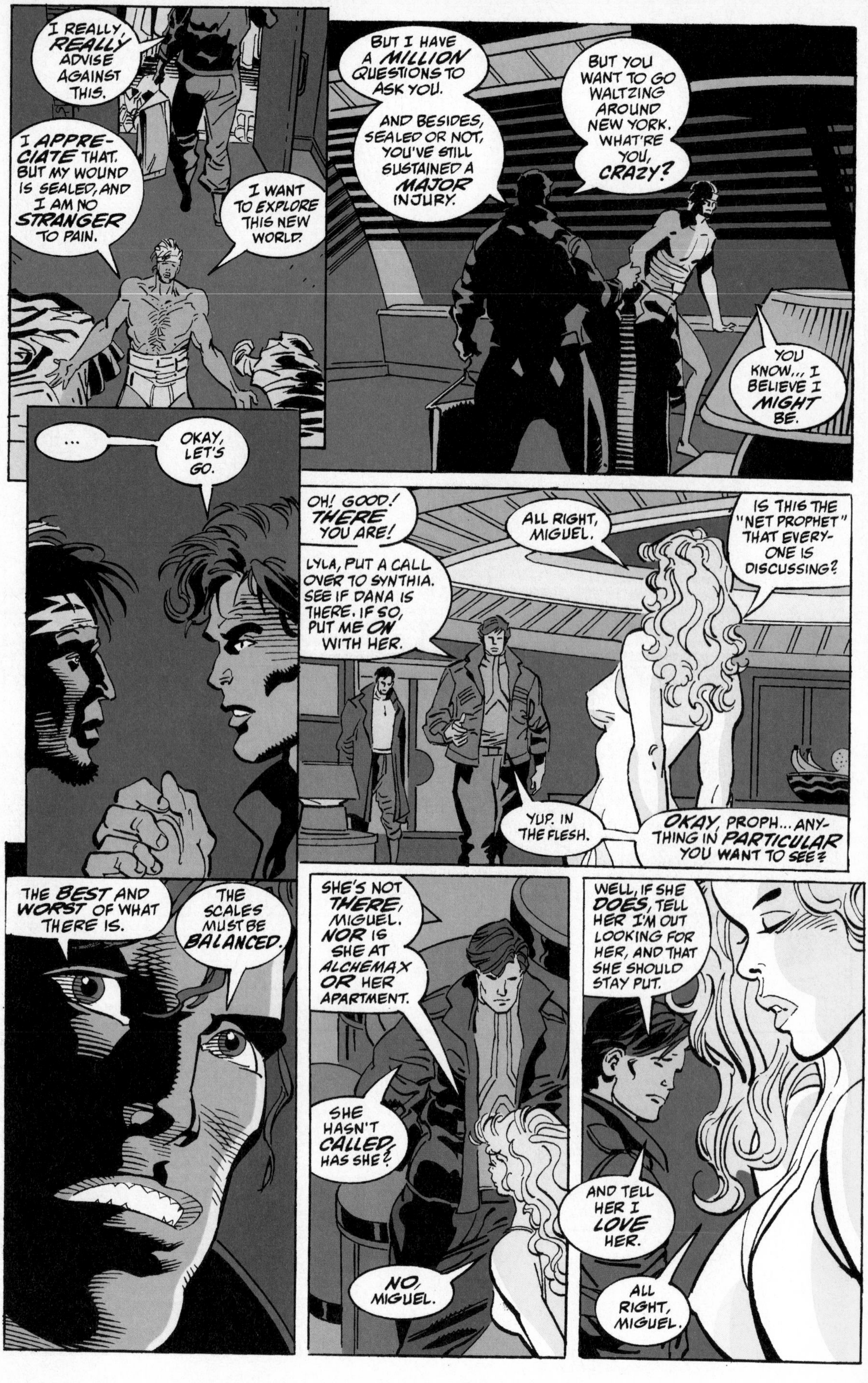
I REALLY, REALLY ADVISE AGAINST THIS.
I APPRECIATE THAT. BUT MY WOUND IS SEALED, AND I AM NO STRANGER TO PAIN.
I WANT TO EXPLORE THIS NEW WORLD.
BUT I HAVE A MILLION QUESTIONS TO ASK YOU.
AND BESIDES, SEALED OR NOT, YOU'VE STILL SUSTAINED A MAJOR INJURY.
BUT YOU WANT TO GO WALTZING AROUND NEW YORK. WHAT'RE YOU, CRAZY?
YOU KNOW... I BELIEVE I MIGHT BE.
...
OKAY, LET'S GO.
OH! GOOD! THERE YOU ARE!
LYLA, PUT A CALL OVER TO SYNTHIA. SEE IF DANA IS THERE. IF SO, PUT ME ON WITH HER.
ALL RIGHT, MIGUEL.
IS THIS THE "NET PROPHET" THAT EVERYONE IS DISCUSSING?
YUP. IN THE FLESH.
OKAY, PROPH... ANYTHING IN PARTICULAR YOU WANT TO SEE?
THE BEST AND WORST OF WHAT THERE IS.
THE SCALES MUST BE BALANCED.
SHE'S NOT THERE, MIGUEL. NOR IS SHE AT ALCHEMAX OR HER APARTMENT.
SHE HASN'T CALLED, HAS SHE?
NO, MIGUEL.
WELL, IF SHE DOES, TELL HER I'M OUT LOOKING FOR HER, AND THAT SHE SHOULD STAY PUT.
AND TELL HER I LOVE HER.
ALL RIGHT, MIGUEL.

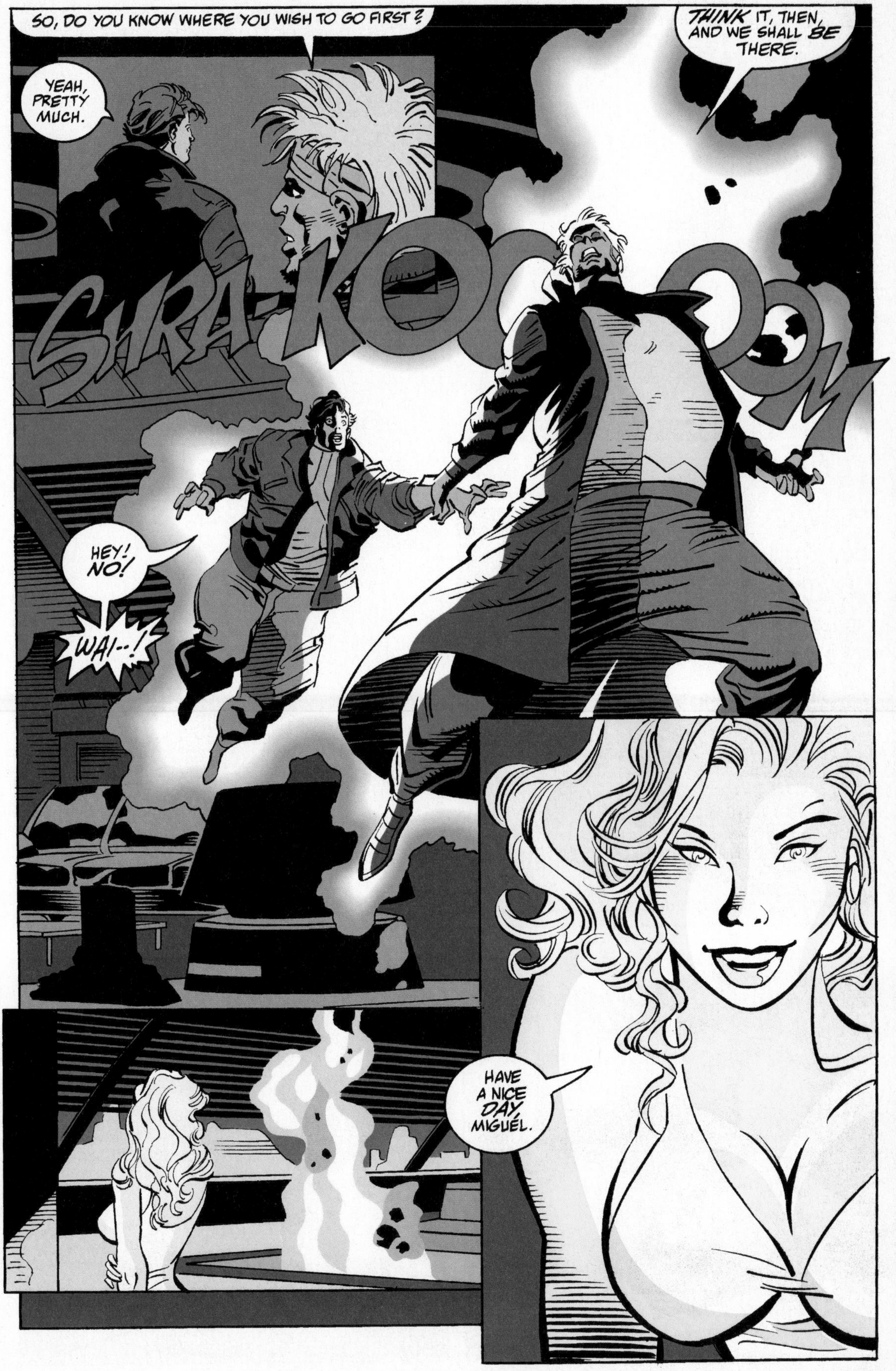
SO, DO YOU KNOW WHERE YOU WISH TO GO FIRST?
YEAH, PRETTY MUCH.
THINK IT, THEN, AND WE SHALL BE THERE.
SHRA-KOOOOOM
HEY! NO!
WAI--!
HAVE A NICE DAY, MIGUEL.

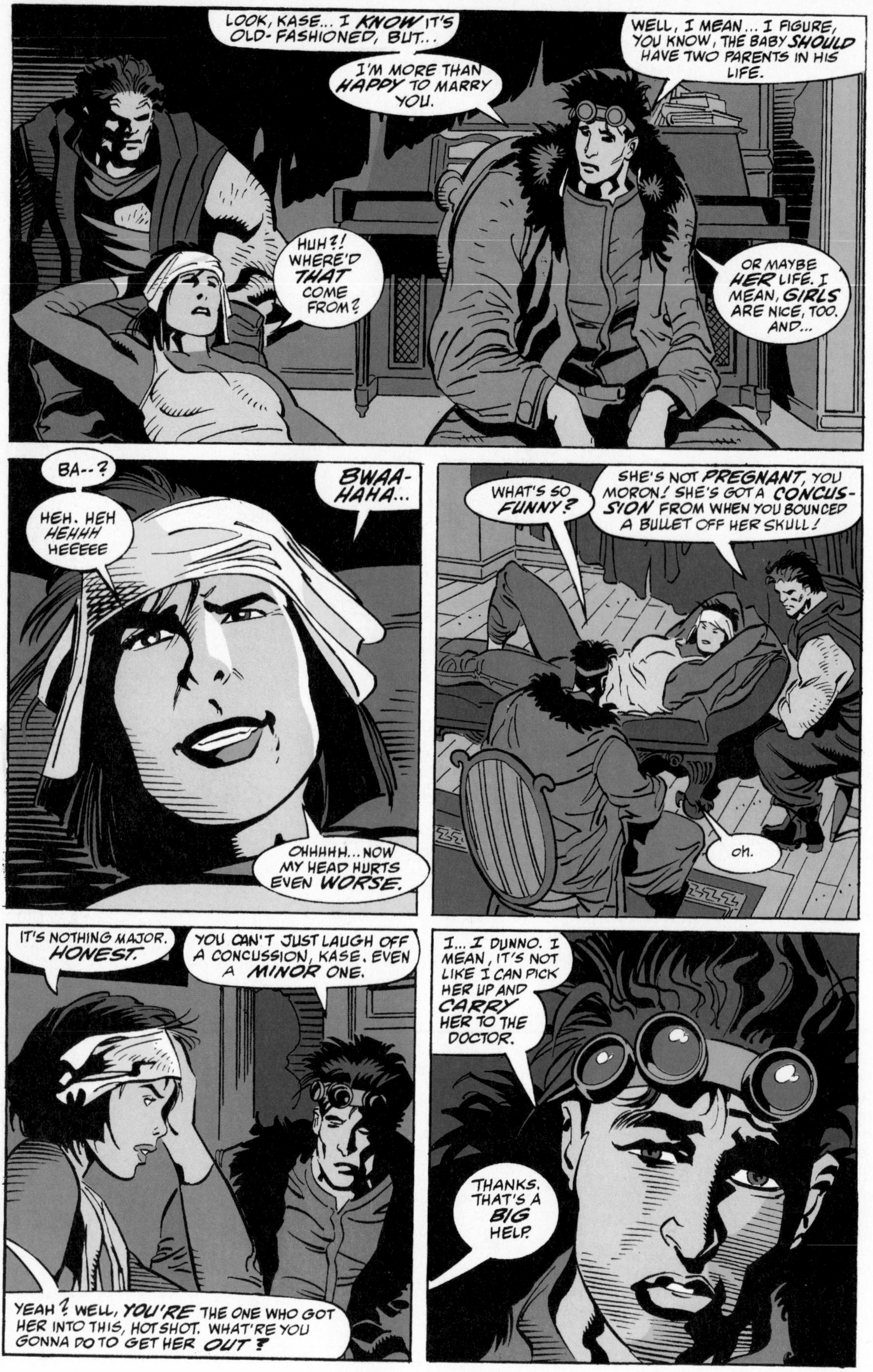
LOOK, KASE... I KNOW IT'S OLD-FASHIONED, BUT...
I'M MORE THAN HAPPY TO MARRY YOU.
WELL, I MEAN... I FIGURE, YOU KNOW, THE BABY SHOULD HAVE TWO PARENTS IN HIS LIFE.
HUH?! WHERE'D THAT COME FROM?
OR MAYBE HER LIFE. I MEAN, GIRLS ARE NICE, TOO. AND...
BA--?
HEH. HEH HEHHH HEEEEE
BWAA-HAHA...
OHHHHH... NOW MY HEAD HURTS EVEN WORSE.
WHAT'S SO FUNNY?
SHE'S NOT PREGNANT, YOU MORON! SHE'S GOT A CONCUSSION FROM WHEN YOU BOUNCED A BULLET OFF HER SKULL!
oh.
IT'S NOTHING MAJOR. HONEST.
YOU CAN'T JUST LAUGH OFF A CONCUSSION, KASE. EVEN A MINOR ONE.
YEAH? WELL, YOU'RE THE ONE WHO GOT HER INTO THIS, HOT SHOT. WHAT'RE YOU GONNA DO TO GET HER OUT?
I... I DUNNO. I MEAN, IT'S NOT LIKE I CAN PICK HER UP AND CARRY HER TO THE DOCTOR.
THANKS. THAT'S A BIG HELP.

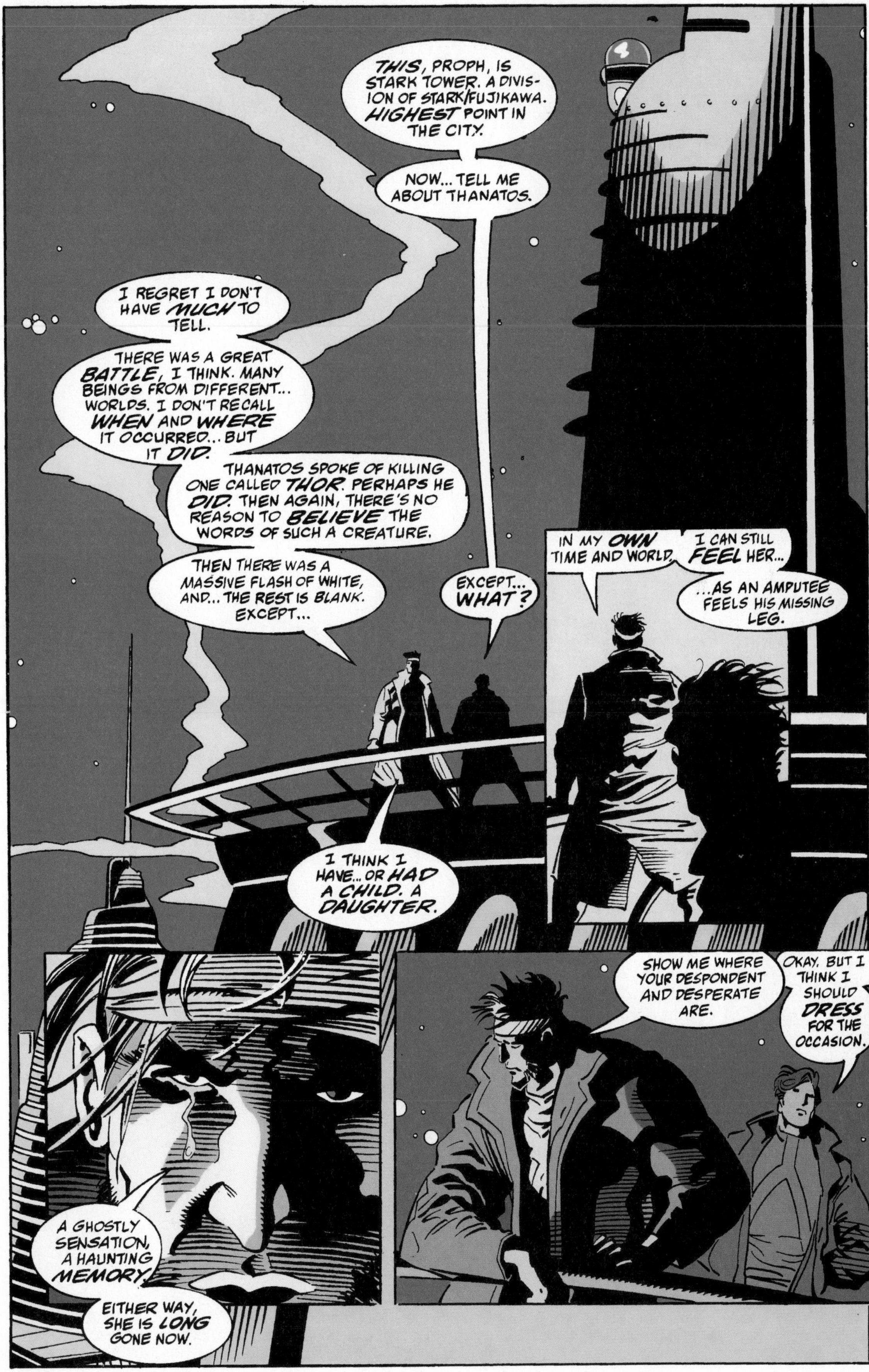

THIS, PROPH, IS STARK TOWER. A DIVISION OF STARK/FUJIKAWA. HIGHEST POINT IN THE CITY.
NOW... TELL ME ABOUT THANATOS.
I REGRET I DON'T HAVE MUCH TO TELL.
THERE WAS A GREAT BATTLE, I THINK. MANY BEINGS FROM DIFFERENT... WORLDS. I DON'T RECALL WHEN AND WHERE IT OCCURRED... BUT IT DID.
THANATOS SPOKE OF KILLING ONE CALLED THOR. PERHAPS HE DID. THEN AGAIN, THERE'S NO REASON TO BELIEVE THE WORDS OF SUCH A CREATURE.
THEN THERE WAS A MASSIVE FLASH OF WHITE, AND... THE REST IS BLANK. EXCEPT...
EXCEPT... WHAT?
I THINK I HAVE... OR HAD A CHILD. A DAUGHTER.
IN MY OWN TIME AND WORLD,
I CAN STILL FEEL HER...
...AS AN AMPUTEE FEELS HIS MISSING LEG.
A GHOSTLY SENSATION, A HAUNTING MEMORY.
EITHER WAY, SHE IS LONG GONE NOW.
SHOW ME WHERE YOUR DESPONDENT AND DESPERATE ARE.
OKAY. BUT I THINK I SHOULD DRESS FOR THE OCCASION.

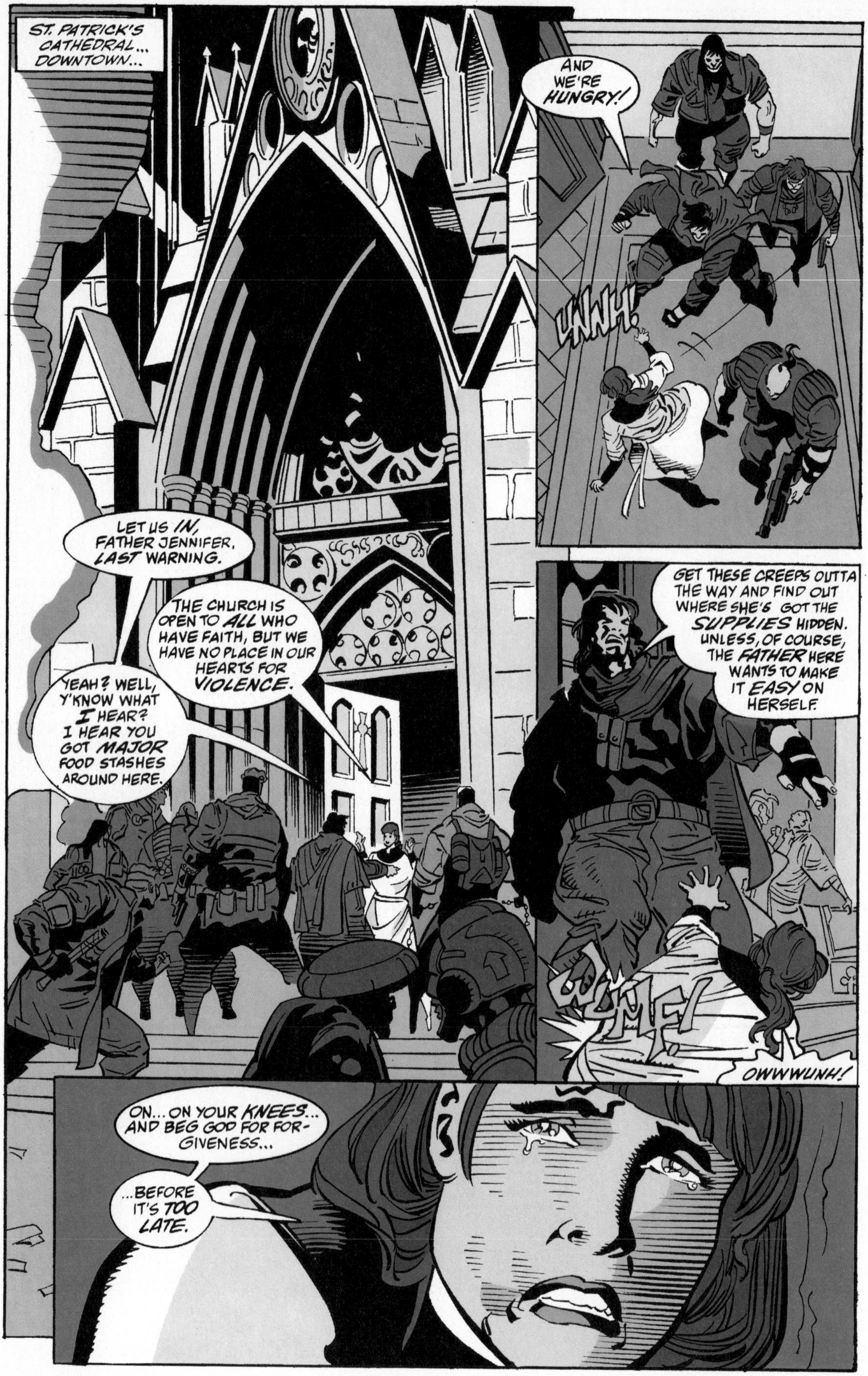
ST. PATRICK'S CATHEDRAL... DOWNTOWN...
AND WE'RE HUNGRY!
UNNH!
LET US IN, FATHER JENNIFER, LAST WARNING.
THE CHURCH IS OPEN TO ALL WHO HAVE FAITH, BUT WE HAVE NO PLACE IN OUR HEARTS FOR VIOLENCE.
YEAH? WELL, Y'KNOW WHAT I HEAR? I HEAR YOU GOT MAJOR FOOD STASHES AROUND HERE.
GET THESE CREEPS OUTTA THE WAY AND FIND OUT WHERE SHE'S GOT THE SUPPLIES HIDDEN. UNLESS, OF COURSE, THE FATHER HERE WANTS TO MAKE IT EASY ON HERSELF.
WUMF!
OWWWUNH!
ON... ON YOUR KNEES... AND BEG GOD FOR FOR-GIVENESS...
...BEFORE IT'S TOO LATE.

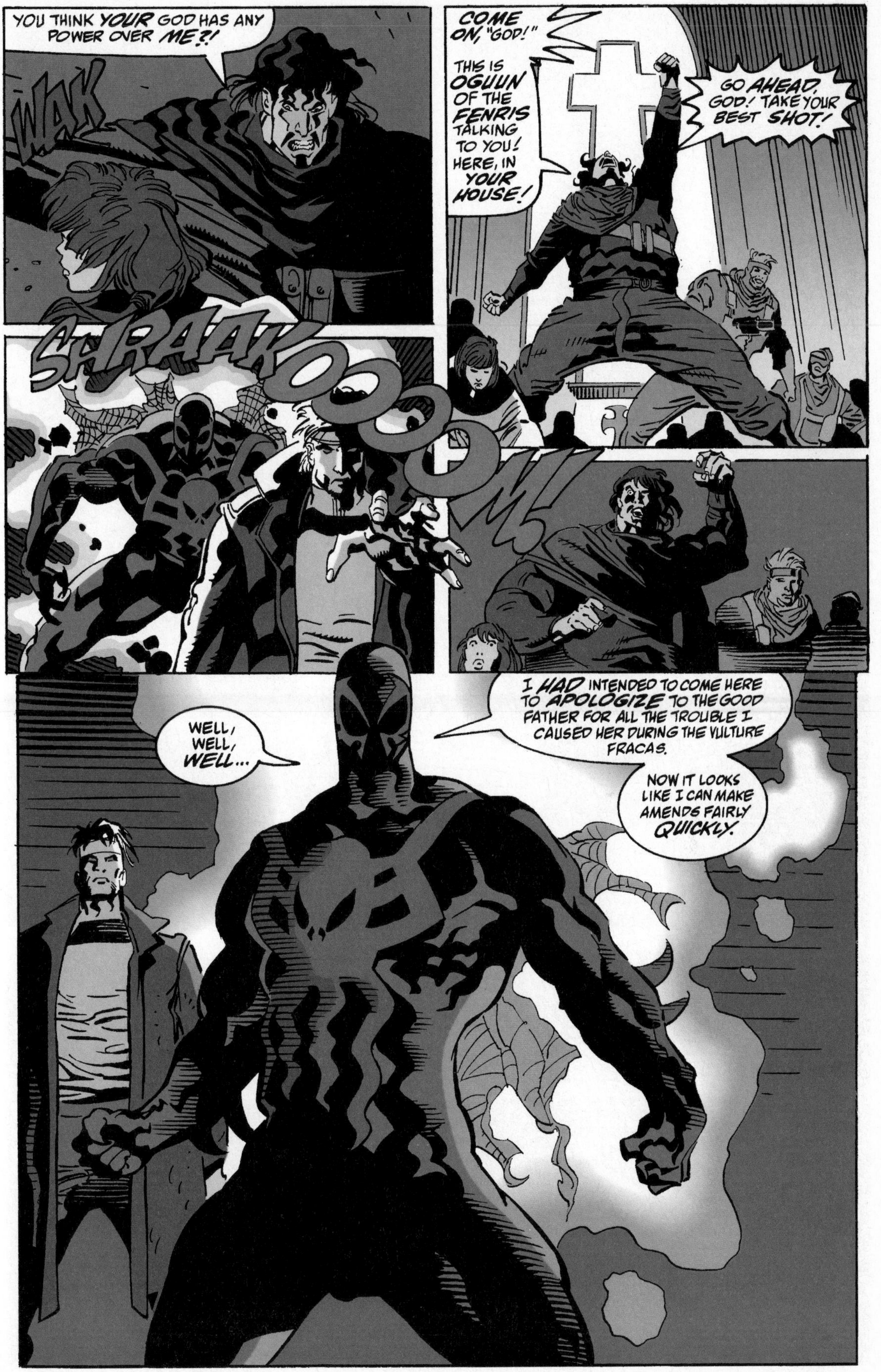
YOU THINK YOUR GOD HAS ANY POWER OVER ME?!
WAK
COME ON, "GOD!"
THIS IS OGUUN OF THE FENRIS TALKING TO YOU! HERE, IN YOUR HOUSE!
GO AHEAD, GOD! TAKE YOUR BEST SHOT!
SHRAAKOOOOOM!
WELL, WELL, WELL...
I HAD INTENDED TO COME HERE TO APOLOGIZE TO THE GOOD FATHER FOR ALL THE TROUBLE I CAUSED HER DURING THE VULTURE FRACAS.
NOW IT LOOKS LIKE I CAN MAKE AMENDS FAIRLY QUICKLY.

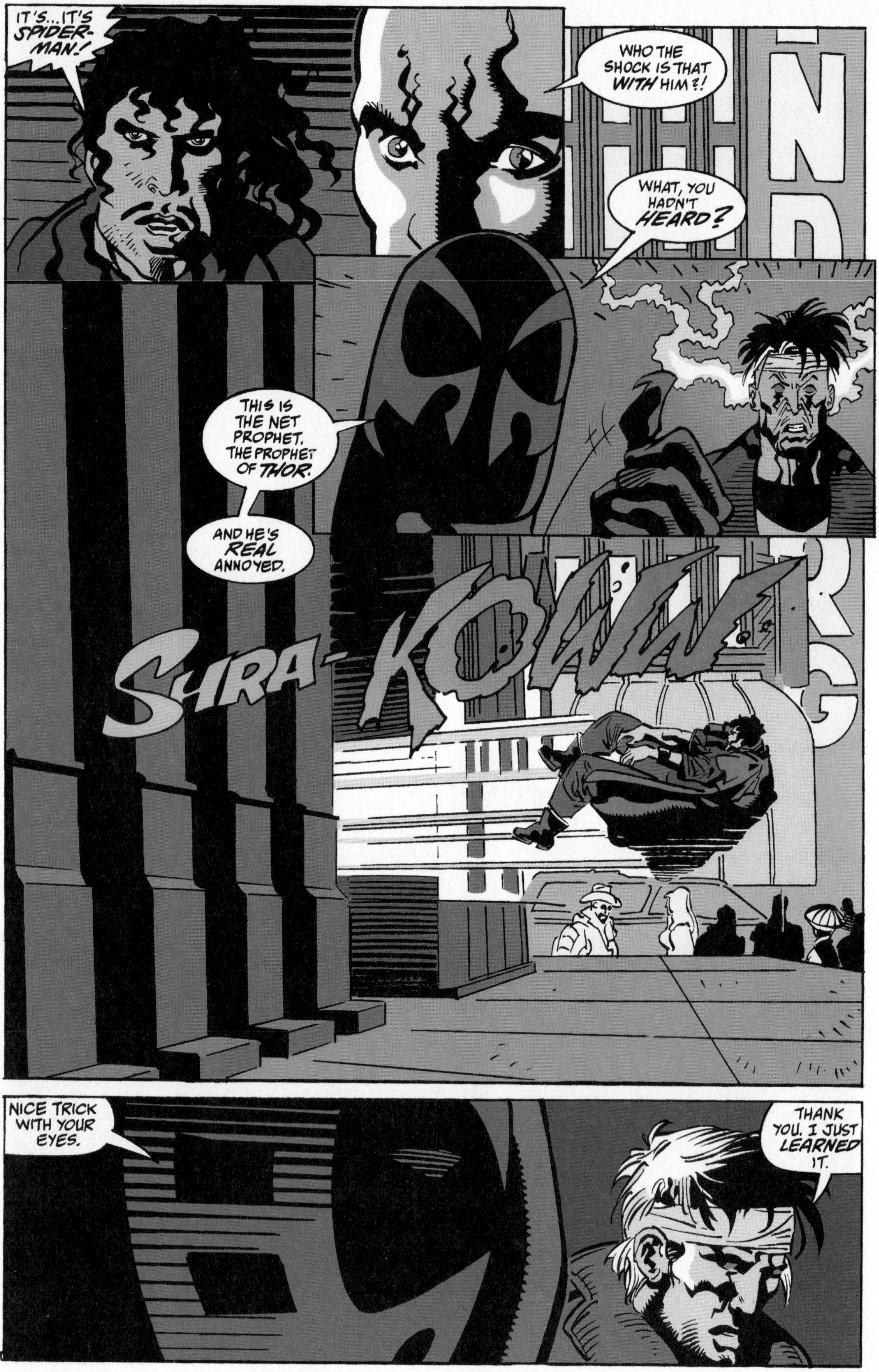
IT'S...IT'S SPIDER-MAN!
WHO THE SHOCK IS THAT WITH HIM?!
WHAT, YOU HADN'T HEARD?
THIS IS THE NET PROPHET. THE PROPHET OF THOR.
AND HE'S REAL ANNOYED.
SHRA-KOWW
NICE TRICK WITH YOUR EYES.
THANK YOU. I JUST LEARNED IT.

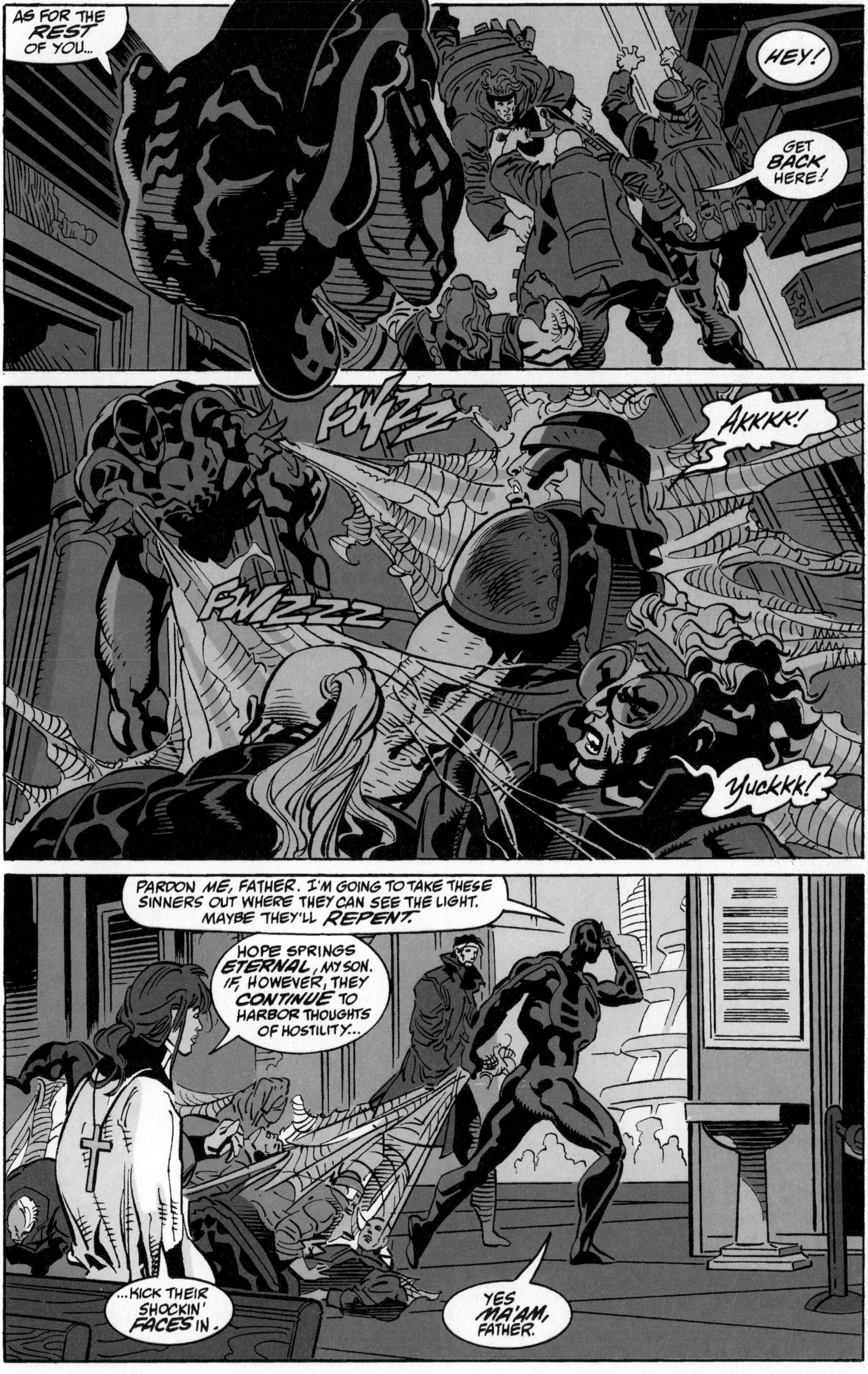
AS FOR THE REST OF YOU...
HEY!
GET BACK HERE!
FWZZZ
AKKKK!
FWIZZZ
YUCKKK!
PARDON ME, FATHER. I'M GOING TO TAKE THESE SINNERS OUT WHERE THEY CAN SEE THE LIGHT. MAYBE THEY'LL REPENT.
HOPE SPRINGS ETERNAL, MY SON. IF, HOWEVER, THEY CONTINUE TO HARBOR THOUGHTS OF HOSTILITY...
...KICK THEIR SHOCKIN' FACES IN.
YES MA'AM, FATHER.

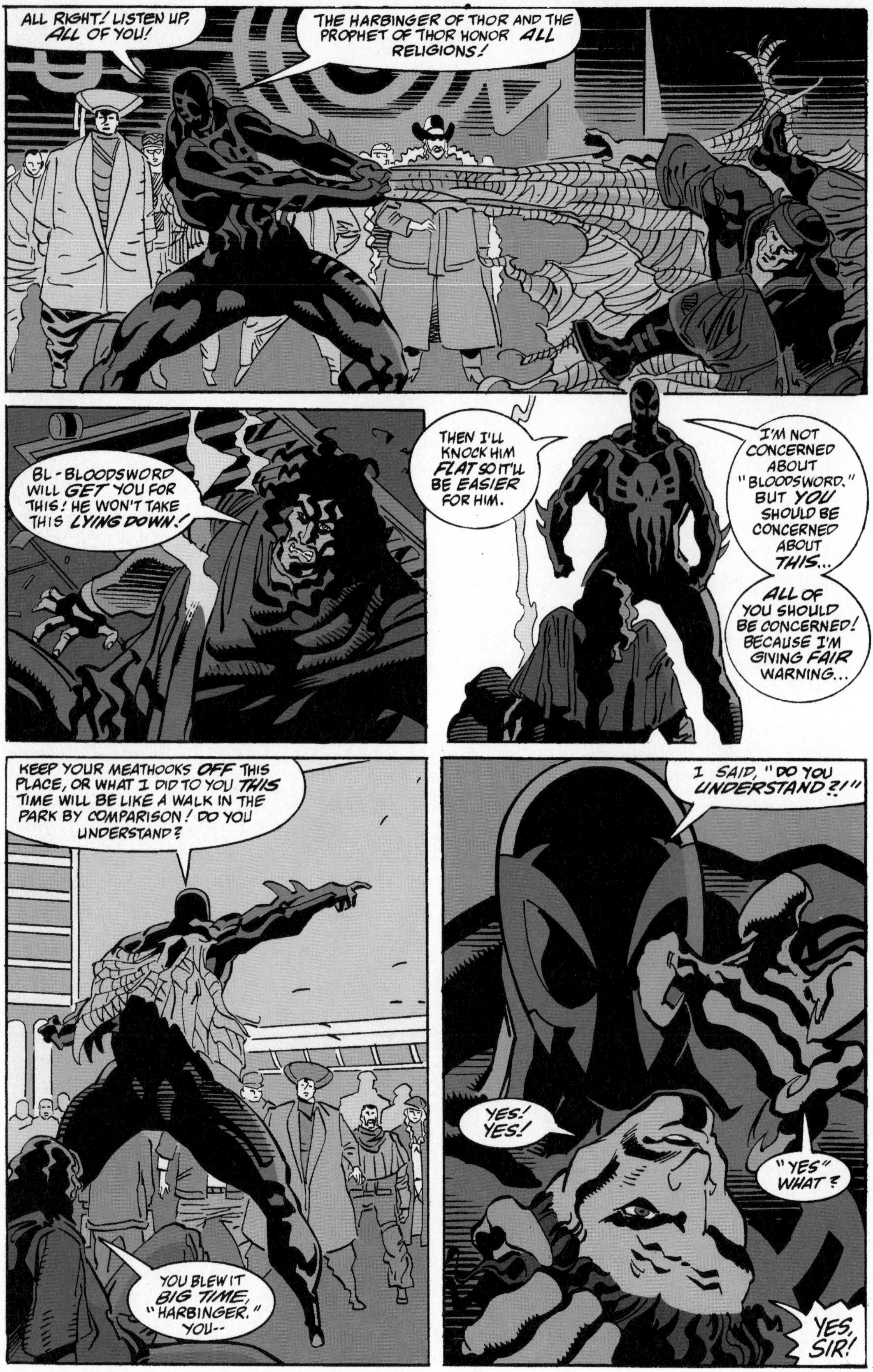
ALL RIGHT! LISTEN UP, ALL OF YOU!
THE HARBINGER OF THOR AND THE PROPHET OF THOR HONOR ALL RELIGIONS!
BL-BLOODSWORD WILL GET YOU FOR THIS! HE WON'T TAKE THIS LYING DOWN!
THEN I'LL KNOCK HIM FLAT SO IT'LL BE EASIER FOR HIM.
I'M NOT CONCERNED ABOUT "BLOODSWORD." BUT YOU SHOULD BE CONCERNED ABOUT THIS...
ALL OF YOU SHOULD BE CONCERNED! BECAUSE I'M GIVING FAIR WARNING...
KEEP YOUR MEATHOOKS OFF THIS PLACE, OR WHAT I DID TO YOU THIS TIME WILL BE LIKE A WALK IN THE PARK BY COMPARISON! DO YOU UNDERSTAND?
YOU BLEW IT BIG TIME, "HARBINGER." YOU--
I SAID, "DO YOU UNDERSTAND?!"
YES! YES!
"YES" WHAT?
YES, SIR!

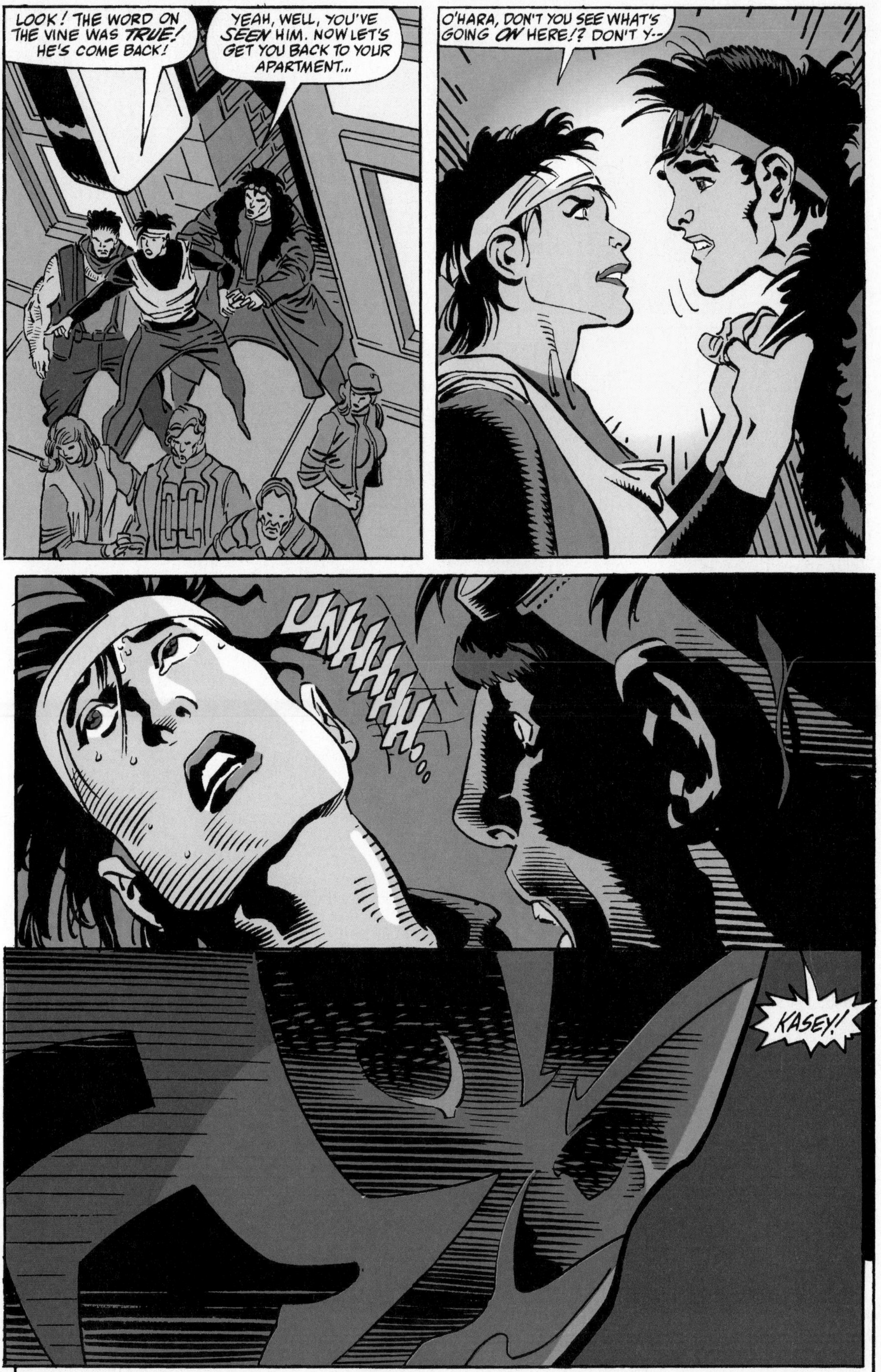
LOOK! THE WORD ON THE VINE WAS TRUE! HE'S COME BACK!
YEAH, WELL, YOU'VE SEEN HIM. NOW LET'S GET YOU BACK TO YOUR APARTMENT...
O'HARA, DON'T YOU SEE WHAT'S GOING ON HERE!? DON'T Y--
UNHHHH...
KASEY!

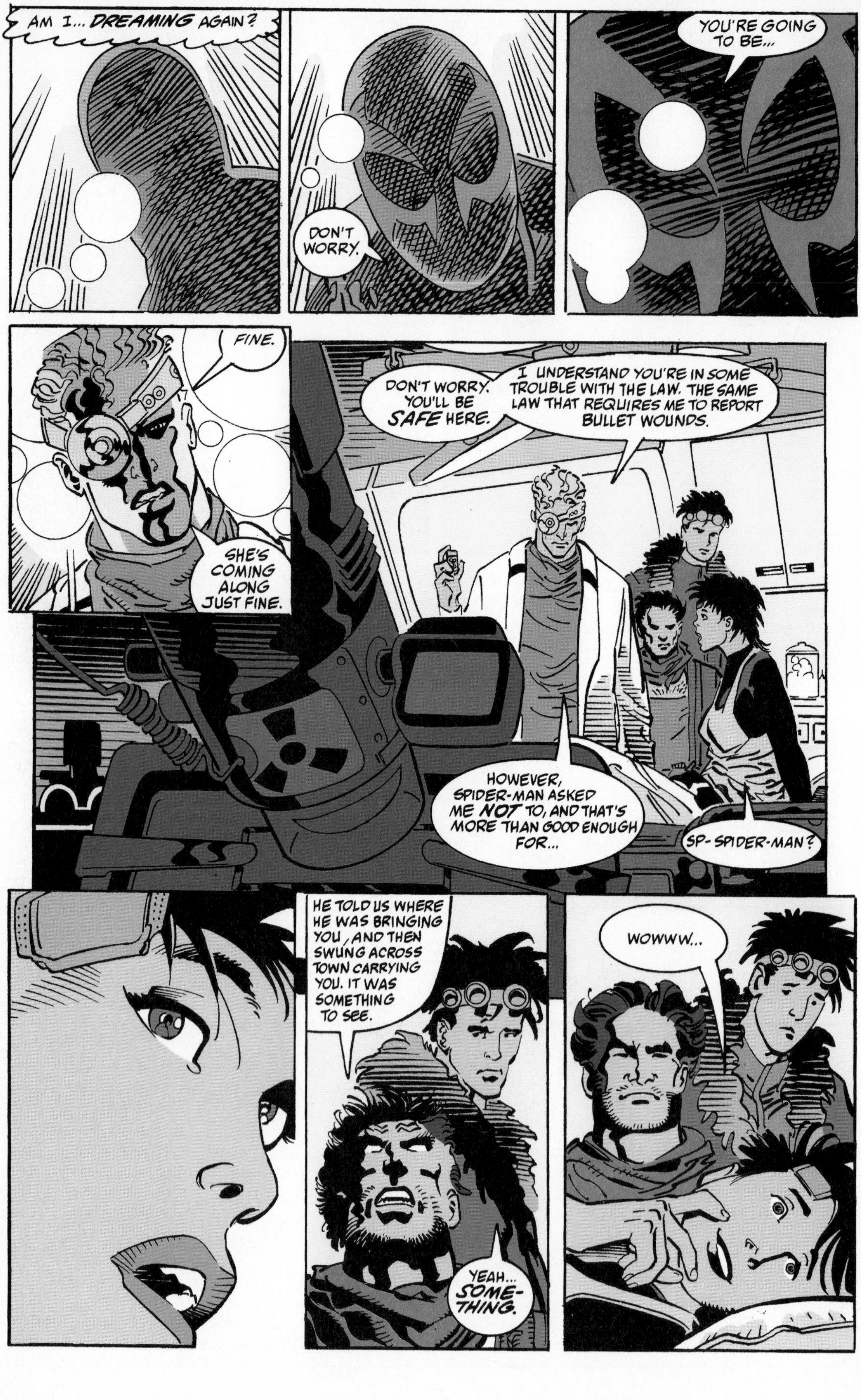

AM I... DREAMING AGAIN?
DON'T WORRY.
YOU'RE GOING TO BE...
FINE.
SHE'S COMING ALONG JUST FINE.
DON'T WORRY. YOU'LL BE SAFE HERE.
I UNDERSTAND YOU'RE IN SOME TROUBLE WITH THE LAW. THE SAME LAW THAT REQUIRES ME TO REPORT BULLET WOUNDS.
HOWEVER, SPIDER-MAN ASKED ME NOT TO, AND THAT'S MORE THAN GOOD ENOUGH FOR...
SP- SPIDER-MAN?
HE TOLD US WHERE HE WAS BRINGING YOU, AND THEN SWUNG ACROSS TOWN CARRYING YOU. IT WAS SOMETHING TO SEE.
YEAH... SOME-THING.
WOWWW...

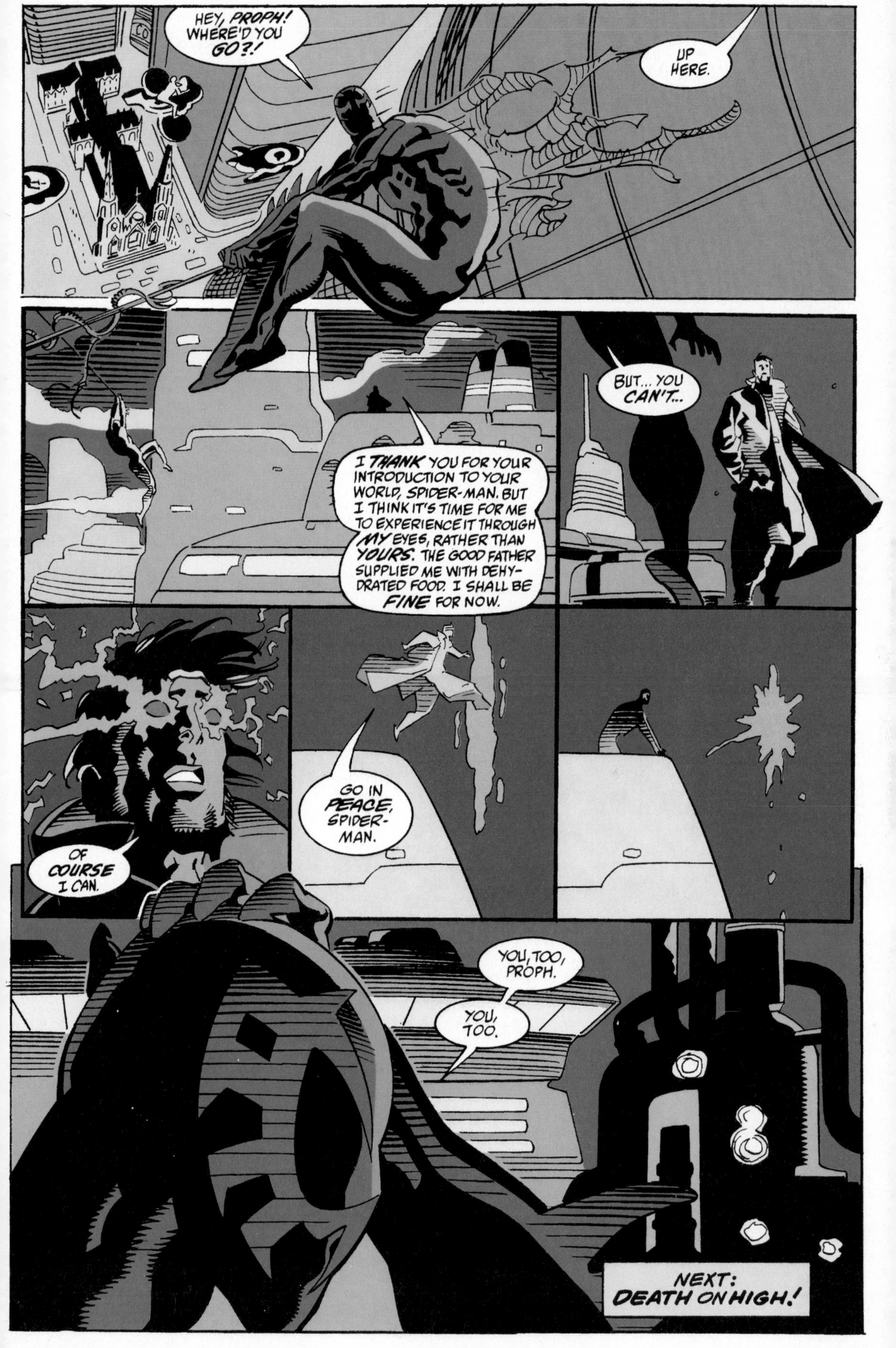
HEY, PROPH! WHERE'D YOU GO?!
UP HERE.
I THANK YOU FOR YOUR INTRODUCTION TO YOUR WORLD, SPIDER-MAN. BUT I THINK IT'S TIME FOR ME TO EXPERIENCE IT THROUGH MY EYES, RATHER THAN YOURS. THE GOOD FATHER SUPPLIED ME WITH DEHY-DRATED FOOD. I SHALL BE FINE FOR NOW.
BUT... YOU CAN'T...
OF COURSE I CAN.
GO IN PEACE, SPIDER-MAN.
YOU, TOO, PROPH.
YOU, TOO.
NEXT: DEATH ON HIGH!

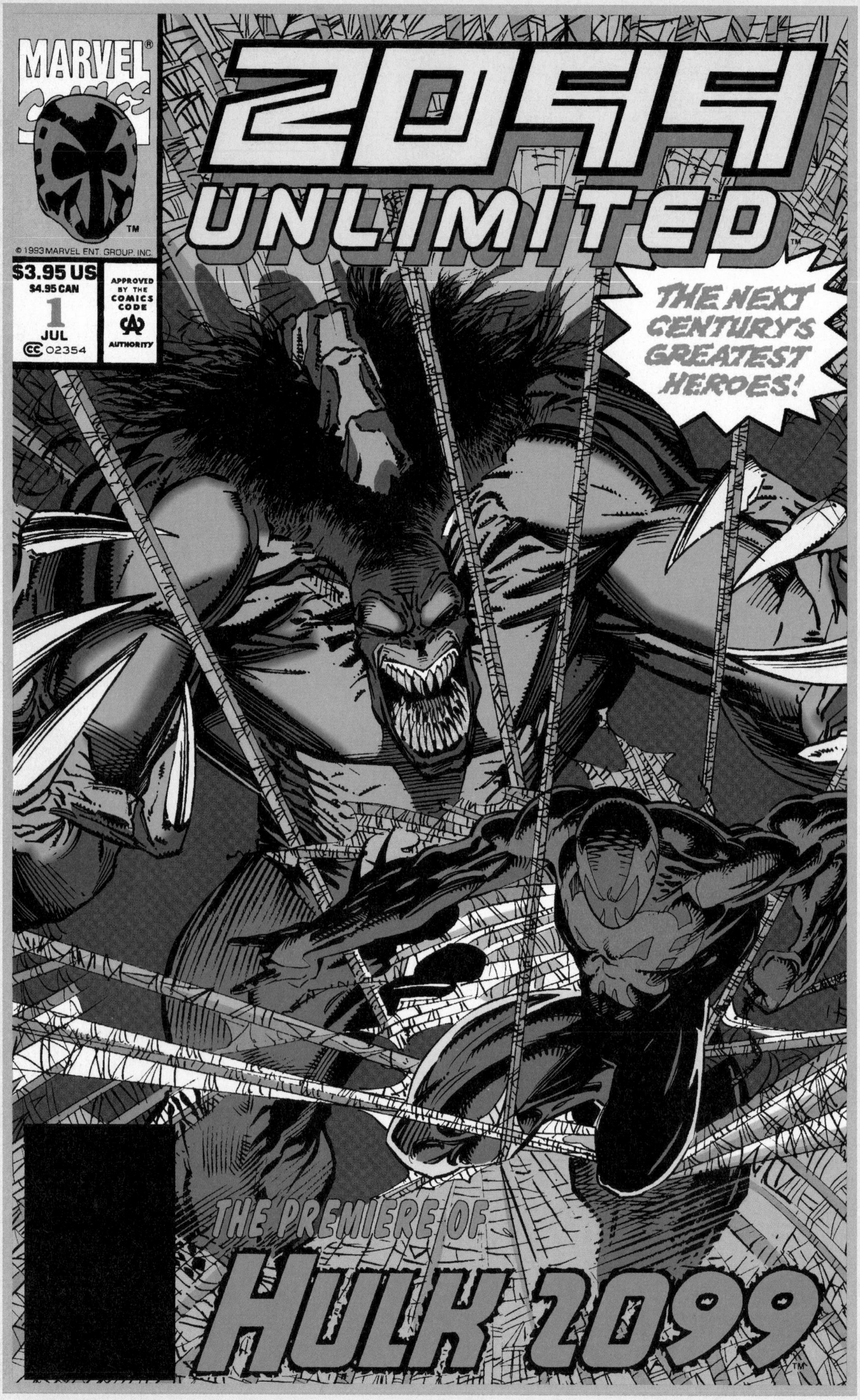

MARVEL COMICS
2099 UNLIMITED
© 1993 MARVEL ENT. GROUP, INC.
$3.95 US
$4.95 CAN
1
JUL
02354
APPROVED BY THE COMICS CODE AUTHORITY
THE NEXT CENTURY'S GREATEST HEROES!
THE PREMIERE OF
HULK 2099

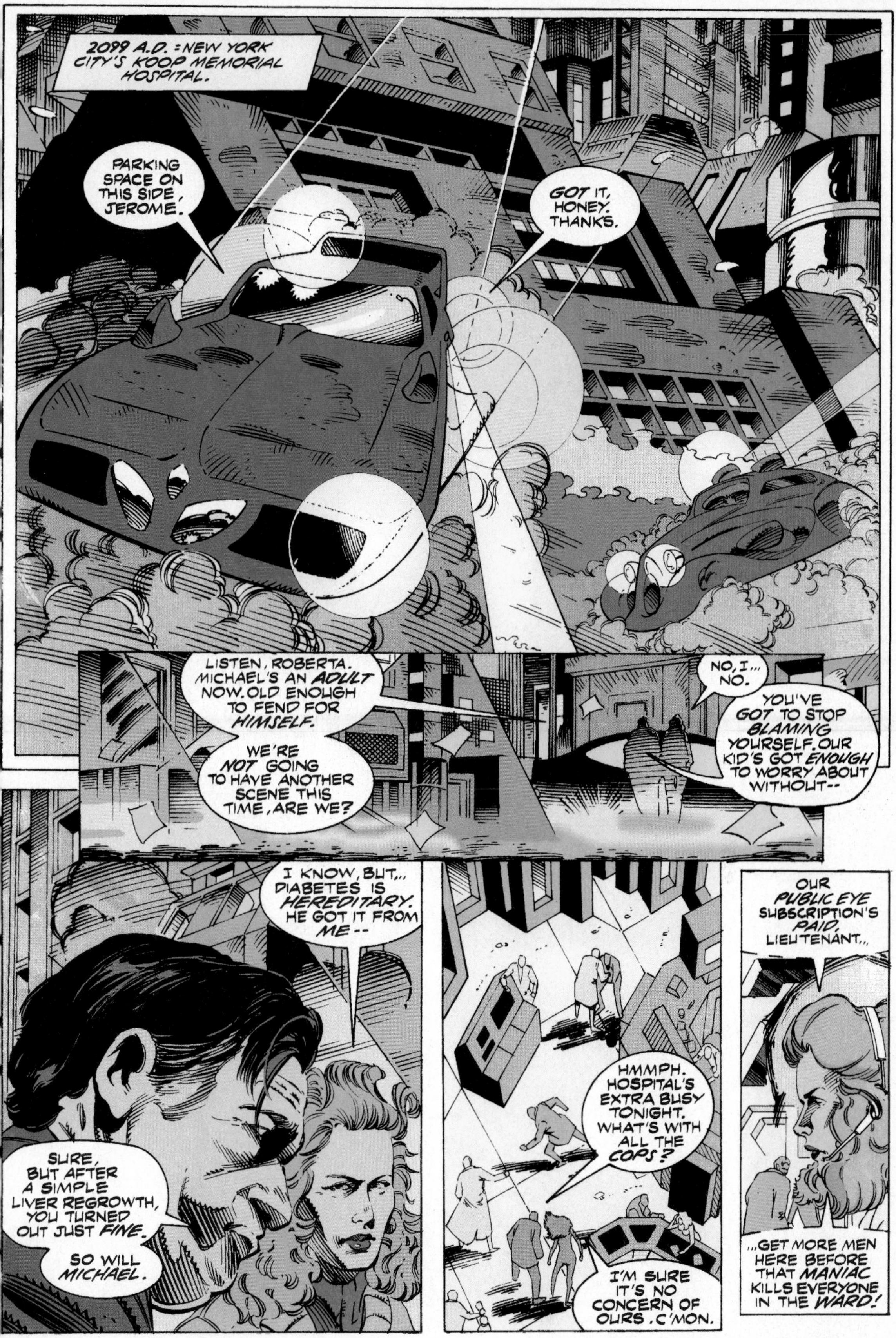
2099 A.D. = NEW YORK CITY'S KOOP MEMORIAL HOSPITAL.
PARKING SPACE ON THIS SIDE, JEROME.
GOT IT, HONEY. THANKS.
LISTEN, ROBERTA. MICHAEL'S AN ADULT NOW. OLD ENOUGH TO FEND FOR HIMSELF.
WE'RE NOT GOING TO HAVE ANOTHER SCENE THIS TIME, ARE WE?
NO, I... NO.
YOU'VE GOT TO STOP BLAMING YOURSELF. OUR KID'S GOT ENOUGH TO WORRY ABOUT WITHOUT--
I KNOW, BUT... DIABETES IS HEREDITARY. HE GOT IT FROM ME--
SURE, BUT AFTER A SIMPLE LIVER REGROWTH, YOU TURNED OUT JUST FINE.
SO WILL MICHAEL.
HMMPH. HOSPITAL'S EXTRA BUSY TONIGHT. WHAT'S WITH ALL THE COPS?
I'M SURE IT'S NO CONCERN OF OURS. C'MON.
OUR PUBLIC EYE SUBSCRIPTION'S PAID, LIEUTENANT...
...GET MORE MEN HERE BEFORE THAT MANIAC KILLS EVERYONE IN THE WARD!

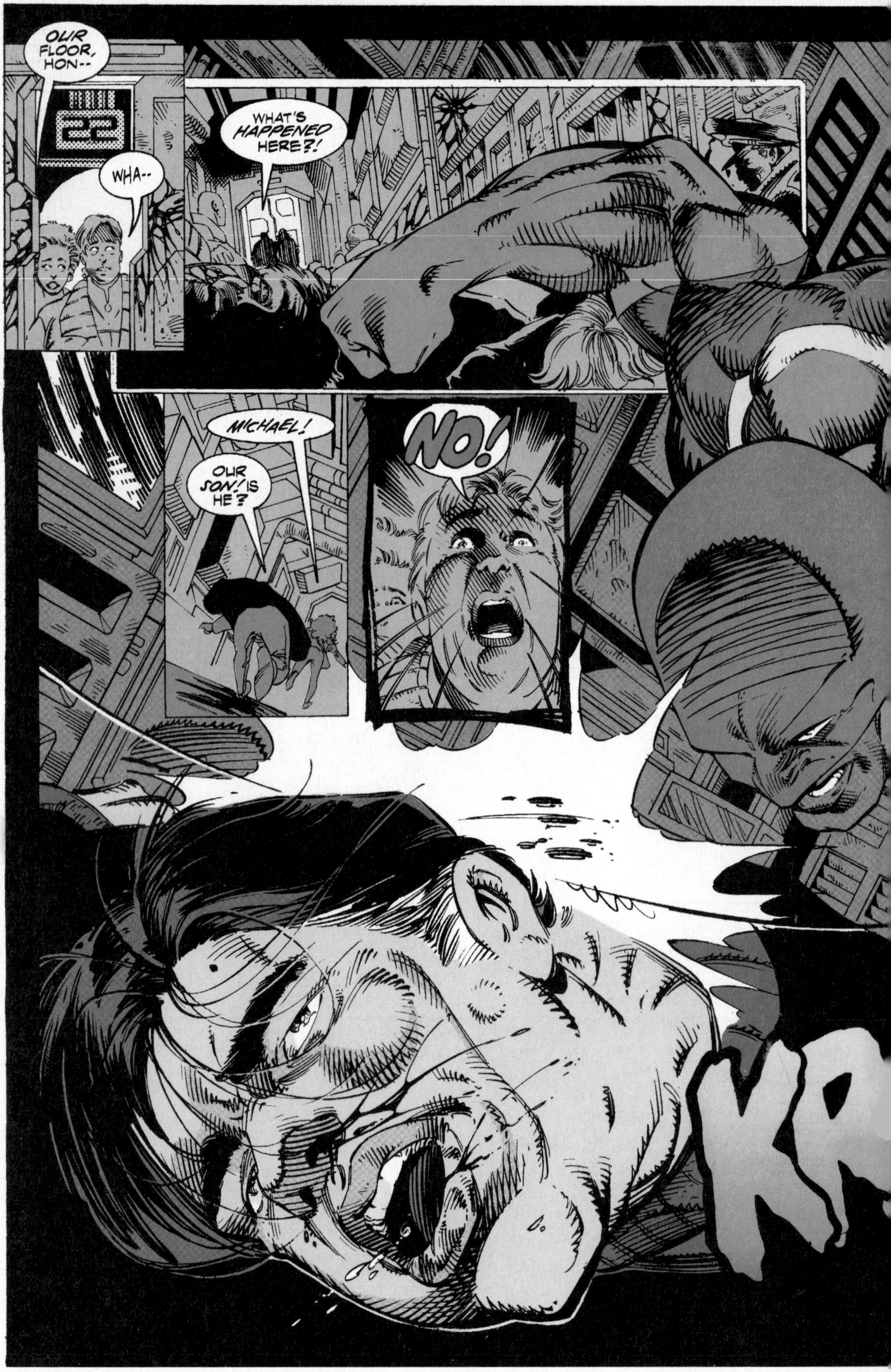
OUR FLOOR, HON--
22
WHA--
WHAT'S HAPPENED HERE?!
MICHAEL!
OUR SON! IS HE?
NO!
KR

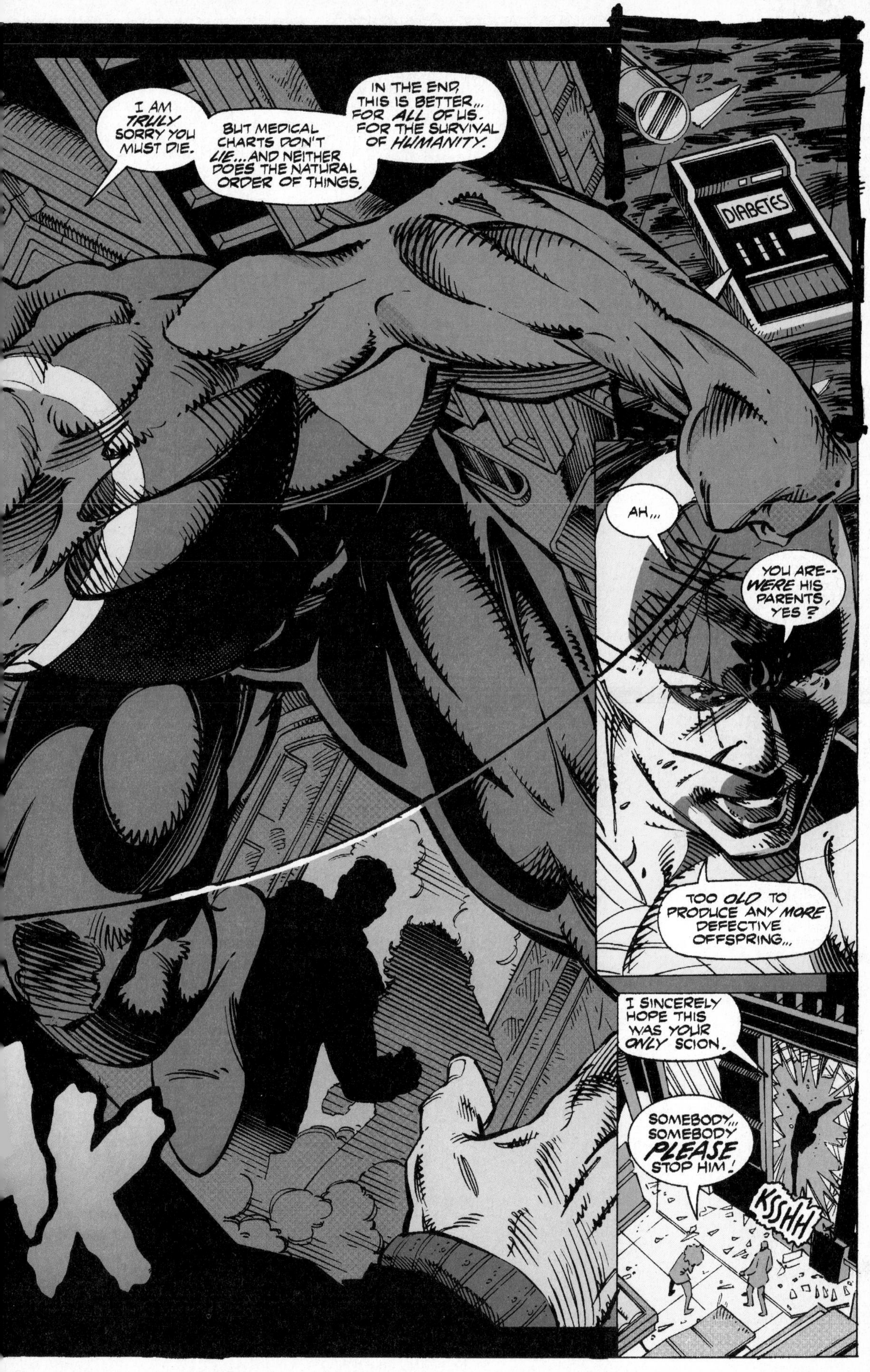
I AM TRULY SORRY YOU MUST DIE.
BUT MEDICAL CHARTS DON'T LIE... AND NEITHER DOES THE NATURAL ORDER OF THINGS.
IN THE END, THIS IS BETTER... FOR ALL OF US. FOR THE SURVIVAL OF HUMANITY.
DIABETES
AH...
YOU ARE-- WERE HIS PARENTS, YES?
TOO OLD TO PRODUCE ANY MORE DEFECTIVE OFFSPRING...
I SINCERELY HOPE THIS WAS YOUR ONLY SCION.
SOMEBODY... SOMEBODY PLEASE STOP HIM!
KSSHH

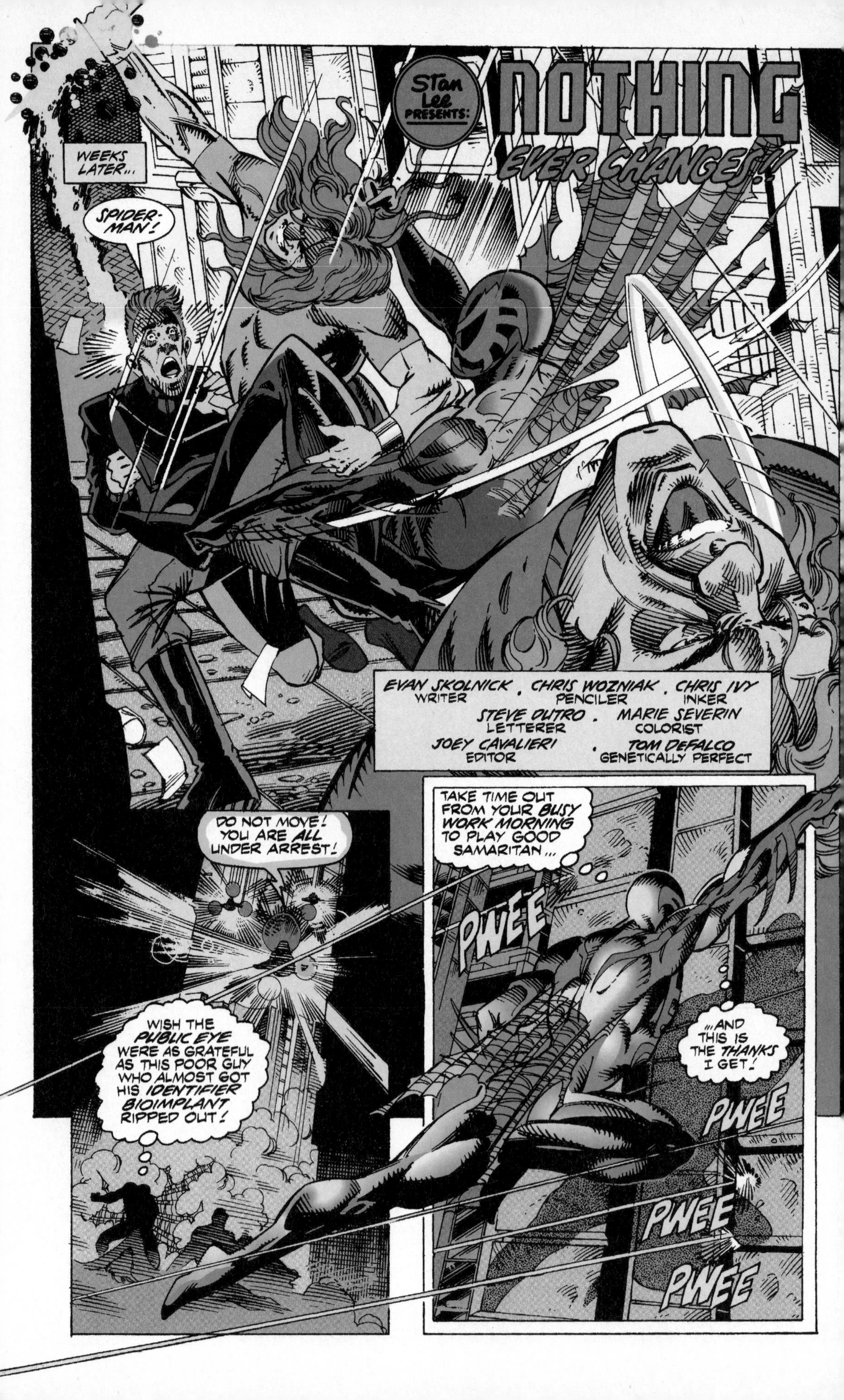
STAN LEE PRESENTS:
NOTHING EVER CHANGES!!
WEEKS LATER...
SPIDER-MAN!
EVAN SKOLNICK WRITER . CHRIS WOZNIAK PENCILER . CHRIS IVY INKER
STEVE DUTRO LETTERER . MARIE SEVERIN COLORIST
JOEY CAVALIERI EDITOR . TOM DEFALCO GENETICALLY PERFECT
DO NOT MOVE! YOU ARE ALL UNDER ARREST!
WISH THE PUBLIC EYE WERE AS GRATEFUL AS THIS POOR GUY WHO ALMOST GOT HIS IDENTIFIER BIOIMPLANT RIPPED OUT!
TAKE TIME OUT FROM YOUR BUSY WORK MORNING TO PLAY GOOD SAMARITAN...
PWEE
...AND THIS IS THE THANKS I GET!
PWEE
PWEE
PWEE

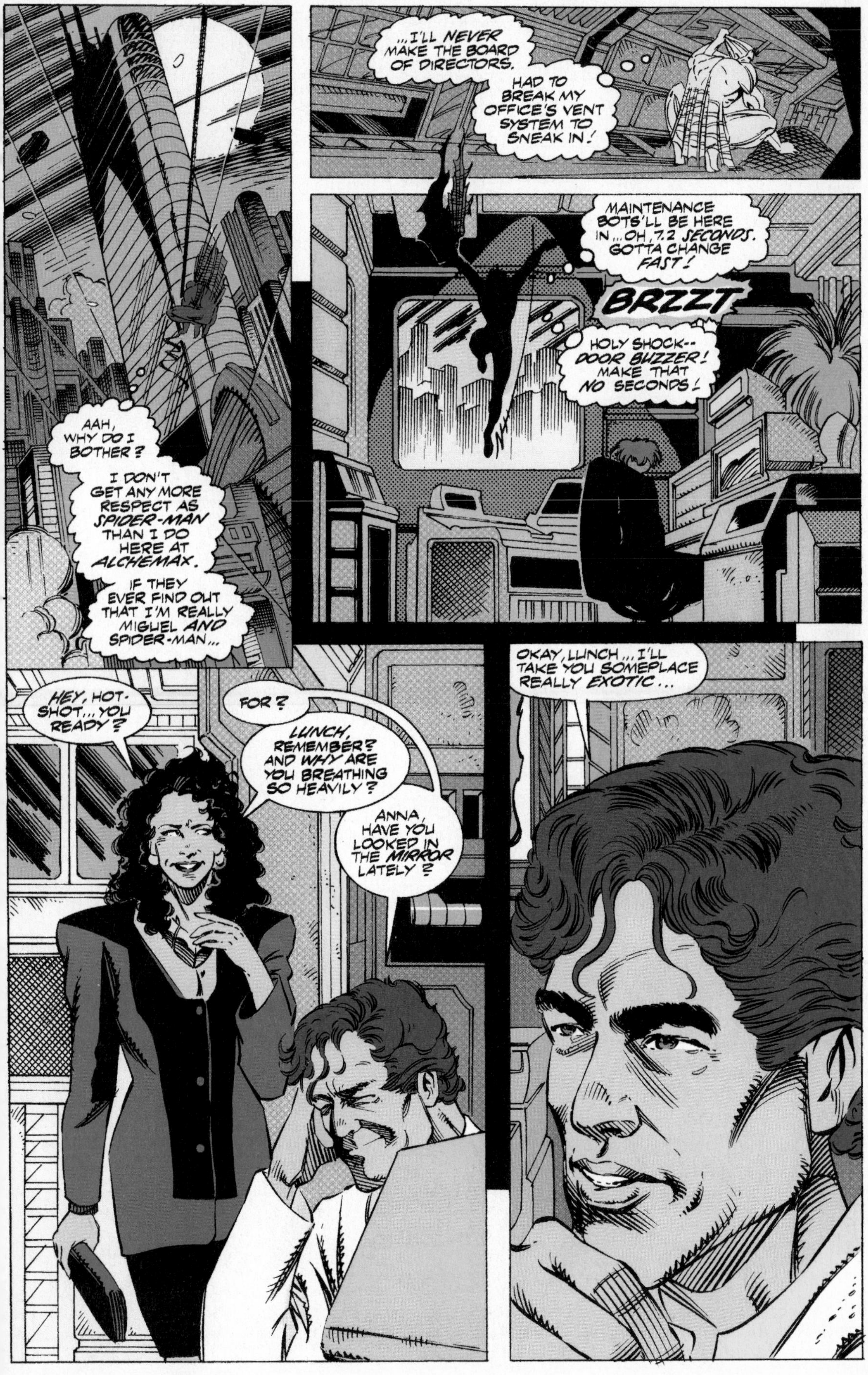

AAH, WHY DO I BOTHER?
I DON'T GET ANY MORE RESPECT AS SPIDER-MAN THAN I DO HERE AT ALCHEMAX.
IF THEY EVER FIND OUT THAT I'M REALLY MIGUEL AND SPIDER-MAN...
...I'LL NEVER MAKE THE BOARD OF DIRECTORS.
HAD TO BREAK MY OFFICE'S VENT SYSTEM TO SNEAK IN!
MAINTENANCE BOTS'LL BE HERE IN...OH, 7.2 SECONDS. GOTTA CHANGE FAST!
BRZZT
HOLY SHOCK--DOOR BUZZER! MAKE THAT NO SECONDS!
HEY, HOT-SHOT...YOU READY?
FOR?
LUNCH, REMEMBER? AND WHY ARE YOU BREATHING SO HEAVILY?
ANNA, HAVE YOU LOOKED IN THE MIRROR LATELY?
OKAY, LUNCH... I'LL TAKE YOU SOMEPLACE REALLY EXOTIC...

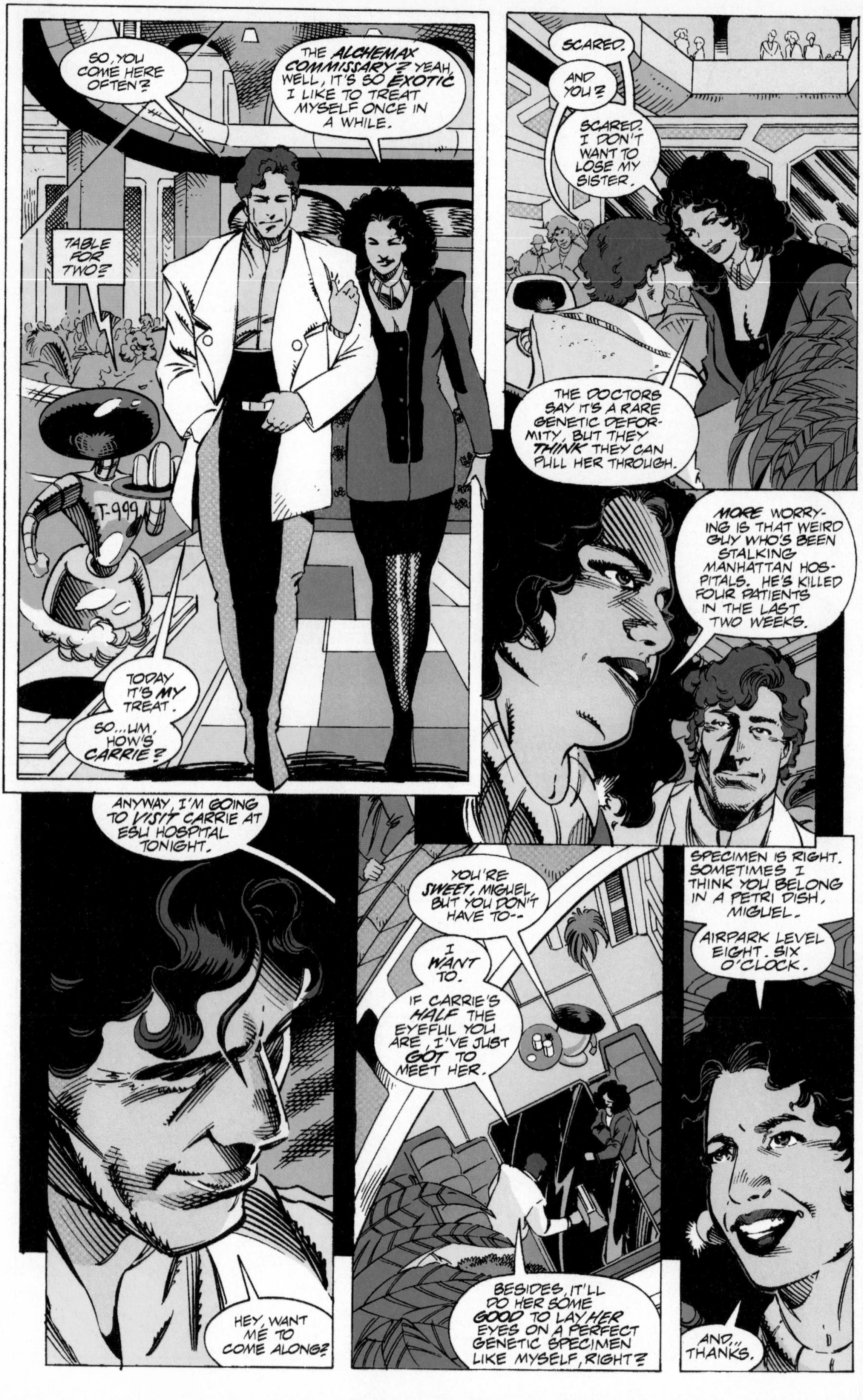
SO, YOU COME HERE OFTEN?
THE ALCHEMAX COMMISSARY? YEAH, WELL, IT'S SO EXOTIC I LIKE TO TREAT MYSELF ONCE IN A WHILE.
TABLE FOR TWO?
T-999
TODAY IT'S MY TREAT.
SO...UM, HOW'S CARRIE?
SCARED.
AND YOU?
SCARED. I DON'T WANT TO LOSE MY SISTER.
THE DOCTORS SAY IT'S A RARE GENETIC DEFORMITY, BUT THEY THINK THEY CAN PULL HER THROUGH.
MORE WORRYING IS THAT WEIRD GUY WHO'S BEEN STALKING MANHATTAN HOSPITALS. HE'S KILLED FOUR PATIENTS IN THE LAST TWO WEEKS.
ANYWAY, I'M GOING TO VISIT CARRIE AT ESU HOSPITAL TONIGHT.
HEY, WANT ME TO COME ALONG?
YOU'RE SWEET, MIGUEL, BUT YOU DON'T HAVE TO--
I WANT TO.
IF CARRIE'S HALF THE EYEFUL YOU ARE, I'VE JUST GOT TO MEET HER.
BESIDES, IT'LL DO HER SOME GOOD TO LAY HER EYES ON A PERFECT GENETIC SPECIMEN LIKE MYSELF, RIGHT?
SPECIMEN IS RIGHT. SOMETIMES I THINK YOU BELONG IN A PETRI DISH, MIGUEL.
AIRPARK LEVEL EIGHT. SIX O'CLOCK.
AND... THANKS.

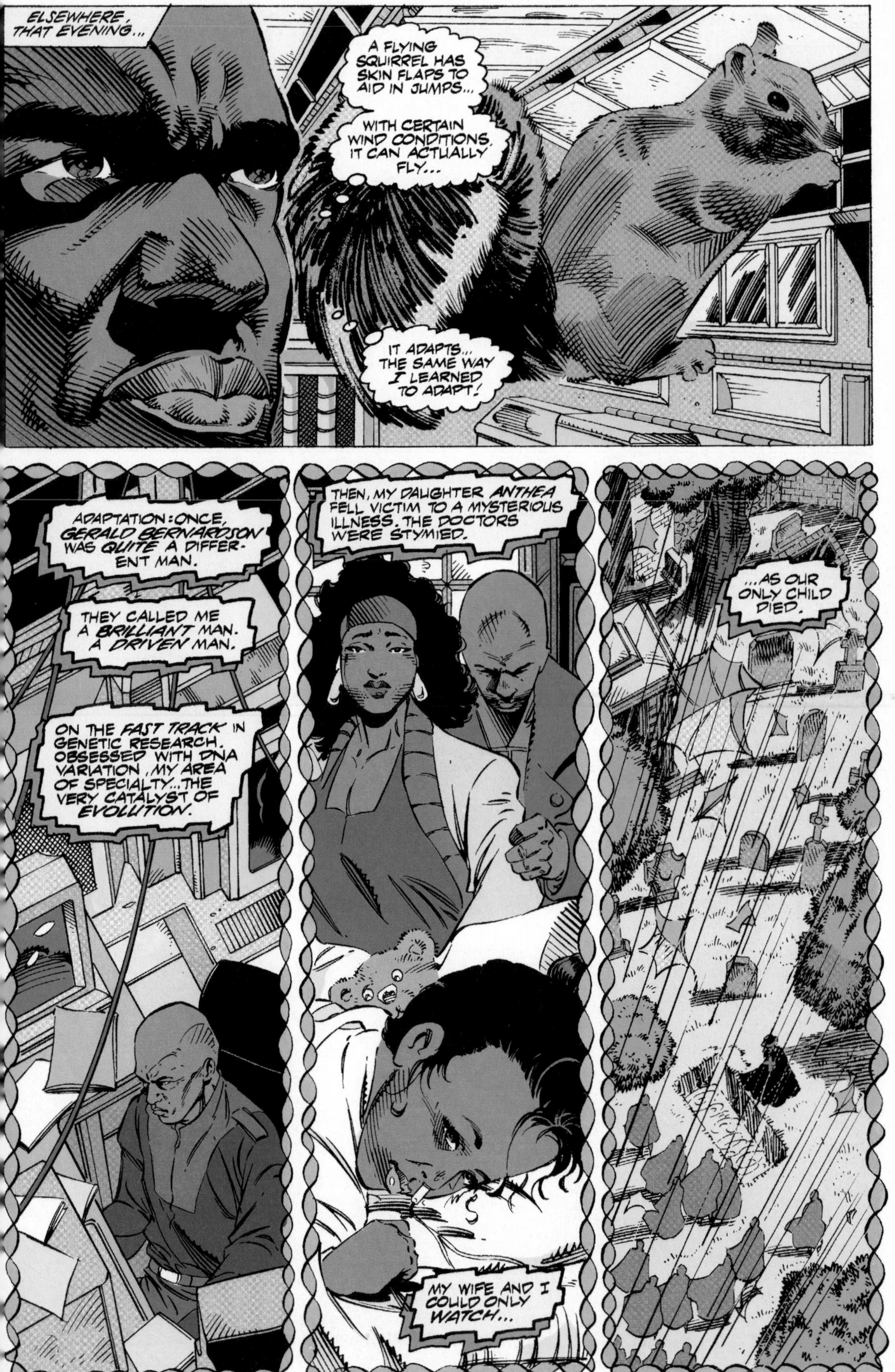

ELSEWHERE, THAT EVENING...
A FLYING SQUIRREL HAS SKIN FLAPS TO AID IN JUMPS...
WITH CERTAIN WIND CONDITIONS, IT CAN ACTUALLY FLY...
IT ADAPTS... THE SAME WAY I LEARNED TO ADAPT!
ADAPTATION: ONCE, GERALD BERNARDSON WAS QUITE A DIFFERENT MAN.
THEY CALLED ME A BRILLIANT MAN. A DRIVEN MAN.
ON THE FAST TRACK IN GENETIC RESEARCH. OBSESSED WITH DNA VARIATION, MY AREA OF SPECIALTY...THE VERY CATALYST OF EVOLUTION.
THEN, MY DAUGHTER ANTHEA FELL VICTIM TO A MYSTERIOUS ILLNESS. THE DOCTORS WERE STYMIED.
MY WIFE AND I COULD ONLY WATCH...
...AS OUR ONLY CHILD DIED.

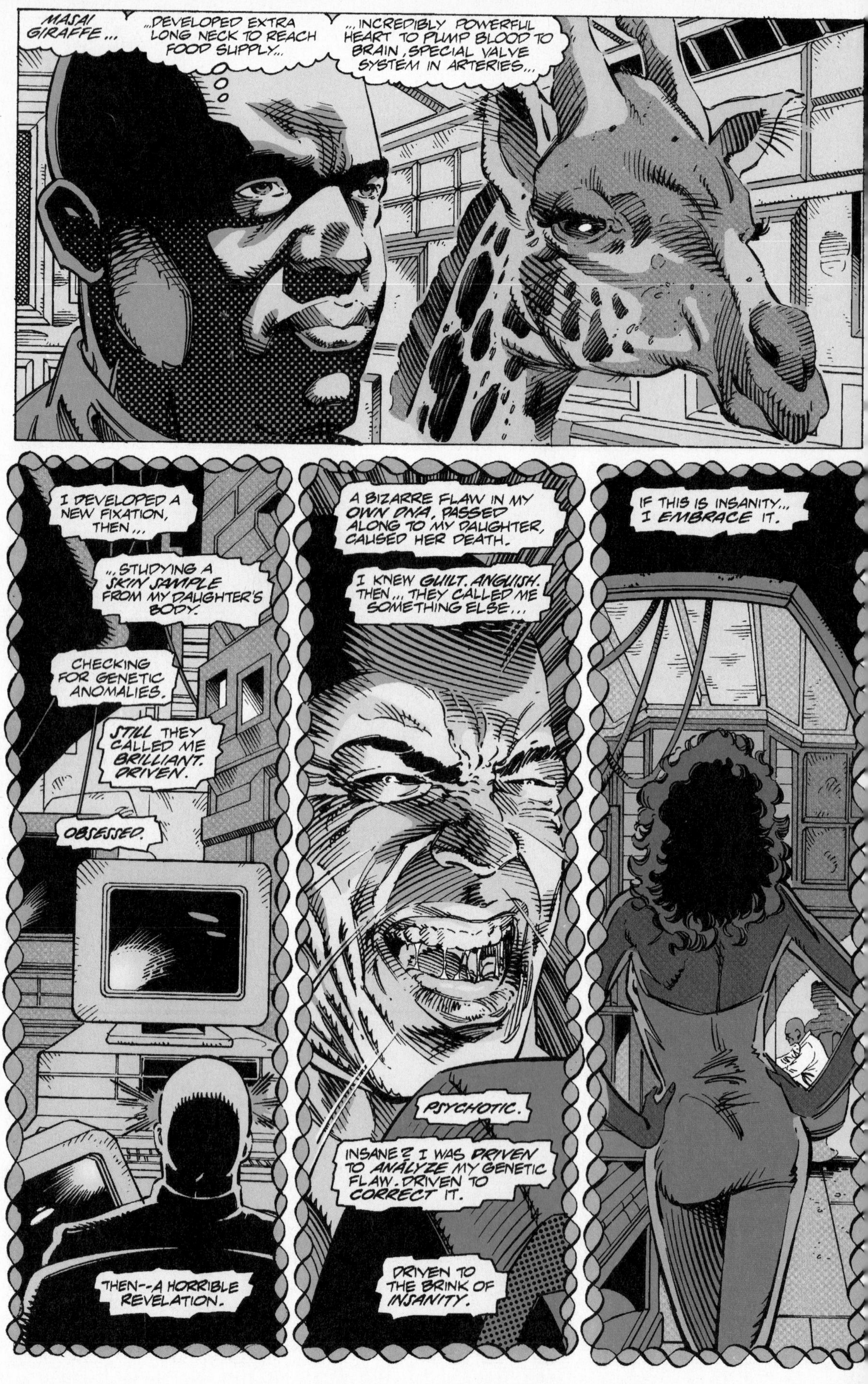
MASAI GIRAFFE...
...DEVELOPED EXTRA LONG NECK TO REACH FOOD SUPPLY...
...INCREDIBLY POWERFUL HEART TO PUMP BLOOD TO BRAIN, SPECIAL VALVE SYSTEM IN ARTERIES...
I DEVELOPED A NEW FIXATION, THEN...
...STUDYING A SKIN SAMPLE FROM MY DAUGHTER'S BODY.
CHECKING FOR GENETIC ANOMALIES.
STILL THEY CALLED ME BRILLIANT. DRIVEN.
OBSESSED.
THEN--A HORRIBLE REVELATION.
A BIZARRE FLAW IN MY OWN DNA, PASSED ALONG TO MY DAUGHTER, CAUSED HER DEATH.
I KNEW GUILT. ANGUISH. THEN... THEY CALLED ME SOMETHING ELSE...
PSYCHOTIC.
INSANE? I WAS DRIVEN TO ANALYZE MY GENETIC FLAW. DRIVEN TO CORRECT IT.
DRIVEN TO THE BRINK OF INSANITY.
IF THIS IS INSANITY... I EMBRACE IT.

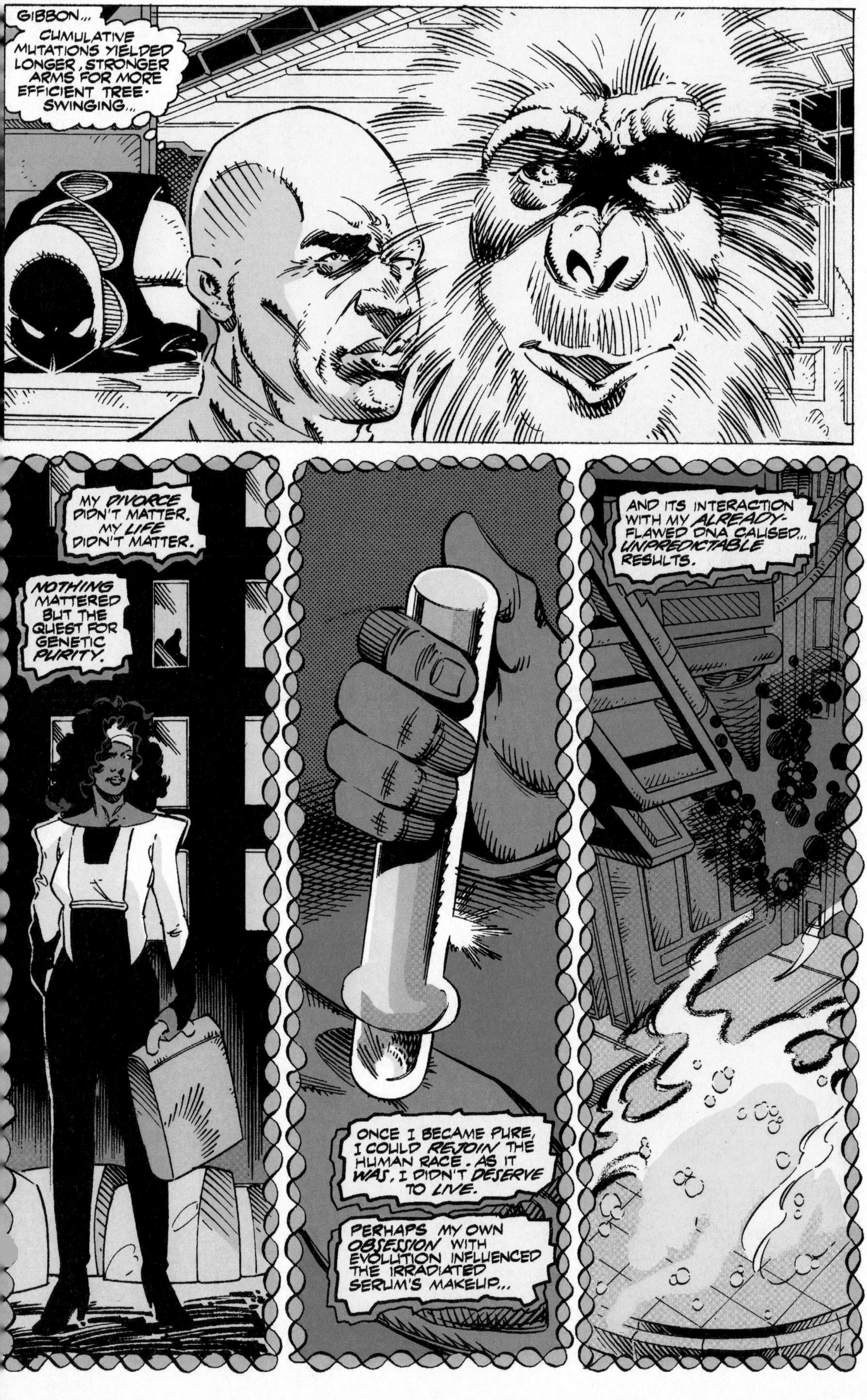
GIBBON...
CUMULATIVE MUTATIONS YIELDED LONGER, STRONGER ARMS FOR MORE EFFICIENT TREE-SWINGING...
MY DIVORCE DIDN'T MATTER. MY LIFE DIDN'T MATTER.
NOTHING MATTERED BUT THE QUEST FOR GENETIC PURITY.
ONCE I BECAME PURE, I COULD REJOIN THE HUMAN RACE. AS IT WAS, I DIDN'T DESERVE TO LIVE.
PERHAPS MY OWN OBSESSION WITH EVOLUTION INFLUENCED THE IRRADIATED SERUM'S MAKEUP...
AND ITS INTERACTION WITH MY ALREADY-FLAWED DNA CAUSED... UNPREDICTABLE RESULTS.

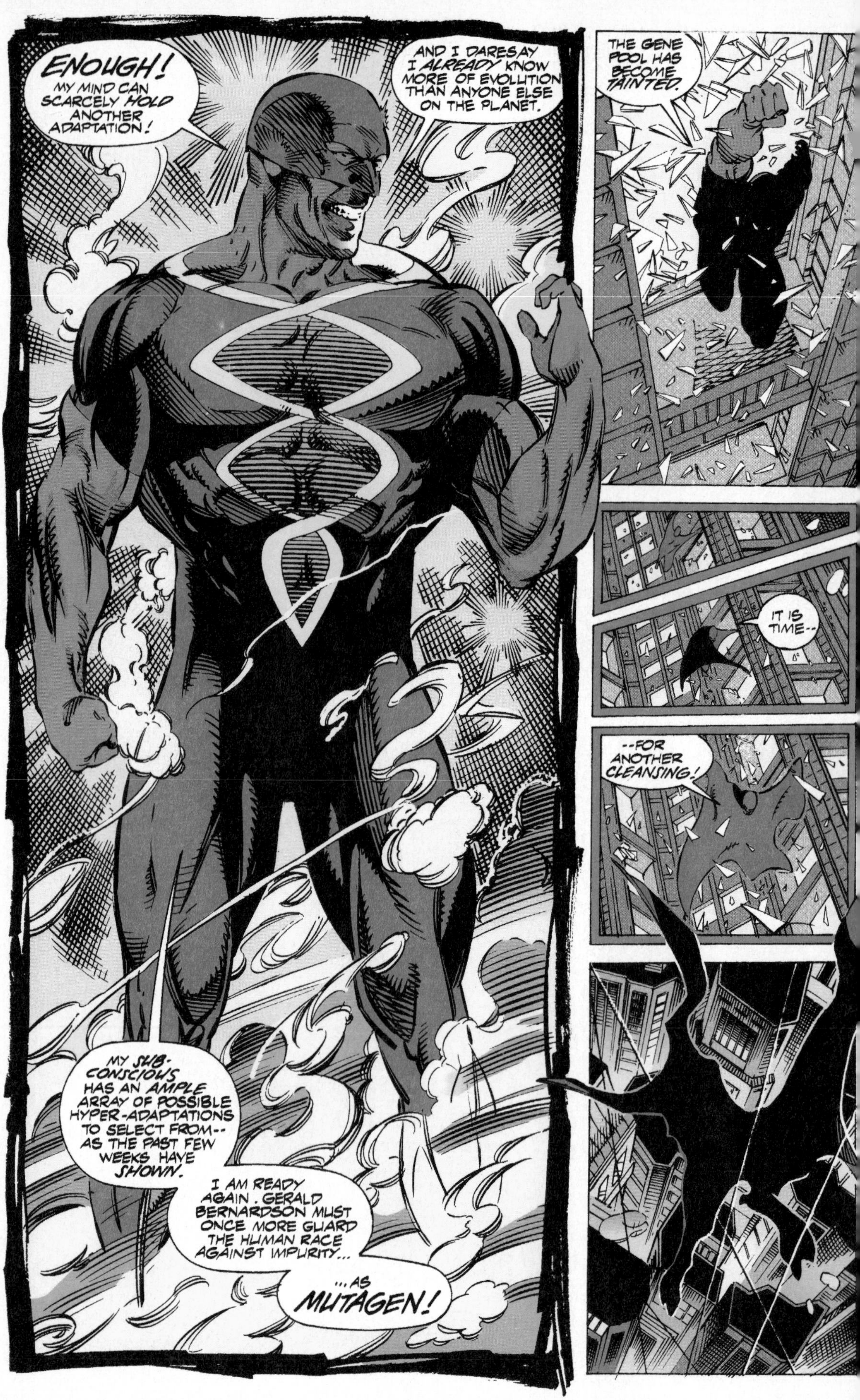
ENOUGH! MY MIND CAN SCARCELY HOLD ANOTHER ADAPTATION!
AND I DARESAY I ALREADY KNOW MORE OF EVOLUTION THAN ANYONE ELSE ON THE PLANET.
THE GENE POOL HAS BECOME TAINTED.
IT IS TIME--
--FOR ANOTHER CLEANSING!
MY SUB-CONSCIOUS HAS AN AMPLE ARRAY OF POSSIBLE HYPER-ADAPTATIONS TO SELECT FROM--AS THE PAST FEW WEEKS HAVE SHOWN.
I AM READY AGAIN. GERALD BERNARDSON MUST ONCE MORE GUARD THE HUMAN RACE AGAINST IMPURITY...
...AS MUTAGEN!

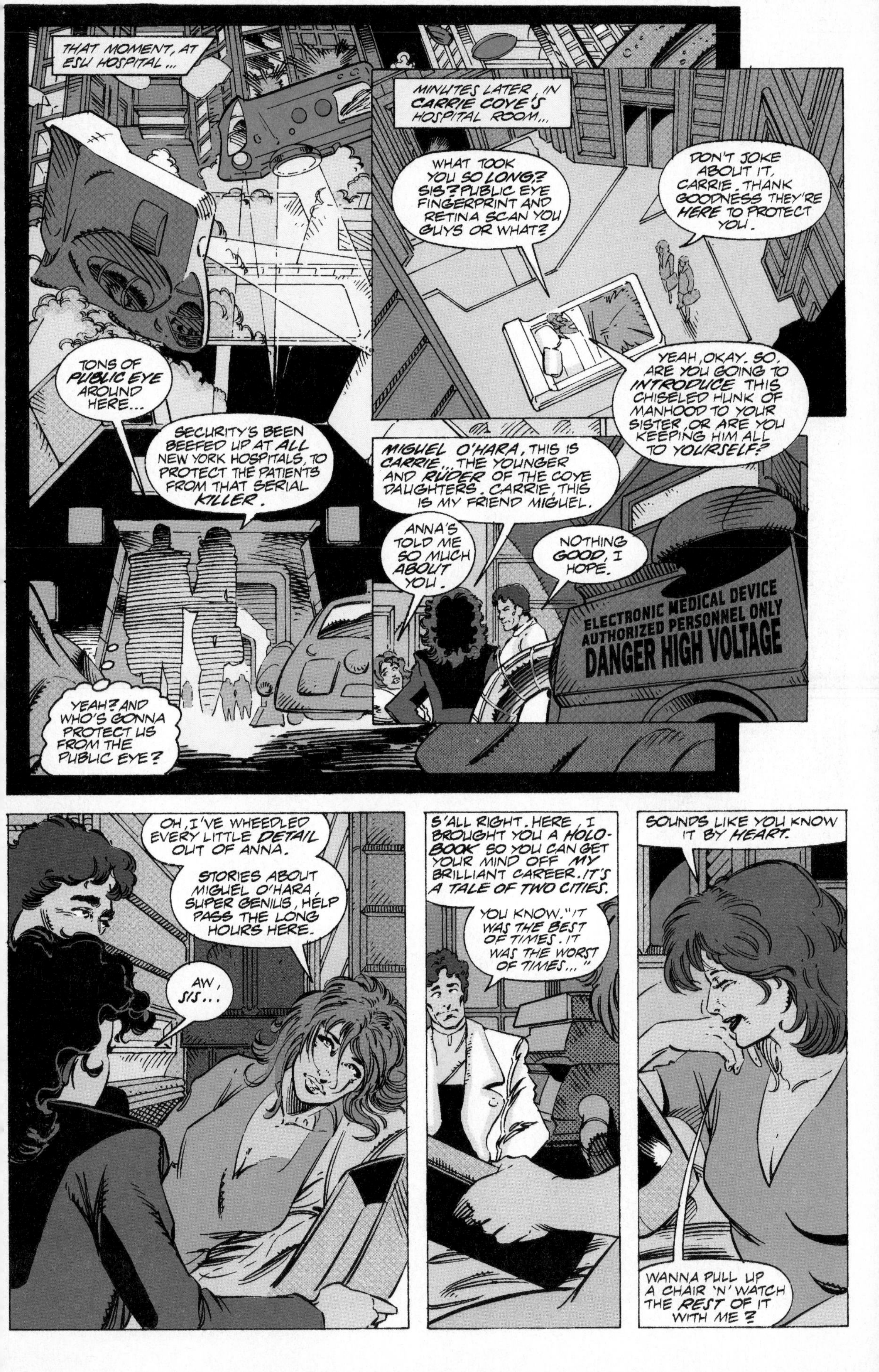
THAT MOMENT, AT ESU HOSPITAL...
TONS OF PUBLIC EYE AROUND HERE...
SECURITY'S BEEN BEEFED UP AT ALL NEW YORK HOSPITALS, TO PROTECT THE PATIENTS FROM THAT SERIAL KILLER.
YEAH? AND WHO'S GONNA PROTECT US FROM THE PUBLIC EYE?
MINUTES LATER, IN CARRIE COYE'S HOSPITAL ROOM...
WHAT TOOK YOU SO LONG? SIS? PUBLIC EYE FINGERPRINT AND RETINA SCAN YOU GUYS OR WHAT?
DON'T JOKE ABOUT IT, CARRIE. THANK GOODNESS THEY'RE HERE TO PROTECT YOU.
YEAH, OKAY. SO, ARE YOU GOING TO INTRODUCE THIS CHISELED HUNK OF MANHOOD TO YOUR SISTER, OR ARE YOU KEEPING HIM ALL TO YOURSELF?
MIGUEL O'HARA, THIS IS CARRIE... THE YOUNGER AND RUDER OF THE COYE DAUGHTERS. CARRIE, THIS IS MY FRIEND MIGUEL.
ANNA'S TOLD ME SO MUCH ABOUT YOU.
NOTHING GOOD, I HOPE.
ELECTRONIC MEDICAL DEVICE
AUTHORIZED PERSONNEL ONLY
DANGER HIGH VOLTAGE
OH, I'VE WHEEDLED EVERY LITTLE DETAIL OUT OF ANNA.
STORIES ABOUT MIGUEL O'HARA, SUPER GENIUS, HELP PASS THE LONG HOURS HERE.
AW, SIS...
S'ALL RIGHT. HERE, I BROUGHT YOU A HOLO-BOOK SO YOU CAN GET YOUR MIND OFF MY BRILLIANT CAREER. IT'S A TALE OF TWO CITIES.
YOU KNOW. "IT WAS THE BEST OF TIMES. IT WAS THE WORST OF TIMES..."
SOUNDS LIKE YOU KNOW IT BY HEART.
WANNA PULL UP A CHAIR 'N' WATCH THE REST OF IT WITH ME?

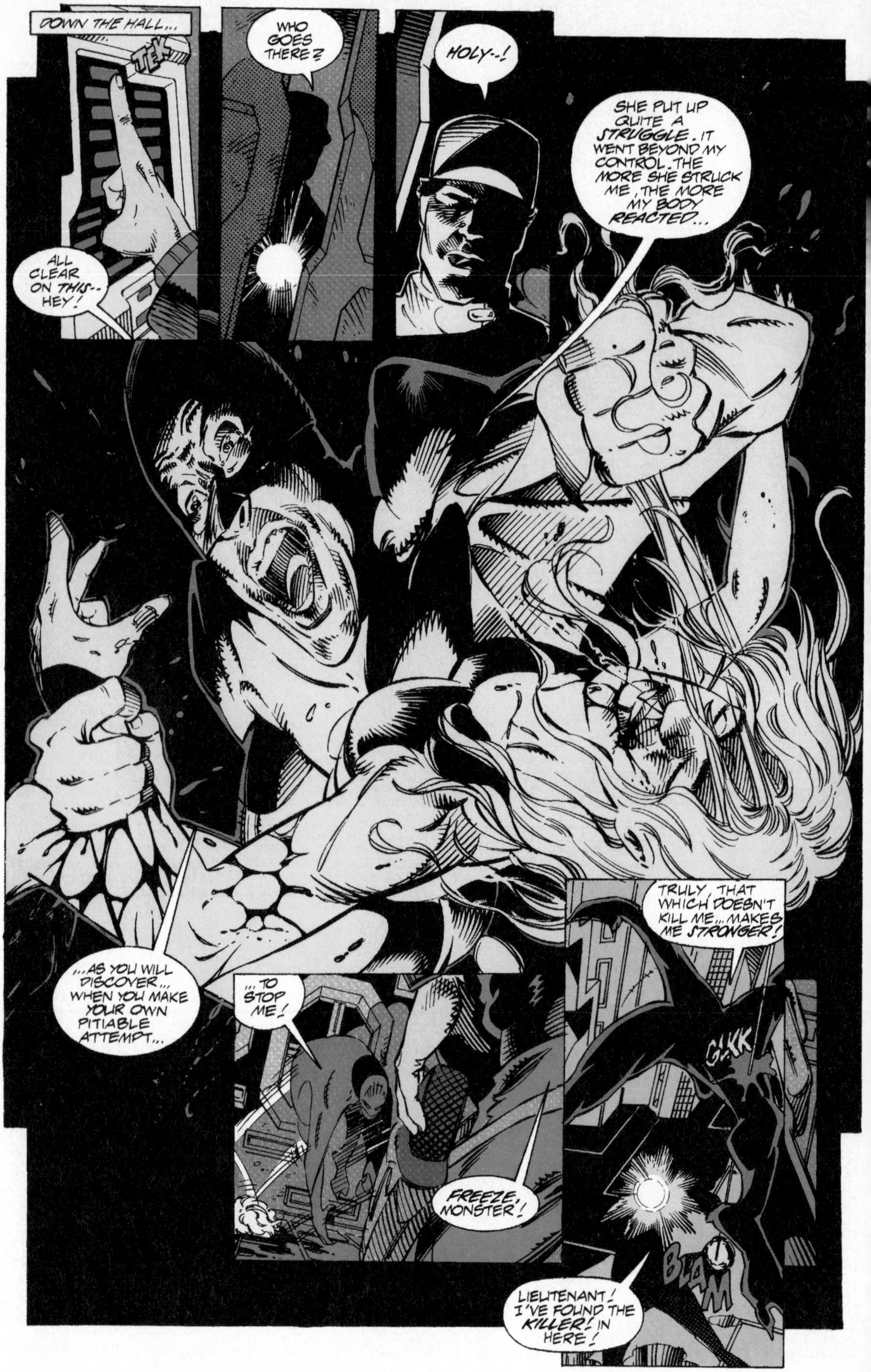
DOWN THE HALL...
TEK
ALL CLEAR ON THIS-- HEY!
WHO GOES THERE?
HOLY--!
SHE PUT UP QUITE A STRUGGLE. IT WENT BEYOND MY CONTROL. THE MORE SHE STRUCK ME, THE MORE MY BODY REACTED...
TRULY, THAT WHICH DOESN'T KILL ME... MAKES ME STRONGER!
...AS YOU WILL DISCOVER... WHEN YOU MAKE YOUR OWN PITIABLE ATTEMPT...
...TO STOP ME!
GAKK
FREEZE, MONSTER!
BLAM
LIEUTENANT! I'VE FOUND THE KILLER! IN HERE!

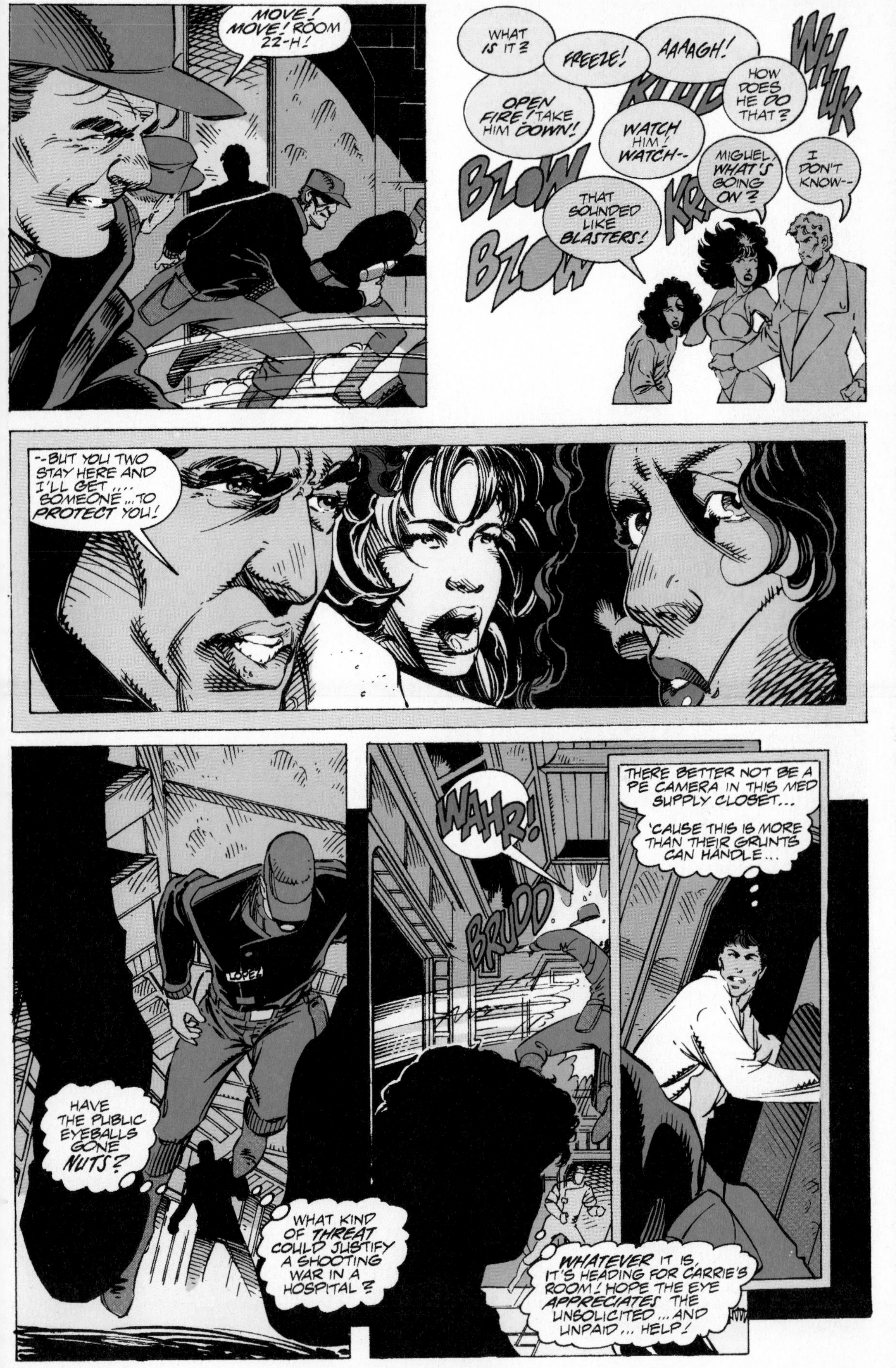

MOVE! MOVE! ROOM 22-H!
WHAT IS IT?
FREEZE!
AAAAGH!
WHUK
HOW DOES HE DO THAT?
OPEN FIRE! TAKE HIM DOWN!
WATCH HIM! WATCH--
BZOW
BZOW
THAT SOUNDED LIKE BLASTERS!
MIGUEL, WHAT'S GOING ON?
I DON'T KNOW--
--BUT YOU TWO STAY HERE AND I'LL GET.... SOMEONE...TO PROTECT YOU!
HAVE THE PUBLIC EYEBALLS GONE NUTS?
LOPEZ
WHAT KIND OF THREAT COULD JUSTIFY A SHOOTING WAR IN A HOSPITAL?
WAHR!
BRUDD
THERE BETTER NOT BE A PE CAMERA IN THIS MED SUPPLY CLOSET...
'CAUSE THIS IS MORE THAN THEIR GRUNTS CAN HANDLE...
WHATEVER IT IS, IT'S HEADING FOR CARRIE'S ROOM! HOPE THE EYE APPRECIATES THE UNSOLICITED... AND UNPAID... HELP!

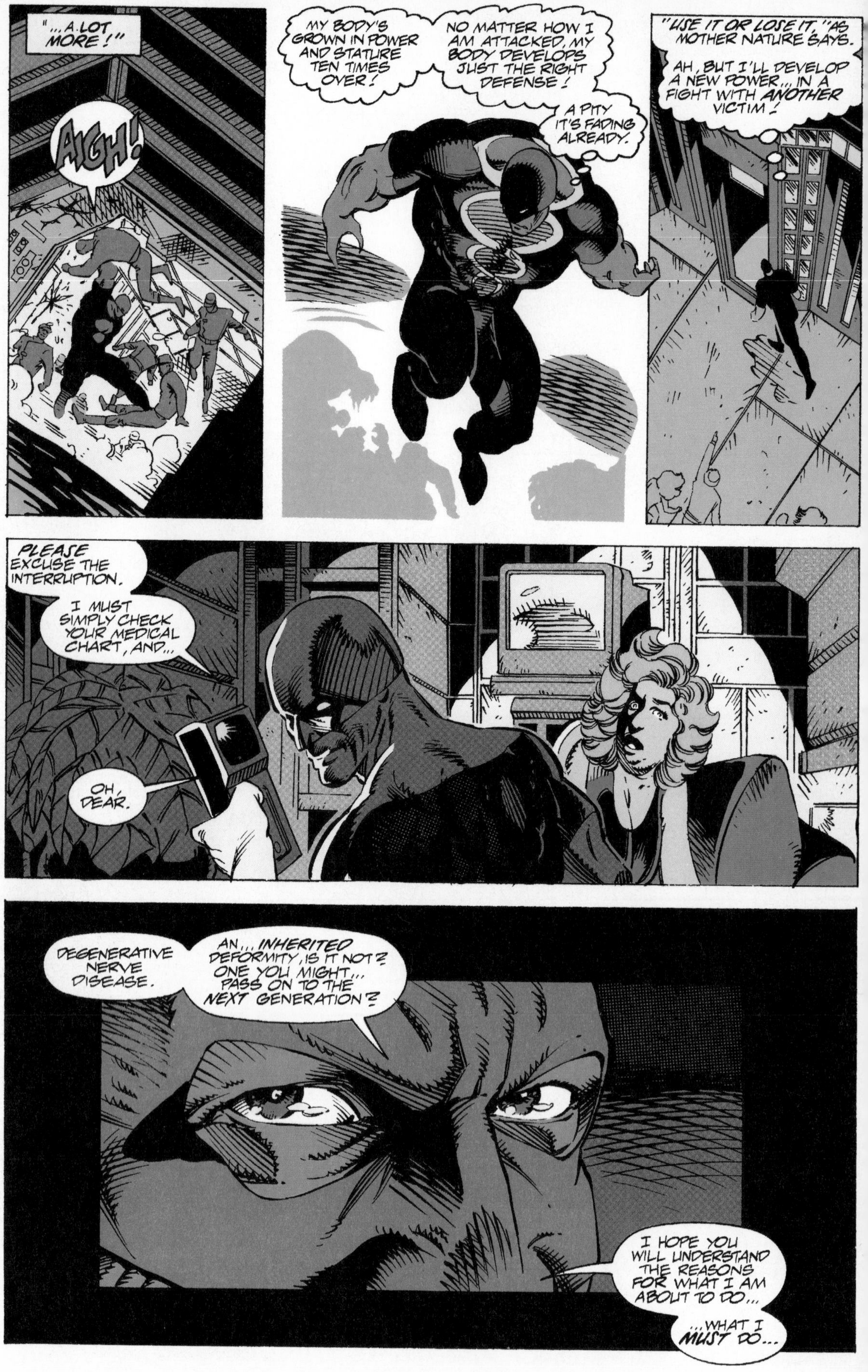
"...A LOT MORE!"
AIGH!
MY BODY'S GROWN IN POWER AND STATURE TEN TIMES OVER!
NO MATTER HOW I AM ATTACKED, MY BODY DEVELOPS JUST THE RIGHT DEFENSE!
A PITY IT'S FADING ALREADY.
"USE IT OR LOSE IT," AS MOTHER NATURE SAYS.
AH, BUT I'LL DEVELOP A NEW POWER... IN A FIGHT WITH ANOTHER VICTIM!
PLEASE EXCUSE THE INTERRUPTION.
I MUST SIMPLY CHECK YOUR MEDICAL CHART, AND...
OH, DEAR.
DEGENERATIVE NERVE DISEASE.
AN... INHERITED DEFORMITY, IS IT NOT? ONE YOU MIGHT... PASS ON TO THE NEXT GENERATION?
I HOPE YOU WILL UNDERSTAND THE REASONS FOR WHAT I AM ABOUT TO DO...
...WHAT I MUST DO...

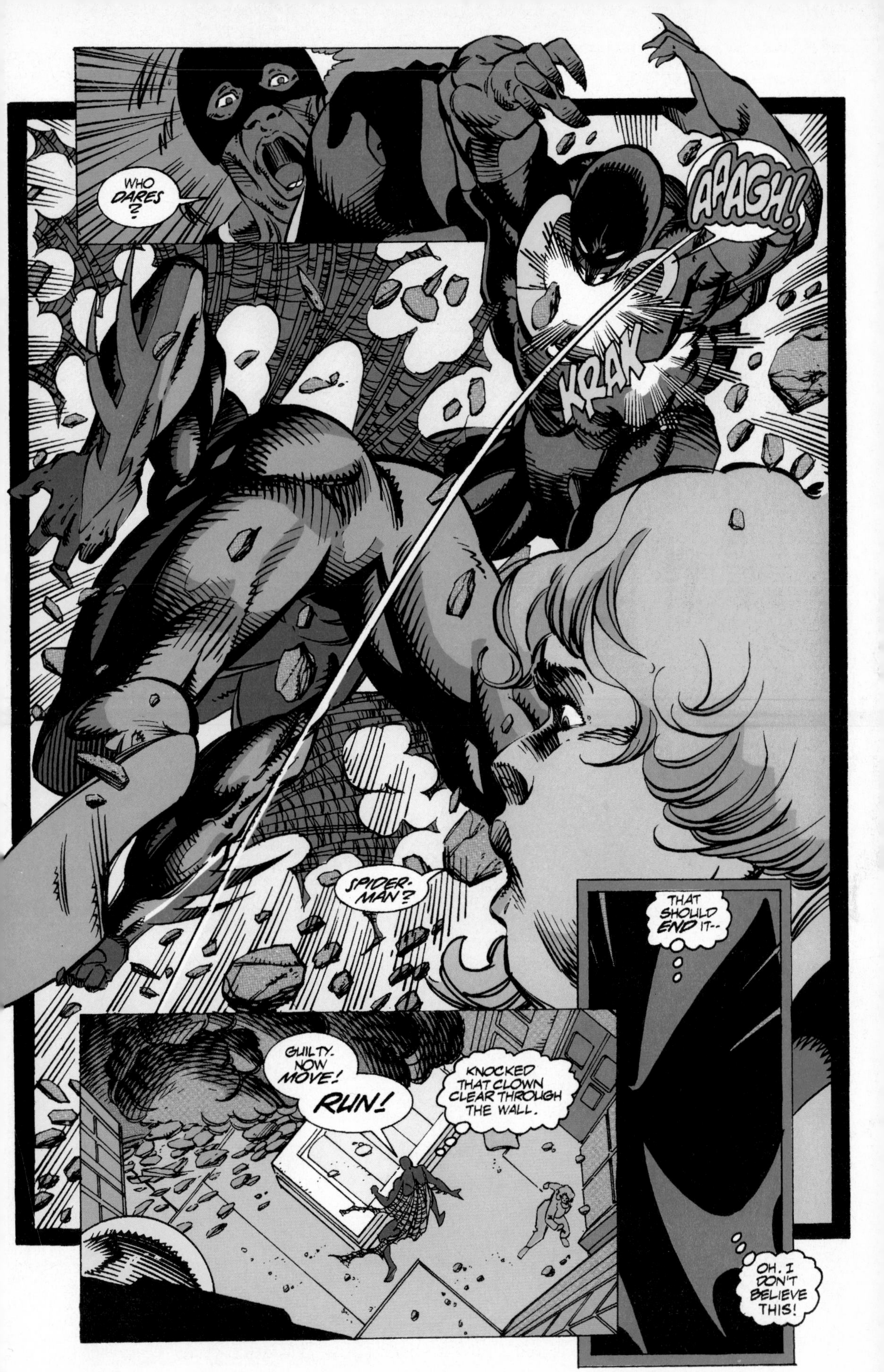
WHO DARES?
AAAGH!
KRAK
SPIDER-MAN?
THAT SHOULD END IT--
GUILTY. NOW MOVE! RUN!
KNOCKED THAT CLOWN CLEAR THROUGH THE WALL.
OH. I DON'T BELIEVE THIS!

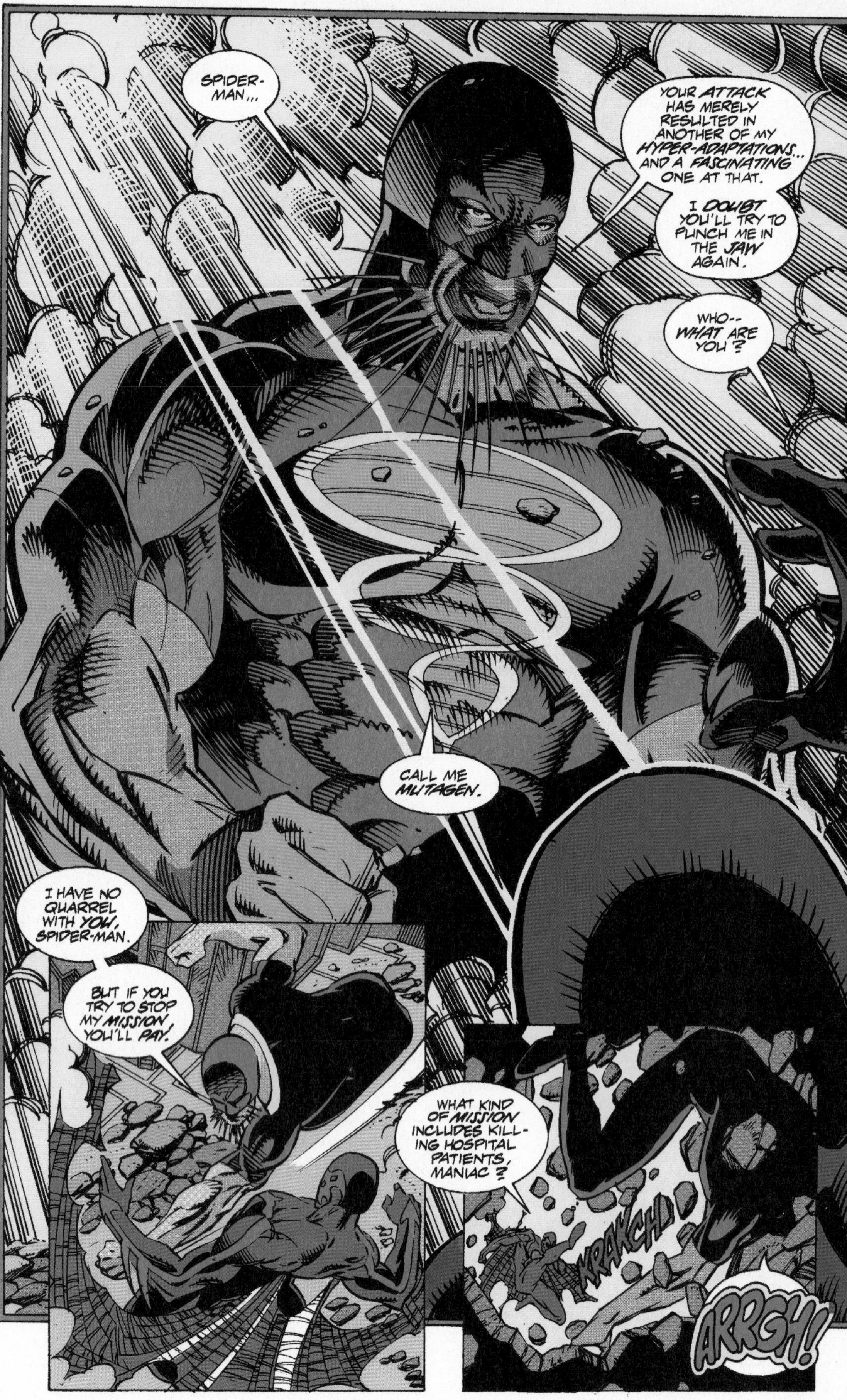
SPIDER-MAN...
YOUR ATTACK HAS MERELY RESULTED IN ANOTHER OF MY HYPER-ADAPTATIONS... AND A FASCINATING ONE AT THAT.
I DOUBT YOU'LL TRY TO PUNCH ME IN THE JAW AGAIN.
WHO-- WHAT ARE YOU?
CALL ME MUTAGEN.
I HAVE NO QUARREL WITH YOU, SPIDER-MAN.
BUT IF YOU TRY TO STOP MY MISSION, YOU'LL PAY.
WHAT KIND OF MISSION INCLUDES KILLING HOSPITAL PATIENTS, MANIAC?
KRAKCH!
ARRGH!

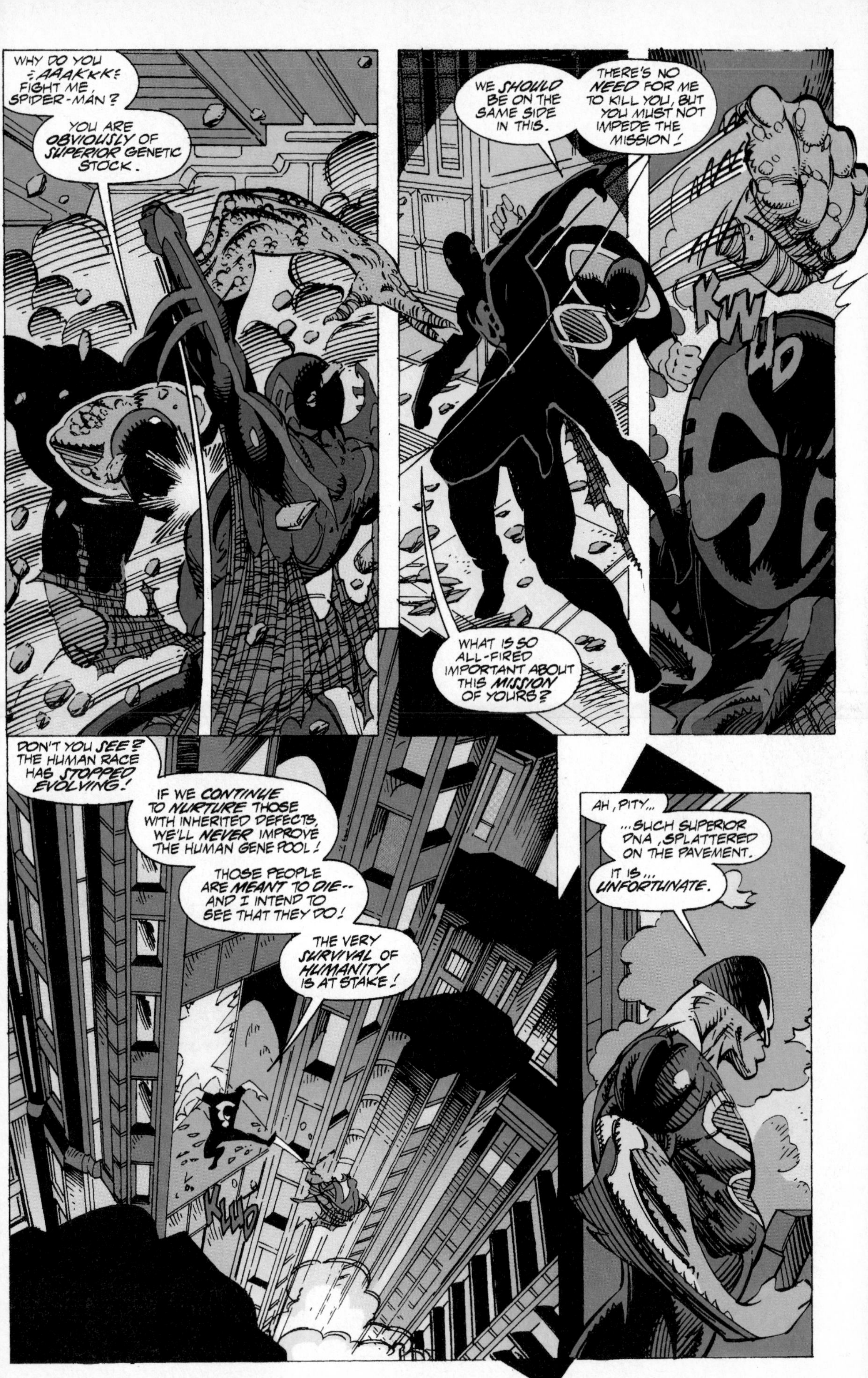
WHY DO YOU =AAAKKK= FIGHT ME, SPIDER-MAN?
YOU ARE OBVIOUSLY OF SUPERIOR GENETIC STOCK.
WE SHOULD BE ON THE SAME SIDE IN THIS.
THERE'S NO NEED FOR ME TO KILL YOU, BUT YOU MUST NOT IMPEDE THE MISSION!
KWUD
WHAT IS SO ALL-FIRED IMPORTANT ABOUT THIS MISSION OF YOURS?
DON'T YOU SEE? THE HUMAN RACE HAS STOPPED EVOLVING!
IF WE CONTINUE TO NURTURE THOSE WITH INHERITED DEFECTS, WE'LL NEVER IMPROVE THE HUMAN GENE POOL!
THOSE PEOPLE ARE MEANT TO DIE-- AND I INTEND TO SEE THAT THEY DO!
THE VERY SURVIVAL OF HUMANITY IS AT STAKE!
KLUD
AH, PITY...
...SUCH SUPERIOR DNA, SPLATTERED ON THE PAVEMENT.
IT IS... UNFORTUNATE.

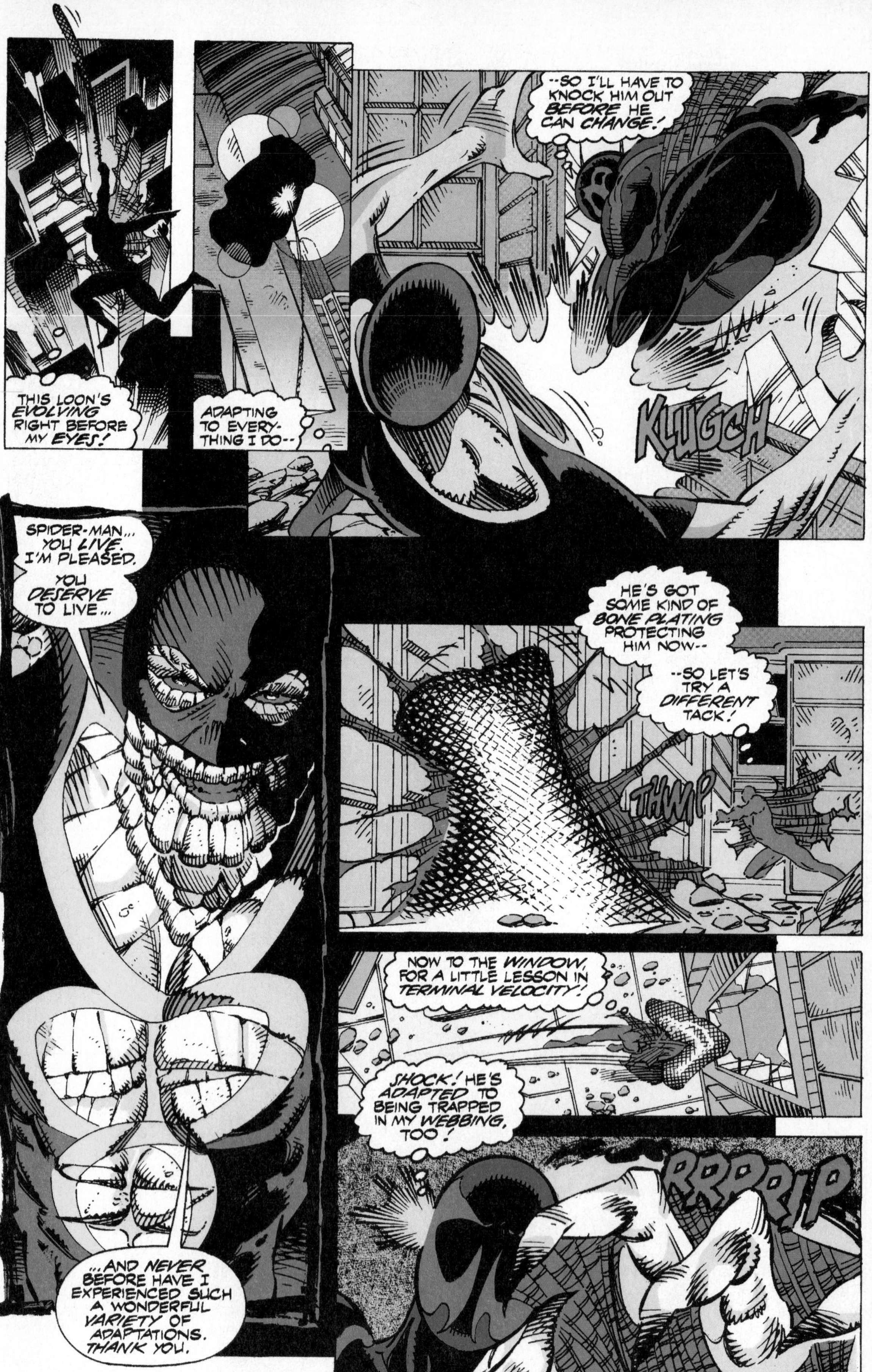
THIS LOON'S EVOLVING RIGHT BEFORE MY EYES!
ADAPTING TO EVERY-THING I DO--
--SO I'LL HAVE TO KNOCK HIM OUT BEFORE HE CAN CHANGE!
KLUGCH
SPIDER-MAN... YOU LIVE. I'M PLEASED.
YOU DESERVE TO LIVE...
...AND NEVER BEFORE HAVE I EXPERIENCED SUCH A WONDERFUL VARIETY OF ADAPTATIONS. THANK YOU.
HE'S GOT SOME KIND OF BONE PLATING PROTECTING HIM NOW--
--SO LET'S TRY A DIFFERENT TACK!
THWIP
NOW TO THE WINDOW, FOR A LITTLE LESSON IN TERMINAL VELOCITY!
SHOCK! HE'S ADAPTED TO BEING TRAPPED IN MY WEBBING, TOO!
RRRRIP

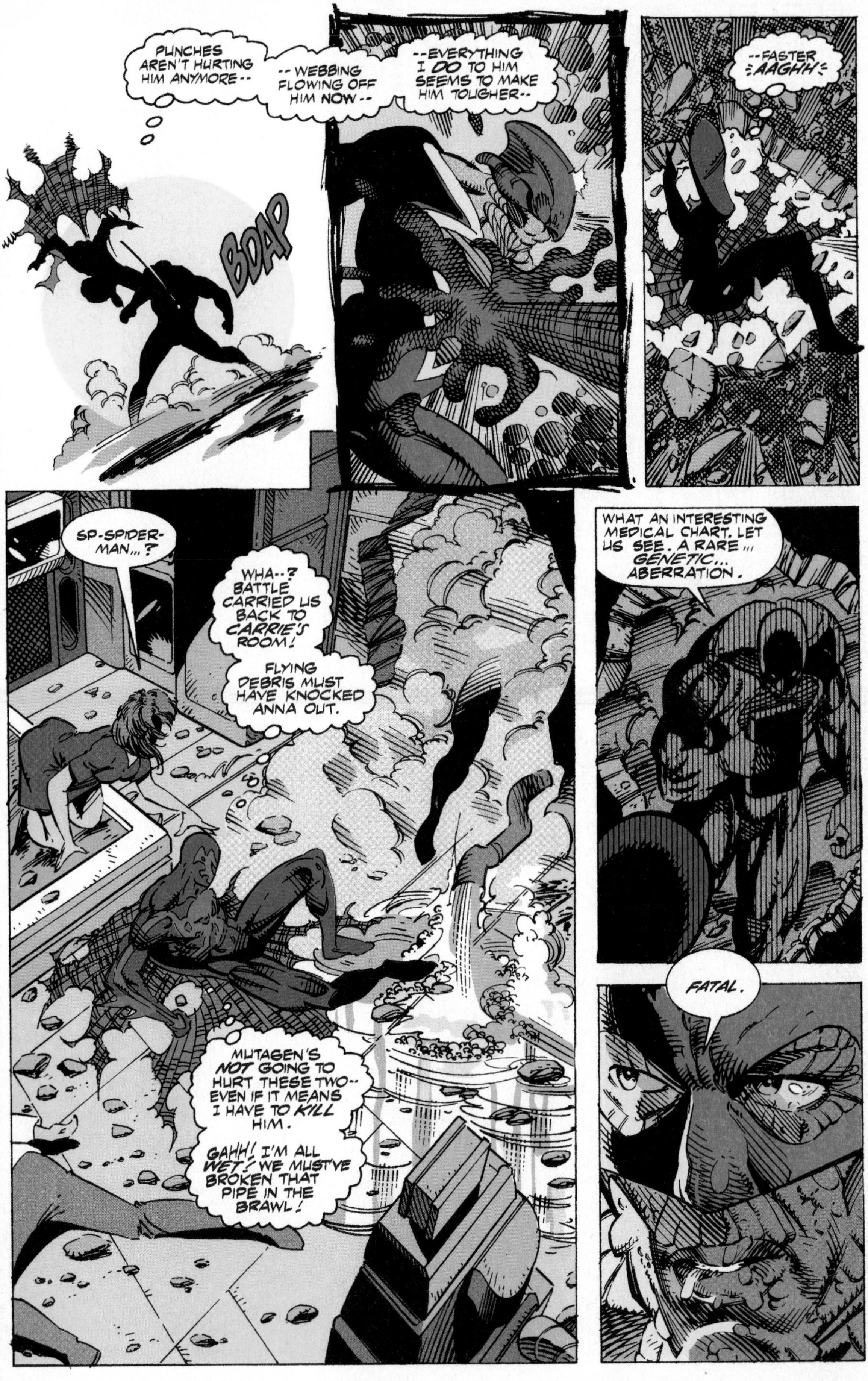
PUNCHES AREN'T HURTING HIM ANYMORE--
--WEBBING FLOWING OFF HIM NOW--
--EVERYTHING I DO TO HIM SEEMS TO MAKE HIM TOUGHER--
BDAP
--FASTER
AAGHH
SP-SPIDER-MAN...?
WHA--? BATTLE CARRIED US BACK TO CARRIE'S ROOM!
FLYING DEBRIS MUST HAVE KNOCKED ANNA OUT.
MUTAGEN'S NOT GOING TO HURT THESE TWO-- EVEN IF IT MEANS I HAVE TO KILL HIM.
GAHH! I'M ALL WET! WE MUST'VE BROKEN THAT PIPE IN THE BRAWL!
WHAT AN INTERESTING MEDICAL CHART. LET US SEE. A RARE... GENETIC... ABERRATION.
FATAL.

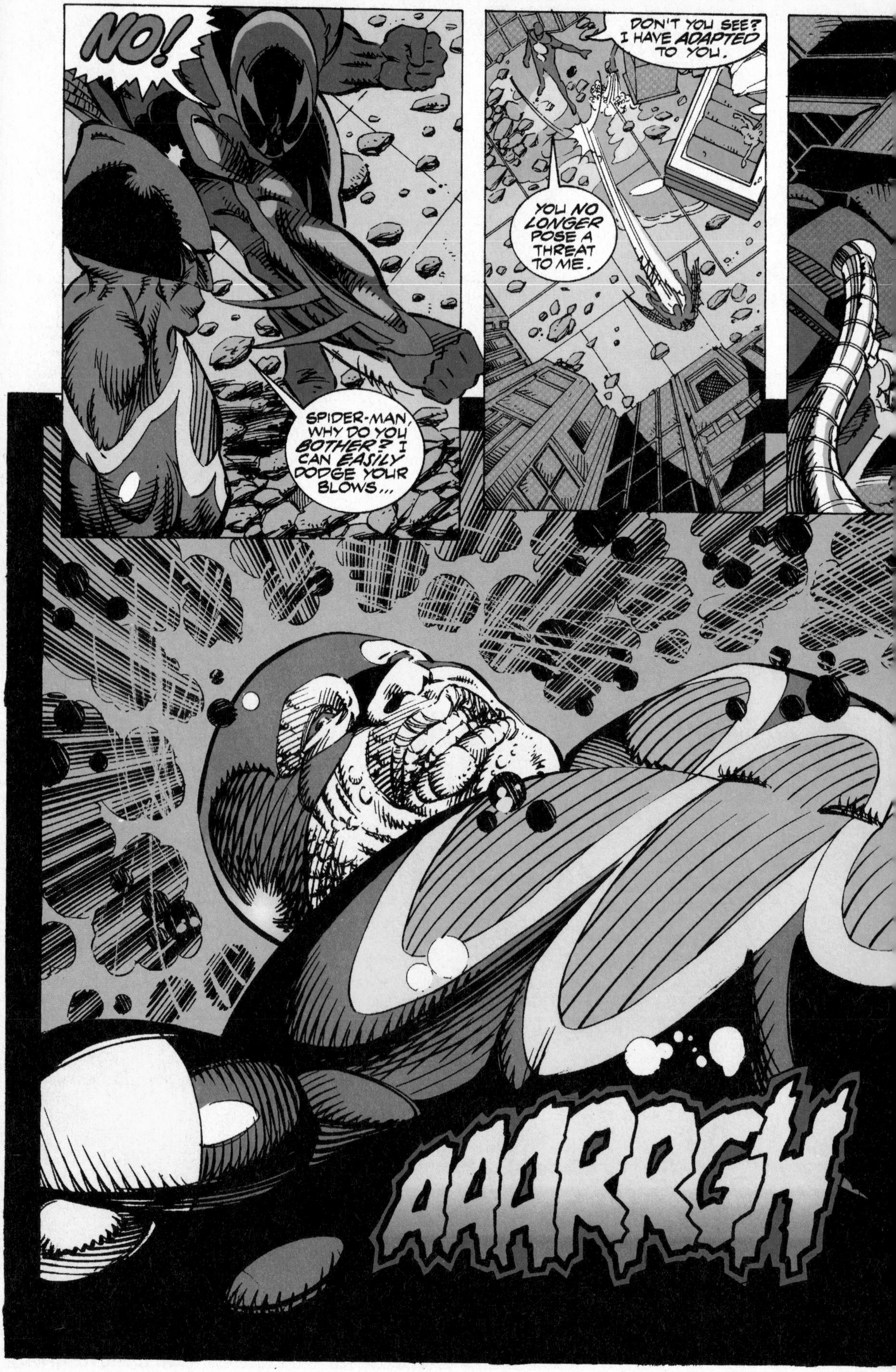
NO!
SPIDER-MAN, WHY DO YOU BOTHER? I CAN EASILY DODGE YOUR BLOWS...
DON'T YOU SEE? I HAVE ADAPTED TO YOU.
YOU NO LONGER POSE A THREAT TO ME.
AAARRGH

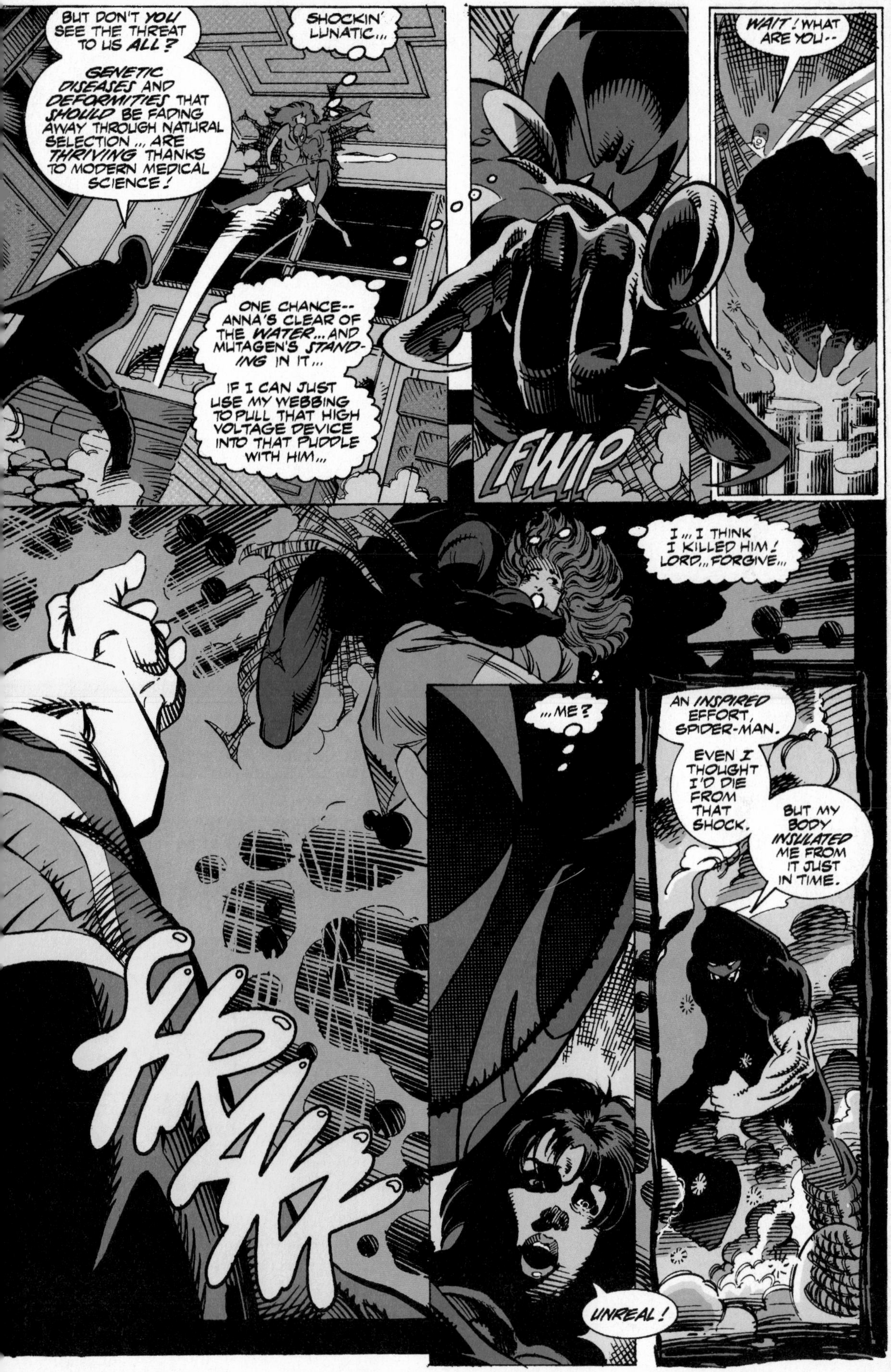
BUT DON'T YOU SEE THE THREAT TO US ALL?
GENETIC DISEASES AND DEFORMITIES THAT SHOULD BE FADING AWAY THROUGH NATURAL SELECTION... ARE THRIVING THANKS TO MODERN MEDICAL SCIENCE!
SHOCKIN' LUNATIC...
ONE CHANCE-- ANNA'S CLEAR OF THE WATER... AND MUTAGEN'S STANDING IN IT...
IF I CAN JUST USE MY WEBBING TO PULL THAT HIGH VOLTAGE DEVICE INTO THAT PUDDLE WITH HIM...
FWIP
WAIT! WHAT ARE YOU--
I... I THINK I KILLED HIM! LORD... FORGIVE...
...ME?
AN INSPIRED EFFORT, SPIDER-MAN.
EVEN I THOUGHT I'D DIE FROM THAT SHOCK.
BUT MY BODY INSULATED ME FROM IT JUST IN TIME.
UNREAL!

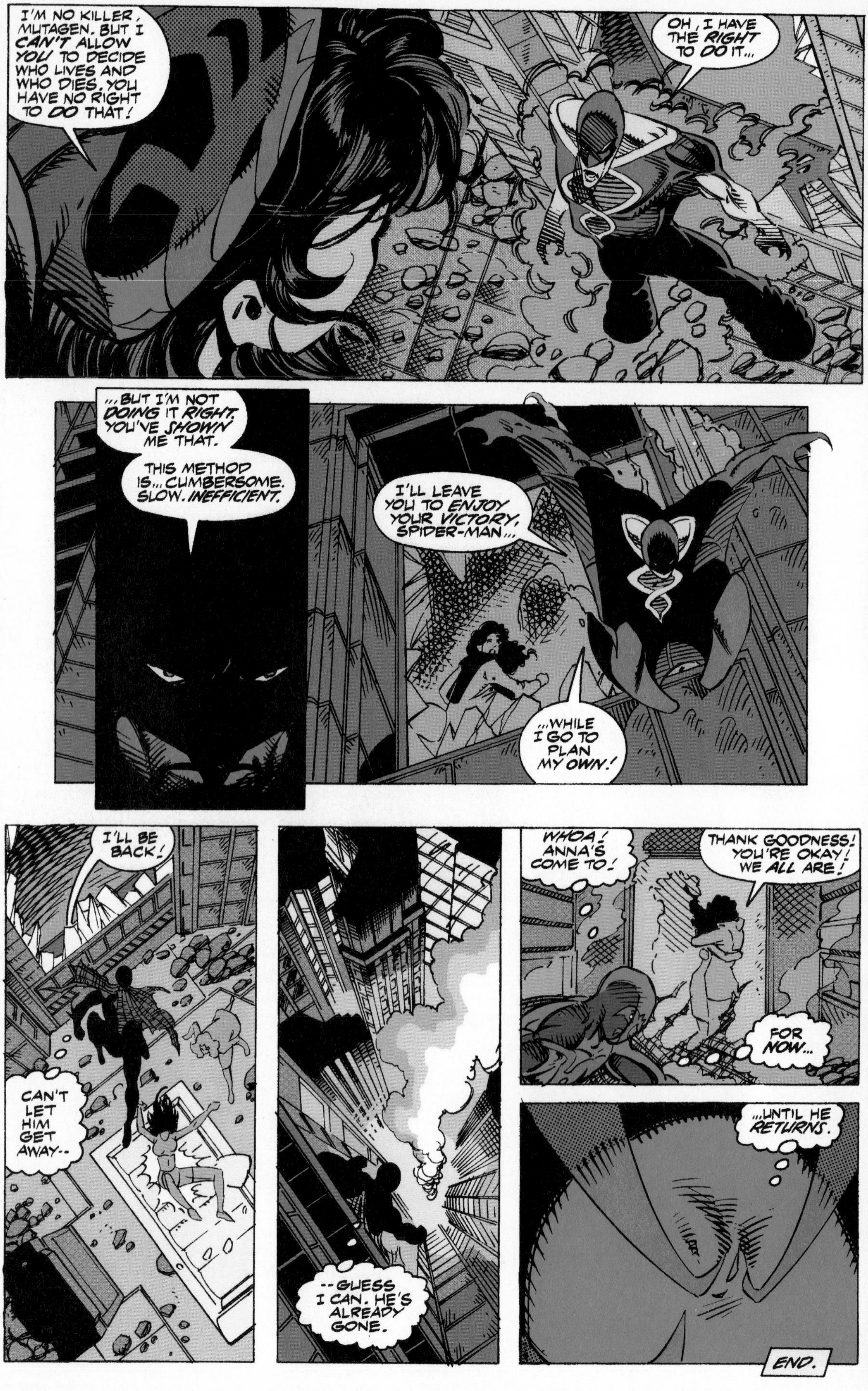
I'M NO KILLER, MUTAGEN. BUT I CAN'T ALLOW YOU TO DECIDE WHO LIVES AND WHO DIES. YOU HAVE NO RIGHT TO DO THAT!
OH, I HAVE THE RIGHT TO DO IT...
...BUT I'M NOT DOING IT RIGHT. YOU'VE SHOWN ME THAT.
THIS METHOD IS... CUMBERSOME. SLOW. INEFFICIENT.
I'LL LEAVE YOU TO ENJOY YOUR VICTORY, SPIDER-MAN...
...WHILE I GO TO PLAN MY OWN!
I'LL BE BACK!
CAN'T LET HIM GET AWAY--
--GUESS I CAN. HE'S ALREADY GONE.
WHOA! ANNA'S COME TO!
THANK GOODNESS! YOU'RE OKAY! WE ALL ARE!
FOR NOW...
...UNTIL HE RETURNS.
END.

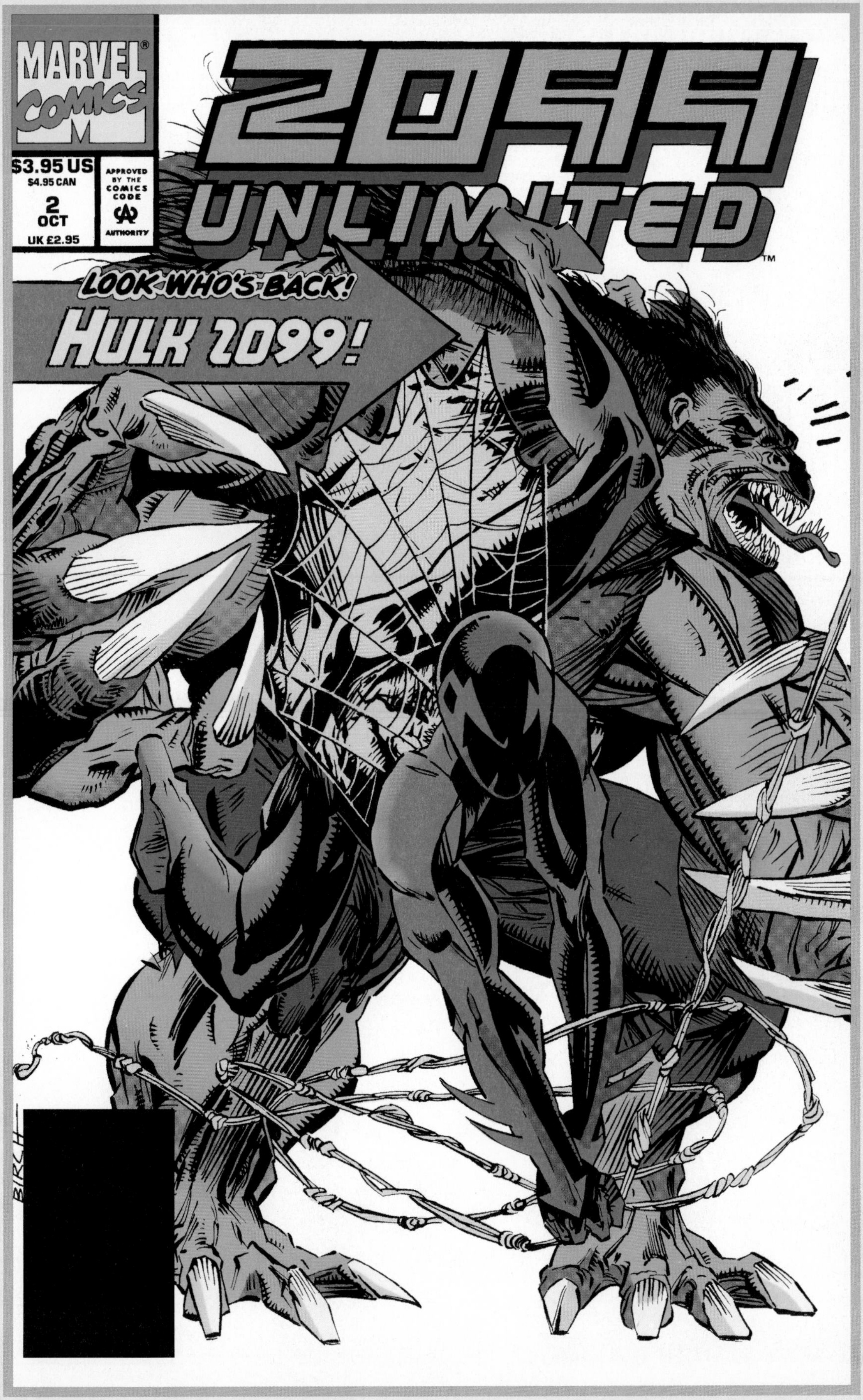
MARVEL COMICS
2099 UNLIMITED™
$3.95 US
$4.95 CAN
2
OCT
UK £2.95
APPROVED BY THE COMICS CODE AUTHORITY
LOOK WHO'S BACK!
HULK 2099!™
BIRCH

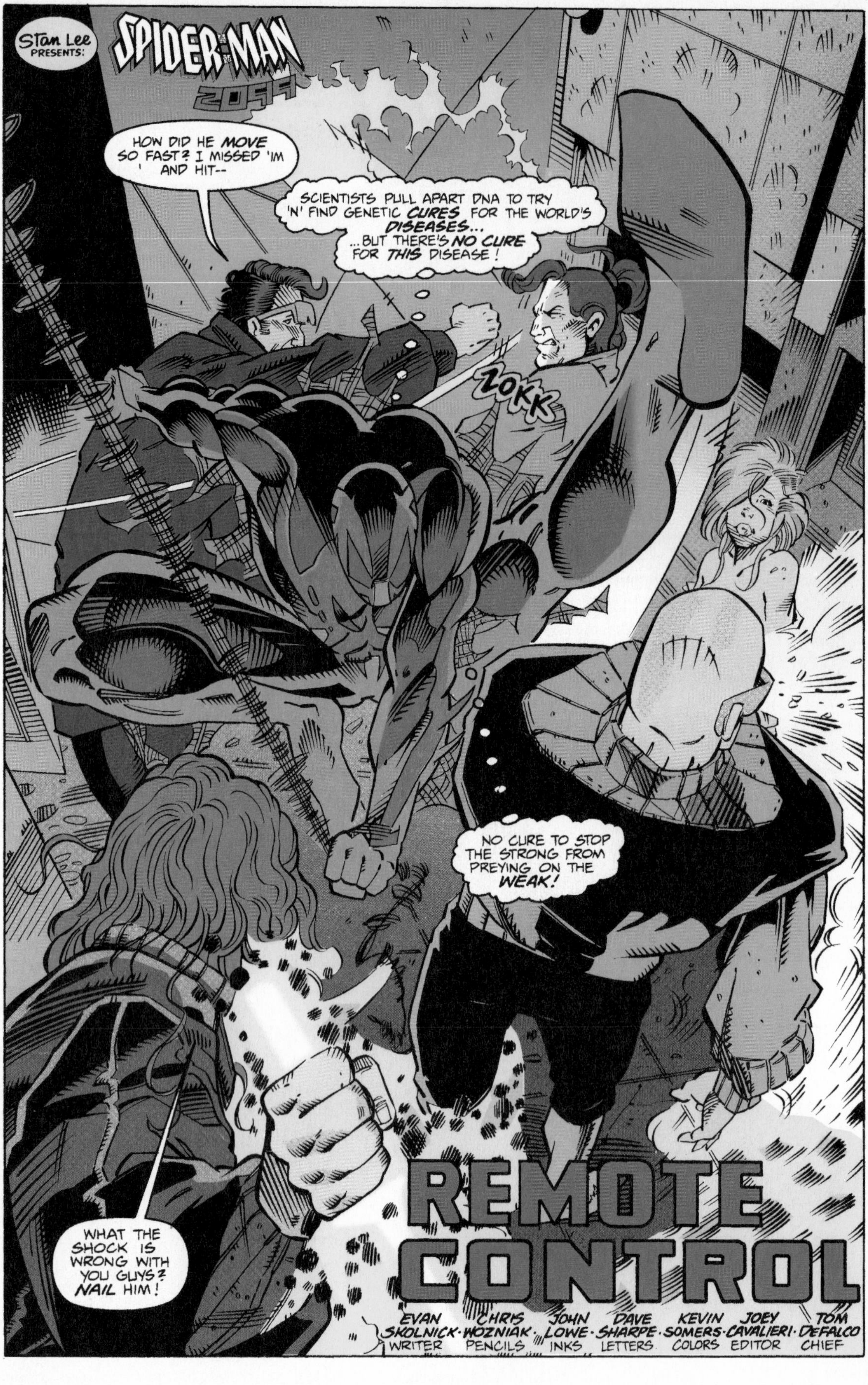
Stan Lee PRESENTS:
SPIDER-MAN 2099
HOW DID HE MOVE SO FAST? I MISSED 'IM AND HIT--
SCIENTISTS PULL APART DNA TO TRY 'N' FIND GENETIC CURES FOR THE WORLD'S DISEASES...
...BUT THERE'S NO CURE FOR THIS DISEASE!
ZOKK
NO CURE TO STOP THE STRONG FROM PREYING ON THE WEAK!
WHAT THE SHOCK IS WRONG WITH YOU GUYS? NAIL HIM!
REMOTE CONTROL
EVAN SKOLNICK · WRITER
CHRIS WOZNIAK · PENCILS
JOHN LOWE · INKS
DAVE SHARPE · LETTERS
KEVIN SOMERS · COLORS
JOEY CAVALIERI · EDITOR
TOM DEFALCO CHIEF

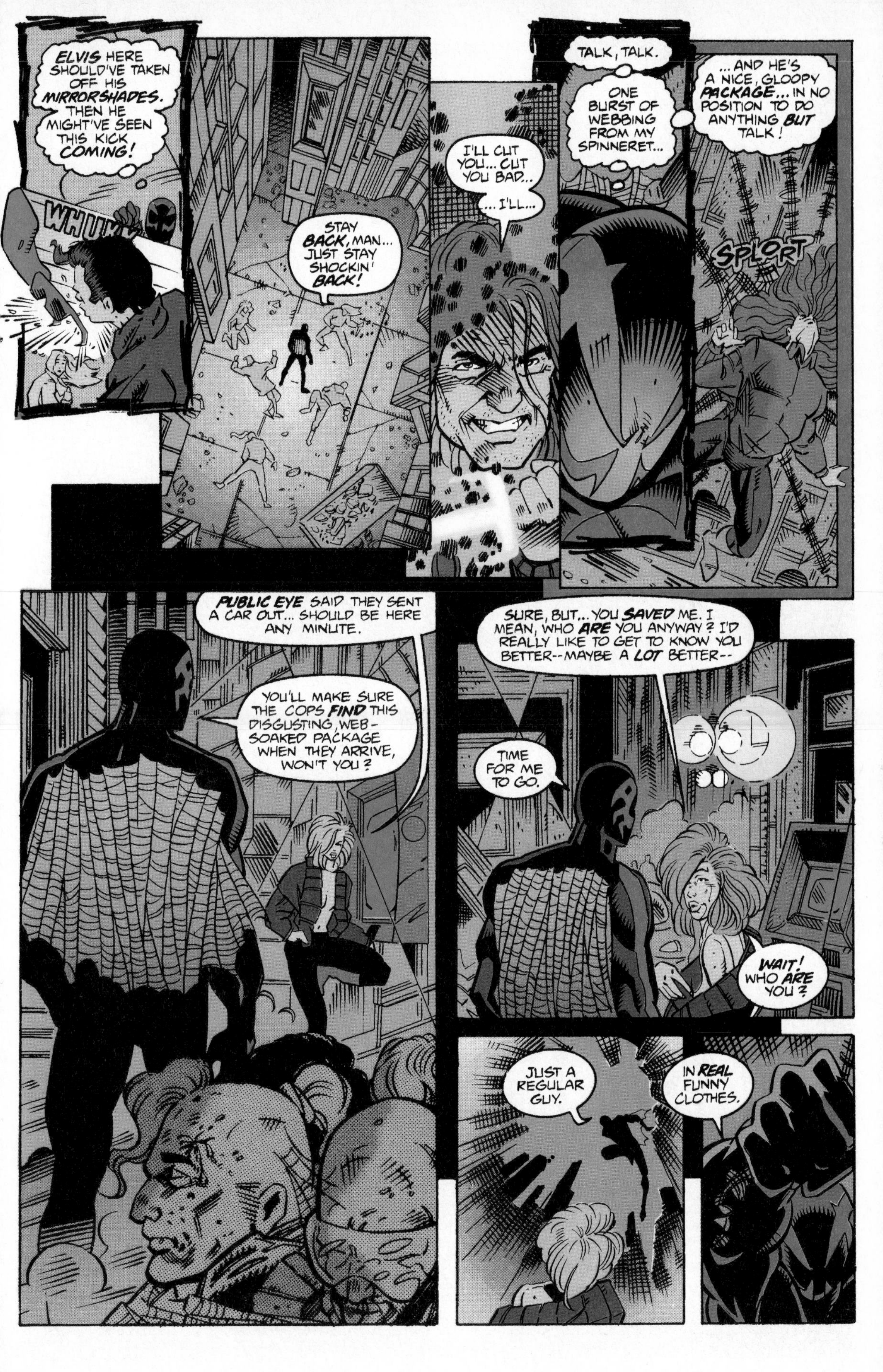
ELVIS HERE SHOULD'VE TAKEN OFF HIS MIRRORSHADES. THEN HE MIGHT'VE SEEN THIS KICK COMING!
WHUMP
STAY BACK, MAN... JUST STAY SHOCKIN' BACK!
I'LL CUT YOU... CUT YOU BAD...
... I'LL...
TALK, TALK.
ONE BURST OF WEBBING FROM MY SPINNERET...
... AND HE'S A NICE, GLOOPY PACKAGE... IN NO POSITION TO DO ANYTHING BUT TALK!
SPLORT
PUBLIC EYE SAID THEY SENT A CAR OUT... SHOULD BE HERE ANY MINUTE.
YOU'LL MAKE SURE THE COPS FIND THIS DISGUSTING, WEB-SOAKED PACKAGE WHEN THEY ARRIVE, WON'T YOU?
SURE, BUT... YOU SAVED ME. I MEAN, WHO ARE YOU ANYWAY? I'D REALLY LIKE TO GET TO KNOW YOU BETTER--MAYBE A LOT BETTER--
TIME FOR ME TO GO.
WAIT! WHO ARE YOU?
JUST A REGULAR GUY.
IN REAL FUNNY CLOTHES.

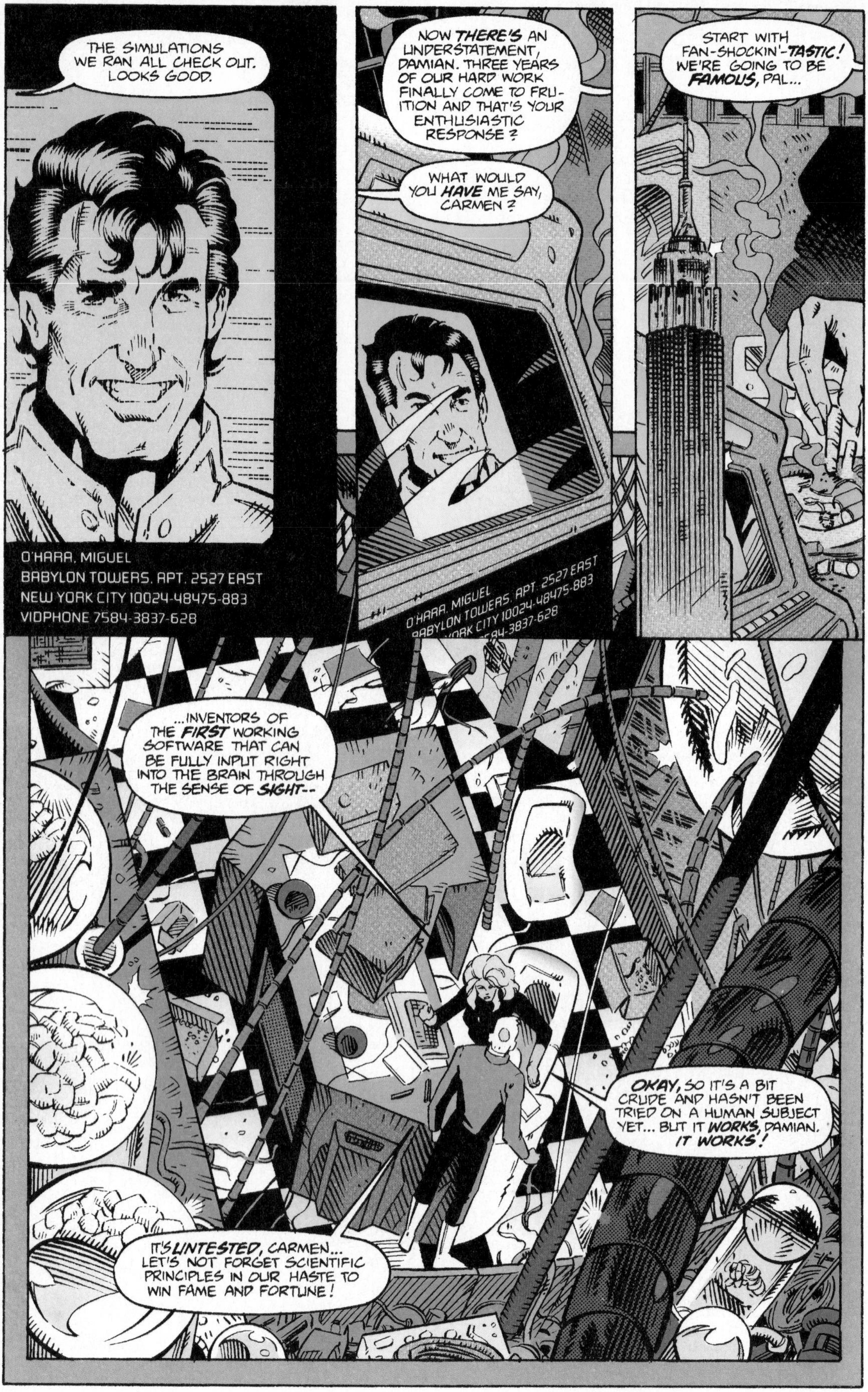

THE SIMULATIONS WE RAN ALL CHECK OUT. LOOKS GOOD.
O'HARA, MIGUEL
BABYLON TOWERS, APT. 2527 EAST
NEW YORK CITY 10024-48475-883
VIDPHONE 7584-3837-628
NOW THERE'S AN UNDERSTATEMENT, DAMIAN. THREE YEARS OF OUR HARD WORK FINALLY COME TO FRUITION AND THAT'S YOUR ENTHUSIASTIC RESPONSE?
WHAT WOULD YOU HAVE ME SAY, CARMEN?
O'HARA, MIGUEL
BABYLON TOWERS, APT. 2527 EAST
START WITH FAN-SHOCKIN'-TASTIC! WE'RE GOING TO BE FAMOUS, PAL...
...INVENTORS OF THE FIRST WORKING SOFTWARE THAT CAN BE FULLY INPUT RIGHT INTO THE BRAIN THROUGH THE SENSE OF SIGHT--
OKAY, SO IT'S A BIT CRUDE AND HASN'T BEEN TRIED ON A HUMAN SUBJECT YET... BUT IT WORKS, DAMIAN. IT WORKS!
IT'S UNTESTED, CARMEN... LET'S NOT FORGET SCIENTIFIC PRINCIPLES IN OUR HASTE TO WIN FAME AND FORTUNE!

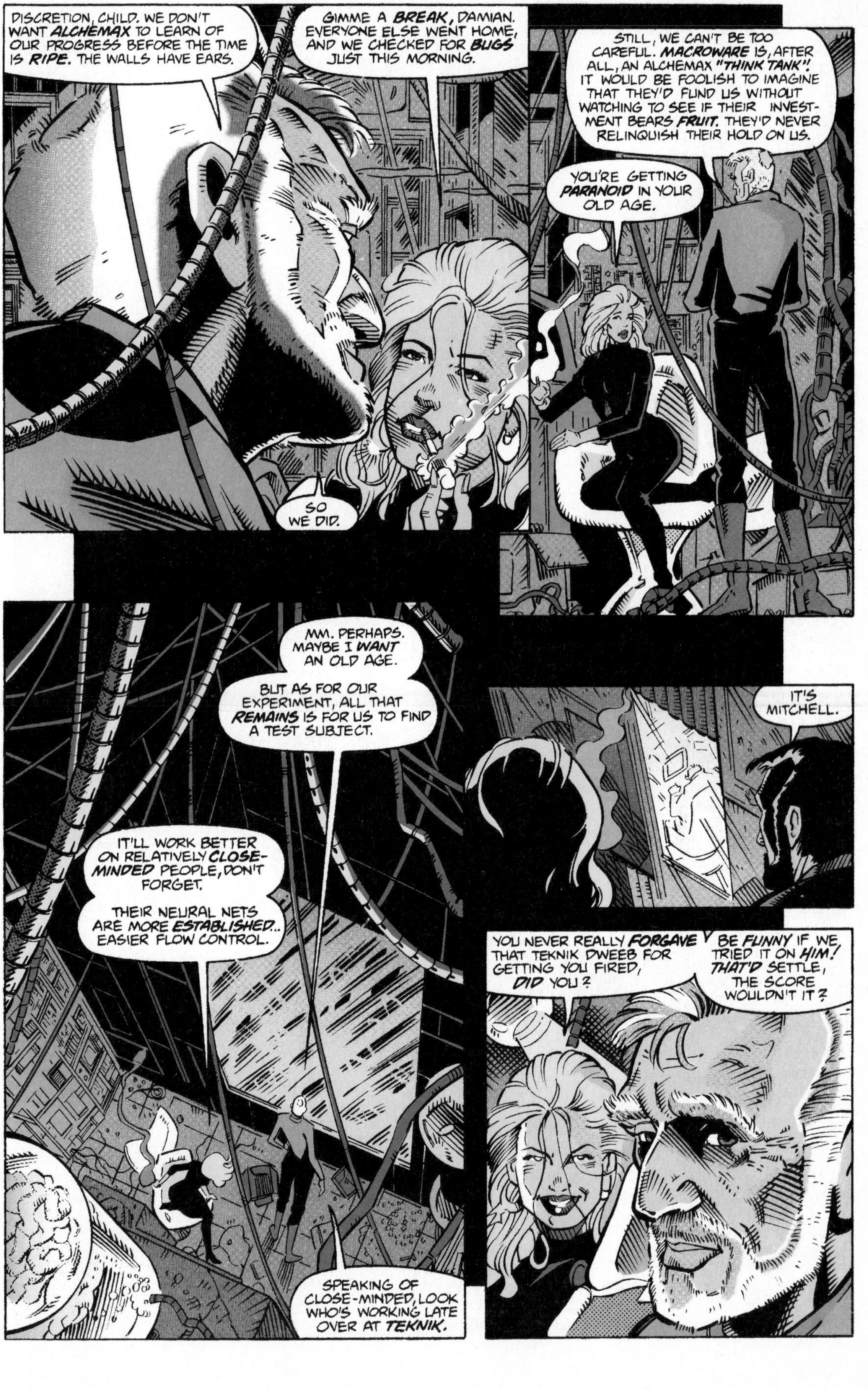
DISCRETION, CHILD. WE DON'T WANT ALCHEMAX TO LEARN OF OUR PROGRESS BEFORE THE TIME IS RIPE. THE WALLS HAVE EARS.
GIMME A BREAK, DAMIAN. EVERYONE ELSE WENT HOME, AND WE CHECKED FOR BUGS JUST THIS MORNING.
SO WE DID.
STILL, WE CAN'T BE TOO CAREFUL. MACROWARE IS, AFTER ALL, AN ALCHEMAX "THINK TANK"! IT WOULD BE FOOLISH TO IMAGINE THAT THEY'D FUND US WITHOUT WATCHING TO SEE IF THEIR INVESTMENT BEARS FRUIT. THEY'D NEVER RELINQUISH THEIR HOLD ON US.
YOU'RE GETTING PARANOID IN YOUR OLD AGE.
MM. PERHAPS. MAYBE I WANT AN OLD AGE.
BUT AS FOR OUR EXPERIMENT, ALL THAT REMAINS IS FOR US TO FIND A TEST SUBJECT.
IT'LL WORK BETTER ON RELATIVELY CLOSE-MINDED PEOPLE, DON'T FORGET.
THEIR NEURAL NETS ARE MORE ESTABLISHED... EASIER FLOW CONTROL.
SPEAKING OF CLOSE-MINDED, LOOK WHO'S WORKING LATE OVER AT TEKNIK.
IT'S MITCHELL.
YOU NEVER REALLY FORGAVE THAT TEKNIK DWEEB FOR GETTING YOU FIRED, DID YOU?
BE FUNNY IF WE TRIED IT ON HIM! THAT'D SETTLE THE SCORE, WOULDN'T IT?

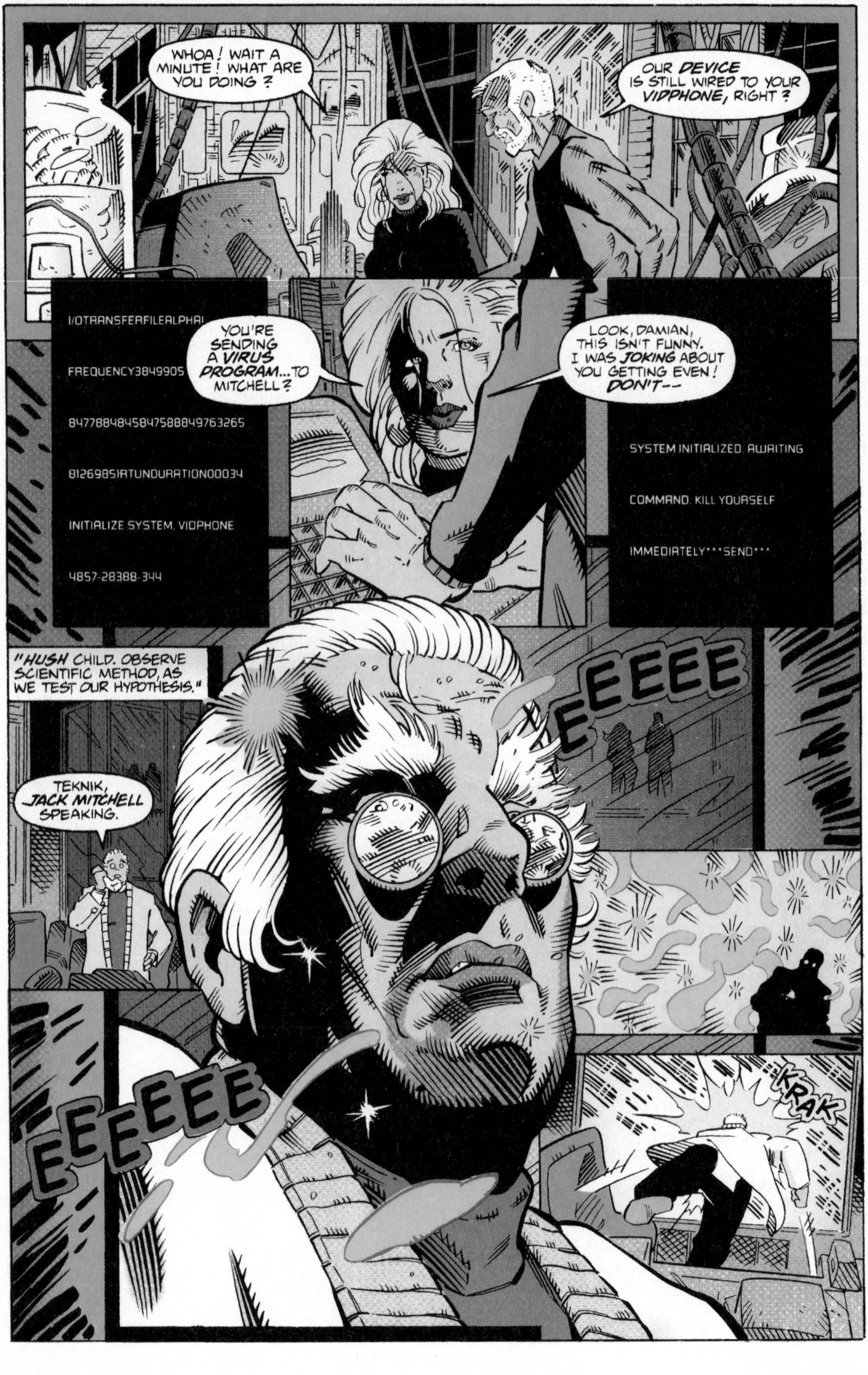
WHOA! WAIT A MINUTE! WHAT ARE YOU DOING?
OUR DEVICE IS STILL WIRED TO YOUR VIDPHONE, RIGHT?
I/OTRANSFERFILEALPHAI
FREQUENCY3849905
8477884845847588849763265
8126985IRTUNDURATION00034
INITIALIZE SYSTEM, VIDPHONE
4857-28388-344
YOU'RE SENDING A VIRUS PROGRAM...TO MITCHELL?
LOOK, DAMIAN, THIS ISN'T FUNNY. I WAS JOKING ABOUT YOU GETTING EVEN! DON'T--
SYSTEM INITIALIZED. AWAITING
COMMAND: KILL YOURSELF
IMMEDIATELY***SEND***
"HUSH CHILD. OBSERVE SCIENTIFIC METHOD, AS WE TEST OUR HYPOTHESIS."
EEEEE
TEKNIK, JACK MITCHELL SPEAKING.
EEEEEE
KRAK

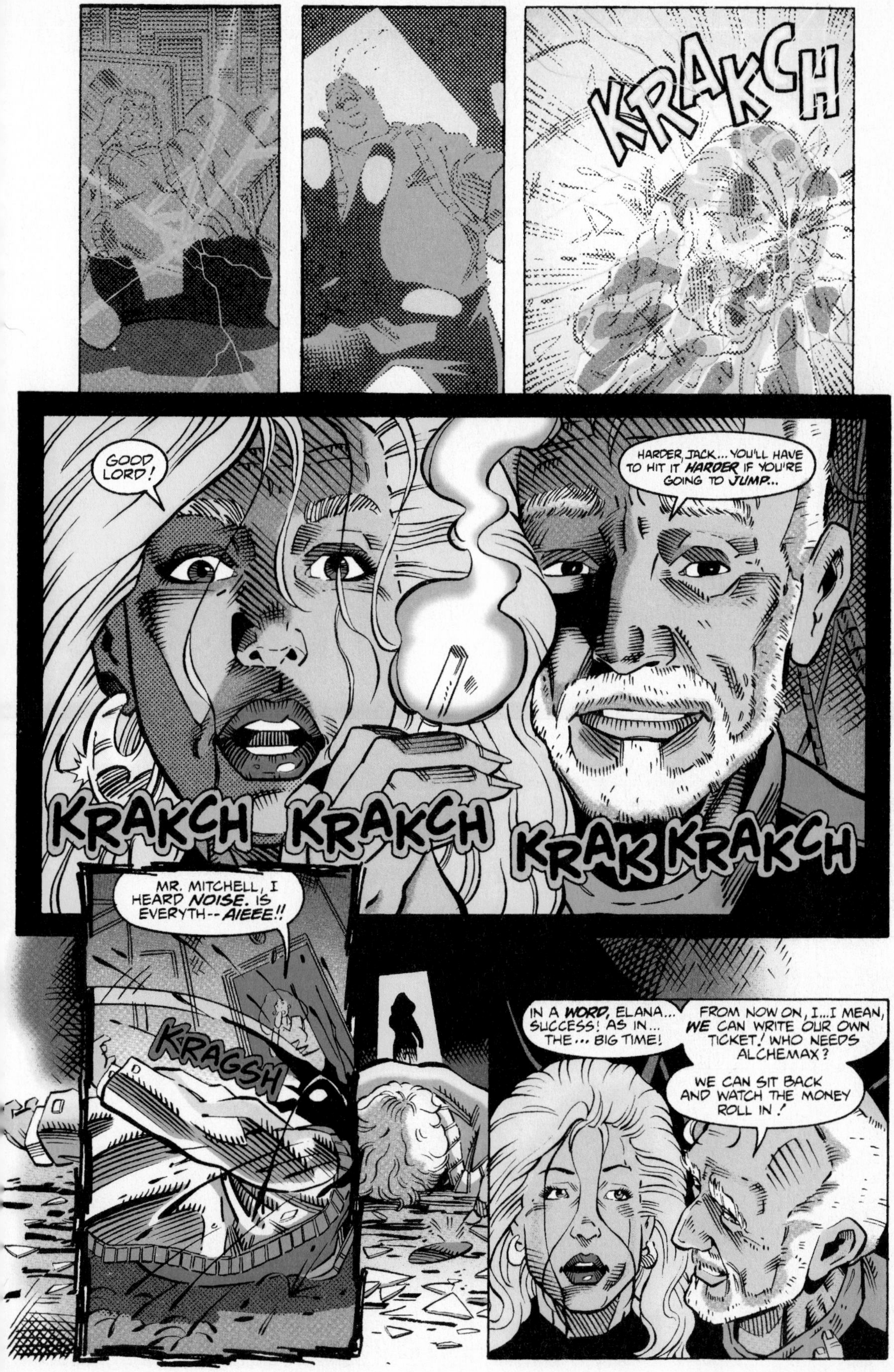
KRAKCH
GOOD LORD!
HARDER, JACK... YOU'LL HAVE TO HIT IT HARDER IF YOU'RE GOING TO JUMP...
KRAKCH KRAKCH KRAK KRAKCH
MR. MITCHELL, I HEARD NOISE. IS EVERYTH-- AIEEE!!
KRAGSH
IN A WORD, ELANA... SUCCESS! AS IN... THE... BIG TIME!
FROM NOW ON, I...I MEAN, WE CAN WRITE OUR OWN TICKET! WHO NEEDS ALCHEMAX?
WE CAN SIT BACK AND WATCH THE MONEY ROLL IN!

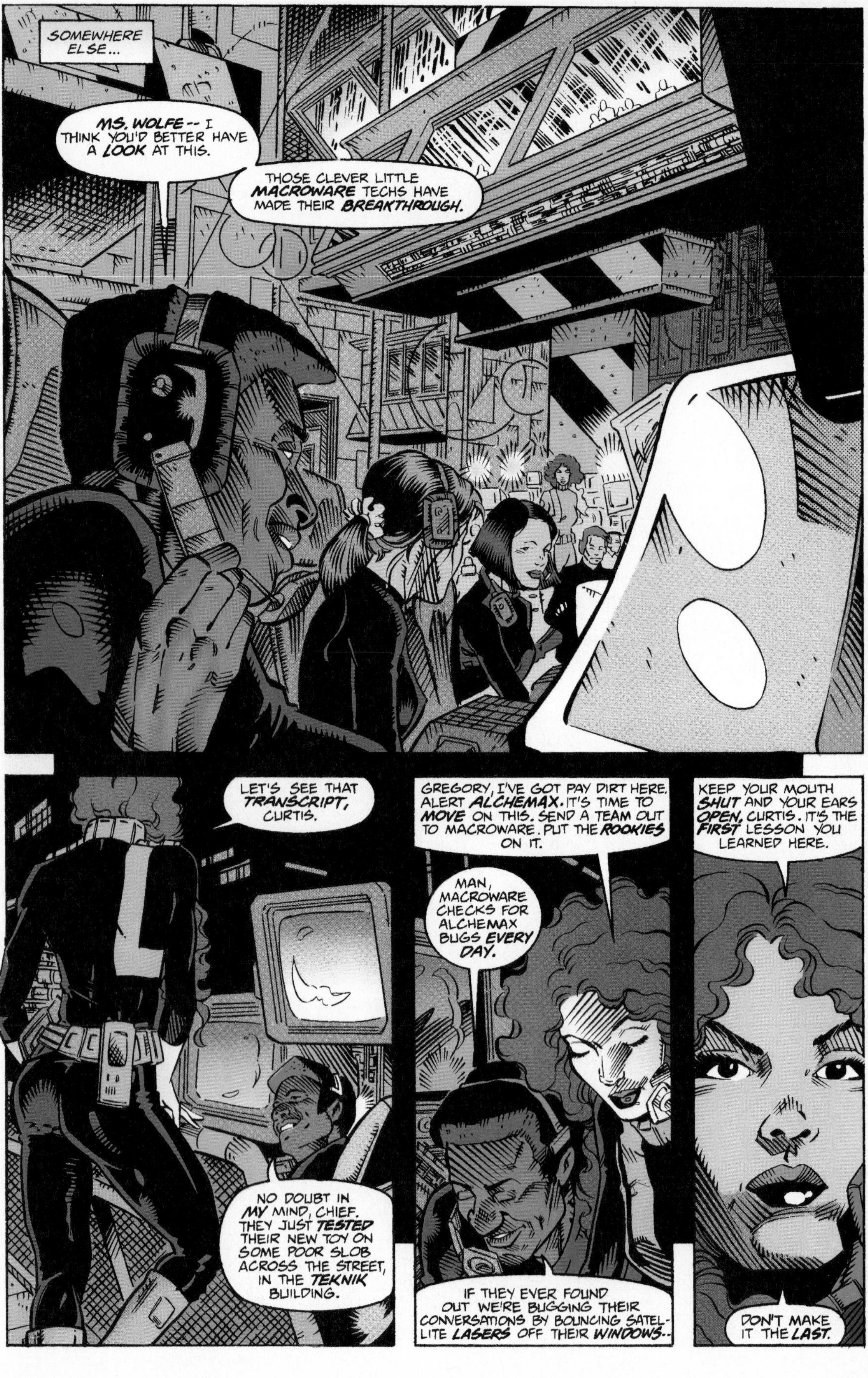
SOMEWHERE ELSE...
MS. WOLFE-- I THINK YOU'D BETTER HAVE A LOOK AT THIS.
THOSE CLEVER LITTLE MACROWARE TECHS HAVE MADE THEIR BREAKTHROUGH.
LET'S SEE THAT TRANSCRIPT, CURTIS.
NO DOUBT IN MY MIND, CHIEF. THEY JUST TESTED THEIR NEW TOY ON SOME POOR SLOB ACROSS THE STREET, IN THE TEKNIK BUILDING.
GREGORY, I'VE GOT PAY DIRT HERE. ALERT ALCHEMAX. IT'S TIME TO MOVE ON THIS. SEND A TEAM OUT TO MACROWARE. PUT THE ROOKIES ON IT.
MAN, MACROWARE CHECKS FOR ALCHEMAX BUGS EVERY DAY.
IF THEY EVER FOUND OUT WE'RE BUGGING THEIR CONVERSATIONS BY BOUNCING SATEL-LITE LASERS OFF THEIR WINDOWS--
KEEP YOUR MOUTH SHUT AND YOUR EARS OPEN, CURTIS. IT'S THE FIRST LESSON YOU LEARNED HERE.
DON'T MAKE IT THE LAST.

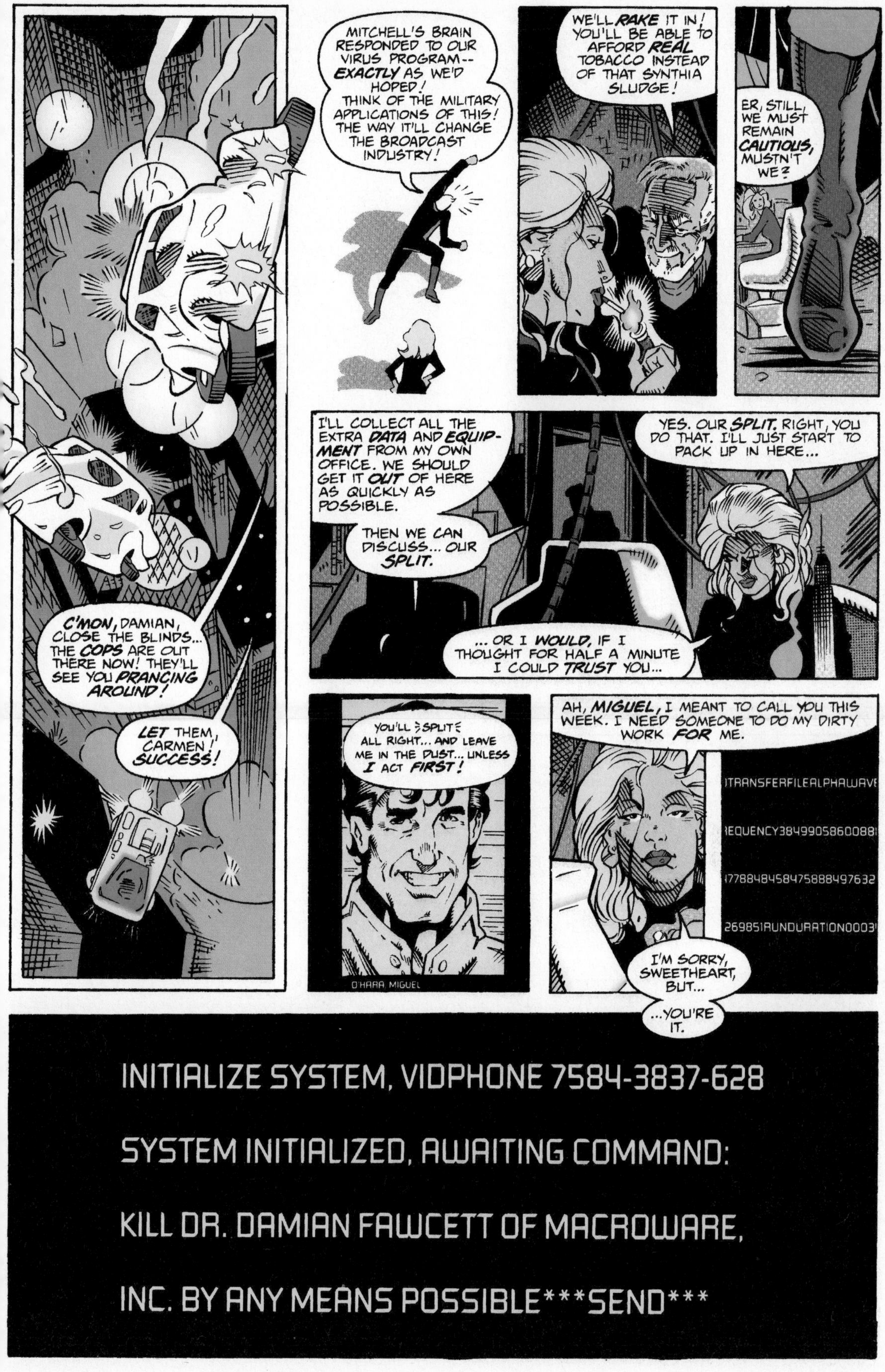
C'MON, DAMIAN, CLOSE THE BLINDS... THE COPS ARE OUT THERE NOW! THEY'LL SEE YOU PRANCING AROUND!
LET THEM, CARMEN! SUCCESS!
MITCHELL'S BRAIN RESPONDED TO OUR VIRUS PROGRAM-- EXACTLY AS WE'D HOPED! THINK OF THE MILITARY APPLICATIONS OF THIS! THE WAY IT'LL CHANGE THE BROADCAST INDUSTRY!
WE'LL RAKE IT IN! YOU'LL BE ABLE TO AFFORD REAL TOBACCO INSTEAD OF THAT SYNTHIA SLUDGE!
ER, STILL, WE MUST REMAIN CAUTIOUS, MUSTN'T WE?
I'LL COLLECT ALL THE EXTRA DATA AND EQUIPMENT FROM MY OWN OFFICE. WE SHOULD GET IT OUT OF HERE AS QUICKLY AS POSSIBLE.
THEN WE CAN DISCUSS... OUR SPLIT.
YES. OUR SPLIT. RIGHT, YOU DO THAT. I'LL JUST START TO PACK UP IN HERE...
...OR I WOULD, IF I THOUGHT FOR HALF A MINUTE I COULD TRUST YOU...
YOU'LL SPLIT ALL RIGHT... AND LEAVE ME IN THE DUST... UNLESS I ACT FIRST!
O'HARA, MIGUEL
AH, MIGUEL, I MEANT TO CALL YOU THIS WEEK. I NEED SOMEONE TO DO MY DIRTY WORK FOR ME.
TRANSFERFILEALPHAWAVE
EQUENCY38499058600888
778848458475888497632
269851AUNDURATION0003
I'M SORRY, SWEETHEART, BUT...
...YOU'RE IT.

INITIALIZE SYSTEM, VIDPHONE 7584-3837-628

SYSTEM INITIALIZED, AWAITING COMMAND:

KILL DR. DAMIAN FAWCETT OF MACROWARE,

INC. BY ANY MEANS POSSIBLE***SEND***

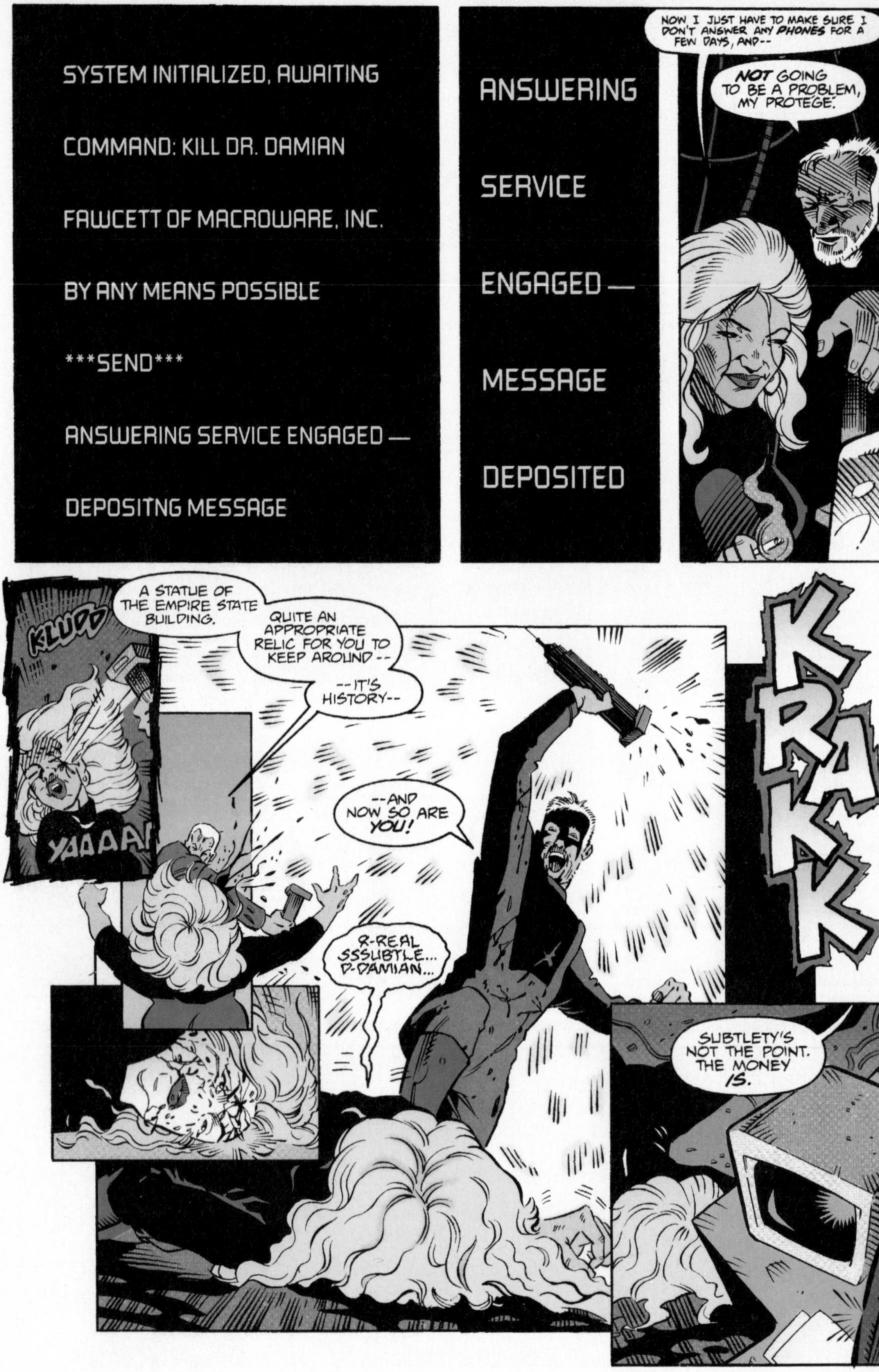
SYSTEM INITIALIZED, AWAITING
COMMAND: KILL DR. DAMIAN
FAWCETT OF MACROWARE, INC.
BY ANY MEANS POSSIBLE
SEND
ANSWERING SERVICE ENGAGED —
DEPOSITNG MESSAGE
ANSWERING
SERVICE
ENGAGED —
MESSAGE
DEPOSITED
NOW I JUST HAVE TO MAKE SURE I DON'T ANSWER ANY PHONES FOR A FEW DAYS, AND--
NOT GOING TO BE A PROBLEM, MY PROTEGE.
KLUDD
YAAAA!
A STATUE OF THE EMPIRE STATE BUILDING.
QUITE AN APPROPRIATE RELIC FOR YOU TO KEEP AROUND--
--IT'S HISTORY--
--AND NOW SO ARE YOU!
KRAKK
R-REAL SSSUBTLE... D-DAMIAN...
SUBTLETY'S NOT THE POINT. THE MONEY IS.

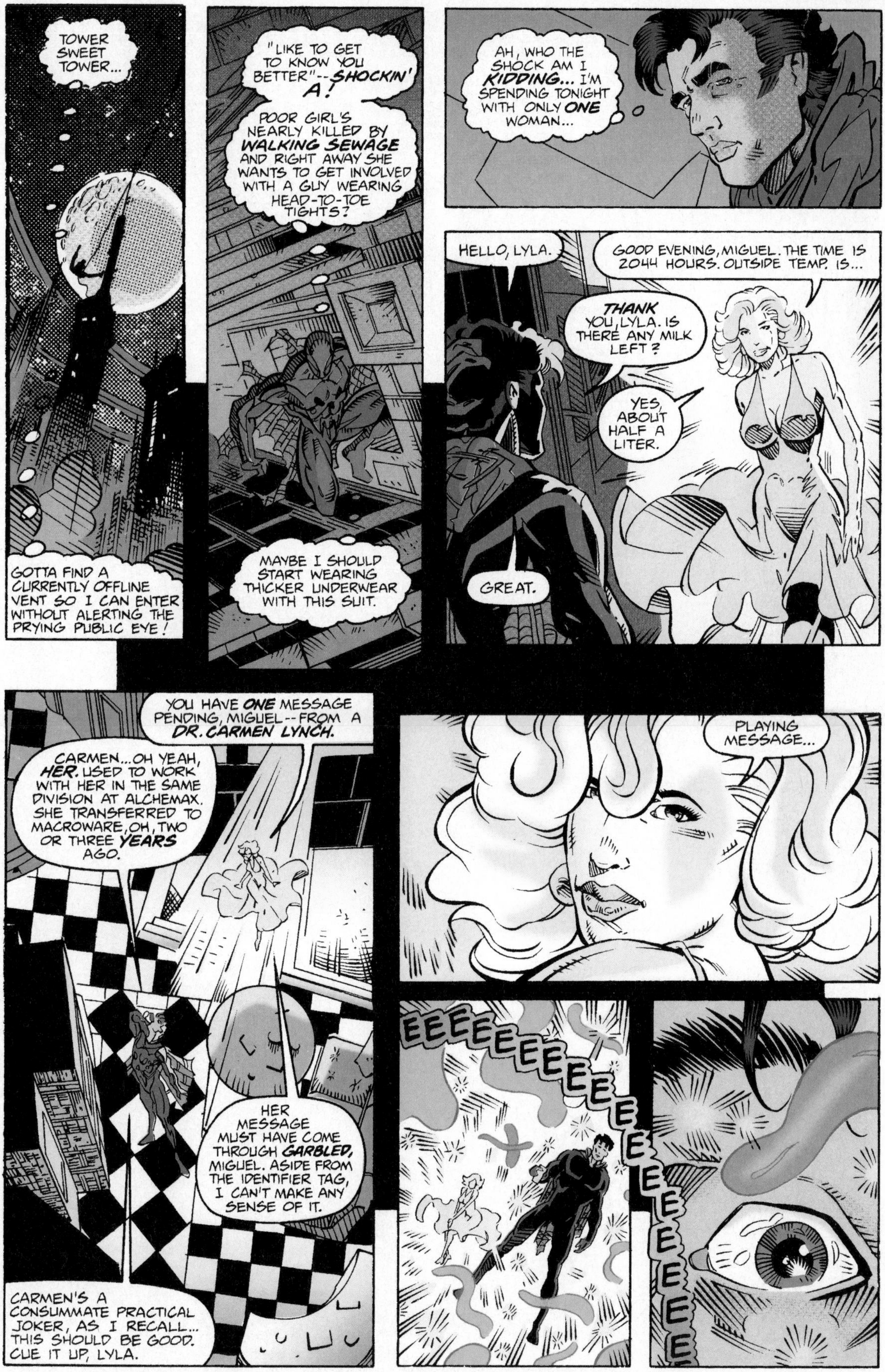
TOWER SWEET TOWER...
GOTTA FIND A CURRENTLY OFFLINE VENT SO I CAN ENTER WITHOUT ALERTING THE PRYING PUBLIC EYE!
"LIKE TO GET TO KNOW YOU BETTER"--SHOCKIN' A!
POOR GIRL'S NEARLY KILLED BY WALKING SEWAGE AND RIGHT AWAY SHE WANTS TO GET INVOLVED WITH A GUY WEARING HEAD-TO-TOE TIGHTS?
MAYBE I SHOULD START WEARING THICKER UNDERWEAR WITH THIS SUIT.
AH, WHO THE SHOCK AM I KIDDING... I'M SPENDING TONIGHT WITH ONLY ONE WOMAN...
HELLO, LYLA.
GOOD EVENING, MIGUEL. THE TIME IS 2044 HOURS. OUTSIDE TEMP. IS...
THANK YOU, LYLA. IS THERE ANY MILK LEFT?
YES, ABOUT HALF A LITER.
GREAT.
YOU HAVE ONE MESSAGE PENDING, MIGUEL--FROM A DR. CARMEN LYNCH.
CARMEN...OH YEAH, HER. USED TO WORK WITH HER IN THE SAME DIVISION AT ALCHEMAX. SHE TRANSFERRED TO MACROWARE, OH, TWO OR THREE YEARS AGO.
HER MESSAGE MUST HAVE COME THROUGH GARBLED, MIGUEL. ASIDE FROM THE IDENTIFIER TAG, I CAN'T MAKE ANY SENSE OF IT.
CARMEN'S A CONSUMMATE PRACTICAL JOKER, AS I RECALL... THIS SHOULD BE GOOD. CUE IT UP, LYLA.
PLAYING MESSAGE...
EEEEEEEEEEEEEEEEEEEE

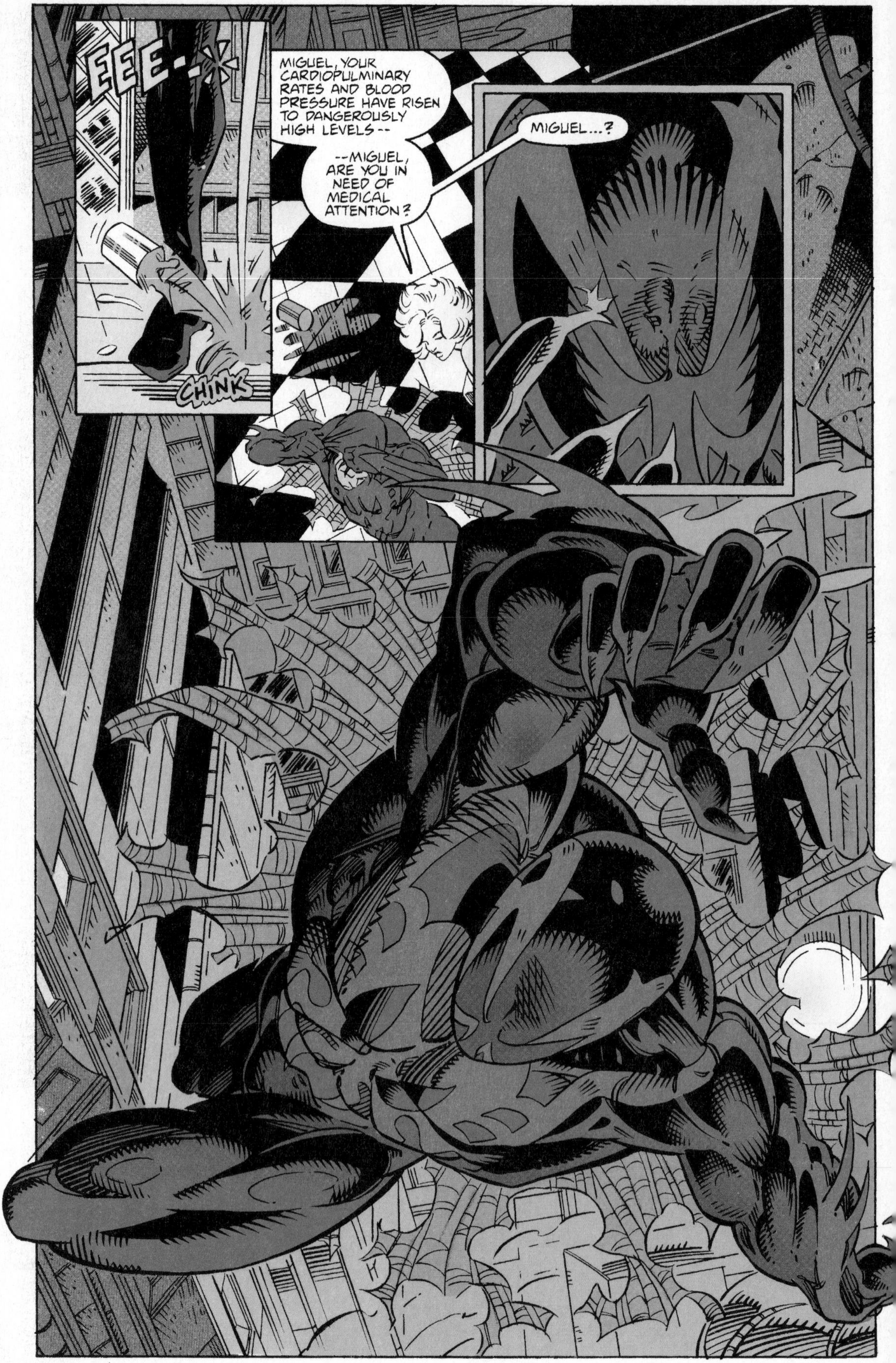
EEE...!
CHINK
MIGUEL, YOUR CARDIOPULMINARY RATES AND BLOOD PRESSURE HAVE RISEN TO DANGEROUSLY HIGH LEVELS --
--MIGUEL, ARE YOU IN NEED OF MEDICAL ATTENTION?
MIGUEL...?

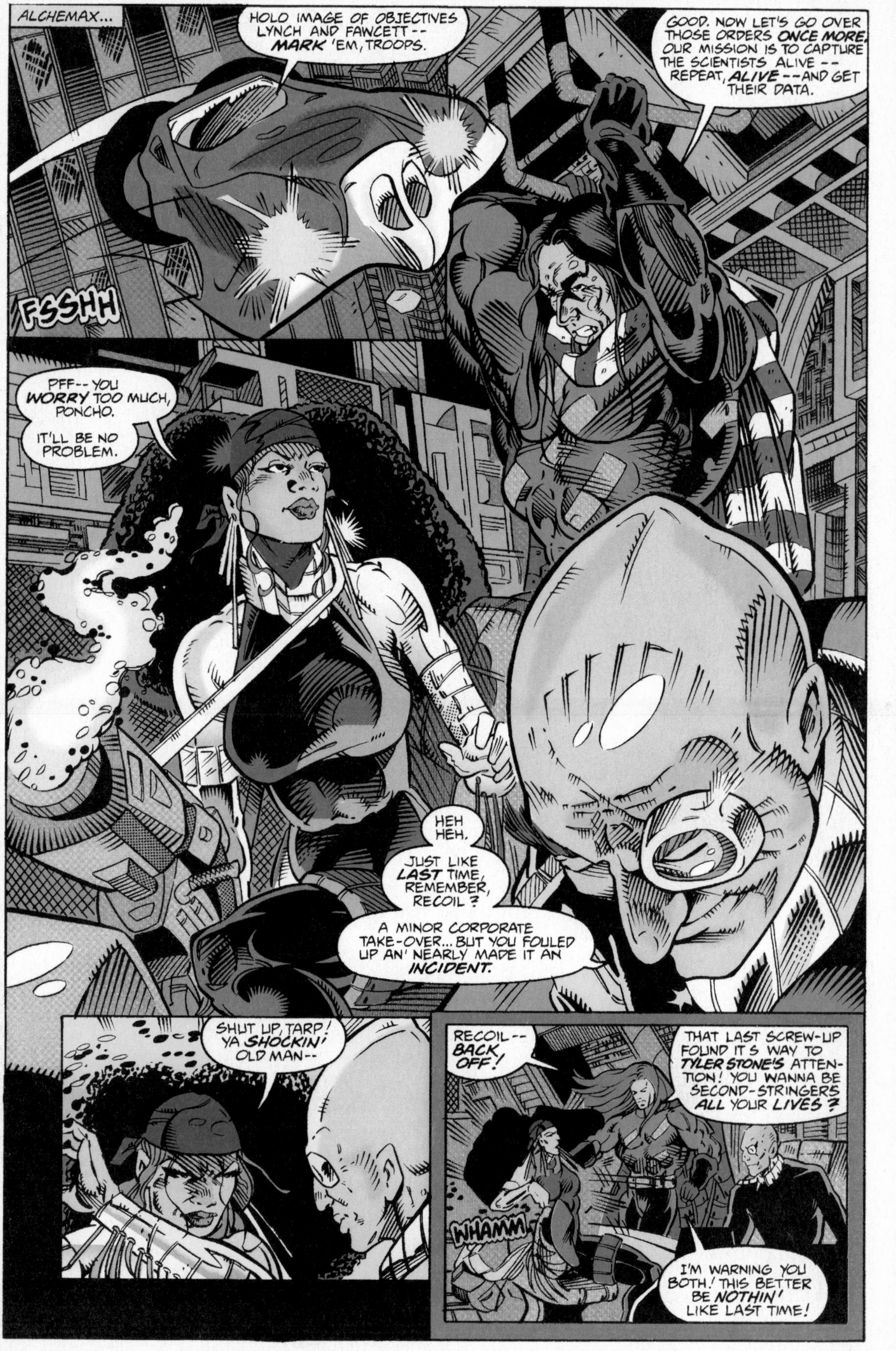
ALCHEMAX...
HOLO IMAGE OF OBJECTIVES LYNCH AND FAWCETT-- MARK 'EM, TROOPS.
GOOD. NOW LET'S GO OVER THOSE ORDERS ONCE MORE. OUR MISSION IS TO CAPTURE THE SCIENTISTS ALIVE -- REPEAT, ALIVE --AND GET THEIR DATA.
FSSHH
PFF--YOU WORRY TOO MUCH, PONCHO.
IT'LL BE NO PROBLEM.
HEH HEH.
JUST LIKE LAST TIME, REMEMBER, RECOIL?
A MINOR CORPORATE TAKE-OVER... BUT YOU FOULED UP AN' NEARLY MADE IT AN INCIDENT.
SHUT UP, TARP! YA SHOCKIN' OLD MAN--
RECOIL-- BACK OFF!
THAT LAST SCREW-UP FOUND IT S WAY TO TYLER STONE'S ATTENTION! YOU WANNA BE SECOND-STRINGERS ALL YOUR LIVES?
WHAMM
I'M WARNING YOU BOTH! THIS BETTER BE NOTHIN' LIKE LAST TIME!

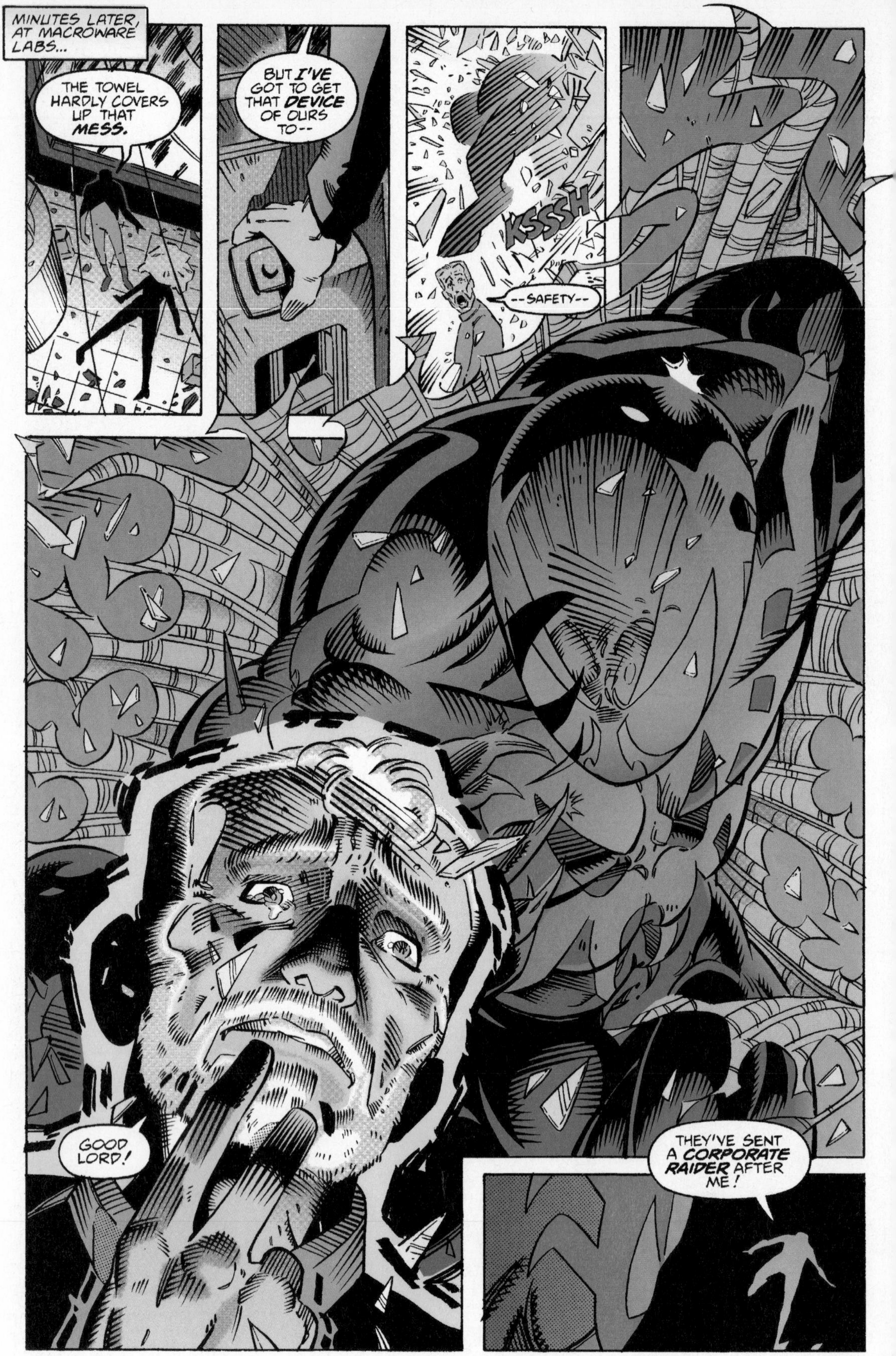
MINUTES LATER, AT MACROWARE LABS...
THE TOWEL HARDLY COVERS UP THAT MESS.
BUT I'VE GOT TO GET THAT DEVICE OF OURS TO--
KSSSH
--SAFETY--
GOOD LORD!
THEY'VE SENT A CORPORATE RAIDER AFTER ME!

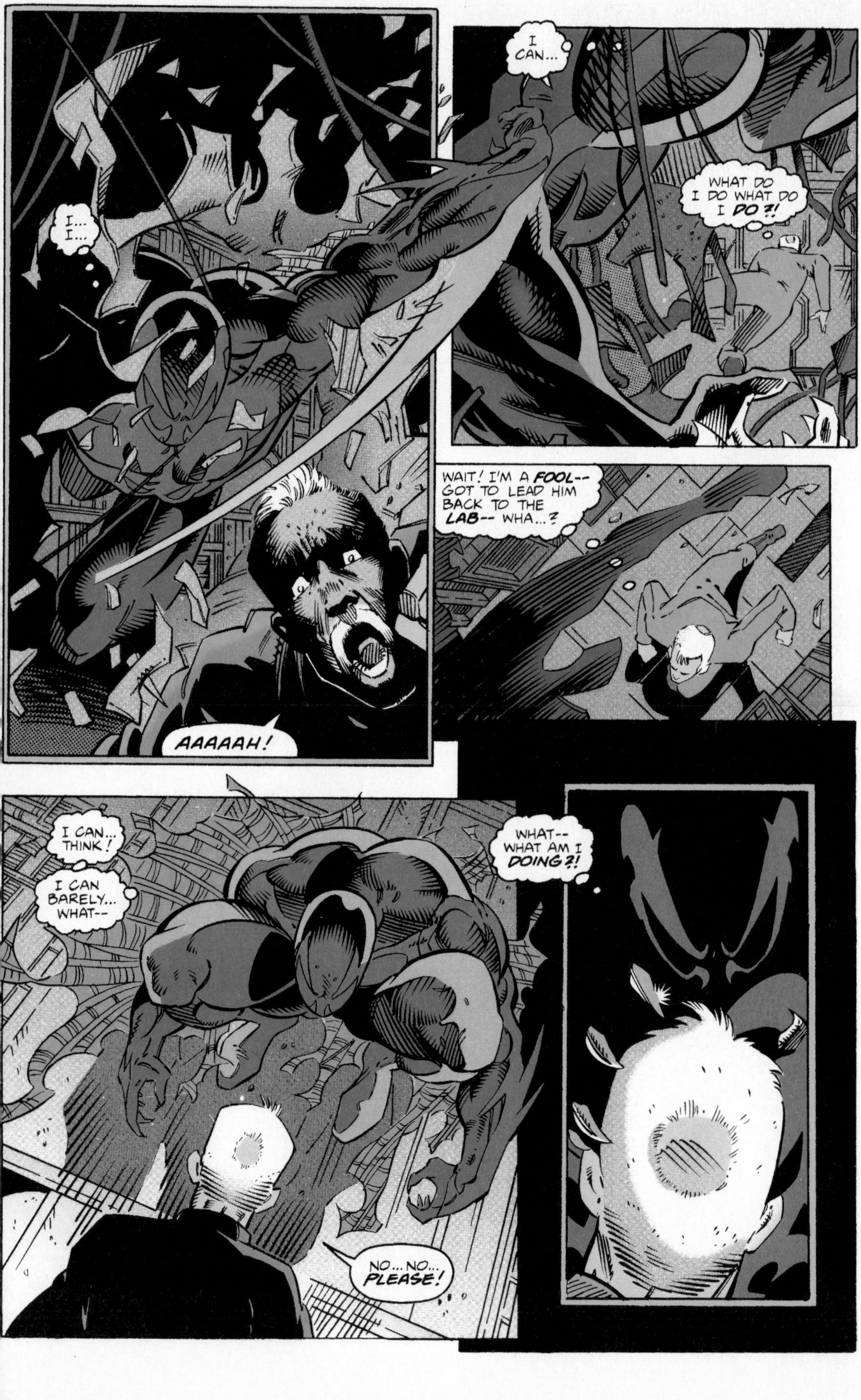
I CAN...
I... I...
WHAT DO I DO WHAT DO I DO?!
AAAAAH!
WAIT! I'M A FOOL-- GOT TO LEAD HIM BACK TO THE LAB-- WHA...?
I CAN... THINK!
I CAN BARELY... WHAT--
WHAT-- WHAT AM I DOING?!
NO... NO... PLEASE!

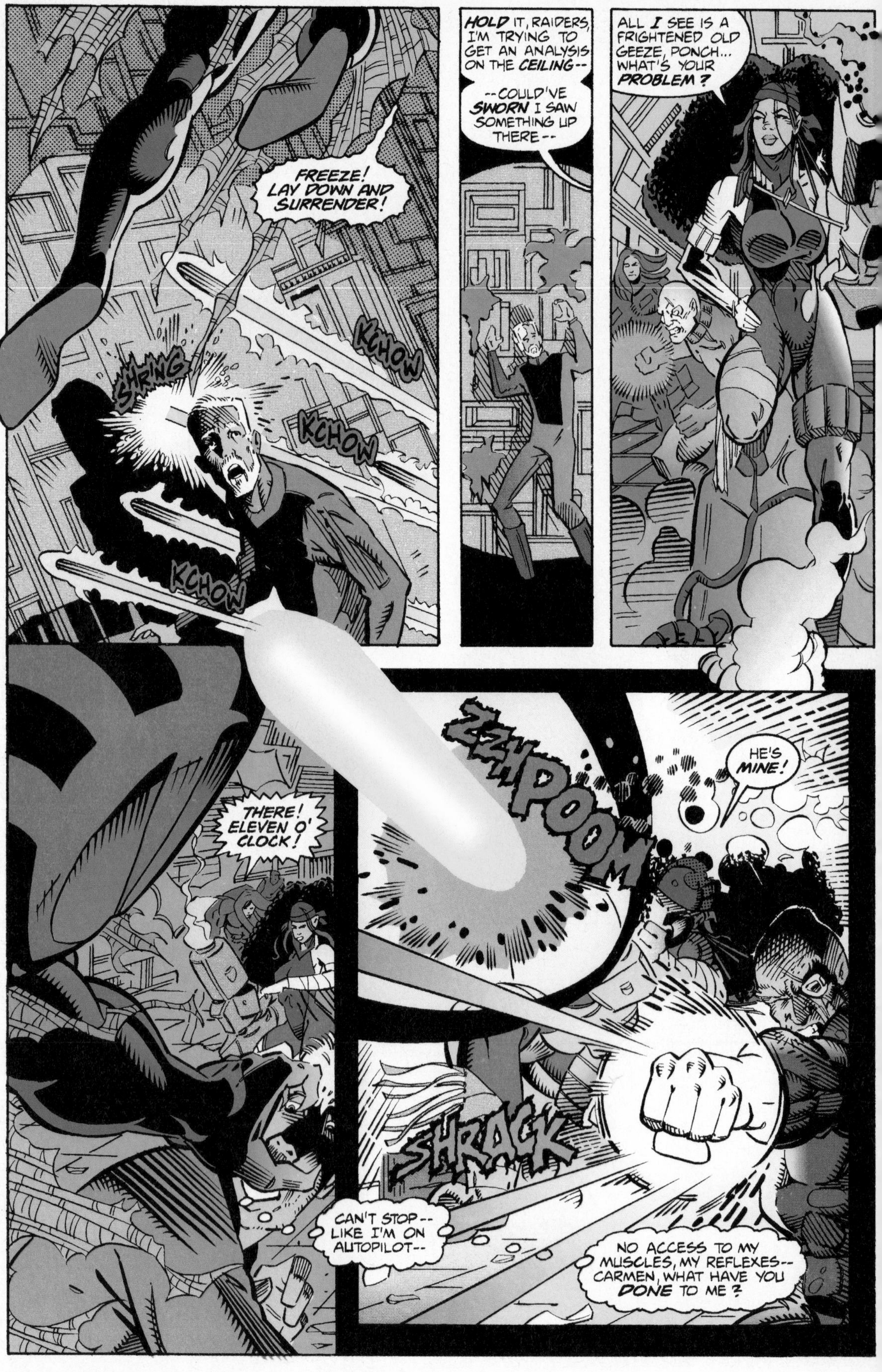
FREEZE! LAY DOWN AND SURRENDER!
SHRNG
KCHOW
KCHOW
KCHOW
HOLD IT, RAIDERS, I'M TRYING TO GET AN ANALYSIS ON THE CEILING--
--COULD'VE SWORN I SAW SOMETHING UP THERE--
ALL I SEE IS A FRIGHTENED OLD GEEZE, PONCH... WHAT'S YOUR PROBLEM?
THERE! ELEVEN O' CLOCK!
ZZHPOOOM
HE'S MINE!
SHRACK
CAN'T STOP-- LIKE I'M ON AUTOPILOT--
NO ACCESS TO MY MUSCLES, MY REFLEXES-- CARMEN, WHAT HAVE YOU DONE TO ME?

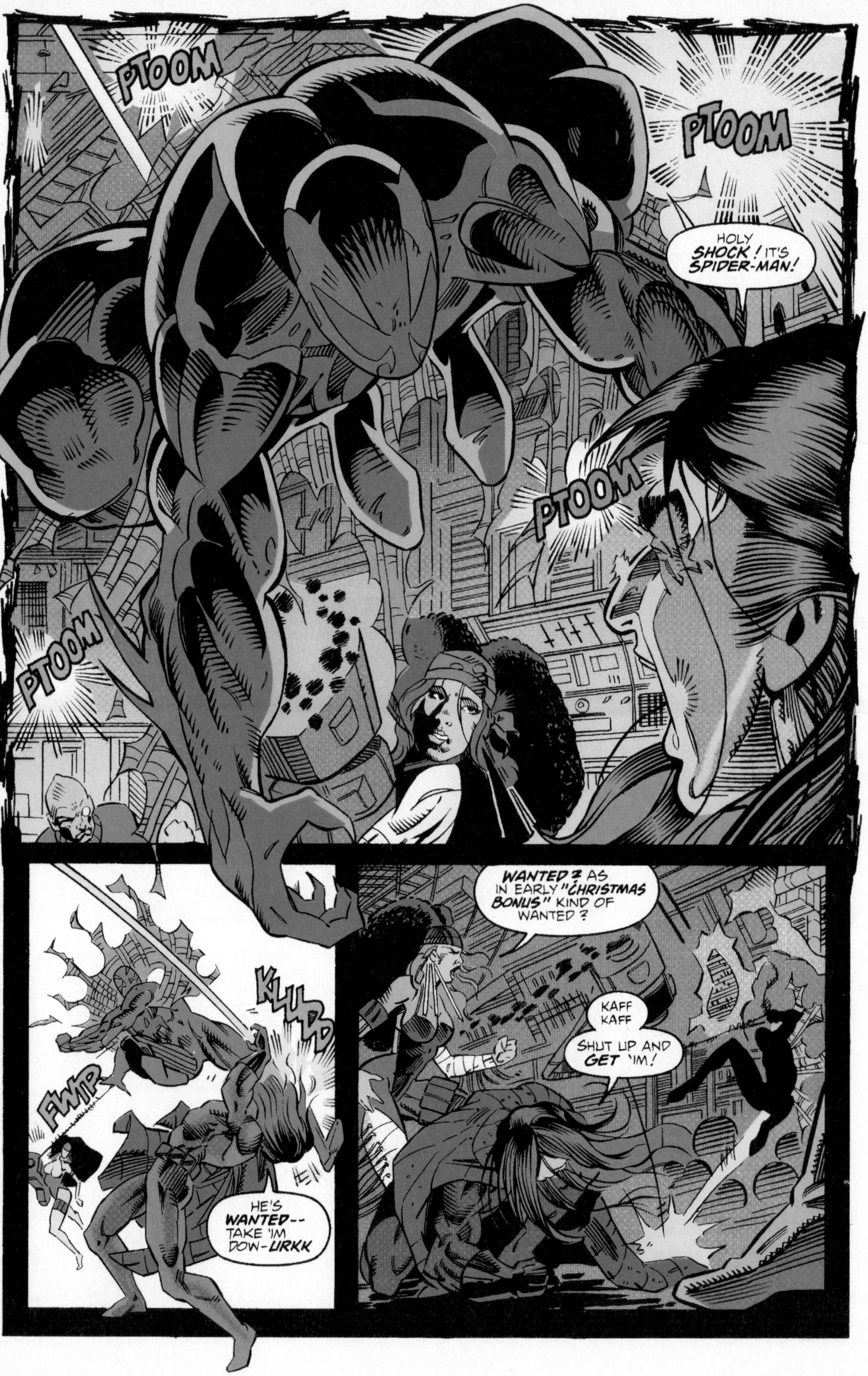
PTOOM
PTOOM
HOLY SHOCK! IT'S SPIDER-MAN!
PTOOM
PTOOM
KLUDD
FWIP
HE'S WANTED-- TAKE 'IM DOW-URKK
WANTED? AS IN EARLY "CHRISTMAS BONUS" KIND OF WANTED?
KAFF KAFF
SHUT UP AND GET 'IM!

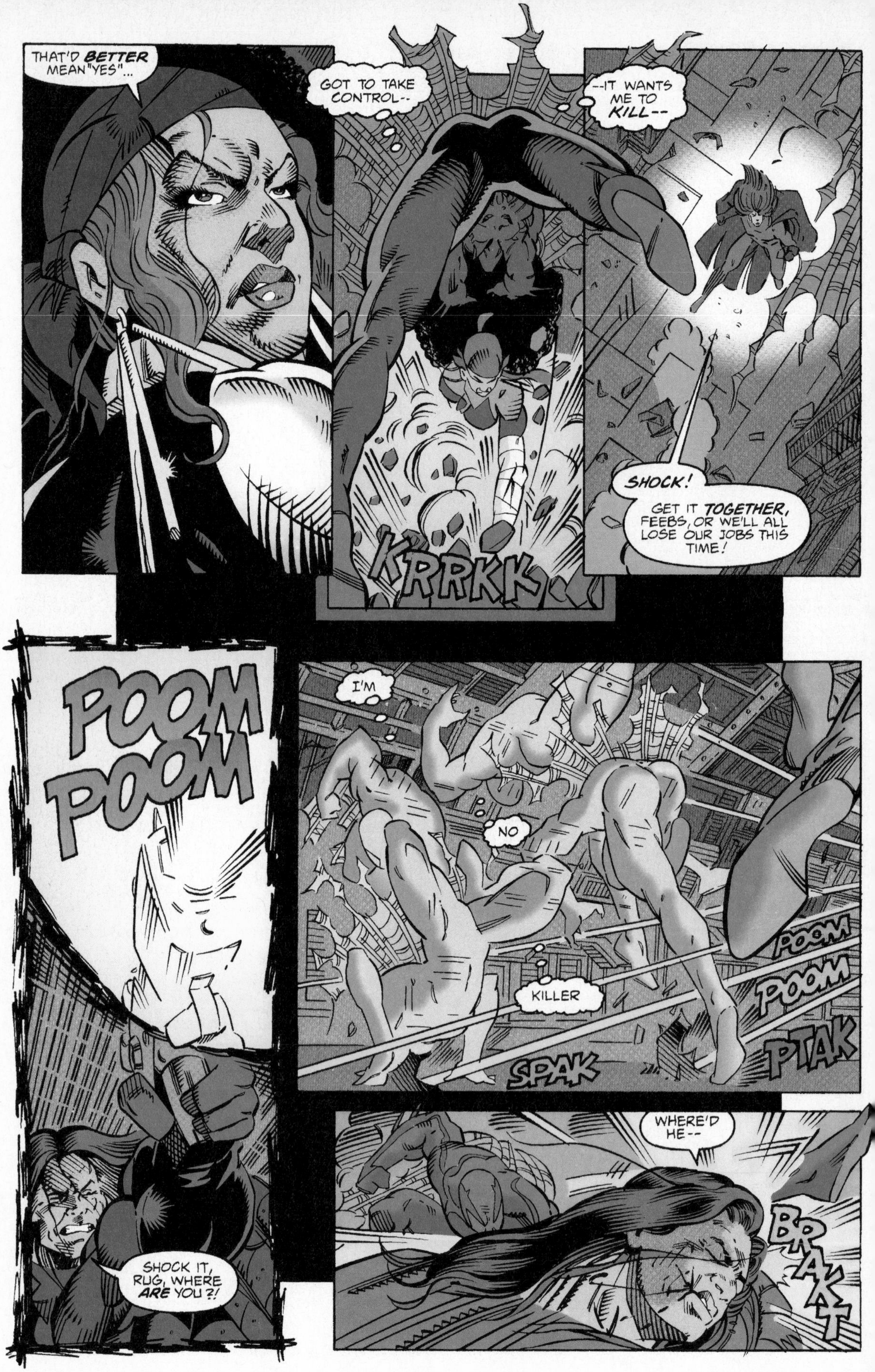
THAT'D BETTER MEAN "YES"...
GOT TO TAKE CONTROL--
--IT WANTS ME TO KILL--
KRRKK
SHOCK!
GET IT TOGETHER, FEEBS, OR WE'LL ALL LOSE OUR JOBS THIS TIME!
POOM POOM
SHOCK IT, RUG, WHERE ARE YOU?!
I'M
NO
KILLER
POOM
POOM
PTAK
SPAK
WHERE'D HE--
BRAKT

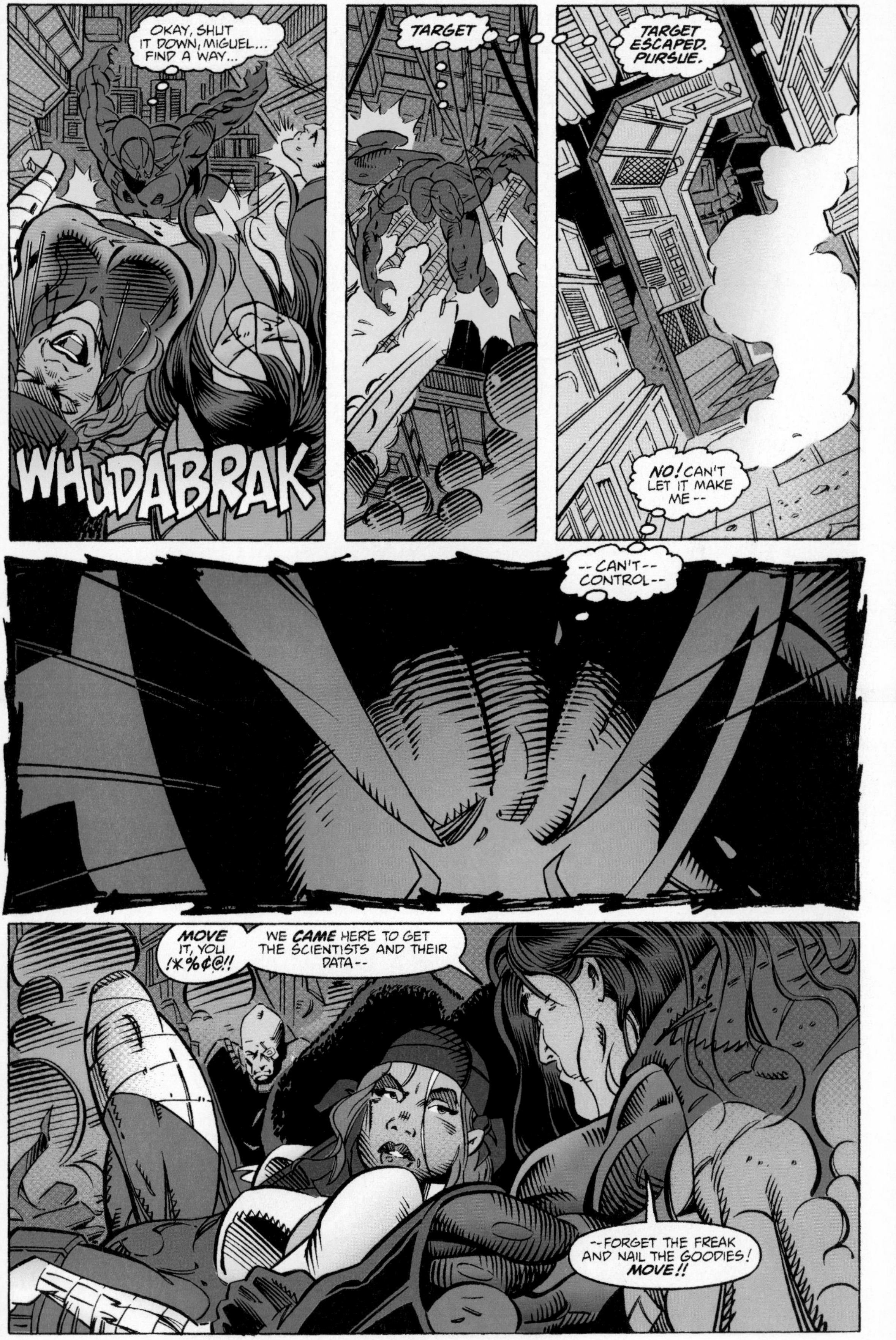
OKAY, SHUT IT DOWN, MIGUEL... FIND A WAY...
WHUDABRAK
TARGET
TARGET ESCAPED. PURSUE.
NO! CAN'T LET IT MAKE ME --
-- CAN'T -- CONTROL --
MOVE IT, YOU !*%¢@!!
WE CAME HERE TO GET THE SCIENTISTS AND THEIR DATA --
-- FORGET THE FREAK AND NAIL THE GOODIES! MOVE!!

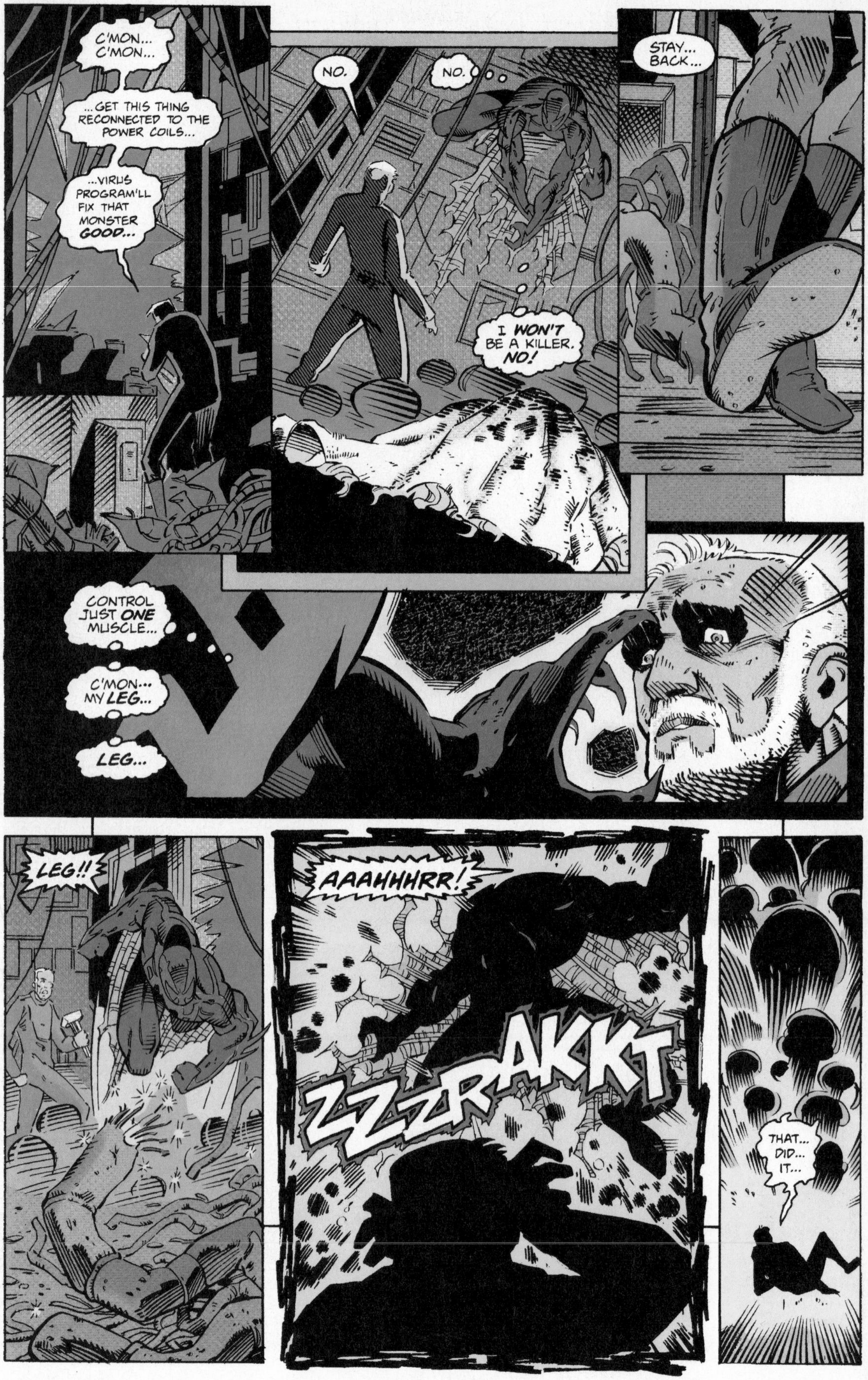
C'MON... C'MON...
...GET THIS THING RECONNECTED TO THE POWER COILS...
...VIRUS PROGRAM'LL FIX THAT MONSTER GOOD...
NO.
NO.
I WON'T BE A KILLER. NO!
STAY... BACK...
CONTROL JUST ONE MUSCLE...
C'MON... MY LEG...
LEG...
LEG!!
AAAHHHRR!
ZZZRAKKT
THAT... DID... IT...

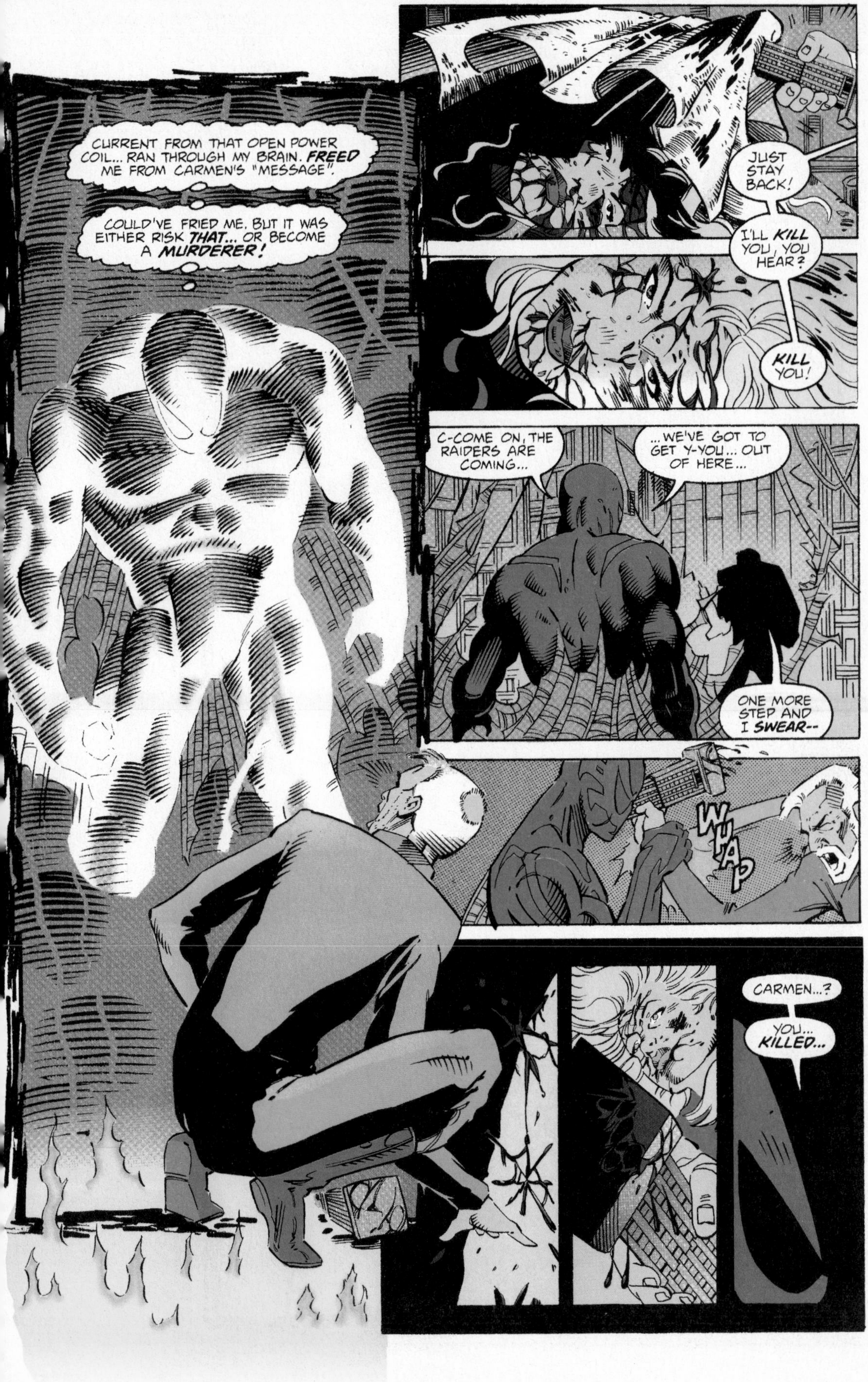

CURRENT FROM THAT OPEN POWER COIL... RAN THROUGH MY BRAIN. **FREED** ME FROM CARMEN'S "MESSAGE".
COULD'VE FRIED ME. BUT IT WAS EITHER RISK **THAT**... OR BECOME A **MURDERER!**
JUST STAY BACK!
I'LL **KILL** YOU, YOU HEAR?
KILL YOU!
C-COME ON, THE RAIDERS ARE COMING...
...WE'VE GOT TO GET Y-YOU... OUT OF HERE...
ONE MORE STEP AND I **SWEAR**--
WHAP
CARMEN...?
YOU... **KILLED**...

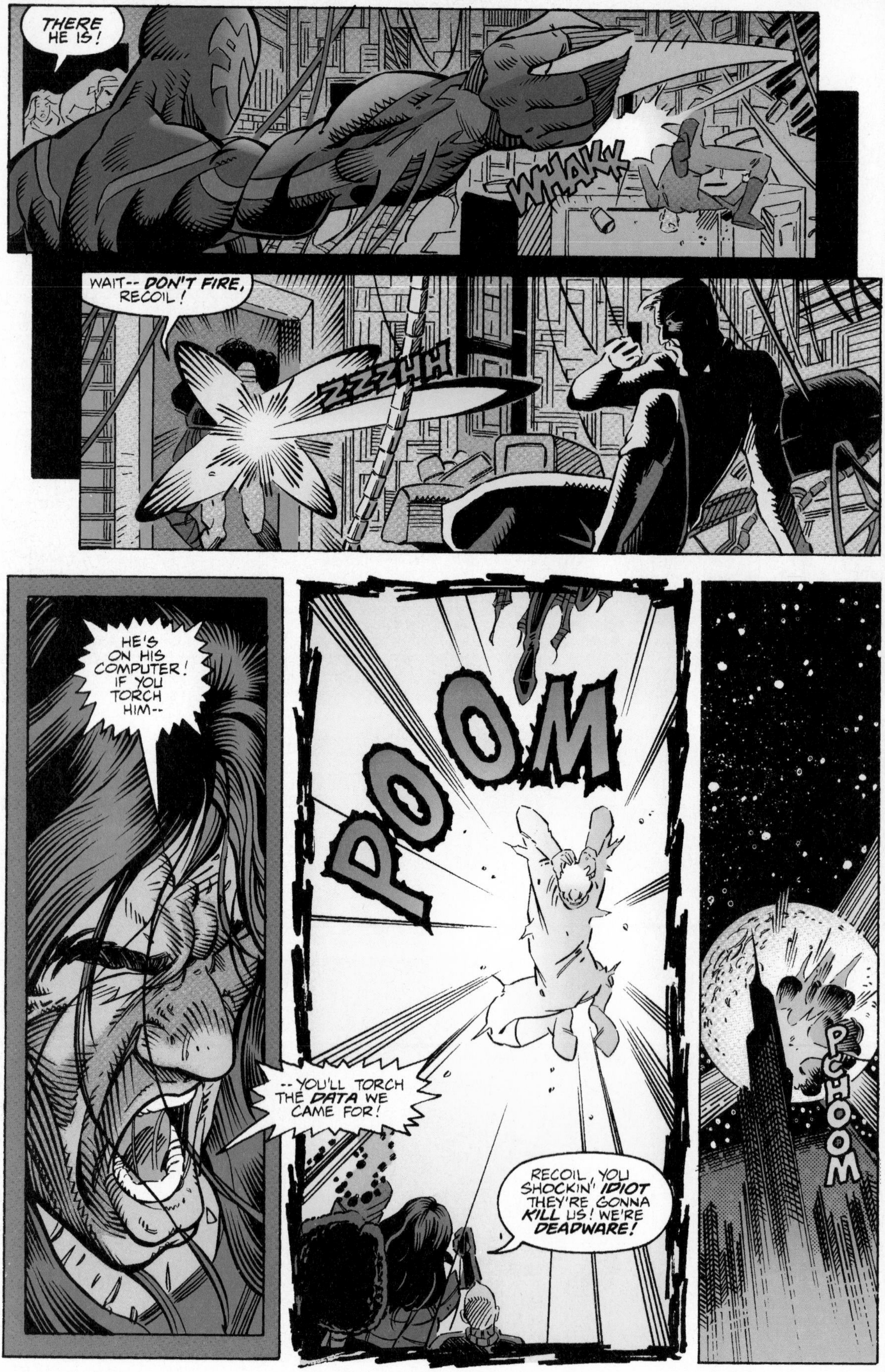
THERE HE IS!
WHAKK
WAIT-- DON'T FIRE, RECOIL!
ZZZHH
HE'S ON HIS COMPUTER! IF YOU TORCH HIM--
--YOU'LL TORCH THE DATA WE CAME FOR!
POOOM
RECOIL, YOU SHOCKIN' IDIOT THEY'RE GONNA KILL US! WE'RE DEADWARE!
PCHOOM

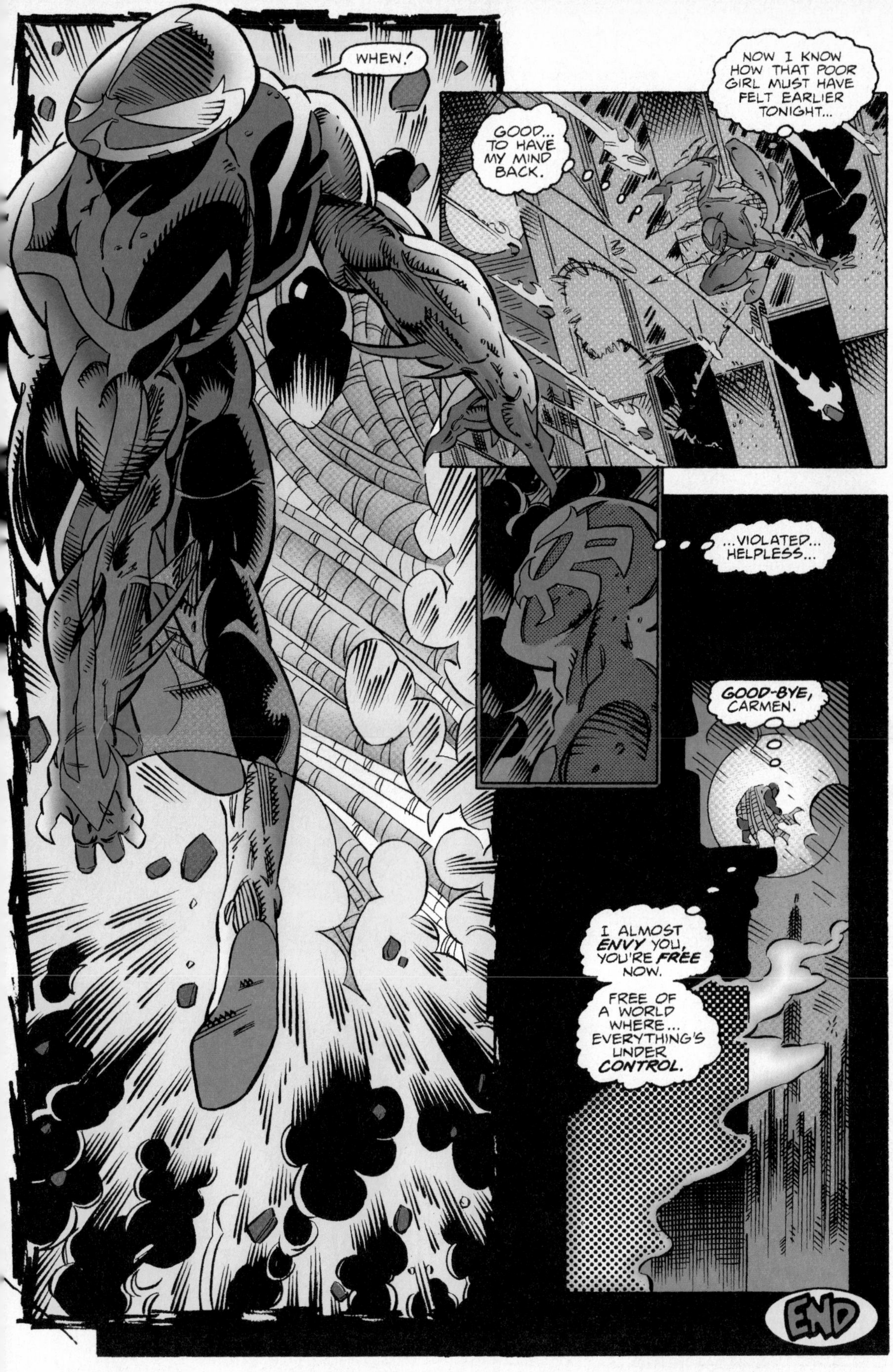
WHEW!
NOW I KNOW HOW THAT POOR GIRL MUST HAVE FELT EARLIER TONIGHT...
GOOD... TO HAVE MY MIND BACK.
...VIOLATED... HELPLESS...
GOOD-BYE, CARMEN.
I ALMOST ENVY YOU, YOU'RE FREE NOW.
FREE OF A WORLD WHERE... EVERYTHING'S UNDER CONTROL.
END

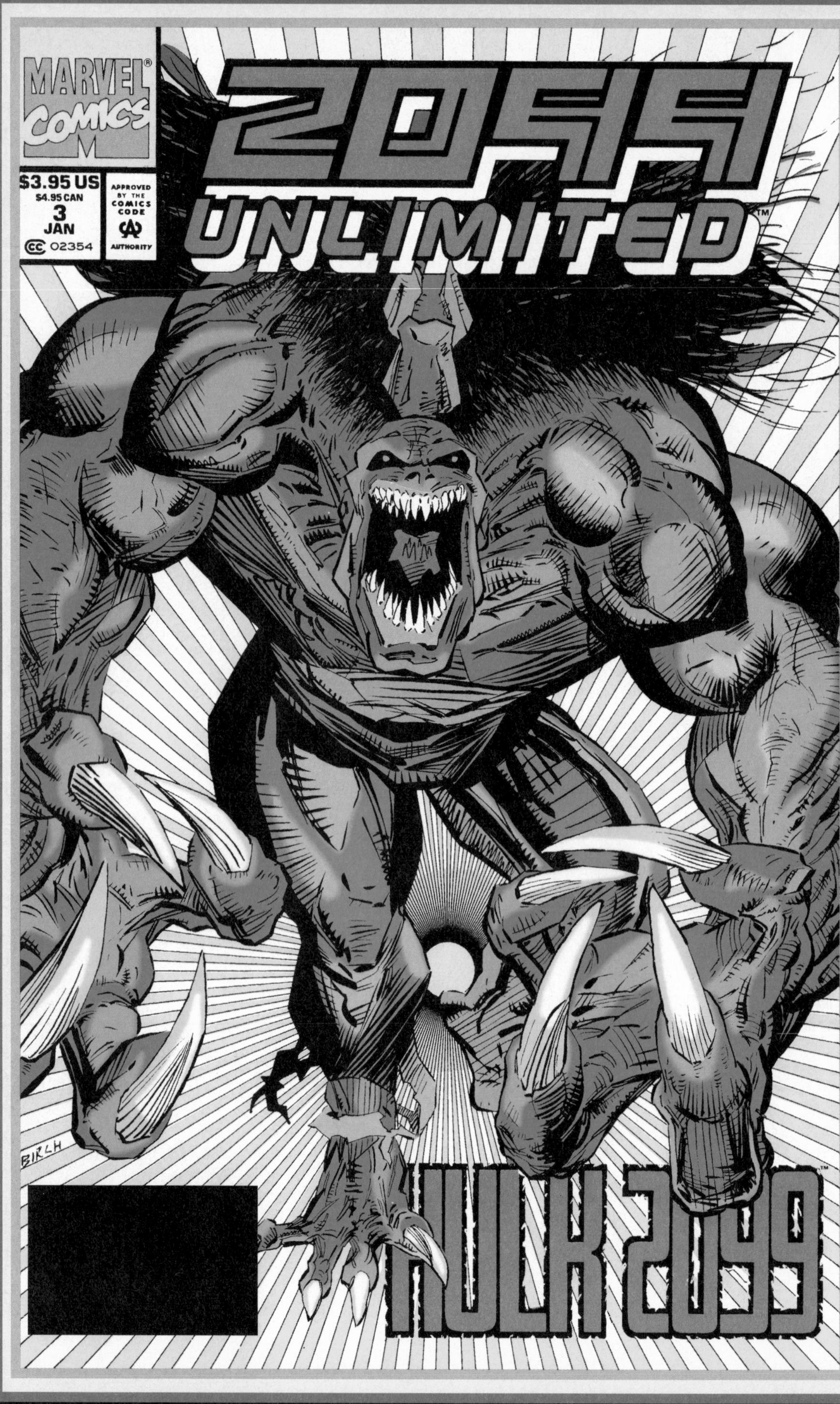

MARVEL COMICS
$3.95 US
$4.95 CAN
3
JAN
CC 02354
APPROVED BY THE COMICS CODE AUTHORITY
2099 UNLIMITED™
BIRCH
HULK 2099™

STAN LEE PRESENTS...

SPIDER-MAN 2099 SPARE CHANGES

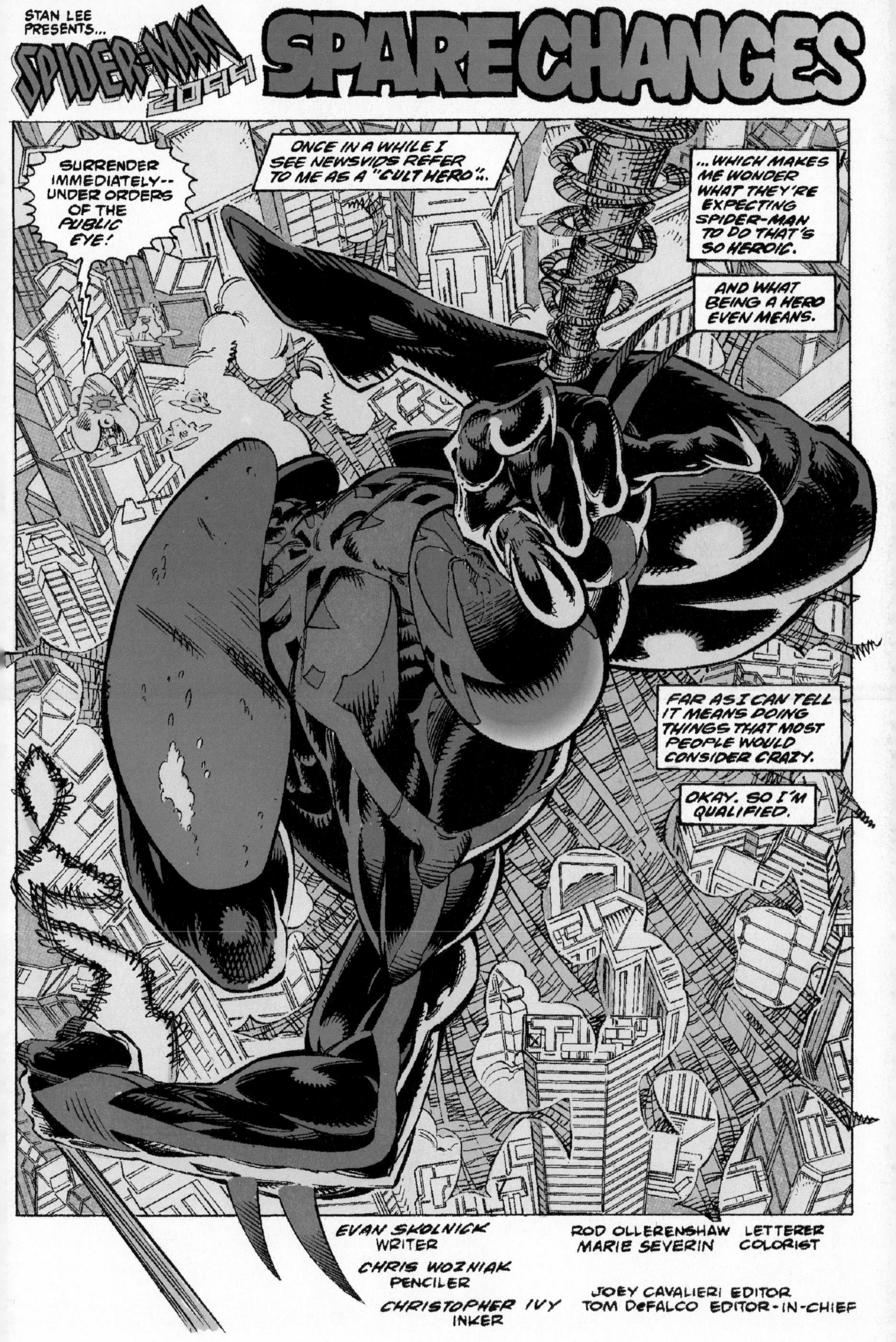

ONCE IN A WHILE I SEE NEWSVIDS REFER TO ME AS A "CULT HERO"...
SURRENDER IMMEDIATELY-- UNDER ORDERS OF THE PUBLIC EYE!
...WHICH MAKES ME WONDER WHAT THEY'RE EXPECTING SPIDER-MAN TO DO THAT'S SO HEROIC.
AND WHAT BEING A HERO EVEN MEANS.
FAR AS I CAN TELL IT MEANS DOING THINGS THAT MOST PEOPLE WOULD CONSIDER CRAZY.
OKAY. SO I'M QUALIFIED.

EVAN SKOLNICK WRITER
CHRIS WOZNIAK PENCILER
CHRISTOPHER IVY INKER
ROD OLLERENSHAW LETTERER
MARIE SEVERIN COLORIST
JOEY CAVALIERI EDITOR
TOM DeFALCO EDITOR-IN-CHIEF

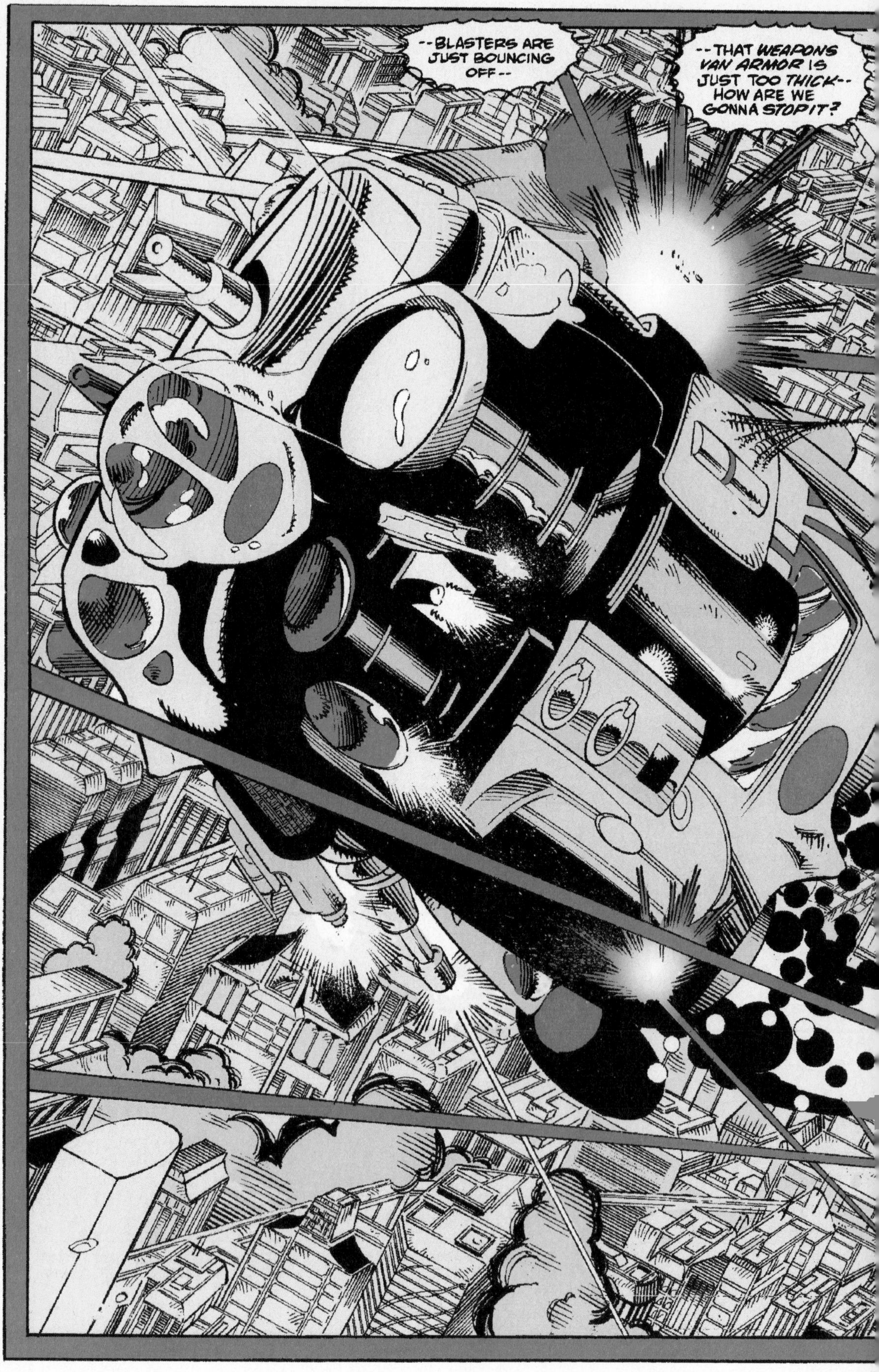
--BLASTERS ARE JUST BOUNCING OFF--
--THAT WEAPONS VAN ARMOR IS JUST TOO THICK-- HOW ARE WE GONNA STOP IT?

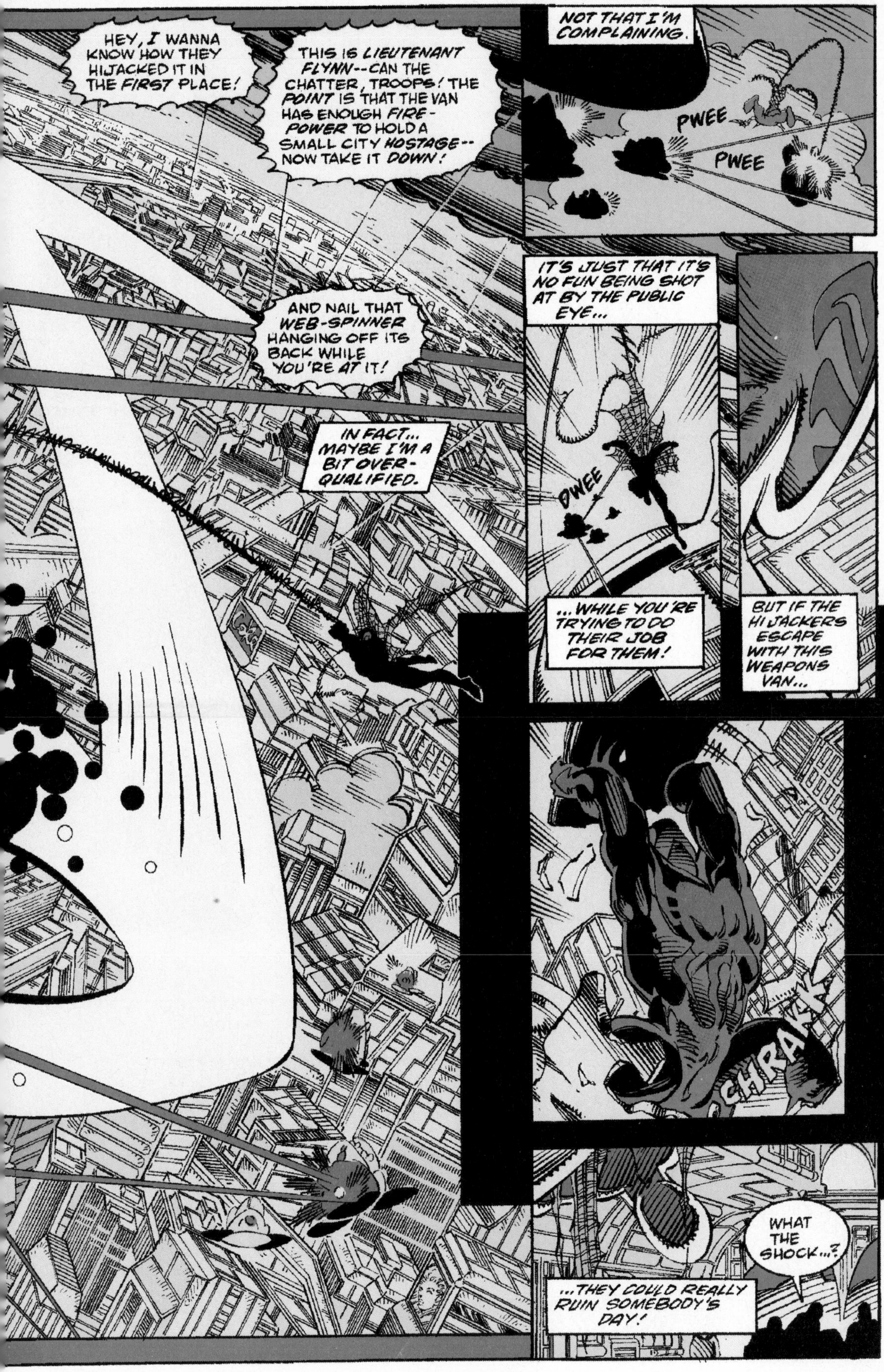
HEY, I WANNA KNOW HOW THEY HIJACKED IT IN THE FIRST PLACE!
THIS IS LIEUTENANT FLYNN--CAN THE CHATTER, TROOPS! THE POINT IS THAT THE VAN HAS ENOUGH FIRE-POWER TO HOLD A SMALL CITY HOSTAGE--NOW TAKE IT DOWN!
AND NAIL THAT WEB-SPINNER HANGING OFF ITS BACK WHILE YOU'RE AT IT!
IN FACT... MAYBE I'M A BIT OVER-QUALIFIED.
NOT THAT I'M COMPLAINING.
PWEE
PWEE
IT'S JUST THAT IT'S NO FUN BEING SHOT AT BY THE PUBLIC EYE...
OWEE
...WHILE YOU'RE TRYING TO DO THEIR JOB FOR THEM!
BUT IF THE HIJACKERS ESCAPE WITH THIS WEAPONS VAN...
CHRAKK
WHAT THE SHOCK...?
...THEY COULD REALLY RUIN SOMEBODY'S DAY!

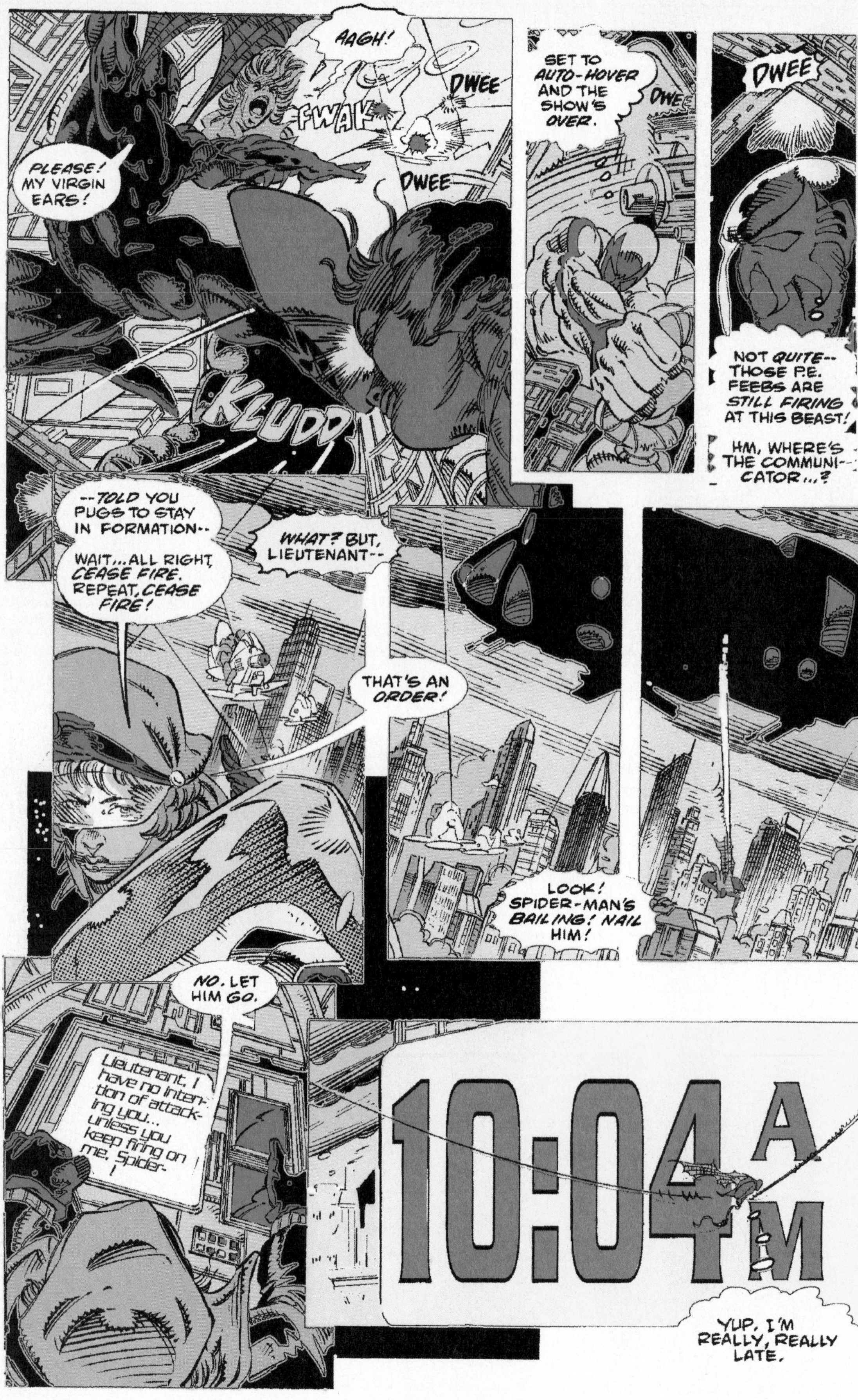
AAGH!
FWAK
DWEE
PLEASE! MY VIRGIN EARS!
DWEE
KLUDD
SET TO AUTO-HOVER AND THE SHOW'S OVER.
DWEE
DWEE
NOT QUITE-- THOSE P.E. FEEBS ARE STILL FIRING AT THIS BEAST!
HM, WHERE'S THE COMMUNICATOR...?
--TOLD YOU PUGS TO STAY IN FORMATION--
WAIT...ALL RIGHT, CEASE FIRE. REPEAT, CEASE FIRE!
WHAT? BUT, LIEUTENANT--
THAT'S AN ORDER!
LOOK! SPIDER-MAN'S BAILING! NAIL HIM!
NO. LET HIM GO.
Lieutenant, I have no intention of attacking you... unless you keep firing on me. Spider-!
10:04 AM
YUP, I'M REALLY, REALLY LATE.

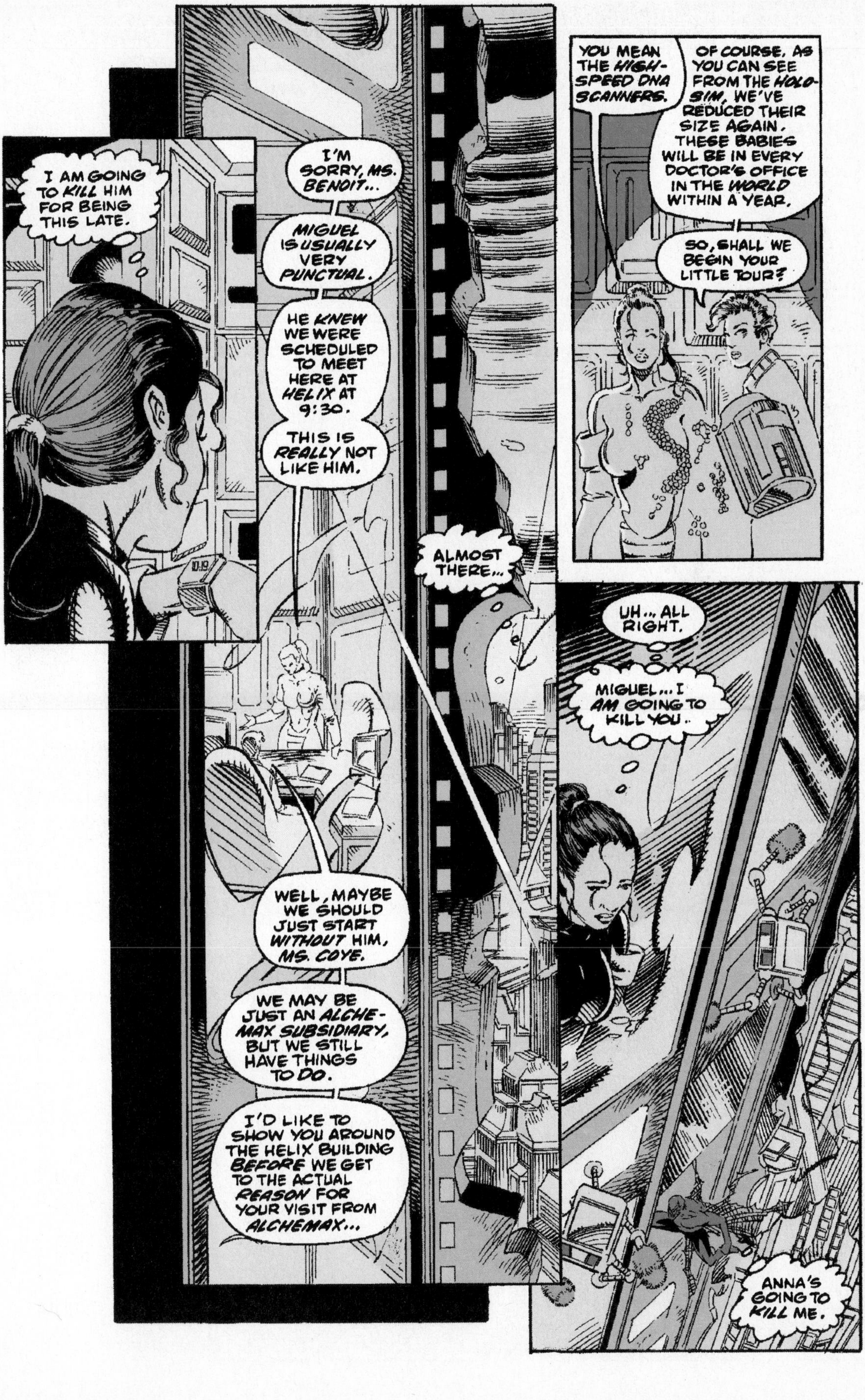
I AM GOING TO KILL HIM FOR BEING THIS LATE.
I'M SORRY, MS. BENOIT...
MIGUEL IS USUALLY VERY PUNCTUAL.
HE KNEW WE WERE SCHEDULED TO MEET HERE AT HELIX AT 9:30.
THIS IS REALLY NOT LIKE HIM.
WELL, MAYBE WE SHOULD JUST START WITHOUT HIM, MS. COYE.
WE MAY BE JUST AN ALCHEMAX SUBSIDIARY, BUT WE STILL HAVE THINGS TO DO.
I'D LIKE TO SHOW YOU AROUND THE HELIX BUILDING BEFORE WE GET TO THE ACTUAL REASON FOR YOUR VISIT FROM ALCHEMAX...
ALMOST THERE...
YOU MEAN THE HIGH-SPEED DNA SCANNERS.
OF COURSE. AS YOU CAN SEE FROM THE HOLO-SIM, WE'VE REDUCED THEIR SIZE AGAIN. THESE BABIES WILL BE IN EVERY DOCTOR'S OFFICE IN THE WORLD WITHIN A YEAR.
SO, SHALL WE BEGIN YOUR LITTLE TOUR?
UH... ALL RIGHT.
MIGUEL... I AM GOING TO KILL YOU.
ANNA'S GOING TO KILL ME.

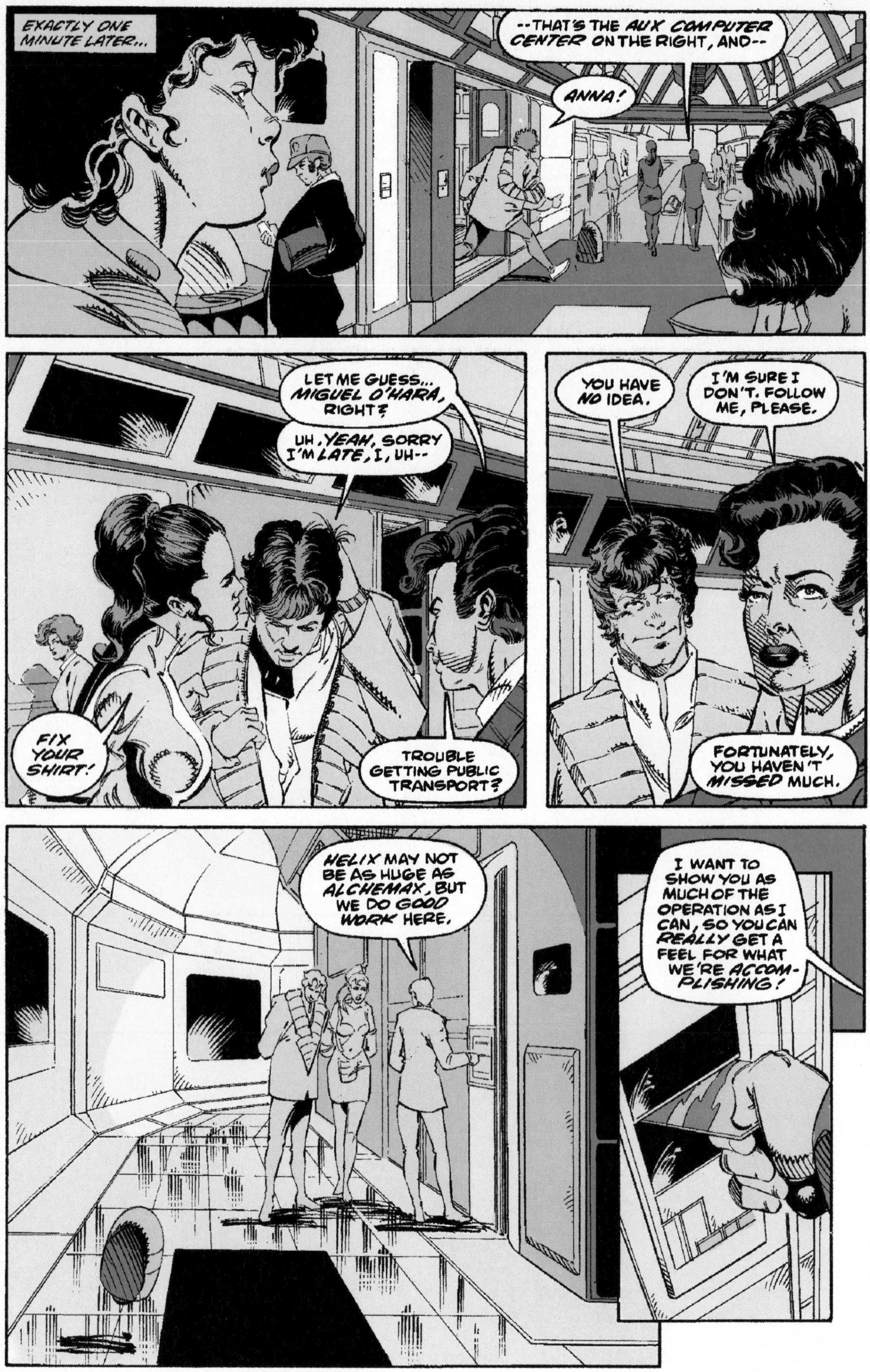
EXACTLY ONE MINUTE LATER...
--THAT'S THE AUX COMPUTER CENTER ON THE RIGHT, AND--
ANNA!
LET ME GUESS... MIGUEL O'HARA, RIGHT?
UH, YEAH, SORRY I'M LATE, I, UH--
FIX YOUR SHIRT!
TROUBLE GETTING PUBLIC TRANSPORT?
YOU HAVE NO IDEA.
I'M SURE I DON'T. FOLLOW ME, PLEASE.
FORTUNATELY, YOU HAVEN'T MISSED MUCH.
HELIX MAY NOT BE AS HUGE AS ALCHEMAX, BUT WE DO GOOD WORK HERE.
I WANT TO SHOW YOU AS MUCH OF THE OPERATION AS I CAN, SO YOU CAN REALLY GET A FEEL FOR WHAT WE'RE ACCOMPLISHING!

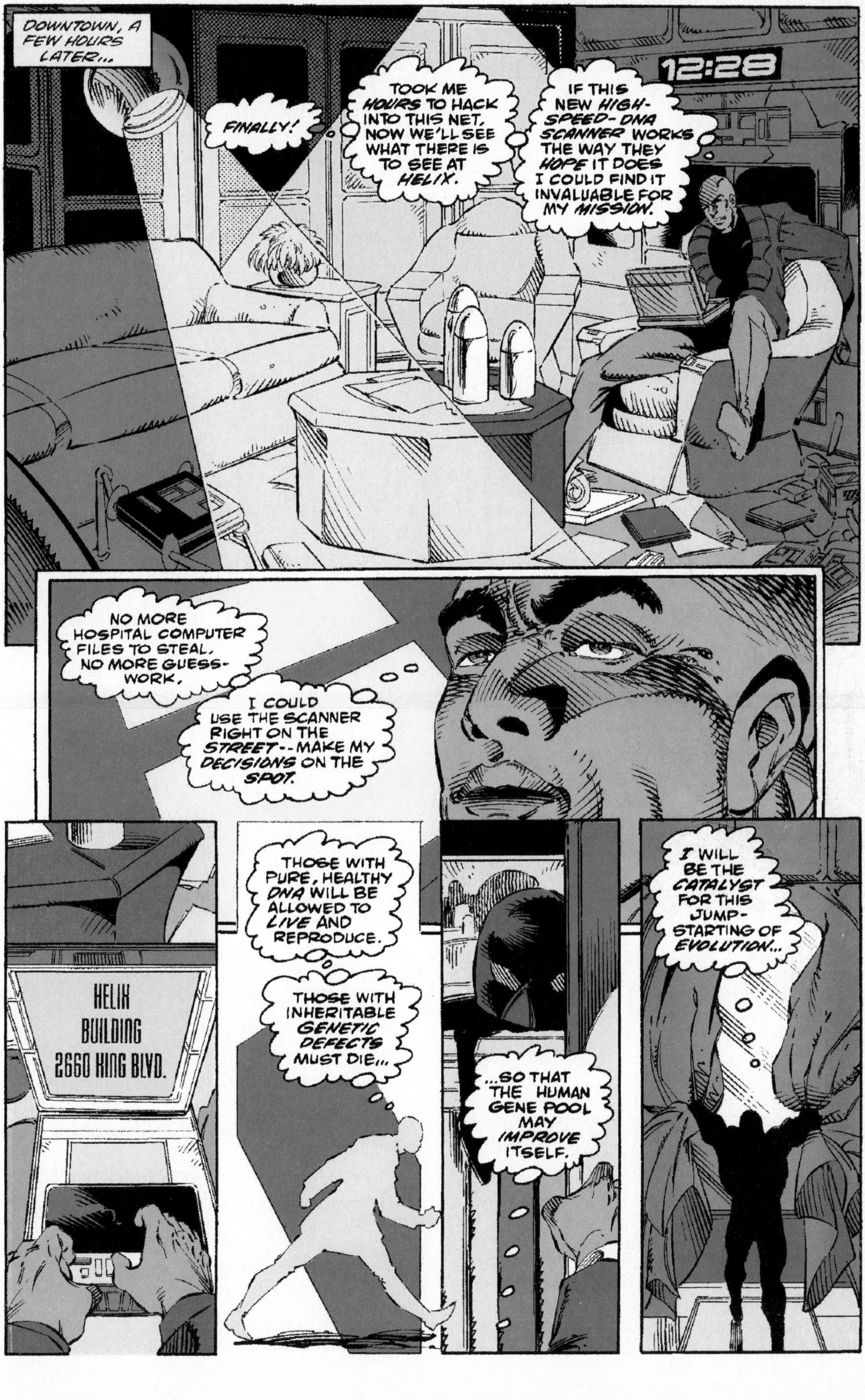
DOWNTOWN, A FEW HOURS LATER...
12:28
FINALLY!
TOOK ME HOURS TO HACK INTO THIS NET. NOW WE'LL SEE WHAT THERE IS TO SEE AT HELIX.
IF THIS NEW HIGH-SPEED-DNA SCANNER WORKS THE WAY THEY HOPE IT DOES I COULD FIND IT INVALUABLE FOR MY MISSION.
NO MORE HOSPITAL COMPUTER FILES TO STEAL. NO MORE GUESS-WORK.
I COULD USE THE SCANNER RIGHT ON THE STREET--MAKE MY DECISIONS ON THE SPOT.
HELIX BUILDING 2660 KING BLVD.
THOSE WITH PURE, HEALTHY DNA WILL BE ALLOWED TO LIVE AND REPRODUCE.
THOSE WITH INHERITABLE GENETIC DEFECTS MUST DIE...
...SO THAT THE HUMAN GENE POOL MAY IMPROVE ITSELF.
I WILL BE THE CATALYST FOR THIS JUMP-STARTING OF EVOLUTION...

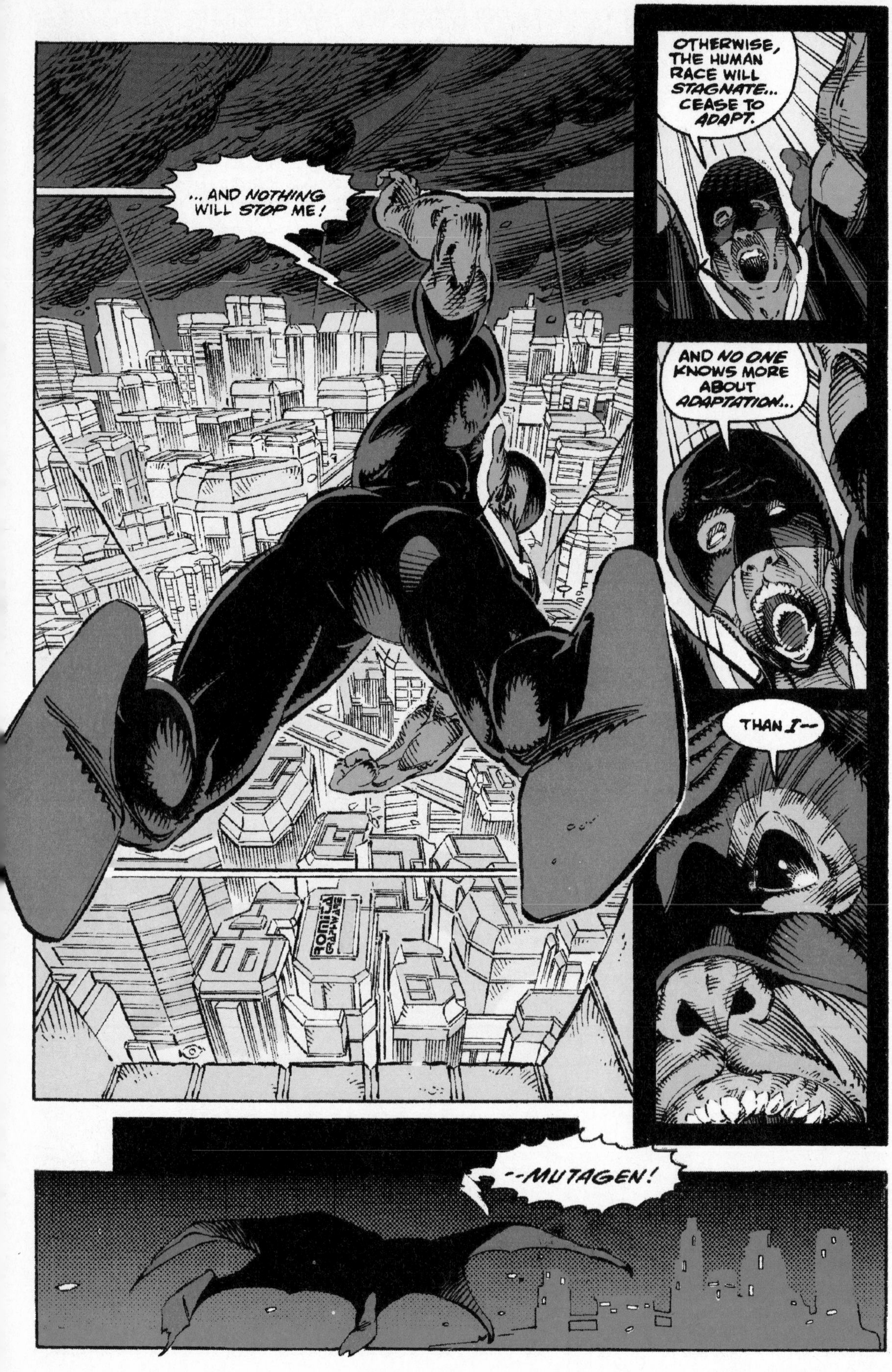
OTHERWISE, THE HUMAN RACE WILL STAGNATE... CEASE TO ADAPT.
...AND NOTHING WILL STOP ME!
AND NO ONE KNOWS MORE ABOUT ADAPTATION...
THAN I--
--MUTAGEN!

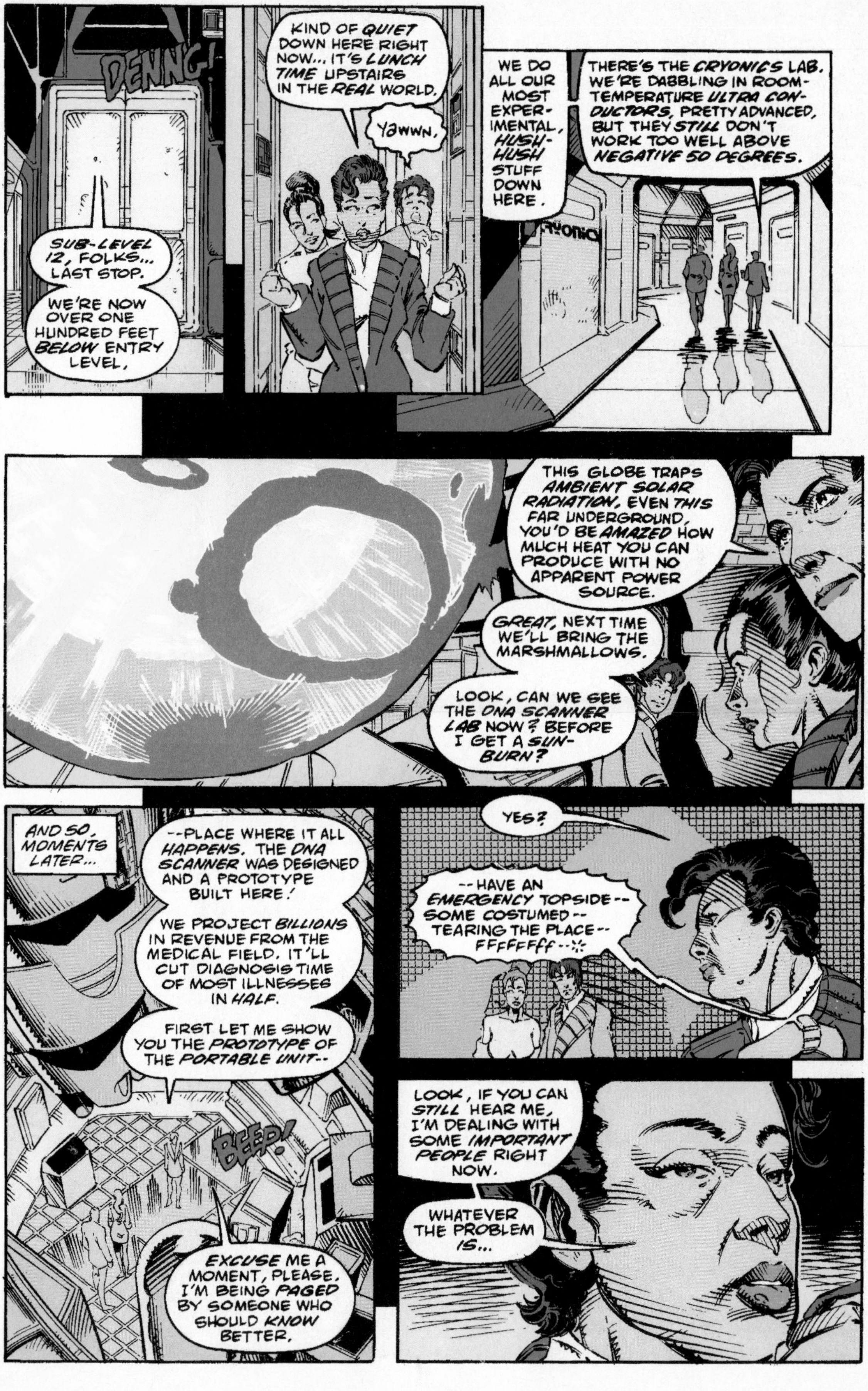

DENNG!
SUB-LEVEL 12, FOLKS... LAST STOP.
WE'RE NOW OVER ONE HUNDRED FEET BELOW ENTRY LEVEL.
KIND OF QUIET DOWN HERE RIGHT NOW... IT'S LUNCH TIME UPSTAIRS IN THE REAL WORLD.
YAWWN.
WE DO ALL OUR MOST EXPERIMENTAL, HUSH-HUSH STUFF DOWN HERE.
THERE'S THE CRYONICS LAB. WE'RE DABBLING IN ROOM-TEMPERATURE ULTRA CONDUCTORS, PRETTY ADVANCED, BUT THEY STILL DON'T WORK TOO WELL ABOVE NEGATIVE 50 DEGREES.
CRYONIC
THIS GLOBE TRAPS AMBIENT SOLAR RADIATION, EVEN THIS FAR UNDERGROUND. YOU'D BE AMAZED HOW MUCH HEAT YOU CAN PRODUCE WITH NO APPARENT POWER SOURCE.
GREAT, NEXT TIME WE'LL BRING THE MARSHMALLOWS.
LOOK, CAN WE SEE THE DNA SCANNER LAB NOW? BEFORE I GET A SUNBURN?
AND SO, MOMENTS LATER...
--PLACE WHERE IT ALL HAPPENS. THE DNA SCANNER WAS DESIGNED AND A PROTOTYPE BUILT HERE!
WE PROJECT BILLIONS IN REVENUE FROM THE MEDICAL FIELD. IT'LL CUT DIAGNOSIS TIME OF MOST ILLNESSES IN HALF.
FIRST LET ME SHOW YOU THE PROTOTYPE OF THE PORTABLE UNIT--
BEEP!
EXCUSE ME A MOMENT, PLEASE. I'M BEING PAGED BY SOMEONE WHO SHOULD KNOW BETTER.
YES?
--HAVE AN EMERGENCY TOPSIDE-- SOME COSTUMED-- TEARING THE PLACE-- FFFFFFFF--
LOOK, IF YOU CAN STILL HEAR ME, I'M DEALING WITH SOME IMPORTANT PEOPLE RIGHT NOW.
WHATEVER THE PROBLEM IS...

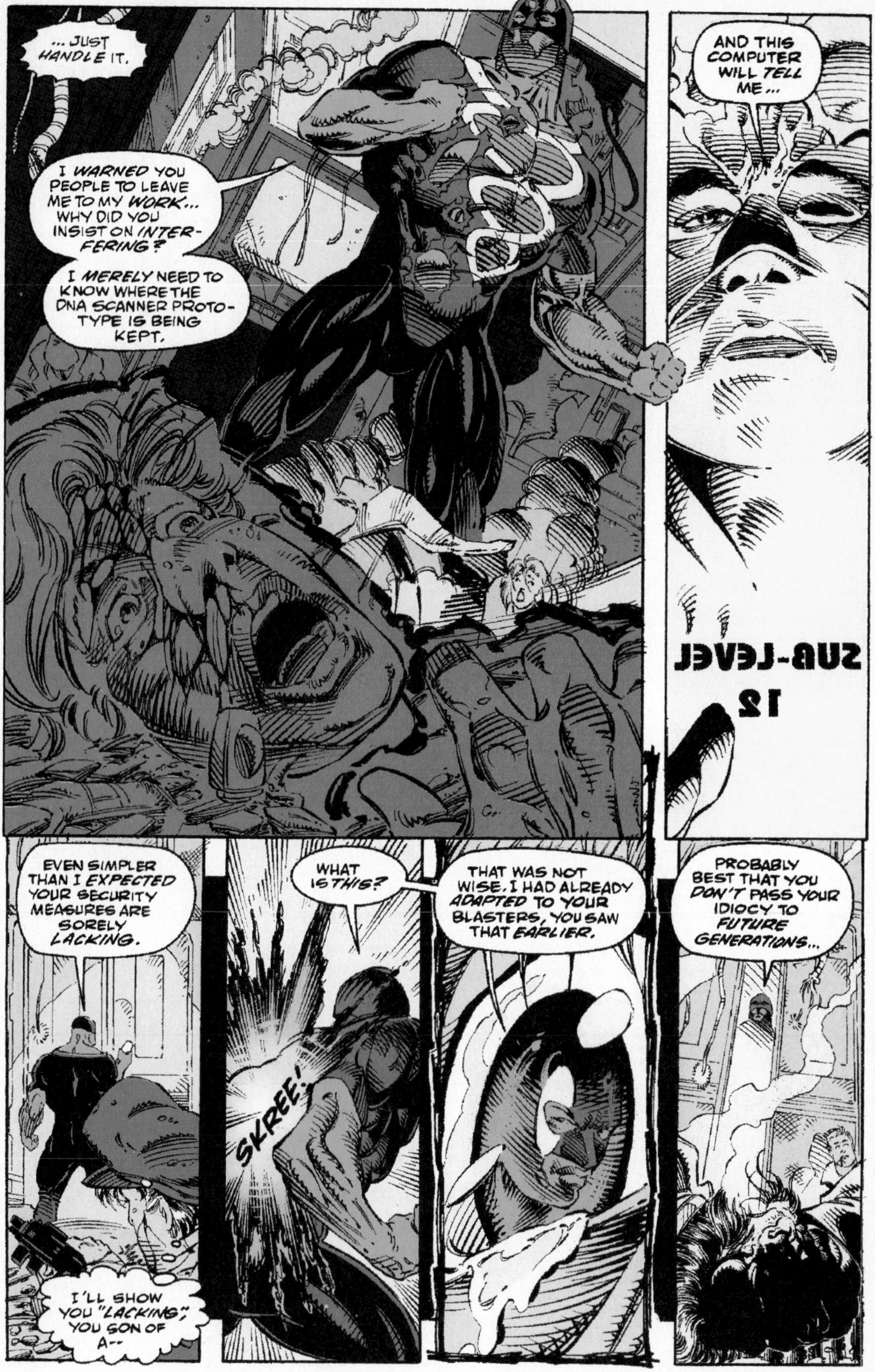

...JUST HANDLE IT.
I WARNED YOU PEOPLE TO LEAVE ME TO MY WORK... WHY DID YOU INSIST ON INTER-FERING?
I MERELY NEED TO KNOW WHERE THE DNA SCANNER PROTO-TYPE IS BEING KEPT.
AND THIS COMPUTER WILL TELL ME...
SUB-LEVEL 12
EVEN SIMPLER THAN I EXPECTED YOUR SECURITY MEASURES ARE SORELY LACKING.
I'LL SHOW YOU "LACKING," YOU SON OF A--
WHAT IS THIS?
SKREE!
THAT WAS NOT WISE. I HAD ALREADY ADAPTED TO YOUR BLASTERS, YOU SAW THAT EARLIER.
PROBABLY BEST THAT YOU DON'T PASS YOUR IDIOCY TO FUTURE GENERATIONS...

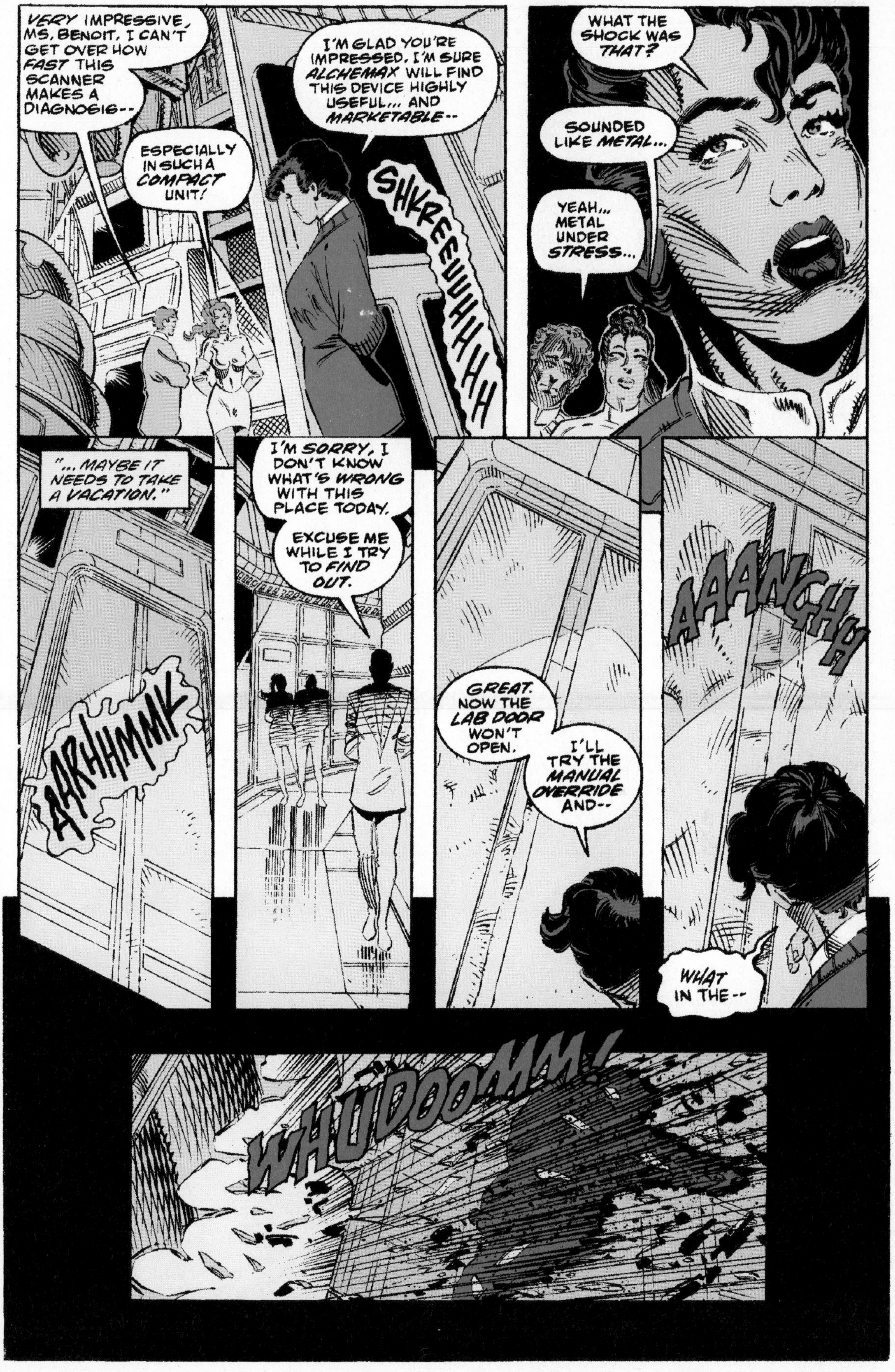
VERY IMPRESSIVE, MS. BENOIT. I CAN'T GET OVER HOW FAST THIS SCANNER MAKES A DIAGNOSIS--
ESPECIALLY IN SUCH A COMPACT UNIT!
I'M GLAD YOU'RE IMPRESSED. I'M SURE ALCHEMAX WILL FIND THIS DEVICE HIGHLY USEFUL... AND MARKETABLE--
SHKREEUUHHHHH
WHAT THE SHOCK WAS THAT?
SOUNDED LIKE METAL...
YEAH... METAL UNDER STRESS...
"...MAYBE IT NEEDS TO TAKE A VACATION."
AARHHMMK
I'M SORRY, I DON'T KNOW WHAT'S WRONG WITH THIS PLACE TODAY.
EXCUSE ME WHILE I TRY TO FIND OUT.
GREAT. NOW THE LAB DOOR WON'T OPEN.
I'LL TRY THE MANUAL OVERRIDE AND--
AAANGHH
WHAT IN THE--
WHUDOOMM!

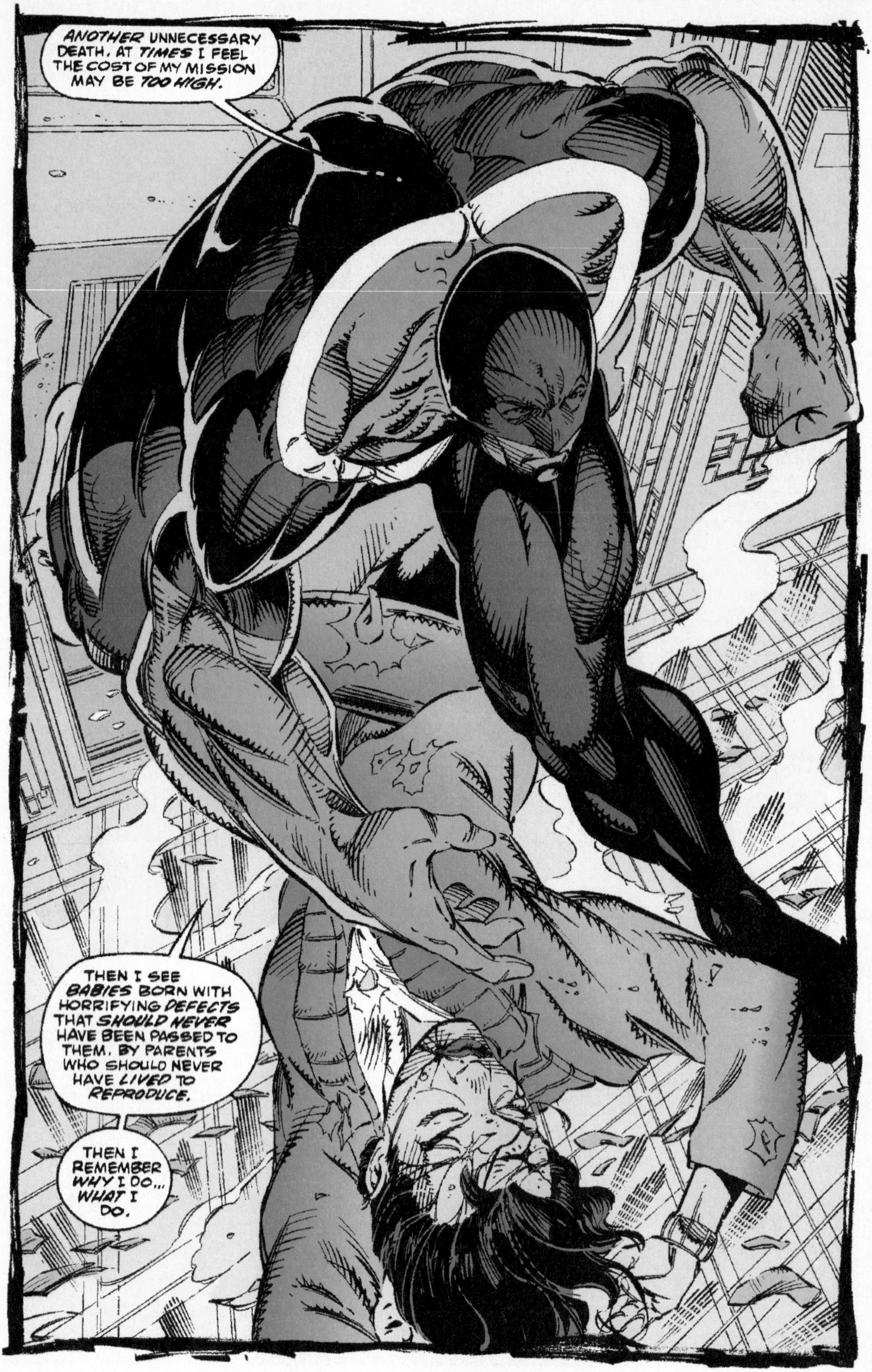
ANOTHER UNNECESSARY DEATH. AT TIMES I FEEL THE COST OF MY MISSION MAY BE TOO HIGH.
THEN I SEE BABIES BORN WITH HORRIFYING DEFECTS THAT SHOULD NEVER HAVE BEEN PASSED TO THEM. BY PARENTS WHO SHOULD NEVER HAVE LIVED TO REPRODUCE.
THEN I REMEMBER WHY I DO... WHAT I DO.

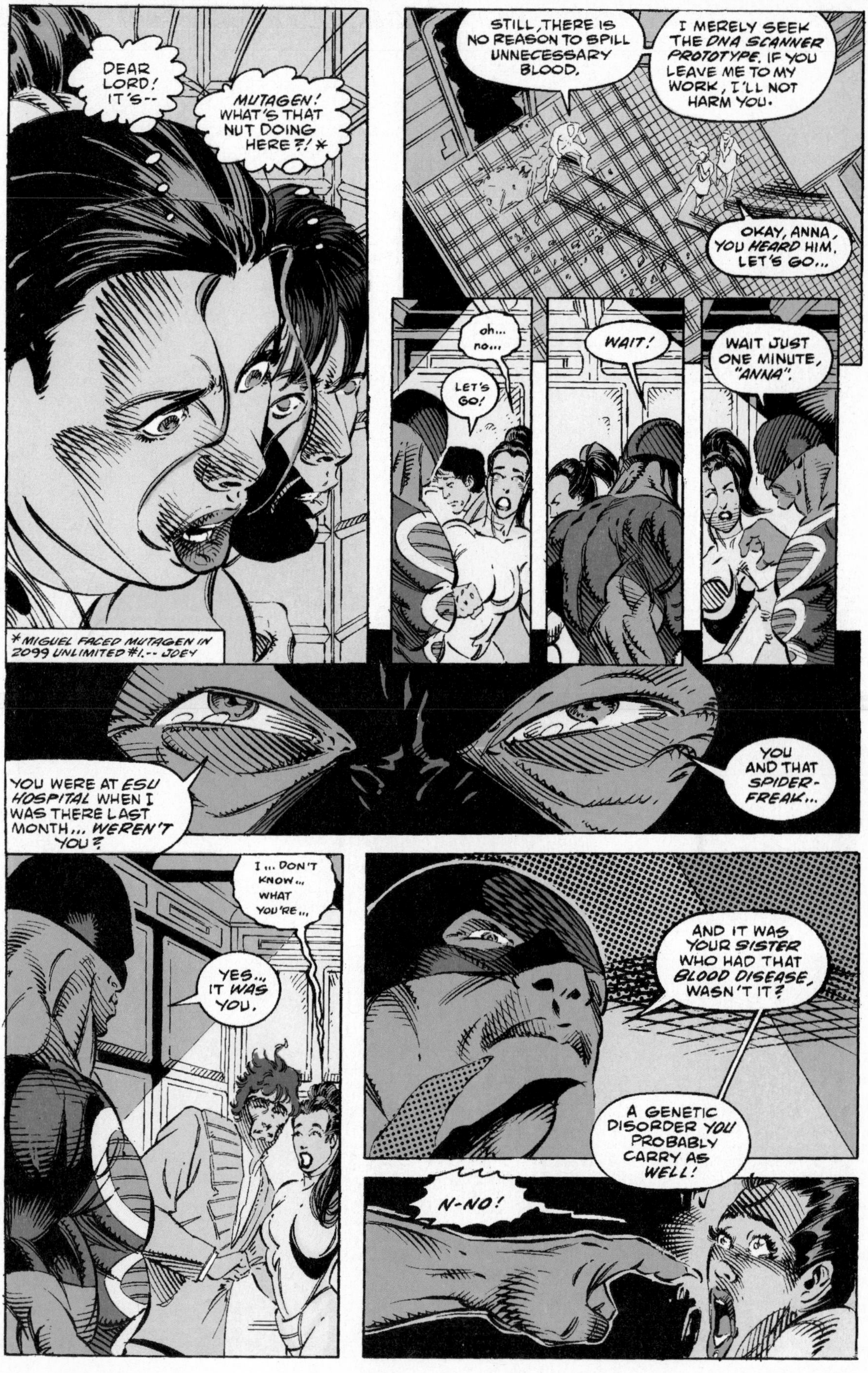
DEAR LORD! IT'S--
MUTAGEN! WHAT'S THAT NUT DOING HERE?!*
*MIGUEL FACED MUTAGEN IN 2099 UNLIMITED #1.-- JOEY
STILL, THERE IS NO REASON TO SPILL UNNECESSARY BLOOD.
I MERELY SEEK THE DNA SCANNER PROTOTYPE. IF YOU LEAVE ME TO MY WORK, I'LL NOT HARM YOU.
OKAY, ANNA, YOU HEARD HIM. LET'S GO...
oh... no...
LET'S GO!
WAIT!
WAIT JUST ONE MINUTE, "ANNA".
YOU WERE AT ESU HOSPITAL WHEN I WAS THERE LAST MONTH... WEREN'T YOU?
YOU AND THAT SPIDER-FREAK...
I... DON'T KNOW... WHAT YOU'RE...
YES... IT WAS YOU.
AND IT WAS YOUR SISTER WHO HAD THAT BLOOD DISEASE, WASN'T IT?
A GENETIC DISORDER YOU PROBABLY CARRY AS WELL!
N-NO!

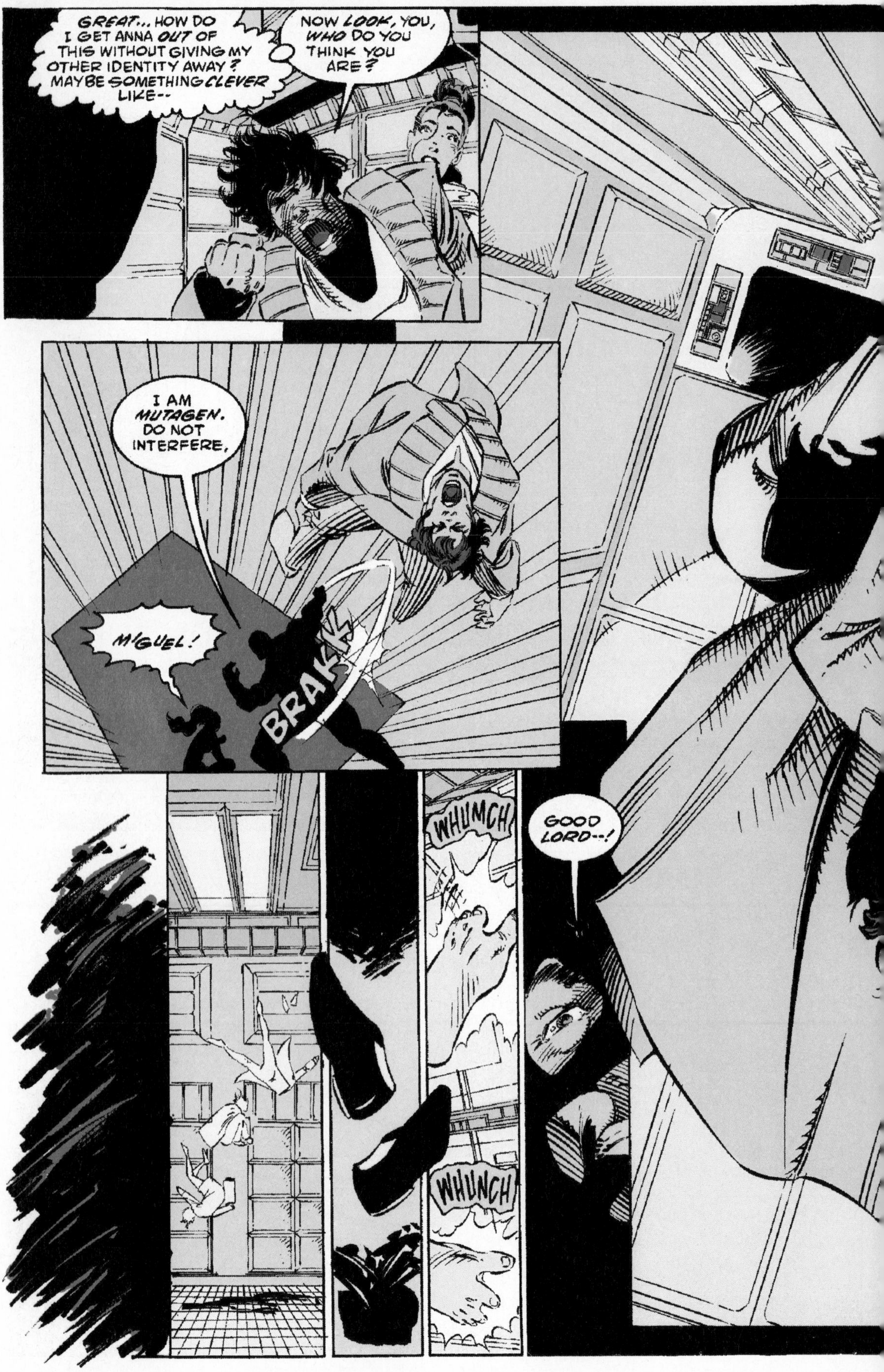
GREAT... HOW DO I GET ANNA OUT OF THIS WITHOUT GIVING MY OTHER IDENTITY AWAY? MAYBE SOMETHING CLEVER LIKE--
NOW LOOK, YOU, WHO DO YOU THINK YOU ARE?
I AM MUTAGEN. DO NOT INTERFERE.
M'GUEL!
BRAK
WHUMCH
WHUNCH
GOOD LORD--!

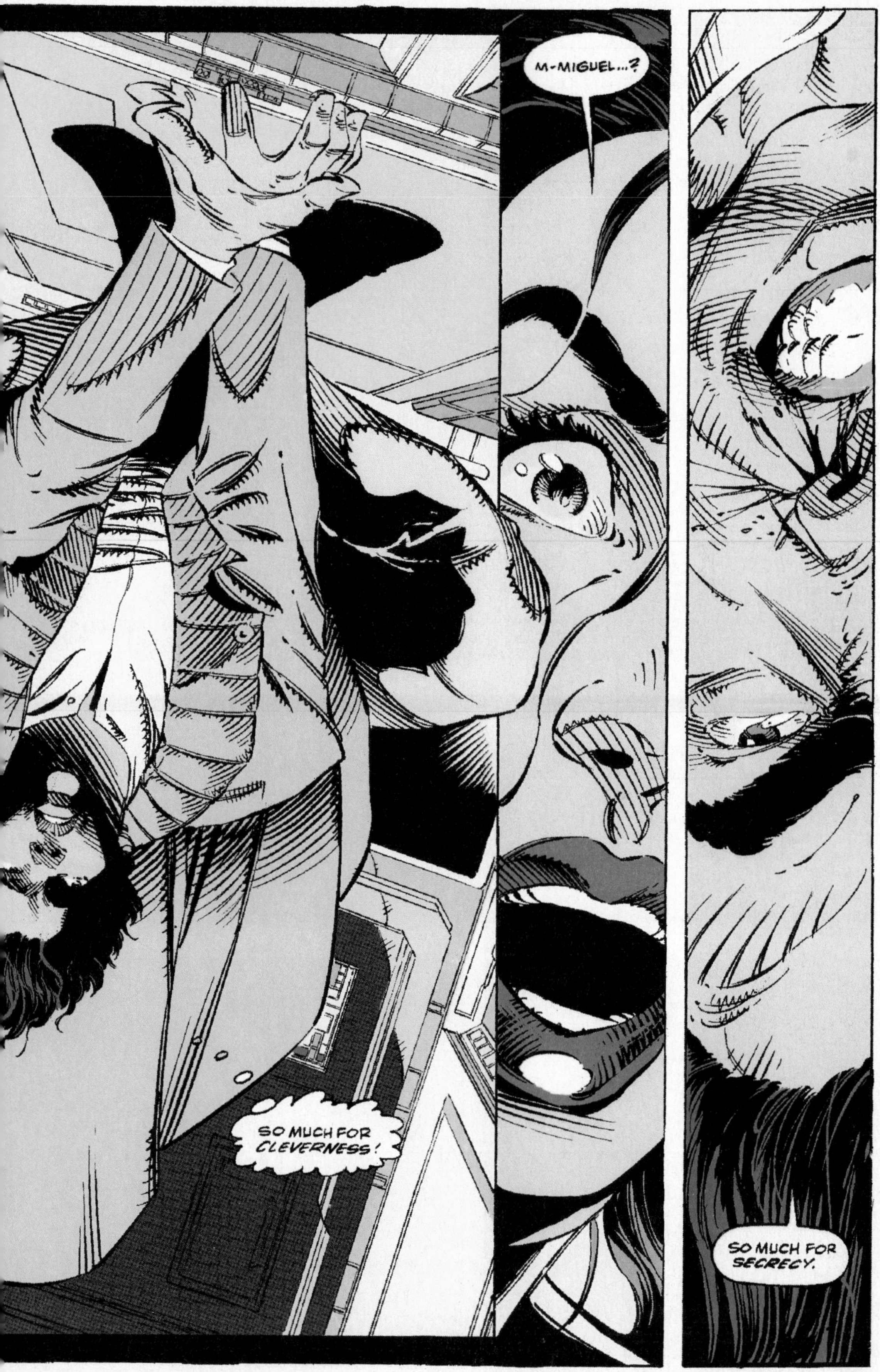

M-MIGUEL...?
SO MUCH FOR CLEVERNESS!
SO MUCH FOR SECRECY.

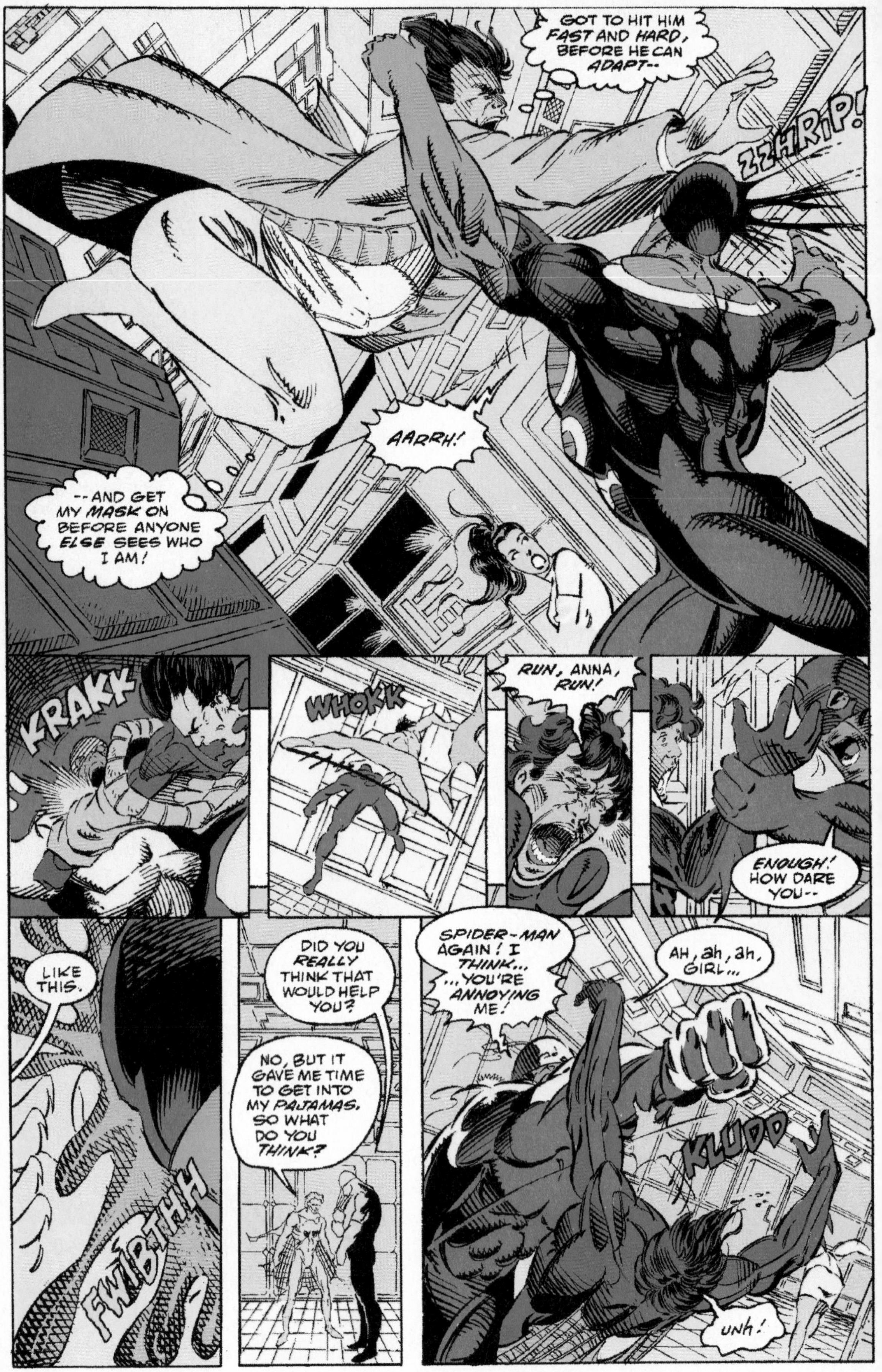
GOT TO HIT HIM FAST AND HARD, BEFORE HE CAN ADAPT--
ZZHRIP!
AARRH!
--AND GET MY MASK ON BEFORE ANYONE ELSE SEES WHO I AM!
KRAKK
WHOKK
RUN, ANNA, RUN!
ENOUGH! HOW DARE YOU--
LIKE THIS.
FWIBTHH
DID YOU REALLY THINK THAT WOULD HELP YOU?
NO, BUT IT GAVE ME TIME TO GET INTO MY PAJAMAS. SO WHAT DO YOU THINK?
SPIDER-MAN AGAIN! I THINK... ...YOU'RE ANNOYING ME!
AH, ah, ah, GIRL...
KLUDD
unh!

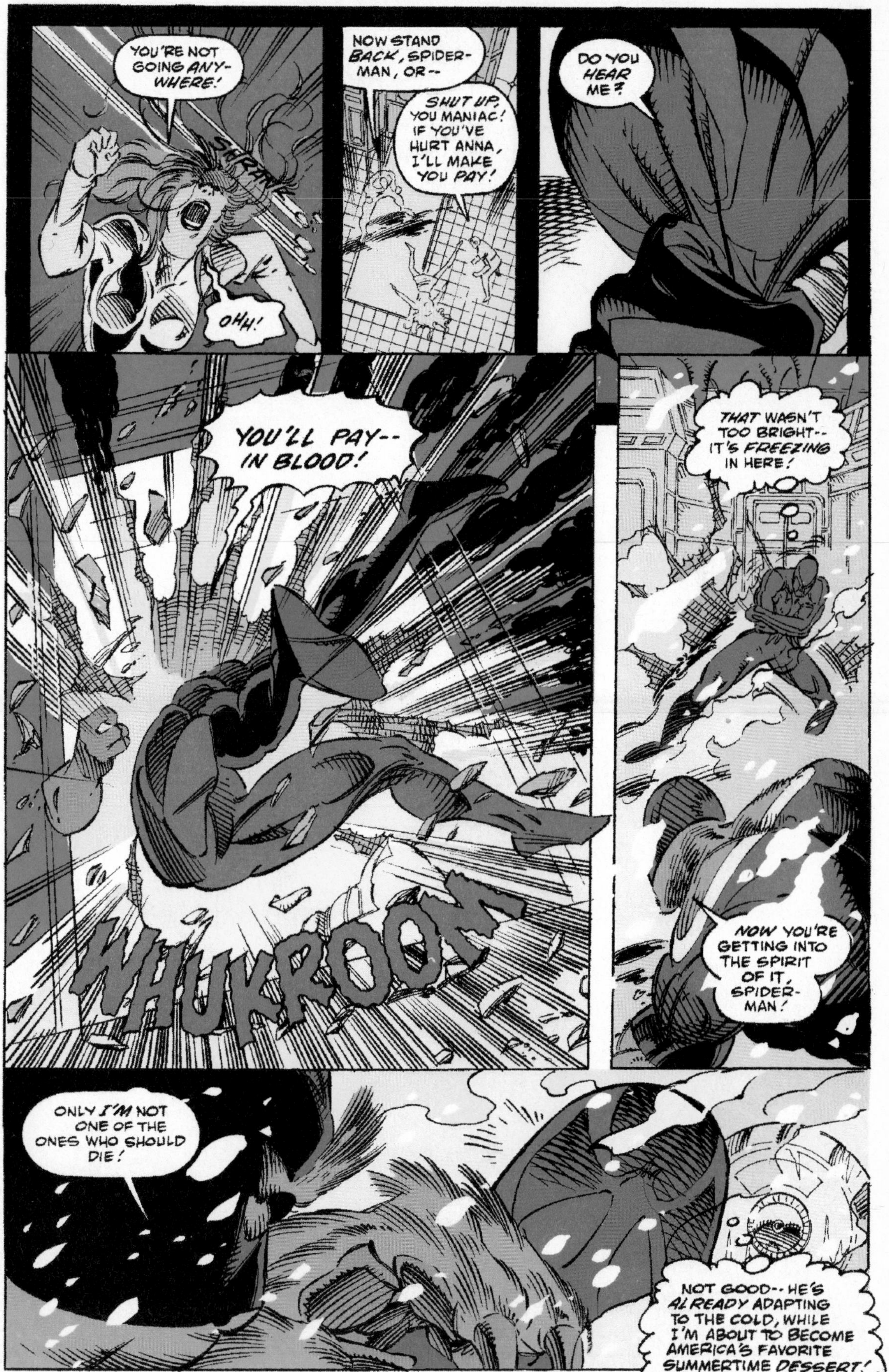
YOU'RE NOT GOING ANY-WHERE!
OHH!
NOW STAND BACK, SPIDER-MAN, OR--
SHUT UP, YOU MANIAC! IF YOU'VE HURT ANNA, I'LL MAKE YOU PAY!
DO YOU HEAR ME?
YOU'LL PAY-- IN BLOOD!
WHUKROOM
THAT WASN'T TOO BRIGHT-- IT'S FREEZING IN HERE!
NOW YOU'RE GETTING INTO THE SPIRIT OF IT, SPIDER-MAN!
ONLY I'M NOT ONE OF THE ONES WHO SHOULD DIE!
NOT GOOD-- HE'S ALREADY ADAPTING TO THE COLD, WHILE I'M ABOUT TO BECOME AMERICA'S FAVORITE SUMMERTIME DESSERT!

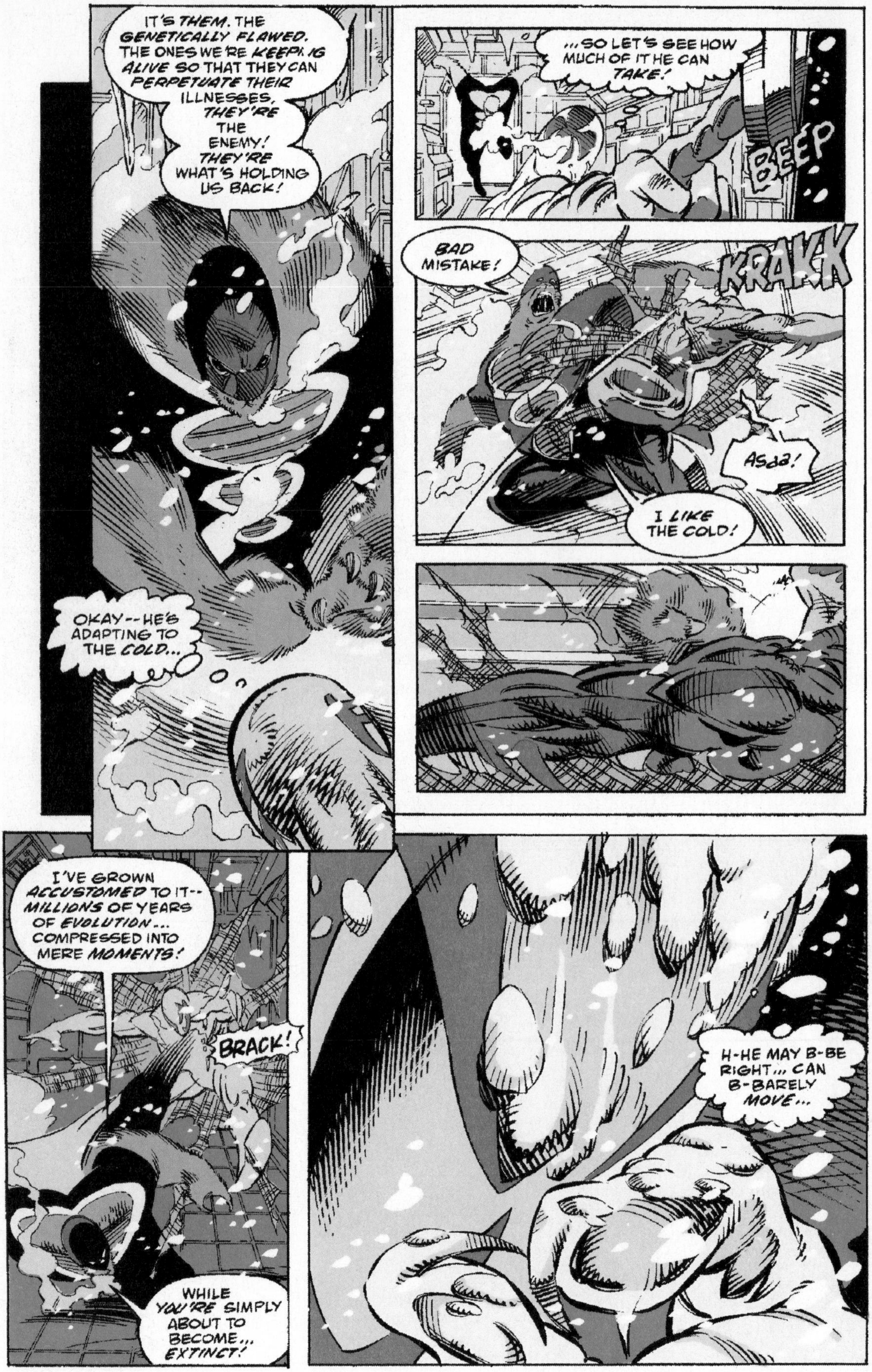
IT'S THEM. THE GENETICALLY FLAWED. THE ONES WE'RE KEEPING ALIVE SO THAT THEY CAN PERPETUATE THEIR ILLNESSES. THEY'RE THE ENEMY! THEY'RE WHAT'S HOLDING US BACK!
...SO LET'S SEE HOW MUCH OF IT HE CAN TAKE!
BEEP
BAD MISTAKE!
KRAKK
ASAA!
I LIKE THE COLD!
OKAY--HE'S ADAPTING TO THE COLD...
I'VE GROWN ACCUSTOMED TO IT-- MILLIONS OF YEARS OF EVOLUTION... COMPRESSED INTO MERE MOMENTS!
BRACK!
WHILE YOU'RE SIMPLY ABOUT TO BECOME... EXTINCT!
H-HE MAY B-BE RIGHT... CAN B-BARELY MOVE...

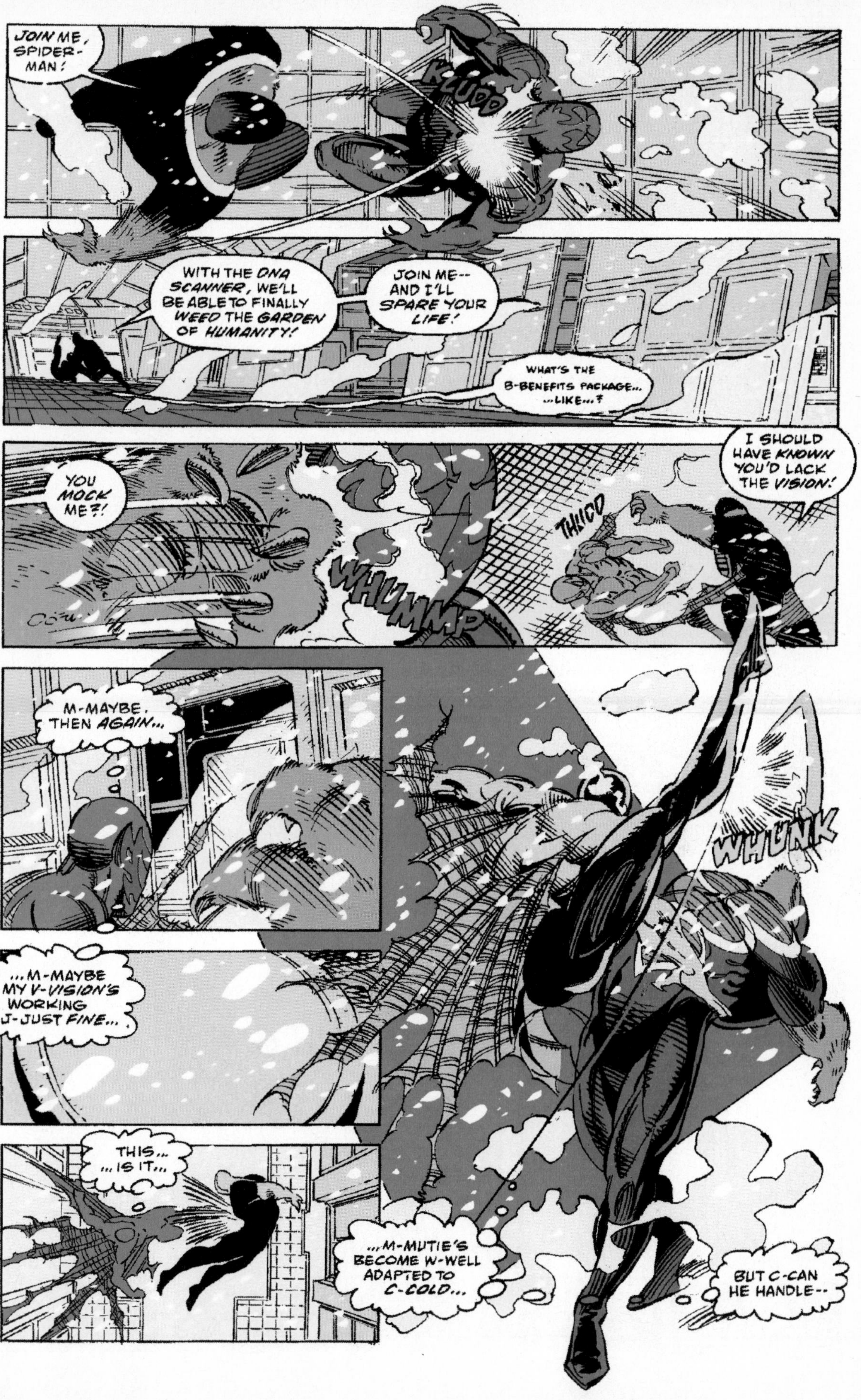

JOIN ME, SPIDER-MAN!
KLUDD
WITH THE DNA SCANNER, WE'LL BE ABLE TO FINALLY WEED THE GARDEN OF HUMANITY!
JOIN ME-- AND I'LL SPARE YOUR LIFE!
WHAT'S THE B-BENEFITS PACKAGE... ...LIKE...?
YOU MOCK ME?!
WHUMMP
THWOD
I SHOULD HAVE KNOWN YOU'D LACK THE VISION!
M-MAYBE, THEN AGAIN...
...M-MAYBE MY V-VISION'S WORKING J-JUST FINE...
WHUNK
THIS... ...IS IT...
...M-MUTIE'S BECOME W-WELL ADAPTED TO C-COLD...
BUT C-CAN HE HANDLE--

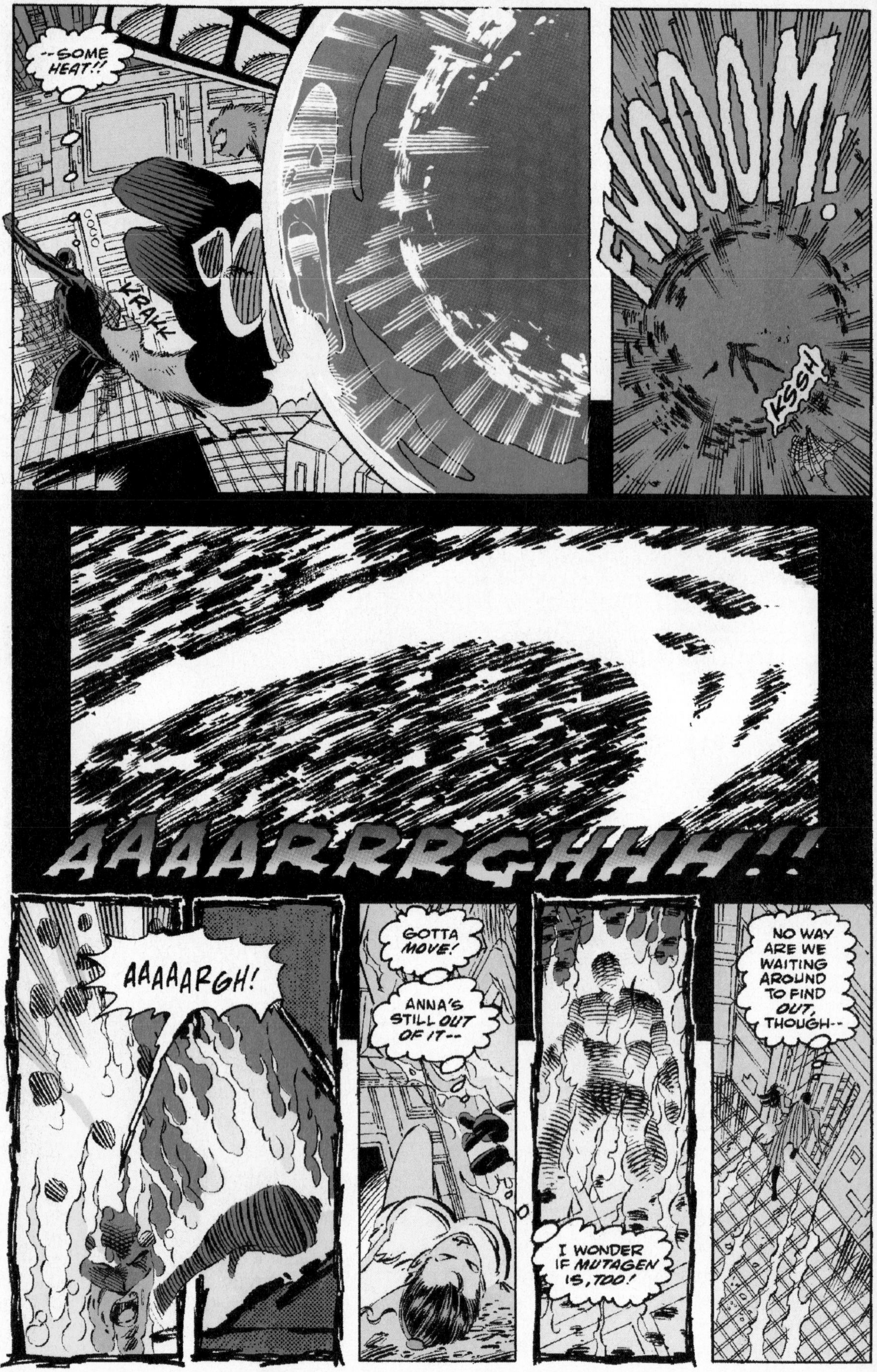
--SOME HEAT!!
KRAKK
FWOOOM!
KSSH
AAAARRRGHHH!!
AAAAARGH!
GOTTA MOVE!
ANNA'S STILL OUT OF IT--
I WONDER IF MUTAGEN IS, TOO!
NO WAY ARE WE WAITING AROUND TO FIND OUT, THOUGH--

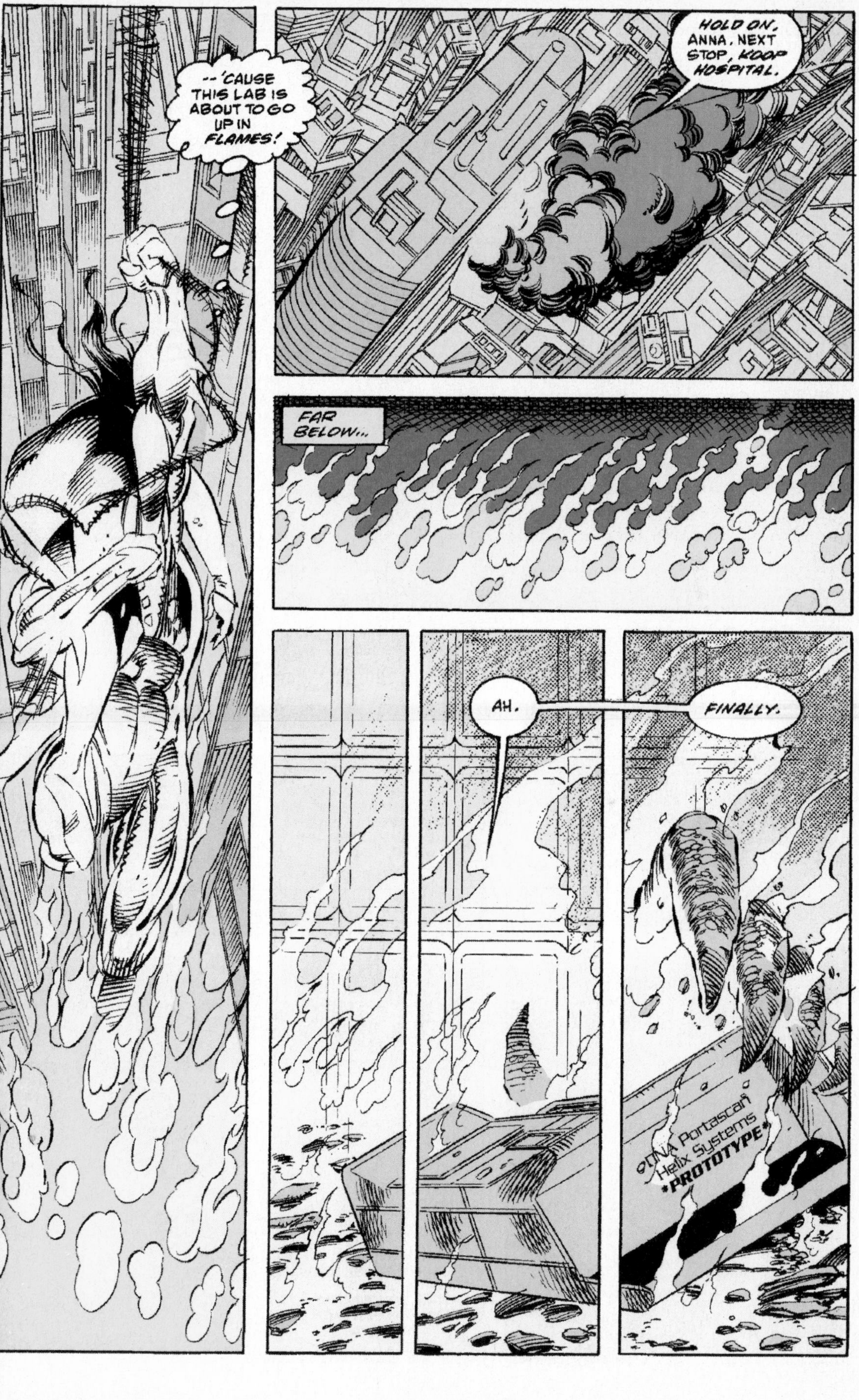
--'CAUSE THIS LAB IS ABOUT TO GO UP IN FLAMES!
HOLD ON, ANNA, NEXT STOP, KOOP HOSPITAL.
FAR BELOW...
AH.
FINALLY.
DNA Portascan
Helix Systems
PROTOTYPE

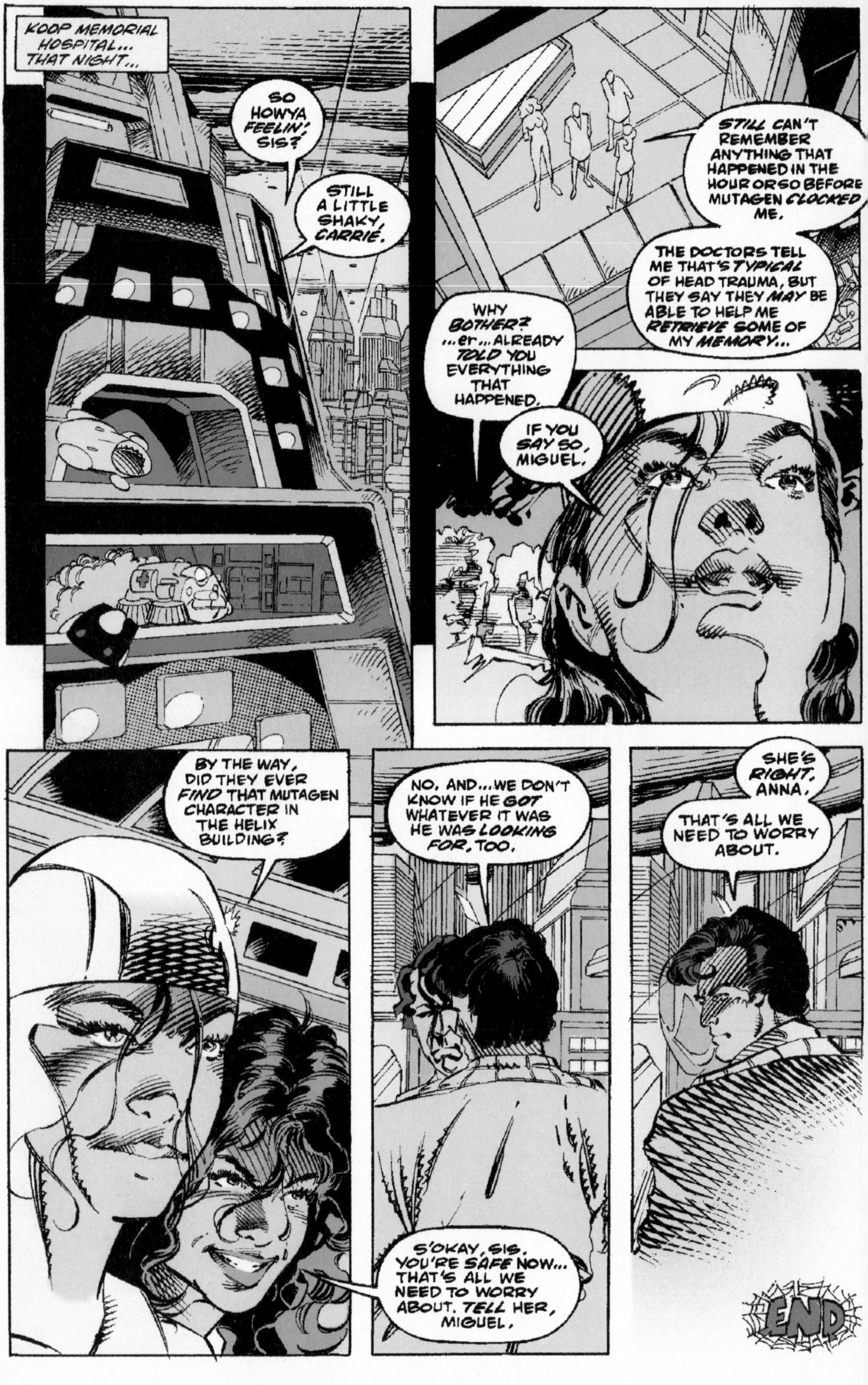

KOOP MEMORIAL HOSPITAL... THAT NIGHT...
SO HOWYA FEELIN', SIS?
STILL A LITTLE SHAKY, CARRIE.
STILL CAN'T REMEMBER ANYTHING THAT HAPPENED IN THE HOUR OR SO BEFORE MUTAGEN CLOCKED ME.
THE DOCTORS TELL ME THAT'S TYPICAL OF HEAD TRAUMA, BUT THEY SAY THEY MAY BE ABLE TO HELP ME RETRIEVE SOME OF MY MEMORY...
WHY BOTHER? ...er... ALREADY TOLD YOU EVERYTHING THAT HAPPENED.
IF YOU SAY SO, MIGUEL.
BY THE WAY, DID THEY EVER FIND THAT MUTAGEN CHARACTER IN THE HELIX BUILDING?
S'OKAY, SIS. YOU'RE SAFE NOW... THAT'S ALL WE NEED TO WORRY ABOUT. TELL HER, MIGUEL.
NO. AND... WE DON'T KNOW IF HE GOT WHATEVER IT WAS HE WAS LOOKING FOR, TOO.
SHE'S RIGHT, ANNA.
THAT'S ALL WE NEED TO WORRY ABOUT.
END

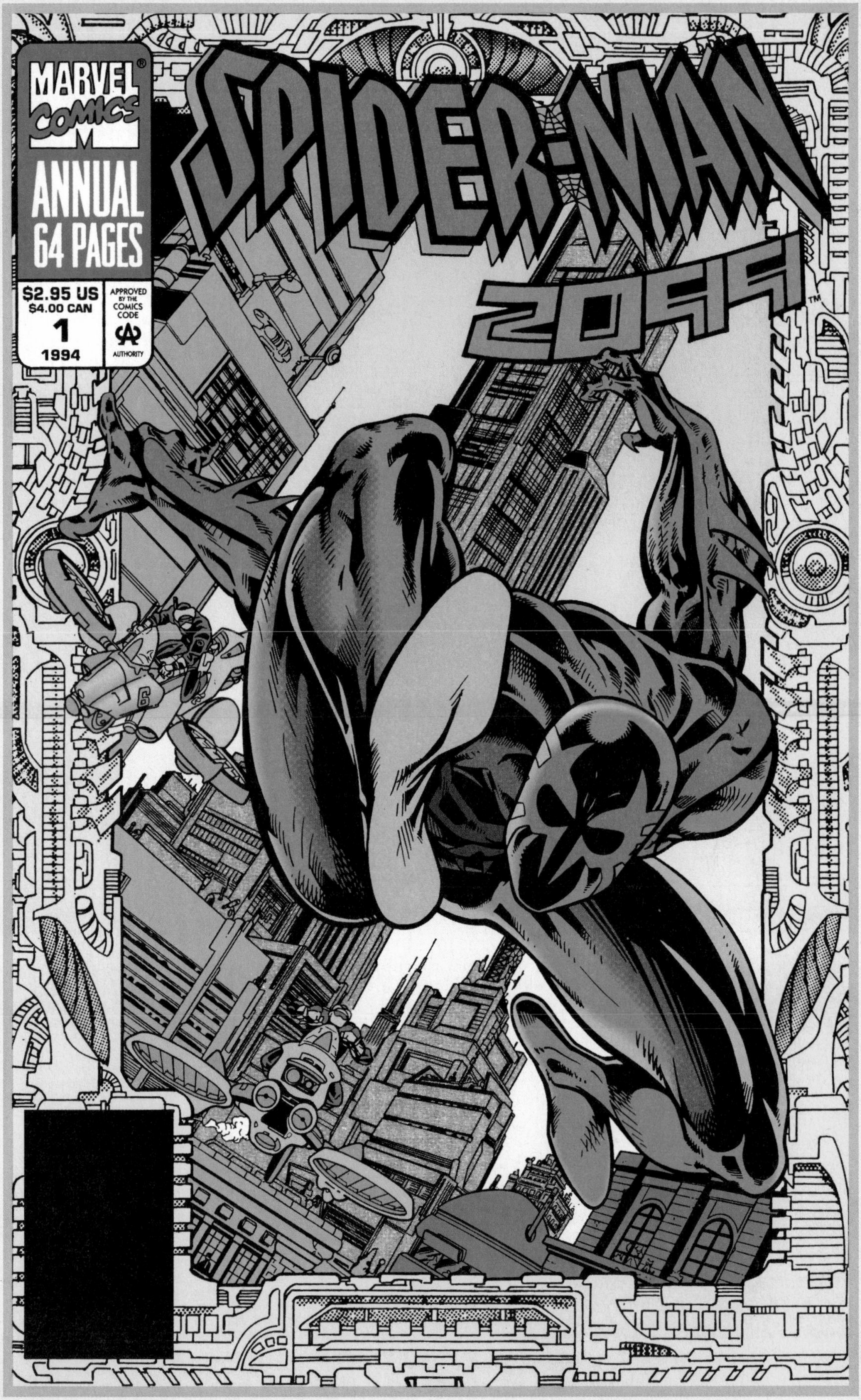
MARVEL COMICS
ANNUAL
64 PAGES
$2.95 US
$4.00 CAN
1
1994
APPROVED BY THE COMICS CODE AUTHORITY
SPIDER-MAN
2099

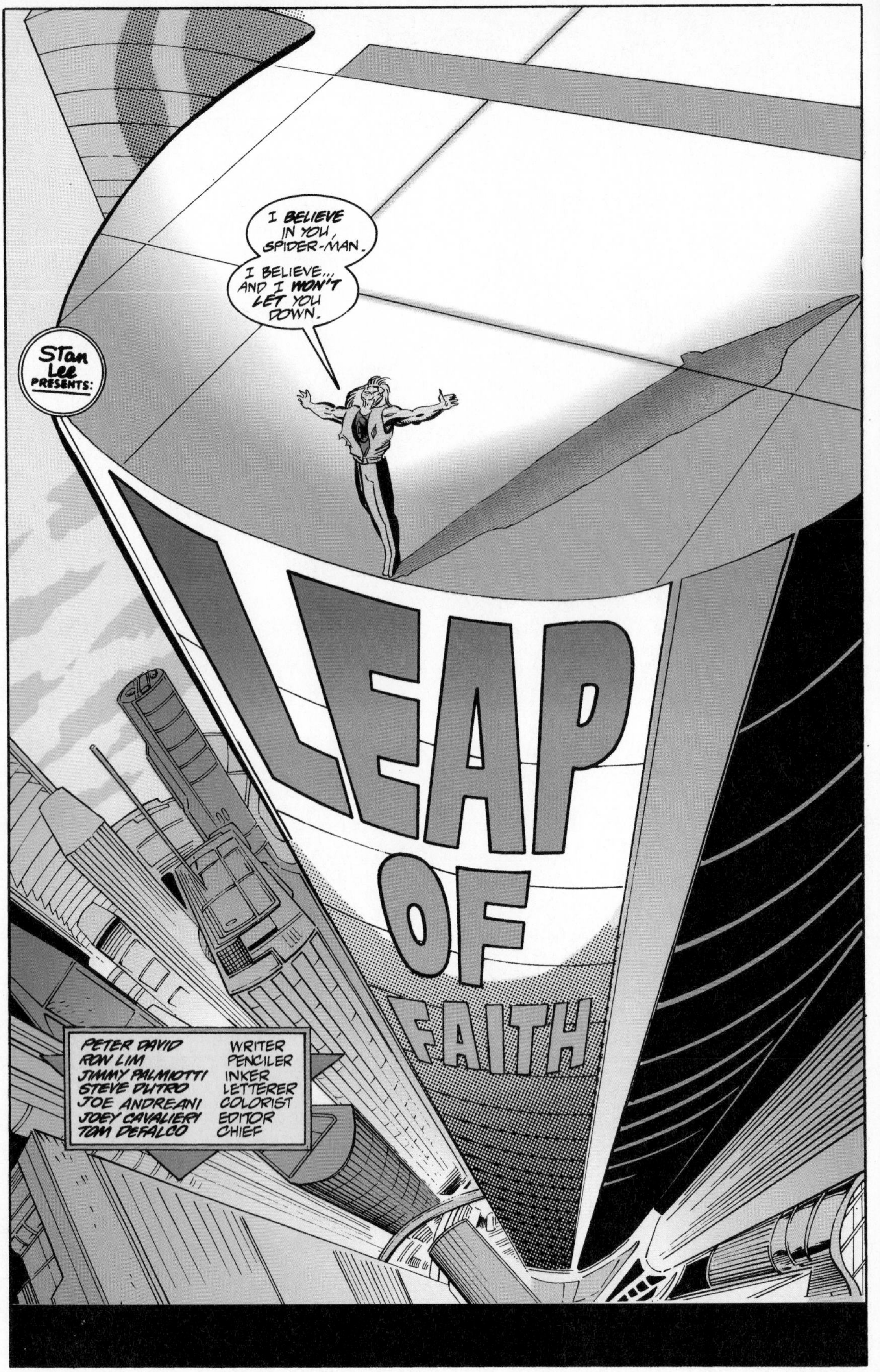
I BELIEVE IN YOU, SPIDER-MAN.
I BELIEVE... AND I WON'T LET YOU DOWN.
STan Lee PRESENTS:
LEAP OF FAITH
PETER DAVID WRITER
RON LIM PENCILER
JIMMY PALMIOTTI INKER
STEVE DUTRO LETTERER
JOE ANDREANI COLORIST
JOEY CAVALIERI EDITOR
TOM DEFALCO CHIEF

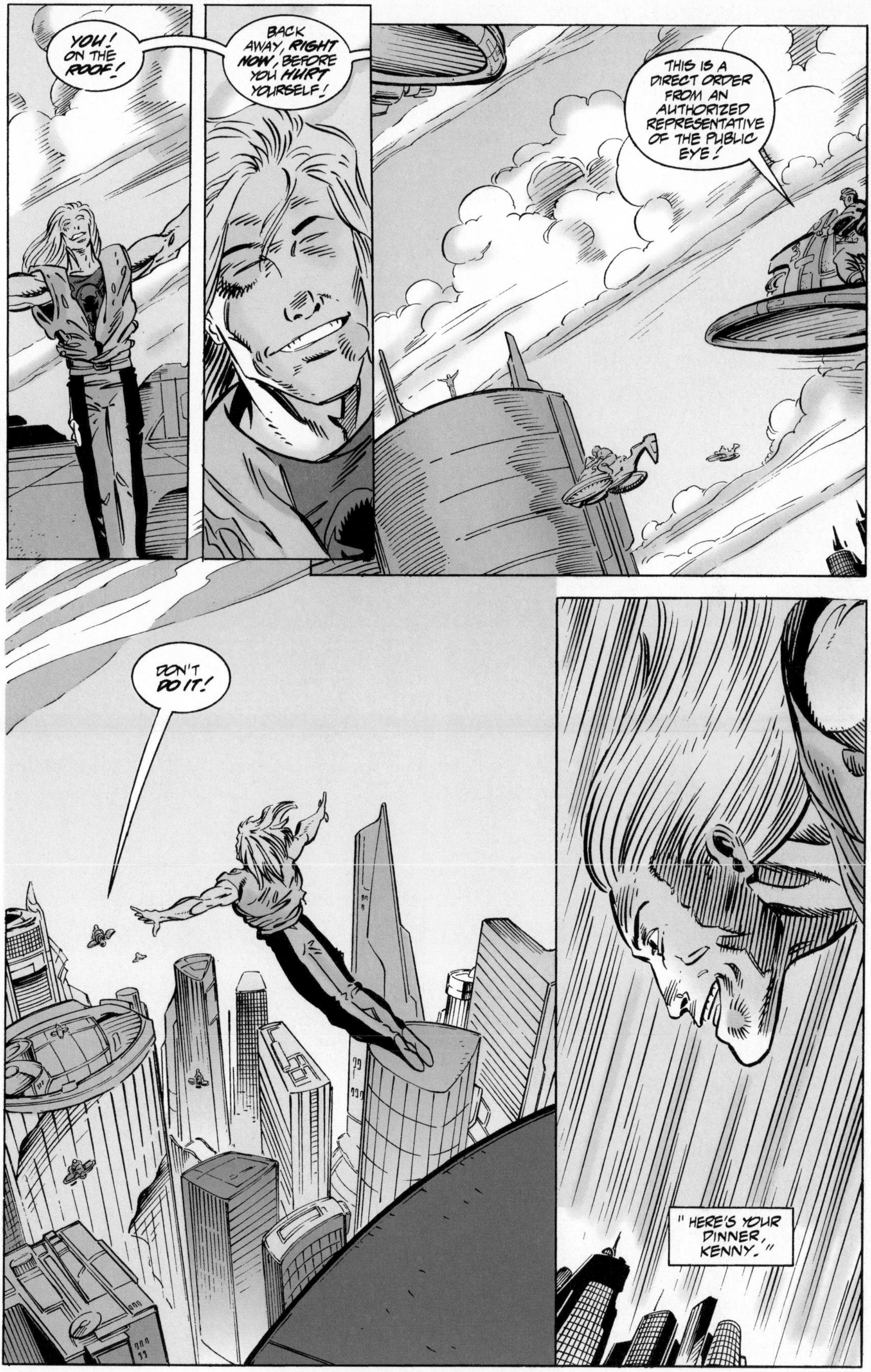
YOU! ON THE ROOF!
BACK AWAY, RIGHT NOW, BEFORE YOU HURT YOURSELF!
THIS IS A DIRECT ORDER FROM AN AUTHORIZED REPRESENTATIVE OF THE PUBLIC EYE!
DON'T DO IT!
"HERE'S YOUR DINNER, KENNY."

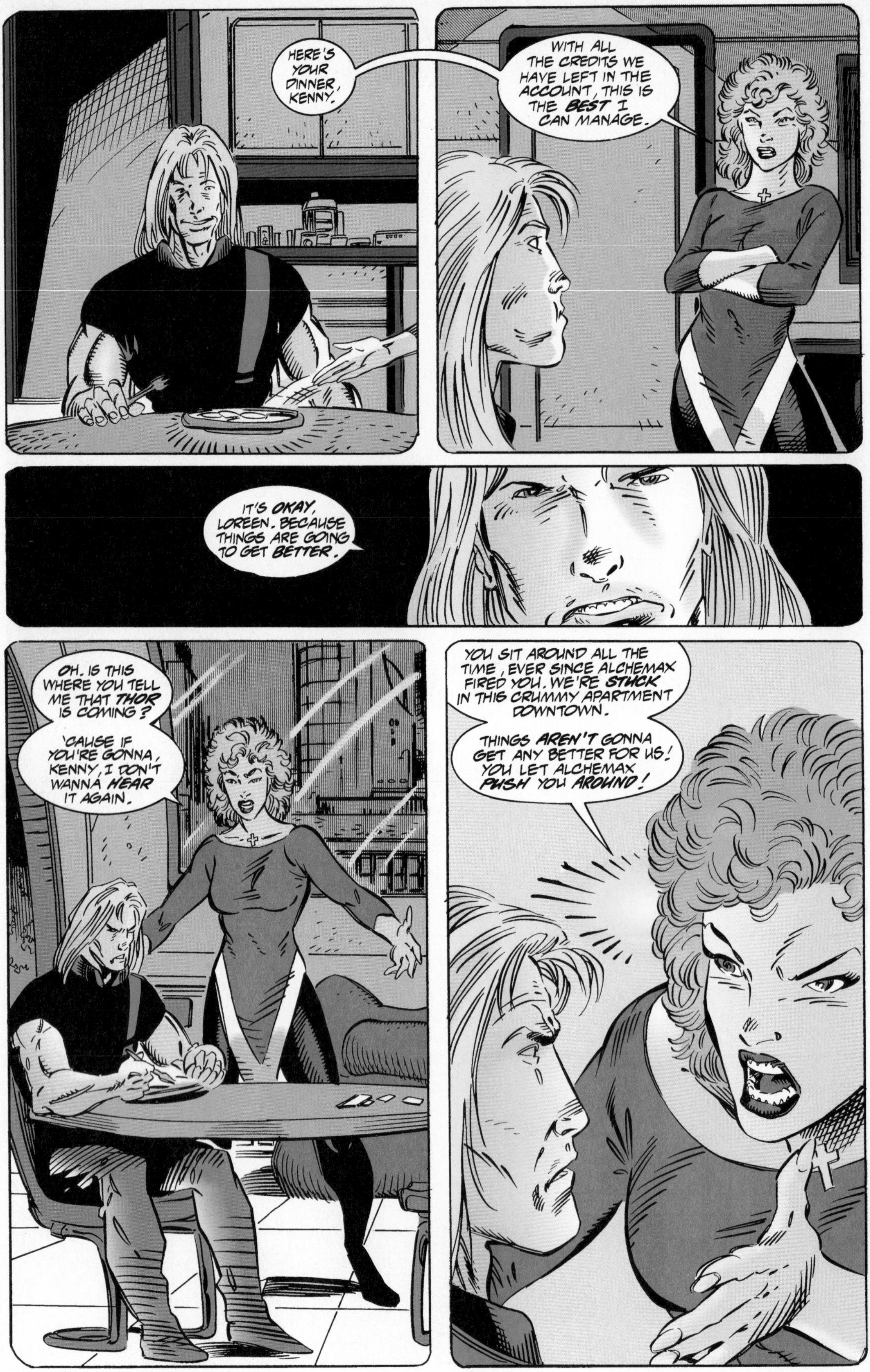
HERE'S YOUR DINNER, KENNY.
WITH ALL THE CREDITS WE HAVE LEFT IN THE ACCOUNT, THIS IS THE BEST I CAN MANAGE.
IT'S OKAY, LOREEN. BECAUSE THINGS ARE GOING TO GET BETTER.
OH. IS THIS WHERE YOU TELL ME THAT THOR IS COMING?
'CAUSE IF YOU'RE GONNA, KENNY, I DON'T WANNA HEAR IT AGAIN.
YOU SIT AROUND ALL THE TIME, EVER SINCE ALCHEMAX FIRED YOU. WE'RE STUCK IN THIS CRUMMY APARTMENT DOWNTOWN.
THINGS AREN'T GONNA GET ANY BETTER FOR US! YOU LET ALCHEMAX PUSH YOU AROUND!

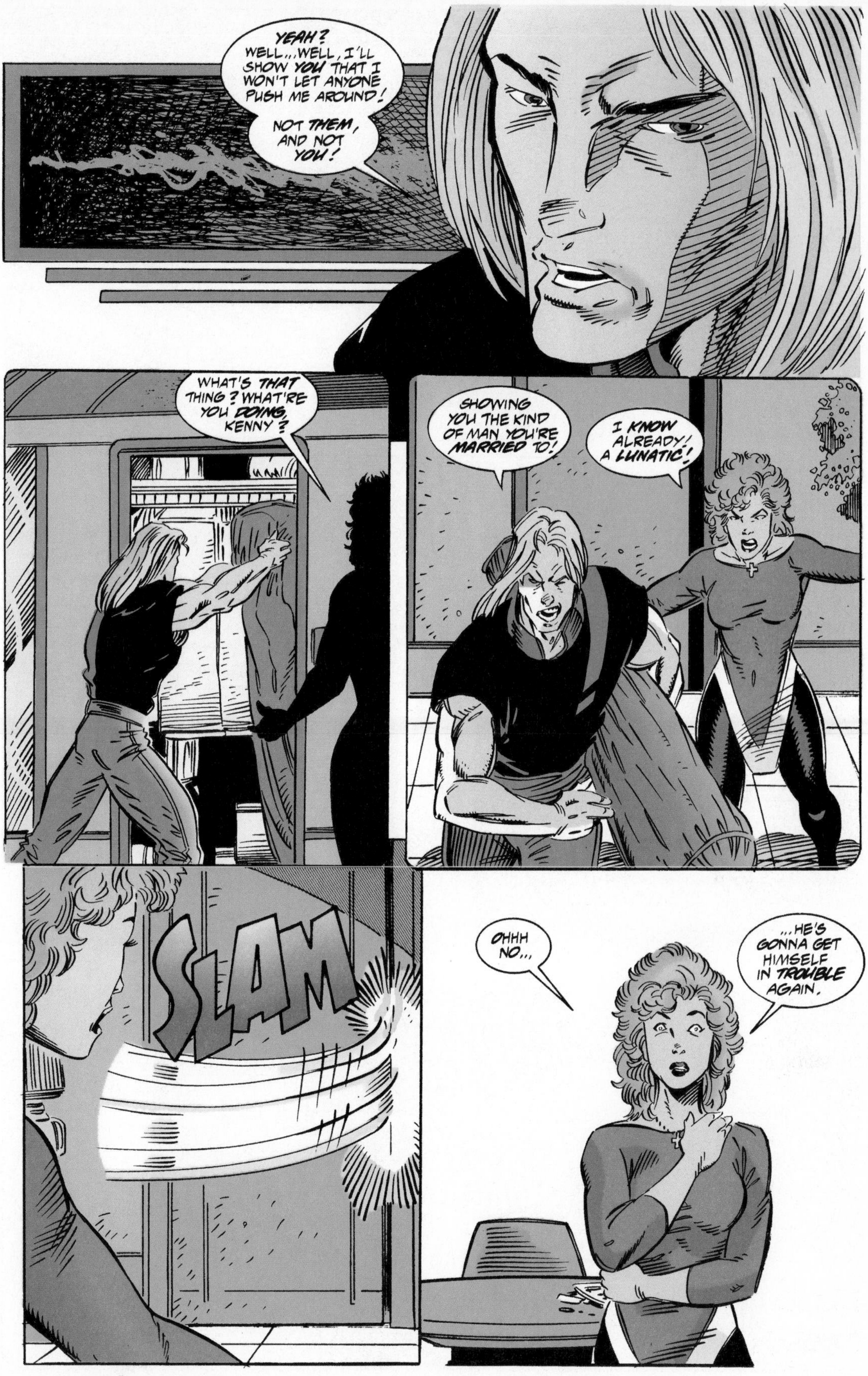
YEAH? WELL... WELL, I'LL SHOW YOU THAT I WON'T LET ANYONE PUSH ME AROUND!
NOT THEM, AND NOT YOU!
WHAT'S THAT THING? WHAT'RE YOU DOING, KENNY?
SHOWING YOU THE KIND OF MAN YOU'RE MARRIED TO!
I KNOW ALREADY! A LUNATIC!
SLAM
OHHH NO...
...HE'S GONNA GET HIMSELF IN TROUBLE AGAIN.

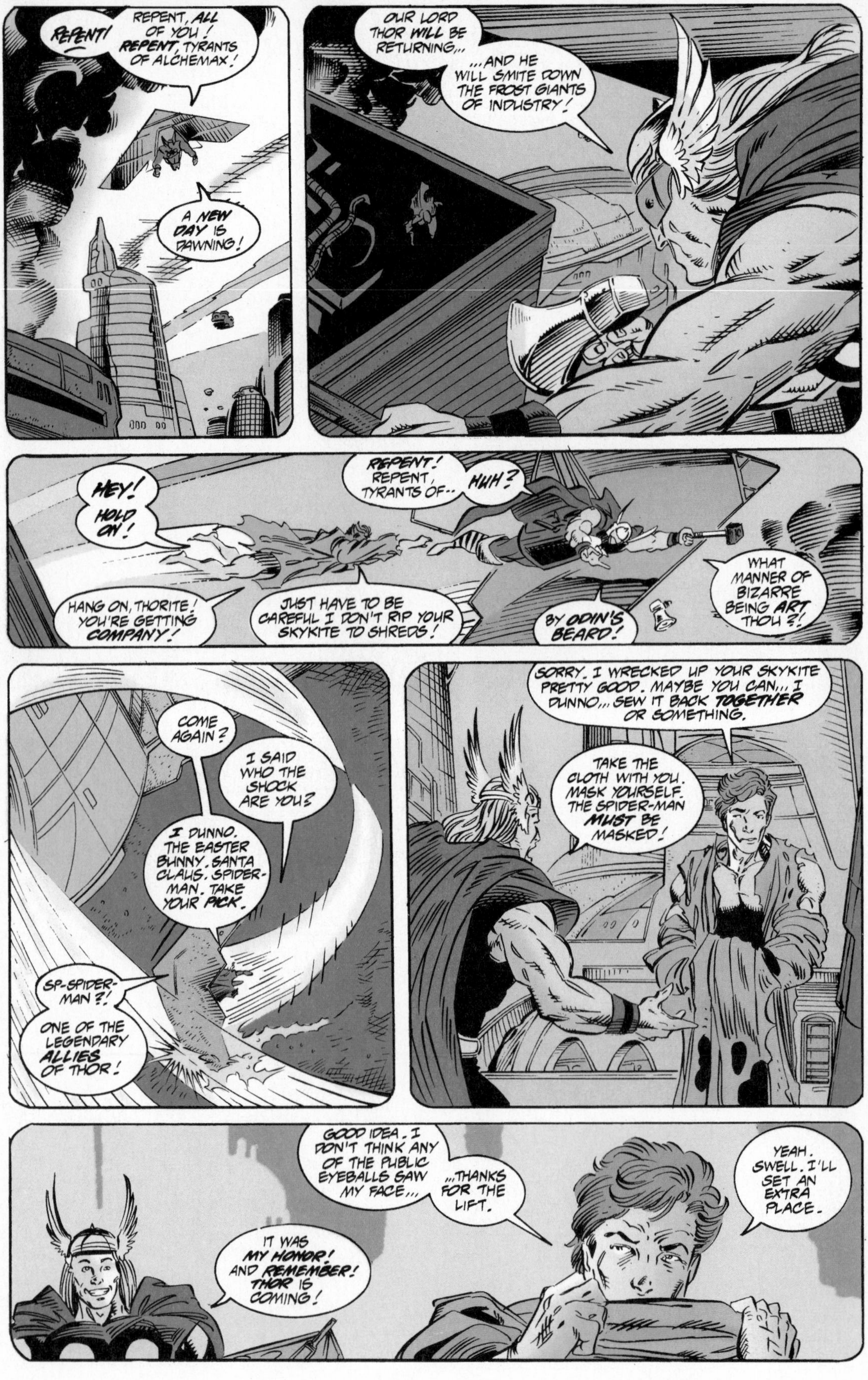
REPENT!
REPENT, ALL OF YOU! REPENT, TYRANTS OF ALCHEMAX!
A NEW DAY IS DAWNING!
OUR LORD THOR WILL BE RETURNING...
...AND HE WILL SMITE DOWN THE FROST GIANTS OF INDUSTRY!
HEY! HOLD ON!
HANG ON, THORITE! YOU'RE GETTING COMPANY!
JUST HAVE TO BE CAREFUL I DON'T RIP YOUR SKYKITE TO SHREDS!
REPENT! REPENT, TYRANTS OF--
HUH?
BY ODIN'S BEARD!
WHAT MANNER OF BIZARRE BEING ART THOU?!
COME AGAIN?
I SAID WHO THE SHOCK ARE YOU?
I DUNNO. THE EASTER BUNNY. SANTA CLAUS. SPIDER-MAN. TAKE YOUR PICK.
SP-SPIDER-MAN?!
ONE OF THE LEGENDARY ALLIES OF THOR!
SORRY. I WRECKED UP YOUR SKYKITE PRETTY GOOD. MAYBE YOU CAN... I DUNNO... SEW IT BACK TOGETHER OR SOMETHING.
TAKE THE CLOTH WITH YOU. MASK YOURSELF. THE SPIDER-MAN MUST BE MASKED!
GOOD IDEA. I DON'T THINK ANY OF THE PUBLIC EYEBALLS SAW MY FACE...
...THANKS FOR THE LIFT.
IT WAS MY HONOR! AND REMEMBER! THOR IS COMING!
YEAH. SWELL. I'LL SET AN EXTRA PLACE.

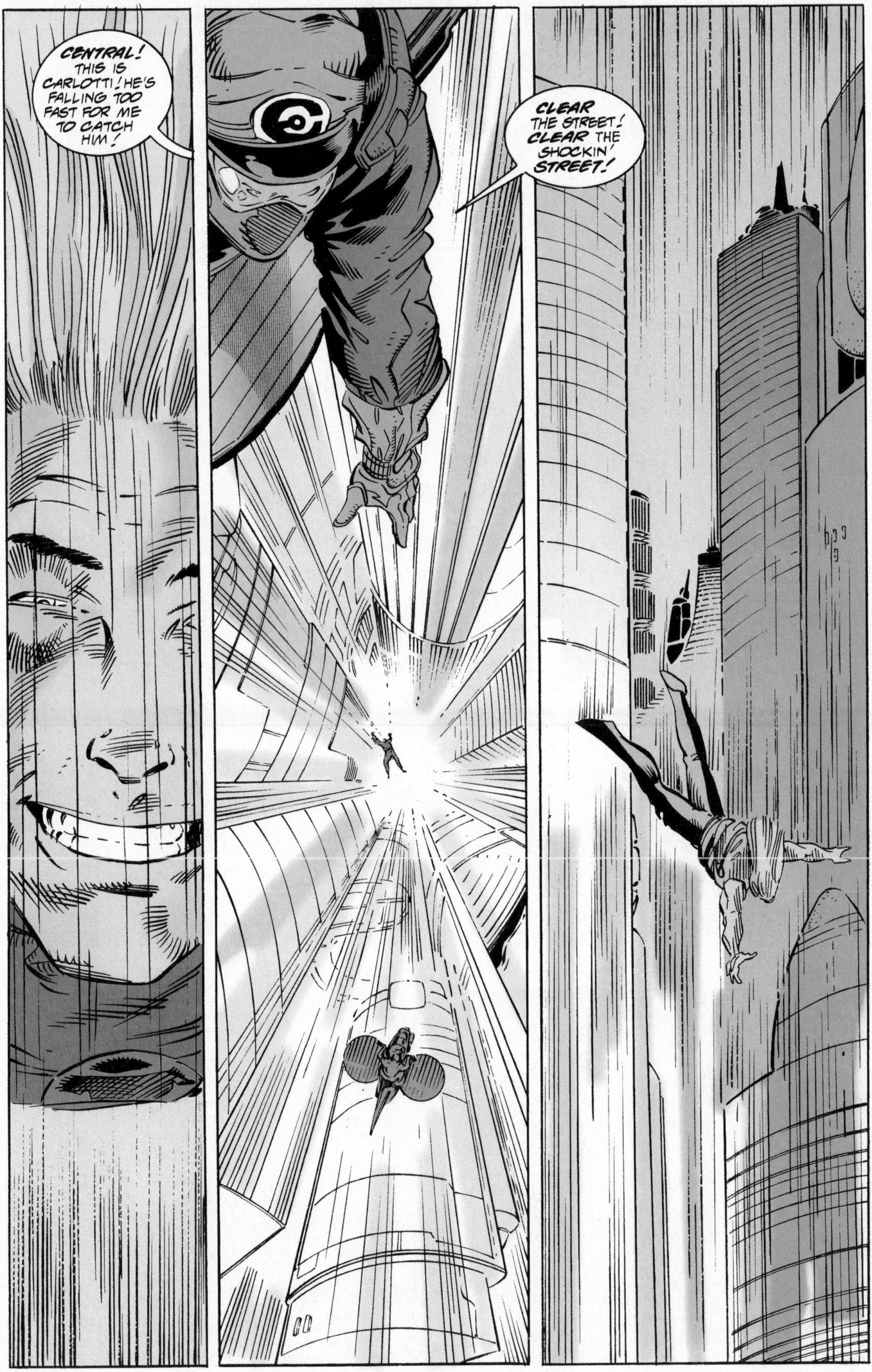
CENTRAL! THIS IS CARLOTTI! HE'S FALLING TOO FAST FOR ME TO CATCH HIM!
CLEAR THE STREET! CLEAR THE SHOCKIN' STREET!

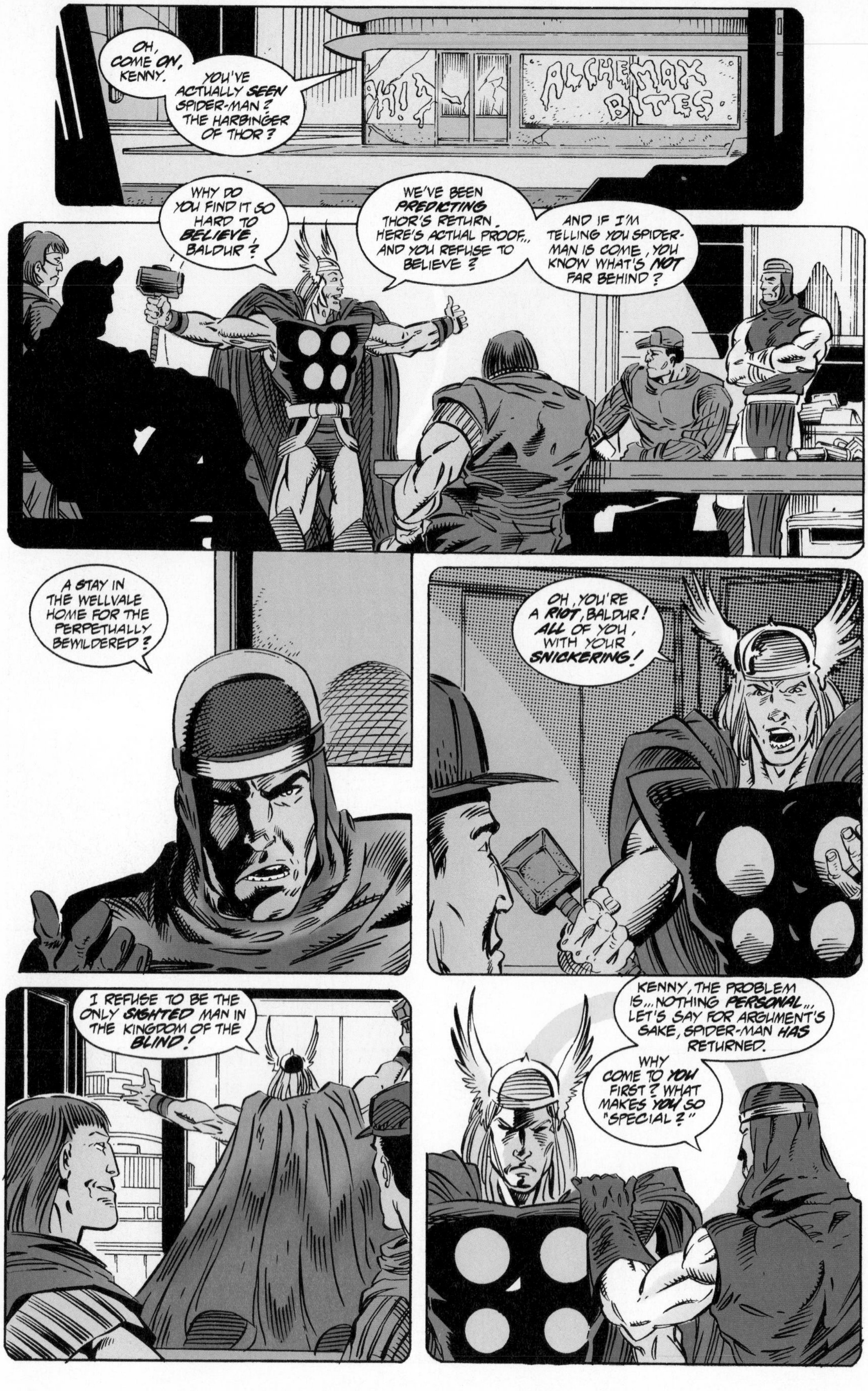
OH, COME ON, KENNY.
YOU'VE ACTUALLY SEEN SPIDER-MAN? THE HARBINGER OF THOR?
ALCHEMAX BITES
WHY DO YOU FIND IT SO HARD TO BELIEVE, BALDUR?
WE'VE BEEN PREDICTING THOR'S RETURN. HERE'S ACTUAL PROOF... AND YOU REFUSE TO BELIEVE?
AND IF I'M TELLING YOU SPIDER-MAN IS COME, YOU KNOW WHAT'S NOT FAR BEHIND?
A STAY IN THE WELLVALE HOME FOR THE PERPETUALLY BEWILDERED?
OH, YOU'RE A RIOT, BALDUR! ALL OF YOU, WITH YOUR SNICKERING!
I REFUSE TO BE THE ONLY SIGHTED MAN IN THE KINGDOM OF THE BLIND!
KENNY, THE PROBLEM IS... NOTHING PERSONAL... LET'S SAY FOR ARGUMENT'S SAKE, SPIDER-MAN HAS RETURNED.
WHY COME TO YOU FIRST? WHAT MAKES YOU SO "SPECIAL?"

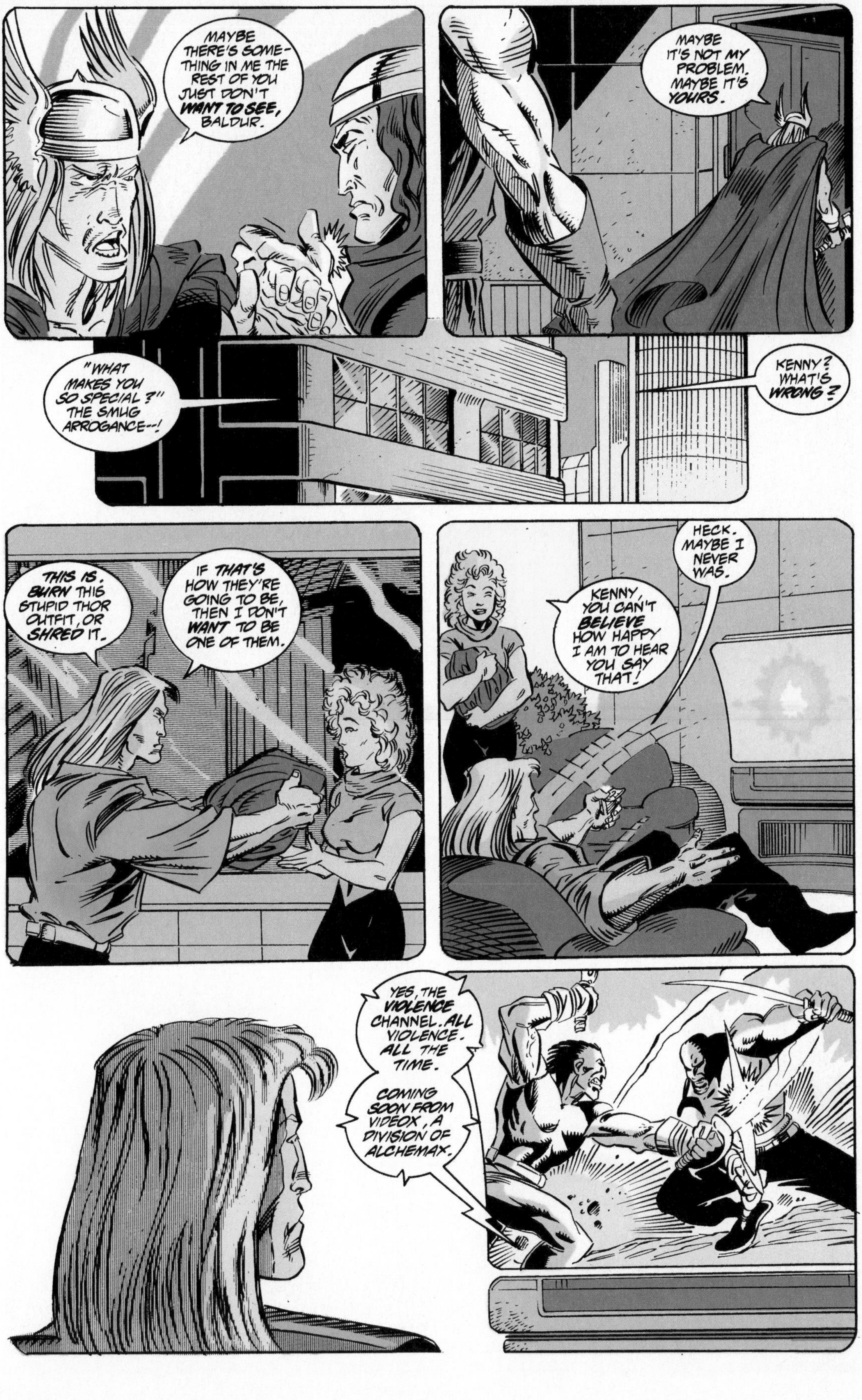
MAYBE THERE'S SOME-THING IN ME THE REST OF YOU JUST DON'T WANT TO SEE, BALDUR.
MAYBE IT'S NOT MY PROBLEM. MAYBE IT'S YOURS.
"WHAT MAKES YOU SO SPECIAL?" THE SMUG ARROGANCE--!
KENNY? WHAT'S WRONG?
THIS IS. BURN THIS STUPID THOR OUTFIT, OR SHRED IT.
IF THAT'S HOW THEY'RE GOING TO BE, THEN I DON'T WANT TO BE ONE OF THEM.
HECK. MAYBE I NEVER WAS.
KENNY, YOU CAN'T BELIEVE HOW HAPPY I AM TO HEAR YOU SAY THAT!
YES, THE VIOLENCE CHANNEL. ALL VIOLENCE. ALL THE TIME.
COMING SOON FROM VIDEOX, A DIVISION OF ALCHEMAX.

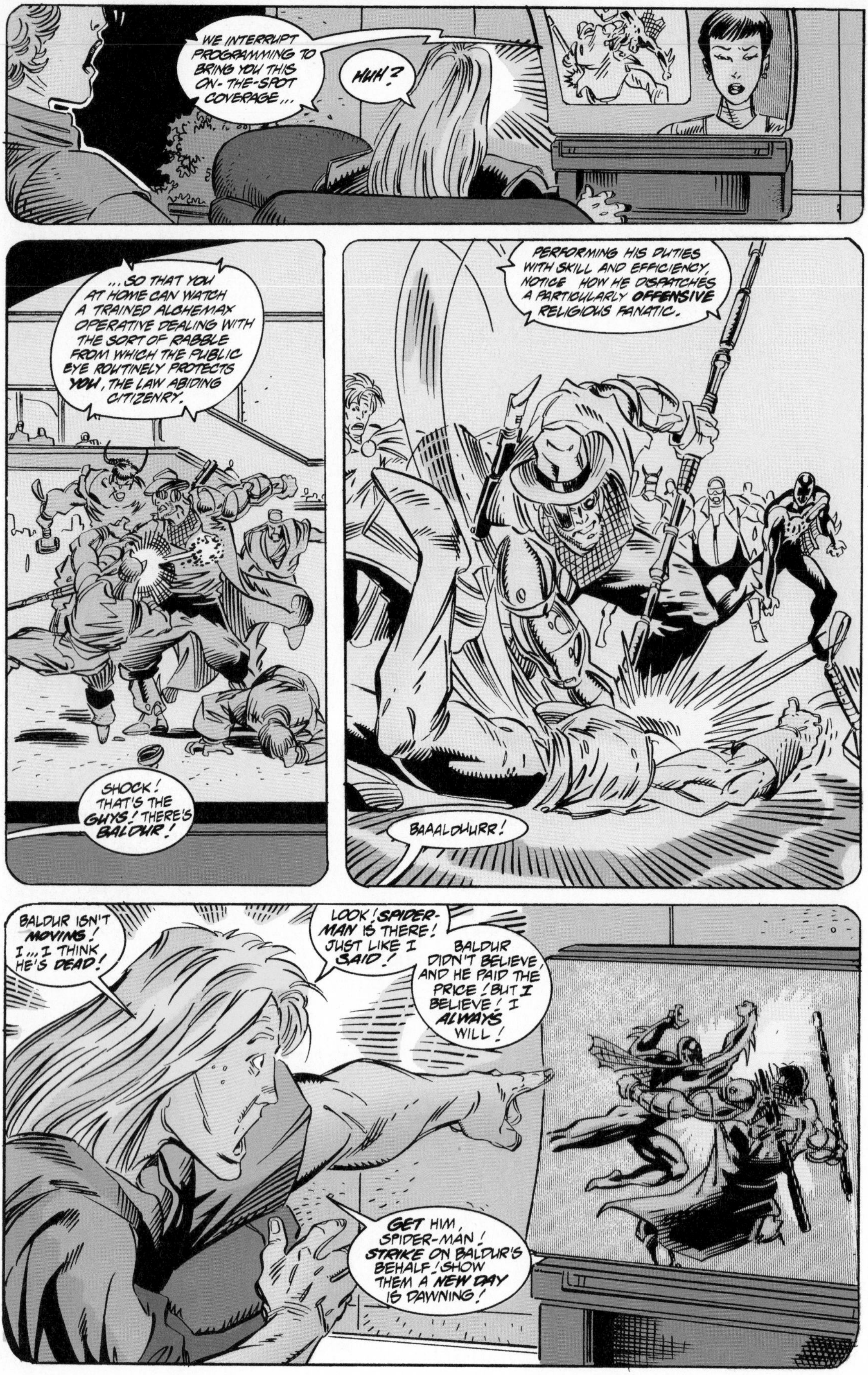

WE INTERRUPT PROGRAMMING TO BRING YOU THIS ON-THE-SPOT COVERAGE...
HUH?
...SO THAT YOU AT HOME CAN WATCH A TRAINED ALCHEMAX OPERATIVE DEALING WITH THE SORT OF RABBLE FROM WHICH THE PUBLIC EYE ROUTINELY PROTECTS YOU, THE LAW ABIDING CITIZENRY.
SHOCK! THAT'S THE GUYS! THERE'S BALDUR!
PERFORMING HIS DUTIES WITH SKILL AND EFFICIENCY, NOTICE HOW HE DISPATCHES A PARTICULARLY OFFENSIVE RELIGIOUS FANATIC.
BAAALDHURR!
BALDUR ISN'T MOVING! I... I THINK HE'S DEAD!
LOOK! SPIDER-MAN IS THERE! JUST LIKE I SAID!
BALDUR DIDN'T BELIEVE AND HE PAID THE PRICE! BUT I BELIEVE! I ALWAYS WILL!
GET HIM, SPIDER-MAN! STRIKE ON BALDUR'S BEHALF! SHOW THEM A NEW DAY IS DAWNING!

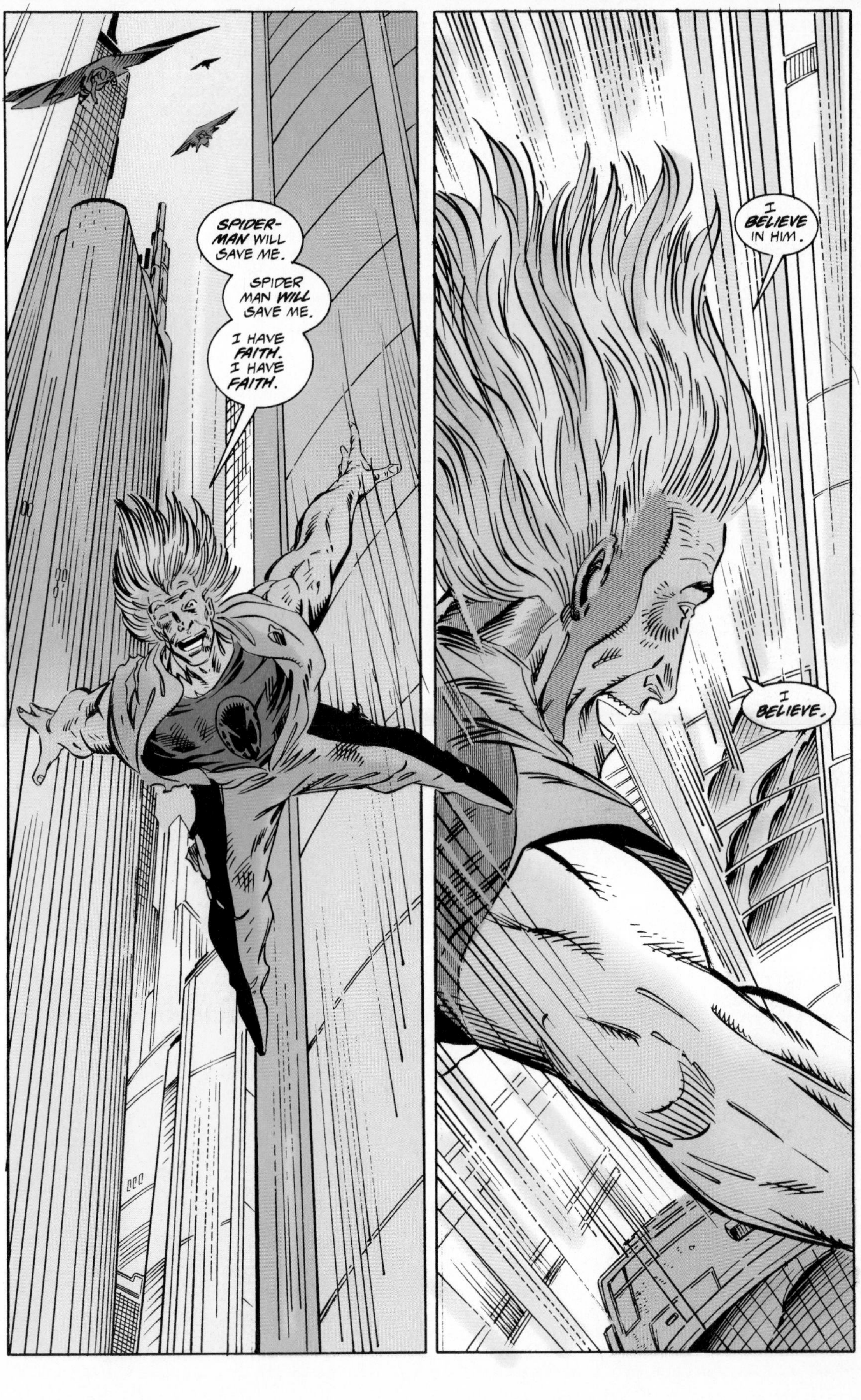
SPIDER-MAN WILL SAVE ME.
SPIDER MAN WILL SAVE ME.
I HAVE FAITH. I HAVE FAITH.
I BELIEVE IN HIM.
I BELIEVE.

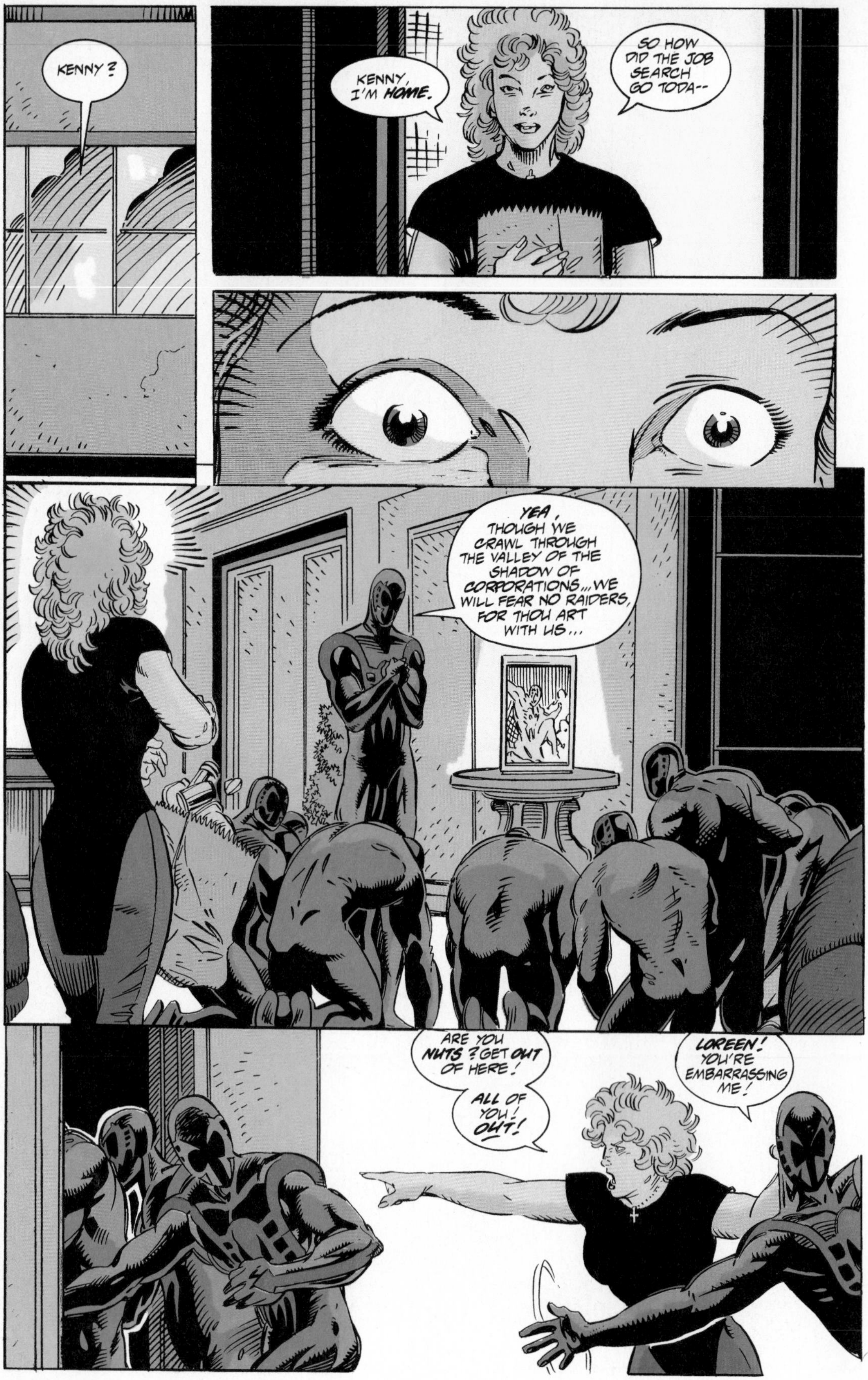
KENNY?
KENNY, I'M HOME.
SO HOW DID THE JOB SEARCH GO TODA--
YEA, THOUGH WE CRAWL THROUGH THE VALLEY OF THE SHADOW OF CORPORATIONS... WE WILL FEAR NO RAIDERS, FOR THOU ART WITH US...
ARE YOU NUTS? GET OUT OF HERE!
ALL OF YOU! OUT!
LOREEN! YOU'RE EMBARRASSING ME!

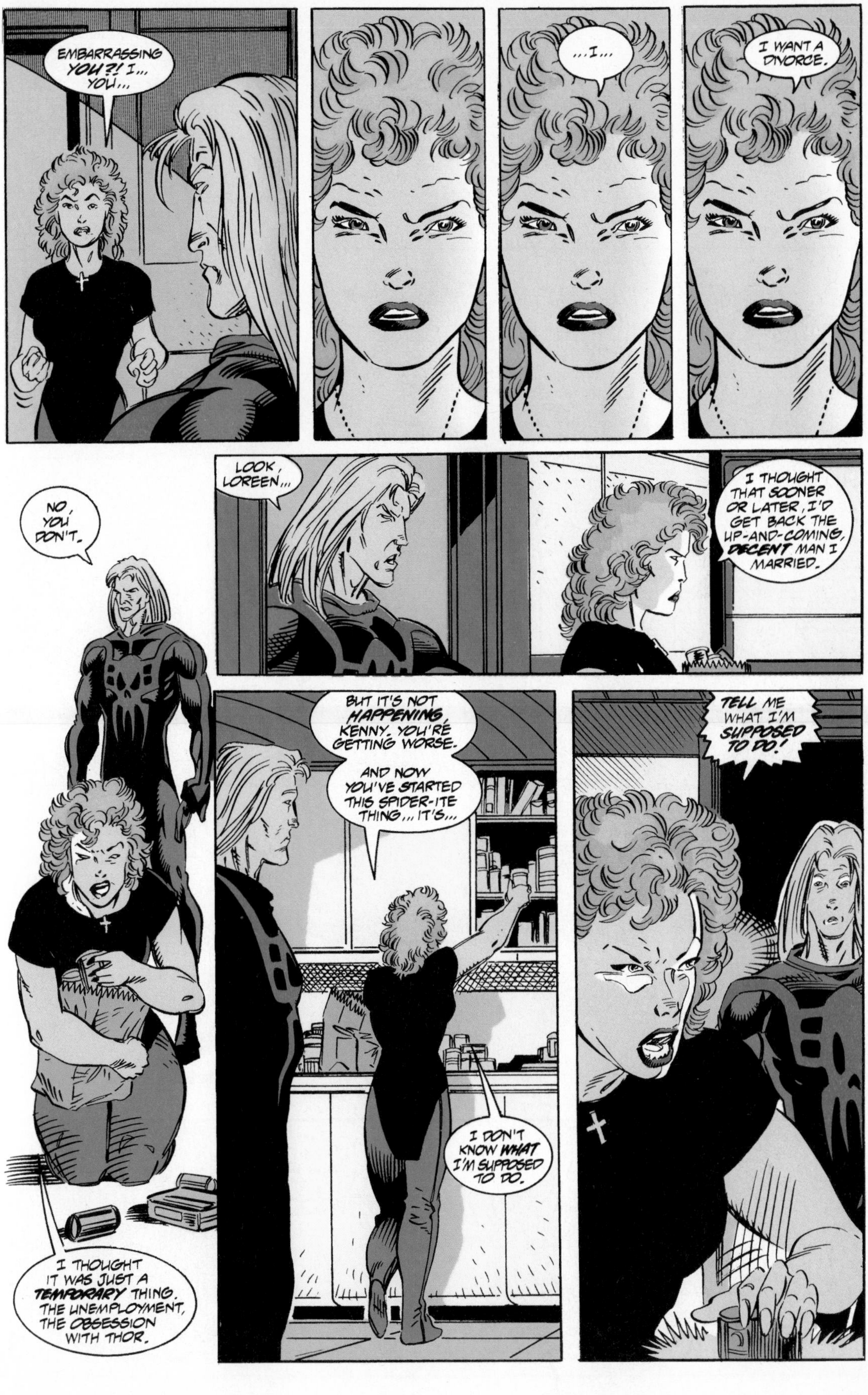
EMBARRASSING YOU?! I... YOU...
...I...
I WANT A DIVORCE.
NO, YOU DON'T.
LOOK, LOREEN...
I THOUGHT THAT SOONER OR LATER, I'D GET BACK THE UP-AND-COMING, DECENT MAN I MARRIED.
I THOUGHT IT WAS JUST A TEMPORARY THING. THE UNEMPLOYMENT, THE OBSESSION WITH THOR.
BUT IT'S NOT HAPPENING, KENNY. YOU'RE GETTING WORSE.
AND NOW YOU'VE STARTED THIS SPIDER-ITE THING... IT'S...
I DON'T KNOW WHAT I'M SUPPOSED TO DO.
TELL ME WHAT I'M SUPPOSED TO DO!

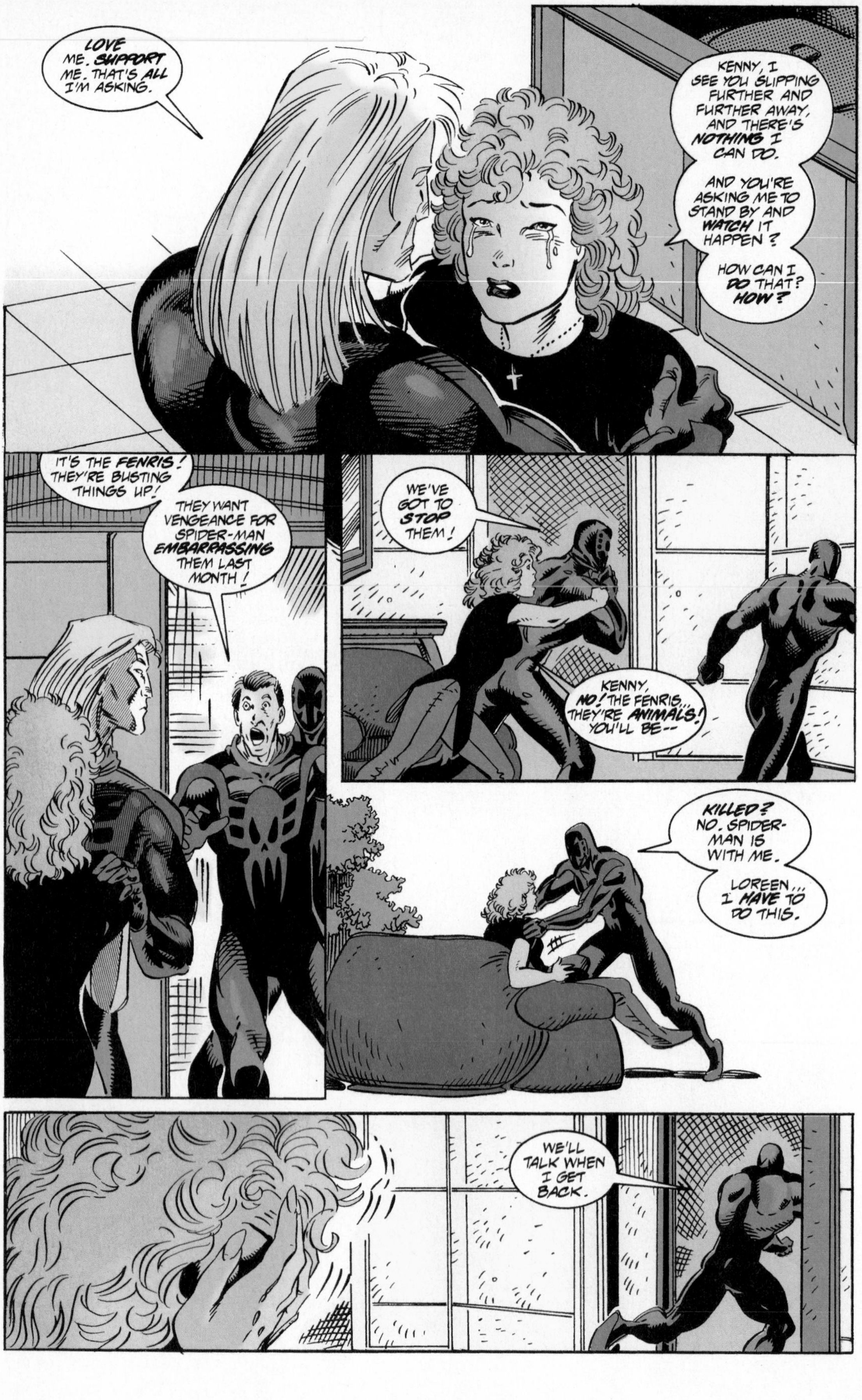
LOVE ME. SUPPORT ME. THAT'S ALL I'M ASKING.
KENNY, I SEE YOU SLIPPING FURTHER AND FURTHER AWAY, AND THERE'S NOTHING I CAN DO.
AND YOU'RE ASKING ME TO STAND BY AND WATCH IT HAPPEN?
HOW CAN I DO THAT? HOW?
IT'S THE FENRIS! THEY'RE BUSTING THINGS UP!
THEY WANT VENGEANCE FOR SPIDER-MAN EMBARRASSING THEM LAST MONTH!
WE'VE GOT TO STOP THEM!
KENNY, NO! THE FENRIS... THEY'RE ANIMALS! YOU'LL BE--
KILLED? NO. SPIDER-MAN IS WITH ME.
LOREEN... I HAVE TO DO THIS.
WE'LL TALK WHEN I GET BACK.

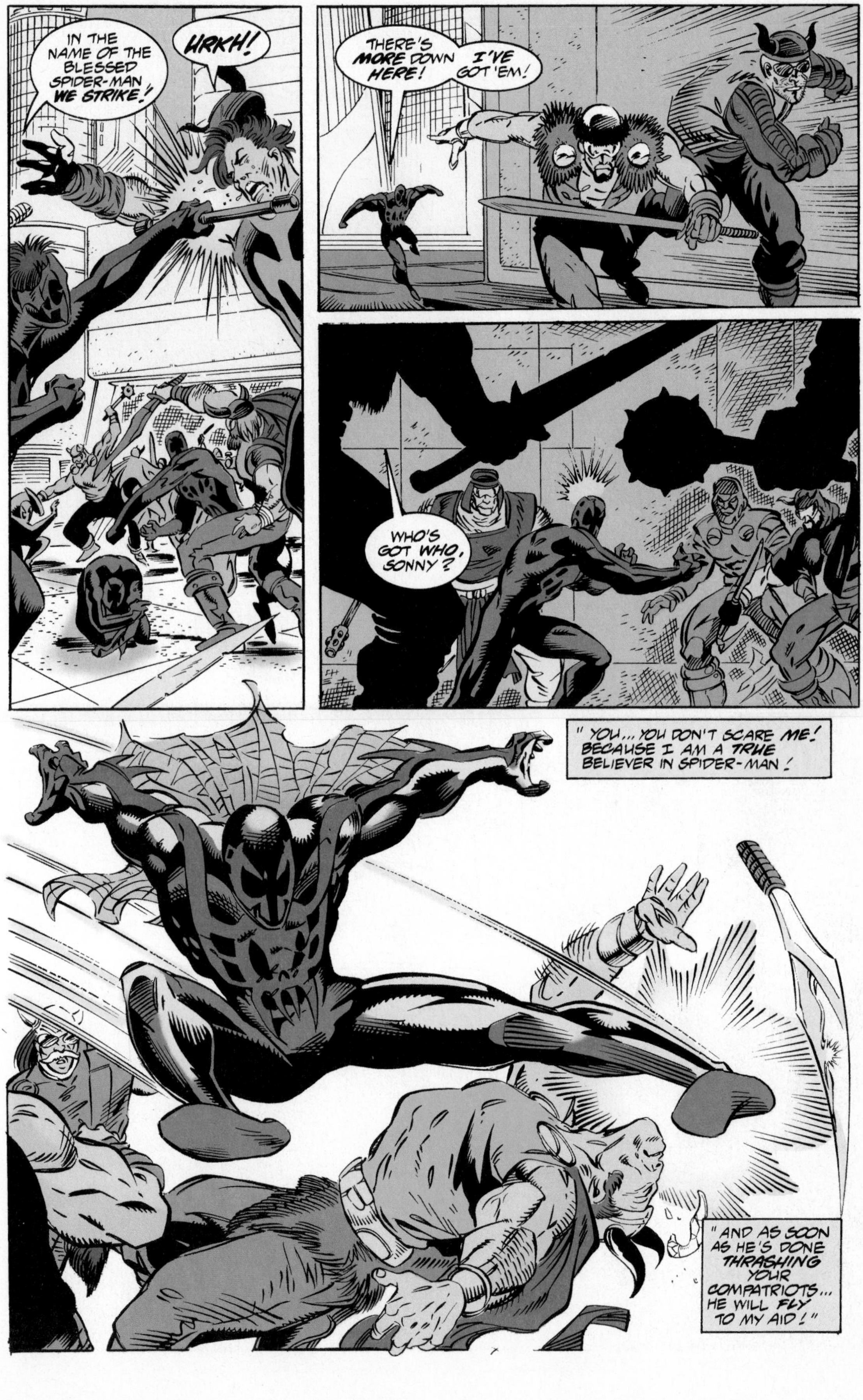

IN THE NAME OF THE BLESSED SPIDER-MAN WE STRIKE!
URKH!
THERE'S MORE DOWN HERE!
I'VE GOT 'EM!
WHO'S GOT WHO, SONNY?
"YOU... YOU DON'T SCARE ME! BECAUSE I AM A TRUE BELIEVER IN SPIDER-MAN!
"AND AS SOON AS HE'S DONE THRASHING YOUR COMPATRIOTS... HE WILL FLY TO MY AID!"

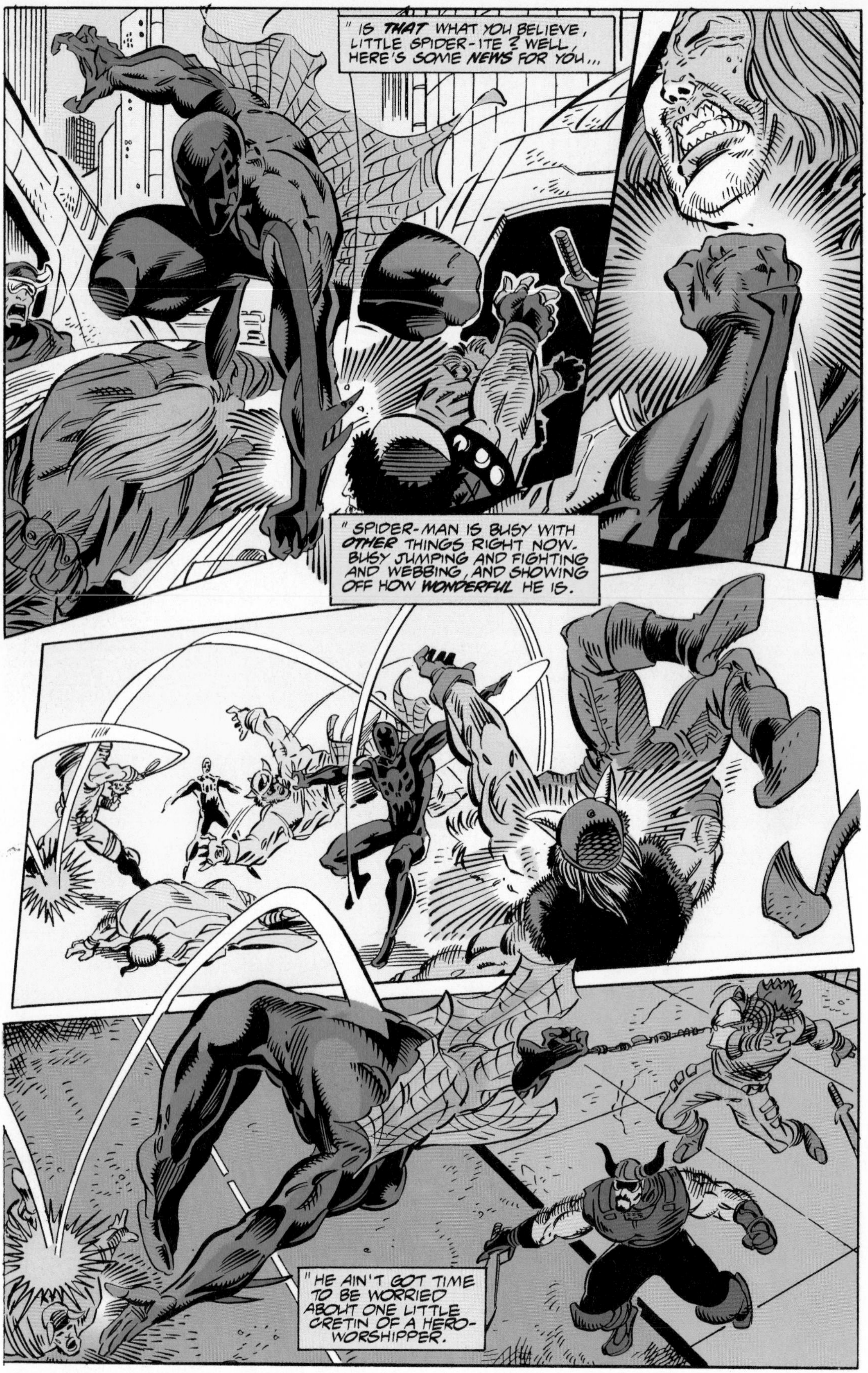
"IS THAT WHAT YOU BELIEVE, LITTLE SPIDER-ITE? WELL, HERE'S SOME NEWS FOR YOU...
"SPIDER-MAN IS BUSY WITH OTHER THINGS RIGHT NOW. BUSY JUMPING AND FIGHTING AND WEBBING, AND SHOWING OFF HOW WONDERFUL HE IS.
"HE AIN'T GOT TIME TO BE WORRIED ABOUT ONE LITTLE CRETIN OF A HERO-WORSHIPPER.

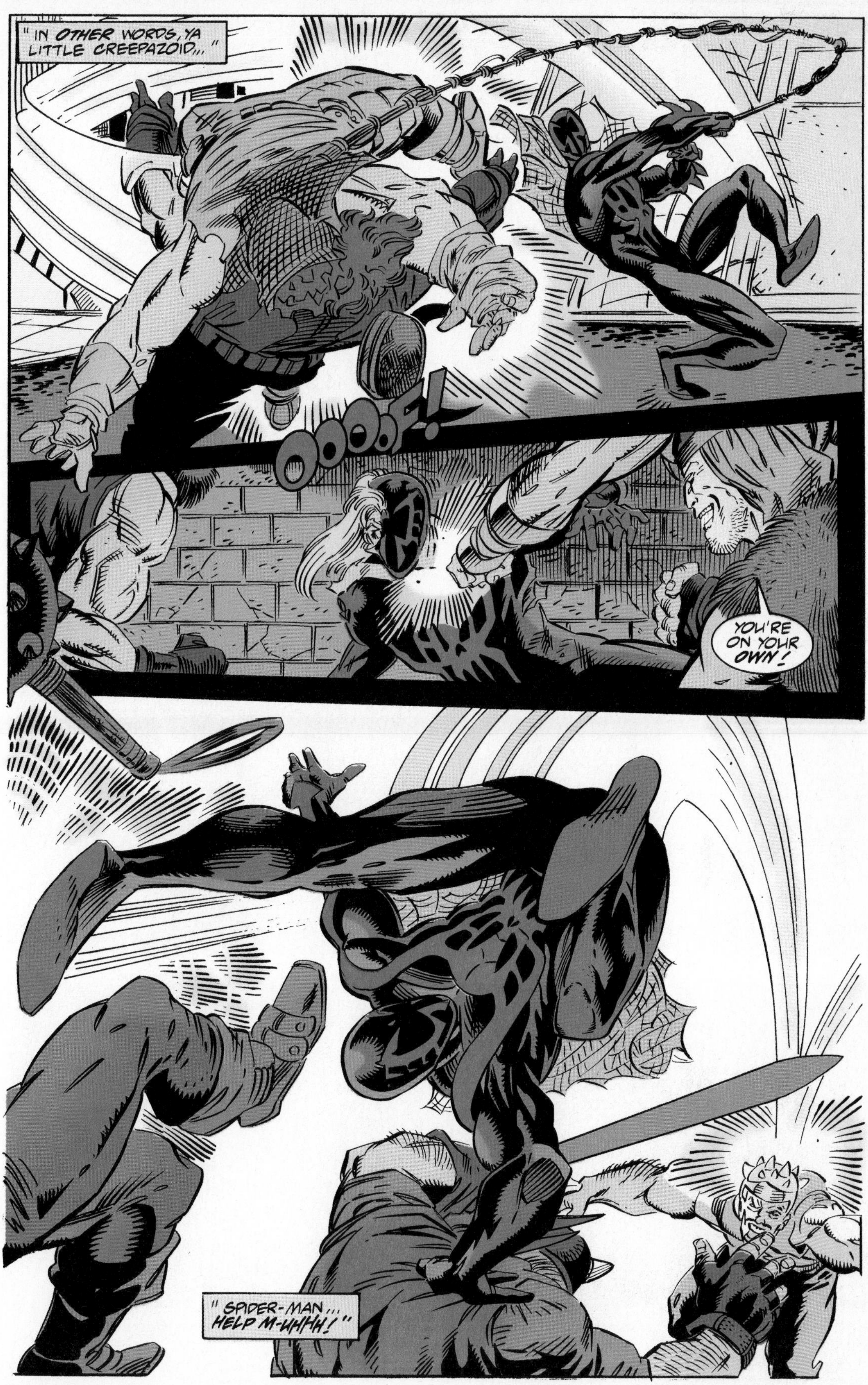
"IN OTHER WORDS, YA LITTLE CREEPAZOID..."
OOOOF!
YOU'RE ON YOUR OWN!
"SPIDER-MAN... HELP M-UHHH!"

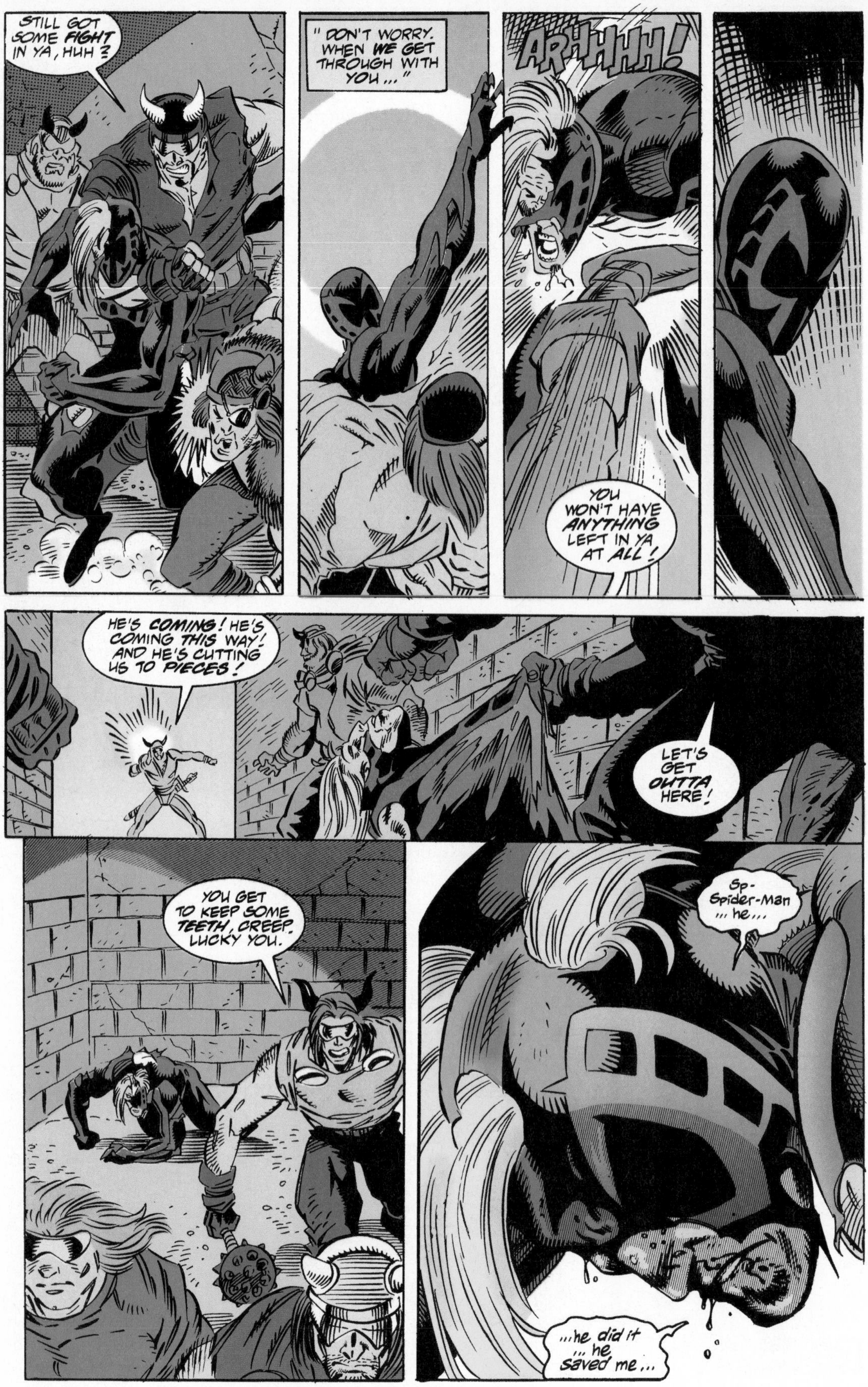
STILL GOT SOME FIGHT IN YA, HUH?
"DON'T WORRY. WHEN WE GET THROUGH WITH YOU..."
ARHHHH!
YOU WON'T HAVE ANYTHING LEFT IN YA AT ALL!
HE'S COMING! HE'S COMING THIS WAY! AND HE'S CUTTING US TO PIECES!
LET'S GET OUTTA HERE!
YOU GET TO KEEP SOME TEETH, CREEP. LUCKY YOU.
Sp-Spider-Man ...he...
...he did it ...he saved me...

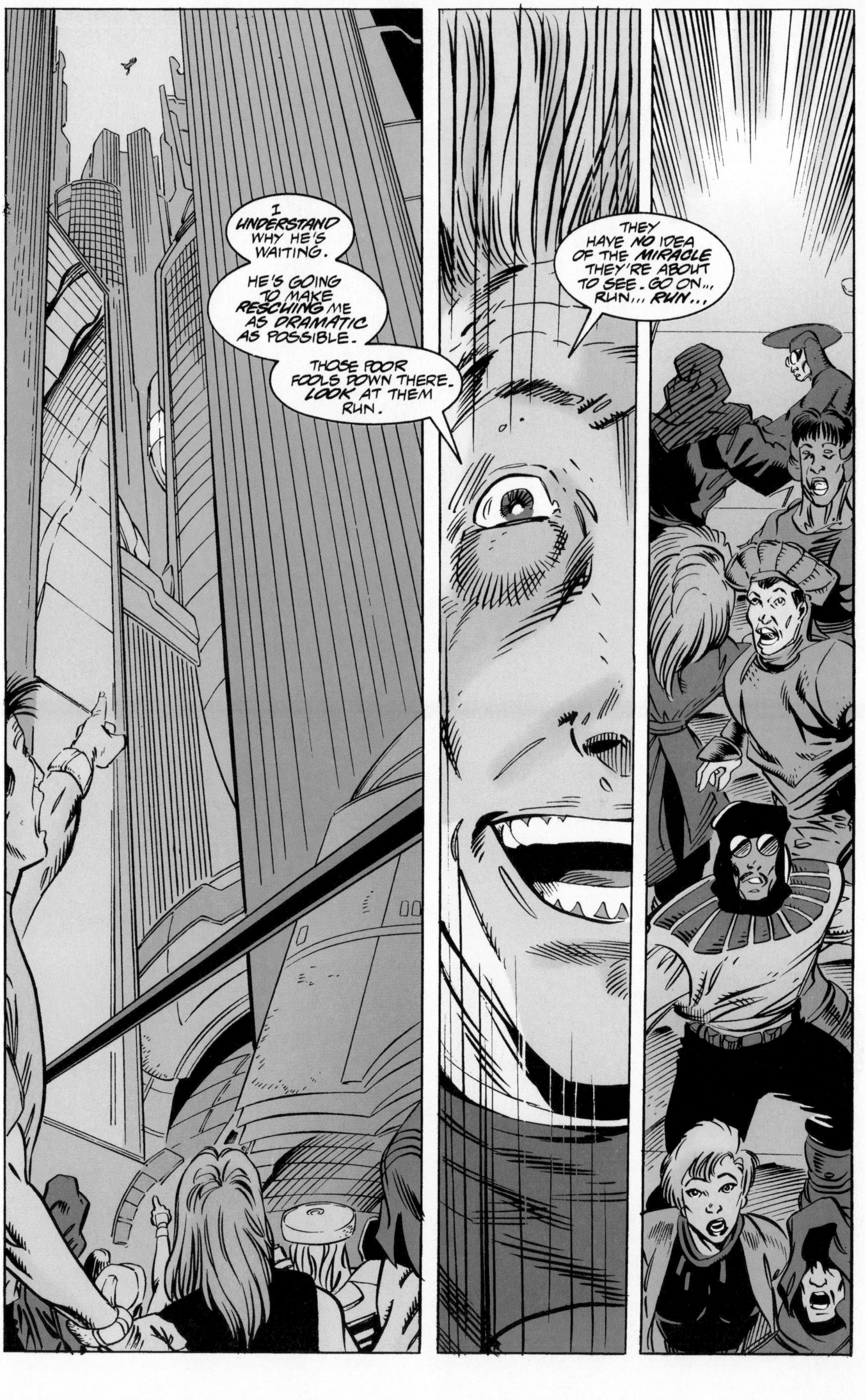

I UNDERSTAND WHY HE'S WAITING.
HE'S GOING TO MAKE RESCUING ME AS DRAMATIC AS POSSIBLE.
THOSE POOR FOOLS DOWN THERE. LOOK AT THEM RUN.
THEY HAVE NO IDEA OF THE MIRACLE THEY'RE ABOUT TO SEE. GO ON... RUN... RUN...

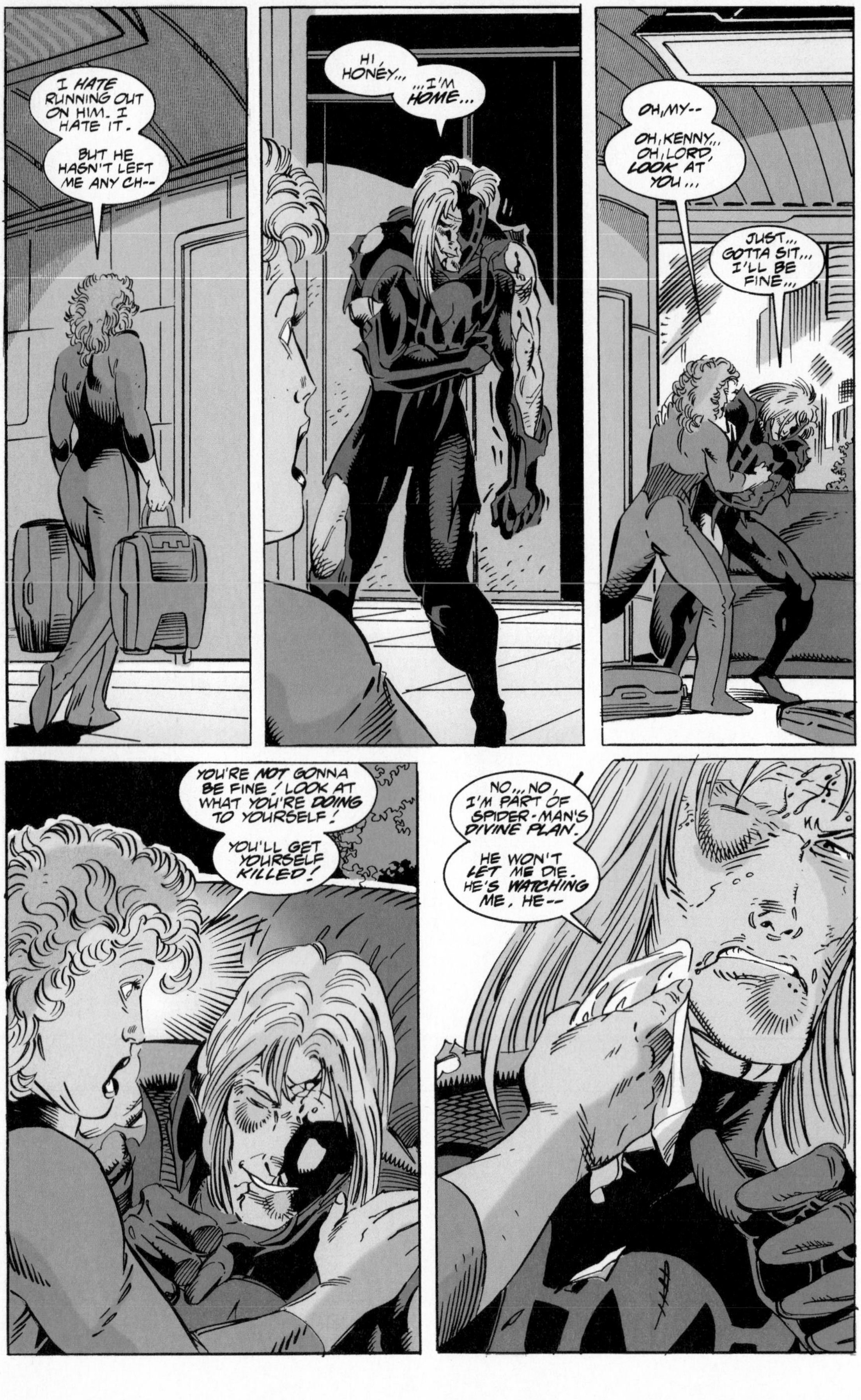
I HATE RUNNING OUT ON HIM. I HATE IT.
BUT HE HASN'T LEFT ME ANY CH--
HI, HONEY... ...I'M HOME...
OH, MY--
OH, KENNY... OH, LORD, LOOK AT YOU...
JUST... GOTTA SIT... I'LL BE FINE...
YOU'RE NOT GONNA BE FINE! LOOK AT WHAT YOU'RE DOING TO YOURSELF!
YOU'LL GET YOURSELF KILLED!
NO... NO, I'M PART OF SPIDER-MAN'S DIVINE PLAN.
HE WON'T LET ME DIE. HE'S WATCHING ME. HE--

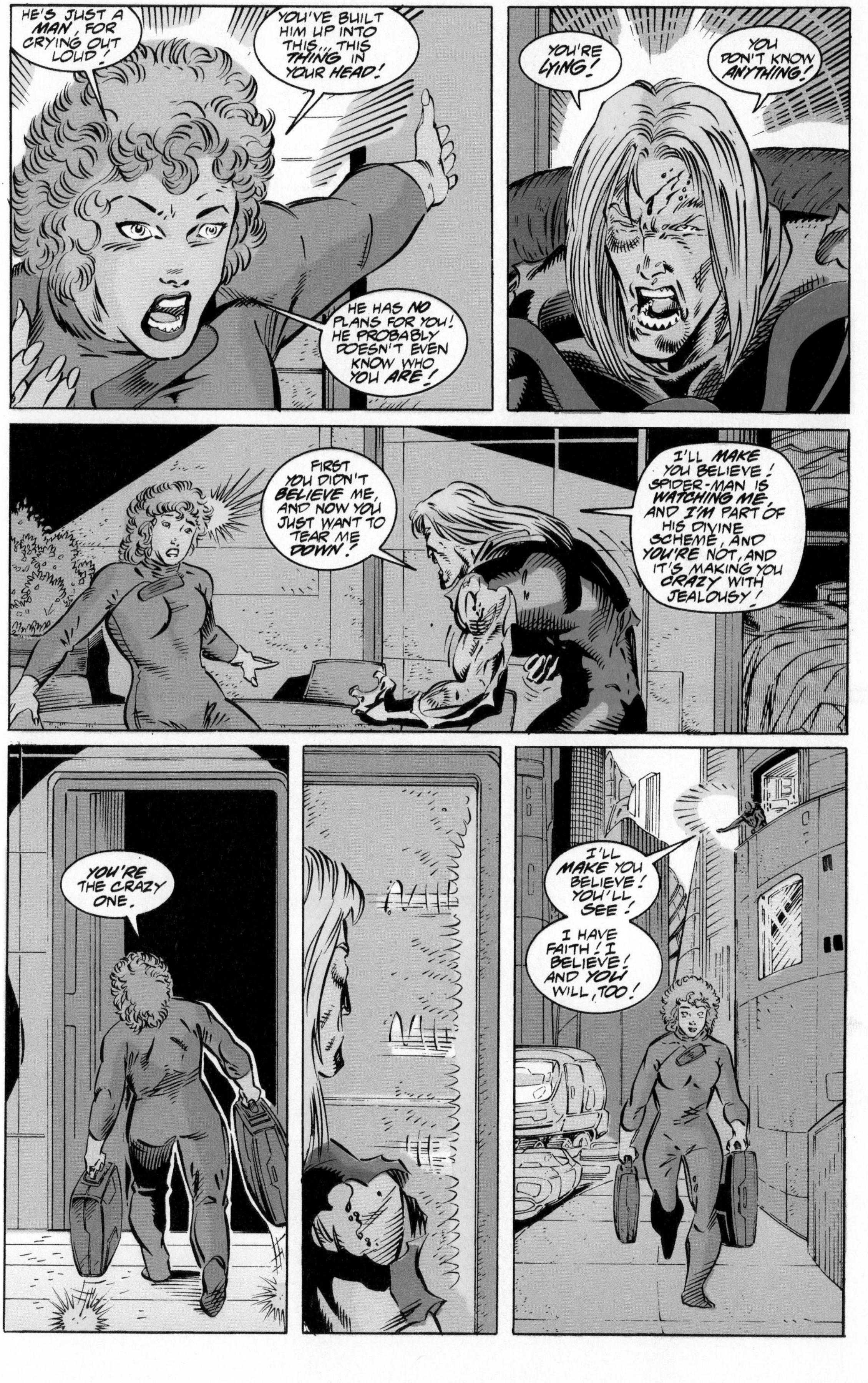
HE'S JUST A MAN, FOR CRYING OUT LOUD!
YOU'VE BUILT HIM UP INTO THIS... THIS THING IN YOUR HEAD!
HE HAS NO PLANS FOR YOU! HE PROBABLY DOESN'T EVEN KNOW WHO YOU ARE!
YOU'RE LYING!
YOU DON'T KNOW ANYTHING!
FIRST YOU DIDN'T BELIEVE ME, AND NOW YOU JUST WANT TO TEAR ME DOWN!
I'LL MAKE YOU BELIEVE! SPIDER-MAN IS WATCHING ME, AND I'M PART OF HIS DIVINE SCHEME, AND YOU'RE NOT, AND IT'S MAKING YOU CRAZY WITH JEALOUSY!
YOU'RE THE CRAZY ONE.
I'LL MAKE YOU BELIEVE! YOU'LL SEE!
I HAVE FAITH! I BELIEVE! AND YOU WILL, TOO!

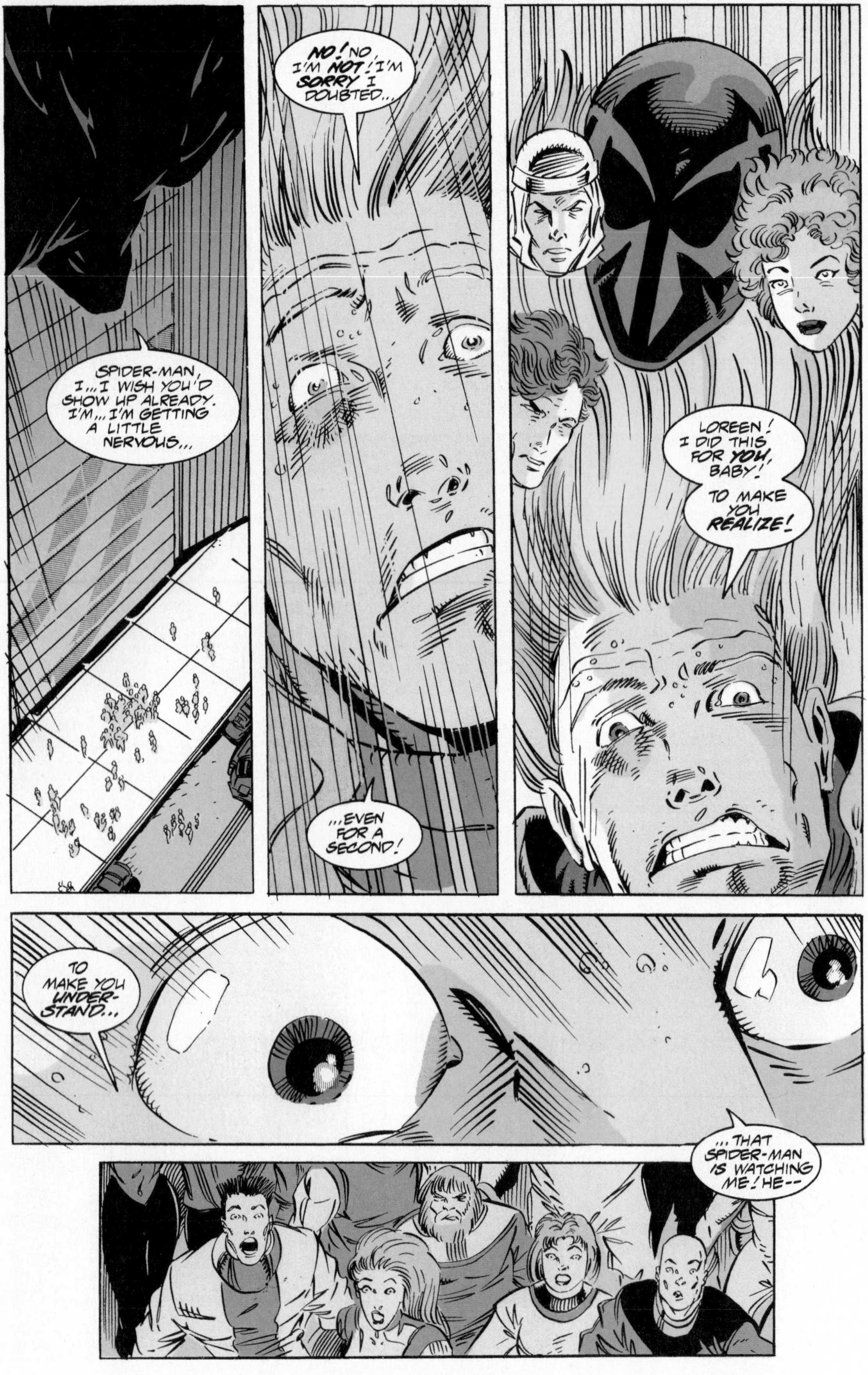
SPIDER-MAN, I... I WISH YOU'D SHOW UP ALREADY. I'M... I'M GETTING A LITTLE NERVOUS...
NO! NO, I'M NOT! I'M SORRY I DOUBTED...
...EVEN FOR A SECOND!
LOREEN! I DID THIS FOR YOU, BABY!
TO MAKE YOU REALIZE!
TO MAKE YOU UNDER-STAND...
...THAT SPIDER-MAN IS WATCHING ME! HE--

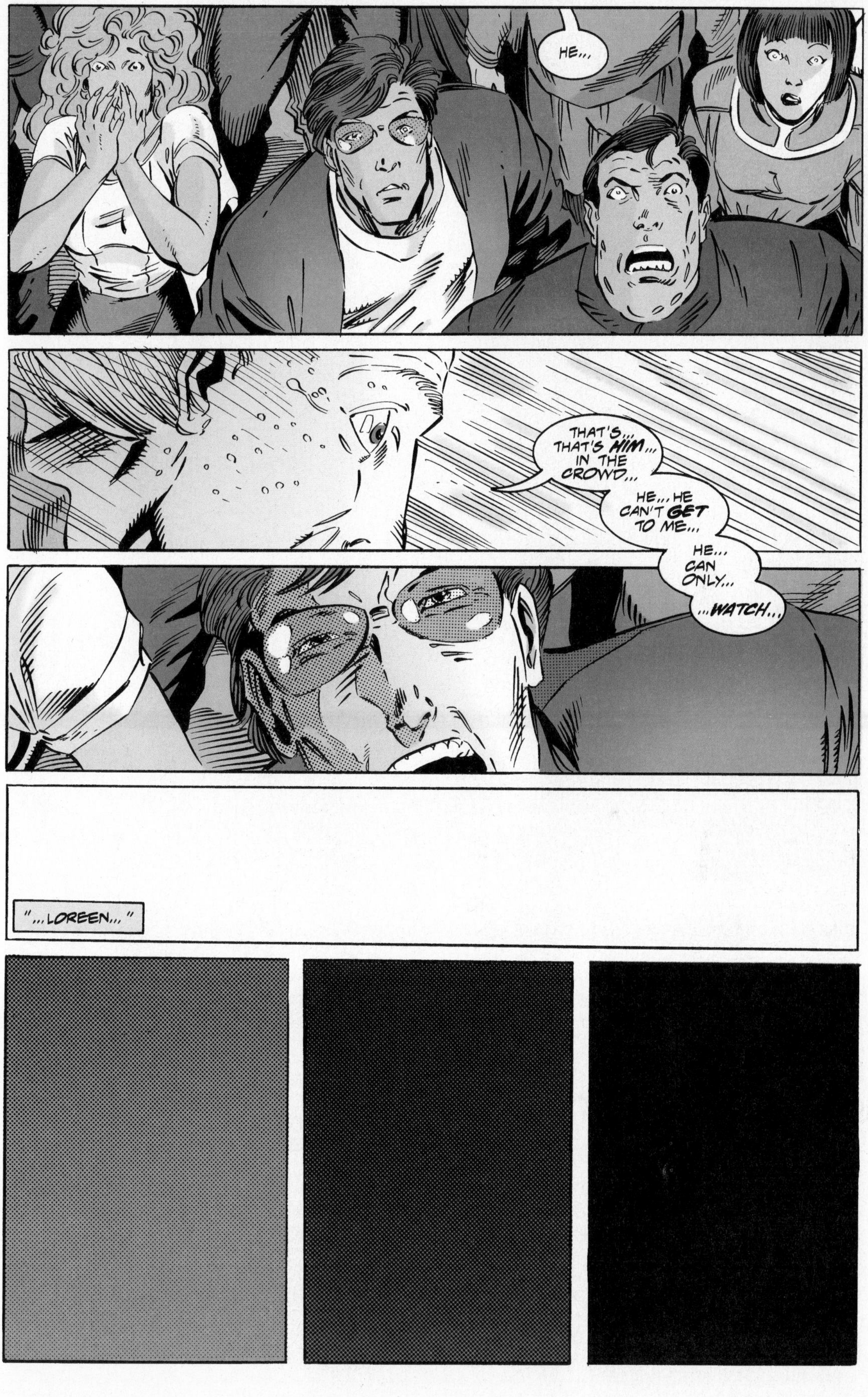
HE...
THAT'S... THAT'S HIM... IN THE CROWD...
HE... HE CAN'T GET TO ME...
HE... CAN ONLY...
...WATCH...
"...LOREEN..."

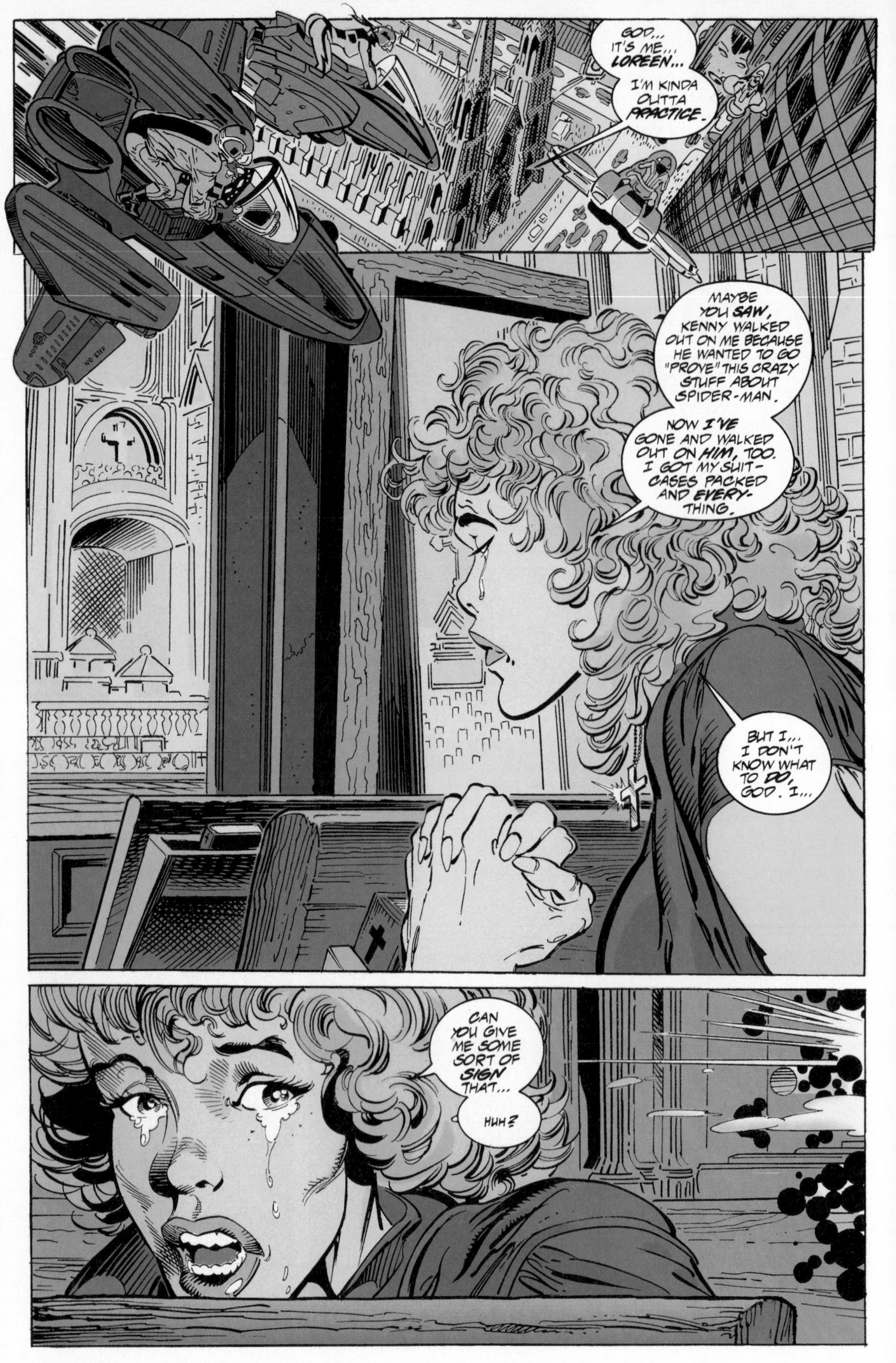
GOD... IT'S ME... LOREEN...
I'M KINDA OUTTA PRACTICE.
NO STEP
MAYBE YOU SAW, KENNY WALKED OUT ON ME BECAUSE HE WANTED TO GO "PROVE" THIS CRAZY STUFF ABOUT SPIDER-MAN.
NOW I'VE GONE AND WALKED OUT ON HIM, TOO. I GOT MY SUIT-CASES PACKED AND EVERY-THING.
BUT I... I DON'T KNOW WHAT TO DO, GOD. I...
CAN YOU GIVE ME SOME SORT OF SIGN THAT...
HUH?

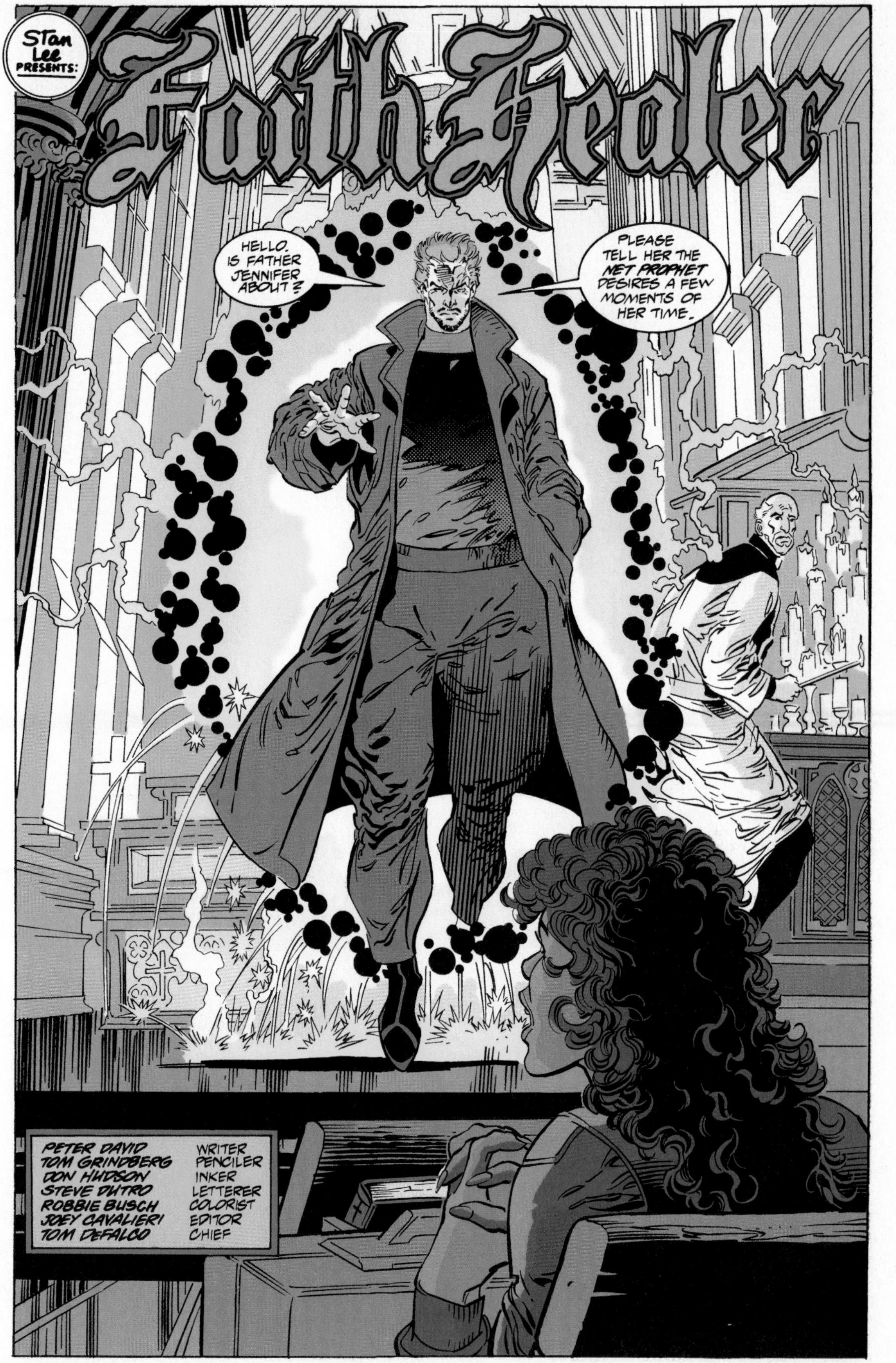
STAN LEE PRESENTS:
Faith Healer
HELLO. IS FATHER JENNIFER ABOUT?
PLEASE TELL HER THE NET PROPHET DESIRES A FEW MOMENTS OF HER TIME.
PETER DAVID WRITER
TOM GRINDBERG PENCILER
DON HUDSON INKER
STEVE DUTRO LETTERER
ROBBIE BUSCH COLORIST
JOEY CAVALIERI EDITOR
TOM DEFALCO CHIEF

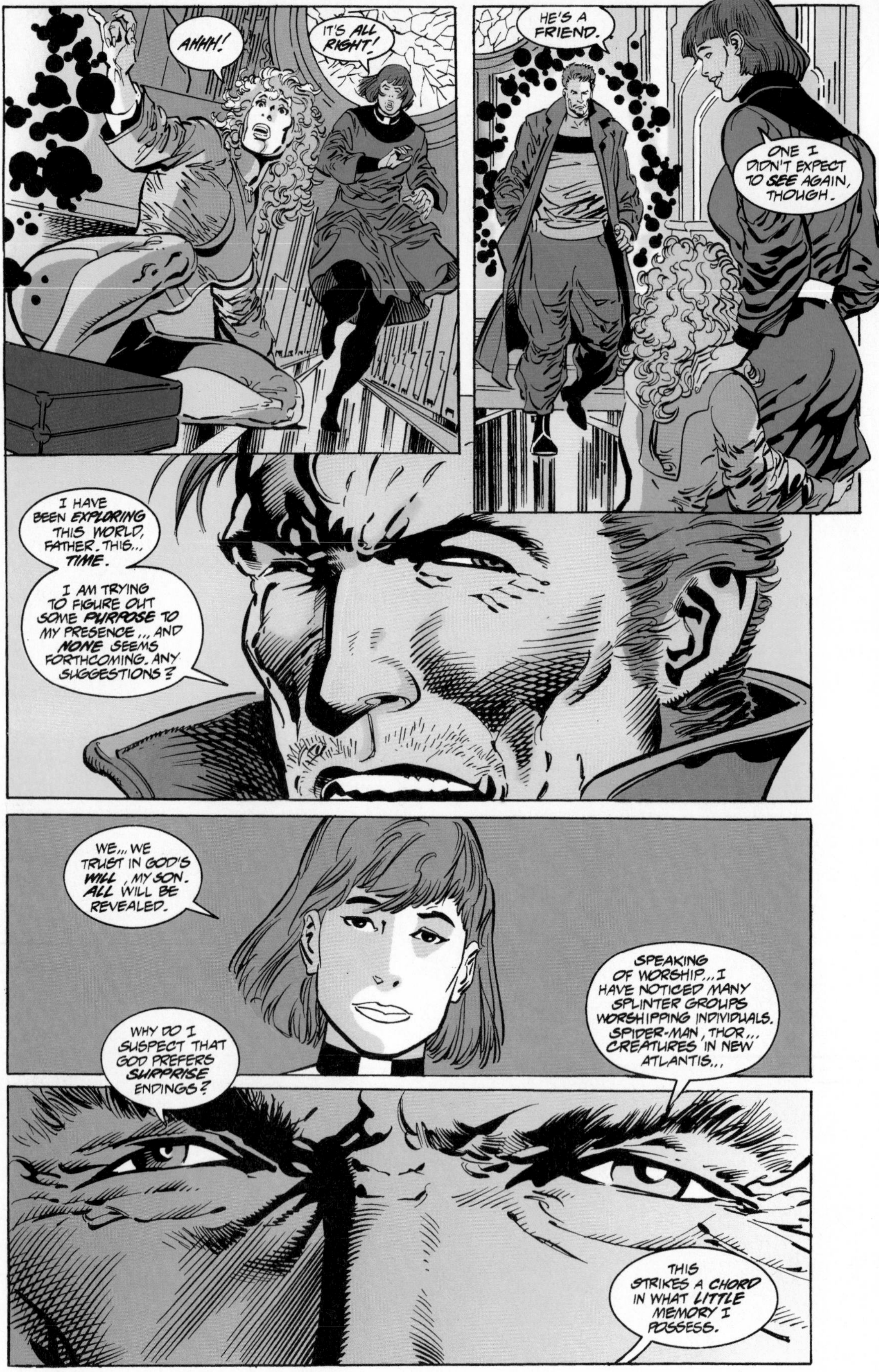
AHHH!
IT'S ALL RIGHT!
HE'S A FRIEND.
ONE I DIDN'T EXPECT TO SEE AGAIN, THOUGH.
I HAVE BEEN EXPLORING THIS WORLD, FATHER. THIS... TIME.
I AM TRYING TO FIGURE OUT SOME PURPOSE TO MY PRESENCE... AND NONE SEEMS FORTHCOMING. ANY SUGGESTIONS?
WE... WE TRUST IN GOD'S WILL, MY SON. ALL WILL BE REVEALED.
WHY DO I SUSPECT THAT GOD PREFERS SURPRISE ENDINGS?
SPEAKING OF WORSHIP... I HAVE NOTICED MANY SPLINTER GROUPS WORSHIPPING INDIVIDUALS. SPIDER-MAN, THOR... CREATURES IN NEW ATLANTIS...
THIS STRIKES A CHORD IN WHAT LITTLE MEMORY I POSSESS.

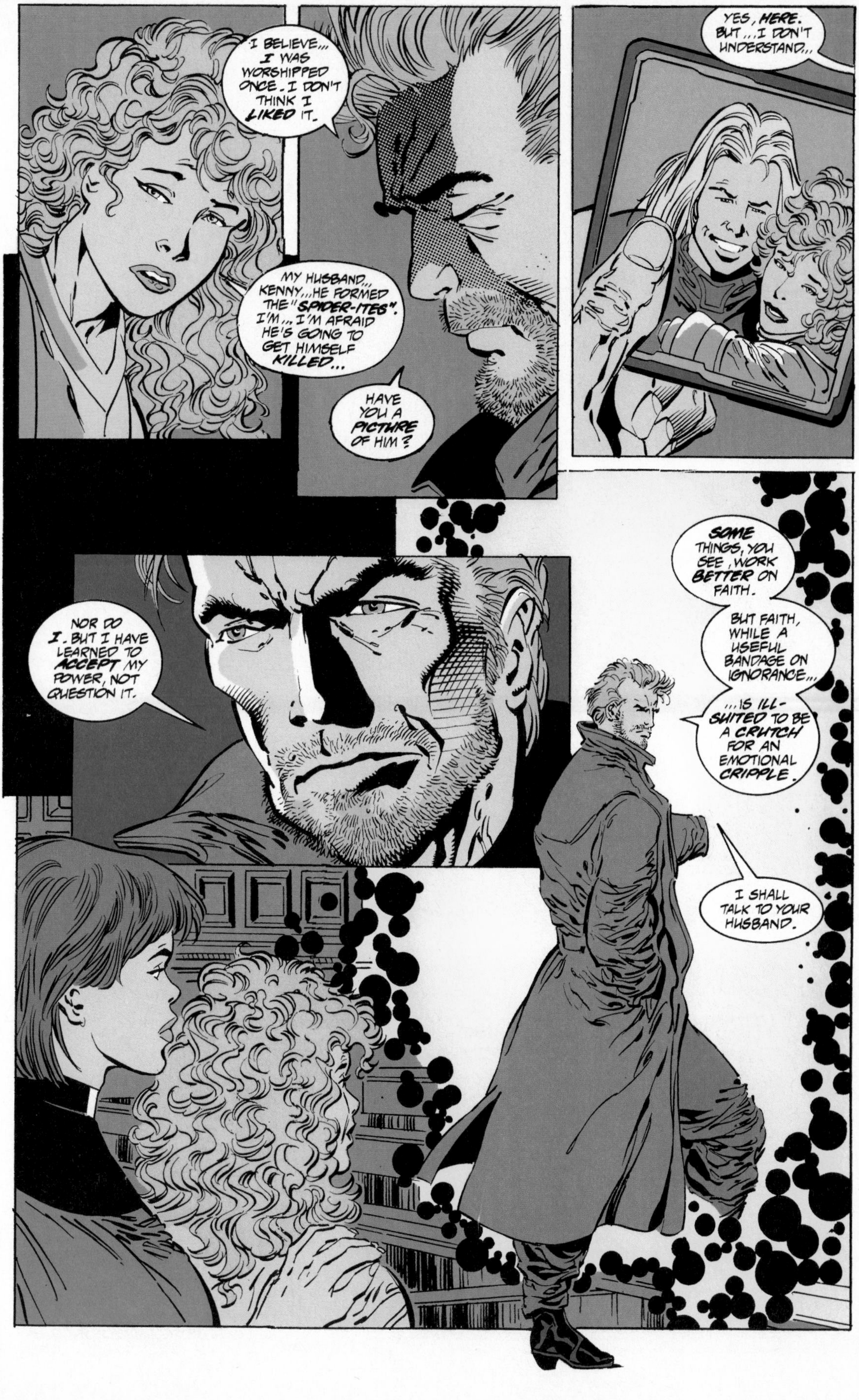
I BELIEVE... I WAS WORSHIPPED ONCE. I DON'T THINK I LIKED IT.
MY HUSBAND... KENNY... HE FORMED THE "SPIDER-ITES". I'M... I'M AFRAID HE'S GOING TO GET HIMSELF KILLED...
HAVE YOU A PICTURE OF HIM?
YES, HERE. BUT... I DON'T UNDERSTAND...
NOR DO I. BUT I HAVE LEARNED TO ACCEPT MY POWER, NOT QUESTION IT.
SOME THINGS, YOU SEE, WORK BETTER ON FAITH.
BUT FAITH, WHILE A USEFUL BANDAGE ON IGNORANCE...
...IS ILL-SUITED TO BE A CRUTCH FOR AN EMOTIONAL CRIPPLE.
I SHALL TALK TO YOUR HUSBAND.

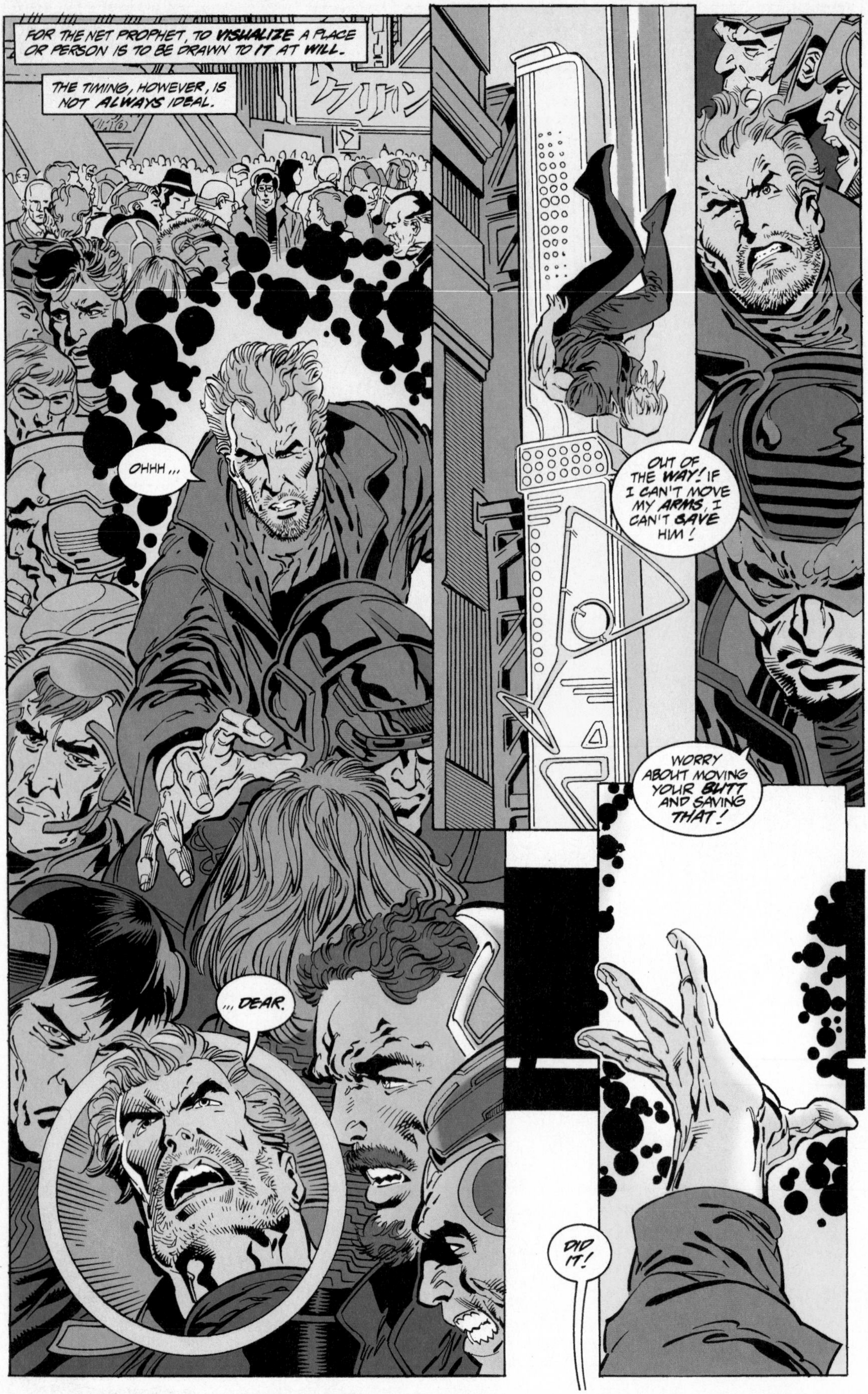
FOR THE NET PROPHET, TO VISUALIZE A PLACE OR PERSON IS TO BE DRAWN TO IT AT WILL.
THE TIMING, HOWEVER, IS NOT ALWAYS IDEAL.
OHHH...
...DEAR.
OUT OF THE WAY! IF I CAN'T MOVE MY ARMS, I CAN'T SAVE HIM!
WORRY ABOUT MOVING YOUR BUTT AND SAVING THAT!
DID IT!

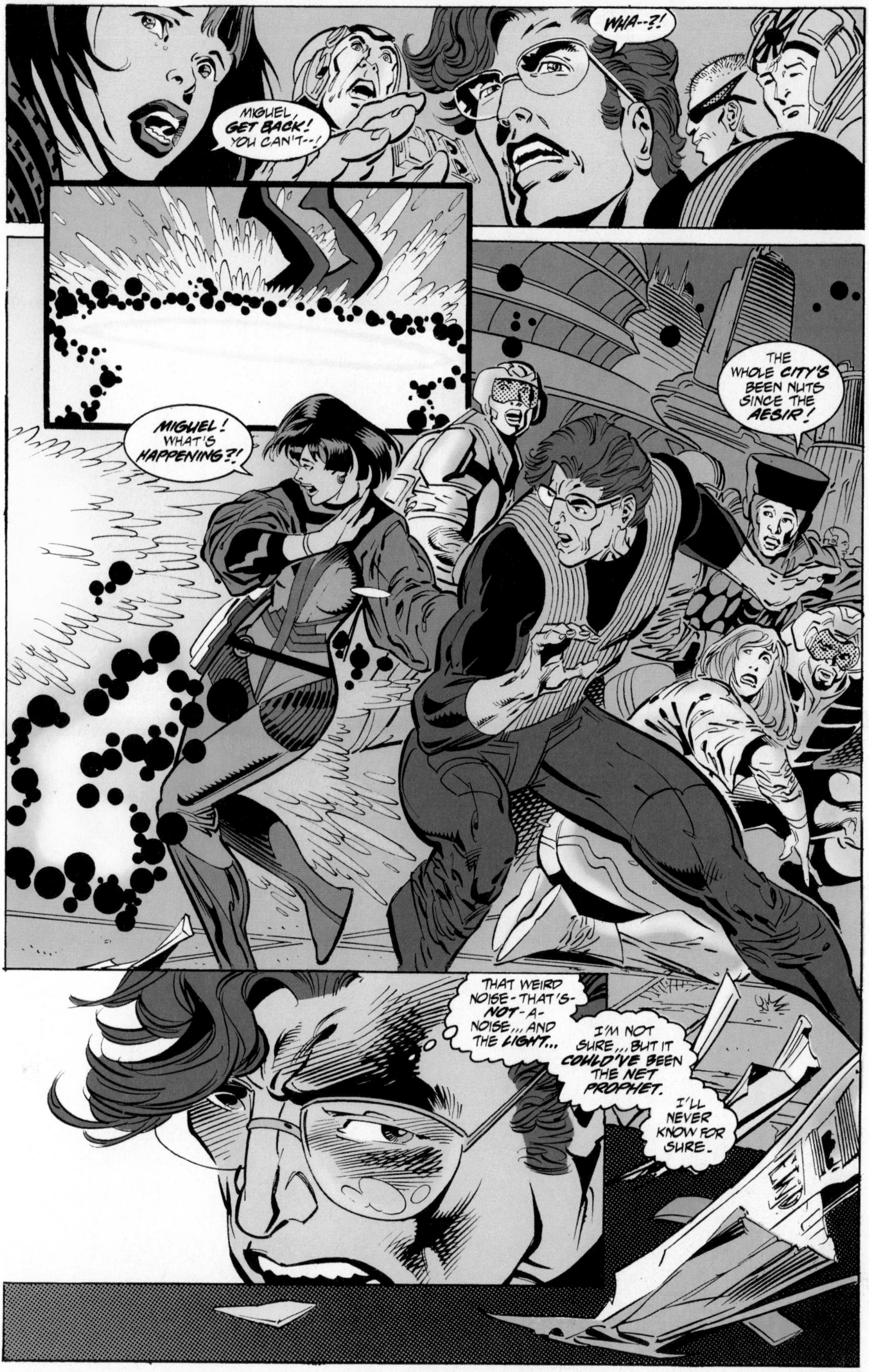
MIGUEL, GET BACK! YOU CAN'T--!
WHA--?!
MIGUEL! WHAT'S HAPPENING?!
THE WHOLE CITY'S BEEN NUTS SINCE THE AESIR!
THAT WEIRD NOISE-THAT'S-NOT-A-NOISE... AND THE LIGHT...
I'M NOT SURE... BUT IT COULD'VE BEEN THE NET PROPHET.
I'LL NEVER KNOW FOR SURE.

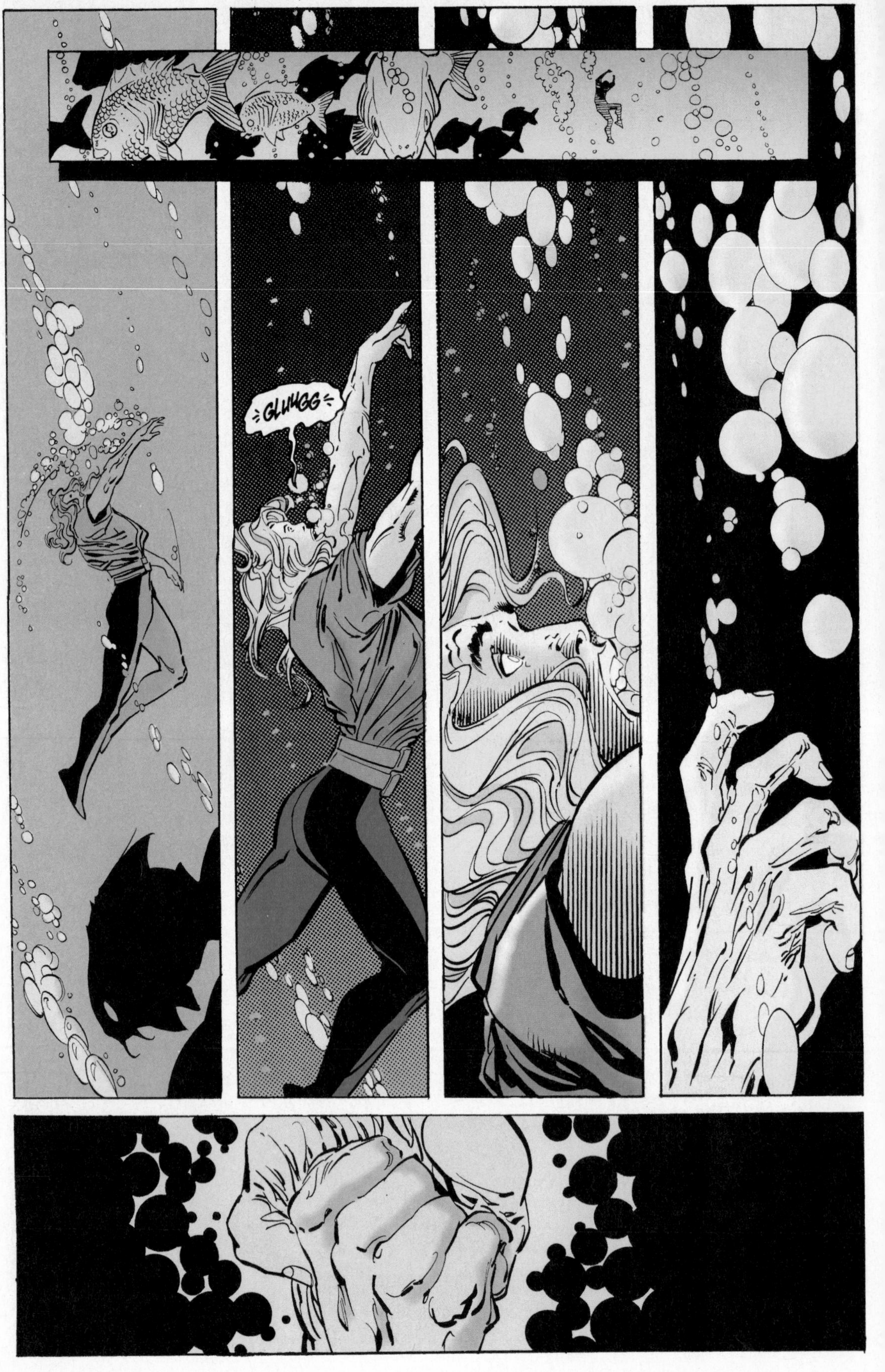
GLUHGG

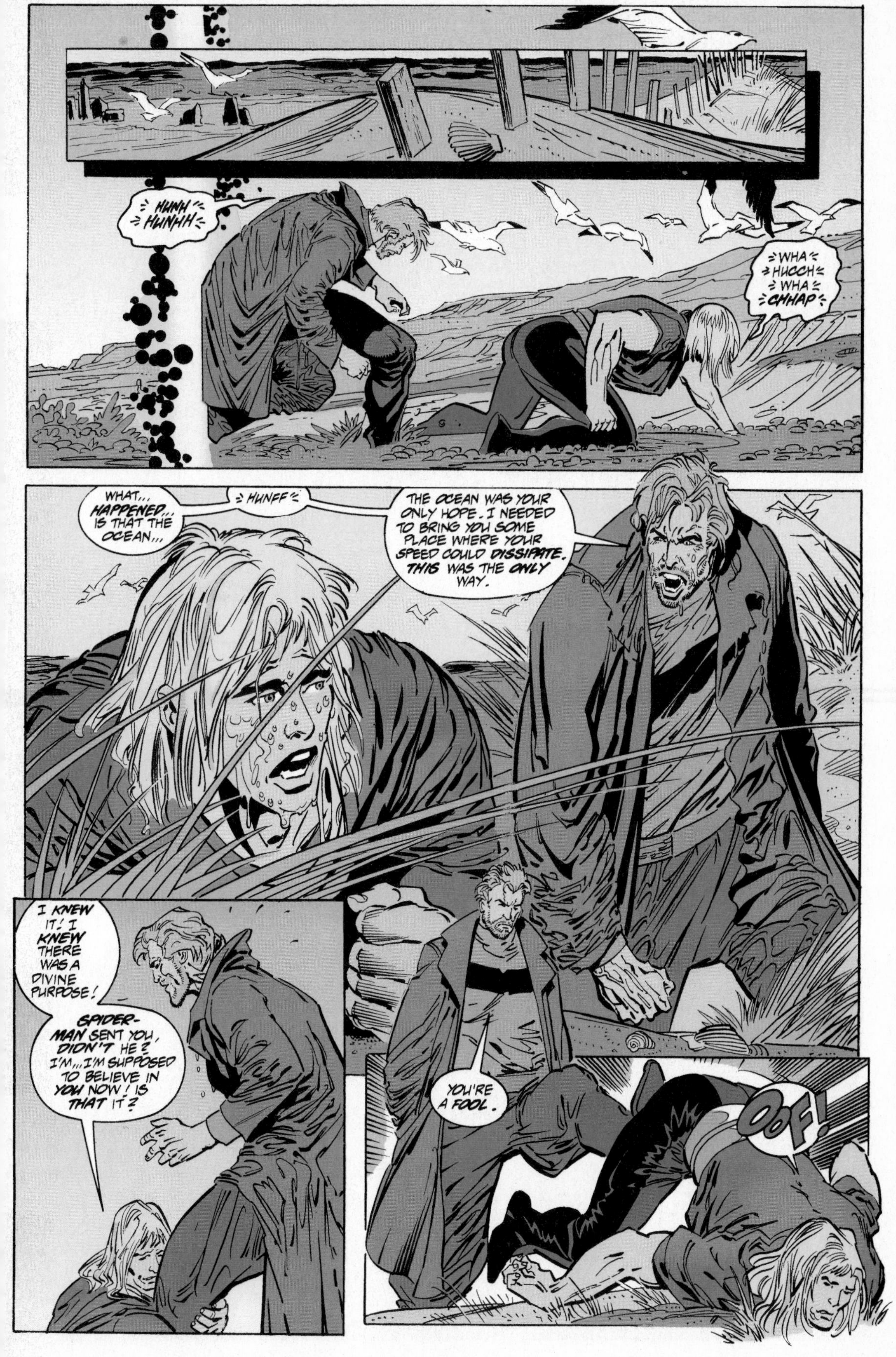
HUNH HUNHH
WHA HUCCH WHA CHHAP
WHAT... HAPPENED... IS THAT THE OCEAN...
HUNFF
THE OCEAN WAS YOUR ONLY HOPE. I NEEDED TO BRING YOU SOME PLACE WHERE YOUR SPEED COULD DISSIPATE. THIS WAS THE ONLY WAY.
I KNEW IT! I KNEW THERE WAS A DIVINE PURPOSE!
SPIDER-MAN SENT YOU, DIDN'T HE? I'M... I'M SUPPOSED TO BELIEVE IN YOU NOW! IS THAT IT?
YOU'RE A FOOL.
OOF!

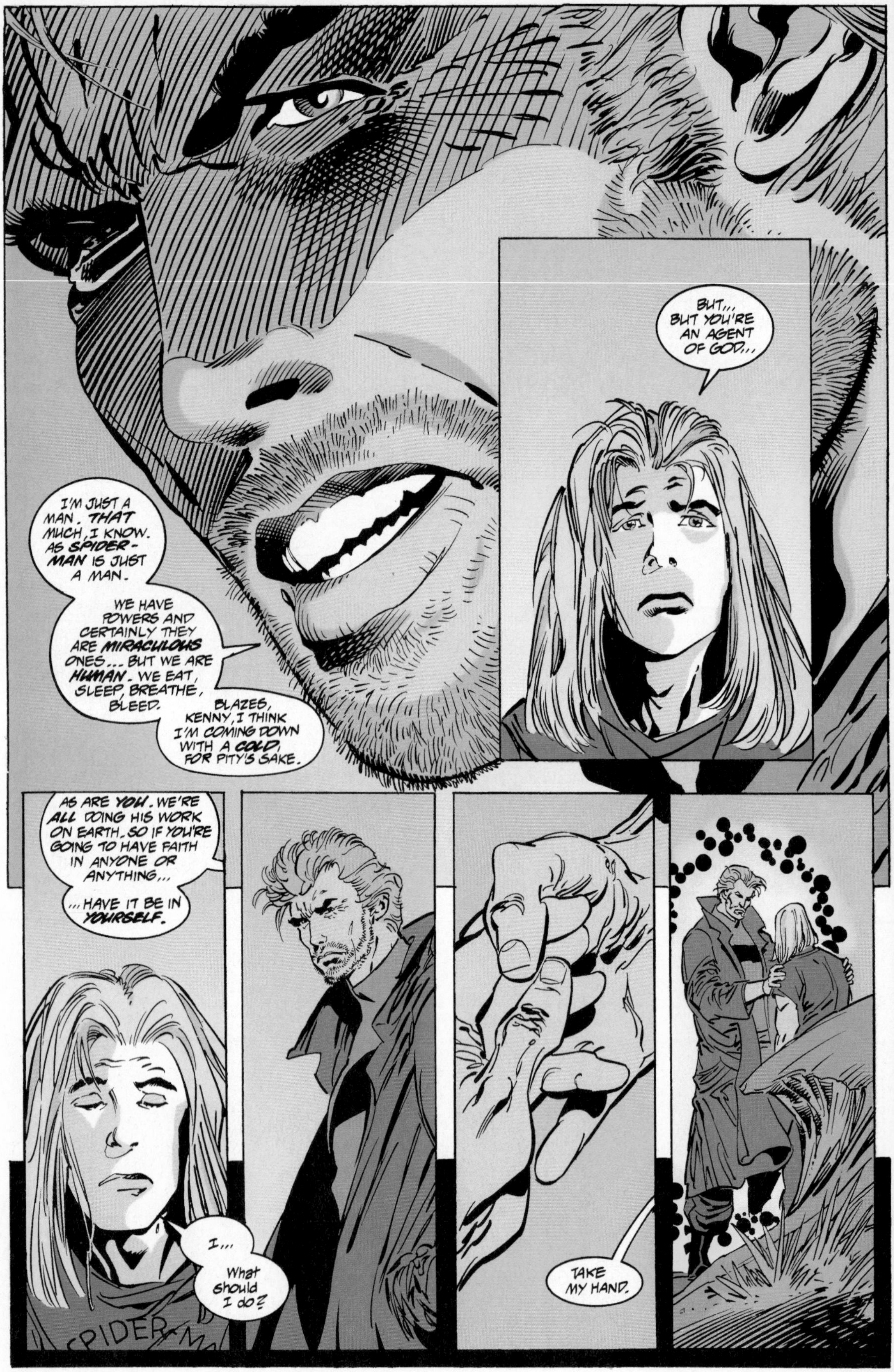
BUT... BUT YOU'RE AN AGENT OF GOD...
I'M JUST A MAN. THAT MUCH, I KNOW. AS SPIDER-MAN IS JUST A MAN.
WE HAVE POWERS AND CERTAINLY THEY ARE MIRACULOUS ONES... BUT WE ARE HUMAN. WE EAT, SLEEP, BREATHE, BLEED.
BLAZES, KENNY, I THINK I'M COMING DOWN WITH A COLD, FOR PITY'S SAKE.
AS ARE YOU. WE'RE ALL DOING HIS WORK ON EARTH. SO IF YOU'RE GOING TO HAVE FAITH IN ANYONE OR ANYTHING...
...HAVE IT BE IN YOURSELF.
I...
What should I do?
TAKE MY HAND.
SPIDER-MA

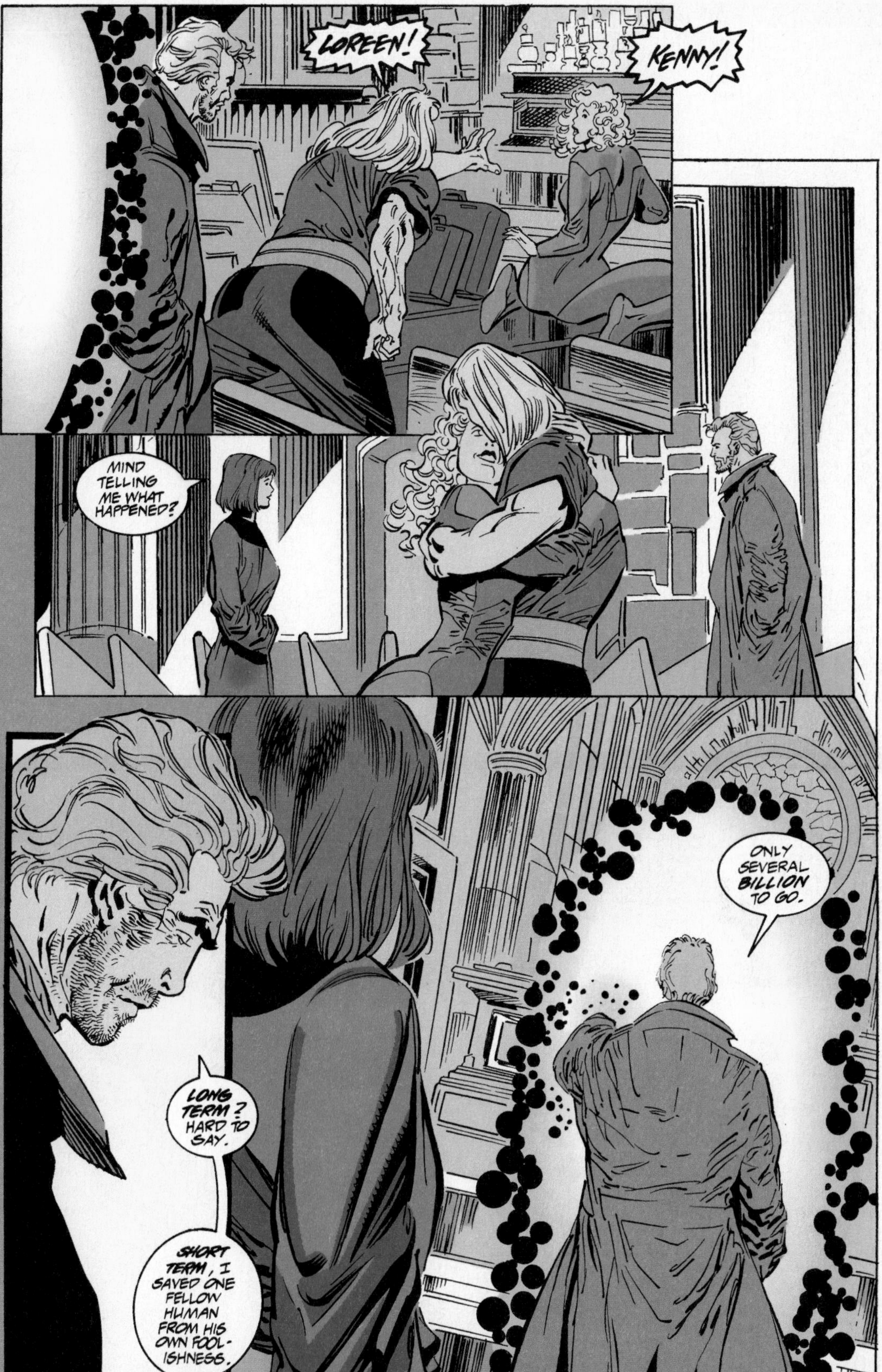
LOREEN!
KENNY!
MIND TELLING ME WHAT HAPPENED?
LONG TERM? HARD TO SAY.
SHORT TERM, I SAVED ONE FELLOW HUMAN FROM HIS OWN FOOL-ISHNESS.
ONLY SEVERAL BILLION TO GO.
END?

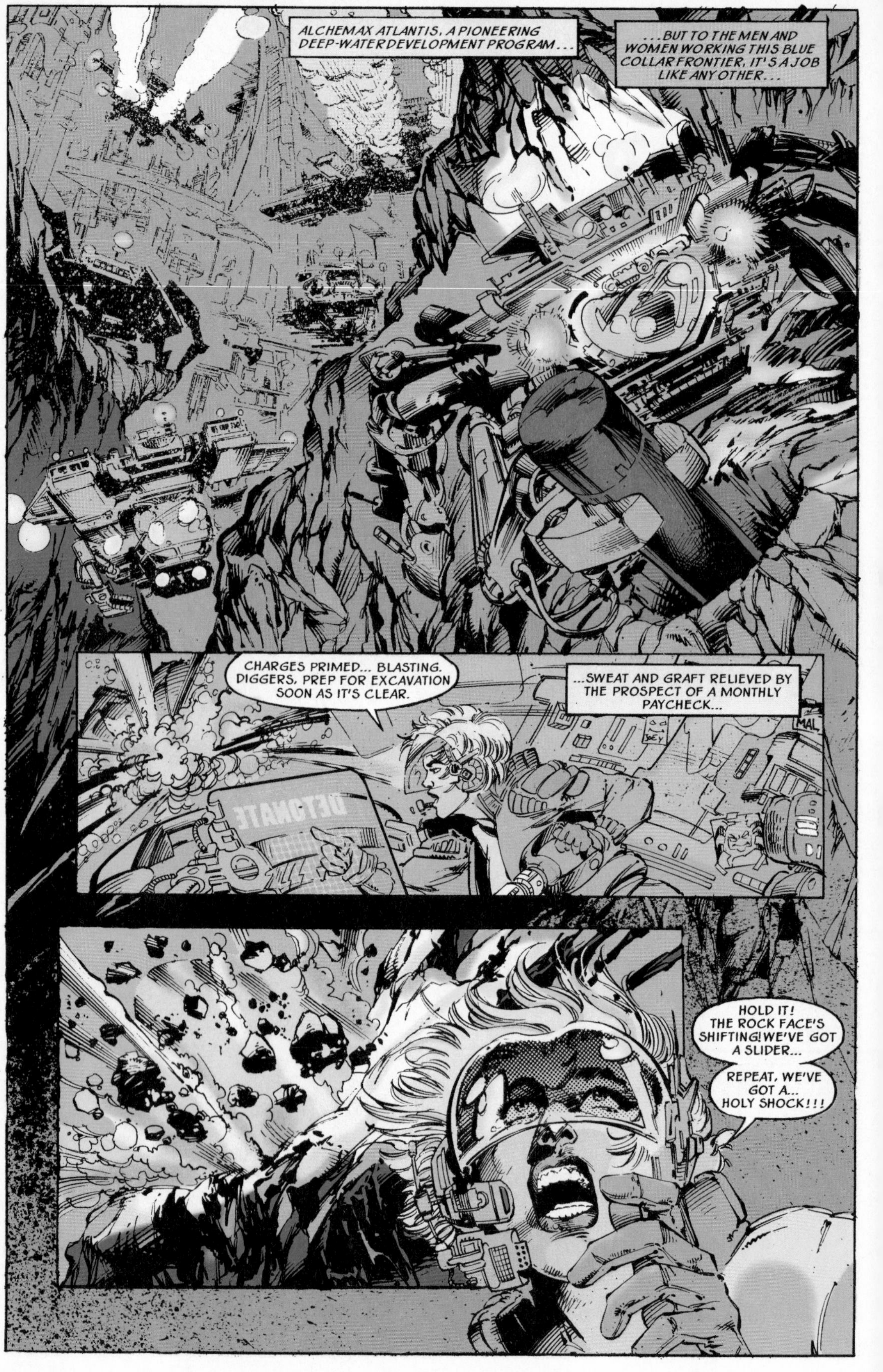
ALCHEMAX ATLANTIS, A PIONEERING DEEP-WATER DEVELOPMENT PROGRAM...
...BUT TO THE MEN AND WOMEN WORKING THIS BLUE COLLAR FRONTIER, IT'S A JOB LIKE ANY OTHER...
CHARGES PRIMED... BLASTING. DIGGERS, PREP FOR EXCAVATION SOON AS IT'S CLEAR.
...SWEAT AND GRAFT RELIEVED BY THE PROSPECT OF A MONTHLY PAYCHECK...
DETONATE
HOLD IT! THE ROCK FACE'S SHIFTING! WE'VE GOT A SLIDER...
REPEAT, WE'VE GOT A... HOLY SHOCK!!!

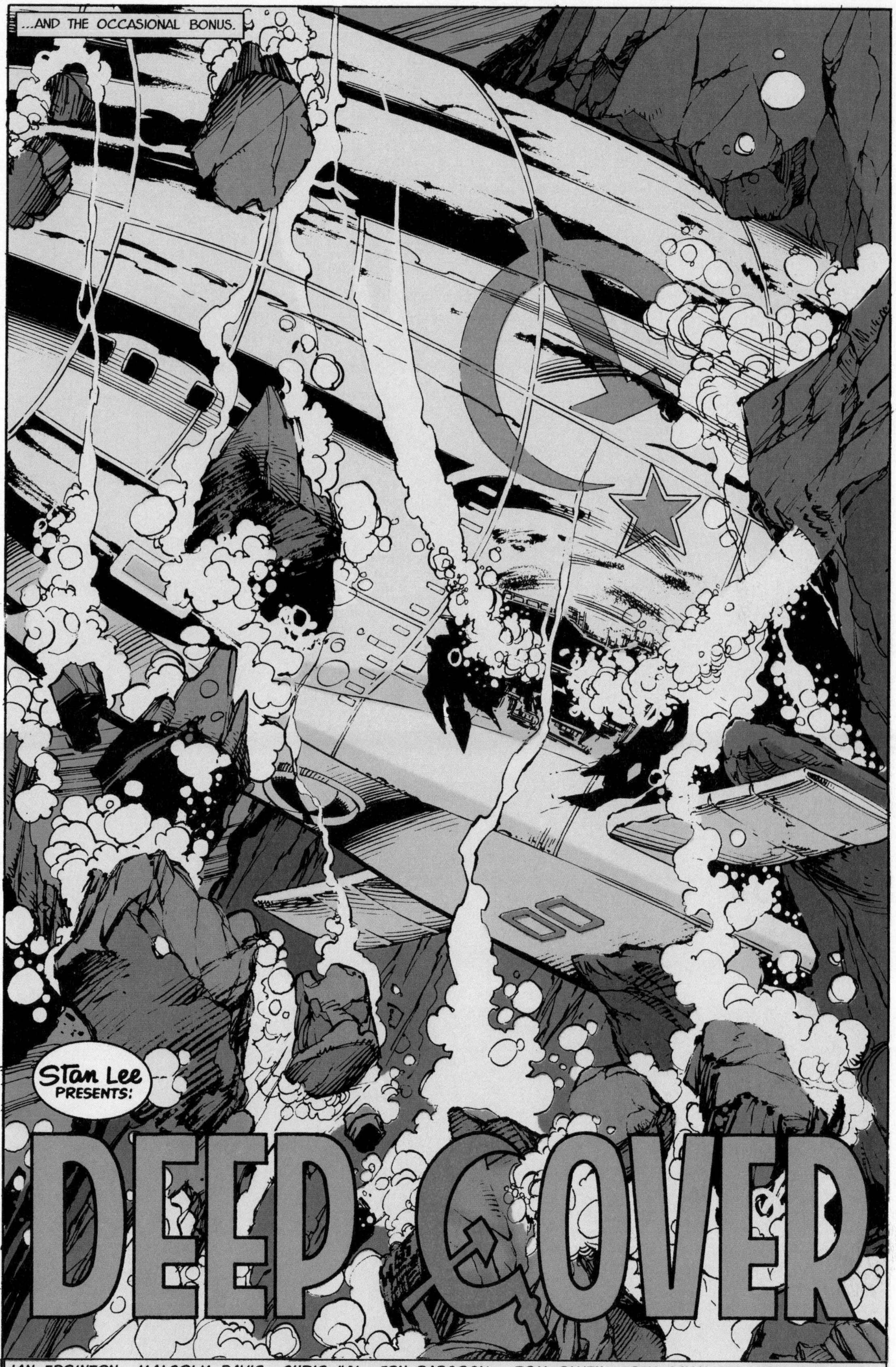
...AND THE OCCASIONAL BONUS.
STAN LEE PRESENTS:
DEEP COVER
IAN EDGINTON STORY
MALCOLM DAVIS PENCILS
CHRIS IVY INKS
JON BABCOCK LETTERS
TOM SMITH COLORS
JOEY CAVALIERI COMRADE
TOM DEFALCO COMISSAR

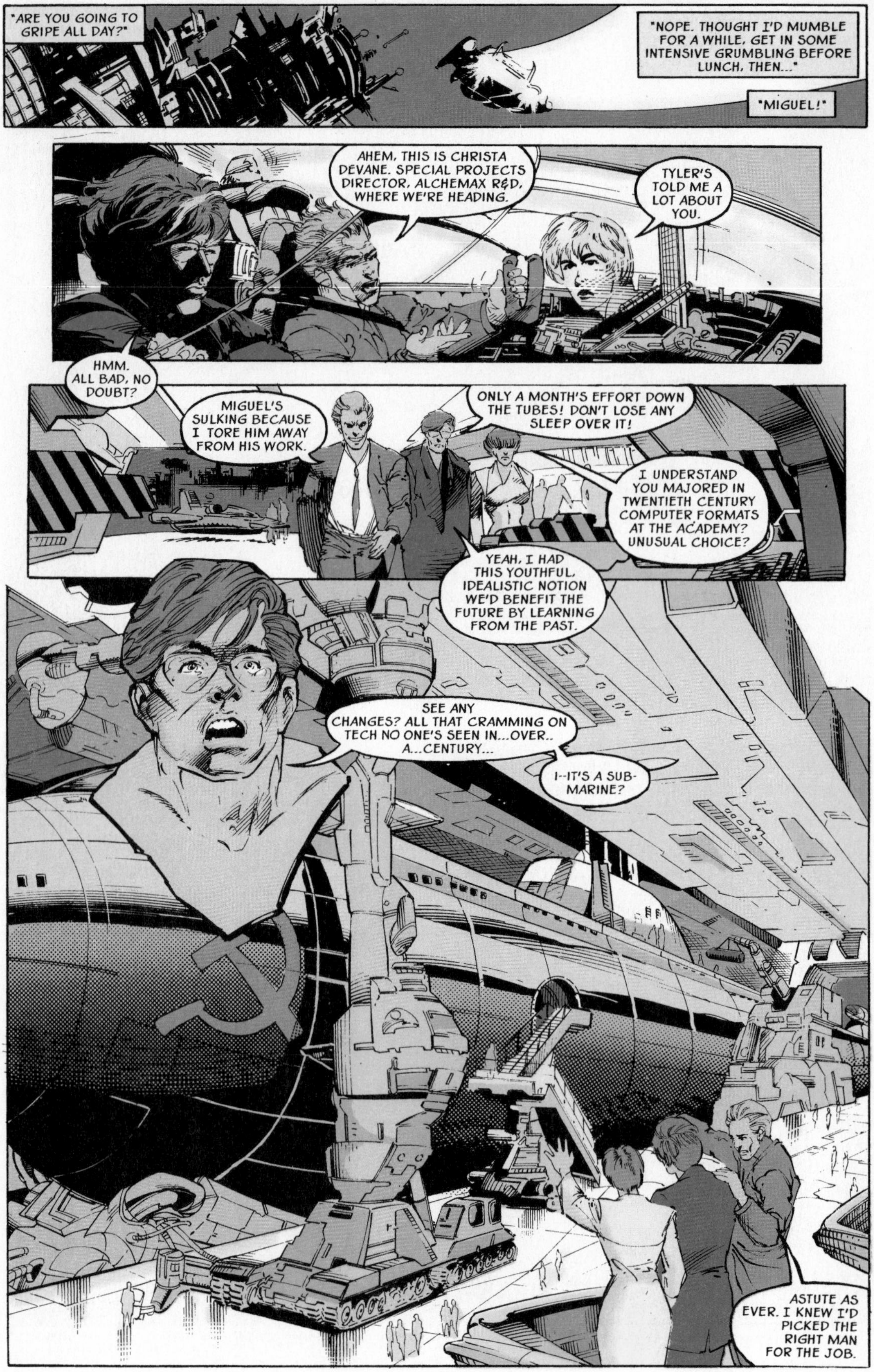
"ARE YOU GOING TO GRIPE ALL DAY?"
"NOPE. THOUGHT I'D MUMBLE FOR A WHILE, GET IN SOME INTENSIVE GRUMBLING BEFORE LUNCH, THEN..."
"MIGUEL!"
AHEM, THIS IS CHRISTA DEVANE. SPECIAL PROJECTS DIRECTOR, ALCHEMAX R&D, WHERE WE'RE HEADING.
TYLER'S TOLD ME A LOT ABOUT YOU.
HMM. ALL BAD, NO DOUBT?
MIGUEL'S SULKING BECAUSE I TORE HIM AWAY FROM HIS WORK.
ONLY A MONTH'S EFFORT DOWN THE TUBES! DON'T LOSE ANY SLEEP OVER IT!
I UNDERSTAND YOU MAJORED IN TWENTIETH CENTURY COMPUTER FORMATS AT THE ACADEMY? UNUSUAL CHOICE?
YEAH, I HAD THIS YOUTHFUL, IDEALISTIC NOTION WE'D BENEFIT THE FUTURE BY LEARNING FROM THE PAST.
SEE ANY CHANGES? ALL THAT CRAMMING ON TECH NO ONE'S SEEN IN...OVER.. A...CENTURY...
I--IT'S A SUB-MARINE?
ASTUTE AS EVER. I KNEW I'D PICKED THE RIGHT MAN FOR THE JOB.

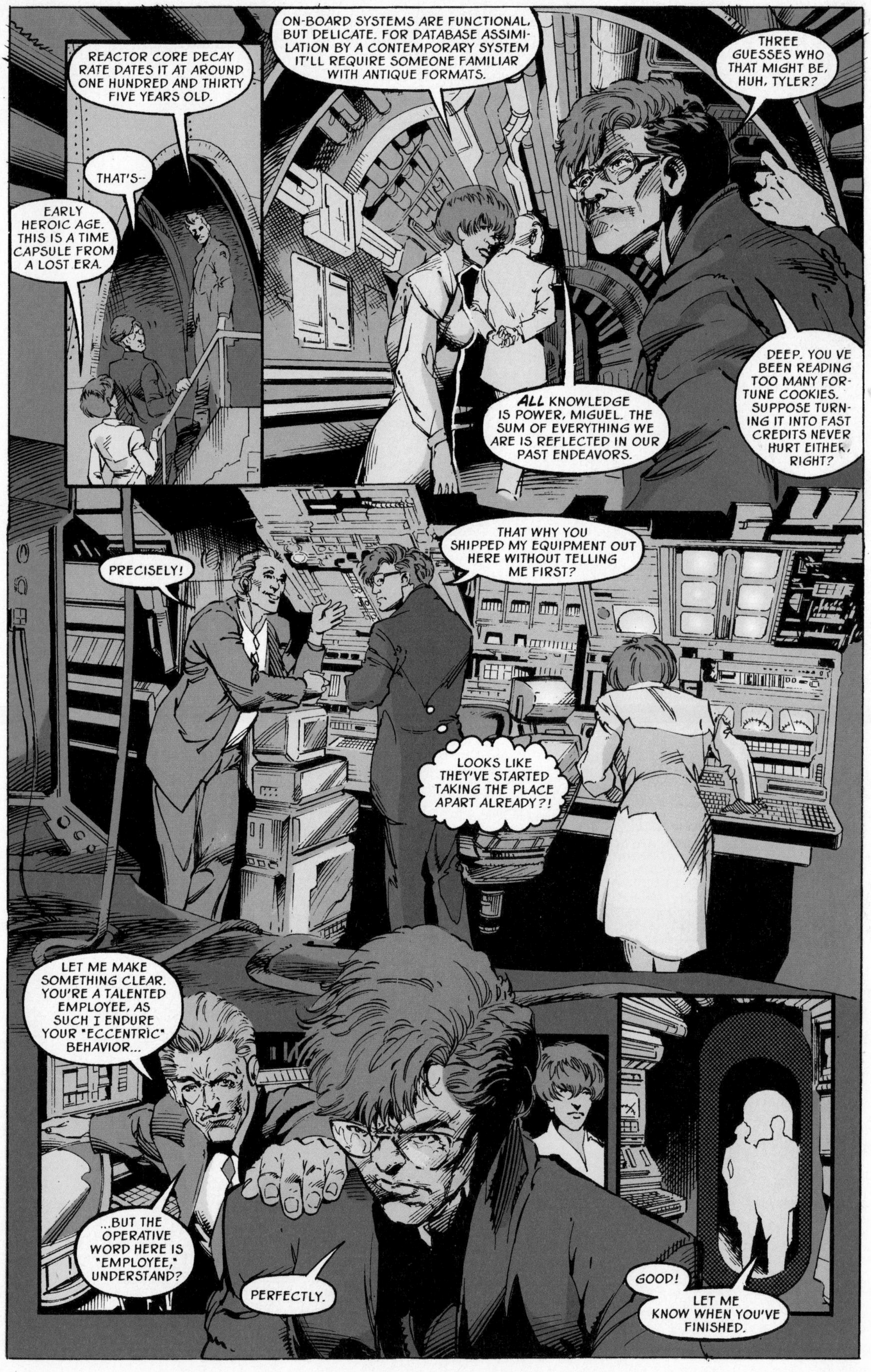
REACTOR CORE DECAY RATE DATES IT AT AROUND ONE HUNDRED AND THIRTY FIVE YEARS OLD.
THAT'S--
EARLY HEROIC AGE. THIS IS A TIME CAPSULE FROM A LOST ERA.
ON-BOARD SYSTEMS ARE FUNCTIONAL, BUT DELICATE. FOR DATABASE ASSIMILATION BY A CONTEMPORARY SYSTEM IT'LL REQUIRE SOMEONE FAMILIAR WITH ANTIQUE FORMATS.
THREE GUESSES WHO THAT MIGHT BE, HUH, TYLER?
ALL KNOWLEDGE IS POWER, MIGUEL. THE SUM OF EVERYTHING WE ARE IS REFLECTED IN OUR PAST ENDEAVORS.
DEEP. YOU VE BEEN READING TOO MANY FORTUNE COOKIES. SUPPOSE TURNING IT INTO FAST CREDITS NEVER HURT EITHER, RIGHT?
PRECISELY!
THAT WHY YOU SHIPPED MY EQUIPMENT OUT HERE WITHOUT TELLING ME FIRST?
LOOKS LIKE THEY'VE STARTED TAKING THE PLACE APART ALREADY?!
LET ME MAKE SOMETHING CLEAR. YOU'RE A TALENTED EMPLOYEE, AS SUCH I ENDURE YOUR "ECCENTRIC" BEHAVIOR...
...BUT THE OPERATIVE WORD HERE IS "EMPLOYEE," UNDERSTAND?
PERFECTLY.
GOOD!
LET ME KNOW WHEN YOU'VE FINISHED.

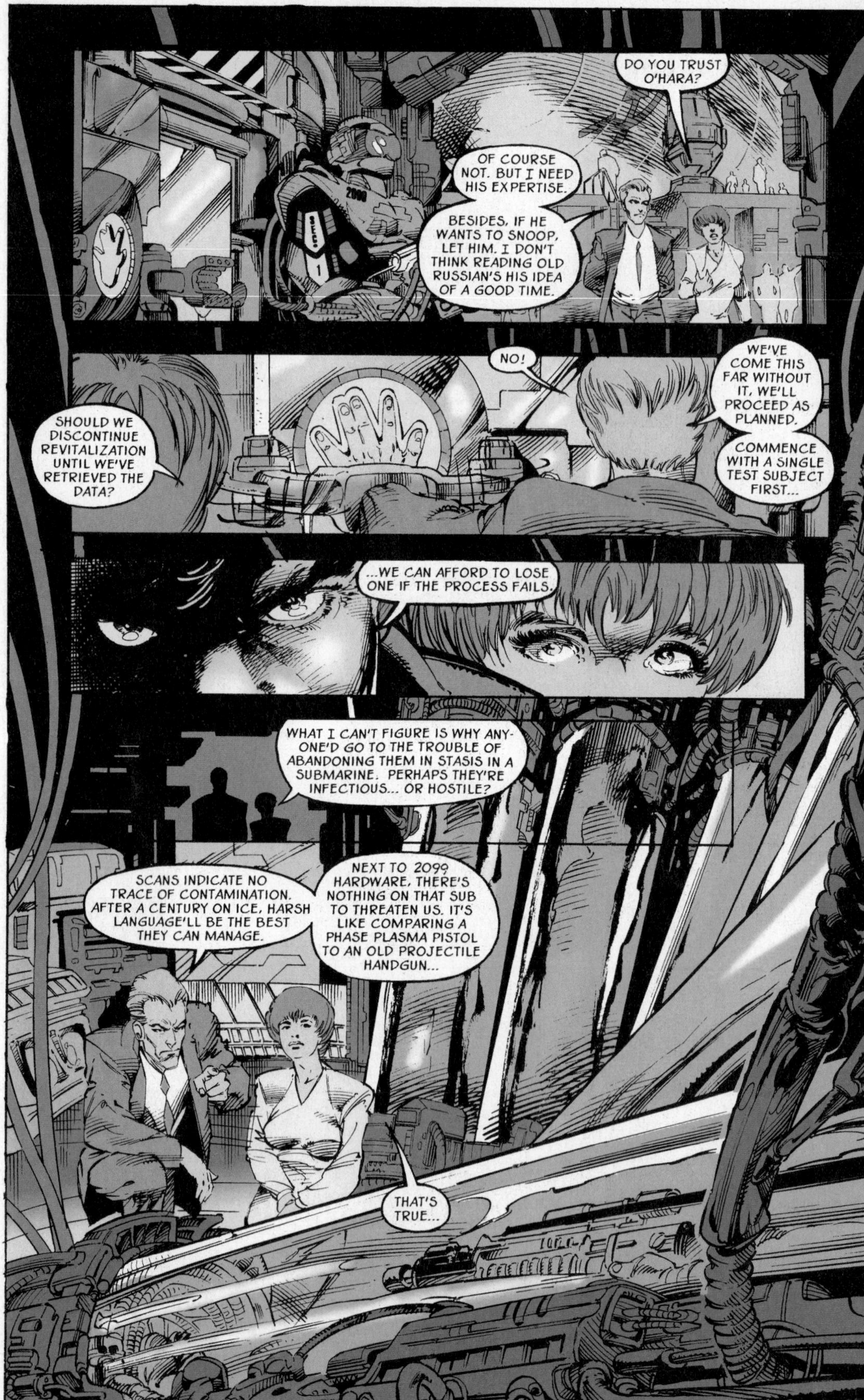
DO YOU TRUST O'HARA?
OF COURSE NOT. BUT I NEED HIS EXPERTISE.
BESIDES, IF HE WANTS TO SNOOP, LET HIM. I DON'T THINK READING OLD RUSSIAN'S HIS IDEA OF A GOOD TIME.
SHOULD WE DISCONTINUE REVITALIZATION UNTIL WE'VE RETRIEVED THE DATA?
NO!
WE'VE COME THIS FAR WITHOUT IT, WE'LL PROCEED AS PLANNED.
COMMENCE WITH A SINGLE TEST SUBJECT FIRST...
...WE CAN AFFORD TO LOSE ONE IF THE PROCESS FAILS.
WHAT I CAN'T FIGURE IS WHY ANYONE'D GO TO THE TROUBLE OF ABANDONING THEM IN STASIS IN A SUBMARINE. PERHAPS THEY'RE INFECTIOUS... OR HOSTILE?
SCANS INDICATE NO TRACE OF CONTAMINATION. AFTER A CENTURY ON ICE, HARSH LANGUAGE'LL BE THE BEST THEY CAN MANAGE.
NEXT TO 2099 HARDWARE, THERE'S NOTHING ON THAT SUB TO THREATEN US. IT'S LIKE COMPARING A PHASE PLASMA PISTOL TO AN OLD PROJECTILE HANDGUN...
THAT'S TRUE...

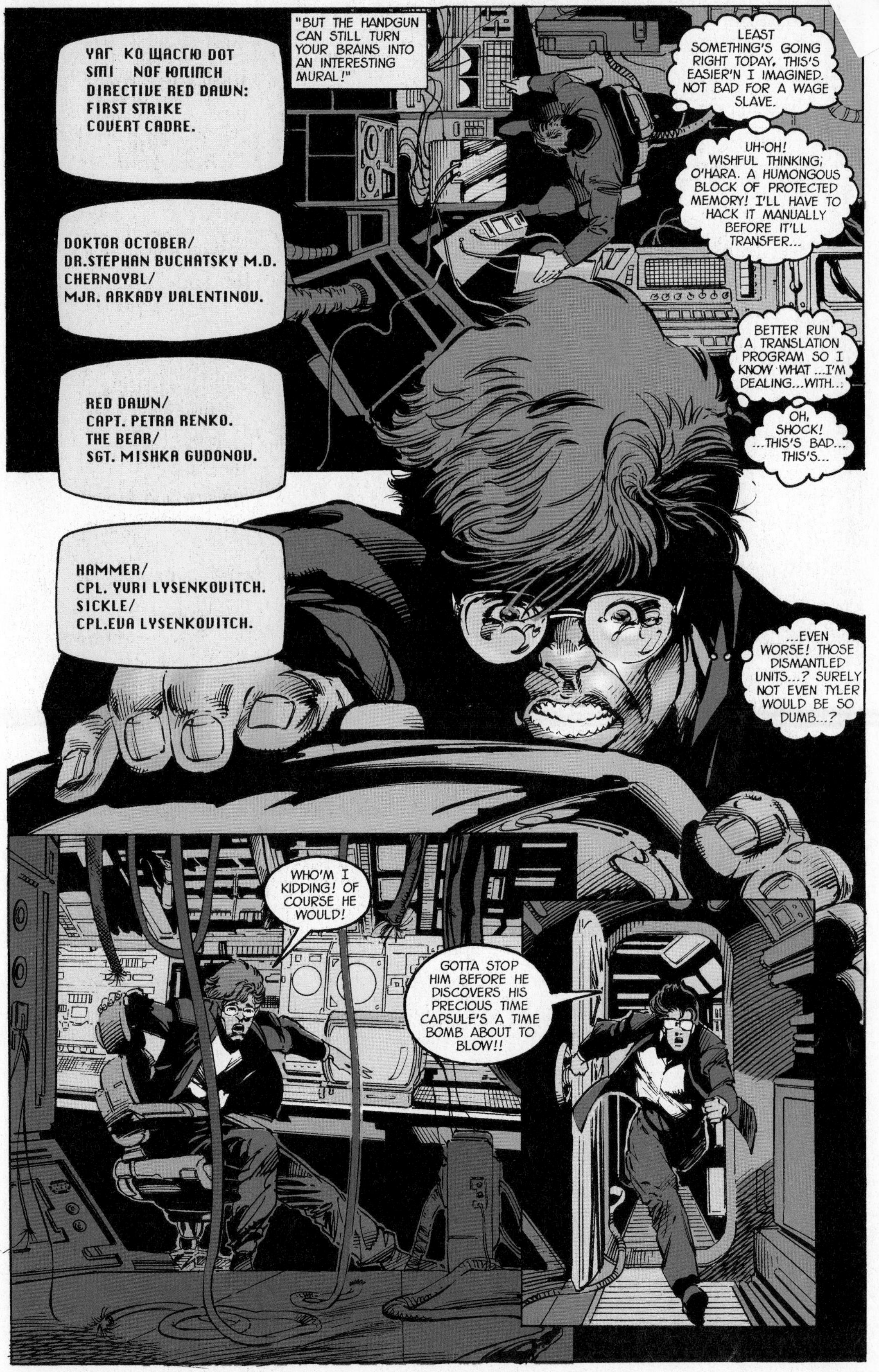
УАГ КО ЩАСГЮ DOT SMI NOF ЮПIПCH DIRECTIVE RED DAWN: FIRST STRIKE COVERT CADRE.
"BUT THE HANDGUN CAN STILL TURN YOUR BRAINS INTO AN INTERESTING MURAL!"
LEAST SOMETHING'S GOING RIGHT TODAY. THIS'S EASIER'N I IMAGINED. NOT BAD FOR A WAGE SLAVE.
UH-OH! WISHFUL THINKING, O'HARA. A HUMONGOUS BLOCK OF PROTECTED MEMORY! I'LL HAVE TO HACK IT MANUALLY BEFORE IT'LL TRANSFER...
DOKTOR OCTOBER/ DR.STEPHAN BUCHATSKY M.D. CHERNOYBL/ MJR. ARKADY VALENTINOV.
BETTER RUN A TRANSLATION PROGRAM SO I KNOW WHAT ...I'M DEALING...WITH...
RED DAWN/ CAPT. PETRA RENKO. THE BEAR/ SGT. MISHKA GUDONOV.
OH, SHOCK! ...THIS'S BAD... THIS'S...
HAMMER/ CPL. YURI LYSENKOVITCH. SICKLE/ CPL.EVA LYSENKOVITCH.
...EVEN WORSE! THOSE DISMANTLED UNITS...? SURELY NOT EVEN TYLER WOULD BE SO DUMB...?
WHO'M I KIDDING! OF COURSE HE WOULD!
GOTTA STOP HIM BEFORE HE DISCOVERS HIS PRECIOUS TIME CAPSULE'S A TIME BOMB ABOUT TO BLOW!!

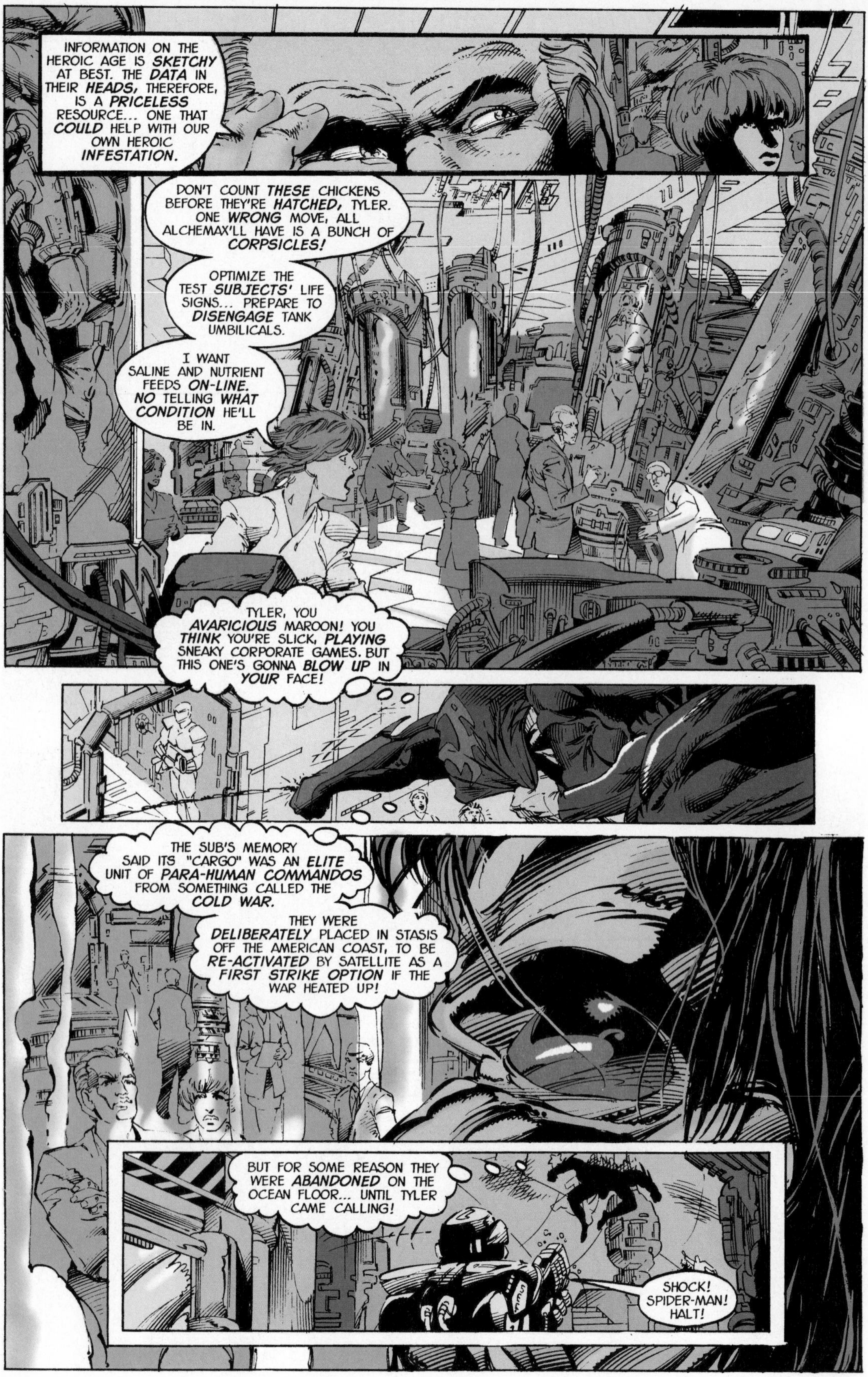
INFORMATION ON THE HEROIC AGE IS SKETCHY AT BEST. THE DATA IN THEIR HEADS, THEREFORE, IS A PRICELESS RESOURCE... ONE THAT COULD HELP WITH OUR OWN HEROIC INFESTATION.
DON'T COUNT THESE CHICKENS BEFORE THEY'RE HATCHED, TYLER. ONE WRONG MOVE, ALL ALCHEMAX'LL HAVE IS A BUNCH OF CORPSICLES!
OPTIMIZE THE TEST SUBJECTS' LIFE SIGNS... PREPARE TO DISENGAGE TANK UMBILICALS.
I WANT SALINE AND NUTRIENT FEEDS ON-LINE. NO TELLING WHAT CONDITION HE'LL BE IN.
TYLER, YOU AVARICIOUS MAROON! YOU THINK YOU'RE SLICK, PLAYING SNEAKY CORPORATE GAMES. BUT THIS ONE'S GONNA BLOW UP IN YOUR FACE!
THE SUB'S MEMORY SAID ITS "CARGO" WAS AN ELITE UNIT OF PARA-HUMAN COMMANDOS FROM SOMETHING CALLED THE COLD WAR.
THEY WERE DELIBERATELY PLACED IN STASIS OFF THE AMERICAN COAST, TO BE RE-ACTIVATED BY SATELLITE AS A FIRST STRIKE OPTION IF THE WAR HEATED UP!
BUT FOR SOME REASON THEY WERE ABANDONED ON THE OCEAN FLOOR... UNTIL TYLER CAME CALLING!
SHOCK! SPIDER-MAN! HALT!

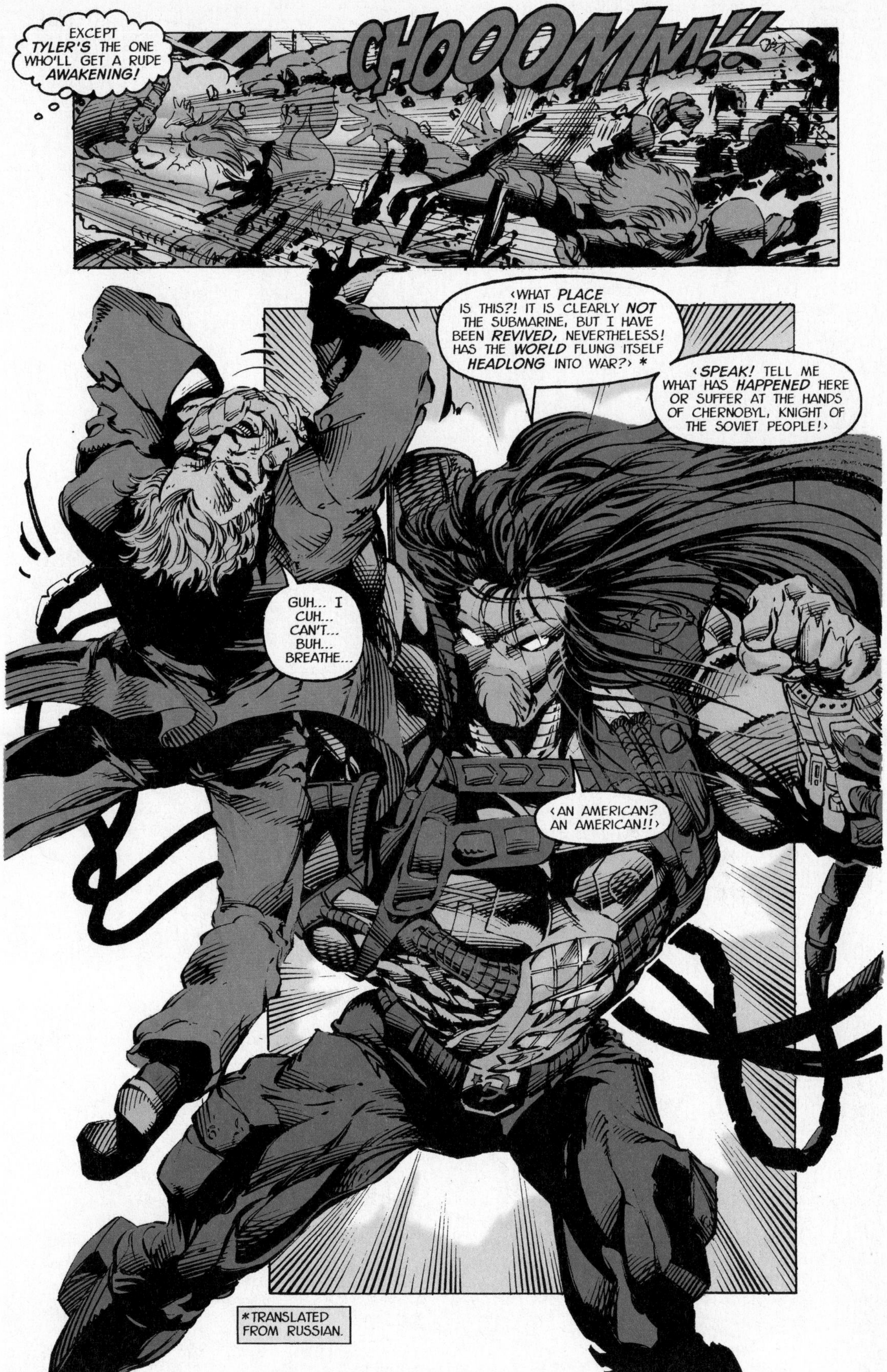
EXCEPT TYLER'S THE ONE WHO'LL GET A RUDE AWAKENING!
CHOOOMM!!
‹WHAT PLACE IS THIS?! IT IS CLEARLY NOT THE SUBMARINE, BUT I HAVE BEEN REVIVED, NEVERTHELESS! HAS THE WORLD FLUNG ITSELF HEADLONG INTO WAR?› *
‹SPEAK! TELL ME WHAT HAS HAPPENED HERE OR SUFFER AT THE HANDS OF CHERNOBYL, KNIGHT OF THE SOVIET PEOPLE!›
GUH... I CUH... CAN'T... BUH... BREATHE...
‹AN AMERICAN? AN AMERICAN!!›
*TRANSLATED FROM RUSSIAN.

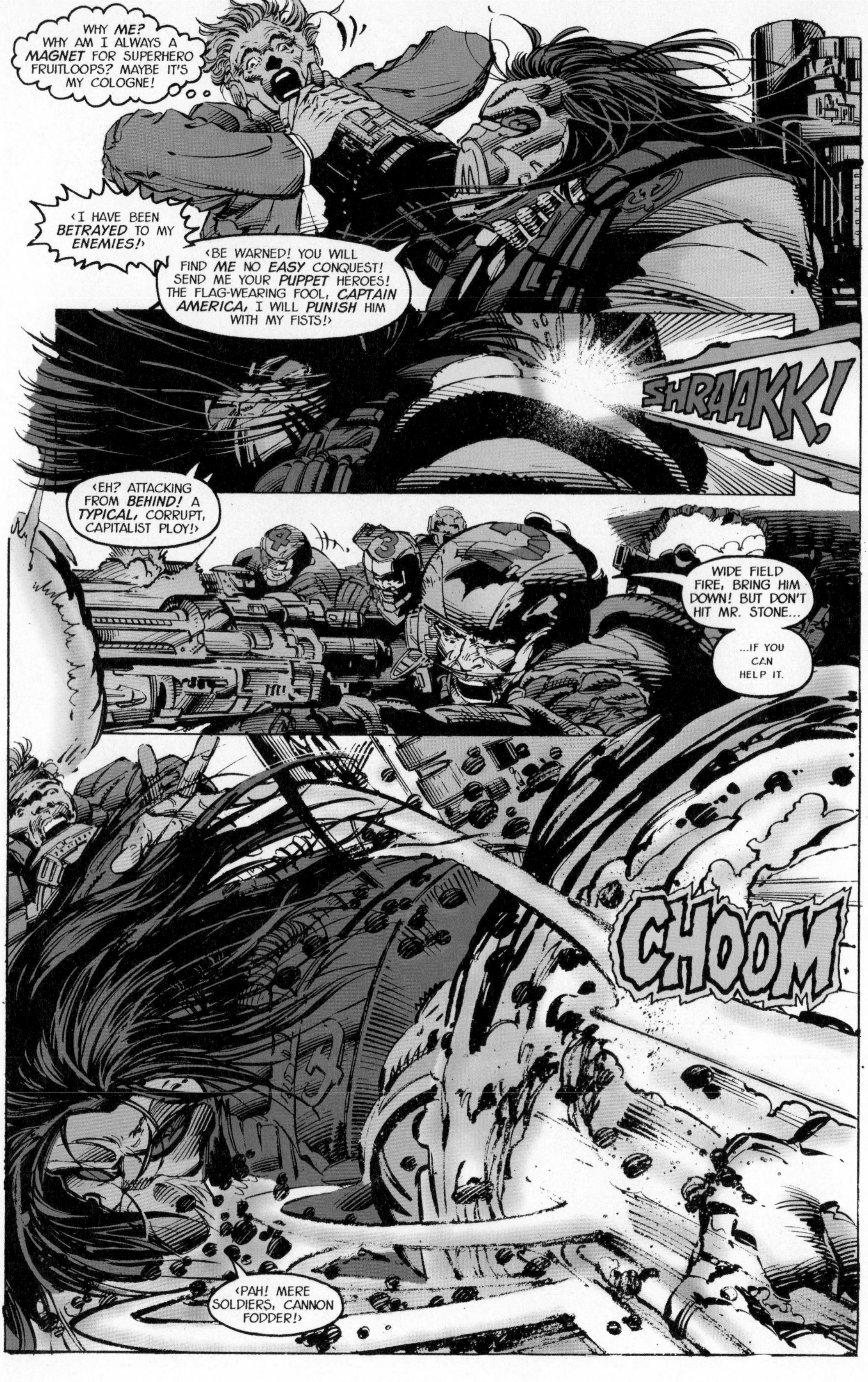

WHY ME? WHY AM I ALWAYS A MAGNET FOR SUPERHERO FRUITLOOPS? MAYBE IT'S MY COLOGNE!
‹I HAVE BEEN BETRAYED TO MY ENEMIES!›
‹BE WARNED! YOU WILL FIND ME NO EASY CONQUEST! SEND ME YOUR PUPPET HEROES! THE FLAG-WEARING FOOL, CAPTAIN AMERICA, I WILL PUNISH HIM WITH MY FISTS!›
SHRAAKK!
‹EH? ATTACKING FROM BEHIND! A TYPICAL, CORRUPT, CAPITALIST PLOY!›
WIDE FIELD FIRE, BRING HIM DOWN! BUT DON'T HIT MR. STONE...
...IF YOU CAN HELP IT.
CHOOM
‹PAH! MERE SOLDIERS, CANNON FODDER!›

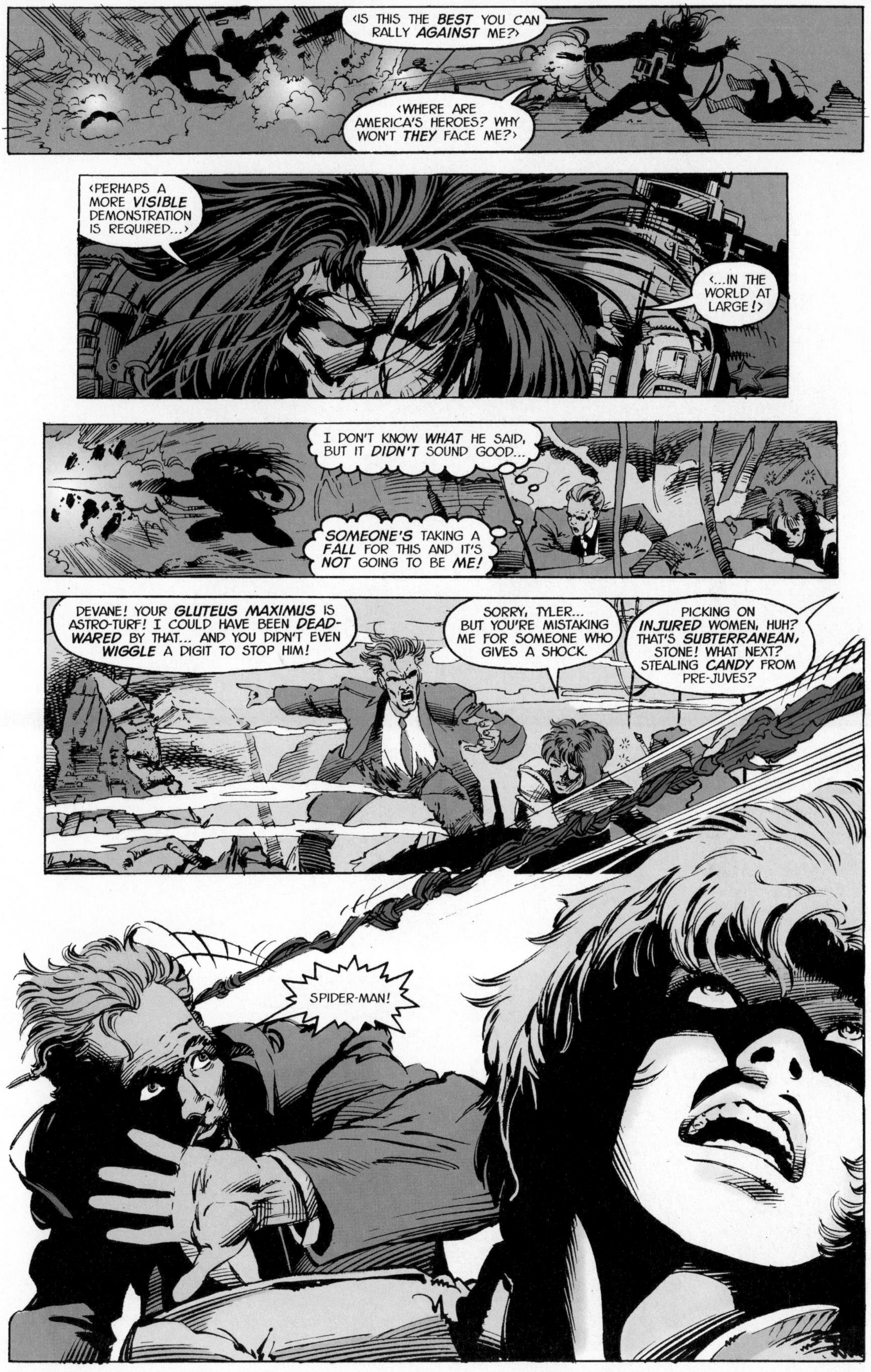
‹IS THIS THE BEST YOU CAN RALLY AGAINST ME?›
‹WHERE ARE AMERICA'S HEROES? WHY WON'T THEY FACE ME?›
‹PERHAPS A MORE VISIBLE DEMONSTRATION IS REQUIRED...›
‹...IN THE WORLD AT LARGE!›
I DON'T KNOW WHAT HE SAID, BUT IT DIDN'T SOUND GOOD...
SOMEONE'S TAKING A FALL FOR THIS AND IT'S NOT GOING TO BE ME!
DEVANE! YOUR GLUTEUS MAXIMUS IS ASTRO-TURF! I COULD HAVE BEEN DEAD-WARED BY THAT... AND YOU DIDN'T EVEN WIGGLE A DIGIT TO STOP HIM!
SORRY, TYLER... BUT YOU'RE MISTAKING ME FOR SOMEONE WHO GIVES A SHOCK.
PICKING ON INJURED WOMEN, HUH? THAT'S SUBTERRANEAN, STONE! WHAT NEXT? STEALING CANDY FROM PRE-JUVES?
SPIDER-MAN!

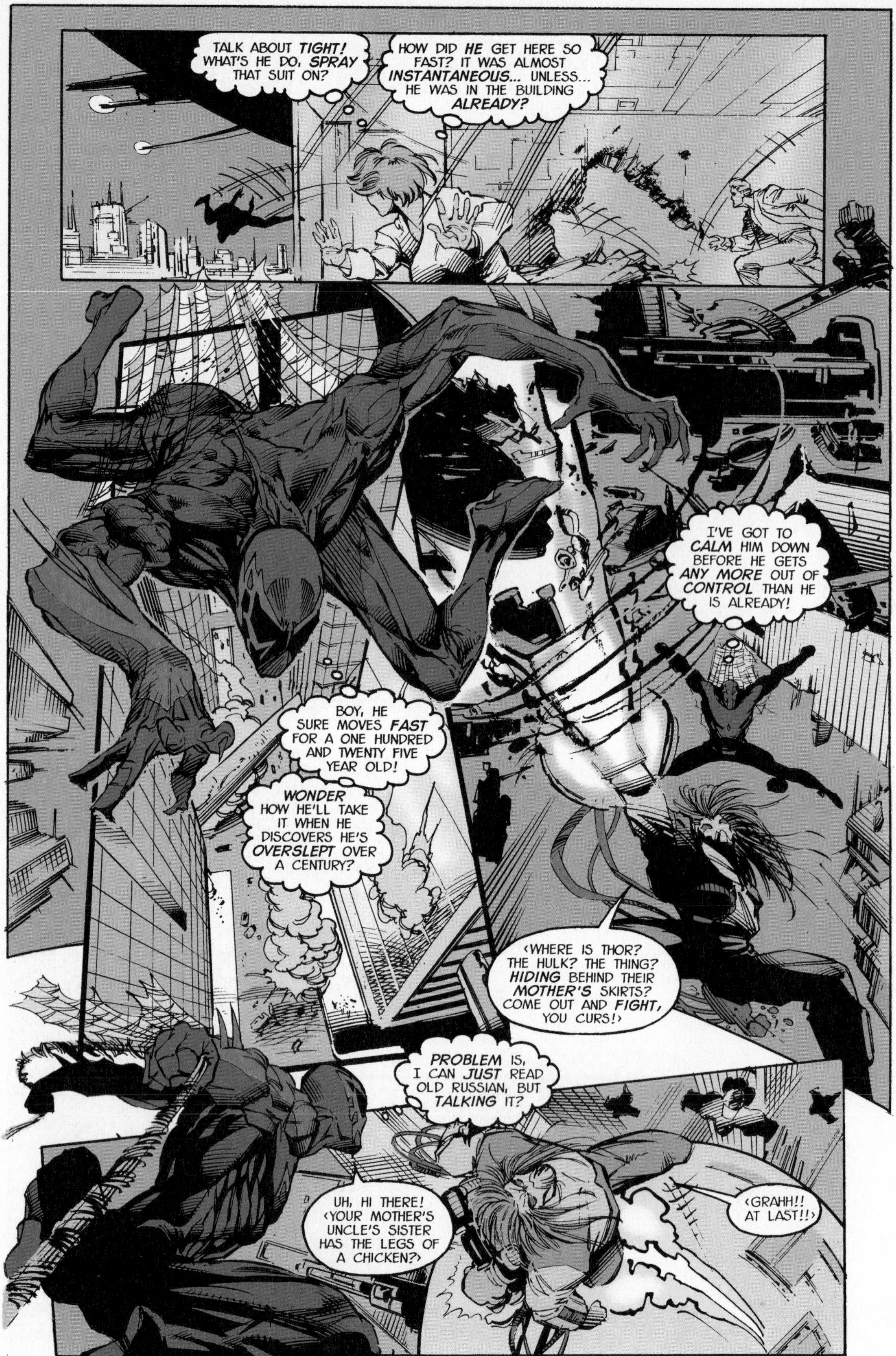

TALK ABOUT TIGHT! WHAT'S HE DO, SPRAY THAT SUIT ON?
HOW DID HE GET HERE SO FAST? IT WAS ALMOST INSTANTANEOUS... UNLESS... HE WAS IN THE BUILDING ALREADY?
I'VE GOT TO CALM HIM DOWN BEFORE HE GETS ANY MORE OUT OF CONTROL THAN HE IS ALREADY!
BOY, HE SURE MOVES FAST FOR A ONE HUNDRED AND TWENTY FIVE YEAR OLD!
WONDER HOW HE'LL TAKE IT WHEN HE DISCOVERS HE'S OVERSLEPT OVER A CENTURY?
‹WHERE IS THOR? THE HULK? THE THING? HIDING BEHIND THEIR MOTHER'S SKIRTS? COME OUT AND FIGHT, YOU CURS!›
PROBLEM IS, I CAN JUST READ OLD RUSSIAN, BUT TALKING IT?
UH, HI THERE! ‹YOUR MOTHER'S UNCLE'S SISTER HAS THE LEGS OF A CHICKEN?›
‹GRAHH!! AT LAST!!›

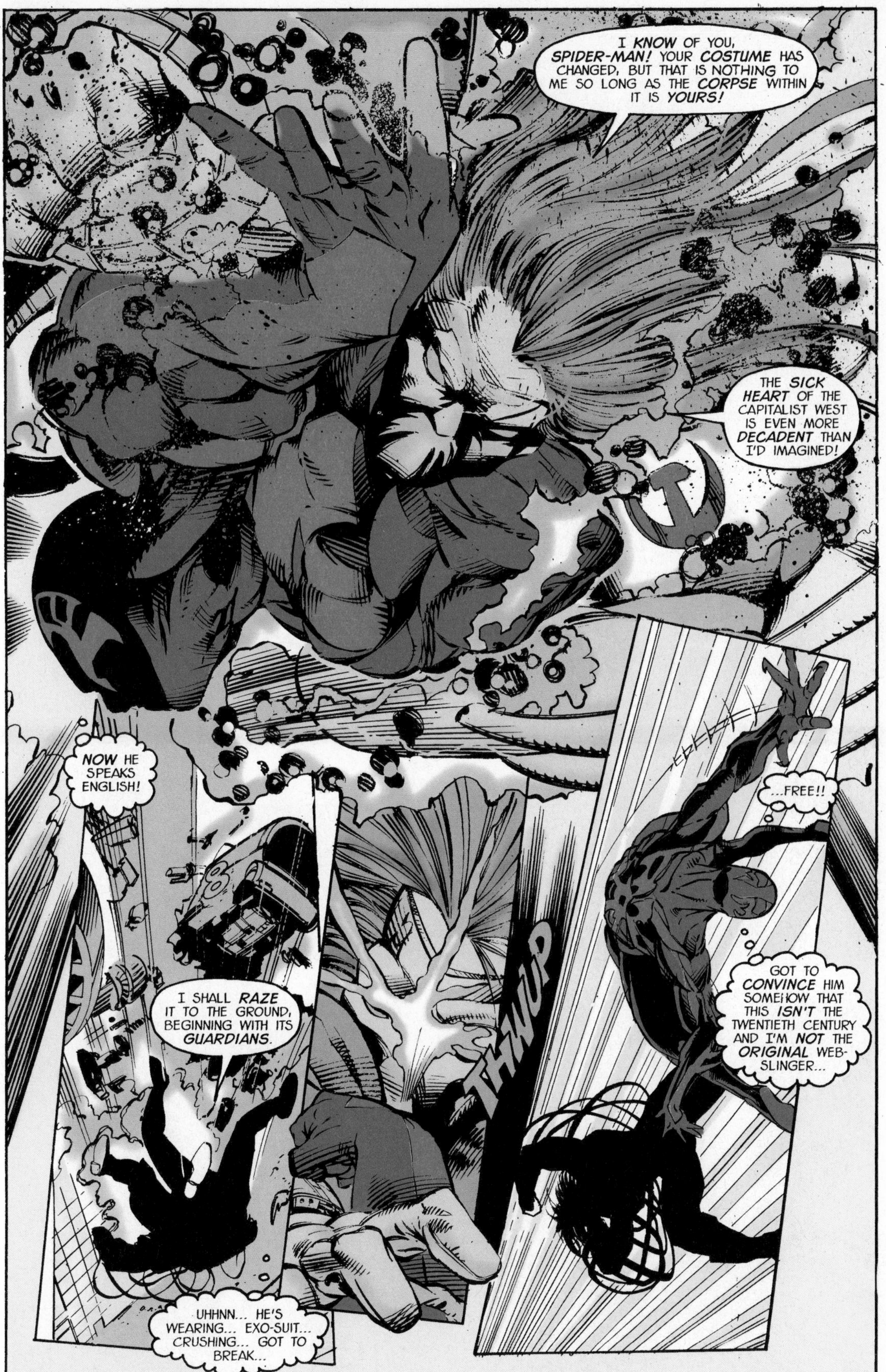
I KNOW OF YOU, SPIDER-MAN! YOUR COSTUME HAS CHANGED, BUT THAT IS NOTHING TO ME SO LONG AS THE CORPSE WITHIN IT IS YOURS!
THE SICK HEART OF THE CAPITALIST WEST IS EVEN MORE DECADENT THAN I'D IMAGINED!
NOW HE SPEAKS ENGLISH!
I SHALL RAZE IT TO THE GROUND, BEGINNING WITH ITS GUARDIANS.
UHHNN... HE'S WEARING... EXO-SUIT... CRUSHING... GOT TO BREAK...
THWUP
...FREE!!
GOT TO CONVINCE HIM SOMEHOW THAT THIS ISN'T THE TWENTIETH CENTURY AND I'M NOT THE ORIGINAL WEB-SLINGER...

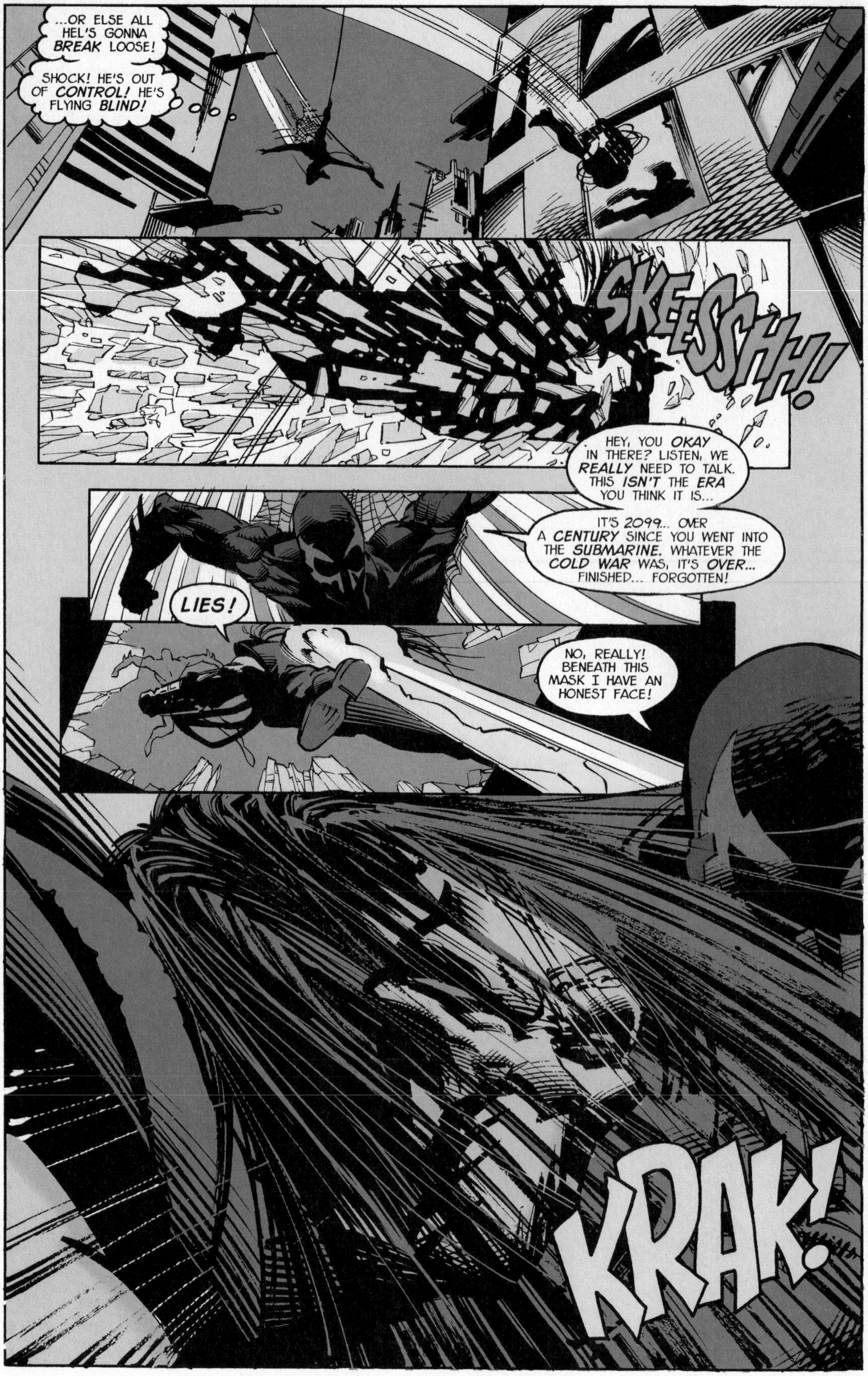
...OR ELSE ALL HEL'S GONNA BREAK LOOSE!
SHOCK! HE'S OUT OF CONTROL! HE'S FLYING BLIND!
SKEESSHH!
HEY, YOU OKAY IN THERE? LISTEN, WE REALLY NEED TO TALK. THIS ISN'T THE ERA YOU THINK IT IS...
IT'S 2099... OVER A CENTURY SINCE YOU WENT INTO THE SUBMARINE. WHATEVER THE COLD WAR WAS, IT'S OVER... FINISHED... FORGOTTEN!
LIES!
NO, REALLY! BENEATH THIS MASK I HAVE AN HONEST FACE!
KRAK!

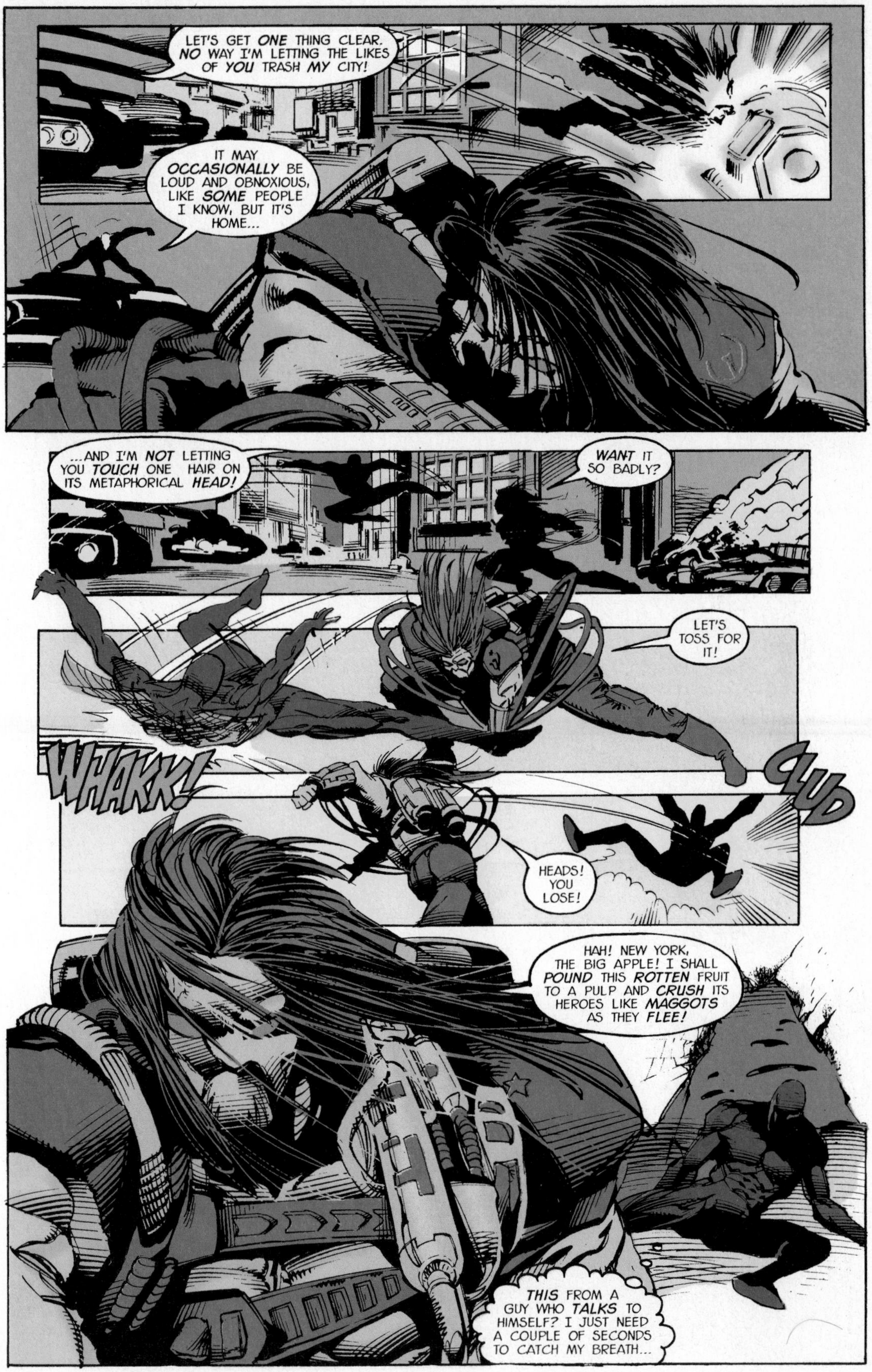
LET'S GET ONE THING CLEAR. NO WAY I'M LETTING THE LIKES OF YOU TRASH MY CITY!
IT MAY OCCASIONALLY BE LOUD AND OBNOXIOUS, LIKE SOME PEOPLE I KNOW, BUT IT'S HOME...
...AND I'M NOT LETTING YOU TOUCH ONE HAIR ON ITS METAPHORICAL HEAD!
WANT IT SO BADLY?
LET'S TOSS FOR IT!
WHAKK!
CLUD
HEADS! YOU LOSE!
HAH! NEW YORK, THE BIG APPLE! I SHALL POUND THIS ROTTEN FRUIT TO A PULP AND CRUSH ITS HEROES LIKE MAGGOTS AS THEY FLEE!
THIS FROM A GUY WHO TALKS TO HIMSELF? I JUST NEED A COUPLE OF SECONDS TO CATCH MY BREATH...

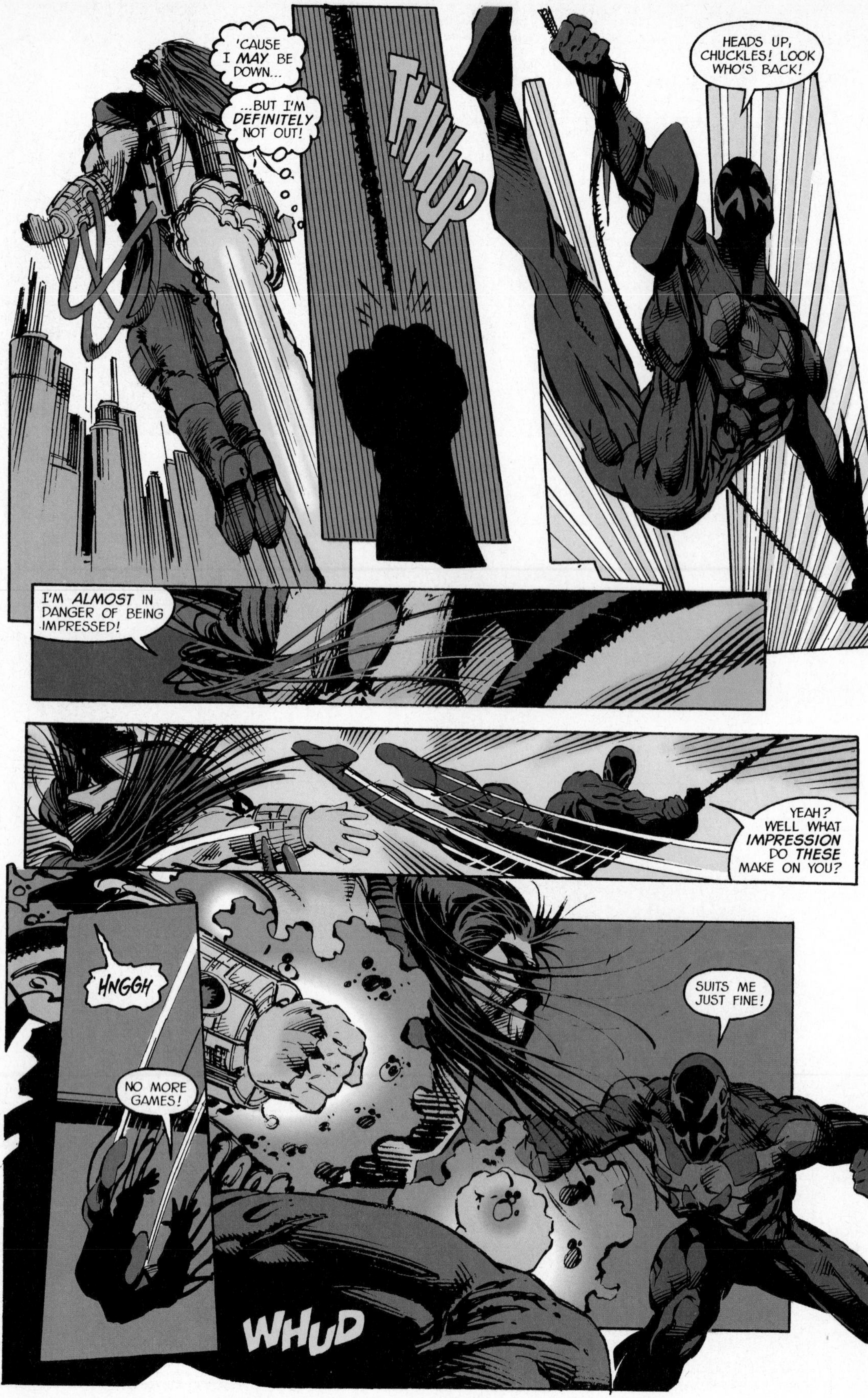
'CAUSE I MAY BE DOWN...
...BUT I'M DEFINITELY NOT OUT!
THWUP
HEADS UP, CHUCKLES! LOOK WHO'S BACK!
I'M ALMOST IN DANGER OF BEING IMPRESSED!
YEAH? WELL WHAT IMPRESSION DO THESE MAKE ON YOU?
HNGGH
NO MORE GAMES!
SUITS ME JUST FINE!
WHUD

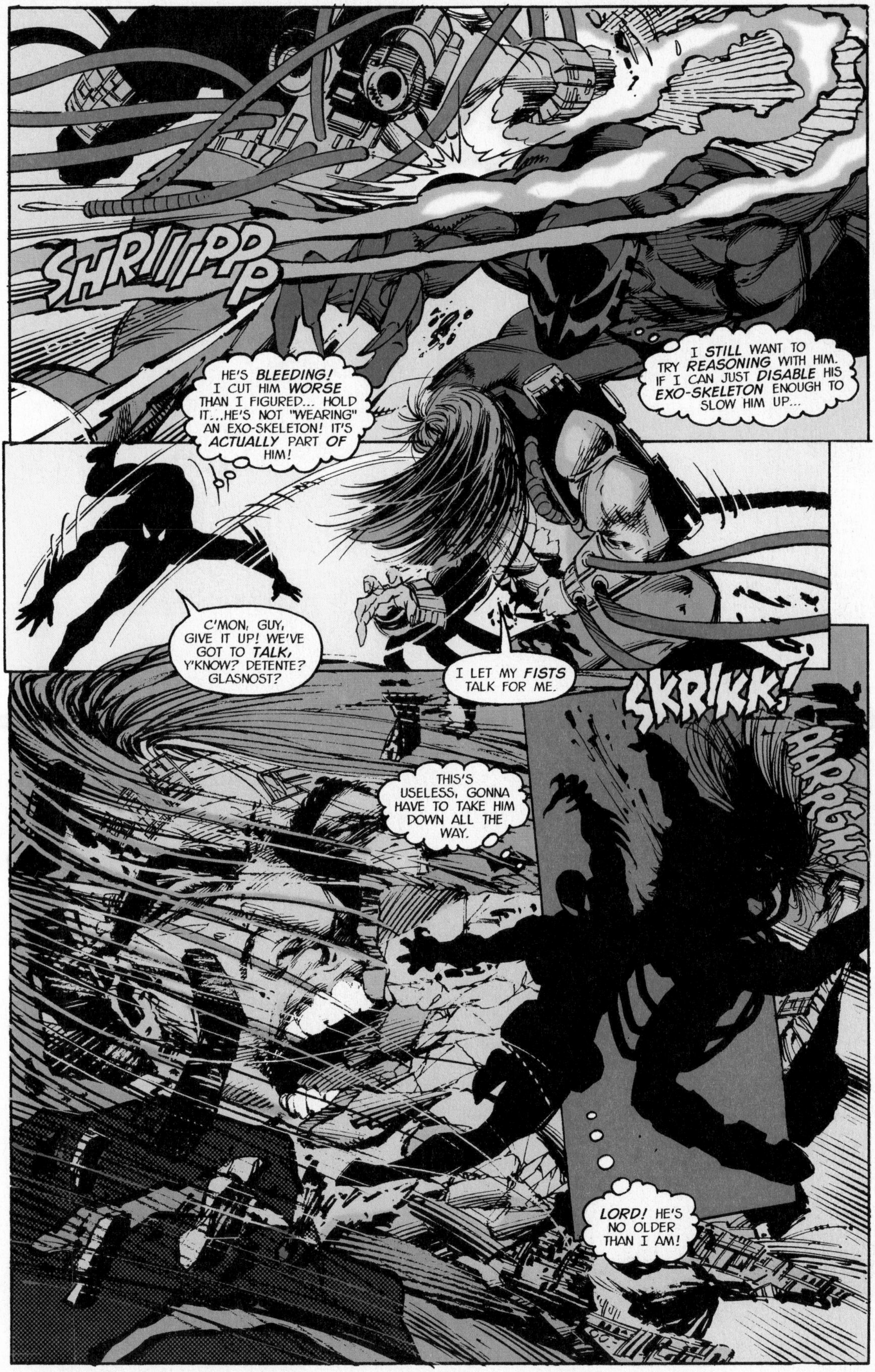
SHRIIIPPP
HE'S BLEEDING! I CUT HIM WORSE THAN I FIGURED... HOLD IT...HE'S NOT "WEARING" AN EXO-SKELETON! IT'S ACTUALLY PART OF HIM!
I STILL WANT TO TRY REASONING WITH HIM. IF I CAN JUST DISABLE HIS EXO-SKELETON ENOUGH TO SLOW HIM UP...
C'MON, GUY, GIVE IT UP! WE'VE GOT TO TALK, Y'KNOW? DETENTE? GLASNOST?
I LET MY FISTS TALK FOR ME.
SKRIKK!
THIS'S USELESS, GONNA HAVE TO TAKE HIM DOWN ALL THE WAY.
LORD! HE'S NO OLDER THAN I AM!

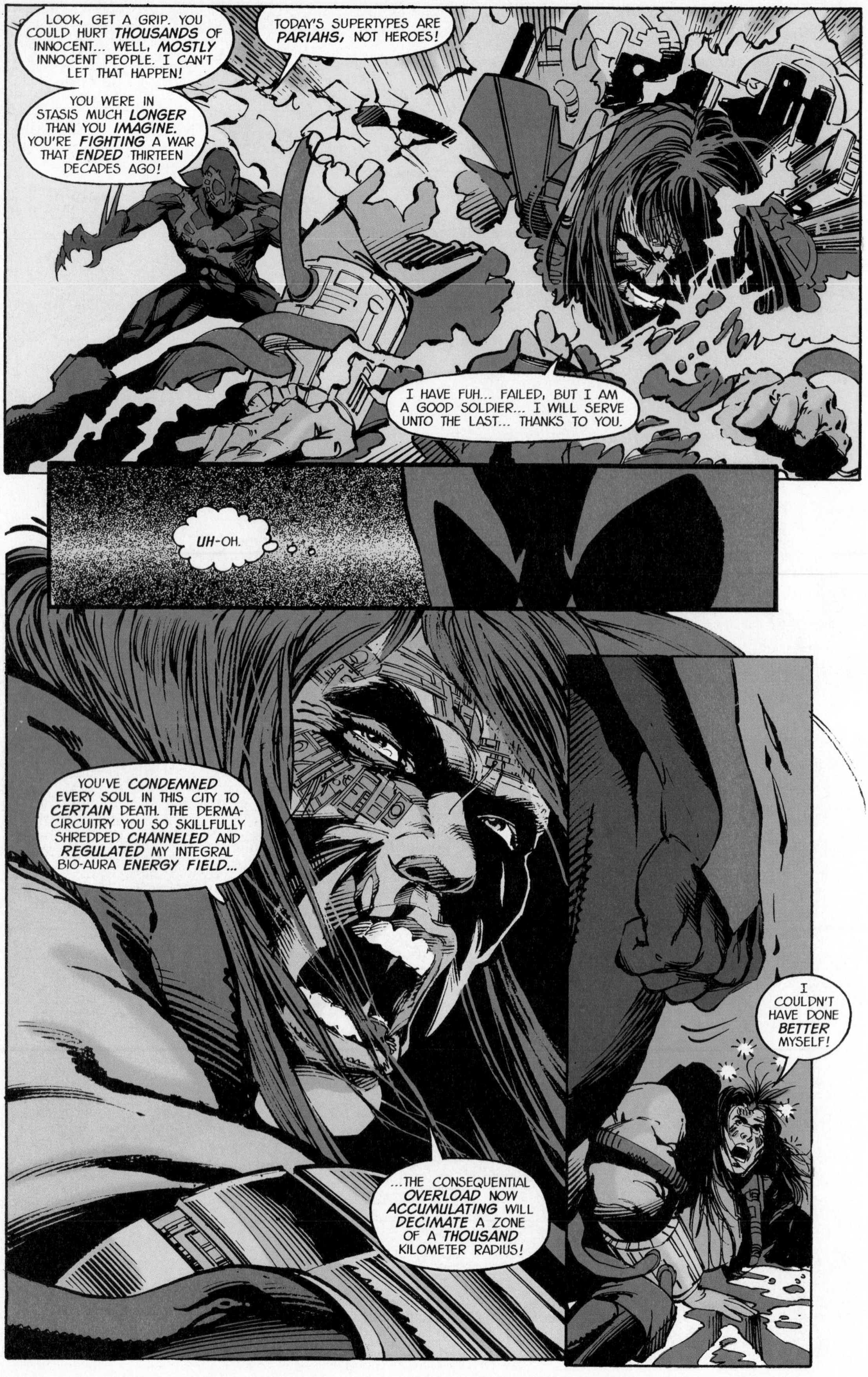
LOOK, GET A GRIP. YOU COULD HURT THOUSANDS OF INNOCENT... WELL, MOSTLY INNOCENT PEOPLE. I CAN'T LET THAT HAPPEN!
TODAY'S SUPERTYPES ARE PARIAHS, NOT HEROES!
YOU WERE IN STASIS MUCH LONGER THAN YOU IMAGINE. YOU'RE FIGHTING A WAR THAT ENDED THIRTEEN DECADES AGO!
I HAVE FUH... FAILED, BUT I AM A GOOD SOLDIER... I WILL SERVE UNTO THE LAST... THANKS TO YOU.
UH-OH.
YOU'VE CONDEMNED EVERY SOUL IN THIS CITY TO CERTAIN DEATH. THE DERMA-CIRCUITRY YOU SO SKILLFULLY SHREDDED CHANNELED AND REGULATED MY INTEGRAL BIO-AURA ENERGY FIELD...
...THE CONSEQUENTIAL OVERLOAD NOW ACCUMULATING WILL DECIMATE A ZONE OF A THOUSAND KILOMETER RADIUS!
I COULDN'T HAVE DONE BETTER MYSELF!

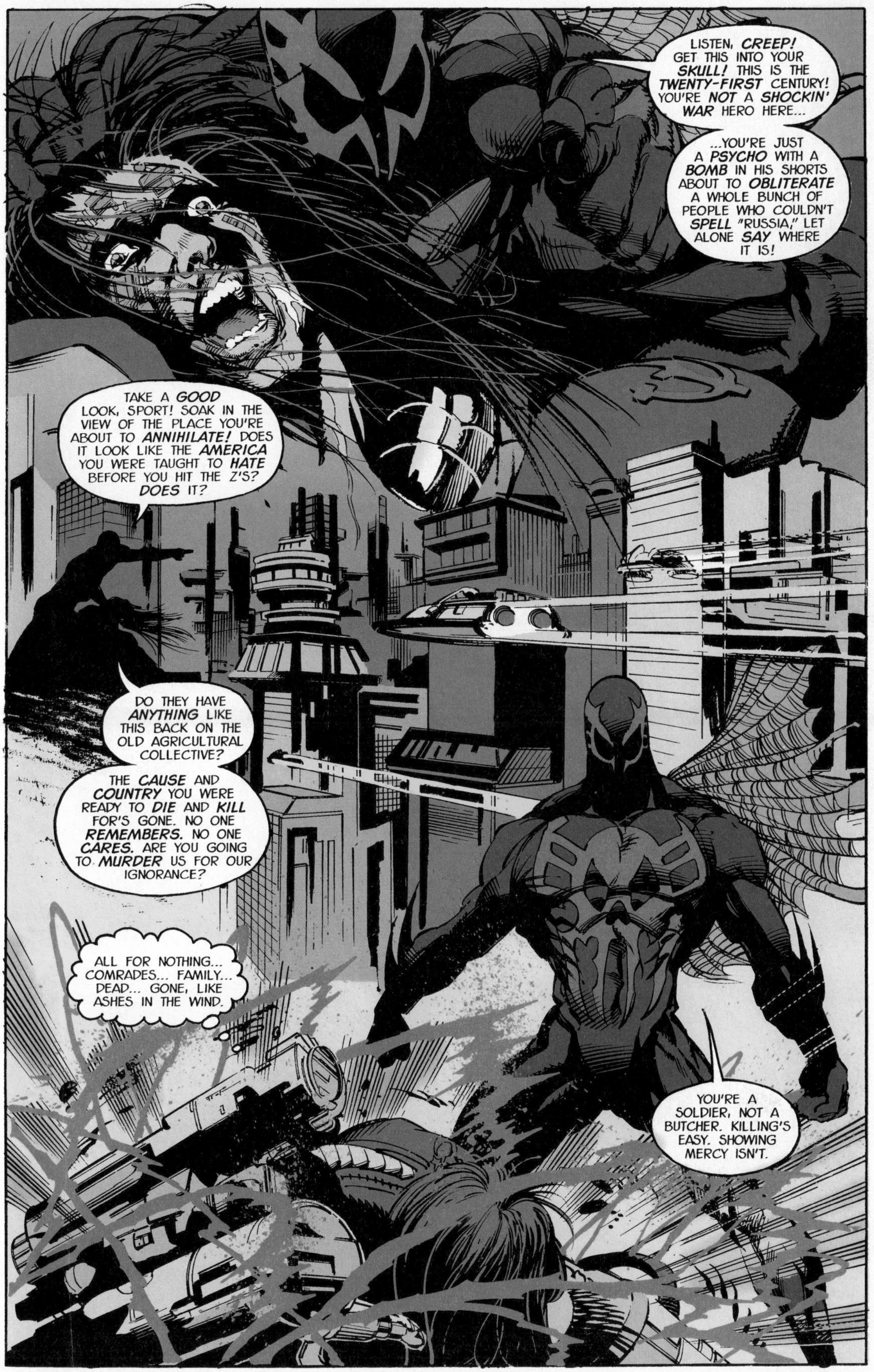
LISTEN, CREEP! GET THIS INTO YOUR SKULL! THIS IS THE TWENTY-FIRST CENTURY! YOU'RE NOT A SHOCKIN' WAR HERO HERE...
...YOU'RE JUST A PSYCHO WITH A BOMB IN HIS SHORTS ABOUT TO OBLITERATE A WHOLE BUNCH OF PEOPLE WHO COULDN'T SPELL "RUSSIA," LET ALONE SAY WHERE IT IS!
TAKE A GOOD LOOK, SPORT! SOAK IN THE VIEW OF THE PLACE YOU'RE ABOUT TO ANNIHILATE! DOES IT LOOK LIKE THE AMERICA YOU WERE TAUGHT TO HATE BEFORE YOU HIT THE Z'S? DOES IT?
DO THEY HAVE ANYTHING LIKE THIS BACK ON THE OLD AGRICULTURAL COLLECTIVE?
THE CAUSE AND COUNTRY YOU WERE READY TO DIE AND KILL FOR'S GONE. NO ONE REMEMBERS. NO ONE CARES. ARE YOU GOING TO MURDER US FOR OUR IGNORANCE?
ALL FOR NOTHING... COMRADES... FAMILY... DEAD... GONE, LIKE ASHES IN THE WIND.
YOU'RE A SOLDIER, NOT A BUTCHER. KILLING'S EASY. SHOWING MERCY ISN'T.

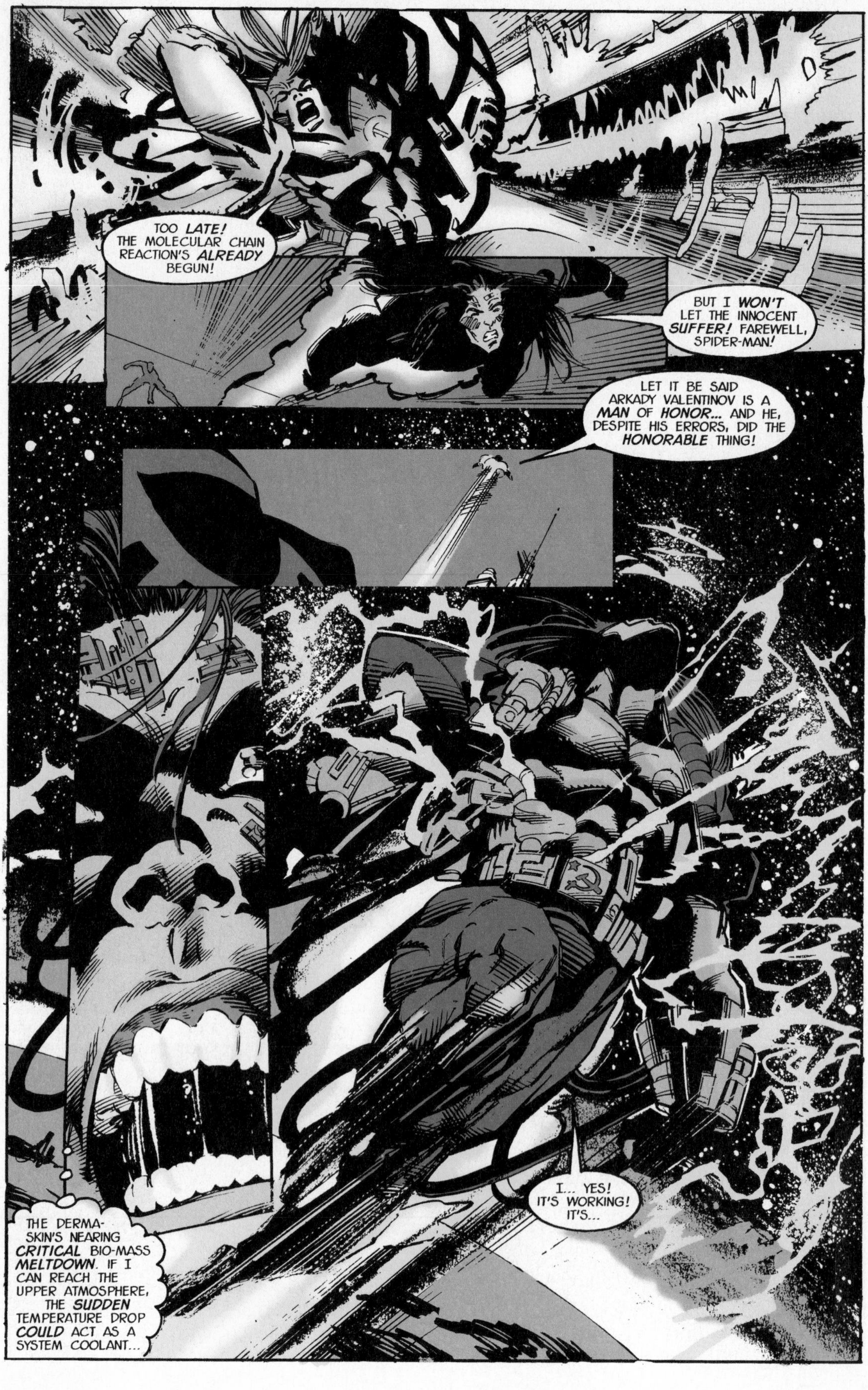
TOO LATE! THE MOLECULAR CHAIN REACTION'S ALREADY BEGUN!
BUT I WON'T LET THE INNOCENT SUFFER! FAREWELL, SPIDER-MAN!
LET IT BE SAID ARKADY VALENTINOV IS A MAN OF HONOR... AND HE, DESPITE HIS ERRORS, DID THE HONORABLE THING!
THE DERMA-SKIN'S NEARING CRITICAL BIO-MASS MELTDOWN. IF I CAN REACH THE UPPER ATMOSPHERE, THE SUDDEN TEMPERATURE DROP COULD ACT AS A SYSTEM COOLANT...
I... YES! IT'S WORKING! IT'S...

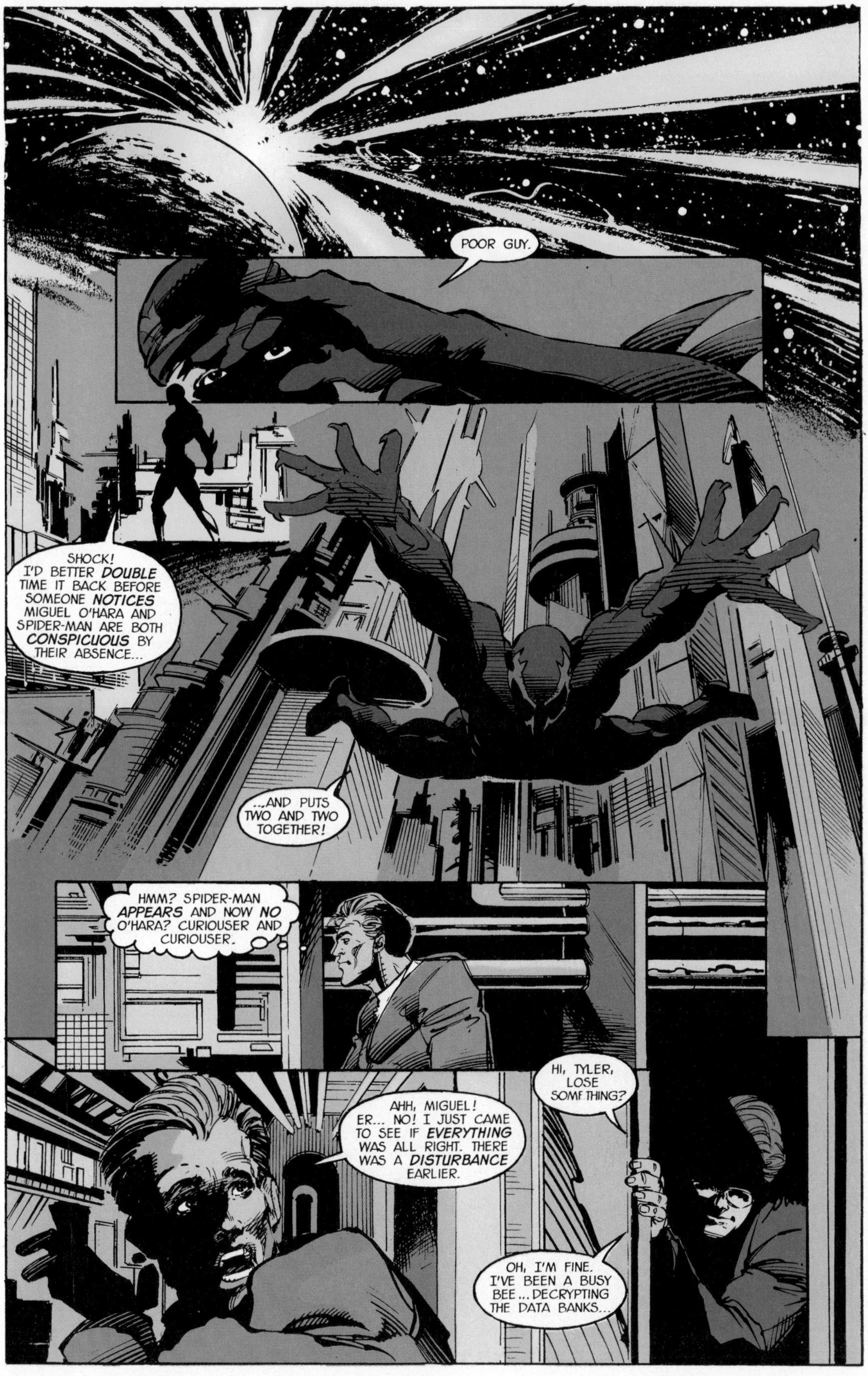
POOR GUY.
SHOCK! I'D BETTER DOUBLE TIME IT BACK BEFORE SOMEONE NOTICES MIGUEL O'HARA AND SPIDER-MAN ARE BOTH CONSPICUOUS BY THEIR ABSENCE...
...AND PUTS TWO AND TWO TOGETHER!
HMM? SPIDER-MAN APPEARS AND NOW NO O'HARA? CURIOUSER AND CURIOUSER.
HI, TYLER, LOSE SOMETHING?
AHH, MIGUEL! ER... NO! I JUST CAME TO SEE IF EVERYTHING WAS ALL RIGHT. THERE WAS A DISTURBANCE EARLIER.
OH, I'M FINE. I'VE BEEN A BUSY BEE... DECRYPTING THE DATA BANKS...

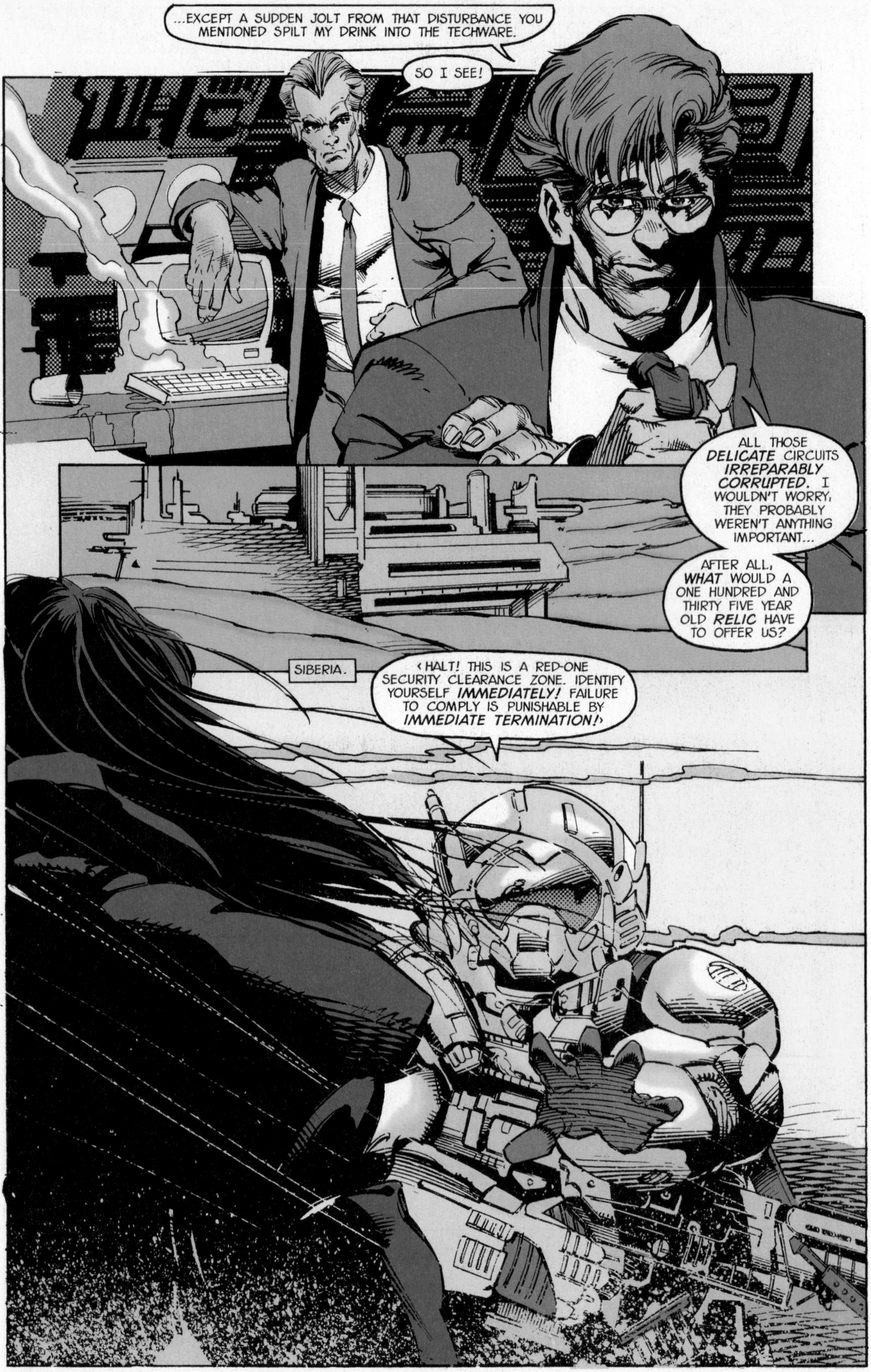
...EXCEPT A SUDDEN JOLT FROM THAT DISTURBANCE YOU MENTIONED SPILT MY DRINK INTO THE TECHWARE.
SO I SEE!
ALL THOSE *DELICATE* CIRCUITS *IRREPARABLY CORRUPTED.* I WOULDN'T WORRY, THEY PROBABLY WEREN'T ANYTHING IMPORTANT...
AFTER ALL, *WHAT* WOULD A ONE HUNDRED AND THIRTY FIVE YEAR OLD *RELIC* HAVE TO OFFER US?
SIBERIA.
‹HALT! THIS IS A RED-ONE SECURITY CLEARANCE ZONE. IDENTIFY YOURSELF *IMMEDIATELY!* FAILURE TO COMPLY IS PUNISHABLE BY *IMMEDIATE TERMINATION!*›

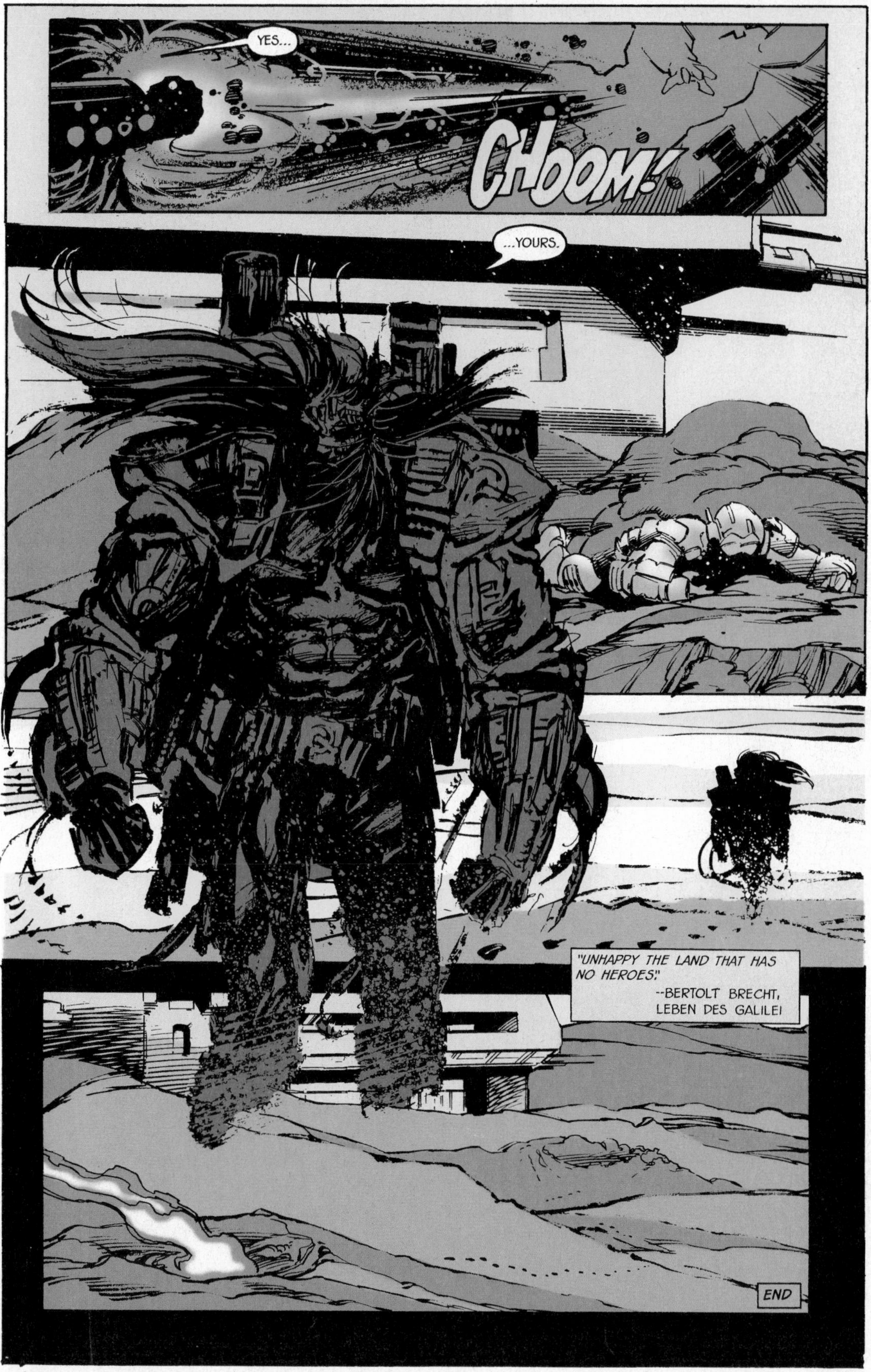

YES...
CHOOM!
...YOURS.
"UNHAPPY THE LAND THAT HAS NO HEROES!"
--BERTOLT BRECHT, LEBEN DES GALILEI
END

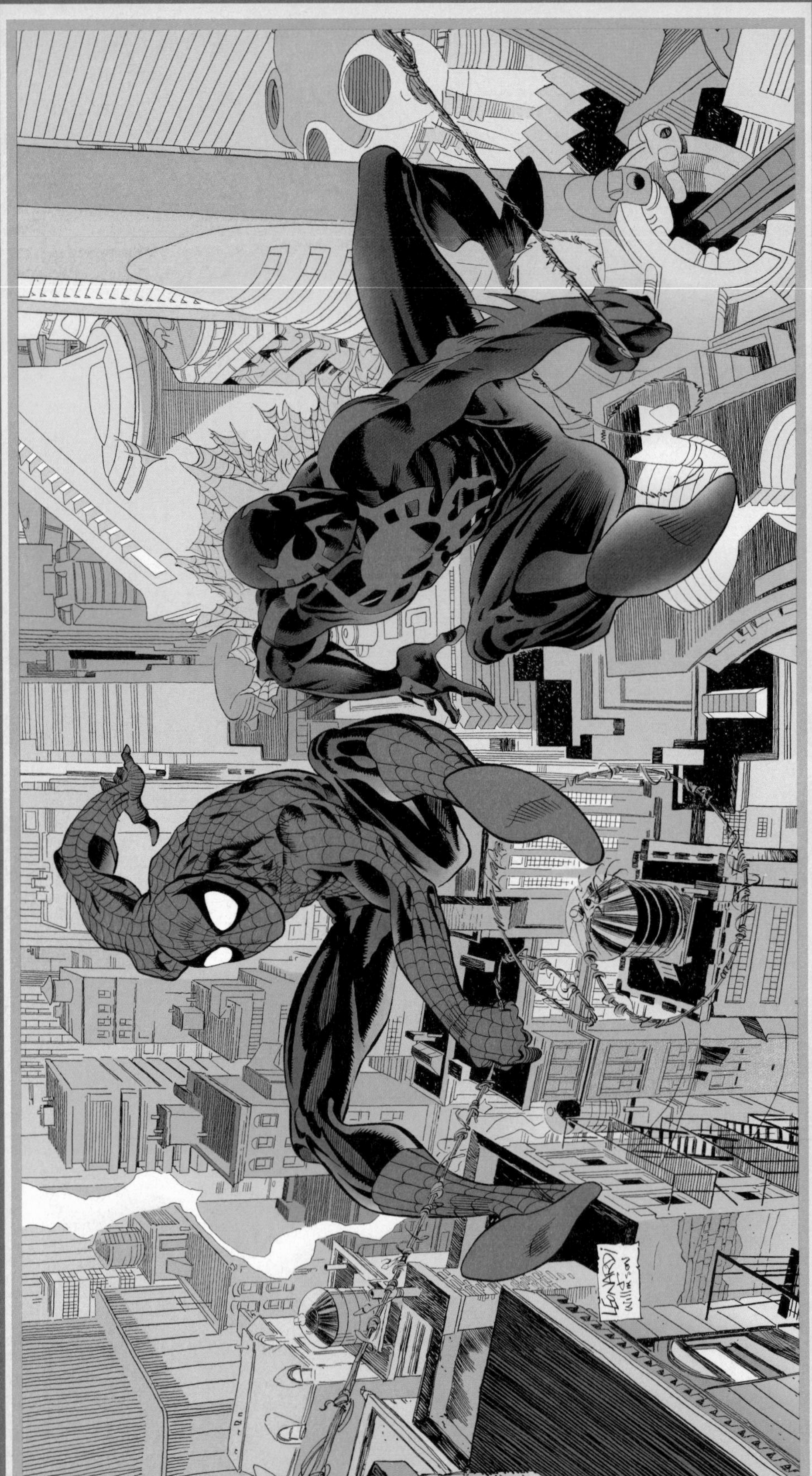

WEB OF SPIDER-MAN HOOPOSTER BY RICK LEONARDI & AL WILLIAMSON

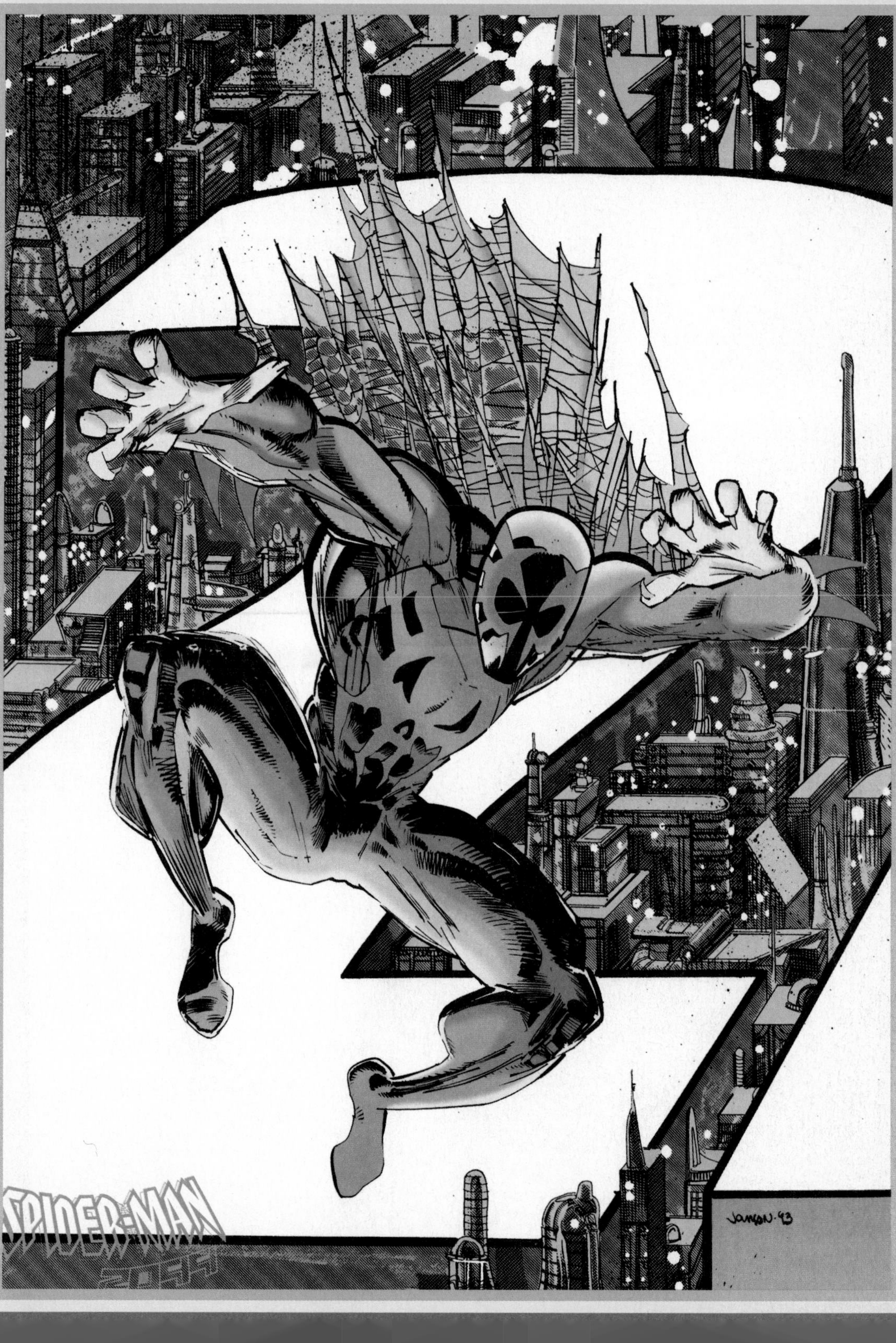
SPIDER-MAN
2099

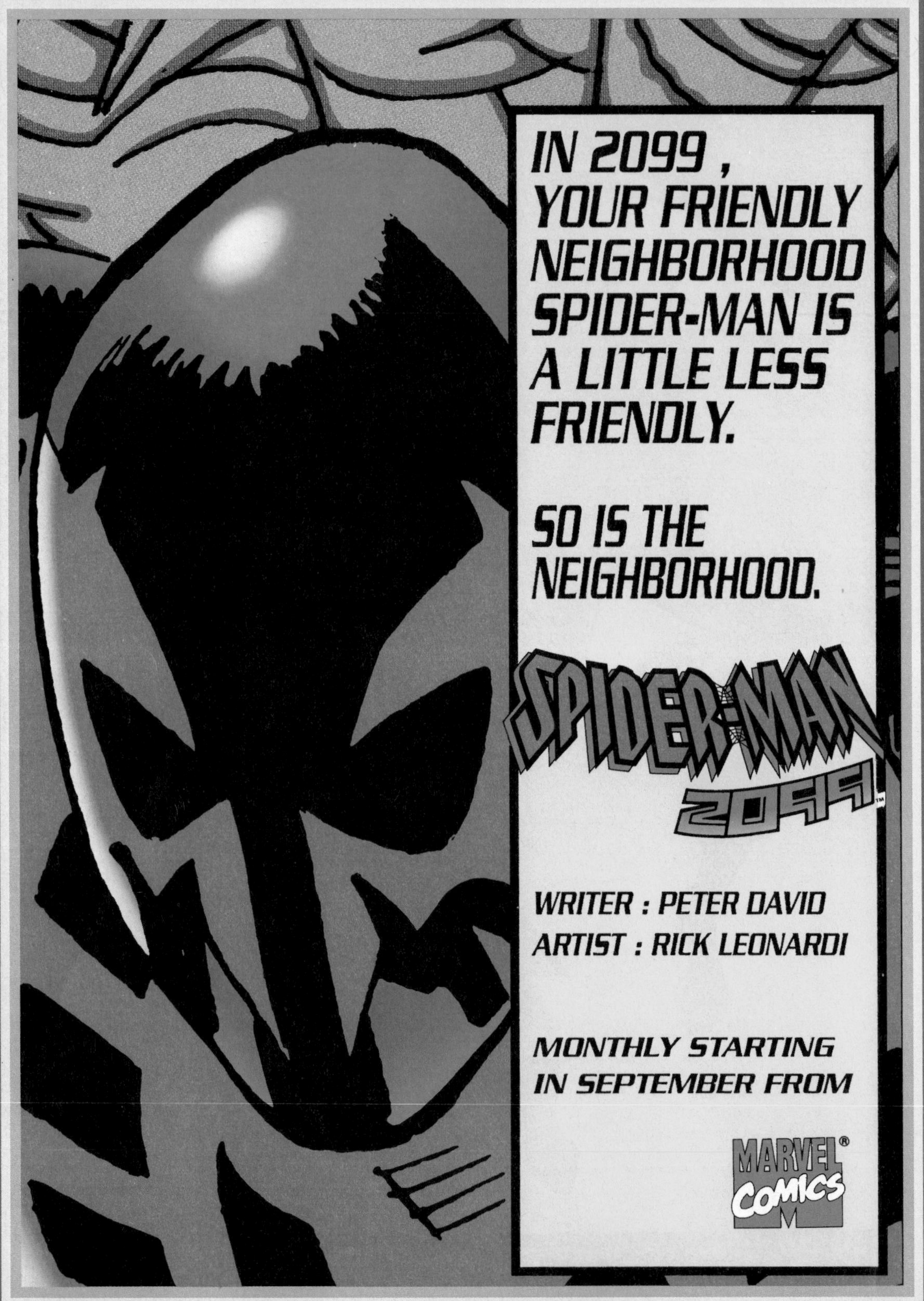

IN 2099 , YOUR FRIENDLY NEIGHBORHOOD SPIDER-MAN IS A LITTLE LESS FRIENDLY.
SO IS THE NEIGHBORHOOD.
SPIDER-MAN 2099™
WRITER : PETER DAVID
ARTIST : RICK LEONARDI
MONTHLY STARTING IN SEPTEMBER FROM
MARVEL® COMICS

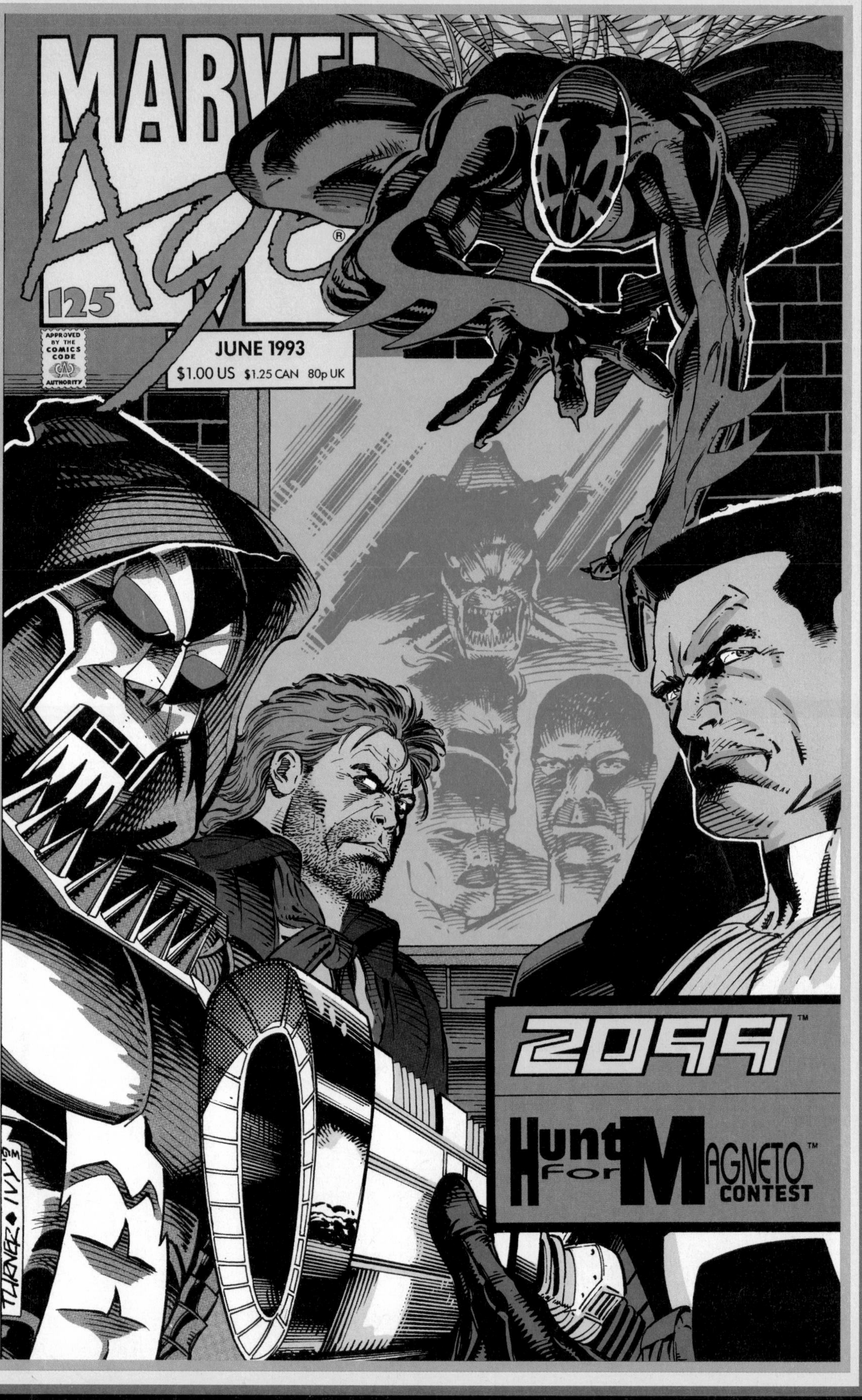
MARVEL Age®
125
APPROVED BY THE COMICS CODE AUTHORITY
JUNE 1993
$1.00 US $1.25 CAN 80p UK
2099™
Hunt for MAGNETO™ CONTEST
TURNER◆IVY

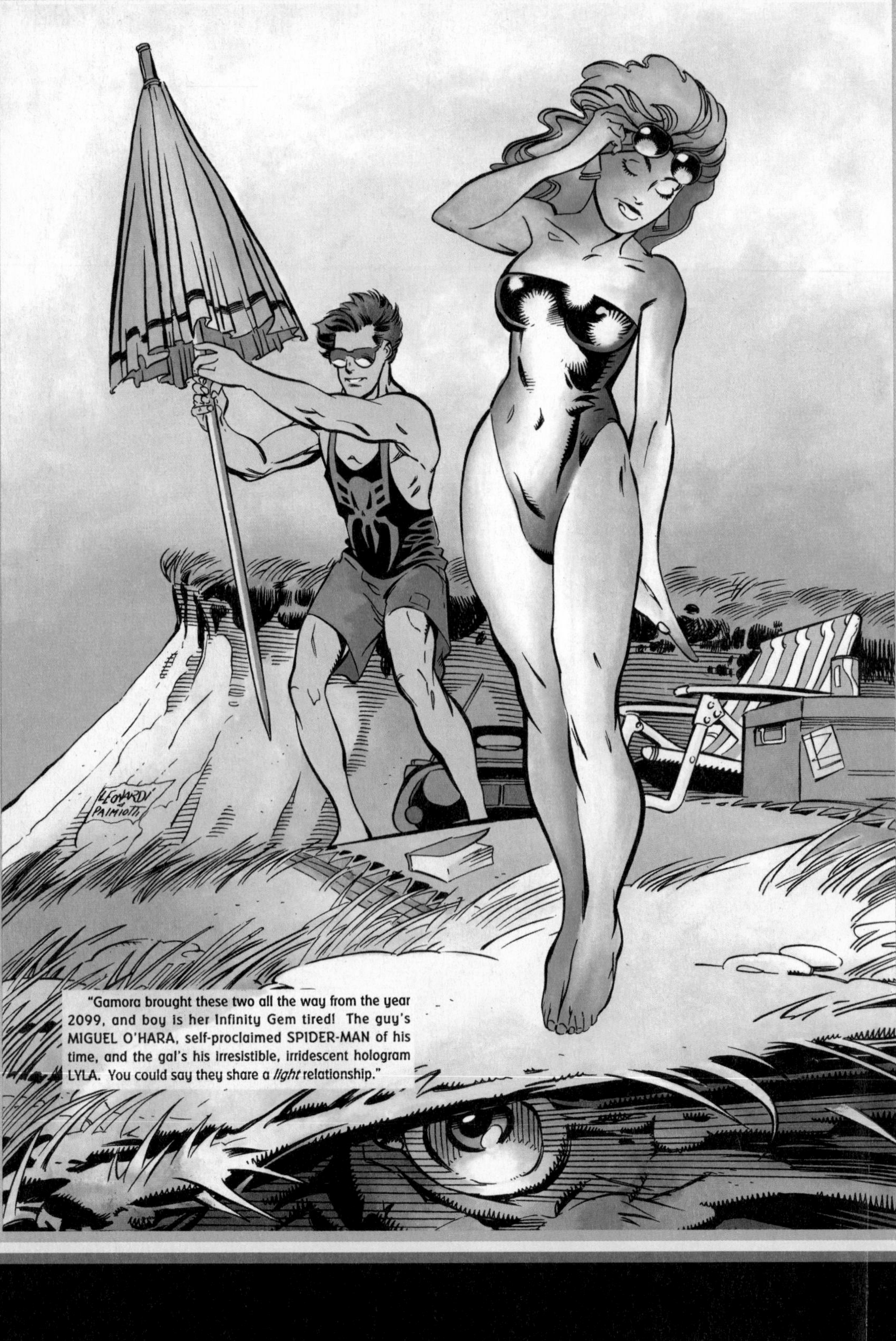
LEONARDI PALMIOTTI
"Gamora brought these two all the way from the year 2099, and boy is her Infinity Gem tired! The guy's MIGUEL O'HARA, self-proclaimed SPIDER-MAN of his time, and the gal's his irresistible, irridescent hologram LYLA. You could say they share a *light* relationship."

MARVEL SWIMSUIT SPECIAL #2 PINUP BY RICK LEONARDI & JIMMY PALMIOTTI

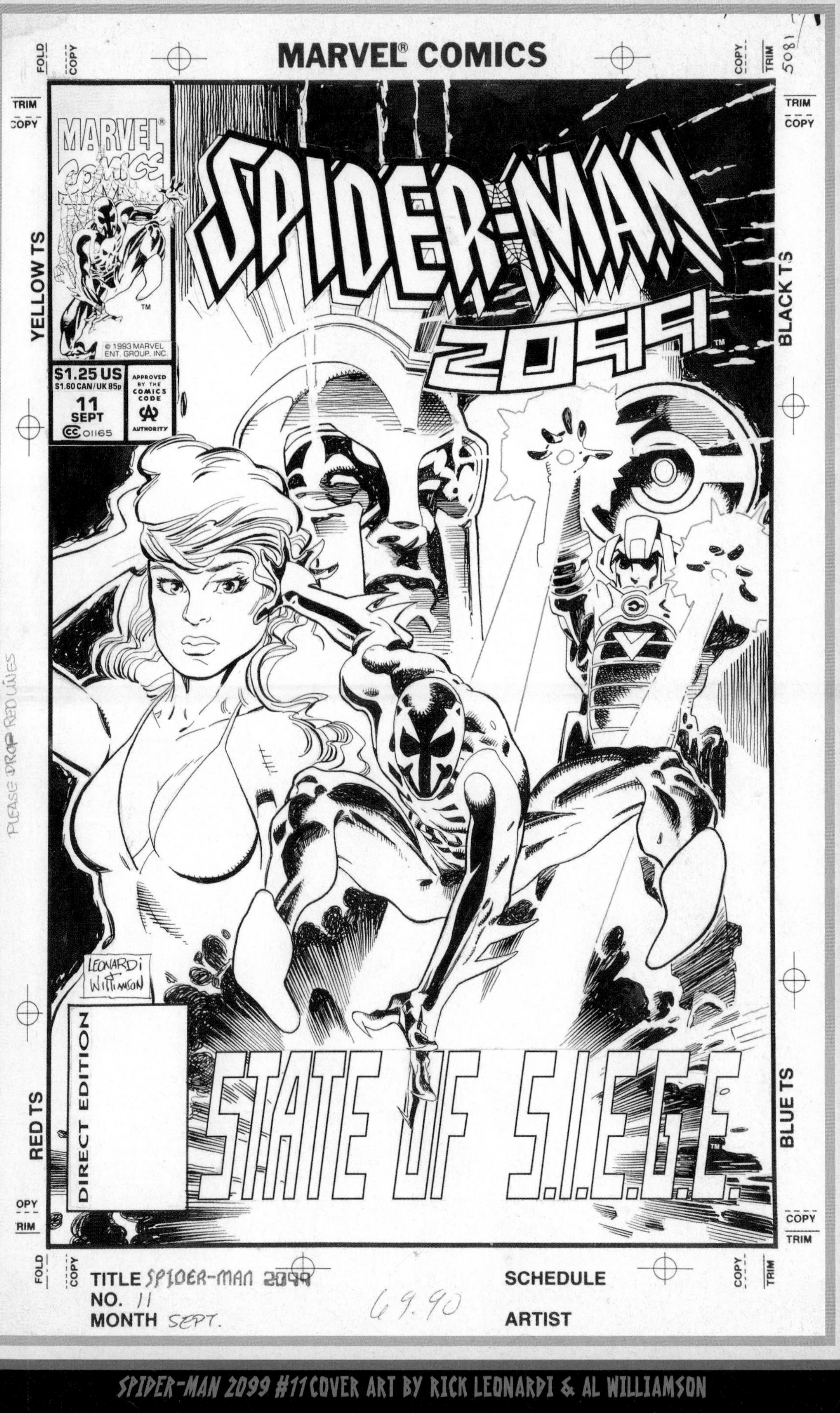

SPIDER-MAN 2099 #11 COVER ART BY RICK LEONARDI & AL WILLIAMSON

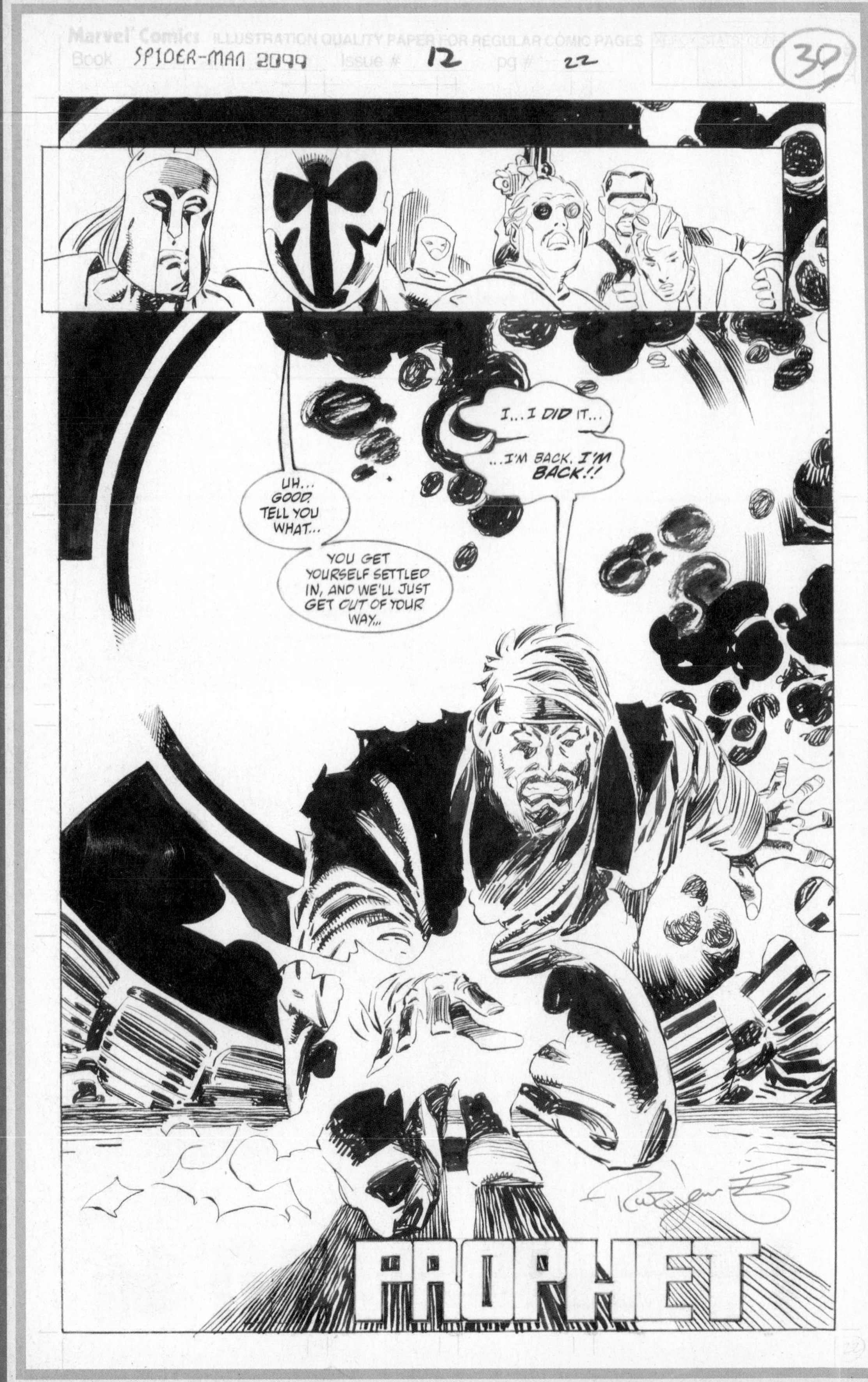
Marvel Comics ILLUSTRATION QUALITY PAPER FOR REGULAR COMIC PAGES
Book SPIDER-MAN 2099 Issue # 12 pg # 22
30
UH... GOOD. TELL YOU WHAT...
YOU GET YOURSELF SETTLED IN, AND WE'LL JUST GET OUT OF YOUR WAY...
I... I DID IT...
...I'M BACK. I'M BACK!!
PROPHET

SPIDER-MAN 2099 #12, PAGE 22 ART BY RICK LEONARDI & AL WILLIAMSON